CONCISE DICTIONARY OF MEDICAL TERMS

Useful for doctors, healthcare professionals and students
appearing for NEET, AIIMS, & other Medical Entrance
Examinations besides school students and general readers

J.S. Aadhyaa

M.SC. Nursing, N.D.D.Y.

V&S PUBLISHERS

Published by:

V&S PUBLISHERS

F-2/16, Ansari road, Daryaganj, New Delhi-110002
☎ 23240026, 23240027 •Fax: 011-23240028
Email: info@vspublishers.com

Branch : Hyderabad
5-1-707/1, Brij Bhawan (Beside Central Bank of India Lane)
Bank Street, Koti, Hyderabad - 500 095
☎ 040-24737290
E-mail: vspublishershyd@gmail.com

Follow us on:

For any assistance sms VSPUB to 56161
All books available at www.vspublishers.com

© Copyright: V&S PUBLISHERS
ISBN 978-93-505703-3-3
Edition: 2013

Printed at: Param Offsetters, Okhla, New Delhi

Contents

	Publisher's Note	5
	Introduction	7
1.	A	9
2.	B	37
3.	C	63
4.	D	93
5.	E	123
6.	F	147
7.	G	174
8.	H	198
9.	I	234
10.	J	267
11.	K	277
12.	L	288
13.	M	309
14.	N	363
15.	O	388
16.	P	400
17.	Q	413
18.	R	416
19.	S	437
20.	T	462
21.	U	478
22.	V	488
23.	W	497
24.	X	503
25.	Y	505
26.	Z	507
	Glossary of abbreviation	510
	Appendices	516

Publisher's Note

This Dictionary of Medical Terms is in line with the best-selling compilations of V&S Publishers' reference dictionaries. It is a new reference work for everyone concerned with medicine and health care, including those working in allied fields of law, insurance, and alternative health. It combines the professional and scientific expertise in technical writing for non-technical readers.

V&S Publishers has so far come out with seven dictionaries of terms; science, physics, chemistry, biology, mathematics, commerce and economics. Dictionaries on other subjects are in works awaiting completion and publication.

Innumerable books are available in the market on medical science, both as a textbook and reference manual. Quite a number of these reference books, especially for non-medical readers, come replete with jargon-filled terms, give short explanations to the 'term' being discussed. and fail to connect with readers' ability to understand. On top of that, research keeps throwing new words that find their way into the books every other day. Each new addition of words adds to complexity needing simplification. An average reader is interested only in knowing what a specific word means without getting lost in technical explanations.

The book gives simplified meaning of popular terms and notations so that an average reader, including average college/medical student can grasp them easily. For easy reference terms have been arranged alphabetically. Clear images, illustrations and examples, where appropriate, have been added along with appropriate appendices at the end of the book.

Medicinal world is undergoing a 'revolution, where getting a clear picture of a medical word is difficult for non-medical people. The author has been selective in choosing entries so that the balance of the book is maintained at the target audience.

Some may think, the book has omitted some important entries while others may see it as having included a number of frivolous ones. To this end, all criticism and suggestions for improvement are welcome.

Introduction

Medical world is perhaps the most intensively researched field in the development of new cure for ailments, preventive medicines, and control of disease, etc. This dictionary provides full coverage of all the important terms and theories used in medicine today. It is intended primarily for people in the medical and paramedical fields: practicing doctors, health workers, hospital administrators, technicians, radiologists, pharmacists, physiotherapists, speech therapists, social workers, and so on. It is equally useful for those working in the fields of law, insurance, and alternative health. Tempered with scientific expertise in technical writing for non-technical readers; it is in line with the best-selling compilations of V&S Publishers' reference dictionaries. For this reason the book will also be of interest and value to the general reader who needs a simplified medical dictionary in everyday language.

Each entry contains a basic definition in clear and concise manner in a medical jargon-free language. The dictionary defines terms specific to anatomy, physiology, biochemistry, genetics, as well as other major surgical and medical specialties. Coverage of psychology and psychiatry, public health & medicine, obstetrics & gynaecology, paediatrics, nephrology, dentistry, cardiology, oncology, genetics, medical ethics as well as other medical and surgical specialties is given in short notes: and exhaustive, where considered necessary. Important features include: more than 10,000 entries. New terms used regularly have also been included. Popular terms from other systems of treatment have also been included, for example, yoga, homeopathy, ayurved, siddha, unani and other oriental methods including acupressure & reflexology.

Cross-reference entries refer the reader to another entry, mentioning that they are either synonyms, or abbreviations; or that more detailed explanation appears elsewhere. Inclusion of illustrations and tables simplify understanding the terms.

Biochemical reference values for blood, urine, faeces, cerebrospinal fluid, haematological & paediatric reference values, baby milk formulas, and abbreviations & symbols are included as appendices.

While every attempt has been made to keep the dictionary accurate, simple and straight forward, we go by the conviction that even the best of the books have scope for improvement. If you feel that some matter needs modification or addition to text or even deletion, please inform us of the action to be taken. We would be grateful for your contribution.

A

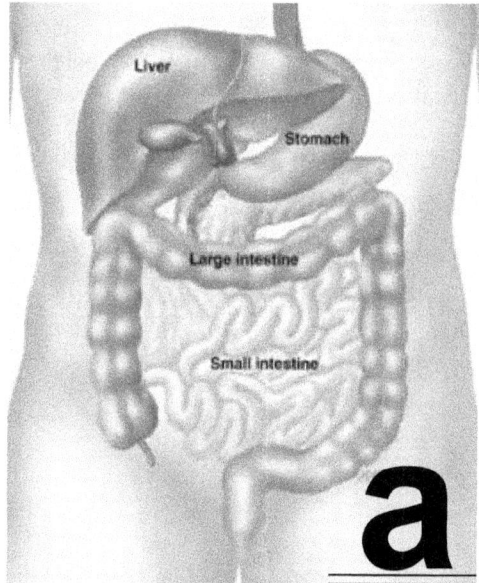

A-alphalipoprotein Neuropathy A rare autosomal recessive familial disorder of cholesterol metabolism, characterised by extremely low HDL-cholesterol, reduced total cholesterol, and increased triglyceride levels in serum.

Aarskog-Scott syndrome A syndrome of wide spaced eyes (ocular hypertelorism), front-facing (anteverted) nostrils, a broad upper lip, a malformed ("saddle-bag") scrotum, and laxity of the ligaments resulting in bending back of the knees (genu recurvatum), flat feet, and overly extensible fingers. There are X-linked and autosomal forms of the disease.

Abate To lessen or decrease. For example, after a boil is lanced, the pus can drain and the pain and tenderness abate. From the French abbatre, to beat down.

Abatement A diminution, decrease or easing. In medicine there may be abatement of pain or any other symptom or sign. In the environment there may be abatement in the degree of pollution

Abarelix A drug used to reduce the amount of testosterone made in patients with advanced symptomatic prostate cancer for which no other treatment options are available. It belongs to the family of drugs called gonadotropin-releasing hormone (GnRH) antagonists.

ABCD rating A staging system for prostate cancer that uses ABCD. 'A' and 'B' refer to cancer that is confined to the prostate. 'C' refers to cancer that has grown out of the prostate but has not spread to lymph nodes or other places in the body. 'D' refers to cancer that has spread to lymph nodes or to other places in the body. Also called Jewett staging system and Whitmore-Jewett staging system.

Abdomen The area of the body that contains the pancreas, stomach, intestines, liver, gallbladder, and other organs.

Abdominal bloating Abdominal bloating is felt by patients as a feeling of fullness, tightness or distension in the abdomen.

Abdominal CT scan An abdominal CT scan is an imaging method that uses x-rays to create cross-sectional pictures of the belly area. CT stands for computed tomography.

Abdominal Pain The abdominal area (the area between your chest and groin) is often referred to as the stomach region or belly.

Abdominal ultrasound A procedure used to examine the organs in the abdomen. An ultrasound transducer (probe) is pressed firmly against the skin of the abdomen. High-energy sound waves from the transducer bounce off tissues and create echoes. The echoes are sent to a computer, which makes a picture called a sonogram. Also called trans-abdominal ultrasound.

Abdominal X-ray An x-ray of the organs inside the abdomen. An x-ray is a type of radiation that can pass through the body and onto film, making pictures of areas inside the body. X-rays may be used to help diagnose disease.

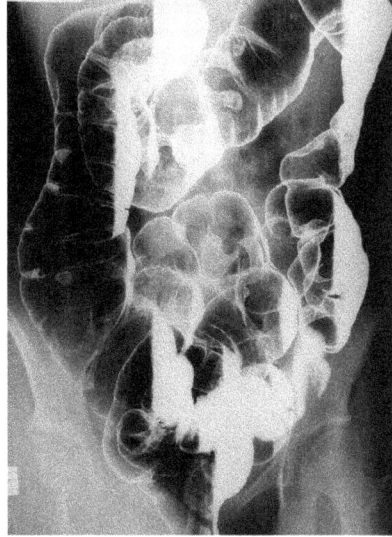

Fig. *Abdominal X-ray*

Abdominoperineal resection Surgery to remove the anus, the rectum, and part of the sigmoid colon through an incision made in the abdomen. The end of the intestine is attached to an opening in the surface of the abdomen and body waste is collected in a disposable bag outside of the body. This opening is called a colostomy. Lymph nodes that contain cancer may also be removed during this operation.

Abduct Movement of any extremity away from the midline of the body.

Abductor Any muscle which moves a body part away from the midline of the body.

Ablation In medicine, the removal or destruction of a body part or tissue or its function. Ablation may be performed by surgery, hormones, drugs, radio-frequency, heat, or other methods.

Abnormal   Not normal. An abnormal lesion or growth may be cancer, premalignant (likely to become cancer), or benign (not cancer).

Abnormal posturing It is an involuntary flexion or extension of the arms and legs, indicating severe brain injury.

Abnormality In psychological terms, any mental, emotional, or behavioural activity that deviates from culturally or scientifically accepted norms.

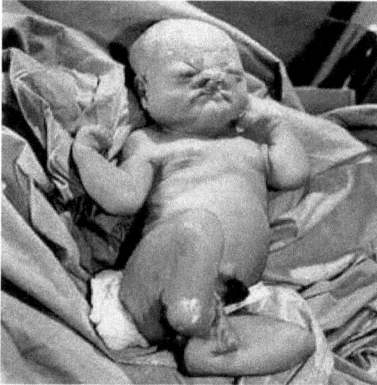

Fig. *Abnormality*

ABO blood group system A system used to group human blood into different types, based on the presence or absence of certain markers on the surface of red blood cells.

The four main blood types are A, B, O, and AB. For a blood transfusion, the ABO blood group system is used to match the blood type of the donor and the person receiving the transfusion. People with blood type O can donate blood to anyone and are called universal donors. People with blood type AB can accept blood from all donors

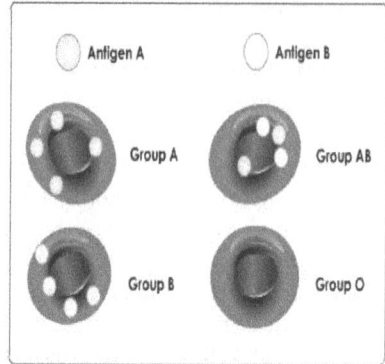

Fig. *ABO blood group system*

and are called universal recipients. People with type A or B can receive matching blood or type O blood.

Abortifacient Induces the premature expulsion (abortion) of a foetus. Same meaning as Ecbolic, e.g., pennyroyal.

Abrasion Any injury which rubs off the surface of the skin.

Abraxane A drug used to treat breast cancer that has spread or that has come back within 6 months after chemotherapy. It is also being studied in the treatment of newly diagnosed breast cancer and other types of cancer. Abraxane is a type of mitotic inhibitor.

Abreaction Emotional release or discharge after recalling a painful experience that has been repressed because it was not consciously tolerable. A therapeutic effect sometimes occurs through partial or repeated discharge of the painful affect.

Abscess An enclosed collection of pus in tissues, organs, or confined spaces in the body. An abscess is a sign of infection and is usually swollen and inflamed.

Absorption The process of taking nutrients from the digestive system into the blood so they can be used in the body.

Abstinence Foregoing some kind of gratification; in the area of alcohol or drug dependence, being without the substance on which the subject had been dependent.

Abuse, substance Impairment in social and occupational functioning resulting from the pathological and 'compulsive' use of a substance. The concept is closely related to the definition of substance dependence, which has similar symptoms of impairment but may include evidence of physiological tolerance or withdrawal. Typical symptoms of abuse include failure to fulfill major role obligations at work, school, or home; recurrent use of the substance in situations where such use is physically hazardous; substance-related legal problems; and continued use even though it causes or exaggerates interpersonal problems.

Abused child A child or infant who has suffered repeated injuries, which may include bone fractures, neurologic and psychological damage, or sexual abuse at the hands of a parent, parents, or parent surrogate(s). The abuse takes place repeatedly and is often precipitated, in the case of physical abuse, by the child's minor and normally irritating behaviour. Child abuse also includes child neglect.

A-C Joint The acromioclavicular (or AC) joint is the joint created by the end of the collar bone (clavicle) connecting to the acromion of the shoulder blade (scapula).

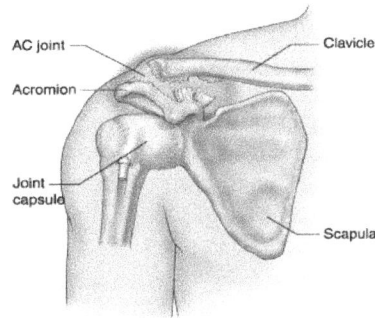

Fig. *A-C Joint*

Pain in this region of the shoulder is most commonly caused by trauma, specifically falling on either an outstretched arm or a fall landing directly on the tip of the AC joint.

Academic disorders In DSM-IV, this is a major group of infancy, childhood, and adolescence disorders that includes reading disorder, mathematics disorder, and disorder of written expression.

Academic problem School difficulty that is not due to a mental disorder. Examples are failing grades or significant underachievement in a person with adequate intellectual capacity.

Accelerated Death Benefits Some life insurance companies offer life insurance policies with a special feature that allows payment of the death benefit when the insured person is still alive. Such payment usually is limited to situations in which the individual is terminally ill. The benefits are available to cover the costs of long term care services.

Accident-proneness Susceptibility to accidents based on psychological causes or motivations, usually unconscious.

Accountable Health Plans Under the Managed Care Act, providers and insurance companies would be encouraged (through tax incentives) to form AHPs, similar to HMOs, PPOs, and other group practices. Accountable health plans would compete on the basis of offering high-quality, low-cost care and would offer insurance and health care as a single product. They would be responsible for looking after the total health of members and reporting medical outcomes in accordance with Federal guidelines.

Accoucheur A male obstetrician. An accoucheuse is a woman obstetrician, or sometimes a midwife.

Accreditation A seal of approval given by a governing body to a housing and/or service provider. To become accredited, the community or provider must meet specific requirements set by the accreditation entity and is then generally required to undergo a thorough review process by a team of evaluators to ensure certain standards of quality. The accrediting organizations are not government agencies or regulatory bodies. Examples of some accreditation bodies for the senior housing and care industry include CCAC (Continuing Care Accreditation Commission), CARF (Commission on Accreditation of Rehabilitation Facilities) and JCAHO (Joint Commission on Accreditation of Health care Organizations).

Accredited To meet the standards set by a non-governmental, state or national peer group.

Accrete The addition of new enrollee to a health plan, usually used in reference to medicare.

Accessory nerve The eleventh cranial nerve, which emerges from the skull and receives an additional (accessory) root from the upper part of the spinal cord. It supplies the sternoclei-domastoid and trapezius muscles.

Acculturation difficulty A problem in adapting to or finding an appropriate way to adapt to a different culture or environment. The problem is not based on any coexisting mental disorder.

ACF Clusters of abnormal tubelike glands in the lining of the colon and rectum. ACF form before colorectal polyps and are one of the earliest changes that can be seen in the colon that may lead to cancer. It is also called aberrant crypt foci.

Achalasia is a disorder of swallowing resulting from the inability

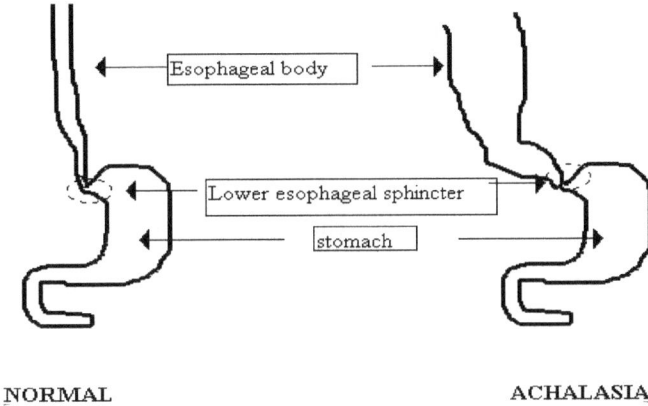

NORMAL   ACHALASIA
Fig. *Achalasia*

of the muscle of the esophagus (food pipe) to relax, preventing food and liquids to get to the stomach. The muscle affected is called the lower esophageal sphincter: this is a ring of muscle at the junction of the oesophagus and stomach, which normally stays shut (to prevent stomach acid from coming back) and opens during swallowing to allow food down. In patients with achalasia, this ring stays shut. In addition, the rest of the esophagus loses its ability to pump material down (a process called peristalsis). This combination of defects results in great difficulty in swallowing.

Achlorhydria A lack of hydrochloric acid in the digestive juices in the stomach. Hydrochloric acid helps digest food.

Acid A chemical that gives off hydrogen ions in water and forms salts by combining with certain metals. Acids have a sour taste and turn certain dyes red. Some acids made by the body, such as gastric acid, can help the body work the way it should. An example of an acid is hydrochloric acid.

Acid-base balance In medicine, the state of having the right amount of acid and base in the blood and other body fluids. Keeping a normal acid-base balance is important for the body to work the way it should. Also called acid-base equilibrium.

Acid-base equilibrium In medicine, the state of having the right amount of acid and base in the blood and other body fluids. Keeping a normal acid-base equilibrium is important for the body to work the way it should. Its also called acid-base balance.

Acidification The process of making or becoming an acid. An acid is a substance that gives off hydrogen ions in water and forms salts by combining with certain metals.

Acidity It refers to the amount of acid in a substance. An acid is a

14

chemical that gives off hydrogen ions in water and forms salts by combining with certain metals.

Acoustic Having to do with sound or hearing. The acoustic nerve (the 8th cranial nerve) is concerned with hearing and the sense of balance and head position. An acoustic neuroma is a benign tumour on the acoustic nerve.

Acromegaly A condition in which the pituitary gland makes too much growth hormone after normal growth of the skeleton is finished. This causes the bones of the hands, feet, head, and face to grow larger than normal. Acromegaly can be caused by a pituitary gland tumour.

Acrylonitrile A substance used to make plastics, rubber, and textiles. Being exposed to acrylonitrile may increase the risk of developing certain cancers, such as lung, brain, or prostate cancer.

ACTH A hormone made in the pituitary gland. ACTH acts on the outer part of the adrenal gland to control its release of cortico-steroid hormones. More ACTH is made during times of stress. It is also called adreno-corticotropic hormone and corti-cotropin.

Actimid A substance being studied in the treatment of prostate cancer, multiple myeloma, and other types of cancer. Actimid is a form of the drug thalidomide. It stops the growth of blood vessels, stimulates the immune system, and may kill cancer cells. Actimid is a type of angiogenesis inhibitor and a type of immuno-modulatory agent.

Actinex A drug put on the skin to treat growths caused by sun exposure. A form of Actinex that is taken by mouth is being studied in the treatment of prostate cancer. Actinex is an antioxidant, and it may block certain enzymes needed for tumour growth. Also called masoprocol, NDGA, and nor-dihydroguaiaretic acid.

Acting out Expressions of unconscious emotional conflicts or feelings in actions rather than words. The person is not consciously aware of the meaning of such acts. Acting out may be harmful or, in controlled situations, therapeutic (e.g., children's play therapy).

Activities director The activities director is trained in social, recreational, or therapeutic programming. The director provides an ongoing programme of meaningful activities to promote self-care and the physical, social, and mental well being of residents.

Activities of daily living Physical functions that an independent person performs each day, including bathing, dressing, eating, toileting, walking or wheeling, and transferring into and out of bed.

Actual charge The amount a physician or other provider actually bills a patient for a particular medical service, procedure or supply in a specific instance. The actual charge may differ from the usual, customary, prevailing, and/or reasonable charge.

Actuarial analysis The statistical calculations used to determine the managed care company's rates and premiums charged to their customers based on projections of utilization and cost for a defined population.

Actuarial cost of coverage The expected dollar value of a health plan's benefits. The method of determining this value may be based entirely on a plan's provisions, or may adjust for the geographic location and demographic characteristics of enrollees, the actual health care utilization level by plan participants, or the type of plan under which the benefits are provided.

Actuarial soundness The requirement that the development of capitation rates meet common actuarial principles and rules.

Actuary A person in the insurance field who decides policy rates and conducts various other statistical studies.

Acupressure The application of pressure or localized massage to specific sites on the body to control symptoms such as pain or nausea. It is a type of complementary and alternative medicine.

Acupressure is the most effective method for self-treatment of tension-related ailments by using the power and sensitivity of the human hand. It deals with all the aspects of a person as a whole: body, emotions, mind, and spirit as one, not as separate parts. It relaxes muscular tension and balances the vital life forces of the body.

Acupuncture The technique of inserting thin needles through the skin at specific points on the body to control pain and other symptoms. It is a type of complementary and alternative

Fig. *Acupressure*

medicine. It is a very old medical art, and there are many approaches to learning and practicing it. Medical acupuncture is the term used to describe acupuncture performed by a doctor trained and licensed in Western medicine who has also had thorough training in acupuncture as a specialty practice. Such a doctor can use one or the other approach, or a combination of both as the need arises, to treat an illness.

Acupuncture needle A stainless steel needle that is slightly thicker than a human hair. Acupuncture needles are inserted through the skin at specific points on the body to control pain and other symptoms.

Acupuncture point A specific spot on the body where an acupuncture needle may be inserted to control pain and other symptoms.

Acupuncture point injection A procedure in which drugs, vitamins, herbal extracts, or other fluids are injected into the body at an acupuncture point using a syringe and needle.

Acute A sudden and severe condition.

Acute angle-closure glaucoma Increased pressure in the front chamber (anterior chamber) of the eye due to sudden (acute) blockage of the normal circulation of fluid within the eye. The block takes place at the angle of the anterior chamber – the space at the junction of the cornea with the iris. This angle can

be seen by looking at one's eye from the side with the slit lamp.

Acute bronchitis inflammation of the breathing tubes within the lungs (bronchial tubes or bronchi) as a result of an infection (viral or bacterial) or a chemical irritant (such as smoke or gastric acid reflux). The inflammation causes swelling of the lining of these breathing tubes, narrowing the tubes and promoting secretion of inflammatory fluid. Most commonly, acute bronchitis is due to a viral infection. Common viruses that cause bronchitis include the rhinovirus, respiratory syncytial virus (RSV), and the influenza virus.

Acute fatty liver of pregnancy Abbreviated AFLP, liver failure in late pregnancy, usually of unknown cause. Symptoms include nausea and vomiting, abdominal pain, yellowing of the skin and eyes (jaundice), frequent thirst (polydipsia), increased urination (polyuria), headache, and altered mental state.

Acute care bed A formula used to determine hospital bed needs.

Acute care hospital Care given to patients who generally require a stay of up to seven days and that focuses on a physical or mental condition requiring immediate intervention and constant medical attention, equipment and personnel.

Acute rehabilitation Early rehabilitation phase as soon as medically stable. Primary emphasis is to provide intensive physical and cognitive restorative services in the early months following injury. Typical stay 3-4 months (short term). Based in medical facility.

ADA deficiency Lack of normal adenosine deaminase (ADA) activity, a genetic (inherited) condition causing one form of severe combined immuno-deficiency ((SCID) disease. It is said to be "combined" in that there is dysfunction of both B and T lymphocytes with impaired cellular immunity and decreased production of immunoglobulins. Adenosine deaminase is an enzyme that plays a key role in salvaging pur-ine molecules.

Adam's apple The familiar feature on the front of the neck that is the forward protrusion of the thyroid cartilage, the largest cartilage of the larynx. It tends to enlarge at adolescence, particularly in males. It is usually said to take its name from the extrabiblical story that a piece of the forbidden fruit stuck in Adam's throat.

Fig. *Adam's apple.*

Addison disease Long-term under-function of the outer portion of the adrenal gland. In medical terms, chronic insufficiency of the adrenal cortex. This may be due to a number of different insults to the adrenal including physical trauma, hemorrhage, and tuberculosis of the adrenal, and destruction of the cells in the pituitary gland that secrete ACTH (adrenocorticotropic hormone) which normally drives the adrenal.

Adaptogenic Helping the human organism adapt to stressful conditions.

Adaptation Fitting one's behaviour to meet the needs of one's environment, which often involves a modification of impulses, emotions, or attitudes.

Adaptive/assistive equipment An appliance or gadget which assists user in the operation of self-care, work or leisure activities.

Adenopathy Large or swollen lymph nodes. Lymph nodes can become enlarged as a result of inflammatory diseases, infection, or cancer. Synonymous with lympha-denopathy.

Addiction Dependence on a chemical substance to the extent that a physiological and/or psychological need is established. This may be manifested by any combination of the following symptoms: tolerance, preoccupation with obtaining and using the substance, use of the substance despite anticipation of probable adverse consequences, repeated efforts to cut down or control substance use, and withdrawal symptoms when the substance is unavailable or not used.

ADHD Attention-deficit/hyperactivity disorder.

Adjusted average per capita cost A county-level estimate of the average cost incurred by medicare for each beneficiary in the fee-for-service system.

Adjusted community rating Community rating impacted by group specific demo-graphics.

Adjustment carer payment A one-off payment helping families with increased costs following a sudden accident, illness or disability involving a child aged under seven year.

Adjustment disorder An imprecise term referring to emotional or behavioural symptoms that develop in response to an identifiable stressor. The symptoms, which may include anxiety, depressed mood, and disturbance of conduct, are clinically significant in that the distress exceeds what would be expected under the circumstances, or significant impairment in social or occupational functioning is produced. Duration of symptoms tends to be self-limited, not persisting more than 6 months after termination of the stressor or its consequences. Sometimes the disorder is designated as 'acute' if duration is 6 months or less, and as 'persistent' or 'chronic' if symptoms endure beyond 6 months.

Adjustment Often transitory functional alteration or accommodation by which one can better adapt oneself to the immediate environment and to one's inner self.

Adjuvant therapy During cancer treatment, additional or adjuvant treatment is given to destroy any cancer cells that may have spread. Adjuvant treatment is usually systemic, meaning a treatment that affects the entire body. This allows the treatment to attack cancerous cells wherever they are present. The most common example of adjuvant therapy is chemotherapy given after a tumour has been surgically removed.

Administration on aging An agency of the U.S. Department of Health and Human Services. AOA is an advocate agency for older persons and their concerns at the federal level. AOA works closely with its nation-wide network of state and Area Agencies on Aging (AAA).

Administrative costs Savings Reductions in expenditures related to changes in the administrative costs associated with the provision of health care coverage and services.

Administrative loading The amount added to the prospective actuarial cost of the health care services (pure premium) for administrative, marketing expenses and profit.

Administrative reform Reducing paperwork though simplified universal forms or electronic filing and processing of claims.

Administrative services An agency that delivers administrative services to an employer group. This type of arrangement usually requires the employer to be at risk for the cost of health care services provided.

Administrative services organization An entity which only provides administrative services (including claims adjudication, member services, and management information reporting).

Administrator An administrator is licensed by the state to supervise a nursing home. This person is ultimately responsible for all nursing home activities.

Adult day care A programme of social and health-related services provided during the day in a community group setting. The purpose of the programme is to support frail or impaired elderly, or other disabled adults who can benefit from care in a group setting outside the home.

Adult day health care Provision of care and services in a residential health care facility or approved extension site, on an outpatient basis, under the medical direction of a physician. Services are in accord with a comprehensive assessment of care needs and individualized health care plan.

Adult foster care An elderly person's placement with another family when independent living is no longer possible, but nursing care is not necessary.

Adult protective services Social service interventions for impaired adults at risk of abuse, neglect or exploitation.

Advanced directives A written statement of an individual's preferences and directions regarding health care. Advanced Directives protect a person's rights even if he or she becomes mentally or physically unable to choose or communicate his or her wishes.

Advanced Practice Nurse A regis-

Fig. *Adult day care*

tered nurse who is approved by the Board of Nursing to practice nursing in a specified area of advanced nursing practice. APN is an umbrella term given to a registered nurse who has met advanced educational and clinical practice requirements beyond the two to four years of basic nursing education required for all RNs.

Advanced Registered Nurse Practitioner (ARNP) In addition to professional nursing, the ARNP may perform acts of medical diagnosis and treatment, prescription, and operation, which are identified and approved in their identified protocols as signed by the physician and by their license in the state of florida.

Adverse selection Among applicants for a given group or individual health insurance program, the tendency for those with an impaired health status, or who are prone to higher-than-average utilization of benefits, to be enrolled in disproportionate numbers in lower deductible plans.

Aerobic bacteria are bacteria that can grow and live in the presence of oxygen.

Aerophagy An excess of air in the alimentary canal that is relieved through burping or flatulence.

Aflatoxins are toxins produced by a mold that grows in nuts, seeds, and legumes. Although afla-toxins are known to cause cancer in animals, the U.S. Food and Drug Administration (FDA) al-lows them at low levels in nuts, seeds, and legumes because they are considered "unavoidable contaminants."

Affect Behaviour that expresses a subjectively experienced feeling state (emotion); affect is responsive to changing emotional states, whereas mood refers to a pervasive and sustained emotion. Common affects are euphoria, anger, and sadness.

Affective disorder A disorder in which mood change or disturbance is the primary manifestation. Now referred to as mood disorder. See depression.

Affective Psychosis Affective psychosis produces intense changes in mood, either to severe depression with diminution in levels of activity or elation with excessive activity.

Aflatoxin A harmful substance made by certain types of mold (Aspergillus flavus and Aspergillus parasiticus) that is often found on poorly stored grains and nuts. Consumption of foods contaminated with afla-toxin is a risk factor for primary liver cancer.

Age-Associated Memory Impairment Mild memory loss that increases with age. Mild memory loss is normal and should not be confused with forms of dementia, which are progressive and affect every day living.

Aging changes in the face The typical appearance of the face and neck changes with age. Muscle tone may be lost, causing a flabby or droopy appear-

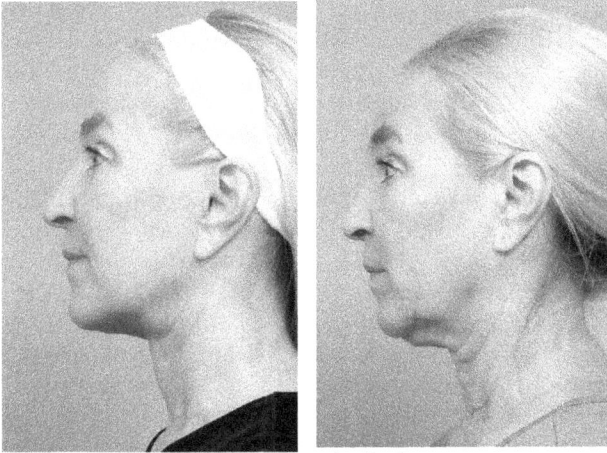

Fig. *Aging changes in the face*

ance. The jowls may begin to sag, leading to a "double chin" in some people. In some people the nose lengthens slightly and may look more prominent. There also may be an increase in the number, size, and colour of coloured spots on the face. This is largely due to sun exposure. The skin may thin, become dryer, and develop wrinkles. Although wrinkles are inevitable to some extent, sun exposure and cigarette smoking are likely to make them develop faster.

Agency for health care policy and research A Federal agency within the Public Health Service responsible for research on quality, appropriateness, effectiveness and cost of health care.

Agranulocytosis means a failure of the bone marrow to make enough white blood cells (neutrophils). Bone marrow is the soft tissue inside bones that helps form blood cells.

Aggression Forceful physical, verbal, or symbolic action. May be appropriate and self- protective, including healthy self-assertiveness, or inappropriate as in hostile or destructive behaviour. May also be directed toward the environment, toward another person or personality, or toward the self, as in depression.

Agitation Excessive motor activity, usually nonpurposeful and associated with internal tension. Examples include inability to sit still, fidgeting, pacing, wringing of hands, and pulling of clothes.

Agoraphobia Anxiety about being in places or situations in which escape might be difficult or embarrassing or in which help may not be available should a panic attack occur. The fears typically relate to venturing into the open, of leaving the familiar setting of one's home, or of being in a crowd, standing in line, or traveling in a car or train. Although agoraphobia usually occurs as a part of panic disorder, agoraphobia without a history of panic disorder has been described.

Ague An intermittent fever, sometimes with chills, as in malaria.

Aid to families with dependant children A Federally supported, state-administered program established by the Social Security Act of 1935 that provides financial support for children under the age of 18 (and their caretakers) who have been deprived of parental support or care because of the parent's death, continued absence from the home, unemployment, or physical or mental illness.

Albinism is a defect of melanin production that results in little or no colour (pigment) in the skin, hair, and eyes.

Alcohol dependence Dependence on alcohol characterized by either tolerance to the agent or development of withdrawal phenomena on cessation of, or reduction in, intake. Other aspects of the syndrome are psychological dependence and impairment in social and/or vocational functioning. This is also called alcoholism.

Alcohol hallucinosis An organic mental disorder consisting of auditory hallucinations occurring in a clear sensorium, developing shortly after the reduction or cessation of drinking, usually within 48 hours. The disorder commonly follows prolonged and heavy alcohol use.

Alcohol psychosis A group of major mental disorders associated with organic brain dysfunction due to alcohol; in DSM-IV, categorized as alcohol-induced psychotic disorder. Includes delirium tremens and alcohol hallucinosis.

Alcohol use disorders In DSM-IV, this group includes alcohol dependence, alcohol abuse, alcohol intoxication, alcohol withdrawal, alcohol delirium, alcohol persisting dementia, alcohol persisting amnestic disorder, alcohol psychotic disorder, alcohol mood disorder, alcohol anxiety disorder, alcohol sleep disorder, and alcohol sexual dysfunction. See abuse, substance; dependence, substance; intoxication, alcohol; withdrawal symptoms, alcohol.

Alcohol, drug abuse, and mental health administration An agency in the U.S. Department of Health and Human Services that was replaced in 1992 by the Substance Abuse and Mental Health Services Administration (SAM-HSA). In reorganizing ADAM-HA into SAMHSA, the three ADAMHA research institutes, the National Institute on Alcohol Abuse and Alcoholism (NIA-AA), the National institute on Drug Abuse (NIDA), and the National Institute of Mental Health (NIMH), were moved to the National Institutes of Health. What remain in

SAMHSA are the substance abuse and mental health services programmes.

Aldosterone A steroid hormone made by the adrenal cortex (the outer layer of the adrenal gland). It helps control the balance of water and salts in the kidney by keeping sodium in and releasing potassium from the body. Too much aldosterone can cause high blood pressure and a build-up of fluid in body tissues.

Aldolase test Aldolase is a protein (called an enzyme) that helps break down certain sugars into energy. It is found in high amounts in muscle tissue. A test can be done to measure the amount of aldolase in your blood.

Alkaptonuria is a rare condition in which a person's urine turns a dark brownish-black colour when exposed to air.

Allergic conjunctivitis is inflammation of the tissue lining the eyelids (conjunctiva) due to a reaction from allergy-causing substances such as pollen and

dander. Symptoms may be seasonal and can include:
- Intense itching or burning eyes.
- Puffy eyelids, especially in the morning.
- Red eyes.
- Stringy eye discharge.
- Tearing (watery eyes).
- Widened (dilated) vessels in the clear tissue covering the white of the eye.

Lubricating eye drops can help decrease symptoms. You can relieve discomfort by applying cool compresses to the eyes. Over-the-counter oral antihistamines can provide more relief. However, they can sometimes make the eyes dry.

Allergic reactions are sensitivities to substances called allergens that come into contact with the skin, nose, eyes, respiratory tract, and gastrointestinal tract. They can be breathed into the lungs, swallowed, or injected.

Allergic rhinitis is a group of symptoms affecting the nose. These symptoms occur when you breathe in something you are allergic to, such as dust, dander, insect venom, or pollen.

Allergy skin tests are tests used to find out which substances cause a person to have an allergic reaction.

Alopecia areata is a medical condition in which hair is lost from some or all areas of the body, usually from the scalp. Because it causes bald spots on the scalp,

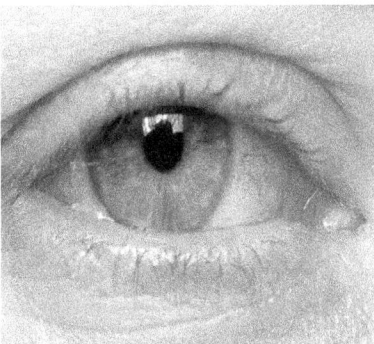
Fig. *Allergic conjunctivitis*

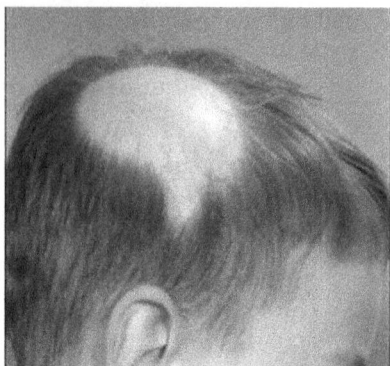

Fig. *Alopecia areata*

especially in the first stages, it is sometimes called spot baldness. Typical first symptoms of alopecia areata are small bald patches. The underlying skin is unscarred and looks superficially normal. These patches can take many shapes, but are most usually round or oval. Alopecia areata most often affects the scalp and beard, but may occur on any hair-bearing part of the body. Different skin areas can exhibit hair loss and regrowth at the same time.

ALP–blood test Alkaline phosphatase (ALP) is a protein found in all body tissues. Tissues with particularly high amounts of ALP include the liver, bile ducts, and bone. A blood test can be done to measure the level of ALP.

Allopathic One of two schools of medicine that treats disease by inducing effects opposite to those produced by the disease. The other school of medicine is osteopathic.

Allowable charge Generic term referring to the maximum fee that a third party will use in de-

termining reimbursement for a given service or supply. An allowable charge may not always be the same as the actual charge.

Allowable costs Charges for services rendered or supplies furnished by a health care provider, which qualify as covered expenses for insurance purposes.

All-payer system A plan to impose uniform prices on medical services, regardless of who's paying.

Alterative A medicinal substance that gradually restores health and the nutritional state of the body.

Alternative delivery sites Substitute for traditional inpatient sites for care such as ambulatory care centers, surgicenters, home care, hospice care, or alternative delivery and financing systems such as health maintenance organizations (HMOs), or preferred provider arrangements.

Alternative delivery system (ADS) An alternative to traditional inpatient care such as ambulatory care, home health care and same day surgery. Also used as an expression to describe all forms of health care delivery systems other than traditional fee-for-service indemnity health care.

Alternative levels of care Alternatives to traditional acute impatient care, such as ambulatory care centers, surgicenters, home care, skilled nursing facilities, and hospices.

Alzheimer's degenerative Age-related disease that impairs an individual's cognitive ability. Symptoms may include forgetfulness, wandering, and inability to recognize others. The disease is caused by neuron dysfunction and death in specific brain regions responsible for cognitive functions. Both genetic and environmental factors likely play a role in the development of Alzheimer's.

Alternative medicine refers to treatments that are used instead of conventional (standard) ones. If you use an alternative treatment along with conventional medicine or therapy, it's considered complementary therapy. There are many forms of alternative medicine. For many people, acupuncture is an effective means of relieving pain. This may be particularly true for back pain and headache pain.

Alveolar abnormalities are changes in the tiny air sacs in the lungs, called alveoli. The alveoli allow oxygen to enter the blood. They are very thin to let oxygen move from the lungs to the blood vessels, and for carbon dioxide to be removed from the blood vessels to the lungs. Alveolar abnormalities are changes in the tiny air sacs in the lungs, called alveoli. The alveoli allow oxygen to enter the blood. They are very thin to let oxygen move from the lungs to the blood vessels, and for carbon dioxide to be removed from the blood vessels to the lungs.

Alzheimer's disease A progressive and irreversible organic disease, typically occurring in the elderly and characterized by degeneration of the brain cells, leading to dementia, of which Alzheimer's is the single most common cause.

Progresses from forgetfulness to severe memory loss and disorientation, lack of concentration, loss of ability to calculate numbers and finally to increased severity of all symptoms and significant personality changes.

Amaurosis fugax is loss of vision in one eye due to a temporary lack of blood flow to the retina. It may be a sign of an impending stroke.

Amblyopia, or 'lazy eye,' is the loss of one eye's ability to see details. It is the most common cause of vision problems in children. Amblyopia occurs when the nerve pathway from one eye to the brain does not develop during childhood.

Ambivalence The coexistence of contradictory emotions, attitudes, ideas, or desires with respect to a particular person, object, or situation. Ordinarily, the ambivalence is not fully conscious and suggests psychopathology only when present in an extreme form.

Ambulance restocking The practice of hospital replenishing certain drugs and supplies used by an ambulance service during transport of a patient to the hospital.

Ambulatory Able to get from one place to another independently (even if using assistive devices such as manual wheelchairs, canes or walkers).

Ambulatory care Care given to patients who do not require overnight hospitalization.

Ambulatory patient group A payment system that pays a fixed price for certain types of outpatient procedures.

Ambulatory setting An institutional health setting in which organized health services are provided on an outpatient basis, such as surgery centre, clinic or other outpatient facility. Ambulatory care settings also may be mobile units of services, e.g., mobile mammography, MRI.

Ambulatory surgical centre Free-standing centres that perform surgeries which do not require an overnight stay.

Ambulatory The ability to walk liberally and independently not confined to bed.

Ambulatory utilization management Review prior to service against established standards to determine the medical necessity and appropriateness of the care to be provided in an ambulatory setting. The selection of treatment plans subject to pre-service review may be based upon criteria such as proposed care that would require frequent visits, expensive therapy, an extended course of therapy, or costly technology. Concurrent review would be applied as appropriate.

Amebic liver abscess is a collection of pus in the liver in response to an intestinal parasite. Amebic liver abscess is caused by Entamoeba histolytica, the same parasite that causes amebiasis, an intestinal infection that is also called amebic dysentery. After an infection has occurred, the parasite may be carried by the blood from the intestines to the liver.

Amitriptyline hydrochloride overdose is a type of prescription medicine called a *tricyclic antidepressant*. Amitriptyline hydrochloride overdose occurs when someone accidentally or intentionally takes more than the normal or recommended amount of this medication. This is for information only and not for use in the treatment or management of an actual poison exposure.

Amniotic fluid is a clear, slightly yellowish liquid that surrounds the developing foetus within the amniotic sac, a membranous structure that forms inside the uterus in pregnancy. It is contained in the amniotic sac.

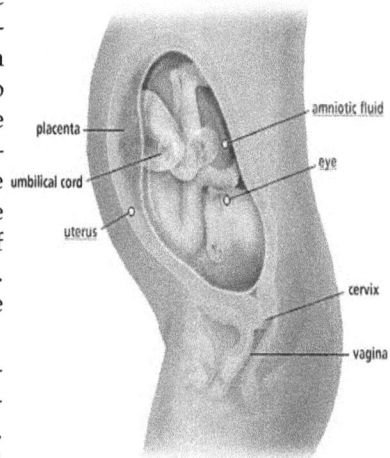

Fig. *Amniotic fluid*

Amniotic fluid is "inhaled" and "exhaled" by the fetus. It is essential that fluid be breathed into the lungs in order for them to develop normally. Swallowed amniotic fluid also creates urine and contributes to the formation of meconium. As well, amniotic fluid protects the developing baby by cushioning against blows to the mother's abdomen, allows for easier fetal movement, and promotes muscular/skeletal development. Amniotic fluid is essential not only to protect the fetus but also for proper fetal development.

Amylase – blood Amylase is an enzyme that helps digest carbohydrates. It is produced in the pancreas and the glands that make saliva. When the pancreas is diseased or inflamed, amylase releases into the blood. A test can be done to measure the level of this enzyme in your blood.

Amylase-urine This is a test that measures the amount of amylase in urine. Amylase is an enzyme that helps digest carbohydrates. It is produced mainly in the pancreas and the glands that make saliva.

American accreditation healthcare commission Formerly known as the Utilization Review Accreditation Commission, AAHC/URAC is an independent not-for-profit corporation which develops national standards for utilization review and managed care organizations.

American association of homes and services for the aging It represents not-for-profit organizations dedicated to providing high quality health care, housing and services to the nation?s elderly. Its memberships consists of over 5,000 not-for-profit nursing homes, continuing care retirement communities, senior housing facilities, assisted living and community services.

AAHSA organizations serve more than one million older persons of all income levels, creed and races. It serves these members by representing the concerns of not-for-profit organizations that serve the elderly through interaction with Congress and Federal agencies. It also strives to enhance the professionalism of practitioners and facilities through the Certification Program for Retirement Housing professionals, the Continuing Care Accreditation Commission, conferences and programmes offered by the AAHSA Professional Development Institute and publications representing current thinking in the long-term care and retirement housing fields.

American college of healthcare executives An international professional society of nearly 30,000 healthcare executives. ACHE is known for it's prestigious credentialing and educational programmes. ACHE is also known for its journal and magazines as well as groundbreaking research and career development and public policy programmes. ACHE' publishing division is a major publisher of books and journals on all aspects of health services management in addition to textbooks for use in college and university courses. Through its efforts, ACHE works toward its goal of improving the health status of society by advancing healthcare management excellence.

American health care association A trade association representing nursing homes and long term care facilities in the United States; based in Washington, D.C.

American hospital association A national association that represents allopathic and osteopathic hospitals in the United States; based in Washington, D.C. with operational offices in Chicago.

American Medical Association A national association organized into local and regional societies that represent over 700,000 medical doctors in the United States; based in Chicago. American with Disabilities Act (ADA) A Federal law which prohibits employers of more than 25 employees from discriminating against any individual with a disability who can perform the essential functions, with or without accommodations, of the job that the individual holds or wants.

Amenorrhoea is the absence of a menstrual period in a woman of reproductive age. Physiological states of amenorrhoea are seen during pregnancy and lactation (breastfeeding), the latter also forming the basis of a form of contraception known as the *lactational amenorrhoea* method.

Amnesia Pathologic loss of memory; a phenomenon in which an area of experience becomes inaccessible to conscious recall. The loss in memory may be organic, emotional, dissociative, or of mixed origin, and may be permanent or limited to a sharply circumscribed period of time.

Amphetamine use disorders In DSM-IV, this group includes amphetamine (or related substance) dependence, amphetamine abuse, amphetamine intoxication, amphetamine withdrawal, amphetamine delirium, amphetamine psychotic disorder, amphetamine mood disorder, amphetamine anxiety disorder, amphetamine sexual dysfunction, and amphetamine sleep disorder.

Amphetamines A group of chemicals that stimulate dopamine release in the central nervous system; often misused by adults and adolescents to control normal fatigue and to induce euphoria. Used clinically to treat hyper-kinetic disorder and narcolepsy.

Anaesthetic Numbs the nerves and causes loss of sensation.

Analgesic A medicine which relieves or reduces pain.

Anal fissure An anal fissure is a small split or tear in the thin moist tissue (mucosa) lining the lower rectum (anus). Anal fissures are extremely common in young infants but may occur at any age.

Analgesic nephropathy involves damage to one or both kidneys caused by overexposure to mixtures of medications, especially over-the-counter pain remedies (analgesics).

Anaphrodisiac or antiaphrodisiac is something that quells or blunts the libido. It is the opposite of an aphrodisiac, something that enhances sexual appetite.

Anaplastic thyroid cancer grows very rapidly and is an invasive type of thyroid cancer. It occurs most often in people over age 60. Anaplastic cancer accounts for only about 1% of all thyroid cancers.

Ancillary care A term used to describe additional services performed related to care, such as lab work, X-ray and anesthesia.

Ancillary charge Its also referred to as hospital 'extras' or miscellaneous hospital charges. They are supplementary to a hospital's daily room and board charge. They include such items as charges for drugs, medicines and dressings; laboratory services; x-ray examinations; and use of the operating room.

Androgyny A combination of male and female characteristics in one person.

Anesthetic A drug used to prevent pain during surgery or other procedure. A general anesthetic makes the person unconscious. A local anesthetic numbs the area where the surgery is to be performed. Local anesthetics may be combined with sedatives to make a person relax and sleepy but not unconscious.

Aneurysm An aneurysm is an abnormal widening or ballooning of a portion of an artery due to weakness in the wall of the blood vessel.

Aneurysm in the brain An aneurysm is a weak area in the wall of a blood vessel that causes the blood vessel to bulge or balloon out. When an aneurysm occurs in a blood vessel of the brain, it is called a cerebral aneurysm.

Anisocoria is unequal pupil size. The pupil is the black part in the center of the eye. It gets larger in dim light and smaller in bright light.

Ankylosing spondylitis is a long-term disease that involves inflammation of the joints between the spinal bones, and the joints between the spine and pelvis. These joints become swollen and inflamed. Over time, the affected spinal bones join together.

Anhedonia Inability to experience pleasure from activities that usually produce pleasurable feelings.

Anhydrotic Stops sweating.

Anniversary reaction An emotional response to a previous event occurring at the same time of year. Often the event involved a loss and the reaction involves a depressed state. The reaction can range from mild to severe and may occur at any time after the event.

Anodyne A pain-relieving medicine, milder than analgesic.

Anomie Apathy, alienation, and personal distress resulting from the loss of goals previously valued. Emile Durkheim popularized this term when he listed it as a principal reason for suicide.

Anonymous testing site a location designated by the 'Ontario Ministry of Health' where doctors are exempt from reporting the identity of people having HIV tests to public health; you do not have to use your real name or produce a health card.

Anorexia nervosa An eating disorder characterized by refusal or inability to maintain minimum normal weight for age and height combined with intense fear of gaining weight, denial of the seriousness of current low weight, undue influence of body weight or shape on self-evaluation, and, in females, amenorrhea or failure to menstruate. Weight is typically 15% or more below normal, and bility is characteristic, such as excessive familiarity with relative strangers or lack of selectivity in choice of attachment figures. The majority of children who develop this disorder (either type) are from a setting in which care has been grossly pathogenic. Either the caregivers have continually disregarded the child's basic physical and emotional needs, or repeated changes of the primary caregiver have prevented the formation of stable attachments.

Anorectal abscess An anorectal abscess is a collection of pus in the area of the anus and rectum.

Anterior cruciate ligament An anterior cruciate ligament injury is the over-stretching or tearing of the anterior cruciate ligament (ACL) in the knee. A tear may be partial or complete.

Anti-insulin antibody test The anti-insulin antibody test checks to see if your body has produced antibodies against insulin.

This test may be performed if you have, or are at risk for, type 1 diabetes. It also may be done if you appear to have an allergic response to insulin, or if insulin no longer seems to control your diabetes.

Blood is typically drawn from a vein, usually from the inside of the elbow or the back of the hand. The site is cleaned with a germ-killing medicine (antiseptic). The health care provider wraps an elastic band around the upper arm to apply pressure to the area and make the vein swell with blood.

The health care provider gently inserts a needle into the vein. The blood collects into an airtight vial or tube attached to the needle. The elastic band is removed from your arm. Once the blood has been collected, the needle is removed, and the puncture site is covered to stop any bleeding.

In infants or young children, a

sharp tool called a lancet may be used to puncture the skin and make it bleed. The blood collects into a small glass tube called a pipette, or onto a slide or test strip. A bandage may be placed over the area if there is any bleeding.

Anti-reflux surgery is surgery to correct a problem with the muscles at the bottom of the oesophagus (the tube from your mouth to the stomach). Problems with these muscles allow gastro-esophageal reflux disease (GERD) to happen.

Antidiarroheal drugs are medications used to treat loose, watery, and frequent stools.

Antigen An antigen is any substance that causes your immune system to produce antibodies against it. An antigen may be a foreign substance from the environment such as chemicals, bacteria, viruses, or pollen. An antigen may also be formed within the body, as with bacterial toxins or tissue cells.

Antithyroglobulin antibody is a test to measure antibodies to a protein called thyroglobulin, which is found in thyroid cells.

Attendant Term used most often by the disability community to refer to an aide who provides personal assistance in the community.

Attending physician A physician is the person responsible for the residents' medical care. A physician must visit residents in a skilled nursing facility once a month for the first three months, then every 60 days, and then every 90 days.

Aortic insufficiency is a heart valve disease in which the aortic valve does not close tightly. This leads to the backward flow of blood from the aorta (the largest blood vessel) into the left ventricle (a chamber of the heart).

Apoplexy is bleeding into an organ or loss of blood flow to an organ. For example, adrenal apoplexy is bleeding into the adrenal glands, pituitary apoplexy is bleeding into the pituitary gland, and so on.

Appendectomy An appendectomy is surgery to remove the appendix. The appendix is a small, finger-shaped organ that comes out from the first part of the large intestine. It is removed when it becomes swollen (inflamed) or infected. An appendix that has a hole in it (perforated) can leak and infect the entire abdomen area, which can be life threatening. An appendectomy is done using either—

Spinal anesthesia. Medicine is put into your back to make you numb below your waist. You will also get medicine to make you sleepy.

General anesthesia. You will be asleep and not feel any pain during the surgery.

The surgeon makes a small cut in the lower right side of your belly area and removes the appendix.

The appendix can also be removed using small surgical cuts

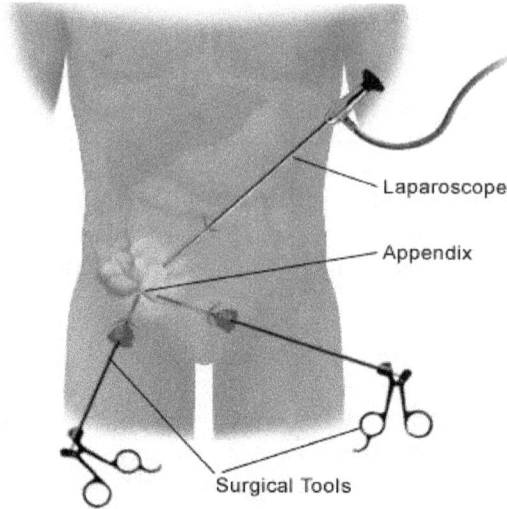

Fig. *Appendectomy*

and a camera. This is called a laparoscopic appendectomy.

If the appendix broke open or a pocket of infection (abscess) formed, your abdomen will be washed out during surgery. A small tube may be left in the belly area to help drain out fluids or pus.

Appendicitis means inflammation of the appendix. It is thought that appendicitis begins when the opening from the appendix into the cecum becomes blocked. The blockage may be due to a build-up of thick mucus within the appendix or to stool that enters the appendix from the cecum. The mucus or stool hardens, becomes rock-like, and blocks the opening. This rock is called a fecalith (literally, a rock of stool).At other times, the lymphatic tissue in the appendix might swell and block the appendix. After the blockage occurs, bacteria which normally are found within the appendix begin to invade (infect) the wall of the appendix. The body re-

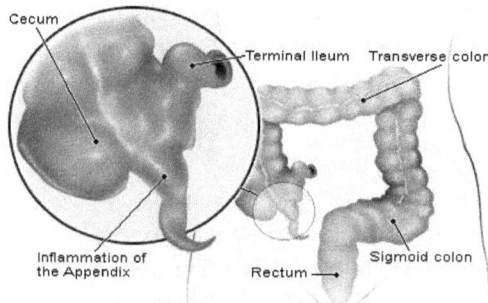

Fig. *Appendicitis*

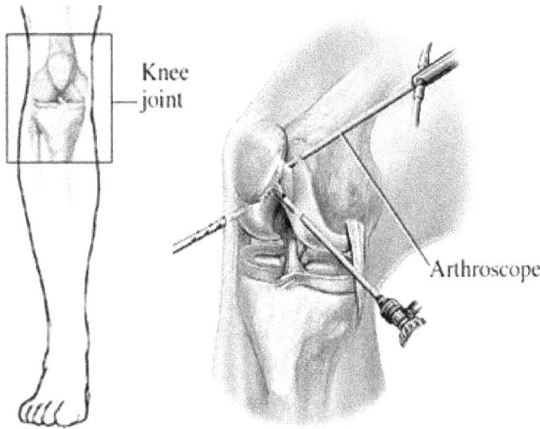

Fig. *Arthroscopy*

sponds to the invasion by mounting an attack on the bacteria, an attack called inflammation.

Arthroscopy is a pen-shaped instrument to which a tiny video camera and light source is attached. Anthroscope is a minimally invasive surgical procedure that allows an orthopedic surgeon to see and operate inside a joint using a device called an arthroscope. The arthroscope is inserted through very small incisions in the skin.

Asbestosis is a lung disease that occurs from breathing in asbestos fibres. Breathing in asbestos fibres can cause scar tissue (fibrosis) to form inside the lung. Scarred lung tissue does not expand and contract normally.

Audiologist/Audiology Health care professionals specializing in the measurement of hearing and the correction of hearing impairment or hearing loss.

Auditory hallucination Perception of sound, most frequently of voices but sometimes of clicks or other noises.

Autism is a developmental disorder that appears in the first 3 years of life, and affects the brain's normal development of social and communication skills.

Authorization As it applies to managed care, authorization is the approval of care, such as hospitalization. Pre-authorization may be required before a patient is admitted or care is given by (or reimbursed to) non-HMO providers.

Auto-assignment A term used with Medicaid mandatory managed care enrollment plans. Medicaid recipients who do not specify their choice for a contracted plan within a specified time frame are assigned to a plan by the state. They can also refer to assignment to primary care physicians.

Autonomic nervous system The

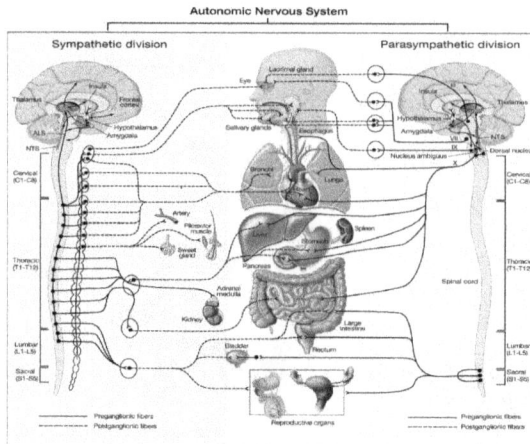

Fig. *Autonomic nervous system*

part of the nervous system that controls muscles of internal organs (such as the heart, blood vessels, lungs, stomach, and intestines) and glands (such as salivary glands and sweat glands). One part of the autonomic nervous system helps the body rest, relax, and digest food and another part helps a person fight or take flight in an emergency. It is also called ANS and involuntary nervous system.

AV node A small nodular mass of specialized muscle fibres located in the interatrial septum near the opening of the coronary sinus. It gives rise to the atrioventricular bundle of the conduction system of the heart.

Avoidance learning A response to a cue that is instrumental in avoiding a noxious experience.

Average length of stay (ALOS) A standard hospital statistic used to determine the average amount of time between admis-

sion and discharge for patients in a diagnosis related group (DRG), an age group, a specific hospital or other factors.

Aversion therapy is a form of psychological conditioning. The theory is the mind can be conditioned to respond a certain way by creating negative associations with 'unacceptable' behavioural patterns. These patterns include addiction or phobias.

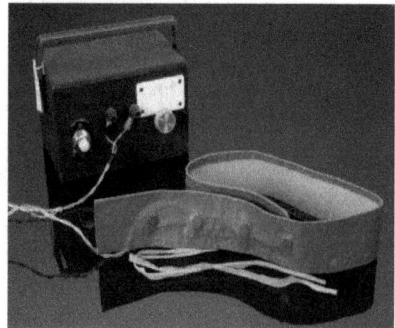

Fig. *Aversion therapy*

Awakening epilepsy A disorder characterized by recurrent episodes of paroxysmal brain dysfunction due to a sudden, disorderly, and excessive neuronal discharge. Epilepsy classification systems are generally based upon:

(i) clinical features of the seizure episodes (e.g., motor seizure),

(ii) etiology (e.g., post-traumatic),

(iii) anatomic site of seizure origin (e.g., frontal lobe seizure),

(iv) tendency to spread to other structures in the brain, and

(v) temporal patterns (e.g., nocturnal epilepsy).

Axon Nerve fibres that are capable of rapidly conducting impulses away from the neuron cell body.

Ayurvedic medicine The traditional Hindu system of medicine which is based on customs, beliefs, and practices of the Hindu culture. Ayurveda means 'the science of Life': veda-science, ayur-life.

B

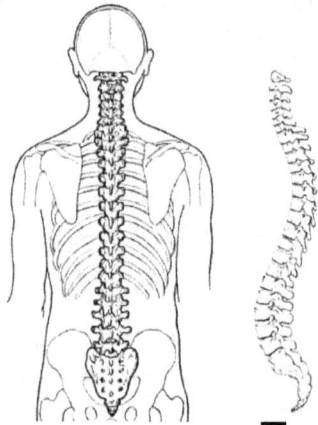

B12, Vitamin A Cobalt-containing coordination compound produced by intestinal micro-organisms and found also in soil and water. Higher plants do not concentrate vitamin B12 from the soil and so are a poor source of the substance as compared with animal tissues. Intrinsic factor is important for the assimilation of vitamin B12.

B7 Antigen A family of cell-surface proteins found on antigen-presenting cells. B7 antigens are ligands for specific cell surface receptor subtypes found on T-cells. They play an immuno-modulatory role by stimulating or inhibiting the T-cell activation process.

B Antibodies, hepatitis Antibodies to the hepatitis B antigens, including antibodies to the surface (Australia) and core of the dane particle and those to the "e" Antigens.

B Cells Lymphoid Cells concerned with Humoral Immunity. They are short-lived Cells resembling bursa-derived Lymphocytes of Birds in their production of Immunoglobulin upon appropriate stimulation.

B Cell activating factor A tumour necrosis factor superfamily member that plays a role in the regulation of B-lymphocyte survival. It occurs as a membrane-bound protein that is cleaved to release an biologically active soluble form with specificity to transmembrane activator and CAML interactor protein; B-cell activation factor receptor; and B-cell maturation antigen.

B Cell epitope Antigenic determinants recognized and bound by the B-cell receptor. Epitopes rec-

37

ognized by the B-cell receptor are located on the surface of the Antigen.

B Cell leukemia A malignant disease of the B-lymphocytes in the bone marrow and/or blood.

B Esterase Carboxylesterase is a serine-dependent esterase with wide substrate specificity. The enzyme is involved in the detoxification of Xenobiotics and the activation of ester and of amide prodrugs.

B Fibres Type B fibres are the small myelinated fibres with a diameter up to 3 um and neural conduction rates of 3-15 m/sec. They are mainly associated with the visceral autonomic nerves.

B Lymphocytes Lymphoid cells concerned with humoral immunity. They are short-lived cells resembling bursa-derived lymphocytes of birds in their production of immunoglobulin upon appropriate stimulation.

B Virus A species of simplexvirus that causes vesicular lesions of the mouth in monkeys. When the virus is transmitted to man it causes an acute encephalitis or encephalomyelitis, which is nearly always fatal.

B Vitamins A group of water-soluble Vitamins, some of which are coenzymes.

Babesia A genus of tick-borne protozoan parasites that infests the red blood cells of mammals, including humans. There are many recognized species, and the distribution is world-wide.

Bacillus A genus of bacillaceae that are spore-forming, rod-shaped cells. Most species are saprophytic soil forms with only a few species being pathogenic.

Bacillus phage Viruses whose host is bacillus. Frequently encountered bacillus-phages include bacteriophage phi 29 and bacteriophage phi 105.

Backache Acute or chronic pain located in the posterior regions of the thorax; lumbosacral region; or the adjacent regions.

Backbone The bones, muscles, tendons, and other tissues that reach from the base of the skull to the tailbone. The backbone encloses the spinal cord and the fluid surrounding the spinal cord. It is also called spinal column, spine, and vertebral column.

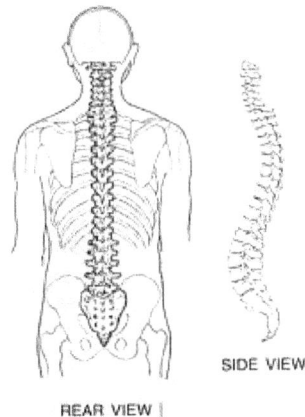

SIDE VIEW

REAR VIEW

Fig. *Backbone*

Back injuries General or unspecified injuries to the posterior part of the trunk. It includes injuries to the muscles of the back.

Bacterial vaccine Suspensions of attenuated or killed bacteria administered for the prevention or treatment of infectious bacterial disease.

Bacteria One of the three domains of life (the others being Eukarya and Archaea), also called *Eubacteria*. They are unicellular prokaryotic microorganisms which generally possess rigid cell walls, multiply by cell division, and exhibit three principal forms: *round* or coccal, *rodlike* or bacillary, and *spiral* or spirochetal. Bacteria can be classified by their response to oxygen— *aerobic, anaerobic,* or facultatively anaerobic; by the mode by which they obtain their energy— *chemotrophy* (via chemical reaction) or *phototrophy* (via Light reaction); for chemotrophs by their source of chemical energy: *Chemolithotrophy* (from inorganic compounds) or chemo-organotrophy (from organic compounds); and by their source for Carbon; Nitrogen; etc.; *hetrotrophy* (from organic sources) or *autotrophy* (from carbon dioxide). They can also be classified by whether or not they stain (based on the structure of their cell walls) with crystal violet dye— *gram-negative* or *gram-positive.*

Bacterial chromosome Structures within the nucleus of bacterial cells consisting of or containing DNA, which carry genetic information essential to the cell.

Bacterial conjunctivitis Purulent infections of the conjunctiva by several species of gram-negative, gram-positive, or acid-fast organisms. Some of the more commonly found genera causing conjunctival infections are Haemo-philus, Streptococcus, Neisseria, and Chlamydia.

Bacterial eye infections Infections in the inner or external eye caused by microorganisms belonging to several families of Bacteria. Some of the more common genera found are haemo-philus, Neisseria, Staphylo-coccus, Streptococcus, and Chla-mydia.

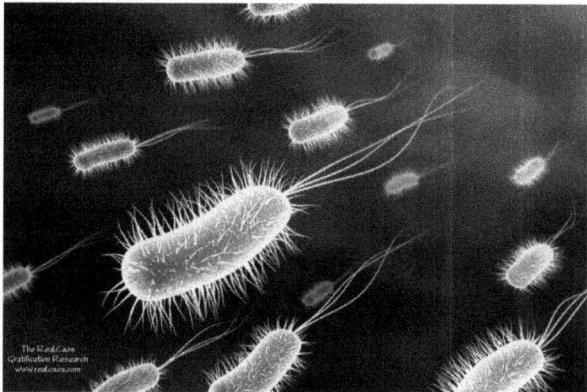

Fig. *Bacteria*

Bacterial inoculant Beneficial microorganisms (Bacteria or Fungi) encapsulated in carrier material and applied to the environment for remediation and enhancement of agricultural productivity.

Bacterial meningitis Bacterial Infections of the leptomeninges and subarachnoid space, frequently involving the cerebral cortex, cranial nerves, cerebral blood vessels, spinal cord, and nerve roots.

Bacterial pneumonia Inflammation of the lung parenchyma that is caused by bacterial infections.

Bacterial transformation The heritable modification of the properties of a competent bacterium by naked DNA from another source. The uptake of naked DNA is a naturally occuring phenomenon in some bacteria. It is often used as a gene transfer technique.

Bacterial translocation The passage of viable bacteria from the gastrointestinal tract to extraintestinal sites, such as the mesenteric lymph node complex, liver, spleen, kidney, and blood. Factors that promote bacterial translocation include overgrowth with gram-negative enteric bacilli, impaired host immune defenses, and injury to the Intestinal mucosa resulting in increased intestinal permeability. Bacterial translocation from the lung to the circulation is also possible and sometimes accompanies mechenical ventilation.

Bacterial vaccine Suspensions of attenuated or killed bacteria administered for the prevention or treatment of infectious bacterial disease.

Bacterial vaginitis Polymicrobial, nonspecific vaginitis associated with positive cultures of Gardnerella vaginalis and other anaerobic organisms and a decrease in lactobacilli. It remains unclear whether the initial pathogenic event is caused by the growth of anaerobes or a primary decrease in lacto-bacilli.

Bacterial venereal disease Bacterial diseases transmitted or propagated by sexual conduct.

Bacteriology The study of the structure, growth, function, genetics, and reproduction of bacteria, and bacterial infections.

Bacteriophage Viruses whose hosts are bacterial cells.

Bacteroides gingivalis A species of gram-negative, anaerobic, rod-shaped bacteria originally classified within the bacteroides genus. This bacterium produces a cell-bound, oxygen-sensitive collagenase and is isolated from the human mouth.

Bachelor of science in nursing A four-year program offered at colleges and universities that prepares nurses to practice across all health care settings. BSN graduates have the greatest opportunity for advancement. For instance, a BSN is required for entry into a master's program, which may in turn lead to a career in management, or on to more specialized nursing positions such as clinical nurse specialist, nurse practitioner, nurse educator, or nurse researcher.

Bag of waters The sac or "bag of waters" filled with amniotic fluid in which the developing baby grows. The membranes which make up the sac may occasionally rupture naturally as labour begins, but usually remain intact until the end of the first stage of labour. The membranes may also be broken by a midwife or doctor to speed up labour.

Baker cysts A synovial cyst located in the back of the knee, in the popliteal space arising from the semimembranous bursa or the knee joint.

Baker yeasts A species of the genus saccharomyces, family saccharomycetaceae, order saccharomycetales, known as "baker's" or "brewer's" yeast. The dried form is used as a dietary Supplement.

Balaenoptera A genus of whales in the family balaenopteridae, consisting of five species—blue whale, bryde's whale, fin whale, sei whale, and minke whale. They are distinguished by a relatively slender body, a compressed tail stock, and a pointed snout.

Baldness Absence of hair from areas where it is normally present.

Balkan nephropathy A form of chronic interstitial nephritis that is endemic to limited areas

of bulgaria, the former Yugoslavia, and romania. It is characterized by a progressive shrinking of the kidneys that is often associated with uroepithelial tumours.

Ballistocardiography Technique of graphic representation of the movements of the body imparted by the ballistic forces (recoil and impact) associated with cardiac contraction and ejection of blood and with the deceleration of blood flow through the large blood vessels. These movements, quantitatively very minute, are translated by a pickup device (Transducer) into an electrical potential which is suitably amplified and recorded on a conventional electrocardiograph or other recording machine.

Balloon angioplasty is a non-surgical procedure that relieves narrowing and obstruction of the arteries to the muscle of the heart (coronary arteries). This allows more blood and oxygen to be delivered to the heart mus-

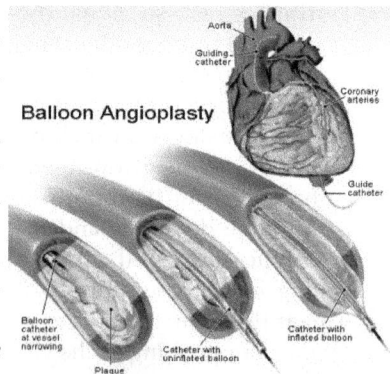

Balloon Angioplasty

Fig. *Balloon angioplasty*

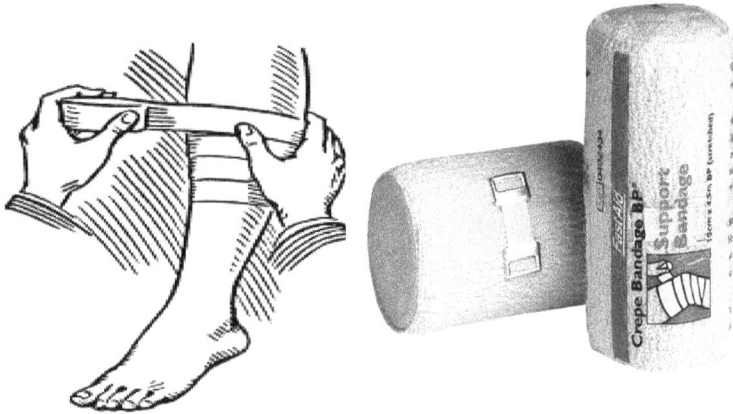

Fig. *Bandage*

cle. PTCA, is now referred to as percutaneous coronary intervention, or PCI, as this term includes the use of balloons, stents, and atherectomy devices. Percutaneous coronary intervention is accomplished with a small balloon catheter inserted into an artery in the groin or arm, and advanced to the narrowing in the coronary artery. The balloon is then inflated to enlarge the narrowing in the artery. When successful, percutaneous coronary intervention can relieve chest pain of angina, improve the prognosis of individuals with unstable angina, and minimize or stop a heart attack without having the patient undergo open heart coronary artery bypass graft (CABG) surgery.

Balloon tamponade The use of an inflatable sac to apply pressure in a lumen to stop the flow of blood or hemorrhage.

Balloon valvotomy Widening of a stenosed heart valve by the insertion of a balloon catheter into the valve and inflation of the balloon.

Bandage A bandage is a piece of material used either to support a medical device such as a dressing or splint, or on its own to provide support to the body; they can also be used to restrict a part of the body. During heavy bleeding or following a poisonous bite it is important to slow the flow of blood, tight bandages accomplish this task very well. Bandages are available in a wide range of types, from generic cloth strips, to specialized shaped bandages designed for a specific limb or part of the body, although bandages can often be improvised as the situation demands, using clothing, blankets or other material.

Band-aid surgery Surgery done through very small incisions that sometimes are covered with adhesive bandage strips; a common name for minimally invasive surgery

Bang disease A disease of cattle caused by bacteria of the genus brucella leading to abortion in late pregnancy. Brucella abortus is the primary infective agent.

Basal ganglia Groups of hundreds of thousands of neurons at the base of the cerebrum and in the upper brainstem; they help control well-learned movements (like walking) and sensation.

Basal thermometer A very accurate thermometer that measures a person's temperature to one tenth of a degree, e.g., 36.8 degrees. Basal thermometer provides Fahrenheit temperature readings to 1/100th of a degree – perfect for fertility charting and predicting ovulation. Other features include: a beeper to indicate peak temperature reading; an easy-to-read digital display; and memory recall of your last reading. The digital basal thermometer comes with a clear storage case, replaceable battery, and ovulation chart for recording and interpreting your results.

Base A set dollar amount to cover

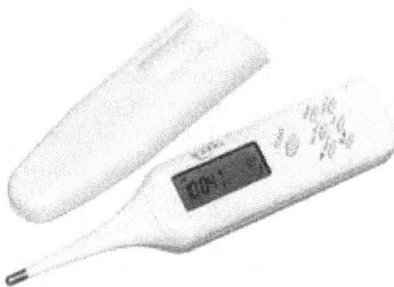

Fig. *Basal thermometer*

the cost of health care per covered person excluding mental health/substance abuse services, pharmacy and administrative charges.

BCG A weakened form of the bacterium *mycobacterium bovis* (bacillus calmette-guérin) that does not cause disease. BCG is used in a solution to stimulate the immune system in the treatment of bladder cancer and as a vaccine to prevent tuberculosis.

Bechterew disease A chronic inflammatory condition affecting the axial joints, such as the sacroiliac joint and other inter-vertebral or costovertebral joints. It occurs predominantly in young males and is characterized by pain and stiffness of joints (ankylosis) with inflammation at tendon insertions.

Bechterew syndrome Heterogeneous group of arthritic diseases sharing clinical and radiologic features. They are associated with the HLA-B27 antigen and some with a triggering infection. Most involve the axial joints in the spine, particularly the sacroiliac joint, but can also involve asymmetric peripheral joints. subsets include— ankylosing spondylitis; reactive arthritis; psoriatic arthritis; and others.

Bedrest Confinement of an individual to bed for therapeutic or experimental reasons.

Bedwetting It is involuntary urination while asleep after the age at which bladder control usually occurs. It is considered *pri-*

mary (PNE) when a child has not yet had a prolonged period of being dry. *Secondary* nocturnal enuresis (SNE) is when a child or adult begins wetting again after having stayed dry. It is also called *Nocturnal enuresis* or *night time urinary incontinence.*

Bedwetting children and adults can suffer emotional stress or psychological injury if they feel shamed by the condition. Treatment guidelines recommend that the physician counsel the parents, warning about psychological damage caused by pressure, shaming, or punishment for a condition children cannot control.

Behaviour disorder, REM A disorder characterized by episodes of vigorous and often violent motor activity during REM sleep (sleep, REM). The affected individual may inflict self injury or harm others, and is difficult to awaken from this condition. Episodes are usually followed by a vivid recollection of a dream that is consistent with the aggressive behaviour. This condition primarily affects adult males.

Behaviour modification The application of modern theories of learning and conditioning in the treatment of behaviour disorders.

Behaviour therapy The application of modern theories of learning and conditioning in the treatment of behaviour disorders.

Behaviour, compulsive The behaviour of performing an act persistently and repetitively without it leading to reward or pleasure. The act is usually a small, circumscribed Behaviour, almost ritualistic, yet not pathologically disturbing. Examples of compulsive behaviour include twirling of hair, checking something constantly, not wanting pennies in change, straightening tilted pictures, etc.

Behaviours, impulsive An act performed without delay, reflection, voluntary direction or obvious control in response to a stimulus.

Behaviour, obsessive Persistent, unwanted idea or impulse which is considered normal when it does not markedly interfere with mental processes or emotional adjustment.

Behaviours, paranoid Behaviour exhibited by individuals who are overly suspicious, but without the constellation of symptoms characteristic of paranoid personality disorder or paranoid type of *schizophrenia.*

Belly button surgery A common name for laparo-scopy, minimally invasive surgery on the abdomen

Benign breast disease A common condition marked by benign (not cancer) changes in breast tissue. These changes may include irregular lumps or cysts, breast discomfort, sensitive nipples, and itching. These symptoms may change throughout the menstrual cycle and usually stop after menopause. Also called fibrocystic breast changes, fibrocystic breast disease, and mammary dysplasia.

Benign essential blepharospasm Neurological disorder causing involuntary muscle contractions, with eyelid muscle spasms.

Bennett's fracture The Bennett's fracture is the most common type of fracture to the thumb metacarpal base. A Bennett's fracture is an intra-articular fracture, or one that extends into the joint between the metacarpal and wrist bone ("trapezium"). This injury most often occurs in contact sports such as football, rugby, and boxing.

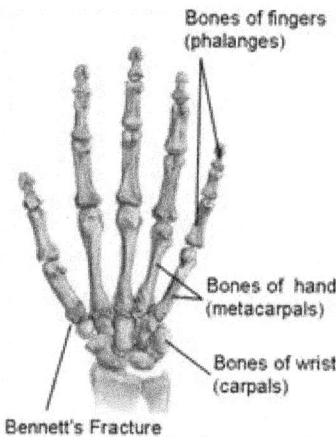

Bones of fingers (phalanges)

Bones of hand (metacarpals)

Bones of wrist (carpals)

Bennett's Fracture

Fig. *Bennett's fracture*

Beriberi A syndrome characterized by inflammation of multiple nerves (polyneuritis), heart disease (cardiopathy), and edema (swelling) due to a deficiency of thiamine (vitamin B1) in the diet.

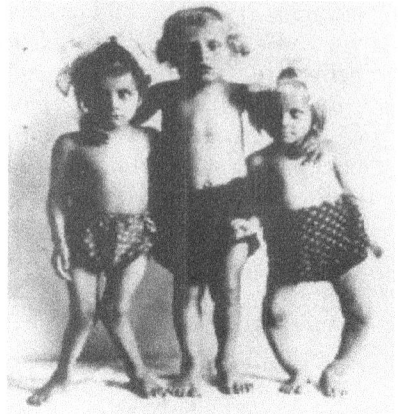

Fig. *Beriberi*

Bicuspid valve One of the four valves of the heart, this valve is situated between the left atrium and the left ventricle. It permits blood to flow one way only, from the left atrium into the left ventricle This valve is more commonly called the mitral valve because it has two flaps (cusps) and looks like a bishop's miter or headdress.

Bid (on prescription) Seen on a prescription, bid means twice (two times) a day. It is an abbreviation for "bis in die" which in Latin means twice a day. The abbreviation bid is sometimes written without a period either in lower-case letters as "bid" or in capital letters as "BID" or with periods as "b.i.d." However it is written, it is one of a number of hallowed abbreviations of Latin terms that have been traditionally used in prescriptions to specify the frequency with which medicines should be taken. Other examples include:
- q.d. (qd or QD) is once a day;

q.d. stands for "quaque die" (which means, in Latin, once a day).

- t.i.d. (or tid or TID) is three times a day ; t.i.d. stands for "ter in die" (in Latin, 3 times a day).
- q.i.d. (or qid or QID) is four times a day; q.i.d. stands for "quater in die" (in Latin, 4 times a day).
- q_h: If a medicine is to be taken every so-many hours, it is written "q_h"; the "q" standing for "quaque" and the "h" indicating the number of hours. So, for example, "2 caps q4h" means "Take 2 capsules every 4 hours."

Best corrected visual acuity (BCVA) The best vision you can achieve with correction (such as glasses), as measured on the standard Snellen eye chart. For example, if your uncorrected eyesight is 20/200, but you can see 20/20 with glasses, your BCVA is 20/20.

Beta blocker Drug that widens or dilates blood vessels, thus enabling more normal flow of blood. Topical beta blockers applied as eye drops also can lessen fluid production and lower internal eye pressure (intraocular pressure) in eye diseases such as glaucoma to reduce the possibility of optic nerve damage. Beta blockers also are used to control high blood pressure (hypertension). Side effects can include respiratory problems.

Bile A digestive chemical that is produced in the liver, stored in the gall bladder, and secreted into the small intestine.

Bile duct is green like the gall-bladder, because of bile stains. A bile duct is any of a number of long tube-like structures that carry bile.

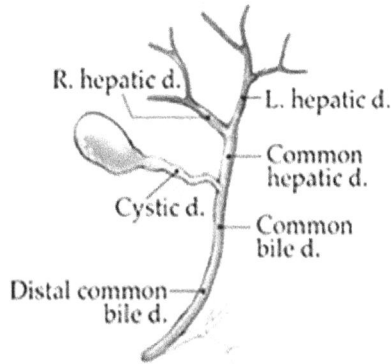

Fig. *Bile duct*

Bile duct cancer Patients with bile duct cancer most often become symptomatic when the cancer obstructs (blocks) the drainage of bile. Because bile cannot be excreted into the bowel, the bilirubin pigments accumulate in the blood, causing jaundice (yellowing of the skin and the whites of the eyes) in 90% of patients. The jaundice is usually associated with itching of the

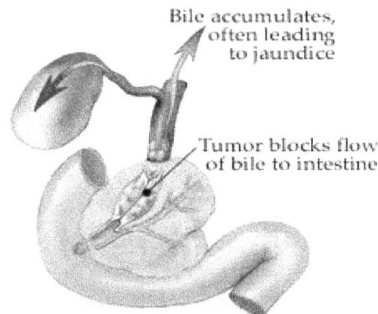

Fig. *Bile duct cancer*

skin (also called "pruritus"). The body compensates partially and excretes some of this bilirubin via the urine, so patients may have dark (cola colored) urine. Because bile cannot reach the intestine, the patient's stools become white (clay colored).

Bilirubin Bilirubin is a by-product of the normal breakdown of old red blood cells. Some newborn babies cannot metabolise it quickly enough, so it builds up under the skin to cause a harmless and temporary type of jaundice. If the bilirubin levels get too high it is stored in the brain and can cause brain damage, which is why some newborns are treated under photo-therapy lamps to break down the bilirubin.

Bifocal lens with one segment for near vision and one segment for far vision. The term "bifocal" can apply to both eyeglass lenses and contact lenses.

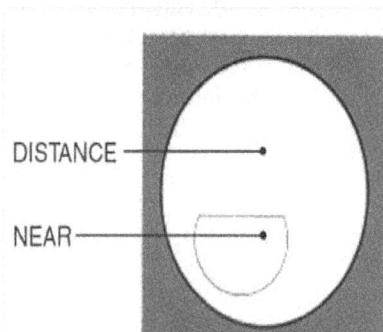

Fig. *Bifocal Lens*

Binocular vision Ability of both eyes to work together to achieve proper focus, depth perception and range of vision.

Biocompatible Able to coexist with living tissues without harming them. For example, artificial lenses are designed to be biocompatible with tissue inside the eye so they won't cause a toxic or immunilogical response that would harm the eye.

Bioptic telescopic lenses A bioptic is a combination two-lens optical system with a telescope(s) attached to a pair of glasses, above one's normal line of sight (see sample bioptic lens system below). These devices are prescription in nature and available through an optometrist or ophthalmologist who practices clinical low vision. These optical low vision aids are available in a number of different styles, sizes and powers. The most common telescopic units used for driving purposes range from 2.0X - 5.5X ("X" referring to the strength or power of magnification of the telescopic lens unit). For people with low vision who are qualified, telescopic lenses are attached above the driver's line of sight to help magnify objects such as road signs.

Fig. *Bioptic telescopic lenses*

Biological agent A substance that is made from a living organism or its products and is used in the prevention, diagnosis, or treatment of cancer and other diseases. Biological agents include antibodies, inter-leukins, and vaccines. Also called biologic agent and biological drug.

Biopsy Removal of a small amount of tissue for examination under a microscope to find out whether part of the body is diseased. A transrectal prostate biopsy is usually done with a device that contains a spring-loaded needle. The needle enters the prostate gland and removes a tissue sample quickly.

Bipolar disorders In DSM-IV, a group of mood disorders that includes bipolar disorder, single episode; bipolar disorder, recurrent; and cyclothymic disorder. A bipolar disorder includes a manic episode at some time during its course. In any particular patient, the bipolar disorder may take the form of a single manic episode (rare), or it may consist of recurrent episodes that are either manic or depressive in nature (but at least one must have been predominantly manic).

Birth canal The passage between the cervix and the outside world through which the baby travels on the way to being born; usually called the vagina.

Birth centre An alternative to a hospital where a woman can go through labour and delivery for a low-risk birth.

Birthing room A birthing room is a place designed and equipped for women giving birth.

Bisexual A person who is attracted to both men and women

Bisexuality Originally a concept of Freud, indicating a belief that components of both sexes could be found in each person. Today the term is often used to refer to persons who are capable of achieving orgasm with a partner of either sex.

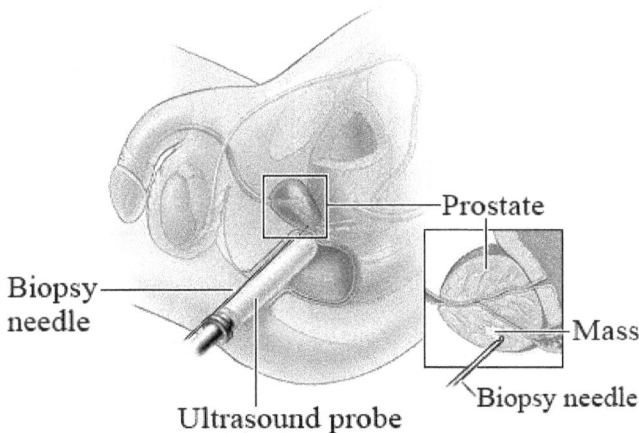

Fig. *Transrectal prostate biopsy*

Black fever A chronic disease caused by leishmania donovani and transmitted by the bite of several sandflies of the genera phlebotomus and lutzomyia. It is commonly characterized by fever, chills, vomiting, anemia, hepato-spleno-megaly, leukopenia, hyper-gammaglo-bulinemia, emaciation, and an earth-gray color of the skin. The disease is classified into three main types according to geographic distribution—Indian, mediterranean (or infantile), and African.

Black lung disease A diffuse parenchymal lung disease caused by accumulation of inhaled carbon or coal dust. The disease can progress from asymptomatic anthracosis to massive lung fibrosis. This lung lesion usually occurs in coal miners, but can be seen in urban dwellers and tobacco smokers.

Black water fever A complication of Malaria, Falciparum characterized by the passage of dark red to black urine.

Bladder A musculomembranous sac along the urinary tract. Urine flows from the kidneys into the bladder via the ureters (ureter), and is held there until *urination.*

Bladder stone Stones in the urinary Bladder; also known as vesical clculi, bladder stones, or cysto-liths.

Bladder tumour Tumours or cancer of the urinary bladder.

Bladder, neurogenic Dysfunction of the urinary bladder due to disease of the central or peripheral nervous system pathways involved in the control of urination. This is often associated with spinal cord diseases, but may also be caused by brain diseases or peripheral nerve diseases.

Blast injury Injuries resulting when a Person is struck by particles impelled with violent force from an explosion. Blast causes pulmonary concussion and hemor-rhage, laceration of other thoracic and abdominal viscera, ruptured ear drums, and minor effects in the central nervous system.

Blast phase An advanced phase of chronic myelogenous leukemia, characterized by a rapid increase in the proportion of immature white blood cells (blasts) in the blood and bone marrow to greater than 30%.

Blastocyst A post-morula preimplantation mammalian embryo

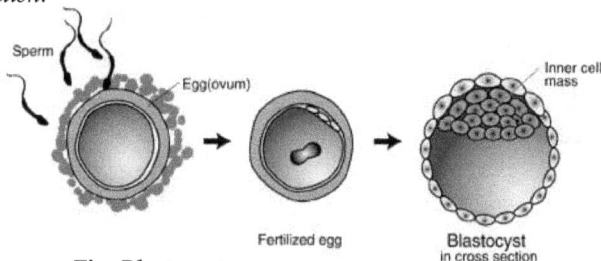

Fig. *Blastocyst*

that develops from a 32-cell stage into a fluid-filled hollow ball of over a hundred cells. A blasto-cyst has two distinctive tissues. The outer layer of tropho-blasts gives rise to extra-embryonic tissues. The inner cell mass gives rise to the embryonic disc and eventual embryo proper.

Blastocyst transfer The delayed transfer of embryos at the blastocyst stage provides a means to eliminate unhealthy embryos that do not develop normally. The selection and Transfer of superior blastocysts reduces the need for multiple-embryo transfer and the risks of high-order multiple gestation.

Bleeding Bleeding or escape of Blood from a vessel.

Blepharitis Inflammation of the eyelid(s), typically around the eyelashes. Various types of dermatitis, rosacea and allergic reactions can cause blepharitis. Symptoms include a red or pink eyelid, crusty lid or lashes, burning, foreign body sensation, eye or eyelid pain or discomfort, dry eyelid, dry eye, eyelash loss, grittiness, stickiness, eyelid swelling and tearing.

Blepharochalasis Excessive, drooping eyelid skin caused by recurring swelling. Blepharochalasis typically occurs in young people.

Blepharoconjunctivitis Inflammation of the eyelid and conjunctiva. Infections and allergic reactions are among the causes. Symptoms include a red or pink eye, a red or pink eyelid, pain or discomfort of the eye or around the eye, tearing, burning, eye dryness and eye stickiness.

Blepharospasm Involuntary increased blinking that progresses to spasms in both eyes. The exact cause is unknown, but doctors believe it to be a central nervous system disorder. It can produce a functional blindness since the patient can't open his or her eyes long enough to function visually.

Blind deaf disorders The absence of both hearing and vision.

Blindness The inability to see or the loss or absence of perception of visual stimuli. This condition may be the result of eye diseases; optic nerve diseases; optic chiasm diseases; or brain diseases affecting the visual pathways or occipital lobe.

Block, autonomic nerve Interruption of sympathetic pathways, by local injection of an anesthetic agent, at any of four levels—peripheral nerve block, sympathetic ganglion block, extradural block, and subarachnoid block.

Blockaders, ganglionic Agents having as their major action the interruption of neural transmission at nicotinic receptors on postganglionic autonomic neurons. Because their actions are so broad, including blocking of sympathetic and parasym-pathetic systems, their therapeutic use has been largely supplanted by more specific drugs. They may still be used in the control of blood pressure in patients with acute dissecting aortic aneurysm and for the induction of hypotension in surgery.

Blood The body fluid that circulates in the vascular system (Blood Vessels). Whole blood includes plasma and blood cells.

Blood cell The cells found in the body fluid circulating throughout the cardiovascular system.

Blood cell count A test to check the number of red blood cells, white blood cells, and platelets in a sample of blood. Also called CBC and complete blood count.

Blood circulation The movement of the blood as it is pumped through the cardiovascular system.

Blood clot A mass of blood that forms when blood platelets, proteins, and cells stick together. When a blood clot is attached to the wall of a blood vessel, it is called a thrombus. When it moves through the bloodstream and blocks the flow of blood in another part of the body, it is called an *embolus.*

Blood coagulation The process of the interaction of blood coagulation factors that results in an insoluble fibrin clot.

Blood coagulation disorder Hemor-rhagic and thrombotic disorders that occur as a consequence of abnormalities in blood coagulation due to a variety of factors such as coagulation protein disorders; blood

platelet disorders; blood nutritional conditions.

Blood coagulation factor Endogenous substances, usually proteins, that are involved in the blood coagulation process.

Blood coagulation factor deficiencies Hemorrhagic and thrombotic disorders resulting from abnormalities or deficiencies of coagulation proteins.

Blood coagulation factor inhibitors Substances, usually endogenous, that act as inhibitors of blood coagulation. They may affect one or multiple enzymes throughout the process. As a group, they also inhibit enzymes involved in processes other than blood coagulation, such as those from the complement system, fibrinolytic enzyme system, blood cells, and bacteria.

Blood component removal Any procedure in which Blood is withdrawn from a donor, a portion is separated and retained and the remainder is returned to the donor.

Blood component transfusion The Transfer of Blood components such as erythrocytes, leukocytes, platelets, and plasma from a donor to a recipient or back to the donor. This process differs from the procedures undertaken in plasmapheresis and types of cytapheresis; (plateletpheresis and leukapheresis) where, following the removal of plasma or the specific cell components, the remainder is transfused back to the donor.

Blood corpuscle The cells found in the body fluid circulating throughout the cardiovascular system.

Blood corpuscle, red Red Blood cells. Mature erythrocytes are non-nucleated, biconcave disks containing hemoglobin whose function is to transport oxygen.

Blood corpuscles, white White blood cells. These include granular leukocytes (basophils; eosi-nophils; and neutrophils) as well as non-granular leukocytes (lymphocytes and monocytes).

Blood dialysers Devices which can substitute for normally functioning kidneys in removing components from the blood by dialysis that are normally eliminated in the urine.

Blood diseases Disorders of the blood and blood forming tissues.

Blood gas analysis Measurement of oxygen and carbon dioxide in the Blood.

Blood glucose The main sugar that the body makes from the food in the diet. Glucose is carried through the bloodstream to provide energy to all cells in the body. Cells cannot use glucose without the help of insulin.

Glucose is a simple sugar (a monosaccharide). The body produces it from protein, fat and, in largest part, carbohydrate. Ingested glucose is absorbed directly into the blood from the intestine and results in a rapid increase in blood glucose.

Blood glucose self monitoring Self evaluation of whole blood glucose levels outside the clinical laboratory. A digital or battery-operated reflectance meter may be used. It has wide application in controlling unstable insulin-dependent diabetes.

Blood group antigens Sets of cell surface antigens located on blood cells. They are usually membrane glycoproteins or glycolipids that are antigenically distinguished by their carbohydrate moieties.

Blood group incompatibilities An antigenic mismatch between donor and recipient blood. Antibodies present in the recipient's serum may be directed against antigens in the donor product. Such a mismatch may result in a transfusion reaction in which, for example, donor blood is hemo-lysed.

Blood grouping and cross-matching testing Erythrocytes to determine presence or absence of Blood-group antigens, testing of serum to determine the presence or absence of antibodies to these antigens, and selecting biocom-patible blood by cross-matching samples from the donor against samples from the recipient. crossmatching is performed prior to transfusion.

Blood groups The classification systems (or schemes) based on the different antigens located on erythrocytes. The most well-known and medically important blood types are in the ABO click this icon to hear the pre-

ABO Blood Type	Antigen A	Antigen B	Antibody anti-A	Antibody Anti-B
A	yes	no	no	yes
B	no	yes	yes	no
O	no	no	yes	yes
AB	yes	yes	no	no

Fig. *Blood groups*

ceding term pronounced group. They were discovered in 1900 and 1901 at the University of Vienna by *Karl Landsteiner* in the process of trying to learn why blood transfusions sometimes cause death and at other times save a patient. In 1930, he belatedly received the Nobel Prize for his discovery of blood types. All humans and many other primates can be typed for the ABO blood group. There are four principal types: A, B, AB, and O. There are two antigens and two antibodies that are mostly responsible for the ABO types. The specific combination of these four components determines an individual's type in most cases. The table below shows the possible permutations of antigens and antibodies with the corresponding ABO type ("yes" indicates the presence of a component and "no" indicates its absence in the blood of an individual).

Blood nerve barrier The barrier between the perineurium of peripheral nerves and the endothelium (endothelium,

vascular) of endo-neurial capillaries. The perine-urium acts as a diffusion barrier, but ion permeability at the blood-nerve barrier is still higher than at the blood-brain barrier.

Blood physiology Physiological processes and properties of the blood.

Blood plasma The residual portion of blood that is left after removal of blood cells by centrifugation without prior blood coagulation.

Blood plasma volume Volume of plasma in the circulation. It is usually measured by indicator dilution techniques.

Blood platelets Non-nucleated disk-shaped cells formed in the megakaryocyte and found in the Blood of all mammals. They are mainly involved in blood coagulation.

Blood platelet count The number of platelets per unit volume in a sample of venous blood.

Blood preservation The process by which blood or its components are kept viable outside of the organism from which they are derived (i.e., kept from decay by means of a chemical agent, cooling, or a fluid substitute that mimics the natural state within the organism).

Blood poisoning Disease caused by the spread of bacteria and their toxins in the bloodstream. Also called septicemia and toxemia.

Blood pressure The force of circulating blood on the walls of the arteries. Blood pressure is taken using two measurements: systolic (measured when the heart beats, when blood pressure is at its highest) and diastolic (measured between heart beats, when blood pressure is at its lowest).

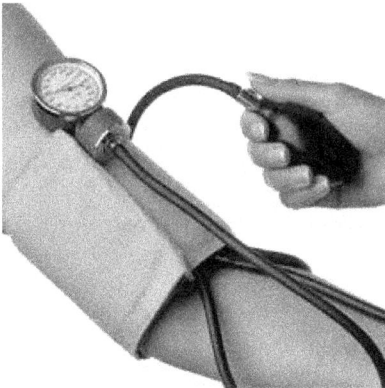

Fig. *Blood pressure*

Blood pressure is written with the systolic blood pressure first, followed by the diastolic blood pressure (for example 120/80).

Blood pressure monitor Devices for continuously measuring and displaying the arterial blood pressure.

Blood pressure, aortic Blood Pressure within Aorta.

Blood pressure, arterial The blood pressure in the arteries. It is commonly measured with a Sphyg-momanometer on the upper arm which represents the arterial pressure in the brachial artery.

Blood pressure, high Persistently high systemic arterial blood pressure. Based on multiple readings (blood pressure determination), hypertension is currently defined as when systolic pressure is consistently greater than 140 mm Hg or when diastolic pressure is consistently 90 mm Hg or more.

Blood pressure, low Abnormally low blood pressure that can result in inadequate blood flow to the Brain and other vital organs. common symptom is dizziness but greater negative impacts on the body occur when there is prolonged depravation of oxygen and nutrients.

Blood pressure, venous The blood pressure in the veins. It is usually measured to assess the filling pressure to the heart ventricle.

Blood proteins Proteins that are present in blood serum, including serum albumin; blood coagulation factors; and many other types of proteins.

Blood serum The clear portion of Blood that is left after blood coagulation to remove blood cells and clotting proteins.

Blood stain Antigenic characteristics and DNA fingerprint patterns identified from blood stains. Their primary value is in criminal cases.

Blood sugar The blood sugar concentration or blood glucose level is the amount of glucose (sugar) present in the blood of a human or animal. The body naturally tightly regulates blood glucose levels as a part of metabolic homeostasis.

Blood sugar self monitoring Self evaluation of whole blood glucose levels outside the clinical laboratory. A digital or battery-operated reflectance meter may be used. It has wide application in controlling unstable Insulin-dependent diabetes.

Blood test Tests used in the analysis of the hoemic system.

Blood transfusions The introduction of whole blood or blood component directly into the blood stream.

Blood urea nitrogen The urea concentration of the blood stated in terms of nitrogen content. Serum (plasma) urea nitrogen is approximately 12% higher than blood urea nitrogen concentration because of the greater protein content of red blood cells. Increases in blood or serum urea nitrogen are referred to as azotemia and may have prerenal, renal, or postrenal causes.

Blood vessels The blood vessels are the part of the circulatory system that transport blood throughout the body. There are three major types of blood vessels: the arteries, which carry the blood away from the heart, the capillaries, which enable the actual exchange of water and chemicals between the blood and the tissues; and the veins, which carry blood from the capillaries back towards the heart.

Blood vessel tumour Neoplasms composed of vascular tissue. This concept does not refer to neoplasms located in blood vessels.

Blood viscosity The internal resistance of the blood to shear forces. The in vitro measure of whole blood viscosity is of limited clinical utility because it bears little relationship to the actual viscosity within the circulation, but an increase in the viscosity of circulating blood can contribute to morbidity in patients suffering from disorders such as sickle cell anemia and polycythemia.

Blood volume Volume of circulating blood. It is the sum of the plasma volume and erythrocyte volume.

Blood volume determination Method for determining the circulating blood volume by introducing a known quantity of foreign substance into the blood and determining its concentration some minutes later when thorough mixing has occurred. From these two values the blood volume can be calculated by dividing the quantity of injected material by its concentration in the Blood at the time of uniform mixing. Generally expressed as cubic centimeters or liters per kilogram of body weight.

Blood-brain barrier The blood-brain barrier protects the brain from chemical intrusion from the rest of the body. Blood flowing into the brain is filtered so that many harmful chemicals cannot enter the brain.

Blood pool scintigraphy Radionuclide ventriculography where scintigraphic data is acquired during repeated cardiac cycles at specific times in the cycle, using an electrocardiographic synch-ronizer or gating device. Analysis of right ventricular function is difficult with this technique; that is best evaluated by first-pass ventriculography.

Blue mussel A species of mussel in the genus mytilus, family mytilidae, class bivalvia, known as the common mussel. It has a bluish-black shell and is highly edible.

Blue light Found in the light spectrum next to violet, which has the shortest wavelength of visible light. Also known as High Energy Visible (HEV) light, blue light has been linked to eye damage and diseases such as age-related macular degeneration.

Blue shields Health Insurance plan for costs of physicians' services.

Bocavirus A genus in the subfamily parvovirinae comprising three species—bovine parvovirus, canine minute virus, and human bocavirus.

Body composition The relative amounts of various components in the body, such as percentage of body fat.

Body constitution The physical characteristics of the body, including the mode of performance of functions, the activity of metabolic processes, the manner and degree of reactions to stimuli, and Power of resistance to the attack of pathogenic organisms.

Body fluids These are liquids that are inside the bodies of living. Fluids such as blood, semen, vaginal secretion, saliva, gastric juice, breast milk. Body fluids consist of the water of the body and substances dissolved in it. Water is the main component of the human body, and, in any individual, the body water content stays remarkably constant from day to day.

Boeck disease An idiopathic systemic inflammatory granulomatous disorder comprised of epithelioid and multinucleated giant cells with little necrosis. It usually invades the lungs with fibrosis and may also involve lymph nodes, skin, liver, spleen, eyes, phalangeal bones, and parotid glands.

Body mass index A measure that relates body weight to height. BMI is sometimes used to measure total body fat and whether a person is a healthy weight. Excess body fat is linked to an increased risk of some diseases including heart disease and some cancers.

Bone cancer Primary bone cancer is cancer that forms in cells of the bone. Some types of primary bone cancer are osteo-sarcoma, Ewing sarcoma, malignant fibrous histio-cytoma, and chondro-sarcoma. Secondary bone cancer is cancer that spreads to the bone from another part of the body (such as the prostate, breast, or lung).

Bone density A measure of the amount of minerals (mostly calcium and phosphorous) contained in a certain volume of bone. Bone density measurements are used to diagnose osteoporosis (a condition marked by decreased bone mass), to see how well osteoporosis treatments are working, and to predict how likely the bones are to break. Low bone density can occur in patients treated for cancer. It is also called BMD, bone mass, and bone mineral density.

Bone marrow ablation The destruction of bone marrow using radiation or drugs.

Bone marrow aspiration The removal of a small sample of bone marrow (usually from the hip) through a needle for examination under a microscope.

Bone marrow biopsy is used to study an actual piece of spongy bone marrow. It may be completed at the same time as a bone marrow aspirate. For this test, a needle is placed in a bone (usually the hipbone); a small piece of spongy bone marrow is removed and sent to the laboratory to be tested.

Bone marrow transplantation A procedure to replace bone marrow that has been destroyed by treatment with high doses of anticancer drugs or radiation. Transplantation may be autologous (an individual's own marrow saved before treatment), allogeneic (marrow donated by someone else), or syngeneic (marrow donated by an identical twin).

Bone mass A measure of the amount of minerals (mostly cal-

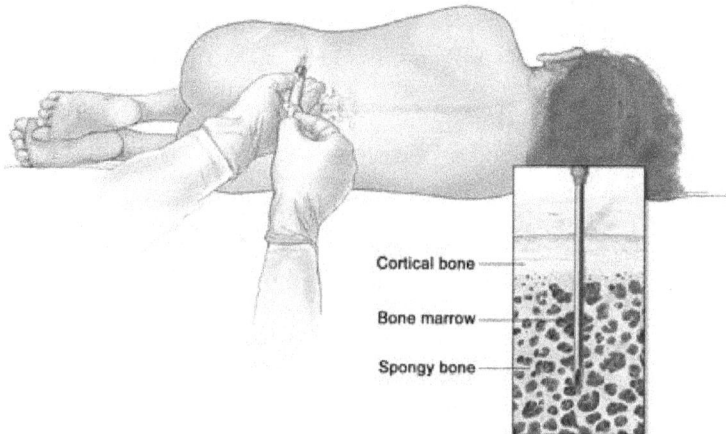

Fig. *Bone marrow biopsy*

cium and phosphorous) contained in a certain volume of bone. Bone mass measurements are used to diagnose osteoporosis (a condition mar-ked by decreased bone mass), to see how well osteoporosis treatments are working, and to predict how likely the bones are to break. Low bone mass can occur in patients treated for cancer. It is also called BMD, bone density, and bone mineral density.

Borderline personality disorder A serious mental illness marked by unstable moods and impulsive behaviour. People with BPD have problems with relationships, family and work life, long-term planning, and self-identity. Symptoms include intense bouts of anger, depression, and anxiety that may lead to self-injury or suicide, drug or alcohol abuse, excessive spending, binge eating, or risky sex. A person with BPD who is diagnosed with cancer may be at an increased risk of suicide.

Botulism Serious illness from a toxin produced by Clostridium bacteria (usually Clostridium botulinum). Infant botulism and food-borne botulism are the most common forms in the United States. Symptoms include double vision, blurred vision, ptosis, muscle weakness, difficulty speaking, difficulty swallowing, difficulty breathing and nausea.

Bowel function The way the intestines work in terms of how often there are bowel move-ments, the ability to control when to have a bowel movement, and whether the stools are hard and dry as in constipation or watery as in diarrhoea.

Bowel movement Movement of feces (undigested food, bacteria, mucus, and cells from the lining of the intestines) through the bowel and out the anus. Also called defecation.

Bowel The long, tube-shaped organ in the abdomen that completes the process of digestion. The bowel has two parts, the small bowel and the large bowel. Also called intestine.

Bowen disease A skin disease marked by scaly or thickened patches on the skin and often caused by prolonged exposure to arsenic. The patches often occur on sun-exposed areas of the skin and in older white men. These patches may become malignant (cancer). Also called precancerous dermatitis and precancerous dermatosis.

Braces Orthopedic appliances used to support, align, or hold parts of the body in correct position.

Brachial artery The continuation of the axillary artery; it branches into the radial and ulnar arteries.

Brachial plexopathy Diseases of the cervical (and first thoracic) roots, nerve trunks, cords, and peripheral nerve components of the brachial plexus. Clinical manifestations include regional pain, paresthesia; muscle weakness, and decreased sensation (Hypesthesia) in the upper extremity. These disorders may be associated with trauma (including birth injuries); thoracic outlet syndrome; neoplasms; neuritis; radiotherapy; and other conditions.

Brachial plexus The brachial plexus is a group of nerves originating from the spinal cord. These nerves are mainly responsible for movement and sensation of the arm and hand. The brachial plexus extends from the neck into the axilla. In humans, the nerves of the plexus usually originate from

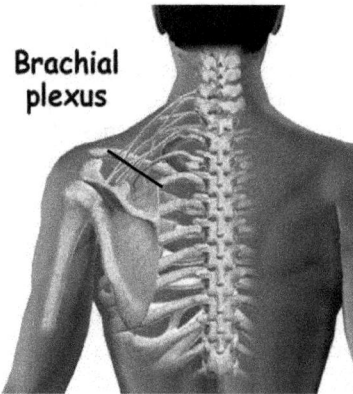

Fig. *Brachial plexus*

the lower cervical and the first thoracic spinal cord segments (C5-C8 and T1), but variations are not uncommon. Brachial plexus injuries are very serious and can cause partial or complete loss of function or sensation of the involved upper extremity. Brachial plexus injuries can happen either because of trauma (accident) or obstetric causes

Brain The part of central nervous system that is contained within the skull (cranium). Arising from the neural tube, the embryonic brain is comprised of three major parts including prosen-cephalon (the forebrain); mesen-cephalon (the midbrain); and rhomben-cephalon (the hind-brain). The developed brain consists of cerebrum; cerebellum; and other structures in the brain stem.

Brain chemistry Changes in the amounts of various chemicals (neuro-transmitters, receptors, enzymes, and other metabolites) specific to the area of the central nervous system contained within the head. These are monitored over time, during sensory stimulation, or under different disease states.

Brain damage is the destruction or degeneration of brain cells. It occur due to a wide range of internal and external factors. Common causes of focal or localized brain damage are physical trauma (traumatic brain injury, stroke, aneurysm, surgery, other neurological disorder), and heavy metals causing poisoning including mercury and its compounds of lead.

Brain disorders Pathologic conditions affecting the brain, which is composed of the intracranial components of the central nervous system. This includes (but is not limited to) the cerebral cortex; intracranial white matter; basal ganglia; thalamus; hypo-thalamus; brain stem; and cerebellum.

Brain injuries Acute and chronic injuries to the brain, including the cerebral hemispheres, cerebellum, and brain stem. Clinical manifestations depend on the nature of injury. Diffuse trauma to the brain is frequently associated with diffuse axonal injury or coma, post-traumatic. Localized injuries may be associated with neurobehavioural manifestations; hemiparesis, or other focal neurologic deficits.

Breast cyst A fluid-filled closed cavity or sac that is lined by an epithelium and found in the breast. It may appear as a single large cyst in one breast, multifocal, or bilateral in *fibrocystic breast disease.*

Breathing The act of breathing with the lungs, consisting of inhalation, or the taking into the lungs of the ambient air, and of exhalation, or the expelling of the modified air which contains more carbon dioxide than the air taken in. This does not include tissue respiration.

Breathing exercises Therapeutic exercises aimed to deepen inspiration or expiration or even to alter the rate and rhythm of respiration.

A 20% reduction in oxygen blood levels may be caused by the aging process and normal breathing habits. Poor breathing robs energy and negatively affects mental alertness. Unless breathing is exercised, aging affects the respiratory system as follows:

Stiffness: The rib cage and surrounding muscles get stiff causing inhalation to become more difficult. Less elasticity and weak muscles leave stale air in the tissues of the lungs and prevents fresh oxygen from reaching the blood stream.

Rapid, Shallow Breathing: This type of breathing, often

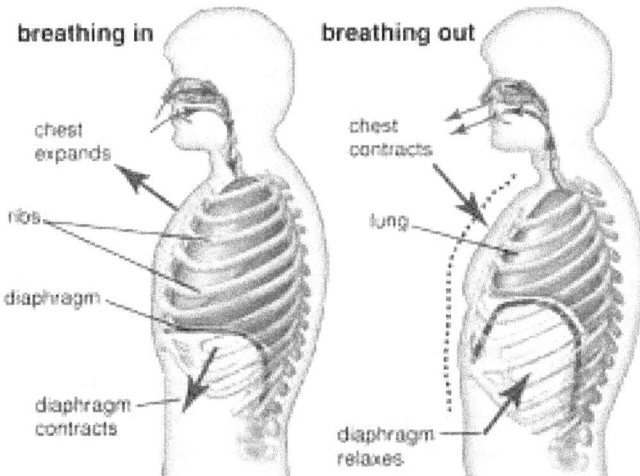

Fig. *Breathing exercises*

caused by poor posture and weak or stiff muscles, leads to poor oxygen supply, respiratory disease, sluggishness, or heart disease.

Buerger disease A non-atherosclerotic, inflammatory thrombotic disease that commonly involves small and medium-sized arteries or veins in the extremities. It is characterized by occlusive thrombosis and Fibrosis in the vascular wall leading to digital and limb Ischemia and ulcerations. Throm-boan-giitis obliterans is highly associated with tobacco smoking.

Build, body Particular categories of body build, determined on the basis of certain physical characteristics. The three basic body types are ectomorph (thin physique), endomorph (rounded physique), and mesomorph (athletic physique).

Bulbar palsies A motor neuron disease marked by progressive weakness of the muscles innervated by cranial nerves of the lower brain stem. Clinical manifestations include dysa-rthria, dysphagia, facial weakness, tongue weakness, and fasciculations of the tongue and facial muscles. The adult form of the disease is marked initially by bulbar weakness which progresses to involve motor neurons throughout the neuroaxis. Eventually this condition may become indistinguishable from Amyotrophic lateral sclerosis.

Burkitt tumour A form of undifferentiated Malignant Lymphoma usually found in Central Africa, but also reported in other parts of the world. It is commonly manifested as a large osteolytic lesion in the jaw or as an abdominal mass. B-Cell Antigens are expressed on the immature Cells that make up the Tumour in virtually all cases of Burkitt Lymphoma. The Epstein-Barr Virus (Herpesvirus 4, Human) has been isolated from Burkitt Lymphoma cases in Africa and it is implicated as the causative agent in these cases; however, most non-African cases are EBV-negative.

Burning mouth syndrome A group of painful oral symptoms associated with a burning or similar sensation. There is usually a significant organic component with a degree of functional overlay; it is not limited to the psychophysiologic group of disorders.

Buruli ulcer A lesion in the skin and subcutaneous tissues due to infections by Mycobacterium ulcerans.

Buschke scleredema A diffuse, non-pitting induration of the skin of unknown etiology that occurs most commonly in association with diabetes mellitus, predominantly in females. It typically begins on the Face or head and spreads to other areas of the body, sometimes involving noncutaneous tissues. Often it is preceded by any of various infections, notably staphylococcal infections.

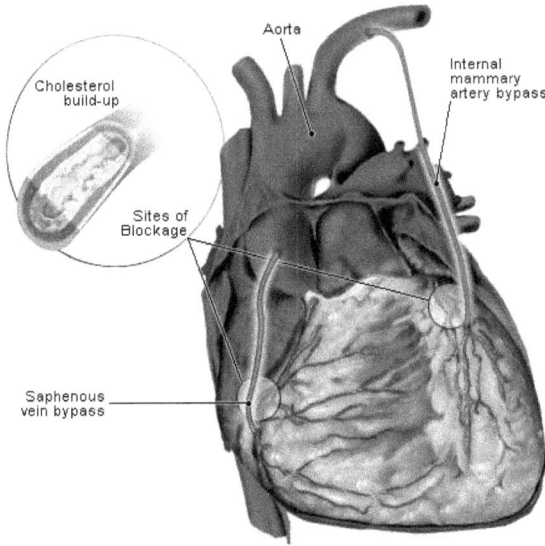

Fig. *Bypass surgery, coronary artery*

Bypass surgery, coronary artery Surgical therapy of ischemic coronary artery disease achieved by grafting a section of saphenous vein, internal mammary artery, or other substitute between the aorta and the obstructed coronary artery distal to the obstructive lesion. In a CABG operation the surgeon grafts other blood vessels onto the patient's coronary artery and bypasses the diseased portion. This creates a new pathway for blood flow that ensures the delivery of oxygen and nutrients to the heart muscle.

Bypass, heart-lung Diversion of the flow of Blood from the entrance of the right atrium directly to the Aorta (or Femoral Artery) via an Oxygenator thus bypassing both the Heart and Lungs.

Byssinosis A condition of Bronchoconstriction resulting from hypersensitive reaction to inhaled Dust during the initial processing of cotton, Flax, or hemp in the Textile Industry. Symptoms include wheezing and tightness in the Chest.

C

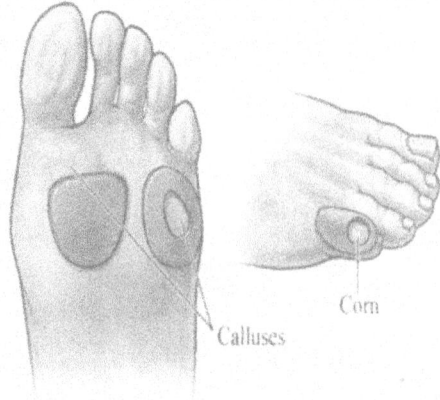

Calluses

Corn

C fibre Type C fibers are peripheral unmyelinated nerve fibres in which several axons are surrounded by a single schwann cell. They constitute more than half of the peripheral sensory nerve fibres as well as all the postganglionic autonomic Fibres.

C peptide The middle segment of proinsulin that is between the N-terminal B-chain and the C-terminal A-chain. It is a pancreatic peptide of about 31 residues, depending on the species. Upon proteolytic cleavage of pro-insulin, equimolar insulin and C-peptide are released. C-peptide immunoassay has been used to assess pancreatic beta cell function in diabetic patients with circulating insulin antibodies or exogenous insulin. Half-Life of C-peptide is 30 min, almost 8 times that of Inured in the serum by means of a radio-immunoassay employing monoclonal antibodies.

Ca sensing receptors A class of G-protein-coupled receptors that react to varying extracellular calcium levels. Calcium-sensing receptors in the para-thyroid glands play an important role in the maintenance of calcium homeostasis by regulating the release of parathyroid hormone. They differ from intracellular calcium-sensing proteins which sense intra-cellular calcium levels.

Caesarean section Extraction of the feotus by means of abdominal hysterotomy. In other sense, it is a surgical procedure in which one or more incisions are made through a mother's abdomen (laparotomy) and uterus (hys-

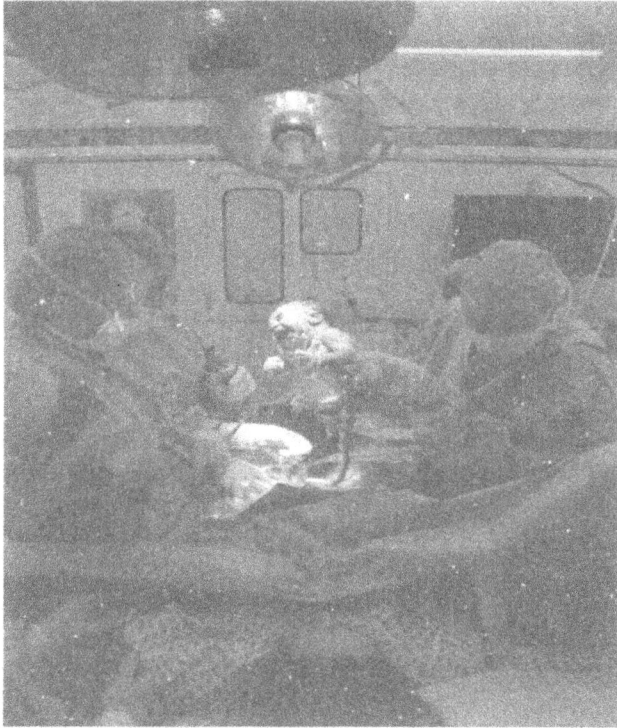

Fig. *Caesarean section*

terotomy) to deliver one or more babies, or, rarely, to remove a dead fetus. A late-term abortion using caesarean section procedures is termed a hysterotomy abortion and is very rarely performed. The first modern caesarean section was performed by German gynecologist Ferdinand Adolf Kehrer in 1881.

A caesarean section is usually performed when a vaginal delivery would put the baby's or mother's life or health at risk, although in recent times it has also been performed upon request for childbirths that could otherwise have been natural

Caffey disease A disease of young Infants characterized by soft tissue swellings over the affected bones, fever, and irritability, and marked by periods of remission and exacerbation.

C.D.E. (Certified Diabetes Educator) A health professional who is certified by the national certification board for diabetes Educators to teach people with diabetes how to manage their condition. The criteria to obtain this certification include:a degree in the health professions such as R.N. (nursing), M.D. or D.O. (physicians), R.D. (dietitians), R.Ph. or Pharm.D. (pharmacists), M.S.W. (social workers), and others.at least two years' experience in diabetes education. successful completion of a comprehensive examination covering the field. Certified diabetes educators must be recredentialed every 5 years.

Calcification Deposits of calcium in the tissues. Calcification in the breast can be seen on a mammogram, but cannot be detected by touch. There are two types of breast calcification—macro-calcification and micro-calcification. Macro-calcifications are large deposits and are usually not related to cancer. Micro-calcifications are specks of calcium that may be found in an area of rapidly dividing cells. Many micro-calcifications clustered together may be a sign of cancer.

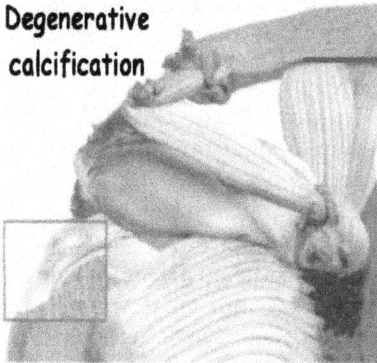

Degenerative calcification

Fig. *Calcification*

Calcinosis A condition in which abnormal amounts of calcium salts are found in soft tissue, such as muscle.

Calcitonin A hormone formed by the C cells of the thyroid gland. It helps maintain a healthy level of calcium in the blood. When the calcium level is too high, calcitonin lowers it.

Calcitriol The active form of vitamin D. Calcitriol is formed in the kidneys or made in the laboratory. It is used as a drug to increase calcium levels in the body in order to treat skeletal and tissue-related calcium deficiencies caused by kidney or thyroid disorders.

CAT scan, 4D Three-dimensional computed tomographic imaging with the added dimension of time, to follow motion during imaging.

CAT Scan, Spiral Computed Tomography where there is continuous X-ray exposure to the Patient while being transported in a spiral or helical pattern through the beam of irradiation. This provides improved three-dimensional contrast and spatial resolution compared to conventional computed tomography, where data is obtained and computed from individual sequential exposures.

CAT Scan, X-Ray Tomography using x-ray transmission and a computer Algorithm to reconstruct the image.

Calcium channel blocker A drug used to lower blood pressure.

Callus Callus is an accumulation of keratocytes that form a thickened area of skin in response to repeated friction or pressure, typically at the site of repeated blistering. A callus may be a different color than the surround-

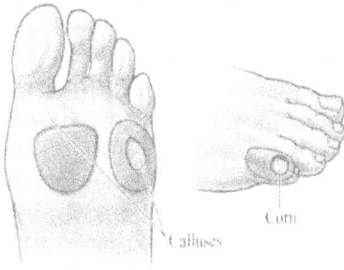

Fig. *Calluses*

ing skin, often grayish or yellowish. Calluses are most likely to develop on the palms, fingers, fingertips, heels, and balls of the feet. Most calluses are not painful and help protect the skin from blisters and other frictionrelated injuries.

Caisson disease A condition occurring as a result of exposure to a rapid fall in ambient pressure. Gases, nitrogen in particular, come out of solution and form bubbles in body fluid and blood. These gas bubbles accumulate in joint spaces and the peripheral circulation impairing tissue oxygenation causing disorientation, severe pain, and potentially death.

Calorie Energy that comes from food. Some foods have more calories than others. Fats have many calories. Most vegetables have few. People with diabetes are advised to follow meal plans with suggested amounts of calories for each meal and/or snack.

Calorimetry The measurement of the quantity of Heat involved in various processes, such as chemical reactions, changes of state, and formations of solutions, or in the determination of the heat capacities of substances. The fundamental unit of measurement is the joule or the calorie

Cancer A term for diseases in which abnormal cells divide without control and can invade nearby tissues. Cancer cells can also spread to other parts of the body through the blood and lymph systems. There are several main types of cancer. Carcinoma is a cancer that begins in the skin or in tissues that line or cover internal organs. Sarcoma is a cancer that begins in bone, cartilage, fat, muscle, blood vessels, or other connective or supportive tissue. Leukemia is a cancer that starts in blood-forming tissue such as the bone marrow, and causes large numbers of abnormal blood cells to be produced and enter the blood. Lymphoma and multiple myeloma are cancers that begin in the cells of the immune system. Central nervous system cancers are cancers that begin in the tissues of the brain and spinal cord. Also called malignancy.

Capacity, mental Refers to the amount of information or mental processing a person can attend to within a given time.

Capillary The smallest of the body's blood vessels. Capillaries have walls so thin that oxygen and glucose can pass through them and enter the

66

cells, and waste products such as carbon dioxide can pass back into the blood to be carried away and taken out of the body.

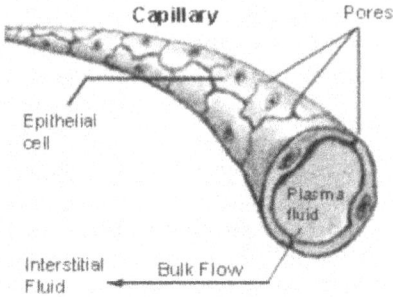

Fig. Capillary

Sometimes people who have had diabetes for a long time find that their capillaries become weak, especially those in the kidney and the retina of the eye.

Capnometer A device to monitor the patient's carbon dioxide levels to assist in providing the appropriate ventilation.

Capsaicin Capsaicin, derived from hot peppers, is the active ingredient in the creams used to relieve the pain of peripheral neuropathy.

Carbohydrate One of the three main classes of foods and a source of energy. Carbohydrates are mainly sugars and starches that the body breaks down into glucose (a simple sugar that the body can use to feed its cells). The body also uses carbohydrates to make a substance called glycogen that is stored in the liver and muscles for future use. If the body does not have enough insulin or cannot use the insulin it has, which

are the basic problems in most forms of diabetes, then the body will not be able to use carbohydrates for energy the way it should.

Carbon dioxide A colourless gas, heavier than air. In small quantities in inhaled air, it stimulates respiration. Careful monitoring of the carbon dioxide levels in the blood is necessary for the brain injured patient. Increases carbon dioxide levels have been shown to increase swelling in the brain and the TBI patient must be "hyperventilated" (maintained with purposely decreased levels of CO2) to prevent brain swelling.

Cardiologist A doctor who sees and takes care of people with heart disease; a heart specialist.

Cardiovascular The essential components of the human cardiovascular system are the heart, blood, and blood vessels. It includes—the pulmonary circulation, a "loop" through the lungs where blood is oxygenated; and the systemic circulation, a "loop" through the rest of the body to provide oxygenated blood.

Carcinoid A slow-crete substances such as serotonin or prostaglandins, causing carcinoid syndrome.

Carcinosarcoma A malignant tumor that is a mixture of carcinoma (cancer of epithelial tissue, which is skin and tissue that lines or covers the internal organs) and sarcoma (cancer of connective tissue, such as bone, cartilage, and fat).

Cardin A plant whose leaves, stems, and flowers have been used in some cultures to treat certain medical problems. Cardin may have anti-inflammatory and anticancer effects. The scientific name is Cnicus benedictus. Also called blessed thistle, holy thistle, spotted thistle, and St. Benedict's thistle.

Cardiac pacemaker An electronic device that is implanted in the body to monitor heart rate and rhythm. It gives the heart electrical stimulation when it does not beat normally. It runs on batteries and has long, thin wires that connect it to the heart. Also called artificial pacemaker and pacemaker.

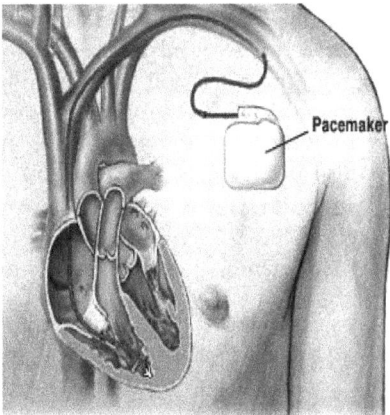

Fig. *Cardiac pacemaker*

Carpal tunnel syndrome A nerve disorder affecting the hand that may occur in people with diabetes; caused by a pinched nerve.

Care coordination benefit A benefit in newer long-term care policies that pays consultation fees for a professional, such as a registered nurse or a medical social worker, to periodically assess and make recommendations about the enrollee's care program. The purpose is to adjust services when and if the individual's care needs change. Also called personal care advisor or personal care advocate benefit.

Caregiver A person who gives care to people who need help taking care of themselves. Examples include children, the elderly, or patients who have chronic illnesses or are disabled. Caregivers may be health professionals, family members, friends, social workers, or members of the clergy. They may give care at home or in a hospital or other health care setting.

Carpal tunnel syndrome A condition associated with swelling and weight gain during pregnancy. The nerves in the wrist become compressed resulting in a tingling, burning or numbness in the hands. It usually goes away after delivery.

Case management Facilitating the access of a patient to appropriate medical, rehabilitation and support programmes, and coordination of the delivery of services. This role may involve liaison with various professionals and agencies, advocacy on behalf of the patient, and arranging for purchase of services where no appropriate programmes are available.

Cataract are cloudy areas in the

lens inside the eye - which is normally clear. Cataracts can develop in one or both eyes. If they develop in both eyes, one will be more severely affected than the other. A normally clear lens allows light to pass through to the back of the eye, so that the patient can see well-defined images. If a part of the lens becomes opaque light does not pass through easily and the patient's vision becomes blurry - like looking through cloudy water or a fogged-up window. The more opaque (cloudier) the lens becomes, the worse the person's vision will be. In people with diabetes, this condition is sometimes referred to as "sugar cataract."

A patient with cataract will eventually find it hard to read, or drive a car - especially during the night. Even seeing people's facial expressions becomes difficult. Cataracts are not usually painful. The patient's long-distance vision is more severely affected at first.

Catatonia Immobility with muscular rigidity or inflexibility and at times excitability.

Catharsis The healthful (therapeutic) release of ideas through "talking out" conscious material accompanied by an appropriate emotional reaction. Also, the release into awareness of repressed ("forgotten") material from the unconscious.

Catheter A hollow flexible tube used to infuse or drain fluids into or from the body. Example: A catheter is used to transfer insulin from an insulin pump to a needle that is placed in the skin of the person using an insulin pump.

Catechol A chemical originally isolated from a type of mimosa tree. Catechol is used as an astringent, an antiseptic, and in photography, electroplating, and making other chemicals. It can also be made in the laboratory.

Catecholamine A type of neurohormone (a chemical that is made by nerve cells and used to

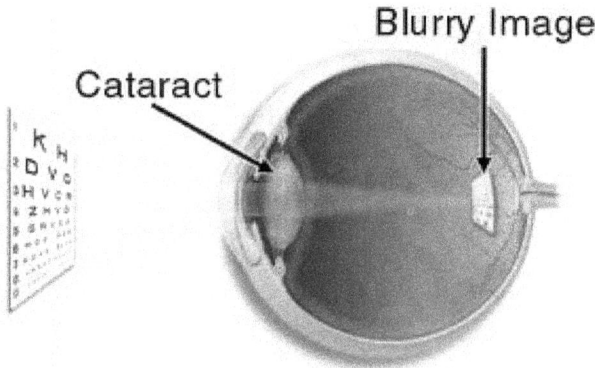

Fig. *Cataract*

send signals to other cells). Catecholamines are important in stress responses. High levels cause high blood pressure which can lead to headaches, sweating, pounding of the heart, pain in the chest, and anxiety. Examples of catecholamines include dopamine, epinephrine (adrenaline), and norepi-nephrine (nor-adrena-line).

Catharsis The healthful (therapeutic) release of ideas through "talking out" conscious material accompanied by an appropriate emotional reaction. Also, the release into awareness of repressed ("forgotten") material from the unconscious.

Cauda equina The bundle of nerve roots below the end of the spinal cord. The cauda equina is a structure within the lower end of the spinal column of most vertebrates, that consists of nerve roots and rootlets from above. The space in which the cerebrospinal fluid is present is actually an extension of the subarachnoid space. In humans, because the spinal cord stops growing in infancy while the bones of the spine continue growing, the spinal cord in adults ends at about the level of the vertebra L1/L2 , and at birth at L3.

Cecum The first part of the large intestine; the appendix is connected to the cecum. The cecum is the part of the colon that sits just below the outlet of the small intestine which expels liquid feces into the colon. This is the part of the colon with the largest diameter. The colon begins in the right lower abdomen where the small intestine ends. This part of the colon is called the cecum.

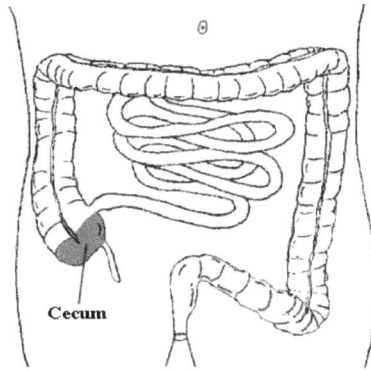

Fig. *Cecum*

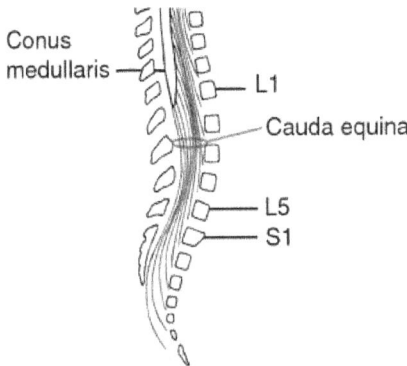

Fig. *Cauda equina*

Celiac disease An autoimmune disorder of the upper intestinal mucosa that is triggered by cereal proteins, especially wheat gluten, and which leads to a malabsorption of all nutrients, primarily of fat. It can be detected by the presence of anti-transglutaminase antibodies. If these are positive it would be justifiable to take a mucosal biopsy and if this is positive, then dietary treatment is all that is required. About 5% of people with autoimmune diabetes have positive anti-transglutaminase antibodies. Celiac syndrome may also be part of the Autoimmune Poly-glandular Syndrome.

Cell culture The growth of microorganisms such as bacteria and yeast, or human, plant, or animal cells in the laboratory. Cell cultures may be used to diagnose infections, to test new drugs, and in research.

Cell cycle The process a cell goes through each time it divides. The cell cycle consists of a series of steps during which the chromosomes and other cell material double to make two copies. The cell then divides into two daughter cells, each receiving one copy of the doubled material. The cell cycle is complete when each daughter cell is surrounded by its own outer membrane. Also called mitotic cycle.

Cell differentiation The process during which young, immature (unspecialized) cells take on individual characteristics and reach their mature (specialized) form and function.

Cell membrane The thin layer of protein and fat that surrounds the cell. The cell membrane is semipermeable, allowing some substances to pass into the cell and blocking others.

Cellular adoptive immunotherapy A treatment used to help the immune system fight cancer. A cancer patient's T cells (a type of white blood cell) are collected and grown in the laboratory to increase the number of T cells that are able to kill the person's cancer cells. These cancer-specific T cells are given back to the patient to help the immune system fight the cancer.

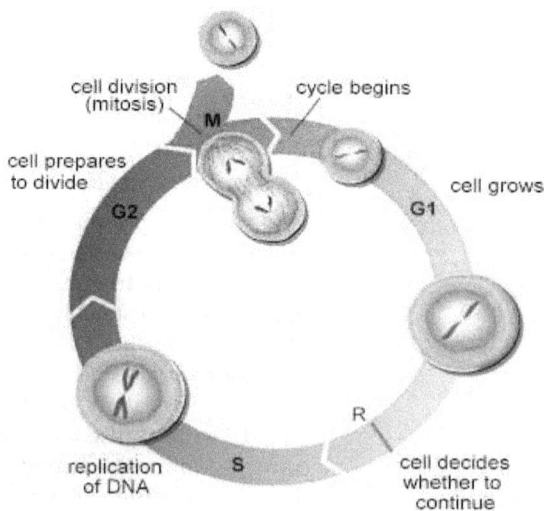

Fig. *Cell cycle*

Cellular metabolism The sum of all chemical changes that take place in a cell through which energy and basic components are provided for essential processes, including the synthesis of new molecules and the breakdown and removal of others.

Centre for medicare and medicaid Formerly the U.S. Health Care Financing Administration, CMS is an element of the Department of Health and Human Services, which finances and administers the Medicare and Medicaid programmes. Among other responsibilities, CMS establishes standards for the operation of nursing facilities that receive funds under the Medicare or Medicaid programmes.

Centres for disease control An agency within the U.S. Department of Health and Human Services that serves as the central point for consolidation of disease control data, health promotion and public health programmes. CDC is also known as the Centres for Disease Control and Prevention, and is based in Atlanta, GA.

Central nervous system The central nervous system (CNS) acts as the command centre of the body. It interprets incoming sensory information, then sends out instructions on how the body should react. The CNS consists of two major parts: the brain and the spinal cord. In vertebrates, the central nervous system is enclosed in the meninges. It contains the majority of

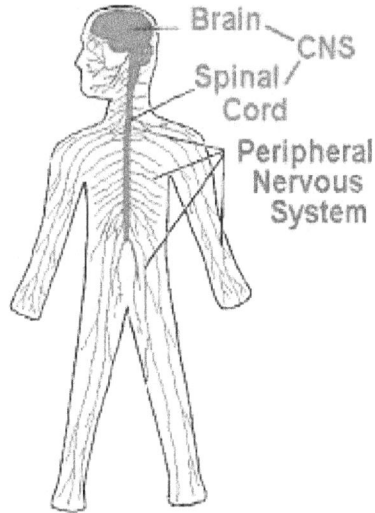

Fig. *Central nervous system*

the nervous system and consists of the brain and the spinal cord. Together with the peripheral nervous system it has a fundamental role in the control of behavior. The CNS is contained within the dorsal cavity, with the brain in the cranial cavity and the spinal cord in the spinal cavity. The brain is protected by the skull, while the spinal cord is protected by the vertebrae

Central sulcus A large groove in the brain that separates the frontal and parietal lobes

Centrosome A small body located near the nucleus - it has a dense centre and radiating tubules. The centrosome is where microtubules are made. During cell division (mitosis), the centrosome divides and the two parts move to opposite sides of the dividing cell. The centriole is the dense centre of the centrosome.

Cephalopelvic disproportion This is when a baby's head is too large to pass through the mother's pelvic opening. It can occur because the baby is disproportionately large, the baby is not in the best position for birth resulting in a larger head diameter than normal, the mother's pelvis is small or abnormally shaped, or as a result of abnormalities of the birth canal. It is a common cause of obstructed labour and can result in delivery by caesarean section.

Cerebral palsy Cerebral palsy (CP) is the term used to describe a physical impairment that affects movement. It is usually caused by brain damage in the developing fetus, during birth, or from illness just after birth.

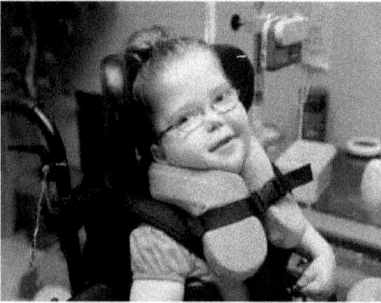

Fig. *Cerebral palsy*

The term is used to describe a variety of conditions depending on which part of the brain was damaged. For example, some people with CP may have learning disabilities, speech problems, hearing impairment or epilepsy.

Cerebrospinal fluid The fluid that flows in and around the hollow spaces of the brain and spinal cord, and between two of the meninges (the thin layers of tissue that cover and protect the brain and spinal cord). Cerebrospinal fluid is made by tissue called the choroid plexus in the ventricles (hollow spaces) in the brain.

Cerebral hemisphere One half of the cerebrum, the part of the brain that controls muscle functions and also controls speech, thought, emotions, reading, writing, and learning. The right hemisphere controls the muscles on the left side of the body, and the left hemisphere controls the muscles on the right side of the body.

Cerebellum The portion of the brain (located at the back) which helps coordinate movement. Damage may result in ataxia.

Cerebral angiography The brain substance is pushed aside and compressed by the presence of a brain tumor, aneurysm, swelling or hematoma.

Cerebral compression The brain substance is pushed aside and compressed by the presence of a brain tumor, aneurysm, swelling or hematoma.

Cerebral infarct When the blood supply is reduced below a critical level to a specific region of the brain and the brain tissue in that region dies.

Cerebrovascular disease Damage to the blood vessels in the brain, resulting in a stroke. The blood vessels become blocked because of fat deposits or they become thick and hard, blocking the flow of blood to the brain. Sometimes, the blood vessels may burst, resulting in a hemorrhagic stroke. People with diabetes are at higher risk of cerebrovascular disease.

Cerebrum The largest and most complex portion of the brain. It controls thought, learning, and many other complex activities. It is divided into the left and right cerebral hemispheres that are joined by the corpus callosum, which communicates between the two hemispheres. The right side of the brain controls the left side of the body, and vice versa. Each cerebral hemisphere is divided into four lobes: the frontal lobe (responsible for reasoning, emotions, judgment, and voluntary movement); the temporal lobe (contains centres of hearing, smells, and memory); the parietal lobe (responsible for touch and spoken language ability), and the occipital lobe (responsible for centres of vision and reading ability).

Certified nursing assistant The CNA provides personal care to residents or patients, such as bathing, dressing, changing linens, transporting and other essential activities. CNAs are trained, tested, certified and work under the supervision of an RN or LPN.

Character neurosis disorder A personality disorder manifested by a chronic, habitual, maladaptive pattern of reaction that is relatively inflexible, limits the optimal use of potentialities, and often provokes the responses from the environment that the person wants to avoid. In contrast to symptoms of neurosis, character traits are typically ego-syntonic.

Cervical cancer Cancer that forms in tissues of the cervix (the organ connecting the uterus and vagina). It is usually a slow-growing cancer that may not have symptoms but can be found with regular Pap tests (a procedure in which cells are scraped from the cervix and

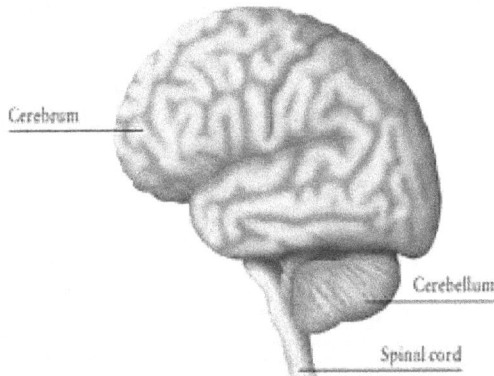

Cerebrum

Cerebellum

Spinal cord

Fig. *Cerebrum*

looked at under microscope. cervical cancer is almost always caused by human papilomavirus(HPV) infection.

Cervical cap A cervical or Dutch cap is a birth control device (similar to a diaphragm, but smaller) which fits over a woman's cervix and keeps sperm from entering. It must be fitted by a doctor or nurse and checked yearly for a proper fit.

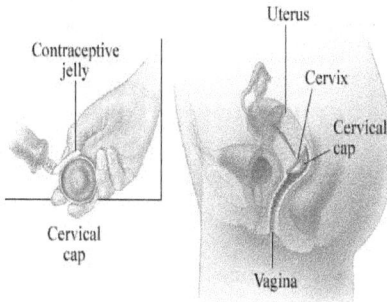

Fig. *Cervical cap*

Cervical dysplasia Cervical dysplasia is the abnormal growth of cervical cells, usually with no symptoms. It has been linked to a sexually transmitted disease called human papillomavirus (genital warts). Mild cases of dysplasia usually resolve by themselves, while more severe cases require surgical removal of the abnormal cells.

Cervical ectropion It occurs when the junction where the cells of the vagina turn into the cells of the uterus hangs out into the vagina. It is very common, especially in younger women and those taking birth control pills. Cervical ectropion usually re-

solves naturally as the cervix matures, some times cervical ectropion may warrent a change in your birth control method.

Cervical incompetence Cervical incompetence is a medical condition in which a pregnant woman's cervix begins to dilate (widen) and efface (thin) before her pregnancy has reached term. Internal os opening more than 1 cm is abnormal and cervical length less than 2 cm is considered diagnostic. Cervical incompetence may cause miscarriage or preterm birth during the second and third trimesters.

In a woman with cervical incompetence, dilation and effacement of the cervix may occur without pain or uterine contractions. In a normal pregnancy, dilation and effacement occurs in response to uterine contractions. Cervical incompetence occurs because of weakness of the cervix, which is made to open by the growing pressure

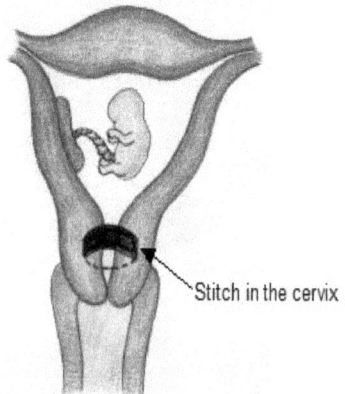

Fig. *Cervical incompetence*

in the uterus as pregnancy progresses. If the responses are not halted, rupture of the membranes and birth of a premature baby can result.

Cervical stitch Cervical stitch is used to close a weak cervix (called an incompetent cervix) to support a pregnancy to term. It is most successful in preventing miscarriage and premature labour when put in during early pregnancy - at about 18 to 20 weeks.

Cervical weakness The condition in which the cervix, under pressure from the growing uterus, painlessly opens before a pregnancy has reached full term. A weak or incompetent cervix can cause miscarriage in the second trimester or premature labour in the third, but can be treated by surgical reinforcement of the cervical muscle (called a cervical stitch).

Cervicitis An inflammation of the cervix, cervicitis can be caused by a bacterial or viral infection,

or irritation of the cervix during childbirth or surgery. Symptoms include abnormal discharge, pain, and spotting.

Charcot foot A foot complication associated with diabetic neuropathy that results in almost painless destruction of joints and soft tissue. Also called "Charcot's joint" and "neuropathic arthropathy."

Chemically dependent Addiction to chemical agents such as prescription medicines, drugs or alcohol.

Chemotherapy The treatment of a condition such as cancer by the systematic administration of chemical compounds.

Chest tubes Tubes inserted into the patient's chest between the lung and ribs to allow fluid and air to drain from the area surrounding the lungs. Removing this fluid and air from around the lungs allows them to more fully expand.

Chlorpropamide A pill taken to lower the level of glucose

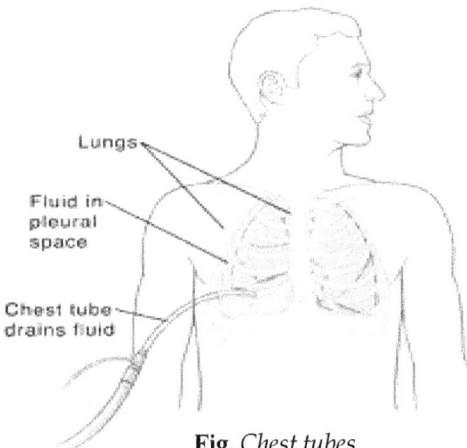

Lungs

Fluid in pleural space

Chest tube drains fluid

Fig. *Chest tubes*

(sugar) in the blood. Only some people with noninsulin-dependent diabetes take these pills.

Chlamydia trachomatis is a common sexually transmitted disease, which often has no visible symptoms. If untreated, chlamydia can make a woman infertile or be passed to a baby during childbirth, causing pneumonia, eye infections and, in severe cases, blindness. Chlamydia is not routinely tested for but can be treated with antibiotics.

Chloasma Brown markings on the skin of a pregnant woman caused by hormonal changes, often seen on the face, in a pattern called "butterfly" marking. These fade after pregnancy.

Cholesterol A fat-like substance found in blood, muscle, liver, brain, and other tissues in people and animals. The body makes and needs some cholesterol. Too much cholesterol, however, may cause fat to build up in the walls of the larger arteries and cause a disease called atherosclerosis. Butter and egg yolks are examples of foods that have a lot of cholesterol. Cholesterol is composed of several components:

HDLCholesterol (high-density lipo-protein cholesterol): This component of cholesterol seems to have protective effects, and higher levels are considered to be good to have.

LDL Cholesterol (low-density lipo-protein cholesterol)

VLDL Cholesterol (very low-density lipoprotein cholesterol) Cholesterol is a lipid.

Choline A nutrient in the vitamin B complex that the body needs in small amounts to function and stay healthy. Choline helps cells make membranes, make a neurotransmitter (a chemical that helps nerve cells communicate with other cells), and remove fat from the liver. It is found in whole milk, beef liver, eggs, soy foods, and peanuts. Choline is water-soluble (can dissolve in water) and must be taken in every day. Not enough choline can cause diseases of the heart and blood vessels and damage to the liver. A form of choline is being studied in the treatment of some types of cancer and to reduce pain and fever. Choline is also being studied together with vitamin B12 in the prevention and treatment of cancer.

Chorionic villus sampling is a diagnostic test carried out in early pregnancy, usually between Week 10 and Week 12 of pregnancy. Some of the cells which line the placenta, the chorionic villi, are removed through the cervix or abdomen using a needle or catheter. The cells are tested to see whether the developing fetus has Down's syndrome or other genetic abnormalities. Early results may help parents decide whether to terminate a pregnancy in the event of severe birth defects.

Chronic care Long-term care for those individual who require medical care, a maintenance program to prevent deterioration of skills, and to provide recreational and social opportunities in a structured environment. Emphasis is on sustaining a reasonable quality of life, and expectations regarding improvements in abilities are limited.

Chronic Present over a long period of time. Diabetes is an example of chronic disease.

Chronic disease A disease which has one or more of the following characteristics: (i) is permanent, leaves residual disability; (ii) is caused by nonrev-ersible pathological alternation; (iii) requires special training of the patient for rehabilitation, or may be expected to require a long period of supervision, observation, or care.

Chronic fatigue syndrome A collection of symptoms including tiredness, weakness and muscle pain is called chronic fatigue syndrome; the cause of this condition is not known, although some suspect it is due to environmental sensitivities

Chronic obstructive pulmonary disease A group of chronic respiratory disorders characterized by the restricted flow of air into and out of the lungs. The most common example is emphysema.

Chromosomal abnormalities A chromosome is a collection of genes which determine how a baby will develop. An abnormal chromosome may result from an inherited problem, or be caused by a mutation, and can lead to disorders such as Down's syndrome. Chromosomal abnormality is the most common cause of miscarriage.

Chyme Food in the stomach that is partly digested and mixed with stomach acids. Chyme goes on to the small intestine for further digestion.

Circulation The flow of blood through the heart and blood vessels of the body.

Circumlocution Use of other words to describe a specific word or idea which cannot be remembered.

Circumstantiality Pattern of speech that is indirect and delayed in reaching its goal because of excessive or irrelevant detail or parenthetical remarks. The speaker does not lose the point, as is characteristic of loosening of associations, and clauses remain logically connected, but to the listener it seems that the end will never be reached.

Clanging A type of thinking in which the sound of a word, rather than its meaning, gives the direction to subsequent associations. Punning and rhyming may substitute for logic, and language may become increasingly a senseless compulsion to associate and decreasingly a vehicle for communication. For example, in response to the statement "That will probably remain a mystery," a patient said, "History is one of my strong points."

Cleft lip Specific congenital anomaly involving incomplete fusion of the lip and gum in the midline of the face. The term (hare lip) is anatomically incorrect and possibly stigmatizing.

Cleft palate A cleft palate is a condition in which the lip, or the lip and palate (roof of the mouth), do not grow together. About one in 600 babies are born with a cleft lip and/or cleft palate. Clefts can be repaired with surgery, usually performed within the first year after birth.

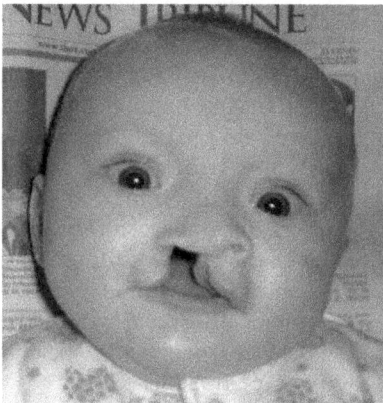

Fig. *Cleft palate*

Client A person under the protection of another, one who engages the professional advice or services of another.

Clinical trial A scientifically controlled study carried out in people, usually to test the effectiveness of a new treatment.

Clonus A sustained series of rhythmic jerks following quick stretch of a muscle.

Cluster suicides Multiple suicides, usually among adolescents, in a circumscribed period of time and area. Thought to have an element of contagion.

Cocaine use disorders In DSM-IV, this group includes cocaine dependence, cocaine abuse, cocaine intoxication, cocaine withdrawal, cocaine delirium, cocaine psychotic disorder with delusions or hallucinations, cocaine mood disorder, cocaine anxiety disorder, cocaine sexual dysfunction, and cocaine sleep disorder.

Codependency A popular term referring to all the effects that people who are dependent on alcohol or other substances have on those around them, including the attempts of those people to affect the dependent person. The term implies that codependence is a psychiatric disorder and hypothesizes that the family's actions tend to perpetuate (enable) the person's dependence. Empirical studies, however, support a stress and coping model for explanation of the family behavior.

Coding A mechanism for identifying and defining physicians' and hospitals' services. Coding provides universal definition and recognition of diagnoses, procedures and level of care. Coders usually work in medical records departments and coding is a function of billing. Medicare fraud investigators look closely at the medical record documentation which supports codes and looks for consistency. Lack of consistency of documentation can earmark a record as "upcoded" which is considered fraud.

Coeliac disease Coeliac disease or gluten-sensitive enteropathy is an inherited disease caused by an allergic reaction to gluten, a protein found in wheat, rye, and barley. The immune system attacks the lining of the intestines in response to the allergy. This common disease, if left untreated, can leave the intestine unable to absorb essential nutrients and vitamins leading to anaemia, bone disease and, rarely, forms of cancer.

Coenzyme Q10 A nutrient that the body needs in small amounts to function and stay healthy. Coenzyme Q10 helps mitochondria (small structures in the cell) make energy. It is an antioxidant that helps prevent cell damage caused by free radicals (highly reactive chemicals). Coenzyme Q10 is fat-soluble (can dissolve in fats and oils) and is found in fatty fish, beef, soybeans, peanuts, and spinach. It is being studied in the prevention and treatment of some types of cancer and heart disease and in the relief of side effects caused by some cancer treatments. Also called CoQ10, Q10, ubiquinone, and vitamin Q10.

Cognition The conscious process of knowing or being aware of thoughts or perceptions, including understanding and reasoning.

Cognitive impairment Difficulty with one or more of the basic functions of the brain: perception, memory, attentional abilities, and reasoning skills.

Cognitive rehabilitation Therapy programmes which aid persons in the management of specific problems in perception, memory, thinking and problem solving. Skills are practiced and strategies are taught to help improve function and/or compensate for remaining deficits. The interventions are based on an assessment and understanding of the person's brain-behavior deficits and services are provided by qualified practitioners.

Cognitive Refers to the mental process of comprehension, judgment, memory, and reasoning, in contrast to emotional and volitional processes.

Cognitive-behavioural psychotherapy Cognitive therapy; a short-term psychotherapy directed at specific target conditions or symptoms. (Depression has been the most intensively investigated to date.) The symptoms themselves are clues to the patient's verbal thoughts, images, and assumptions that account for both the symptomatic state and the psychological vulnerability to that state. Initial treatment is aimed at symptom reduction. The patient is taught to recognize the negative cognitions that contribute significantly to the development or maintenance of symptoms and to evaluate and modify such thinking patterns. The second phase of treatment concerns the underlying problem.

Cohort A group of individuals who share a common trait, such as birth year. In medicine, a cohort is a group that is part of a clinical trial or study and is observed over a period of time.

Cohort study A research study that compares a particular outcome (such as lung cancer) in groups of individuals who are alike in many ways but differ by a certain characteristic (for example, female nurses who smoke compared with those who do not smoke).

Collagen disease A term previously used to describe chronic diseases of the connective tissue (e.g., rheumatoid arthritis, systemic lupus erythematosus, and systemic sclerosis), but now is thought to be more appropriate for diseases associated with defects in collagen, which is a component of the connective tissue.

Collecting duct The last part of a long, twisting tube that collects urine from the nephrons (cellular structures in the kidney that filter blood and form urine) and moves it into the renal pelvis and ureters. Also called renal collecting tubule.

Colon The longest part of the large intestine, which is a tube-like organ connected to the small intestine at one end and the anus at the other. The colon removes water and some nutrients and electrolytes from partially digested food. The remaining material, solid waste called stool, moves through the colon to the rectum and leaves the body through the anus.

Colon cancer Cancer that forms in the tissues of the colon (the longest part of the large intestine). Most colon cancers are adenocarcinomas (cancers that begin in cells that make and release mucus and other fluids).

Colon crypt Tube-like gland found in the lining of the colon and rec-

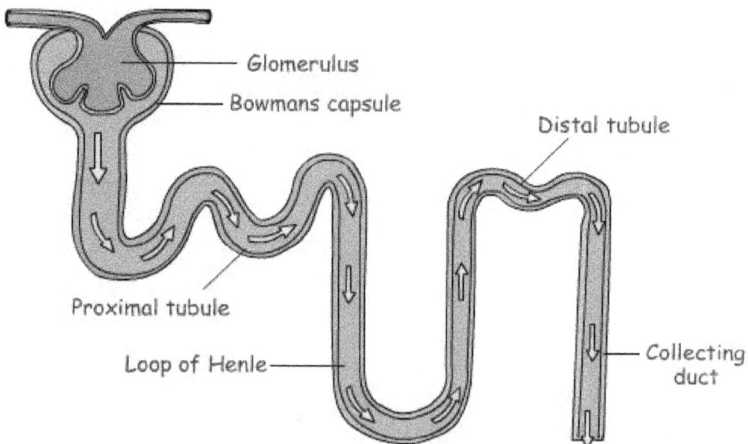

Fig. *Collecting duct*

tum. Colon crypt cells renew the lining of the intestine and make mucus. Also called gland of Lieberkuhn.

Colon polyp An abnormal growth of tissue in the lining of the bowel. Polyps are a risk factor for colon cancer.

Colonoscope A thin, tube-like instrument used to examine the inside of the colon. A colonoscope has a light and a lens for viewing and may have a tool to remove tissue.

Colonoscopy Examination of the inside of the colon using a colonoscope, inserted into the rectum. A colonoscope is a thin, tube-like instrument with a light and a lens for viewing. It may also have a tool to remove tissue to be checked under a microscope for signs of disease.

Colostomy An opening into the colon from the outside of the body.

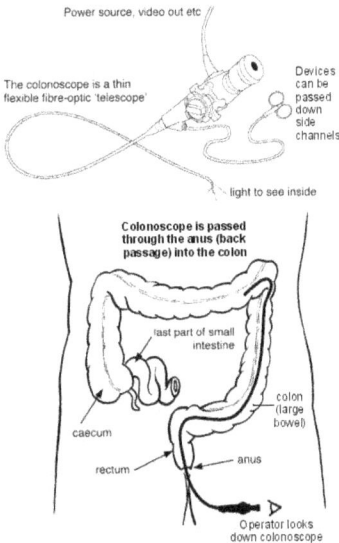

Fig. *Colonoscopy*

A colostomy provides a new path for waste material to leave the body after part of the colon has been removed.

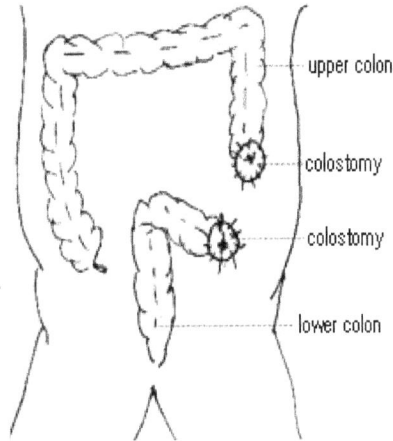

Fig. *Colostomy*

In broad sense, colostomy is an incision (cut) into the colon (large intestine) to create an artificial opening or "stoma" to the exterior of the abdomen. This opening serves as a substitute anus through which the intestines can eliminate waste products until the colon can heal or other corrective surgery can be done. The bowel movements fall into a collection pouch.

Colostrums Colostrum is the first "milk" the breasts produce as a precursor to breast milk. It is rich in fats, protein, and antibodies, which protect the baby against infection and kick-start the immune system. Most women produce colostrum a few days before and after childbirth; some women produce small amounts of it from the fifth or sixth month of pregnancy. It is gradually replaced by breastmilk over the first week or so of breastfeeding.

Coma A sleep-like state; or a state of unconsciousness from which the patient cannot be awakened or aroused, even by powerful stimulation; lack of any response to one's environment. Defined clinically as 'an inability to follow a one-step command consistently; glasgow coma scale score of eight or less. It may be due to a high or low level of glucose (sugar) in the blood.

Coma vigil A patient who has no meaningful interaction with his or her environment but exhibits sleep and wake cycles, spontaneous respiration and heart beat.

Commensurate wage A wage paid to a disabled worker which is comparable to wages paid to a non-disabled worker in the vicinity, performing similar work at a specific quality level, with the quality factor being the main variable.

Communicative disorder An impairment in the ability to:
(i) receive and/or process a symbol system,
(ii) represent concepts or symbol systems, and/or
(iii) transmit and use symbol systems. The impairment may be observed in disorders of hearing, language, and/or speech processes.

Community alternatives Agencies, outside an institutional setting, which provide care, support, and/or services to persons with disabilities.

Community based programmes Programmes for disabled which are located in a community environment, as opposed to an institutional setting.

Community resources Public or private agencies, schools, or programmes offering services, usually funded by governmental bodies, community drives, donations, and fees.

Community skills Those abilities needed to function independently in the community. They may include: telephone skills, money management, pedestrian skills, use of public transportation, meal planning and cooking.

Community based care The blend of health and social services provided to an individual or family in their place of residence (or nearby) for the purpose of promoting, maintaining, or restoring health or minimizing the effects of illness and disability.

Community care networks Systems of health care providers organized to provide access to a comprehensive range of personal health services to members of a geographic area. The "network" may act as a health insurance plan offering its services for a specified premium. In this setting, primary care phy-

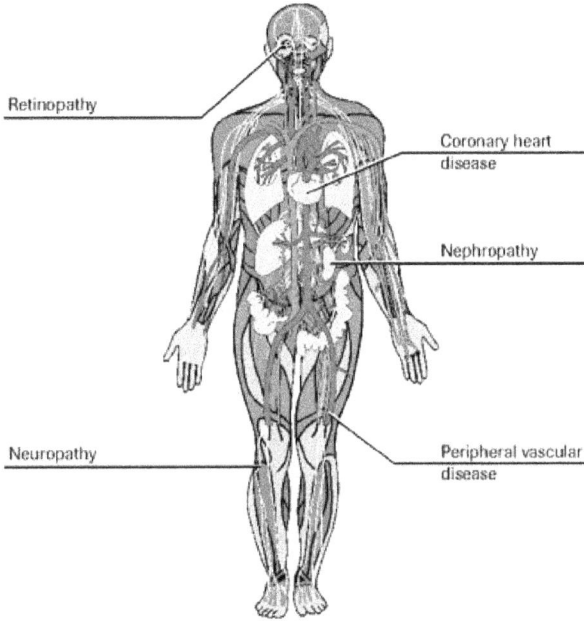

Fig. *Complications of diabetes*

sicians and mid-level professionals are usually used as the entry and referral point for services and a range of services tailored to the needs of the specific community.

Community health centre An ambulatory health care programme usually serving a geographic area which has scarce or nonexistent health services or a population with special health needs (sometimes known as the neighbourhood health centre). community health centres attempt to coordinate federal, state, and local resources into a single organization capable of delivering both health and related social services to a defined population. While such a centre may not directly provide all types of health care, it usually takes responsibility to arrange all medical services needed by its patient population.

Community health purchasing alliance Established by the health care and insurance reform act of 1993. CHPAs are responsible for assisting their members and particularly small employers to be prudent purchasers of health care by analyzing and disseminating data on prices, quality and patient satisfaction. CHPAs annually solicit bids for a variety of state mandated insurance products.

Community integration Term used in the disability community to refer to an individual's ability to share in community life including physical, cultural and social integration as well as self-determination.

Community nursing organization A federal demonstration program that capitates home health and durable medical equipment costs using nurses as care managers.

Community rating by class Modifies community rating principles to establish different premiums based upon the age, sex, marital status, or industry of the individual group. The 1981 amendments to the federal HMO Act allowed federally qualified HMOs to community rate by class. Defined under the Tax Equity and Fiscal Responsibility Act of 1982 (TEFRA), a competitive medical plan (CMP) resembles a health maintenance organization but is not qualified under the federal HMO Act; it must be state-licensed; to be eligible to participate in medicare, the CMP must be federally approved.

Community rating Method of establishing health insurance premiums on a communitywide rather than group-specific basis. The premium is based on a blend of the average cost of actual and anticipated health services use by all enrollees in a geographic area or industry and does not consider variables such as claims experience, age, sex, or health status of the covered population. Community rating spreads the cost of illness more evenly over the whole community. Federally qualified HMOs must community rate.

Comorbidity The simultaneous appearance of two or more illnesses, such as the co-occurrence of schizophrenia and substance abuse or of alcohol dependence and depression. The association may reflect a causal relationship between one disorder and another or an underlying vulnerability to both disorders. Also, the appearance of the illnesses may be unrelated to any common etiology or vulnerability.

Compensation A defence mechanism, operating unconsciously (see unconscious), by which one attempts to make up for real or fancied deficiencies. Also a conscious process in which one tries to make up for real or imagined defects of physique, performance skills, or psychological attributes. The two types frequently merge.

Competitive bid An agreement to perform specified work under specified conditions and for a specified price which has been determined through the use of the same cost estimating procedures as those of competitive private industrial concerns.

Complex A group of associated ideas having a common, strong emotional tone. These ideas are largely unconscious and significantly influence attitudes and associations.

Complications of diabetes Harmful effects that may happen when a person has diabetes. Some effects, such as hypoglycemia, can happen any time.

Others develop when a person has had diabetes for a long time. These include damage to the retina of the eye (retinopathy), the blood vessels (angiopathy), the nervous system (neuropathy), and the kidneys (nephropathy). Studies show that keeping blood glucose levels as close to the normal, nondiabetic range as possible may help prevent, slow, or delay harmful effects to the eyes, kidneys, and nerves.

Comprehension Understanding of spoken, written, or gestural communication.

Compulsion repetitive Ritualistic behavior such as hand washing or ordering or a mental act such as praying or repeating words silently that aims to prevent or reduce distress or prevent some dreaded event or situation. The person feels driven to perform such actions in response to an obsession or according to rules that must be applied rigidly, even though the behaviors are recognized to be excessive or unreasonable.

Concentration Maintaining attention on a task over a period of time; remaining attentive and not easily diverted.

Concrete thinking A style of thinking in which the individual sees each situation as unique and is unable to generalize from the similarities between situations. Language and perceptions are interpreted literally so that a proverb such as "a stitch in time saves nine" cannot be readily grasped.

Concussion The common result of a blow to the head or sudden deceleration usually causing an altered mental state, either temporary or prolonged. Physiologic and/or anatomic disruption of connections between some nerve cells in the brain may occur. Often used by the public to refer to a brief loss of consciousness.

Conduct disorder A disruptive behavior disorder of childhood characterized by repetitive and persistent violation of the rights of others or of age-appropriate social norms or rules. Symptoms may include bullying others, truancy or work absences, staying out at night despite parental prohibition before the age of 13, using alcohol or other substances before the age of 13, breaking into another's house or car, firesetting with the intent of causing serious damage, physical cruelty to people or animals, stealing, or use more than once of a weapon that could cause harm to others (e.g., brick, broken bottle, or gun).

Confabulation Verbalizations about people, places, and events with no basis in reality. May be a detailed account delivered.

Confusion A state in which a person is bewildered, perplexed or unable to self-orient.

Congenital defects Problems or conditions that are present at birth.

Congenital disability A disability that has existed since birth but is not necessarily hereditary.

The term birth defect is less desirable.

Congestive heart failure Heart failure caused by loss of pumping power by the heart, resulting in fluids collecting in the body. Congestive heart failure often develops gradually over several years, although it also can happen suddenly. It can be treated by drugs and in some cases, by surgery.

Conjugate movement Both eyes move simultaneously in the same direction. Convergence of the eyes toward the midline (crossed eyes) is a disconjugate movement.

Consciousness The state of awareness of the self and the environment.

Consumer, health care An individual who, by reason of disability, is eligible for, may require, has received, or is the recipient of some kind of human service, including such services as medical, rehabilitation, housing, transportation.

Continent The ability to control urination and bowel movements.

Contracture Loss of range of motion in a joint due to abnormal shortening of soft tissues.

Contraction The tightening of a muscle. In labour, the strong, rhythmic contractions of the muscles of the uterus open up the cervix and push the baby out. Any contractions before labour begins are usually irregular and don't increase in intensity or duration.

Contraindication A condition that makes a treatment not helpful or even harmful.

Contralateral Opposite side.

Contrecoup Bruising of the brain tissue on the side opposite where the blow was struck.

Control of attention Control refers to a person's ability to guide the selective process by directing and organizing whatever attentional capacity he or she has.

Controlled disease Taking care of oneself so that a disease has less of an effect on the body. People with diabetes can "control" the disease by staying on their diets, by exercising, by taking medicine if it is needed, and by monitoring their blood glucose. This care will help keep the glucose (sugar) level in the blood from becoming either too high or too low.

Contusion, brain A bruise. The result of a blow to the head which bruises the brain.

Conventional therapy A system of diabetes management practiced by most people with diabetes; the system consists of one or two insulin injections each day, daily self-monitoring of blood glucose, and a standard program of nutrition and exercise. The main objective in this form of treatment is to avoid very high and very low blood glucose (sugar). Also called: Standard Therapy. The diabetes control and complications trial has shown that intensive therapy, rather than conventional therapy, can reduce the risk of complications.

Convergence Movement of two eyeballs inward to focus on an object moved closer. The nearer the object, the greater is the degree of convergence necessary to maintain single vision.

Conversion disorder One of the somatoform disorders (but in some classifications called a dissociative disorder), characterized by a symptom suggestive of a neurologic disorder that affects sensation or voluntary motor function. The symptom is not consciously or intentionally produced, it cannot be explained fully by any known general medical condition, and it is severe enough to impair functioning or require medical attention. Commonly seen symptoms are blindness, double vision, deafness, impaired coordination, paralysis, and seizures.

Coping mechanisms Ways of adjusting to environmental stress without altering one's goals or purposes; includes both conscious and unconscious mechanisms.

Coping skills The ability to deal with problems and difficulties by attempting to overcome them or accept them.

Coprophagia Eating of filth or feces.

Core therapies, brain injury Basic therapy services provided by professionals on a brain injury rehabilitation unit. Usually refers to nursing, physical therapy, occupational therapy, speech-language pathology, neuropsychology, social work and therapeutic recreation.

Coronary disease Damage to the heart. Not enough blood flows through the vessels because they are blocked with fat or have become thick and hard; this harms the muscles of the heart. People with diabetes are at a higher risk of coronary disease.

Coronary artery bypass Surgery in which a healthy blood vessel taken from another part of the body is used to make a new path for blood around a blocked artery leading to the heart. This restores the flow of oxygen and nutrients to the heart. Also called aortocoronary bypass and CAB.

Coronary artery disease A disease in which there is a narrowing or blockage of the coronary arteries (blood vessels that carry blood and oxygen to the heart). Coronary artery disease is usually caused by atherosclerosis (a build up of fatty material and plaque inside the coronary arteries). The disease may cause chest pain, shortness of breath during exercise, and heart attacks. The risk of coronary artery disease is increased by having a family history of coronary artery disease before age 50, older age, smoking tobacco, high blood pressure, high cholesterol, diabetes, lack of exercise, and obesity. Also called CAD and coronary heart disease.

Coronary heart disease A disease in which there is a narrowing or blockage of the coronary arteries (blood vessels that carry blood and oxygen to the heart). Coronary heart disease is usually caused by atherosclerosis (a build up of fatty material and plaque inside the coronary arteries). The disease may cause chest pain, shortness of breath during exercise, and heart attacks. The risk of coronary heart disease is increased by having a family history of coronary heart disease before age 50, older age, smoking tobacco, high blood pressure, high cholesterol, diabetes, lack of exercise, and obesity. Also called CAD and coronary artery disease.

Cortical blindness Loss of vision resulting from a lesion of the primary visual areas of the occipital lobe. Light reflex is preserved.

Corpus The body of the uterus.

Corpus callosum A large bundle of nerve fibers that connect the left and right cerebral hemispheres. In the lateral section, it looks a bit like a "C" on its side.

Corpus luteum The corpus luteum (Latin for "yellow body") (plural corpora lutea) is a temporary endocrine structure in mammals, involved in production of estrogen and progestogen, which is needed to maintain the endometrium.

Cortex The outer layer of the cerebrum, composed of six cell layers of deeply folded and ridged gray matter.

Corticosteroid Any steroid hormone made in the adrenal cortex (the outer part of the adrenal gland). They are also made in the laboratory. Cortico-steroids have many different effects in the body, and are used to treat many different conditions. They may be used as hormone replacement, to suppress the

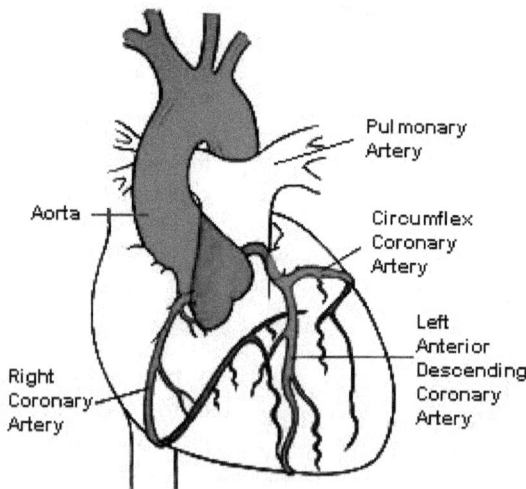

Fig. *Coronary artery disease*

immune system, and to treat some side effects of cancer and its treatment. Corticosteroids are also used to treat certain lymphomas and lymphoid leukemias.

Corticotropin A hormone made in the pituitary gland. Corticotropin acts on the outer part of the adrenal gland to control its release of corticosteroid hormones. More corticotropin is made during times of stress. Also called ACTH and adrenocorticotropic hormone.

Cortisol A hormone made by the adrenal cortex (the outer layer of the adrenal gland). It helps the body use glucose (a sugar), protein, and fats. Cortisol made in the laboratory is called hydrocortisone. It is used to treat many conditions, including inflammation, allergies, and some cancers. Cortisol is a type of glucocorticoid hormone.

Cortisone A natural steroid hormone produced in the adrenal gland. It can also be made in the laboratory. Cortisone reduces swelling and can suppress immune responses.

Cortisol One of several hormones made in the adrenal glands. The primary responsibility of cortisol is to activate the immune system; it also is involved with the metabolism of glucose, and can cause elevation of the blood sugar level.Cortisol is in the class of hormones called corticosteroids (or steroids). It, and synthetic versions such as prednisone, are available as prescription medications for treating severe illnesses including asthma and arthritis; they are sometimes also used for severe cases of minor illnesses like poison ivy rashes.

Counterphobia Deliberately seeking out and exposing oneself to, rather than avoiding, the object or situation that is consciously or unconsciously feared.

Counterregulatory An attempt by the body to correct a perceived abnormality. The correction may be in the form of an endocrine, neuronal, or other mechanism. In diabetes, this is a term that is usually used to describe the body's normal response through other hormones, epinephrine and gluco-corticoids (which are called "counterregulatory hormones") to correct blood sugars that are too low.

Coup damage Damage to the brain at the point of impact.

Coxsackie B4 virus An agent that has been shown to damage the beta cells of the pancreas in lab tests. This virus may be one cause of insulin-dependent diabetes.Be sure to read Common Class of Viruses Implicated as Cause of Type 1 Diabetes.

C-Peptide A substance that the pancreas releases into the bloodstream in equal amounts to insulin. A test of C-peptide levels will show how much insulin the body is making.

Creatinine An end-product of protein metabolism found in the blood and urine, that can be used to help assess if the kidneys are working adequately. A related test, using simultaneous measurements of a timed urine sample plus a blood creatinine test, is called the creatinine clearance.

CSII Continuous Subcutaneous Insulin Infusion

CT scan/computerized axial tomography A series of X-rays taken at different levels of the brain that allows the direct visualization of the skull and intracranial structures. A scan is often taken soon after the injury to help decide if surgery is needed. The scan may be repeated later to see how the brain is recovering.

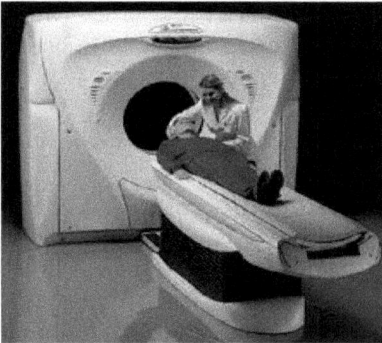

Fig. *CT scan*

Cue A signal or direction used to assist a person in performing an activity (telling a person the initial of your first name serves as a cue when he or she cannot remember your name.)

Cyclamate A man-made chemical that people used instead of sugar. The Food and Drug Administration banned the sale of cyclamates in 1973 because lab tests showed that large amounts of cyclamates can cause bladder cancer in rats.

Cytotoxins Substances that are toxic to Cells; they may be involved in Immunity or may be contained in Venoms. These are distinguished from Cytostatic Agents in degree of effect. Some of them are used as Cytotoxic Antibiotics. The mecha-nism of action of many of these are as Alkylating Agents or Mitosis Modulators.

Cyclothymic disorder In DSM-IV, one of the bipolar disorders characterized by numerous hypomanic episodes and frequent periods of depressed mood or loss of interest or pleasure. These episodes do not meet the criteria for a full manic episode or major depressive disorder.

Cystic fibrosis An inherited disorder occurring in children and young adults, with chronic pulmonary disease (due to production of sticky mucus in the respiratory tract), pancreatic deficiency (leading to diabetes), abnormally high levels of electrolytes in the sweat, and other disorders.

Cystoscope is a thin, lighted viewing tool that is put into the urethra and moved into the bladder.

When the cystoscope is inside your bladder, sterile water or saline is injected through the scope to help expand your bladder and to create a clear view. A medicine may also be injected through the scope to reduce chances of infection. Tiny instruments may be inserted through the scope to collect tissue samples (biopsy) to test.`

Cystoscopy Examination of the bladder and urethra using a cystoscope, inserted into the urethra. A cystoscope is a thin, tube-like instrument with a light and a lens for viewing. It may also have a tool to remove tissue to be checked under a microscope for signs of disease.

Cystoscope

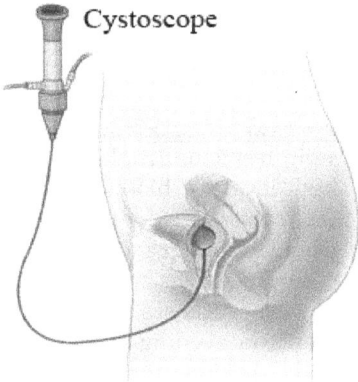

Fig. *Cystoscopy*

Cytomegalovirus infection Cytomegalovirus is a common viral infection transmitted by saliva, breast milk, or urine. Relatively rare and relatively mild, the infection does occasionally cause deafness, visual impairment and neurological problems in a developing foetus.

Cytotec is a drug used to help ripen the cervix. It is put directly on the cervix and the patient is monitored in the hospital while it is on. Usually, it is put in overnight and pitocin is administered in the morning to trigger contractions.

D

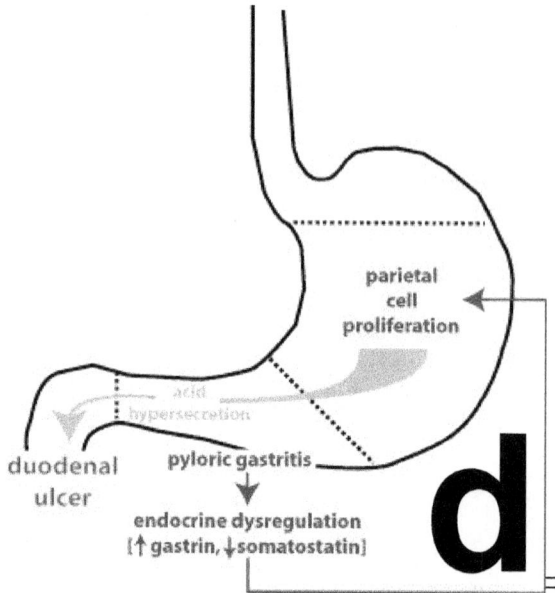

parietal
cell
proliferation

acid
hypersecretion

duodenal
ulcer

pyloric gastritis

endocrine dysregulation
[↑gastrin, ↓somatostatin]

D antigen A red cell antigen of the Rh blood group system.

D Cell Endocrine cells found throughout the gastro-intestinal tract and in islets of the Pancreas. D Cells secrete Somatostatin that acts in both an endocrine and paracrine manner. Somatostatin acts on a variety of tissues including the Pituitary Gland; Gastro-intestinal tract; Pancreas; and kidney by inhibiting the release of hormones, such as growth hormone; gastrin; insulin; and renin.

Dawn phenomenon A sudden rise in blood glucose levels in the early morning hours. This condition sometimes occurs in people with insulin-dependent diabetes and (rarely) in people with noninsulin-dependent diabetes. Unlike the Somogyi effect, it is not a result of an insulin reaction. People who have high levels of blood glucose in the mornings before eating may need to monitor their blood glucose during the night. If blood glucose levels are rising, adjustments in evening snacks or insulin dosages may be recommended.

Day blindness Visual impairments limiting one or more of the basic functions of the eye: visual acuity, dark adaptation, colour vision, or peripheral vision. These may result from eye diseases; optic nerve diseases; visual pathway diseases; occipital lobe diseases; ocular motility disorder; and other conditions. Visual disability refers to inability of the individual to perform specific visual tasks, such as reading, writing, orientation, or traveling unaided.

Day treatment A nonresidential mental health service that provides an integrated set of educational, counseling, and family interventions which involve a child or adolescent for at least 5 hours a day, and that can be provided in a school setting, community mental health centres, hospitals or elsewhere in the community. Day treatment programmes that are provided in hospitals are referred to as partial hospitalization. Day treatment is considered the most intensive of the nonresidential services that can continue over a longer period of time.

Death rate The number of deaths per some portion of a population, usually 100,000 individuals.

Debridement The removal of infected, hurt, or dead tissue.

Decision-making capacity The ability of a person to make decisions for himself or herself. Three types of criteria are generally used to judge an individual's decisionmaking capacity: status criteria (e.g., consciousness or age), outcome criteria (e.g., a judgment about the "reasonableness" of a person's decision), and functional criteria (e.g., evidencing an understanding of relevant information and issues).

Decision-making skills Skills relevant to the ability to make rational, health-promoting decisions about one's life. Often a part of life-skills training interventions.

Decision-specific decisionmaking capacity: An individual's capacity to make a specific decision. A concept that has emerged in the legal and ethical debate about determining individuals' decisionmaking capacity is that an individual's capacity to make a decision may differ for each decision, depending on the characteristics of the decision and the circumstances in which it is made.

Declopramide A substance that blocks the process cells use to repair DNA. It may help anticancer drugs and radiation kill more cancer cells. It is a type of chemosensitizer and a type of radiosensitizer.

Decubitus ulcers or bedsores, are localized injuries to the skin and/or underlying tissue usually over a bony prominence, as a result of pressure, or pressure in combination with shear and/or friction. Most commonly this will be the sacrum, coccyx, heels or the hips, but other sites such as the elbows, knees, ankles or the back of the cranium can be affected.

Deductible An initial expense of a specified amount of approved charges for covered services within a given time period (e.g., $75 per year) payable by an insured person before the insurer assumes liability for any additional costs of covered services. The Part B deductible is the portion of approved charges (for covered services each calendar year) for which a beneficiary is responsible before medicare assumes liability.

Deep tissue bodywork General term for a range of therapies that seek to improve the function of the body's connective tissues and/or muscles. Among the conditions treated are whiplash, low back and neck pain, and degenerative diseases, such as multiple sclerosis.

Deep vein thrombosis A deep vein thrombosis (DVT) is a blood clot in a vein. Blood clots in veins most often occur in the legs but can occur elsewhere in the body, including the arms. This leaflet is about blood clots in leg veins.

The most common cause of a blood clot developing in a vein is immobility. A complication can occur in some cases where part of the blood clot breaks off and travels to the lung (pulmonary embolus). This is usually prevented if you are given anticoagulation treatment.

Deep leg veins are the larger veins that go through the muscles of the calf and thighs. They are not the veins that you can see just below the skin, neither are they the same as varicose veins. When you have a DVT, the blood flow in the vein is partially or completely blocked by the blood clot.

A calf vein is the common site for a DVT. A thigh vein is less commonly affected. Rarely, other deep veins in the body can be blocked by blood clots.

Defecation Movement of feces (undigested food, bacteria, mucus, and cells from the lining of the intestines) through the bowel and out the anus. Also called bowel movement.

Defence mechanism Unconscious intrapsychic processes serving to provide relief from emotional conflict and anxiety. Conscious efforts are frequently made for the same reasons, but true defence mechanisms are uncon-

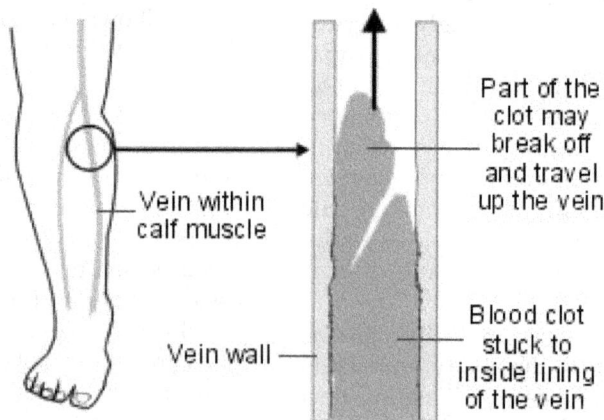

Part of the clot may break off and travel up the vein

Vein within calf muscle

Blood clot stuck to inside lining of the vein

Vein wall

Fig. *Deep vein thrombosis*

scious. Some of the common defence mechanisms defined in this glossary are compensation, conversion, denial, displacement, dissociation, idealization, identification, incorporation, introjection, projection, rationalization, reaction formation, regression, sublimation, substitution, symbolization, and undoing.

Deferred therapy Closely watching a patient's condition but not giving treatment unless symptoms appear or change, or there are changes in test results. Deferred therapy avoids problems that may be caused by treatments such as radiation or surgery. It is used to find early signs that the condition is getting worse. During deferred therapy, patients may be given certain exams and tests. It is sometimes used in prostate cancer. Also called expectant management.

Defibrotide A substance that is being studied in the prevention of veno-occlusive disease, a rare complication of high-dose chemotherapy and stem cell transplantation in which small veins in the liver become blocked.The belief is not part of a cultural tradition such as an article of religious faith. The belief that one's feelings, impulses, thoughts, or actions are not one's own but have been imposed by some external force.

Degenerative disorders Diseases whose progression cannot be arrested. These disorders cause progressive deterioration of mental and neurological function, often over years. Alzheimer's disease is the most prevalent degenerative dementia. The ultimate cause of such disorders is unknown.

Dehydration Great loss of body water. A very high level of glucose (sugar) in the urine causes loss of a great deal of water, and the person becomes very thirsty.

Deja vu A paramnesia consisting of the sensation or illusion that one is seeing what one has seen before.

Delayed-type hypersensitivity An inflammatory reaction that occurs 24 to 48 hours after challenge with antigen and is a result of cell-mediated immunity.

Delinquent behavior As it pertains to adolescence, includes two types of acts: 1) acts committed by minors that would be considered crimes if committed by an adult, and 2) status offenses (i.e., acts that are offenses solely because they are committed by a juvenile, such as running away from home, or truancy).

Delirium tremens Acute, sometimes fatal, psychotic reaction caused by excessive intake of alcoholic beverages over a long period of time. Usually seen after withdrawal from heavy alcohol intake. Symptoms include mental confusion, excitement, hallucinations, anxiety, tremors of the tongue and extremities, fever, sweating and stomach and chest pain.

Delta Cell A type of cell in the pancreas in areas called the islets of Langerhans. Delta cells make somatostatin, a hormone that is believed to control how the beta cells make and release insulin and how the alpha cells make and release glucagon.

Delusion A false belief based on an incorrect inference about external reality and firmly sustained despite clear evidence to the contrary. The belief is not part of a cultural tradition such as an article of religious faith. Among the more frequently reported delusions are the following: (i) *Delusion of control* The belief that one's feelings, impulses, thoughts, or actions are not one's own but have been imposed by some external force. (ii) *Delusion of poverty* The conviction that one is, or will be, bereft of all material possessions. (iii) *Delusion of reference* The conviction that events, objects, or other people in the immediate environment have a particular and unusual significance (usually negative). (iv) *Delusional jealousy* The false belief that one's sexual partner is unfaithful; also called the Othello delusion.

Delusion of reference The conviction that events, objects, or other people in the immediate environment have a particular and unusual significance (usually negative).

Dementia pugilistic Brain damage resulting from repeated head trauma. Also known as boxer's or fighter's dementia or encephalopathy.

Dementia Progressive impairment in mental function and global cognitive abilities of long duration (months to years) in an alert individual due to brain disease. Symptoms include memory loss, loss of ' language function, inability to think abstractly, inability to care for oneself, personality change, emotional instability, a loss of sense of time and place, and behavior problems.

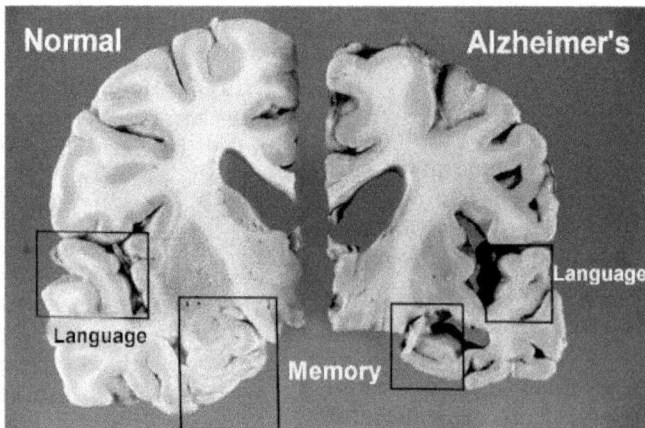

Fig. *Dementia*

Dementing illness, disease, or condition: One of the more than 70 illnesses, diseases, and conditions that can cause dementia. Disease of blood vessels is the second most common cause of dementia. Some of the diseases that cause dementia are AIDS, Down's Syndrome, Creutzfeldt-Jakob disease, Huntington's disease, Binswanger's disease, and normal pressure hydrocephalus (NPH). Many other types of disorders may or may not produce dementia, such as certain infectious, metabolic, and nutritional disorders.

Demonstration project An intevention that is typically in an experimental (unproven) stage of effectiveness and is supported for a limited period with an evaluation component.

Demyelinating disease Outer wrapping (myelin sheath) of the nerves or nerve fibres is destroyed. One example is multiple sclerosis.

Demyelination A disease process that destroys the myelin sheaths surrounding nerve fibres in the central or peripheral nervous system, affecting conduction of nerve impulses (e.g., in multiple sclerosis).

Denaturation The separation of double-stranded DNA into its single strands or of protein into its constituent peptides through treatment with chemicals, heat, or extremes of pH. The narrow range of temperature or chemical concentrations at which DNA and proteins denature is characteristic of the particular molecule and is used to identify their presence. Denaturation also results in loss or reduction of the biological properties of the substance.

Dendrite Any of the shorter branched extensions of the cell body of a neuron, which makes contact - with other neurons and carries nerve impulses into the cell body. Dendrites receive chemical signals from other cells.

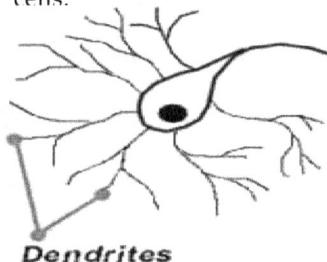

Dendrites

Fig. *Dendrite*

Dengue fever An acute febrile disease caused by an arbovirus, transmitted by mosquitoes of the genus Aedes, and characterized by fever, severe pains in the head, eyes, muscles, and joints, and a skin eruption.

Dendritic cell vaccine A vaccine made of antigens and dendritic antigen-presenting cells (APCs).

Denial In psychiatry, a state in which a person is unable or unwilling to see the truth or reality about an issue or situation. It is a defence mechanism, operating unconsciously, used to resolve emotional conflict and allay anxiety by disavowing thoughts, feelings, wishes,

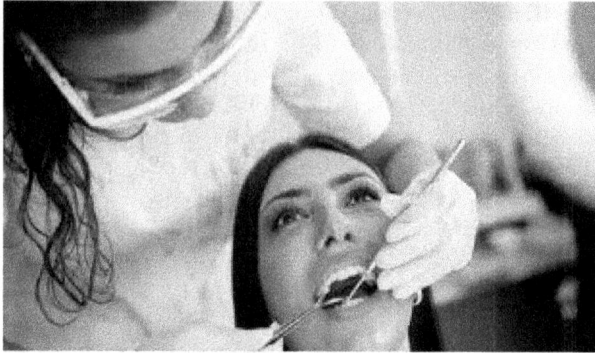

Fig. *Dental and oral health*

needs, or external reality factors that are consciously intolerable.

Dental and oral health The term dental means of or relating to the teeth or dentistry (the health profession that cares for teeth); and the term oral means of or relating to all aspects of the oral cavity (such as the gums and the tongue). Thus, dental and oral health refers to the health of these stuctures.

Dental caries The localized, progressive decay of a tooth, starting on the surface, and if untreated, extending to the inner tooth chamber and resulting in infection.

Dentistry, Wholistic are licensed dentists who bring an interdisciplinary approach to their practice, often incorporating such methods as homeopathy, nutrition and acupuncture into their treatment plans. Most wholistic dentists emphasize wellness and preventive care and avoid silver-mercury fillings.

Denver Developmental Screening Test A standardized test, developed in 1967, for the detection of developmental and behavioral problems in children.

Dependency ratio The number of children and elderly people per every 100 people of working age.

Depersonalization Feelings of unreality or strangeness concerning either the environment, the self, or both. This is characteristic of depersonalization disorder and may also occur in schizotypal personality disorder, schizophrenia, and in those persons experiencing overwhelming anxiety, stress, or fatigue.

Depreciation An estimate of the value of consumption of a fixed asset during a specific period of time.

Deprenyl A drug shown to slow the progression of Parkinson's disease in clinical trials by blocking the activity of MAO-B.

Depo-provera This injected form of birth control requires injections of progesterone every 12 weeks.

Fig. *Depression*

Depression When used to describe a mood, depression refers to feelings of sadness, despair, and discouragement. As such, depression may be a normal feeling state. The overt manifestations are highly variable and may be culture specific. Depression may be a symptom seen in a variety of mental or physical disorders, a syndrome of associated symptoms secondary to an underlying disorder, or a specific mental disorder. Slowed thinking, decreased pleasure, decreased purposeful physical activity, guilt and hopelessness, and disorders of eating and sleeping may be seen in the depressive syndrome. DSM-IV classifies depression by severity, recurrence, and association with hypomania or mania. Other categorizations divide depression into reactive and endogenous depressions on the basis of precipitants or symptom clusters. Depression in children may be indicated by refusal to go to school, anxiety, excessive reaction to separation from parental figures, antisocial behavior, and somatic complaints.

Dermoid cyst A type of benign (not cancer) germ cell tumour (type of tumour that begins in the cells that give rise to sperm or eggs) that often contains several different types of tissue such as hair, muscle, and bone. Also called mature teratoma.

Dermatitis Inflammatory condition of the skin, characterized by redness and pain or itching. The type of skin rash or lesions that occur may suggest a particular allergy, disease or infection. The condition may be chronic or acute; treatment is specific to the cause.

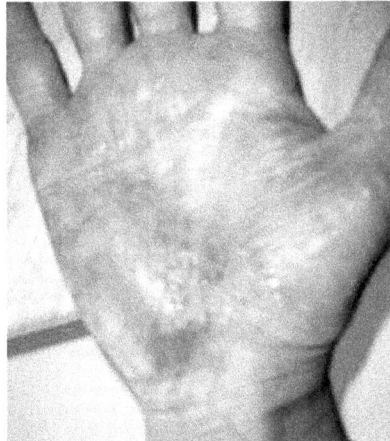

Fig. *Dermatitis*

Dermatofibromas Fibrous, tumour like nodule of the skin most commonly found on the arms or legs. Requires no treatment. It is sometimes associated with systemic lupus erythematosus.

Dermatomyositis Inflammation of connective tissue, with degenerative changes in muscles and skin. This causes weakness and muscle wasting, especially in the arms and legs.

Description Where there is a sale of goods by description, it is a term of the contract that the goods correspond with the description; otherwise the buyer may reject the goods. A sale is by description where the buyer cannot verify the description of the goods before sale (e.g. tinned goods).

Descriptive toxicology A branch of toxicology dealing with phenomena above the molecular level, Descriptive toxicology relies heavily on the techniques of pathology, statistics, and pharmacology to demonstrate the relationship cause and effect (e.g., that certain substances cause liver cancer in certain species within a certain time). It is most often used in regulatory schemes requiring testing.

Desensitization A method to reduce or stop a response such as an allergic reaction to something. For instance, if a person with diabetes has a bad reaction to taking a full dose of beef insulin, the doctor gives the person a very small amount of the insulin at first. Over a period of time, larger doses are given until the person is taking the full dose. This is one way to help the body get used to the full dose and to avoid having the allergic reaction.

Designated driver (programmes) The practice of a group designating a person in the group to not drink alcohol and to be the driver for others who may be drinking alcoholic beverages.

Detached retina Separation or tear of the light-sensitive tissue at the back of the eye (retina) from the eye. Symptoms include light flashes or floating spots in the field of vision, blurred vision, partial loss of vision or gradual vision loss. Often curable with prompt surgical treatment.

Development A process of growth and differentiation by successive changes. In humans, includes physiological development; cognitive development (increasing ability to think critically and engage in higher order reasoning); ego development (qualitatively different psychosocial stages, including internalization of the rules of social intercourse, increasing cognitive complexity and tolerance of ambiguity, and growing objectivity); and moral development (changes in the ability to recognize and reason about moral dilemmas and to make choices based on moral principles and reasoning).

Developmental disorders A set of mental disorders characterized by deviations from the normal path of child development. Such disorders may be pervasive, thereby affecting multiple areas of development (e.g., autism), or specific, affecting only one aspect of development (e.g., arithmetic disorder).

Developmental neurotoxicity tests Experimental studies of the offspring of animals exposed to toxic substances during pregnancy and lactation in order to determine the nature and extent of structural or functional damage to the nervous system of the offspring.

Developmentally appropriate Health promotion, prevention, and treatment services and environments designed so that they fit the emotional, behavioral/experiential, and intellectual levels of the individual who is to benefit from the service.

Device, medical An instrument, apparatus, implant, in vitro reagent, or other similar or related article intended for use in the diagnosis, cure, mitigation, treatment, or prevention of disease, or intended to affect the structure or function of the body, that works through nonchemical, nonmetabolic means.

Dextrose A simple sugar found in the blood. It is the body's main source of energy. Also called glucose.

Diabetes Diabetes is a metabolic disorder during which the body has a reduced ability (or none at all) to produce the hormone insulin or the insulin is inactivated (insulin resistance).

The body insulin is needed for the blood sugar (glucose) to enter cells and provide them with nourishment. Due to the lack of insulin or insulin resistance, protein and fat metabolism is also affected.

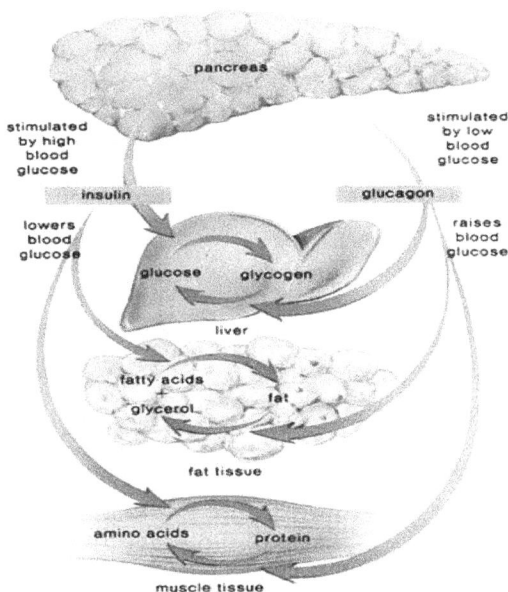

Fig. *Diabetes*

Diabetes is not a single disease, but represents several different diseases with completely different variety of reasons, but the common feature is that blood sugar level is too high.

The two best known and most common forms of diabetes are type 1 and type 2. *Type 1* is also known as children's and juvenile's diabetes because it usually breaks out in childhood or adolescence. *Type 2* is a form of adult-onset diabetes which is almost always present after 40 years of age.

Diabetes control and complications trial A 10-year study (1983-1993) funded by the National Institute of Diabetes and Digestive and Kidney Diseases to assess the effects of intensive therapy on the long-term complications of diabetes. The study proved that intensive management of insulin-dependent diabetes prevents or slows the development of eye, kidney, and nerve damage caused by diabetes.

Diabetes insipidus is often called "water diabetes" to set it apart from "sugar diabetes." It is caused by a deficiency of antidiuretic hormone (ADH) normally secreted by the pituitary gland. Usually a temporary condition. Characterized by passage of large amounts of diluted, colourless urine (up to 15 quarts a day), unquenchable thirst, dry skin and constipation.

Diabetes mellitus A disease that occurs when the body is not able to use sugar as it should. The body needs sugar for growth and energy for daily activities. It gets sugar when it changes food into glucose (a form of sugar). A hormone called *insulin* is needed for the glucose to be taken up and used by the body. Diabetes occurs when the body cannot make use of the glucose in the blood for energy because either the pancreas is not able to make enough insulin or the insulin that is available is not effective. The beta cells in areas of the pancreas called the islets of Langerhans usually make insulin. There are two main types of diabetes mellitus: insulin-dependent (Type 1) and noninsulin-dependent (Type 2). In insulin-dependent diabetes (IDDM), the pancreas makes little or no insulin because the insulin-producing beta cells have been destroyed. This type usually appears suddenly and most commonly in younger people under age 30. Treatment consists of daily insulin injections or use of an insulin pump, a planned diet and regular exercise, and daily self-monitoring of blood glucose. In noninsulin-dependent diabetes (NIDDM), the pancreas makes some insulin, sometimes too much. The insulin, however, is not effective (see Insulin Resistance). NIDDM is controlled by diet and exercise and daily monitoring of glucose levels. Sometimes oral drugs that lower blood glucose levels or insulin injections are needed. This type of diabetes usually develops gradually, most often in people over 40 years of age. NIDDM accounts for 90 to 95 percent of diabetes. The signs of diabetes include having to urinate often, losing weight, getting very thirsty, and being hungry all the time. Other signs are blurred vision, itching, and slow healing of sores. People with untreated or undiagnosed diabetes are thirsty and have to urinate often because glucose builds to a high level in the bloodstream and the kidneys are working hard to flush out the extra amount. People with untreated diabetes often get hungry and tired because the body is not able to use food the way it should. In insulin-dependent diabetes, if the level of insulin is too low for a long period of time, the body begins to break down its stores of fat for energy. This causes the body to release acids (ketones) into the blood. The result is called ketoacidosis, a severe condition that may put a person into a coma if not treated right away. The causes of diabetes are not known. Scientists think that insulin- dependent diabetes may be more than one disease and may have many causes. They are looking at hereditary (whether or not the person has parents or other family members with the disease) and at factors both inside and outside

Diabetes Affects the Nerves

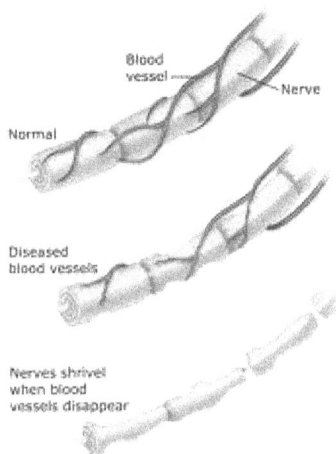

Fig. *Diabetic amyotrophy*

the body, including viruses. Noninsulin-dependent diabetes appears to be closely associated with obesity and with the body resisting the action of insulin.

Diabetic amyotrophy A disease of the nerves leading to the muscles. This condition affects only one side of the body and occurs most often in older men with mild diabetes.

There are different types of diabetic neuropathy. Peripheral neuropathy is a type of diabetic neuropathy that affects the toes, feet, legs, hands, and arms. can develop without notice or pain and develop into ulcers, infections, and cause tissue death .

Diabetic coma A severe emergency in which a person is not conscious because the blood glucose (sugar) is too low or too high. If the glucose level is too low, the person has hypo-glycemia; if the level is too high, the person has

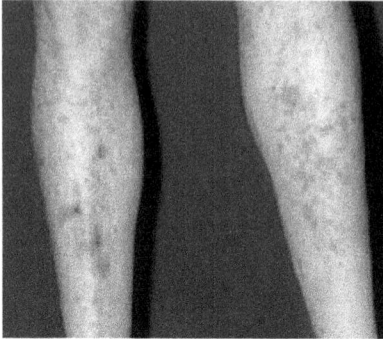

Fig. *Diabetic dermopathy*

hyperglycemia and may develop ketoacidosis.

Diabetic dermopathy A characteristic skin disorder found in up to 50% of male adults and 30% of female adults with diabetes. The lesions may be round or oval and usually are red or reddish brown, and usually measure 1-3 inches. They usually occur on the thigh or shin, but may appear also on the scalp, forearm and trunk. There is not an effective treatment and the lesions tend to disappear spontaneously after several years. The incidence of diabetic dermopathy in patients with all three complications is much higher than in patients with just one complication..

Diabetic ketoacidosis Serious complication of diabetes mellitus in which the body produces acids that cause fluid and electrolyte disorders, dehydration and sometimes coma. It is caused by a profound lack of circulating insulin. This may happen because of illness, taking too little insulin, or getting too little exercise. The body starts using stored fat for energy, and ketone bodies (acids) build up in the blood. Keto-acidosis starts slowly and builds up. The signs include nausea and vomiting, which can lead to loss of water from the body, stomach pain, and deep and rapid breathing. Other signs are a flushed face, dry skin and mouth, a fruity breath odor, a rapid and weak pulse, and low blood pressure. If the person is not given fluids and insulin right away, ketoacidosis can lead to coma and even death.

Diabetic myelopathy Spinal cord damage found in some people with diabetes.

Diabetic osteopathy Loss of foot bone as viewed by x-ray; usually temporary. Also called "disappearing bone disease."

Diabetic retinopathy A disease of the small blood vessels of the retina of the eye. When retinopathy first starts, the tiny blood vessels in the retina become swollen, and they leak a little fluid into the centre of the retina. The person's sight may be blurred. This condition is

Fig. *Diabetic retinopathy*

called background retinopathy. About 80 percent of people with background retinopathy never have serious vision problems, and the disease never goes beyond this first stage. However, if retinopathy progresses, the harm to sight can be more serious. Many new, tiny blood vessels grow out and across the eye. This is called neovascularization. The vessels may break and bleed into the clear gel that fills the centre of the eye, blocking vision. Scar tissue may also form near the retina, pulling it away from the back of the eye. This stage is called proliferative retinopathy, and it can lead to impaired vision and even blindness.

Diabetogenic Causing diabetes; some drugs cause blood glucose (sugar) to rise, resulting in diabetes.

Diabetologist A doctor who sees and treats people with diabetes mellitus.

Diagnosable mental disorders Disorders included in the American Psychiatric Association's Diagnostic and Statistical Manual of Mental Disorders, 3d cd., revised.

Diagnosis The term used when a doctor finds that a person has a certain medical problem or disease.

Diagnostic guidelines A practice guideline targeted at evaluating patients with particular symptoms for the presence of diseases that would benefit from intervention. They are also used to guide the screening of asymptomatic patient populations for early stages of disease.

Diagnostic mammogram X-ray of the breasts used to check for breast cancer after a lump or other sign or symptom of breast cancer has been found.

Diagnostic procedure A specific test or series of steps done to help diagnose a disease or condition. Mammograms and colonscopies are examples of diagnostic procedures.

Diagnostic technique A type of method or test used to help diagnose a disease or condition. Imaging tests and tests to measure blood pressure, pulse, and temperature are examples of diagnostic techniques.

Diagnostic trial A research study that evaluates methods of detecting disease.

Diagnosis-related groups Entries in a taxonomy of types of hospitalizations based on groupings of diagnostic categories drawn from the International Classification of Diseases and modified by the presence of a surgical procedure, patient age, presence or absence of significant comorbidities or complications, and other relevant criteria. DRGs have been mandated for use in establishing payment amounts for individual admissions under Medicare's prospective hospital payment system as required by the Social Security Amendments of 1983 (Public Law 98-21).

Diagnostic inteview schedule for children A child-oriented version of the Diagnostic Interview Schedule, a questionnaire developed for use by the National Institute of Mental Health for its epidemiologic catchment area survey of mental disability in adults.

Diagnostic test A medical test administered to those asymptomatic but high risk individuals identified ' by a screening test, or a test used to identify the cause of abnormal physical signs or symptoms.

Dialysate The sterile fluid used in dialysis to remove toxic substances from the blood. The chemical composition of the dialysate varies according to the types of substances being removed. According to the basic principle of osmosis, the dialysate generally contains low concentrations of the waste substances.

Dialysis A method for removing waste such as urea from the blood when the kidneys can no longer do the job. The two types of dialysis are—hemodialysis and peritoneal dialysis.

In *hemodialysis*, the patient's blood is passed through a tube into a machine that filters out waste products. The cleansed blood is then returned to the body.

In *peritoneal dialysis*, a special solution is run through a tube into the peritoneum, a thin tissue that lines the cavity of the abdomen. The body's waste products are removed through the tube. There are three types of peritoneal dialysis. *Continuous ambulatory peritoneal dialysis* (CAPD), the most common type, needs no machine and can be done at home. *Continuous cyclic peritoneal dialysis* (CCPD) uses a machine and is usually per-

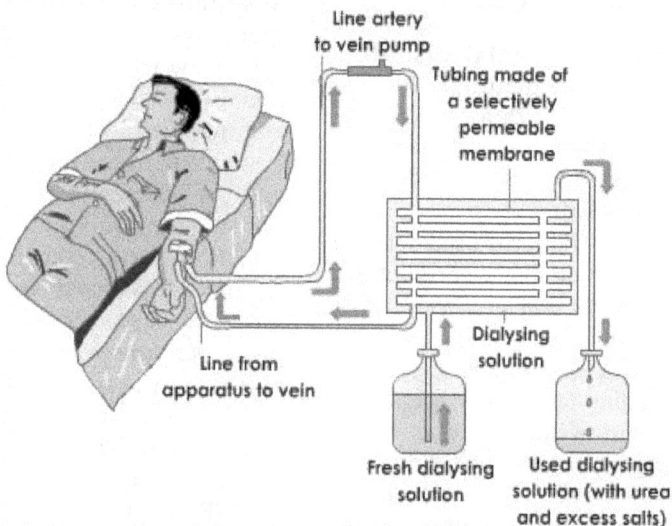

Fig. *Dialysis*

formed at night when the person is sleeping. *Intermittent peritoneal dialysis* (IPD) uses the same type of machine as CCPD, but is usually done in the hospital because treatment takes longer.

Hemodialysis and peritoneal dialysis may be used to treat people with diabetes who have kidney failure.

Dialyzer A device used to effect dialysis. The term is often used synonymously with hemodialyzer. The dialyzer has two spaces separated by a thin membrane. Blood passes on one side of the membrane and dialysis fluid passes on the other. The wastes and excess water pass from the blood through the membrane into the dialysis fluid, which is then discarded. The cleaned blood is returned to our bloodstream.

Diaphoresis Profuse perspiration.

Diaphragm Large, thin muscle that separates the chest cavity from the abdominal cavity.

Diaphragmatic paralysis Complete loss of function of the diaphragm. The diaphragm is used with each breath of air.

Diarrheal diseases Diseases characterized by the passage of loose watery stools, usually at more frequent than normal intervals. The dehydration that accompanies diarrhea is the cause of great morbidity and mortality, particularly among infants and children.

Diathermy is a deep heating device used to promote circulation and control pain. This machine works by generating electromagnetic energy, similar to a microwave oven, but not as intense. These milder "radio waves" are directed into the body area needing treatment, and produce heat from within the tissues. Interestingly, the surface does not get hot, only the deep tissues. Patients only feel a mild, comfortable warm sensation. Diathermy is more effective at promoting circulation in the deep muscle tissues than a surface heater such as a heating pad. The target area is treated directly and comfortably.

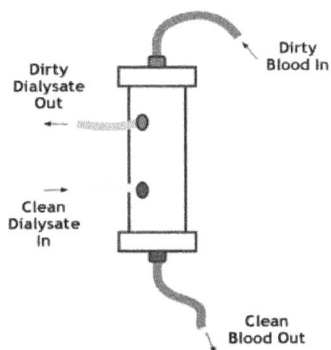

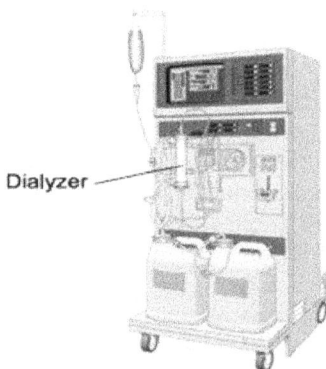

Dirty Blood In

Dirty Dialysate Out

Clean Dialysate In

Clean Blood Out

Dialyzer

Fig. *Dialyzer*

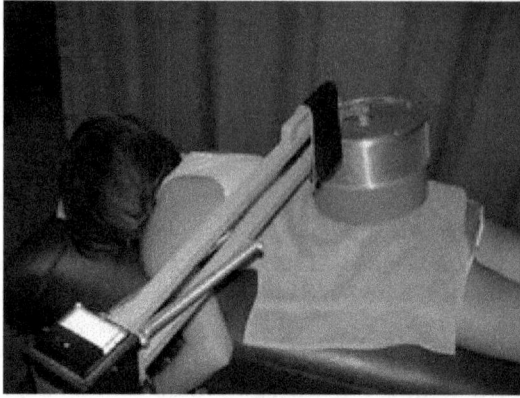

Fig. *Diathermy*

Physical therapists and sports physicians use diathermy to treat arthritis, bursitis, and fractures. It also may help treat gynecological diseases and sinusitis.

Dibromochloropropane The name of a specific chemical used as a pesticide. In the mid- 1970s, a group of male workers discovered that their exposure to DBCP had rendered them sterile. A regulation limiting exposures to DBCP was issued by the Occupational Safety and Health Administration in 1978.

Dietary supplement A product intended to supply nutrients and other healthful substances that may be lacking in a diet. Term used to apply only to vitamins, minerals, and proteins. Herbs are now classified as dietary supplements, and the definition also includes amino acids, glandulars (processed animal glands), enzymes, fish oils, and various extracts, such as flower essences. While their labels may not make any claims to cure, prevent, treat, or mitigate a disease, they can claim to help a structure or function of the body. Unlike food additives and prescription and over-the-counter drugs, dietary supplements do not require FDA approval to be sold on the market.

Dietitian An expert in nutrition who helps people with special health needs plan the kinds and amounts of foods to eat. A registered dietitian (R.D.) has special qualifications. The health care team for diabetes should include a dietitian, preferably an R.D.

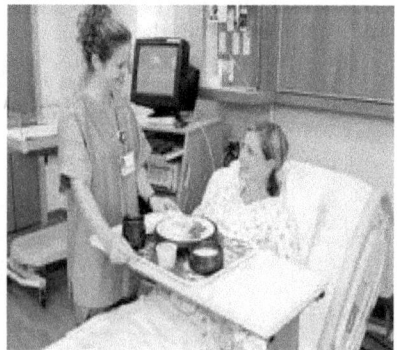

Fig. *Dietitian*

Dietary supervisor A dietary supervisor is trained in planning menus for regular and special diets and in establishing dietary procedures. A dietary supervisor is not necessarily a licensed dietitian.

Differentiation In embryology, the process in which unspecialized cells or tissues become specialized for certain functions. In oncology, the degree of similarity of tumour cells to the cells from which the tumour arose.

DiGeorge's syndrome Congenital disorder characterized by severe immunodeficiency, birth defects and absence of the thymus and parathyroid glands. Death usually occurs by age 2, often caused by infection.

Digital subtraction angiography A radiologic tool used for taking images of arteries, veins and organs of the body using complex computerised x-ray equipment. This usually requires an injection of a special 'dye' to highlight the blood supply to the legs, heart or other organ. The 'dye' is a clear liquid which shows on x-rays due to its high density. This 'dye' is harmless and will pass out of our body in our urine over the hours following our test.

Some of the more common examinations carried out in the DSA suite are listed below:

Angioplasty – This is a treatment to open narrowings or blockages of arteries using a small balloon.

Arterial Stent – This is a treatment to open blockages of arteries using an expanding metal mesh which remains in place to hold the artery open. This is used in the heart, pelvis and abdomen.

Biliary Procedures: This is treatment to relieve a blockage of the bile duct draining the liver.

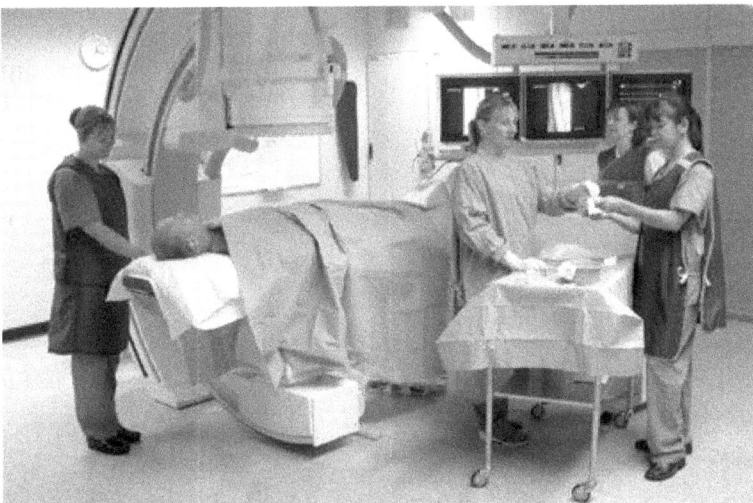

Fig. *Digital subtraction angiography*

Coronary Angiogram: This is an x-ray of the arteries that supply blood to the heart.

Femoral Angiogram: This is an x-ray of the arteries which supply blood to the legs

Nephrostomy: This is a treatment to relieve pain from a blocked kidney. A tube is inserted into the kidney to allow it to drain properly.

Pacemaker: This is a small battery powered box that is implanted under the skin on the chest wall with wires leading to the heart to help it to beat properly.

Dilated pupil examination A necessary part of an examination for diabetic eye disease. Special drops are used to enlarge the pupils, enabling the doctor to view the back of the eye for damage.

Di-methyl adipimidate An experimental compound used to prevent sickling of the red blood cells of patients with sickle-cell anemia.

Dimethyl Sulfoxide An alkyl sulfoxide, a powerful solvent that can dissolve aromatic and unsaturated hydrocarbons, organic compounds, and many other substances. Its biological activities include the ability to penetrate plant and animal tissues and to preserve living cells during freezing. In mainstream medical treatment, it has been shown efficacious for one condition, interstitial cystitis. It is used in a number of unconventional cancer treatments, applied topically in conjunction with other agents.

Diphtheria is a serious bacterial infection. It may affect different organs such as the nose and throat and may be resulted in a bad sore throat, swollen glands, low fever and chills. It is caused by Corynebacterium diphtheriae bacteria. When dealing with diphtheria we notice that the back of your throat is expressed by thick gray covering. It can make breathing difficult. skin may also be infected with diphtheria. Long time ago, before using any vaccines, diphtheria was a major reason for

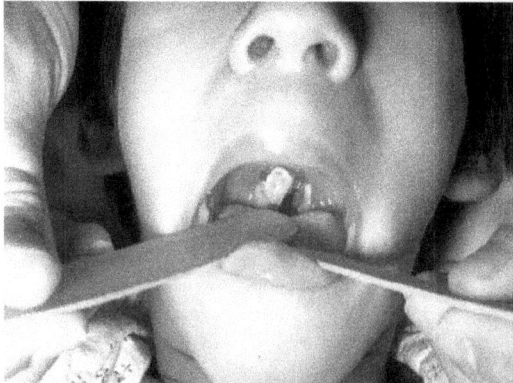

Fig. *Diphtheria*

death among kids. The bacteria causing diphtheria is usually transmitted in droplets of moisture coughed into the air.

Diphtheria, tetanus, pertussis (DTP) vaccine A combination vaccine composed of two toxoids (diphtheria and tetanus) and one inactivated whole-cell bacterial vaccine (pertussis).

Diploid In genetics, refers to a nucleus, cell, or organism with twice the haploid number of chromosomes characteristic of the species, i.e., two half sets of chromosomes are present, one half set from the female parent and the other from the male parent. In humans, all somatic cells are diploid, with 46 chromosomes, and mature reproductive cells are haploid, with 23 chromosomes.

Haploid (N)

Diploid (2N)

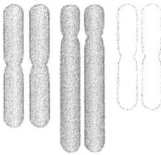

Fig *Diploid*

Diploidy Having two full sets of chromosomes.

Diplopia A vision disorder characterized by the perception of two images of a single object because of, for example, unequal action of the eye muscles. Also called "double vision."

Direct genetic test A DNA-based test capable of identifying a specific disease-causing allele.

Direct reimbursement Payment for services that is submitted directly to the health care practitioner who provided those services.

Directed blood donation Blood donation from identified individuals, such as family and friends, intended to be used as the sole source of blood for the patient for whom the donations were made.

Disability A term used to denote the presence of one or more functional limitations. A person with a disability has a limited ability or an inability to perform one or more basic life functions (e.g., walking) at a level considered "typical."

Fig. *Disability*

Disc A flat, round-like, plate structure usually referring to cartilage between vertebrae. On the other hand the disc between vertebrae in our back is made up of two parts: 1. The so-called "nucleus pulposis", a bubble of gelatine made up of substances called"glycosamino-glycans",

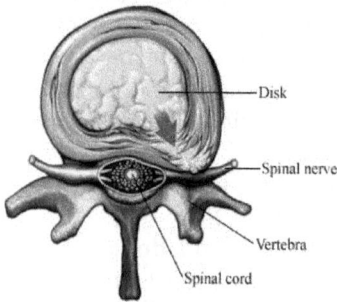

Fig. *Disc*

made from the substrate gluco-samine sulphate. Healthy glucos-amino--glycans are able to bind water, and water is in-compressible. This gives the disc its shock-absorbing properties. 2. The outer ring of the disc is called the "annulus fibrosus". It is made from fibrocartilage, powerful collagen fibres ar-ranged in a criss-cross ring, and attached deep into the endplate of the bone by very strong roots called Sharpey's fibres. Healthy cartilage is able to stretch out-wards. When we lift something heavy, the nucleus bulges into the annulus and, being a liquid and thus incompressible, it also presses back against the verte-brae, pushing them apart. Healthy annular cartilage con-tains this bubble of water-rich, gelatinous gel (it looks a bit like egg-white) as it bulges. But dis-eased cartilage, particularly if we twist as the same time as bending and lifting, may rip, al-low the gel to leak out. Getting the gel back where it belongs, without the use of drugs and surgery.

Discharge abstract Consists of data abstracted from a hospi-talized patient's medical record, usually including specific clini-cal data such as diagnostic and procedure codes as well as other information about the patient, the physician, and the patient's insurance and finan-cial status.

Discounting A procedure used in economic analysis to express as "present values" those costs and benefits that will occur in future years. Discounting is based on two premises—

(i) individuals prefer to receive benefits today rather than in the future; and

(ii) resources invested today in alternative programmes could earn a return over time.

Discretionary adjustment factor The component of the DRG up-date factor that accounts for cost increases or decreases that are not necessarily captured by inflation measures (e.g., quality of care). The discretionary ad-justment factor was originally set at 1 percent per year but was later limited by Congress to 0.25 percent for fiscal years 1985 and 1986.

Discretionary spending programmes Those spending programmes subject to the annual appropriations process.

Discretionary time That portion of time during which individuals are not engaged in mandatory or maintenance activities (e.g., school, work, sleeping, eating).

113

Disease Any deviation from or interruption of the normal structure of function of any part, organ, or system (or combination thereof) of the body that is manifested by a characteristic set of symptoms and signs and whose etiology, pathology, and prognosis may be known or unknown.

Disease prevention The averting of disease, traditionally characterized as primary, secondary, and tertiary prevention. Primary prevention aims at avoiding disease altogether. Secondary prevention strategies detect disease in its early stages of development, with the hope of preventing its progression. Tertiary prevention attempts to arrest further deterioration in individuals who already suffer from a disease.

Disorientation The lack of correct knowledge of person, place, or time (e.g., where a person is, who the people around him or her are, and what time of the day, day of the week, or month it is).

Disruptive behaviour disorder A disturbance of conduct severe enough to produce significant impairment in social, occupational, or academic functioning because of symptoms that range from oppositional defiant to moderate and severe conduct disturbances.oppositional defiantsymptoms may include losing temper; arguing with adults and actively refusing their requests; deliberately annoying others; blaming others for one's mistakes; being easily annoyed, resentful, or spiteful; and physically fighting with other members of the household.conduct disturbance (moderate)symptoms may include truancy or work absences, alcohol or other substance use before the age of 13, stealing with confrontation, destruction of others' property, firesetting with intent of causing serious damage, initiating fights outside of home, and being physically cruel to animals.conduct disturbance (severe)symptoms may include running away from home overnight at least twice, breaking into another's property, being physically cruel to people, stealing with confrontation, repeatedly using a dangerous weapon, and forcing someone into sexual activity.

Disseminated intravascular coagulation Serious disruption of blood clotting mechanisms, resulting in hemorrhaging or internal bleeding. Condition is a complication of an underlying disorder.

Dissociation The splitting off of clusters of mental contents from conscious awareness, a mechanism central to hysterical conversion and dissociative disorder; the separation of an idea from its emotional significance and affect as seen in the inappropriate affect of schizophrenic patients.

Distress Usually the product of pain, anxiety, or fear. However, distress can also occur in the absence of pain. For example, an animal struggling in a restraint device may be free from pain, but may be in distress. Distress can be eased with tranquilizers.

Diuretic A drug that increases the flow of urine to rid the body of extra fluid.

Diverticula Small, pouch-like projections in the wall of the colon.

Diverticulitis Inflammation of diverticula. During periods of inflammation, person experiences crampy pain and fever. White blood cells increase to fight off infection.

DNA The genetic material of most living things (exceptions include some RNA viruses) that determines hereditary characteristics by directing protein synthesis in the cells. DNA is a double-stranded nucleic acid, with an external "backbone" formed by a chain of attempting phosphate and sugar (deoxyribose) units and an internal ladder-like structure formed by nucleotide base-pairs held together by hydrogen bonds. The nucleotide base pairs consist of the bases *adenine* (A), *cytosine* (C), *guanine* (G) and *thymine* (T), whose structures are such that A can hydrogen bond only with T, and C only with G. The sequence of each individual strand can be deduced by knowing that of its partner. This complementary is the key to the information transmitting capabilities of DNA.

DMSO (dimethyl sulphoxide) Solvent capable of passing through body tissues, approved by the FDA to treat one medical condition, interstitial cystitis (an uncommon bladder inflammation). Proponents & manufacturers claim that DMSO heals a wide range of problems (including bruises, pimples, herpes) and relieves pain from conditions such as muscle strains. They credit DMSO with the ability to kill bacteria and fungi, improve circulation, and stimulate the immune system. DMSO produces strong garlic breath in users, even when used topically or intravenously.

DNA adducts Compounds formed from the binding of exogenous and xenobiotic materials to DNA. Their presence may be indicative of exposure to specific toxicants.

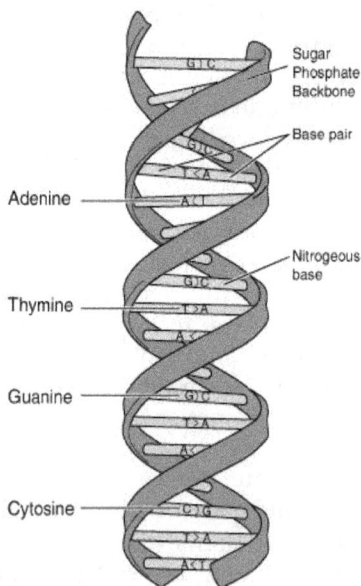

Fig. *DNA*

DNA probes Segments of single-strand DNA that are labeled with a radioactive or other chemical marker and used to identify complementary sequences of DNA by hybridizing with them.

DNA sequence The order of nucleotide bases in the DNA helix.

Domain A discrete portion of a protein with its own function. The combination of domains in a single protein determines its unique overall function.

Domestic discretionary spending As defined by the Budget Enforcement Act of 1990 (Title XIII of OBRA-90 [Public Law 101-508]), discretionary spending that is related to domestic programmes (i.e., not to the military or to assist foreign governments).

Domiciliary care facility A nonmedical residential care facility that provides room and board and variable amounts of protective supevision, personal care, and other services. The term is used for the 29 large residential care facilities currently operated by the Veterans' Administration.

Dominant In genetics, describes an allele, or genetic trait, that is expressed when present in only one copy in the cells of an organism.

Donor gametes Eggs or sperm donated by individuals for medically assisted conception.

Dopamine A catecholamine derived from dopa that is an intermediate in the synthesis of norepinephrine; found in high concentrations in the adrenal medulla and also in the brain, where it functions as a neurotransmitter in insufficient amounts produces the symptoms of Parkinson's disease.

Doppler ultrasonography Doppler ultrasonography evaluates blood flow in the major blood vessels of the arms and legs and in the extracranial cerebrovascular system. A handheld transducer directs high frequency sound waves to the artery or vein being tested. The sound wave strike moving red blood cells and are reflected back to the transducer at frequencies that corresponds to blood flow velocity through the vessel. The transducer then amplifies the sound waves to permit direct listening and graphic recording of blood flow. Measurement of systolic pressure helps detect the presence, location, and extent of peripheral arterial occlusive disease.

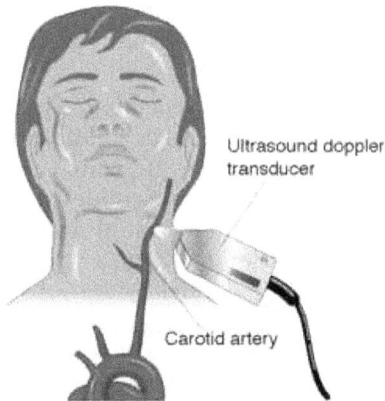

Ultrasound doppler transducer

Carotid artery

Fig. *Doppler ultrasonography*

Dorsal root The portion of the nerve root that brings sensory information from the body to the spinal cord.

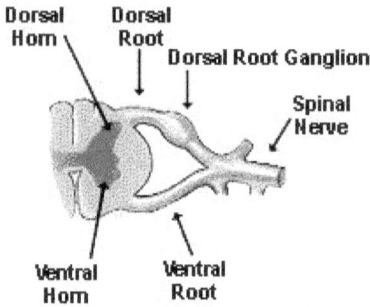

Fig. *Dorsal root*

Dosage The amount, frequency, and number of doses of a substance administered.

Dose The amount of a substance absorbed in a unit volume or in an individual. Dose rate is the dose delivered per unit of time.

Dose-response The quantitative relationship between exposure to a substance, usually expressed as a dose, and the extent of toxic injury or disease.

Dosimeter Device or methodology for measuring the dose of a chemical or ionizing radiation to a biological system.

Double helix In genetics, refers to the Watson-Crick model of DNA structure in which the two chains of nucleotide bases are linked and wound around each other to form a spiral-shaped molecule.

Down syndrome A genetic disorder caused by the presence of three copies of chromosome 21 (called trisomy 21) or by two

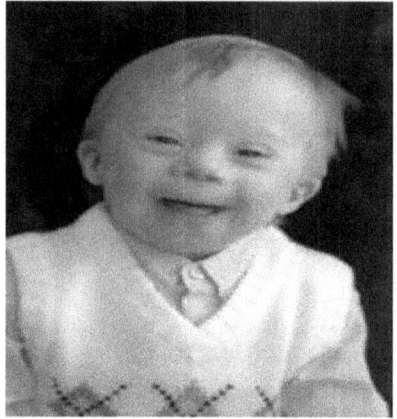

Fig. *Down syndrome*

copies of chromosome 21 and another chromosome 21 translocated to a different chromosome (usually to chromosome 14). The latter is called "translocation Down syndrome." Down syndrome is characterized by mental retardation and may also include congenital heart defects, immune system abnormalities, various morphological abnormalities, and a reduced life expectancy. Down syndrome has been shown to increase in frequency among children born to older mothers and can be detected prenatally by amniocentesis or chononic villi sampling. The disorder is named after the British physician John Down (1828-1896) who studied its incidence.

Downsizing (of hospitals and other health care facilities) Taking actions such as reducing the number of beds and staff according to a reduction in demand for services.

Draize eye irritancy test In toxicology, an experimental test for ocular toxicity of chemical compounds that involves applying a single dose of a chemical directly to one eye of each of several experimental animals (e.g., albino rabbits), with the other eye seining as the control.

Dream therapy mental activity associated with the rapid-eye-movement period of sleep. Generally consists of visual images and may reflect bodily disturbances or external stimuli. In primitive and ancient cultures, dreams played an extensive role in myth and religion. Freud emphasized dreams as keys to the makeup of the individual and distinguished between the experienced content of a dream and the actual meaning of the dream. Jung held that dreams are not limited to the personal unconscious but may also be shaped by archetypes that originate in the collective unconscious of the human species.

DRG outliers Cases with unusually high or low resource use. Defined by the Social Security Amendments of 1983 (Public Law 98-21) as atypical hospital cases that have either an extremely long length of stay or extraordinarily high costs when compared to most discharges classified in the same diagnosis-related group.

DRG weights The weight assigned a DRG represents its assumed resource use relative to other DRGs. The higher the weight is, the larger the Medicare payment.

Dropout rate The proportion of a particular group of individuals (usually an age cohort) who are not enrolled in school and have not finished high school at a particular point in time.

Drug abuse According to the American Psychiatric Association's diagnostic manual (DSM III-R), drug abuse is characterized by maladaptive patterns of psychoactive substance use that have never met the criteria for dependence for that particular class of substance. Drug abuse refers to a pattern of drug use that results in harm to the user; the user continues use despite persistent or recurrent adverse consequences.

Drug dependence A disorder in which a person has impaired control of psychoactive substance use and continues use despite adverse consequences. It is characterized by compulsive behavior and the active pursuit of a lifestyle that centres around searching for, obtaining, and using the drug. According to the American Psychiatric Association, diagnosis of drug dependence is established if at least three out of nine defined symptoms have been persistent for at least one month or have occurred repeatedly over a longer period of time. The range of symptoms include inability to control use, compulsive use, continued use despite knowledge of adverse consequences, tolerance, and physical dependence.

Drug therapy Various drugs are used to alleviate symptoms of some mental illnesses. Lithium is used in alleviating symptoms of manic depression. Tranquilizers are used to reduce anxiety. All drugs have side effects, such as Ritalin, which is prescribed for hyperactive children, and can retard physical growth.

Drug Any chemical or biological substance that maybe applied to, ingested by, or injected into humans in order to prevent, treat, or diagnose disease or other medical conditions.

Dual diagnosis Coexistence of two disorders in the same individual (e.g., drug abuse or dependence and psychiatric disorder).

Duchenne muscular dystrophy Abnormal congenital condition characterized by progressive weakness and wasting of the leg and pelvic muscles. Often involves the heart muscle. Affects only male children. Symptoms usually begin between the ages of 3 and 5. Currently not curable.

Dumping syndrome Group of symptoms that is a complication of surgical removal of all or part of the stomach. Often experienced 1 to 6 months after surgery. It becomes a serious problem in 1 to 2% of all patients. Symptoms include weakness, faintness, decreased blood pressure, abdominal cramping, diarrhea, sweating and anxiety.

Duodenal lesions Abnormalities in the duodenum, such as ulcers, tumours or inflammatory reactions.

Duodenal ulcer Some individuals produce excessive quantities of acid, and this leads to development of a duodenal ulcer. This type of response occurs when gastritis is localized in the pyloric region. The cytokines released in response to inflammation disrupt the regulation of the endocrine cells located in the pylorus.

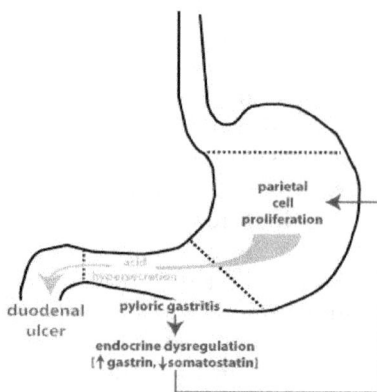

Fig. *Duodenal ulcer*

Duodenitis Inflammation of mucous membrane lining of the duodenum.

Duodenum First portion of the small intestine.

Dupuytren's Contracture A condition that causes the fingers to curve inward and may also affect the palm. The condition is more common in people with diabetes and may precede diabetes.

Dura mater The thickest, outermost membrane surrounding

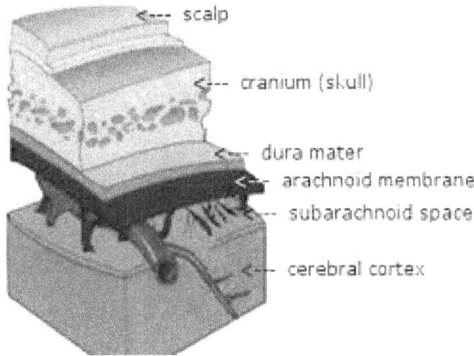

Fig. *Dura mater.*

the brain and spinal cord. The dura has been described as "tough and inflexible" and "leather-like". The dura mater is a sac (aka thecal sac) that envelops the arachnoid mater. It surrounds and supports the dural sinuses (also called dural venous sinuses, cerebral sinuses, or cranial sinuses) and carries blood from the brain toward the heart.

The dura mater has two layers, or lamellae: The superficial layer, which serves as the skull's inner periosteum, called the endocranium; and a deep layer, the actual dura mater.

Durable power of attorney A modification of the standard power of attorney that permits an individual (the principal) to transfer specified powers to another person. The power may be broad in scope or limited. The fundamental difference between standard and durable power of attorney is that the former loses its validity when the principal becomes incompetent and is therefore not useful for people with a dementing illness. A durable power of attorney provides a means of designating a surrogate decision-maker that survives the incompetence of the principal.

Duration of exposure The length of time a person or test animal is exposed to a chemical. Duration of exposure is divided into four categories: acute (exposure to a chemical for less than 24 hours), subacute (exposure for 1 month or less), subchronic (exposure for 1 to 3 months), and chronic (exposure for more than 3 months).

Dwarfism A general term for pathological conditions of ab-

Fig. *Dwarfism*

normally short stature. Some types are caused by chromosome abnormalities, while othes result from disease, metabolic dysfunction (such as kidney or hormone failure), or from fetal exposure to teratogens or chronic malnutrition.

Dwarfism, growth hormone deficiency A form of dwarfism caused by complete or partial growth hormone deficiency, resulting from either the lack of growth hormone-releasing factor from the hypothalamus or from the mutations in the growth hormone gene (GH1) in the pituitary gland. It is also known as type I pituitary dwarfism. Human hypophysial dwarf is caused by a deficiency of human growth hormone during development.

Dye laser Tunable liquid Lasers with organic compounds (i.e., dye) which have a strong Absorption band, used as the active medium. During emission, the dye has to be optically excited by another light source (e.g., another laser or flash lamp). The range of the emission wavelength may be anywhere from the ultraviolet to the near infrared (i.e., from 180 to 1100nm). These lasers are operated in continuous wave and pulsed modes.

Dysentery Inflammation of the intestine, especially the colon; may be caused by chemical irritants, bacteria, viruses, parasites or protozoa. Characterized by frequent, bloody stools, abdominal pain and ineffective, painful straining to have a bowel movement (tenesmus).

Dysentery, amoebic Dysentery caused by intestinal amebic infection, chiefly with Entamoeba histolytica. This condition may be associated with amebic Infection of the liver and other distant sites.

Dysfibrinogenemia Congenital disorder in which fibrinogen is present in the blood, but does not function normally.

Dysmenorrhea is a gynecological medical condition of pain during menstruation that interferes with daily activities.

Dysphoria is a state of feeling unwell or unhappy; a feeling of emotional and mental discomfort as a symptom of discontentment, restlessness, dissatisfaction, malaise, depression, anxiety or indifference.

Dyspnea Difficulty in breathing.

Dysproteinemia Derangement of the protein content of the blood.

Dysthymic disorder One of the depressive disorders, characterized by a chronic course (i.e.,. seldom without symptoms) with lowered mood tone and a range of other symptoms that may include feelings of inadequacy, loss of self-esteem, or self-deprecation: feelings of hopelessness or despair; feelings of guilt,brooding about past events, or self-pity; low energy and chronic tiredness; being less active or talkative than usual; poor concentration and indecisiveness; and inability to enjoy pleasurable activities.

Dysfunction, cerebellar Diseases that affect the structure or function of the cerebellum. Cardinal manifestations of cerebellar dysfunction include —dysmetria, gait ataxia, and muscle hypotonia.

Dystrophies, cone-rod retinal Hereditary, progressive degeneration of the neuroepithelium of the retina characterized by night blindness and progressive contraction of the visual field.

Dystrophy, macular Degenerative changes in the retina usually of older adults which results in a loss of vision in the centre of the visual field (the macula lutea) because of damage to the retina. It occurs in dry and wet forms.

Dysuria Painful urination. It is often associated with Infections of the lower urinary tract.

E

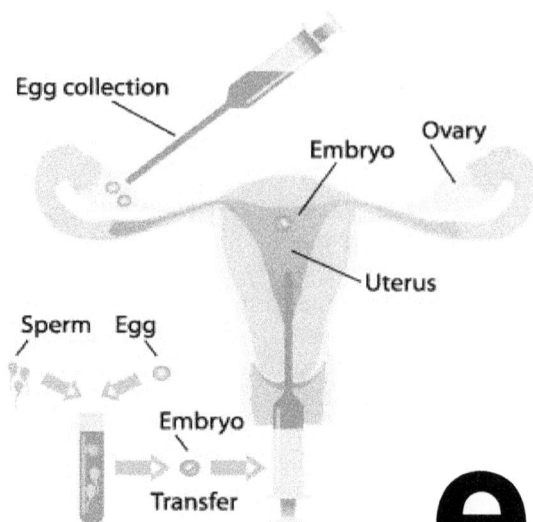

Egg collection

Embryo

Ovary

Uterus

Sperm Egg

Embryo

Transfer

Ear candling It is also called Ear Coning. It involves placing the narrow end of a specially designed hollow candle at the entry of the ear canal, while the opposite end is lit. Primarily used for relieving wax build up and related hearing problems, ear candling is also used for ear infections and sinus infections.

Early adolescence A period encompassing the profound physical and social changes that occur with puberty, as maturation begins and social interactions become increasingly focused on sex (e.g., on members of the opposite sex). Typically takes place from ages 10 through 14.

Early and periodic screening, diagnosis, and treatment program A state and federally funded, state-administered programme under medicaid that is intended to provide preventive screening exams and follow-up services for illnesses, abnormalities, and treatable conditions to medicaid-eligible children under age 21.

Early intervention Treatment services delivered before a problem becomes serious and/or chronic.

Eating disorder Psycho-physiological disorders characterized by disturbances in eating. In DSM-IV, this category includes anorexia nervosa, bulimia nervosa, and eating disorder not otherwise specified.

Echo planar technique A particular type of magnetic resonance imaging in which an image is obtained from an excitation pulse.

Echocardiography Echo-cardiography is the process of mapping the heart through echoes. The

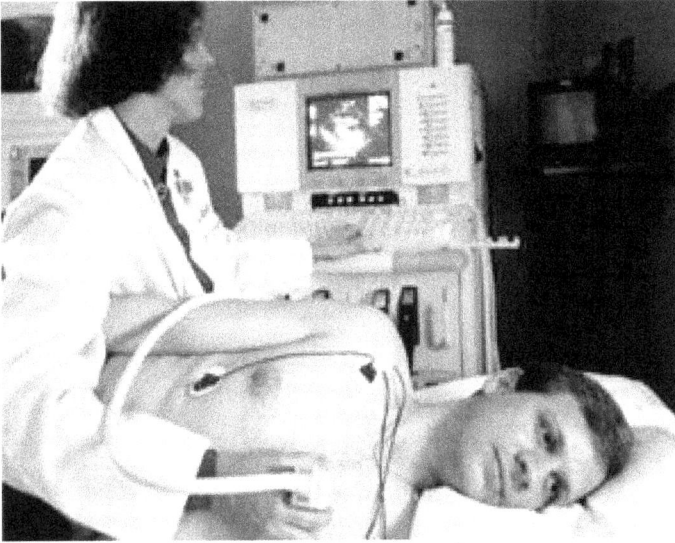

Fig. *Echocardiography*

pulses are sent into the chest and the high-frequency sound waves bounce off of the heart's walls and valves. The returning echoes are electronically plotted to produce a picture of the heart called an echocardiogram.

Echolalia Parrot-like repetition of overheard words or fragments of speech. It may be part of a developmental disorder, a neurologic disorder, orschi-zophrenia. Echolalia tends to be repetitive and persistent and is often uttered with a mocking, mumbling, or staccato intonation.

Eclampsia (Toxemia of pregnancy) Extremely serious disturbance in blood pressure, kidney function and the central nervous system, including seizure and coma. May occur from the 20th week of pregnancy until 7 days after delivery. C

Econometric techniques A group of statistical methods used to estimate and test models of economic behaviour or systems.

Economic efficiency The state in which the greatest direct and indirect gains (benefits) are derived from the resources expended (costs) to achieve a stated objective.

Ectopic ACTH production Adrenocorticotropic hormone production (ACTH) at some site other than the pituitary gland.

Ectopic pregnancy Pregnancy that develops outside the uterus. The most common site is one of the narrow tubes that connect each ovary to the uterus (Fallopian tube). Other sides include the ovary or abdominal cavity. Early symptoms include severe abdominal pain and vaginal bleeding; if untreated, may lead

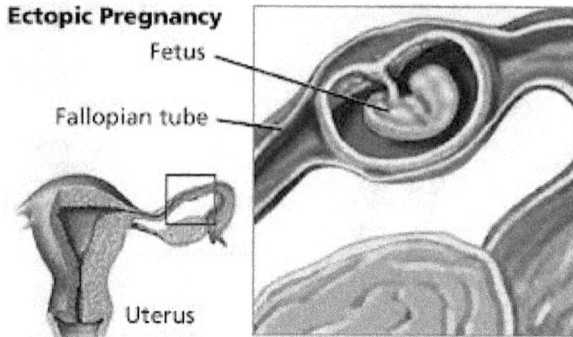

Fig. *Ectopic pregnancy*

to rupture or internal hemorrhage, and shock. In 98% of the cases, the embryo implants in the fallopian tube, while in the rest of the cases, pregnancy might occur in the ovaries, cervix or abdomen. Ectopic pregnancies are very dangerous, because, if left untreated, they can lead to the death of the mother.

Ectropion An abnormal turning out of an eyelid, typically the lower one, which exposes the inner, conjunctival side of the eyelid; usually due to aging. Additional symptoms include eye or lid pain or discomfort, a red or pink eye or eyelid and overflow tearing.

Edema Edema derives from a Greek word 'Oidema' meaning "swelling." Basically, edema is the excessive accumulation of fluid in spaces between the cells caused by either lymphatic system or venous system defect or disorder. The milder form of edema is referred to as 'water retention,' which is common in a lot of people. Symptoms of edema include:

• Inflammation or swelling.
• Stretched skin.
• Shiny skin.
• Skin that's slow to restore to its natural state after being pressed on by an object.

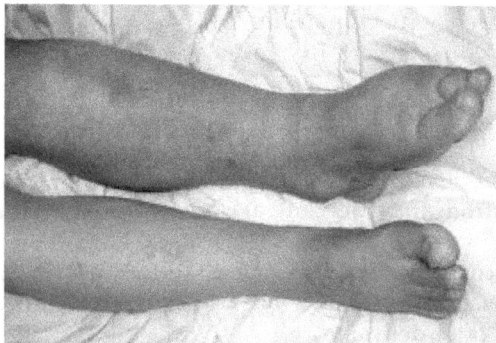

Fig. *Edema*

• Increased size in a limb, body part or abdomen.

• Healing edema naturally.

Diuretic herbs are ideal in reversing or healing edema and other swelling conditions.

Education for all handicapped children Act The education for all handicapped children sct (Public Law 94-142) mandates that all physically and mentally handicapped children be provided a free, appropriate education and the "related services" necessary to obtain an education. The federal government provides a small amount of grant money to States to help them implement this law.

Educational neglect As defined by DHHS'S national center on child abuse and neglect, educational neglect can take several forms: permitted chronic truancy, failure to enroll a school-aged child in school, causing the child to miss school for nonlegitimate reasons, and inattention to special educational need (e.g., refusal to allow or failure to obtain recommended remedial educational services).

Educationally based preventive interventions Preventive interventions that rely primarily on educating the target group.

Educationally disadvantaged Having difficulties in learning not related to sheer exertion of effort (although motivational difficulties can also prove a disadvantage).

Efficacy The probability of benefit to individuals in a defined population from a medical technology applied for a given medical problem under ideal conditions of use. Efficacy is generally evaluated in controlled trials of an experimental therapy and a control condition.

Efficient resource allocation The allocation of resources among alternative social benefits are derived from the resources.

Ejaculation The ejection of sperm from the body. Ejaculation occurs as a two-part spinal reflex that involves emission, when the semen moves into the urethra, and ejaculation proper, when it is propelled out of the urethra at the time of orgasm.

Elderly Individuals over age 65.

Electrocardiogram (EKG or ECG) A graphic tracing of the changes of electrical potential of the heart occurring during each heartbeat; usually performed with the patient supine and at rest. An electrocardiogram monitors your heart rhythm for problems. Electrodes are taped

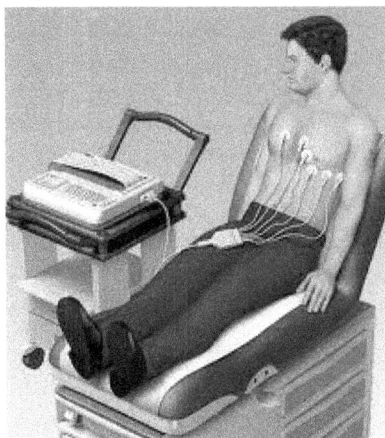

Fig. *Electrocardiogram*

to your chest to record your heart's electrical signals, which cause your heart to beat. The signals are shown as waves on an attached computer monitor or printer.

Electroejaculation Electrical stimulation of the nerve that controls ejaculation, used to obtain semen from men with spinal cord injuries.

Electrolyte Any compound that dissociates into charged ions in solution and can conduct a current of electricity. A balance of electrolytes in body fluids is necessary for the body to function normally.

Electrolyte balance The state in which the body has the correct amount of positively and negatively charged ions (e.g., sodium, potassium, hydrogen, magnesium, bicarbonate, phosphate, and chloride), which play important roles in regulating body processes.

Electromyographic (EMG) signals Electrical changes that accom-

pany muscle contraction.

Electromyography (EMG) and nerve conduction velocity (NCV) studies tests It is used to diagnose neuropathy and check for nerve damage. These tests are usually both run at the same time, using the same equipment.

Electromyography It is used to diagnose various nerve and muscle disorders, to assess progress in recovery from some forms of paralysis, and to test the effects of neurotoxic substances on humans.

Electromyographyr EMG Recording and measuring the electrical activity of muscles by means of electrodes inserted into muscle fibres, with a tracing displayed on an electromyograph.

Electroneurography, ENG Recording and measuring the electrical signals generated by nerves by means of an electromyograph. Electro-neurography is used in testing the ef-

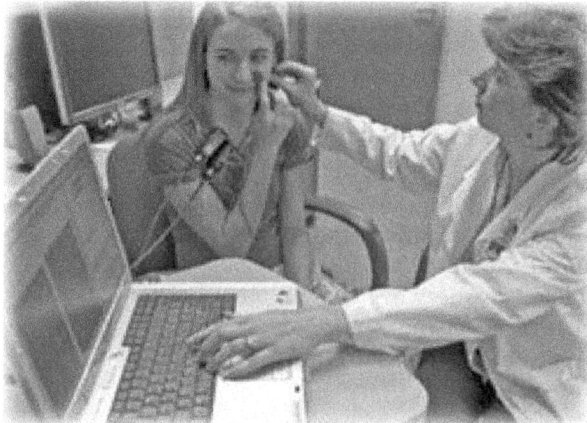

Fig. *Electroneurography*

127

fects of neurotoxic substances on humans.

Electroneurography evaluates acute facial nerve weakness due to Bell's palsy, traumatic injury, or disease. The test determines the percentage of degenerated nerve fibres associated with facial weakness.

Electronic fetal monitoring The use of a device to listen to and record a fetus' heart beat during pregnancy and labor, either externally (using an ultrasound transmitter stropped to the woman's abdomen) or internally (by an electrode attached to the fetal scalp and linked to the recording device by a wire inserted through the vagina).

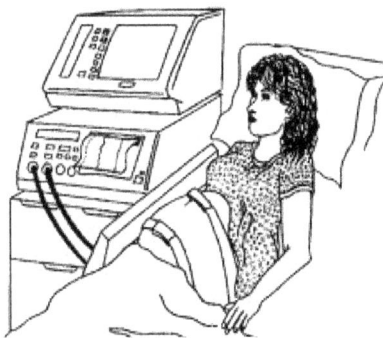

Fig. *Electronic fetal monitoring.*

An abnormal fetal heartbeat detected during labor may be a sign of fetal distress, caused by a lack of oxygen to the fetus.

Electrophoresis A method of separating molecules (such as DNA fragments or proteins) from a mixture of similar molecules, based on differential movement of the molecules through an electric field. An electric current is passed through a medium containing the mixture, and each kind of molecule travels through the medium at a rate detemined by its electrical charge and size.

Electrophysiology Measuring and recoding the electrical activity of the brain or nerve cells by means of electrodes.

Elephantiasis A chronic condition caused by a worm infestation (filariasis); it is characterized by massive swelling of a limb, usually a leg, followed by thickening of the skin and subcutaneous tissues.

Elliptocystosis Hereditary disorder in which red blood cells (erythrocytes) are oval in shape, instead of round, and have pale centers. Disorder may occur in a variety of anemias.

ELISA testing is used to detect the presence of antibodies to HIV in human sera.

Embolism Sudden blockage of a blood vessel by an embolus.

Embolus Clot, foreign object, air, gas or a bit of tissue or fat that circulates in the bloodstream until it becomes lodged in a blood vessel.

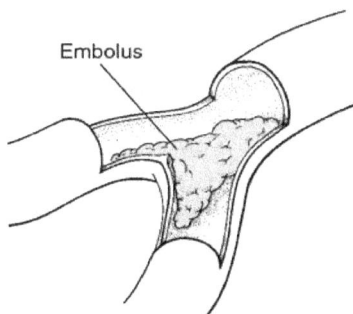

Fig. *Embolus*

Embryo An animal in the earliest stages of its development after conception; in humans, refers to the stages of growth from the second to the ninth week following conception. During this period cell differentiation proceeds rapidly and the brain, eyes, heart, upper and lower limbs, and other organs are formed.

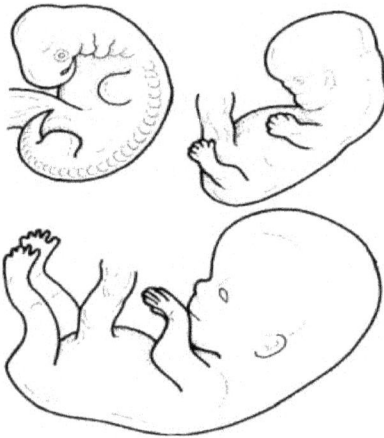

Fig. *Embryo*

Embryo donation The transfer from one woman to another of an embryo obtained by artificial insemination and Iavage or, more commonly, by in vitro fertilization (IVF).

Embryo donation is a form of third party reproduction. In vitro fertilisation, or IVF, often results in a number of frozen, unused embryos after the woman for whom they were originally created has successfully carried one or more pregnancies to term. In embryo donation, these extra embryos are given to other couples or

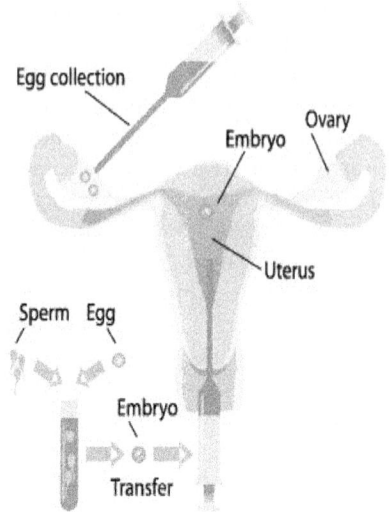

Fig. *Embryo donation.*

women for transfer with the goal of producing a successful pregnancy. The resulting child is considered the child of the woman who carries it and gives birth, and not the child of the donor, the same as occurs with egg donation or sperm donation.

Embryo iavage A flushing of the uterus to recover a pre-implantation embryo.

Embryo transfer The transfer of an in vitro fertilized egg from its Iaboratory dish into the uterus of a woman.

Embryogenesis The process of cell growth that produces an embryo from a zygote, given the proper nutrients and time.

Emergency medical ientification Cards, bracelets, or necklaces with a written message used by people with diabetes or other medical problems to alert others in case of a medical emergency such as coma.

Emergency temporary standard (ETS) A standard that may be issued under section 6(c) of the occupationalsafety and health act (Public Law 91-596) when the occupational safety and health administration determines that workers are exposed to a "grove danger from an occupational hazard and that an emergency standard is necessary to protect them from that danger.

Emesis Vomiting.

Emmetropia The condition of an eye with normal vision, meaning that light rays correctly are focused at the inner back of the eye (retina) where images are processed.

Emotional abuse As defined by DHHS'S national center on child abuse and neglect, emotional abuse takes three different forms: close confinement, such as tying or binding, or other tortuous restriction of movement; verbal or emotional assault (e.g., habitual patterns of belittling, denigrating, or scapegoating); and other overtly punitive, exploitative, or abusive treatment other than those specified

Emotional disorders Mental disorders characterized by the presence of an emotional problem and considerable impairment of a person's ability to function. Such disorders include anxiety and depression.

Emotional neglect As defined by DHHS'S national center on child abuse and neglect, emotional neglect can take several forms: inadequate nurturance and affection; chronic or extreme spouse abuse in the child's presence; encouragement or pemitting of drug or alcohol use by the child; permitting other maladaptive behaviour; refusal of recommended, needed, and available psychological care; delay in psychological care; and other emotional neglect (e.g., other inattention to the child's developmental/emotional needs not classifiable under any of the above forms of emotional neglect, such as inappropriate application of expectations or restrictions).

Emotional problems The mental health problems exhibited in the form of emotional distress (e.g., anxiety and depressive disorders); may include subjective distress.

Empathy Insightful awareness, including the meaning and significance of the feelings, emotions, and behaviour of another person.

Emphysema A disorder of the lungs characterized by an increase beyond the normal in the size of air spaces in the farthest reaches of the lung either from dilation of the alveoli (the tiny sacs in the lung where oxygen from the air and waste carbon dioxide in the blood are exchanged) or from the destruction of their walls; causes shortness of breath and can result in respiratory and/or heart failure. Emphysema is usually caused by cigarette smoking, although other contributors include air pollution and an inherited predisposition (alpha-1-anti-trypsin deficiency).

Employer mandate A requirement imposed by the federal government on the states that requires employers to offer group health insurance policies and pay a significant amount of the premiums for all employees who work more than a specified number of hours per week.

Empowerment Empowerment approaches take as a given that individuals, not just professionals, have a set of competencies, that these competencies are useful in the design and management of services, and, further, that those competencies can be even more fully developed by giving individuals additional opportunities to control their own lives. Empowerment is sometimes viewed as a health promotion strategy.

Encephalins A peptide neurotransmitter found in the brain, spinal cord, nerve cells, and in gut epithelial cells. Encephalins bind to opiate receptors in the brain and their release into the bloodstream is thought to control levels of pain and other sensations.

Encephalitis Acute inflammation of the brain, usually caused by a contagious viral infection. May also be caused by lead poi-

soning, leukemia or as a vaccine reaction. Symptoms in severe cases may include impairment of vision, speech and hearing, vomiting, headache, personality changes, seizures and coma. In mild cases, symptoms include fever and malaise. Death or complications, such as permanent brain damage, are most common in infants and people over 65. People in other age groups usually recover completely.

Encephalomyelitis An inflammation of the brain and spinal cord that is caused by infection with any of a number of viruses.

Encephalopathy Any of several disorder that impair the functioning of the brain.

Encopresis, functional An elimination disorder in a child who is at least 4 years of age, consisting of repeated passage of feces into inappropriate places (clothing, floor, etc.) and not due to a general medical condition.

Encopresis A psychophysiological disorder characterized by defecation in inappropriate places.

Endarterectomy Surgical removal of the inner layer of an artery when the artery is thickened and obstructed.

Endemic Constantly present or persistent within a given geographic area. A term used in reference to a disease or infectious agent.

Endobronchial Within the bronchial tubes.

Endocrine disorders Any disorder involving the endocrine sys-

131

tem. The endocrine system is made up of organs that secrete hormones into the blood to regulate basic functions of cells and tissues. Endocrine organs are pituitary, thyroid, parathyroid, adrenal glands, pancreas, ovaries (in women) and testicles (in men).

Endocrine glands Glands that release hormones into the bloodstream. They affect how the body uses food (metabolism). They also influence other body functions. One endocrine gland is the pancreas. It releases insulin so the body can use sugar for energy.

Endocrine pancreas The part of the pancreas that produces hormones that govern sugar metabolism.

Endocrine system Organs and glands (e.g., thyroid, pituitary, parathyroid, adrenal, ovary, testes, placenta, and part of the pancreas) that secrete hormones (involved in the regulation of growth and sexual development) into the bloodstream.

Endocrinologist A doctor who treats people who have problems with their endocrine glands. Diabetes is an endocrine disorder.

Endogenous antibodies In Type 1 diabetes, several different autoantibodies against normal tissues are found. These antibodies are associated with the destruction of the beta cells of the pancreas, although their exact role is uncertain. Some of the autoantibodies which are found in diabetes patients include islet-cell antibodies (ICA's), anti-insulin antibodies (AIA's) and anti-GAD antibodies.

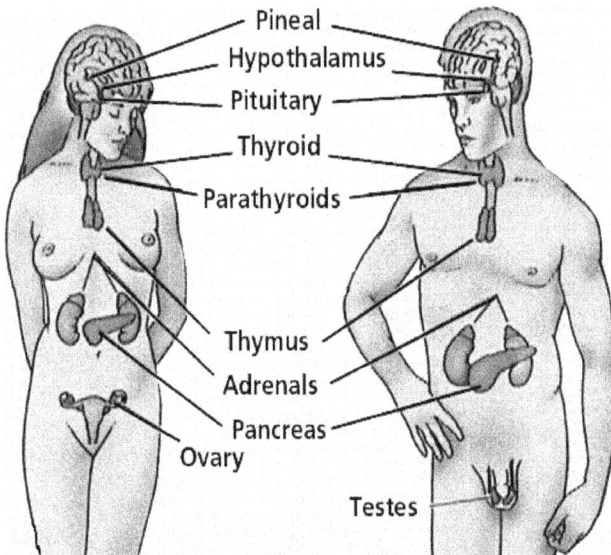

Fig. *Endocrine system*

Endogenous Developing or originating within the organism or other entity, or arising from causes within the entity.

Endometrial biopsy It is a procedure in which a sample of the endometrium (tissue lining the inside of the uterus) is removed for microscopic examination obtained from the lining of the uterus between days 22 and 25 of a normal 28-day menstrual cycle, in order to evaluate ovulatory function. This is usually done to determine whether the abnormal bleeding is secondary to abnormal endometrial cells (hyper-plasia). Sometimes it is done to rule out endometrial cancer. Previously, woman would need to have a D & C (dilatation and curettage) in order to obtain this sample of endometrial cells.

An endometrial biopsy is performed by a physician, usually a gynecologist or a family physician in the doctor's office. It usually takes about 10 minutes. Women, who require an endometrial biopsy, will be asked to lie on their back with feet in stirrups. The doctor first opens the vagina with a speculum (a metal instrument) just as during a *pap test*. Sometimes the doctor will use a local anesthetic to the cervix to help reduce discomfort. A thin, flexible, straw-like tube is inserted through the opening of the uterus and a small amount of fluid or tissue is removed using suction. No cutting or incision is made. Some women experience cramping or pressure during the procedure. It is often suggested to take Ibuprofen or Tylenol prior to the procedure to reduce the discomfort. The sample is sent to the lab for analysis.

Endometriosis Disorder in women in which tissue resembling inner lining of the uterus (endo-

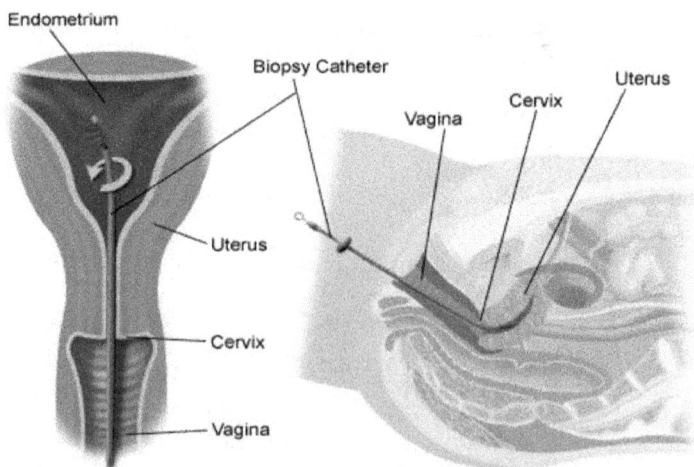

Fig. *Endometrial biopsy*

metrium) is found at unusual locations in the lower abdomen. Tissue may be found on the outside of the ovaries, behind the uterus, low in the pelvic cavity, on the intestinal wall and rarely, at other sites far away.

Endometrium is the mucous membrane that lines the inside of the uterus (womb). The endometrium changes throughout the menstrual cycle. It becomes thick and rich with blood vessels to prepare for pregnancy. If the woman does not get pregnant, part of the endometrium is shed, causing menstrual bleeding.

Endophthalmitis Inflammation of the interior of the eye, typically caused by an infection from eye surgery or trauma. Endophthalmitis is an ocular emergency. Symptoms include floaters, light sensitivity, eye pain or discomfort, a red or pink eye and vision loss.

Endorphins A group of endogenous morphine-like proteins found in the pituitary gland and hypothalamus that bind to specific opiate receptors in the brain to produce painkilling and euphoric effects; also may be involved in the body's response to stress, regulation of intestinal wall activity, influencing mood, and regulating the release of hormones (growth hormone and gonadotropin) from the pituitary. Endorphins can produce the tolerance and addiction characteristic of opiates. They occur in various forms, including alpha, beta, and gamma endorphins and the encephalins. The term derives from "endogenous morphine-like substances."

Endothelial cell A type of cell forming a single layer lining the inner surfaces of the heart, blood vessels, and lymphatic vessels.

Endothelium The cornea's inner layer of cells.

Endotoxin A poison produced by some gram-negative bacteria in the cellular membrane, and released only upon cell rupture or cell death. In the body, endo-tox-

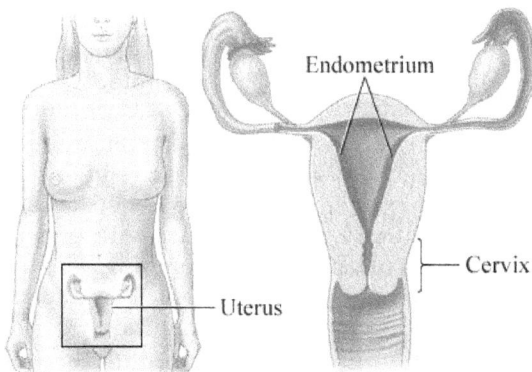

Fig. *Endometrium*

ins can act as antigens, producing an immune response against them.

Endpiece At left and right of the front of an eyeglass frame, the part that attaches to the temples, usually but not always with a screw mounting.

End-stage renal disease (ESRD) The final phase of kidney disease; treated by dialysis or kidney transplantation. Chronic renal failure that occurs when an individual irreversibly loses a sufficient amount of kidney function so that life cannot be sustained without treatment (e.g., hemodialysis, kidney transplant surgery, or continuous ambulatory peritoneal dialysis).

Enema Infusion of a fluid via the rectum, usually for the purpose of clearing out the bowel.

Energy field work Practitioners look for weaknesses in the energy field in and around the clients body and seek to restore its proper circulation and balance. Energy channeled through the practitioner is directed to strengthen the body's natural defences and help the client's physical, mental, emotional and/or spiritual state.

Engineering controls Methods of controlling worker exposure to certain hazardous agents by modifying the source or reducing the amount of contaminants released into the workplace. Engineering controls include process design and modification, equipment design, enclosure

and isolation, and ventilation. Compare administrative controls, personal protective equipment, and work practice.

Enophthalmos The sinking of the eye into the socket. Causes include development problems in utero, trauma and inflammation.

Enteral nutrition The intake of nutrients that undergo at least partial processing in the intestine. Strictly speaking, enteral nutrition includes normal food intake through the mouth. However, the term is often used to indicate more specifically the intake of nutrients through a tube that is passed via the throat or surgical opening (in the esophagus) leading to the stomach or the small intestine.

Enteric nervous system The nerve network controlling the stomach and intestines.

Enteritis Inflammation of the mucous membrane lining of the small intestine.

Enterocolitis or coloenteritis is an inflammation of the digestive tract, involving enteritis of the small intestine and colitis of the colon. It may be caused by various infections, with bacteria, viruses, fungi, parasites, or other causes. Common clinical manifestations of enterocolitis are frequent diarrheal defecations, with or without nausea, vomiting, abdominal pain, fever, chills, alteration of general condition.

Enterocolitis, necrotizing is infection and inflammation of the

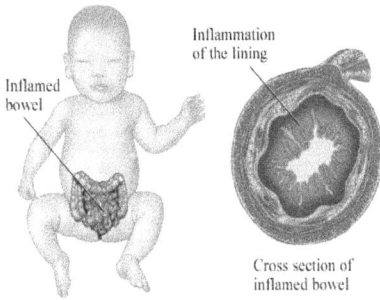

Fig. *Enterocolitis, necrotizing*

bowel (intestines). The disease is most common among premature newborns.

Enterotoxigenic Capable of producing a toxin specific for the cells of the intestine. Some strains of Escherichia coli cause disease by producing such a toxin.

Entitlement programmes Programmes that provide benefits paid out automatically to all who qualify unless there is a change in underlying law (examples include federal employee retirement benefits, medicare, medicaid, unemployment compensation, aid to families With dependent children).

Entomology The scientific study of insects.

Entropion An abnormal turning in of an eyelid, which causes the lashes to rub on the ocular surface; usually due to aging. Additional symptoms include eye or lid pain or discomfort, foreign body sensation, a red or pink eye, itching, tearing and vision loss.

Enuresis, functional An elimination disorder in a child who is at least 5 years of age, consisting of repeated voiding of urine into bed or clothing, and not due to any general medical condition.

Enuresis A psychophysiological disorder in adults characterized by involuntary bedwetting or other lack of control over urination.

Envelope antigens Proteins that constitute the envelope or surface of a virus.

Environmental condition Air pollution, wind and bright light can irritate your eyes and cause symptoms such as burning, dryness and tearing.

Environmental control of disease The control of insects, other vectors of disease, or the pathogens themselves through alteration of the physical environment (to eliminate the conditions necessary for the vectors' or pathogens' survival).

Environmental hypothesis The theory that exposure to toxic substances contributes significantly to neurological disorders such as parkinson's disease, alzheimer's disease, and amyotrophic lateral sclerosis (Lou gehrig's disease).

Enzootic The constant presence or persistence of an animal disease or infectious agent within a given geographic area.

Enzymatic cleaner A cleaner that removes protein deposits and other debris from contact lenses. It's recommended for use either daily, weekly, or monthly. Some enzymatic cleaners are a small tablet dropped into a solution along with the lens; others come in liquid form.

Enzyme deficiency variants Proteins, altered by mutation, reduce or eliminate the biological activity of certain blood enzymes. These mutations may lead to the absence of a specific gene product or the changing of a protein so that they become non-functional or abnormally unstable.

Enzyme immunoassay (EIA) An assay based on antigen-antibody interactions, which uses enzymes to measure the reaction. For example, in EIAs that are used to measure drugs in urine, a reagent that contains antibodies against a specific drug is first added to the urine specimen. A second reagent containing the specific drug attached to an enzyme is then added, and the enzyme-labeled drug combines with any remaining antibody binding sites. This binding decreases the enzyme activity. The residual enzyme activity relates directly to the concentration of drug in the specimen. The active enzyme converts another substance in the reagent, resulting in an absorbance change that is measured spectro-photometrically.

Enzyme therapy A form of therapy that employs supplements of plant and animal enzymes to improve digestive function and other conditions. During digestion, the body's own digestive enzymes are not the only ones at work; the enzymes present in raw fruits and vegetables also contribute to the breakdown of food in the stomach. Enzyme therapy advocates supplementation to reduce the work that the body has to do, and because plant enzymes are destroyed in cooking. Since enzymes can't be synthetically manufactured, supplements are derived from plants or from animal tissues. Some practitioners inject liquid enzymes to treat cancer and multiple sclerosis. Enzyme supplements are available over the counter, singly or in combination, in capsule, tablet, powder, and liquid form.

Enzyme A protein that acts as a catalyst in biochemical reactions in living cells.

Enzyme-linked immunosorbent assay (ELISA) A type of enzyme immunoassay for determining the amount of protein or other antigen in a given sample by means of an enzyme-catalyzed colour change.

Ependymomas Tumour in the brain or spinal cord that is usually benign and slow growing.

Epidemic A sudden increase in the incidence rate of an illness affecting large numbers of people in a defined geographic area.

Epidemiological studies Studies concerned with the relationships of various factors determining the frequency and distribution of specific diseases in a human community.

Epidemiology The scientific study of a distribution and occurrence of human disease that deals with how many people have it, where they are, how many new cases develop, and how to control the disease.

Epididymis A coiled tubular structure in the male that receives sperm moving from the testis to the vas deferens. Sperm are stored and matured for a period of several weeks in the epididymis.

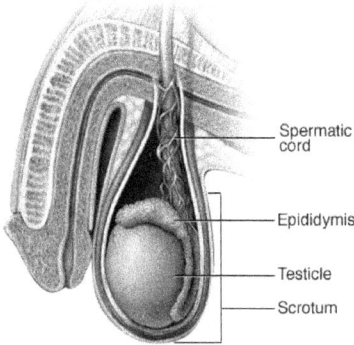

Fig. *Epididymis*

Epididymitis Infection of the epididymis, usually from a sexually transmitted disease such as gonorrhea, that can impair fertility during the course of the infection and cause scarring that can partially or completely block sperm transport.

Epilepsy Disorder of brain function. There are several forms of epilepsy, each with its own characteristics. Cause is usually unknown (75% of the time) but may be due to brain damage at birth, severe head injury, drug or alcohol abuse, brain infection or brain tumour. It is incurable, except in rare cases where brain tumour or infection is treatable. Anti-seizure drugs can prevent most seizures and allow a nearly normal life.

Epilepsy, focal Small part of the body begins twitching uncontrollably. The twitching (seizure) spreads until it may involve the entire body. The person does not lose consciousness.

Epilepsy, grandmal Affects all ages. Person loses consciousness, stiffens, then twitches and jerks uncontrollably and may lose bladder control. Seizure may last several minutes and is often followed by a deep sleep or mental confusion.

Epilepsy, petitmal Affects children mostly. Child stops activity and stares blankly around for a minute or so and is unaware of what is happening.

Epilepsy, temporal lobe Person suddenly behaves out of character or inappropriately, such as becoming suddenly violent or angry, laughing for no reason or making bizarre body movements, including odd chewing movements.

Epinephrine One of several hormones made in the adrenal glands. It helps the liver release glucose (sugar), and limits the release of insulin from the pancreas. Epinephrine is responsible for some of the symptoms of hypoglycemia, including anxiety, sweating, tremor, pallor, nausea, and rapid heart beat. Epinephrine is also called *adrenalin*. It is available as a prescription medication, for treat-

Pituitary gland
Hypothalamus
CRH
ACTH
Adrenal glands
Cortisol

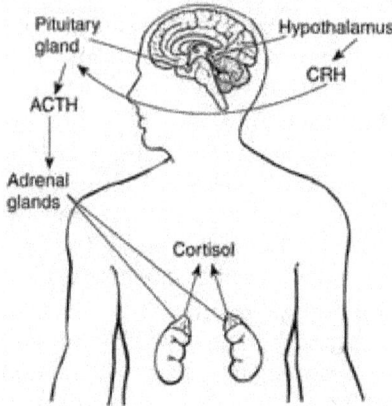

Fig. *Epinephrine*

ing severe allergic reactions by antagonizing the effects of histamine and reducing capillary permeability.

Epiretinal membrane Thin layer of scar tissue on the retina; also called a macular pucker. Epiretinal membranes have a variety of causes, including vitreous detachment, but the cause is often unknown. In its early stages, an epiretinal membrane is often asymptomatic, but some people have blurred vision. You may also develop meta-morphopsia.

Episclera Outer layer of the eye's sclera that loosely connects it to the conjunctiva.

Episcleritis Inflammation of the episclera. The cause is usually unknown, but episcleritis may be associated with some systemic (e.g., autoimmune) diseases. Symptoms include a red or pink eye, eye pain or discomfort, light sensitivity and tearing.

Episome A DNA molecule that may exist either as an integrated part of a chromosomal DNA molecule of the host or as an independently replicating DNA molecule (plasmid) free of the host chromosome (e.g., bacterial plasmids).

Epistasis The interaction of genes at different loci resulting in the-masking of a character.

Epithelium The cornea's outer layer of cells.

Epitope A structural part of an antigen that is responsible for an antibody response against that antigen. Also called "antigenic determinant."

Epizootic Affecting many animals in one region simultaneously and spreading rapidly; the animal counterpart of epidemic. Compare enzootic, epidemic.

Equity fund A fund established through additional congressional appropriations or through a set aside by the Indian Health Service of a portion of its appropriations, and distributed to benefit IHS service units identified as being deficient in resources relative to other IHS service units.

Ergonomics The study of how humans and machines interact. In the occupational setting, one goal of ergonomics is to design the workplace to match the capabilities of workers.

Erythema Abnormal flushing of the skin caused by dilation of blood capillaries.

Erythroblastosis fetalis (Rh-in-compatibility Incompatibility between an infant's blood type and that of its mother. Results in destruction of the infant's red blood cells (hemolytic anemia) after birth by antibodies from mother's blood.

Erythrocytes Red blood cells. These cells contain hemoglobin and are adapted for the transport of oxygen in the blood.

Erythropoiesis Formation of red blood cells.

Erythropoietic porphyrias Inherited disorder in which there is an abnormal increase in the production of porphyrins (chemicals in all living things). Erythropoietic porphyria is characterized by production of large quantities of porphyrins in the blood-forming tissue of bone marrow. The symptoms include sensitivity to light, abdominal pain and neuropathy.

Erythropoietic protoporphyrias Disease characterized by itching, redness and edema after short exposure of the skin to sunlight.

Escherichia coli (E. coli) A species of rod-shaped, gram-negative aerobic bacteria that inhabit the normal intestinal tract of vertebrates. Some strains cause intestinal disease and diarrhea in humans through at least three mechanisms: enterotoxigenic E. coli produces toxins that cause excessive fluid production in the intestine; enteroinvasive E. coli invades the cells of the intestinal wall;

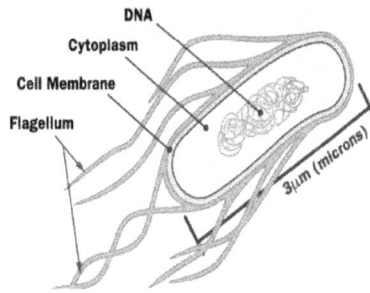

Fig. *E.coli Bacterium*

enteropathogenic E. coli produces a toxin that causes disease in infants. Many non-pathogenic strains of E. coli are used as hosts in recombinant DNA technologies and as experimental organisms in microbiological and genetics research.

E. coli are about as simple as living organisms can get, and because they reproduce so rapidly you can actually see evolution's effects on a normal time scale. In the past several decades, many different types of bacteria have become immune to antibiotics.

Escort service A service in which someone accompanies an individual to a medical appointment, another appointment, or an errand to provide assistance and supervision.

Esophageal rings Muscular fibres that surround the esophagus.

Esophageal varices Enlarged veins on the lining of the esophagus subject to severe bleeding. They often appear in patients with severe liver disease.

Esophagitis Inflammation of the mucous-membrane lining of the esophagus.

Esophagus Hollow tube that provides passage from the back of the throat to the stomach.

Esotropia When one or both eyes point inward, so the eyes are "crossed." This is one type of strabismus.

Essential A nutritional term applied to vitamins, minerals, and amino acids; refers to anything that the body does not manufacture and that must be obtained through the diet.

Essential Access Community Hospital (EACH) A newly designated type of rural hospital created by congress in 1989 (public law 101-239). Limited to hospitals in only a few states, EACHS will be facilities of at least 75 beds that provide backup to rural primary care hospitals as part of a patient referral network. Designated facilities will automatically qualify for medicare's payment roles for sole community hospitals.

Estrogen A group of steroid hormones, produced mainly by the ovaries during the life of a woman from puberty to menopause, essential for normal female sexual development and for normal functioning of the reproductive system.

Ethnicity A term used to indicate national origin (e.g., Hispanic). Most Census and health status information is available for individuals of Hispanic origin.

Etiology The study of what causes a disease.

Eugenics of normalcy Policies and programmes intended to ensure that each individual has at least a minimum number of normal genes.

Eugenics Attempts to improve hereditary qualities through selective breeding and the elimination of harmful genes.

Euglycemia A normal level of glucose (sugar) in the blood.

Eukaryote A cell or organism with membrane-bound, structurally discrete nuclei, and well-developed cell organelles. Eukaryotes include all organisms except viruses, bacteria, and blue-green algae.

Eunuchoidism Deficiency of male hormone, which results in abnormal tallness, small testes and deficient development of secondary sex characteristics, sex drive and potency.

Evaluative and management services Services, such as office visits, that may involve but do not depend in a major way on any medical devices.

Evoked potentials, sensory evoked potentials (EPs) Electrical signals generated by the nervous system in response to a stimulus, whether auditory (brain-stem auditory evoked responses, BAERs), visual (visual evoked potentials, VEPS, which include flash evoked potentials, FEPs, and pattern reversal evoked potentials, PREPs), or somato-sensory (somato-sensory evoked potentials, SEPS). EPs can be measured and the measurements used to identify which senses are affected by neurotoxic substances and how they are affected.

Ex utero Outside the uterus.

Exchange lists A grouping of foods by type to help people on special diets stay on the diet. Each group lists food in serving sizes. A person can exchange, trade, or substitute a food serving in one group for another food serving in the same group. The lists put foods in six groups:

(i) starch

(ii) bread

(iii) meat

(iv) vegetables

(v) fruit

(vi) milk

(vii) fats.

Within a food group, each serving has about the same amount of carbohydrate, protein, fat, and calories.

Exchange transfusion Introduction of whole blood in exchange for 75 to 85% of an infant's circulating blood. Blood is repeatedly withdrawn in small amounts and replaced with equal amounts of donor blood. This procedure is performed in infants to treat erythroblastosis fetalis.

Excimer laser An instrument that uses shorter wave (ultraviolet) light to vaporize and remove tissue from the eye's surface during vision correction procedures.

Excitotoxin A chemical substance (kainic acid, ibotenic acid, or quinolinic acid) that, when injected into the brain, kills nerve cells by overstimulating them.

Exclusion waiver An agreement attached to an insurance policy which eliminates a specified preexisting condition from coverage under the policy.

Number of Exchanges per Day for Various Calories Levels					
Calories	1,200	1,500	1,800	2,000	2,200
Starch/Bread	5	8	10	11	13
Meat	4	5	7	8	8
Vegetable	2	3	3	4	4
Fruit	3	3	3	3	3
Milk	2	2	2	2	2
Fat	3	3	3	4	5

Fig. *Exchange lists*

Exercise tolerance testing (exercise stress testing): Testing the response of the heart to exercise while observing the EKG and other physiological functions of the heart.

Exocrine pancreas: The part of the pancreas that produces enzymes that are needed in intestinal digestion.

Exogenous Produced or made outside the body; for instance, insulin that is commercially produced (made from pork or beef pancreas or by bio-synthetic processes) is exo-genous insulin when given to people.

Exons In genetics, DNA sequences that determine the sequence of amino acids in proteins. Exons are separated on DNA by introns, or intervening sequences, that are transcribed and later removed, or spliced out, during the production of mature mRNA in protein synthesis.

Exotic Describing a species not originating in the place where it is found; a nonnative, introduced species.

Exotoxin A poison excreted by some gram-negative or gram-positive organisms; composed of protein.

Exotropia When one or both eyes point outward; also called "walleyed." This is one type of strabismus. Exotropia is the opposite of esotropia, both of which are disorders of the eye falling under the general category of a strabismus, commonly known as "cross – eyed".

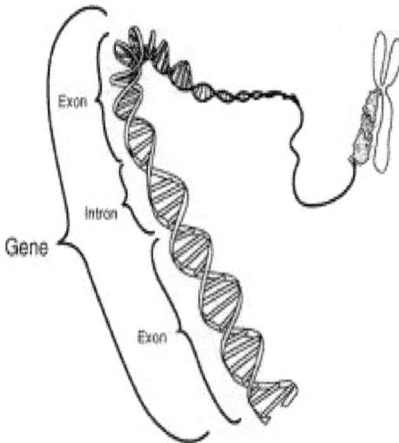

Fig. *Exotropia*

The most common form of exotropia – intermittent exotropia – is found in young children up to the age of seven. Obviously young children are not able to discern what they are experiencing compared to other children, nor are they able to explain adequately what they experience; children in such instances often start to close one eye for improved vision as well as rub and "squint" their eyes.

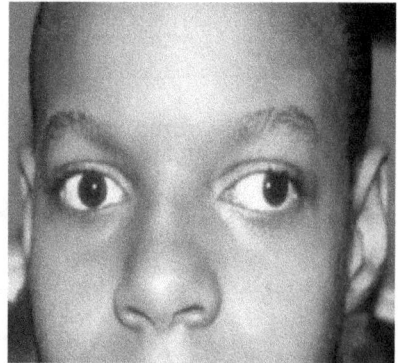

Fig. *Exons.*

Expenses per inpatient day Expenses incurred for inpatient care only, derived by dividing total expenses by the number of inpatient days during a particular period (American Hospital Association definition).

Experience-rating A method of determining group premium rates based on the actual amount of claims payments made on behalf of the group in a prior period, usually the preceding year.

Experimental group In a randomized clinical trial, the group receiving the treatment being evaluated for safety and efficacy. The experimental treatment may be a new technology, an existing technology applied to a new problem, or an accepted treatment about whose safety or efficacy there is doubt.

Experimental use permit An application to EPA by a manufacturer for permission to conduct field tests on a pesticide.

Explant culture Living tissue taken from its original site and placed in an artificial medium for growth.

Explicit review Review of the process of medical care using explicit criteria specified in advance.

Exposure The accidental or intentional contact of a person or animal with a substance, such as a drug or environmental contaminant, or with a factor such as radiation. Exposure is measured by the amount of the substance or factor involved (dose), how often and for how long

contact took place (frequency and duration of exposure), and the means through which contact occurred (route of exposure).

Expressive therapies use the arts to promote physical & mental health and personal growth. Examples of expressive therapies include art therapy, dance therapy, drama therapy, music therapy, poetry, and psychodrama.

Expressivity A term referring to the degree to which a gene is manifest in some traits (e.g., curliness of hair) may vary in the extent or seventy to which an individual. Genes for they are seen in different individuals. Genes known to be manifest in different degrees in different individuals are said to show differential or variable expressivity.

Extended wear Currently, these contact lenses are FDA-approved to be worn without removal for up to seven days (or 30 days in the case of one brand), meaning some people will be comfortable sleeping with them in their eyes. Thirty-day contact lenses are sometimes referred to as "continuous wear."

External catheterization: With regard to urinary functions, a catheter applied to the penis; requires frequent changing and may result in local skin irritations or other complications.

External controls In a clinical trial, individuals not formally enrolled in the trial who have had an alternative treatment, with which the experimentally treated group is compared. External controls may be historical or concurrent.

External validity A measure of the extent to which study results can be generalized to the population that is represented by individuals in the study, assuming that the characteristics of that population are accurately specified.

Extrachromosomal DNA DNA not associated with the chromosome(s) (e.g., plasmid DNA or organelle (mito-chondria or chloroplast) DNA).

Extracorporeal embryo An embryo maintained outside the body.

Extracorporeal shock wave lithotripsy A technique for the disintegrating of upper urinary tract stones that uses shock waves generated outside a patient's body and does not require a surgical incision.

Extremely low birthweight Birthweight of less than 1000 grams (2 lb. 2 oz.).

Exudate Matter that penetrates through vessel walls into adjoining tissue. Production of pus or serum.

Eye care practitioner Optometrists (ODs) and ophthalmologists (MDs) both practice eye care, but in different, though often overlapping, areas: In the United States, ODs (Doctors of Optometry) examine eyes for both vision and health problems, prescribe eyeglasses, pre-scribe and fit contact lenses, and treat some eye conditions and diseases. ODs attend four years of optometry school after attaining their BS or BA college degree. MDs are medical doctors who specialize in the eyes. They examine eyes, treat disease, perform surgery, and prescribe glasses and contacts. Like other physicians, they complete a BS or BA degree, attend four years of medical school, and complete a residency program in their practice specialty. Both ODs and MDs often pursue further subspecialty fellowship training, and they take additional continuing education courses during their careers in order to stay up to date and to maintain state and national board certifications. Other non-doctor eye care practitioners include paraoptometrics, contact lens technicians, and opticians, whose training and continuing education requirements can differ depending on the state in which they practice.

Eye tumour A "tumour" simply means a mass or tissue swell-

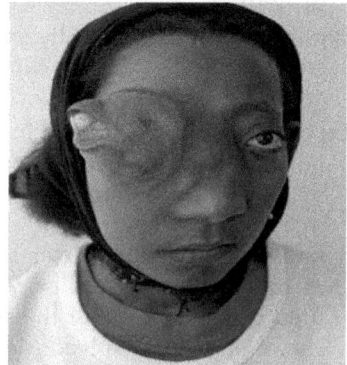

Fig. *Eye tumour*

ing. In other words, a growth or mass that occurs in or next to the eye. Specific tumours, both benign tumours (such as a mole on the skin) as well as malignant tumours (which are referred to as cancer), include— the dermoid cyst, capillary hema-ngioma, cavernous hema-ngioma, cho-roidal melanoma, retino-blas-toma, rhabdo-myo-sarcoma and lymphoma. The cause is dependent on the type of tumour you have. Symptoms can include blurred vision; a bulging eye; double vision; floaters; foreign body sensation; pain or discomfort in the eye, the lid or around the eye; swelling of the lid or around the eye; a red or pink eye; ptosis; vision loss; limited eye or lid movement; a white or cloudy spot on the eye; and an iris defect.

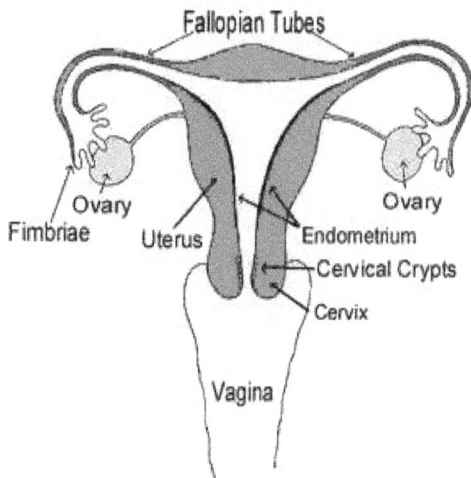

F

Fallopian Tubes

Ovary

Fimbriae   Uterus   Endometrium

Cervical Crypts

Cervix

Ovary

Vagina

f

Fabry disease An X-linked (the gene is located on the X chromosome) hereditary disease of lipid metabolism. Symptoms are a particular type of skin lesion, kidney disease (the usual cause of death) and a variety of neurological and biochemical abnormalities.

The diagnosis of fabry's disease was confirmed by the detection of reduced α-galactosidase A activity in peripheral leukocytes. He received carbamazepine for the neuropathic pain. Testing of renal function when the patient was 38 years of age showed a serum creatinine concentration of 1.1 mg per deciliter (97.2 μmol per litre), a creatinine clearance rate of 92 ml per minute per 1.73 m2 of body-surface area, and a protein excretion rate of 3.9 g per day. Renal biopsy showed an accumulation of toluidine

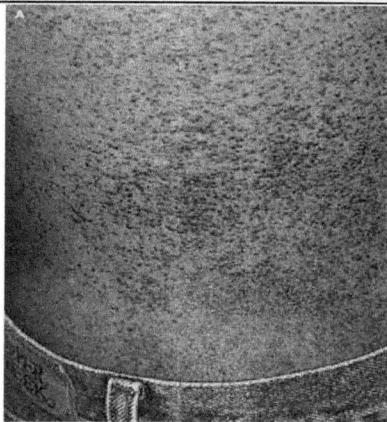

Fig. *Fabry disease*

blue staining in cellular inclusions that was prominent in glomerular podocytes and also present in distal tubular epithelial cells and extra-glomerular vascular cells (Panel C, ×80). Electron-microscopical examination of the glomerulus revealed podocytes bearing electron-dense lamellar bodies that represented secondary lysosomes containing glycolipid (Panel D, ×3800). The patient is being treated with α-galactosidase A administered by intravenous infusion every two weeks. His symptoms have improved, although his renal function has continued to deteriorate, with a serum creatinine concentration now of 2.2 mg per deciliter (194.5 μmol per litre).

Facet joints The joint that occurs between facets of the interior and superior articular processes of adjacent vertebra.

The facet joints, also termed zygapophyseal joints, are located at the back of the spine. There are two joints at each level, one on either side of the spine.

The facet joints are classified as synovial joints and are enclosed within a joint capsule. There is synovial fluid within the capsule and the joint surfaces are covered with hyaline cartilage, the same type of cartilage that is covering, for example, the ankle joint.

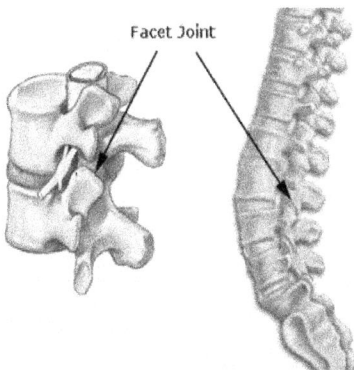

Fig. *Facet joints*

The role of the facet joints is to control excessive movement especially in rotation and extension, and therefore, provide stability for the spine.

Facial bone The facial skeleton, consisting of bones situated between the cranial base and the mandibular region.

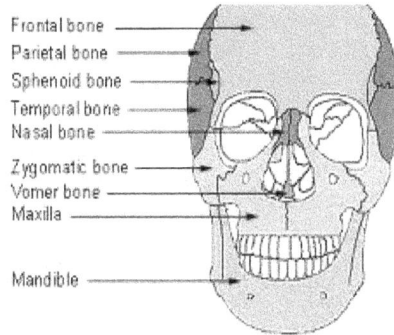

Frontal bone
Parietal bone
Sphenoid bone
Temporal bone
Nasal bone
Zygomatic bone
Vomer bone
Maxilla
Mandible

Fig. *Facial bone.*

While some consider the facial bones to comprise the hyoid, palatine, and zygomatic bones, mandible, and maxilla, others include also the lacrimal and nasal bones, inferior nasal concha, and vomer but exclude the hyoid bone.

Facial injury General or unspecified injuries to the soft tissue or bony portions of the face.

Facial nerve The 7th cranial nerve. The facial nerve has two parts, the larger motor root which may be called the facial nerve proper, and the smaller intermediate or sensory root. Together they provide efferent innervation to the muscles of facial expression and to the lacrimal and salivary glands, and convey afferent informa-

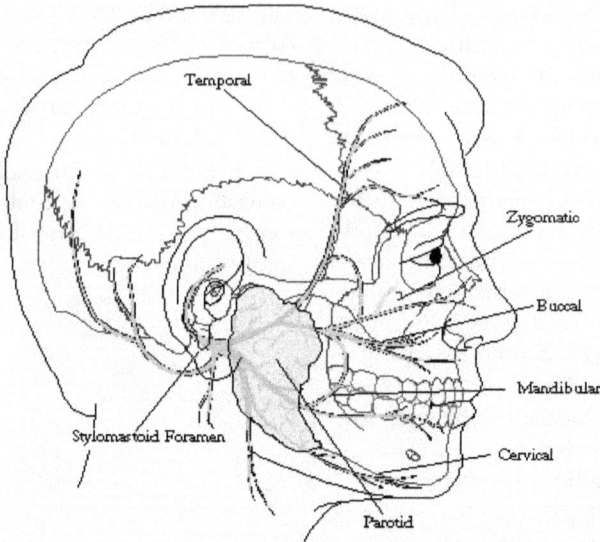

Fig. *Facial nerve*

tion for taste from the anterior two-thirds of the tongue and for touch from the external ear.

Facial nerve disease Diseases of the facial nerve or nuclei. Pontine disorders may affect the facial nuclei or nerve fascicle. The nerve may be involved intra-cranially, along its course through the petrous portion of the temporal bone, or along its extracranial course. Clinical manifestations include facial muscle weakness, loss of taste from the anterior tongue, hyperacusis, and decreased lacrimation.

Facial neuropathy Diseases of the facial nerve or nuclei. Pontine disorders may affect the facial nuclei or nerve fascicle. The nerve may be involved intra-cranially, along its course through the petrous portion of the temporal bone, or along its

extracranial course. Clinical manifestations include facial muscle weakness, loss of taste from the anterior tongue, hyperacusis, and decreased lacrimation.

Facial paralysis Severe or complete loss of facial muscle motor function. This condition may result from central or peripheral lesions. Damage to CNS motor pathways from the cerebral cortex to the facial nuclei in the pons

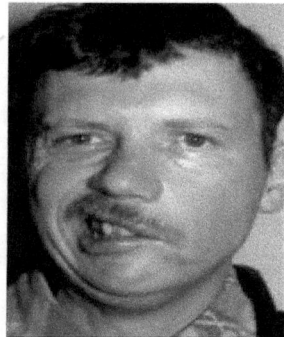

Fig. *Facial paralysis*

149

leads to facial weakness that generally spares the forehead muscles. Facial nerve disease generally results in generalized hemifacial weakness. Neuromuscular junction diseases and muscular diseases may also cause facial paralysis or paresis.

Factor I Fibrinogen needed for blood to clot.

Factor II Prothrombin needed for blood to clot.

Factor III Tissue thromboplastin needed for blood to clot.

Factor IV Calcium needed for blood to clot.

Factor V Proaccelerin needed for blood to clot.

Factor VI Accelerin needed for blood to clot.

Factor VII Proconvertin needed for blood to clot.

Factor VIII Anti-hemophilic factor needed for blood to clot.

Factor VIII concentrate A concentrated preparation of Factor VIII that is used in the treatment of individuals with hemophilia A.

Factor IX Plasma thromboplastin component needed for blood to clot.

Factor X Stuart factor (autoprothrombin C) needed for blood to clot.

Factor XI Plasma thromboplastin antecedent needed for blood to clot.

Factor XII Hageman factor needed for blood to clot.

Factor XIII Fibrin-stabilizing factor needed for blood to clot.

Factored rating Community rating impacted by group-specific demographics. It is also known as adjusted community rating.

Factor-VII deficiency Deficiency of normal clotting factor. Can be inherited or acquired. This deficiency commonly causes nosebleeds, easy bruising and bleeding gums.

Failed sterilisation Wrongful birth is the term the courts use to describe a claim that arises out of the birth of a child who would not have been born without negligent treatment, usually to the child's parents. The claim belongs to the parents, usually primarily to the mother because she is more likely to be the person who received treatment. Wrongful birth claims fall into two main categories. The first is failed sterilisation or failed vasectomy. The second arises where parents have not been warned that a child will be born with a specific disability, and if they had been warned would have terminated the pregnancy. It may include such things as wrong advice about the risks of a child being born with sickle cell disease, or simply forgetting to offer screening for Down's Syndrome to a woman at risk.

Failure to thrive A term which refers to the slow growth and development of a baby, characterised by failure to gain weight, delayed development, unwillingness to interact, and gastrointestinal problems. Failure to thrive is almost always the result of inadequate nutrition.

Fallopian tube The fallopian tubes are a pair of tubes found in every female mammal. These two tubes sometimes referred to as the oviducts or uterine tubes and are found in the pelvic cavity, running between the uterus and the ovaries. Approximately three to four inches long, the fallopian tubes are not directly attached to the ovaries. Instead, the tubes open up into the peritonial (abdominal) cavity, very close to the ovaries. Named after the Italian anatomist Gabriel Fallopius.

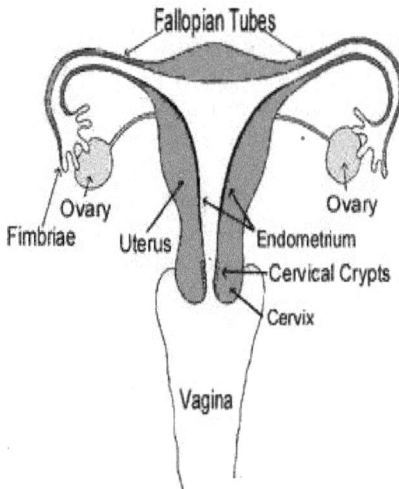

Fig. *Fallopian tube*

Falloposcopy is the inspection of the inner lining of the Fallopian tubes using a narrow flexible fibre-optic tube called a falloposcope, which is introduced via a hysteroscope (an endoscope used for visualization of the interior of the uterus).

False Claims Act A Federal law that imposes liability for treble damages and fines of $5,000 to $10,000 for knowingly submitting a false or fraudulent claim for payment to the Federal government.

False negative A negative test result in an individual who actually has the disease or characteristic being tested for. The patient is incorrectly diagnosed as not having a particular disease or characteristic.

False positive In medical diagnostics, a "false positive" is a positive test result in an individual who does not have the disease or characteristic being tested for (i.e., the individual is incorrectly diagnosed as having a particular disease or characteristic).

Familial hypercholesterolemia An autosomal dominant genetic disease caused by defects in the gene encoding for the low density lipoprotein (LDL) receptor. The defects disrupt the normal control of cholesterol metabolism, leading to accumulation of LDL in arteries and the formation of plaques; manifested by high serum cholesterol levels and heart disease in early life.

Familial hypoproteinemia Inherited abnormal decrease in the amount of protein in the blood.

Familial myoglobinuria Inherited condition in which myoglobin appears in urine. Causes include vigorous, prolonged exercise and severe injuries, such as a broken bone.

Familial xanthurenic aciduria Inherited deficiency disorder of xanthine oxidase that causes physical and mental retardation.

Family consent laws State statutes that authorize family members to make specified types of decisions (e.g., about life-sustaining medical treatments) for relatives who are incapable of making a decision. Such statutes exist in a only a few states.

Family counseling Counselling provided to an entire family rather than solely to an individual.

Family history A record of the relationships among family members along with their medical histories. This includes current and past illnesses. A family history may show a pattern of certain diseases in a family. Also called family medical history.

Family medical history A record of the relationships among family members along with their medical histories. This includes current and past illnesses. A family medical history may show a pattern of certain diseases in a family. Also called family history.

Family medical leave act 1993 Federal law requiring that employers of 50 or more (and public employers of any size) allow employees to take leave to care for ill family members and to return to substantially similar employment conditions following the leave.

Family planning A range of services intended to help individuals plan when to have children, from counseling concerning the advisability of initiating sexual intercourse to the provision of contraceptive methods.

Family planning programmes authorized by Title X of the Public Health Service Act: Title X, established by the Family Planning Services and Population Research Act of 1970, funds public or private nonprofit entities that operate voluntary family planning projects; funds training for personnel to improve the delivery of family planning services; promotes service delivery improvement through research; and develops and disseminates information on family planning. Contraceptives may be distributed without parental consent or notification, but the use of Title X funds for abortion as a method of family planning has been prohibited by statute and regulations. Low-income individuals are targeted as a priority group for receiving services. Although projects funded by Title X do not focus exclusively on adolescents, they are required to offer a broad range of family planning services to all who want them, including adolescents.

Family rest residential care Residential option in Delaware providing less care than assisted living, usually at the "board and care" level (i.e., no direct health or personal care services) but differs from rest residential in that it is provided in the home of a caregiver. Also known as adult foster care.

Family structure Used to describe whether a family consists of children and a single parent, two parents living with their biological children), or children living with a biological parent and a stepparent.

Family survival project An organization in San Francisco that provides public education, information and referral, care coordination, and a variety of other services for brain-impaired adults and their caregivers.

Family therapy A type of psychotherapy based on the idea that a child's problems are manifestations of disturbed interactions within a family rather than problems that lie within the child alone. Treatment heavily involves other family members as well as the child (e.g., in sessions attended by the entire family) because it is believed that a child cannot change if the family as a whole does not change.

Fanconi's syndrome Rare, usually congenital disorder characterized by aplastic anemia, bone abnormalities, olive-brown skin pigmentation, abnormally small head, small gonads and kidney-function abnormalities. Adults can get a form of the syndrome as a result of heavy-metal poisoning. It also may occur after a kidney transplant.

Farinaceous Of the nature of flour or meal. Starchy or containing starch.

Farsightedness It is also called hyperopia. To farsighted people, near objects are blurry, but far objects are in focus.

Fascia A connective tissue sheath consisting of fibrous tissue and fat which unites the skin to the underlying tissues.

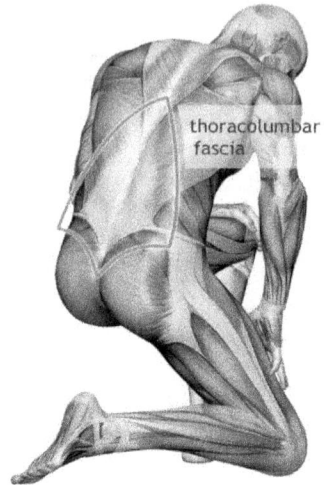

Fig. *Fascia*

Fasting plasma glucose A method for finding out how much sugar (glucose) is in the blood. The test can show if a person has diabetes. A blood sample is taken in a lab or doctor's office. The test is usually done in the morning, after not eating for eight hours. The normal, nondiabetic range for fasting plasma glucose is less than 100 mg/dl (6.1 mmol/L). If the level is 126 mg/dl (7 mmol/L) or higher, it usually means the person has diabetes. Previous name for this test was fasting blood sugar (FBS).

Fat cell Fat-storing cells found mostly in the abdominal cavity and subcutaneous tissue. Fat is usually stored in the form of tryglyceride.

Fatality/catastrophe inspection An Occupational Safety and Health Administration investigation of occupational fatalities or an incident that resulted in the hospitalization of five or more employees.

Fats One of the three main classes of foods and a source of energy in the body. Fats help the body use some vitamins and keep the skin healthy. They also serve as energy stores for the body. In food, there are two types of fats: saturated and unsaturated. Saturated fats are solid at room temperature and come chiefly from animal food products. Some examples are butter, lard, meat fat, solid shortening, palm oil, and coconut oil. These fats tend to raise the level of cholesterol, a fat-like substance in the blood. Unsaturated fats, which include monounsaturated fats and polyunsaturated fats, are liquid at room temperature and come from plant oils such as olive, peanut, corn, cottonseed, sunflower, safflower, and soybean. These fats tend to lower the level of cholesterol in the blood.

Fatty acids A basic unit of fats. When insulin levels are too low or there is not enough glucose (sugar) to use for energy, the body burns fatty acids for energy. The body then makes ketone bodies, waste products that cause the acid level in the blood to become too high. This in turn may lead toketoacidosis, a serious problem.

FDA (food & drug administration) A U.S. government body that oversees medical devices and medications, including contact lenses, intraocular lenses, excimer lasers and eye drops. In the United States, these products must be approved by the FDA before they can be marketed.

Feasibility In the context of evaluations of indicators of medical quality, whether it is practical to use a certain indicator to convey information to the public about quality.

Febrifuge That which reduces or prevents fever. Same as antipyretic or refrigerant.

Febrile convulsions Spontaneous contractions and relaxations of the muscles brought about by a high temperature

Fecal incontinence Involuntary excretion of stool sufficient in frequency to be a social or health problem.

Fecund Able to conceive. A characterization used by demographer to identify couples who have no known physical problem that prevents conception.

Federal medical assistance percentage The percentage of Federal matching dollars available to a state to provide medicaid services. FMAP is calculated annually based on a formula designed to provide a higher federal matching rate to states with lower per capital income. Currently at 50% (minimum FMAP) for delaware.

Federal poverty level Income guidelines established annually by the federal government. Public assistance programmes usually define income limits in relation to FPL or the supplemental security income (SSI) level.

Federal qualified health center A Federal payment option that enables qualified providers in medically underserved areas to receive cost-based medicare and medicaid reimbursement and allows for the direct reimbursement of nurse practitioners, physician assistants and certified nurse midwives. Many outpatient clinics and specialty outreach services are qualified under this provision.

Federal recognition It refers to the relationship between Indian tribes and the Federal Government. Federal recognition can be obtained by satisfying the criteria of the Federal Acknowledgement Process administered through the Department of Interior, by Federal statute enacted by Congress, or by court decree. Federally recognized tribes and their members are eligible for the special programmes provided by the United States to Indians because of their status as Indians.

Federal register An official publication of the Federal government that provides final and proposed regulations of Federal legislation.

Federal tort claims Act Enacted in 1946 [28 U.S.C.A. sec. 1346(b) (Supp. 1988)], the FTCA allows an injured party to sue the United States Government.

Federally qualified HMO An HMO that is certified as meeting the qualification requirements of the Federal Health Maintenance Act of 1973, as amended (42 U.S.C. Sec. 300e et seq.). Federally qualified HMOS must adhere to certain financial, underwriting, and rate-setting standards and provide specified medical services.

Federally qualified HMOs HMOs that meet certain Federally stipulated provisions aimed at protecting consumers, such as providing a broad range of basic health services, assuring financial solvency and monitoring the quality of care. The application process is administered by HCFA's Office of Prepaid Health Care.

Federation of American Health Systems A trade association comprised of proprietary or investor-owned hospitals.

Fee disclosure Physicians and caregivers discussing their charges with patients prior to treatment.

Fee for service Method of charging whereby a physician or other practitioner bills for each encounter or service rendered. This is the usual method of billing by the majority of physicians.

Fee HR service equivalency Quantitative measures of the difference between the amount a provider receives from an alternative reimbursement system (e.g., capitation) compared to fee-for-service reimbursement.

Fee schedule An exhaustive list of medical services in which each entry is associated with a specific monetary amount that represents the approved payment amount for the service under a given insurance plan.

Fee schedule payment area A geographic area within which payment for a given service under the Medicare Fee Schedule will be equal.

Fee screen year The calendar period during which a particular year's CPR limits are in effect. As of September 30, 1984, fee screen years run from October 1 through September 30 of the following calendar year, with fee screen year 1985, for example, beginning on October 1, 1984 and ending on September 30, 1985. Prior to the Deficit Reduction Act of 1984 (Public Law 98-389), fee screen years began on July 1 of a calendar year and continued through June 30 of the next year.

Fee screen A limit used to determine the Medicare approved charge for a particular physician service, such as the physician's customary charge or the locality prevailing charge for the service in question.

Fee-for-service payment A method of paying for medical services in which each service performed by an individual provider beam a related charge. This charge is paid by the indi-

vidual patient receiving the service or by an insurer on behalf of the patient.

Female infertility Diminished or absent ability of a female to achieve conception.

Femtosecond laser Device that creates bursts of laser energy at an extremely fast rate measured in terms of a unit known as a femtosecond (one quadrillionth of a second). These ultra fast energy pulses precisely target and break apart tissue or other substances at a molecular level, without damaging adjacent areas.

Femur A bone of the leg situated between the pelvis and knee in humans. It is the largest and strongest bone in the body.

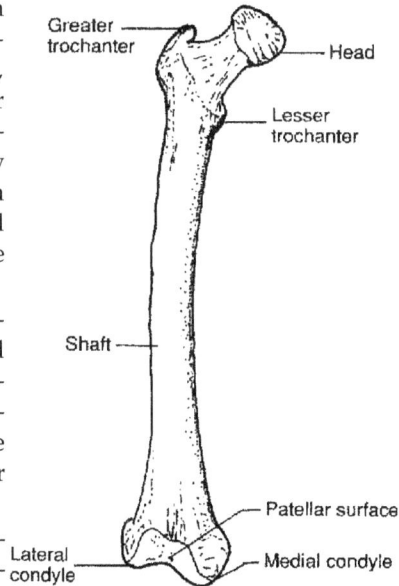

Fig. *Femur*

Femur fracture Fracture of the thigh bone.

Feng shui An ancient Chinese practice of configuring home or work environments to promote health, happiness, prosperity. Feng shui consultants may advise clients to make adjustments in their surroundings, from colour selection to furniture placement, to promote a healthy flow of chi, or vital energy.

Feral Refers to animals existing in the wild (e.g., an undomesticated animal), or to animals that have reverted to the wild state (e.g., a previously domesticated animal).

Fermentation An anaerobic process of growing microorganisms for the production of various chemical or pharmaceutical compounds. Microbes are normally incubated under specific conditions in the presence of nutrients in large tanks called fermenters.

Fern test Evaluation of fern-like pattern of dried cervical mucus for the prediction of ovulation. As ovulation approaches, more ferning can be observed.

Fertilisation The penetration of an oocyte by a sperm and subsequent combining of maternal and paternal DNA during the process of sexual reproduction.

Fertilisation conception It is the moment when sperm and egg meet, join and form a single cell. It usually takes place in the Fallopian tubes. The fertilised egg then travels into the uterus, where it implants in the lining before developing into an embryo and then a fetus.

Fertility drugs Compounds used to treat ovulatory dys-function. these include clomiphene citrate, human gonadotropin, bromo-criptine, gluco-corticoids, and progesterone.

Fertility factor An episome capable of transferring a copy of itself from its host bacterial cell (an F+ cell) to a bacterial cell not harboring an F factor (an F- cell). When the F factor is integrated into the host chromosome (the resulting cell is called an Hfr cell), the factor is capable of mo-

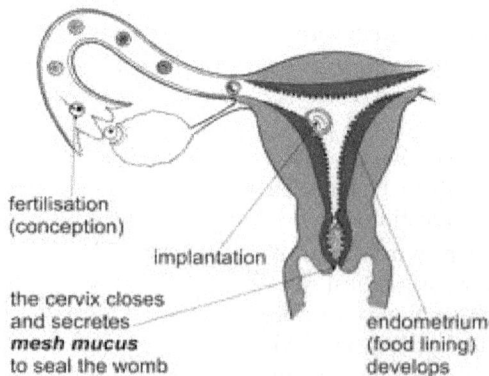

fertilisation
(conception)

implantation

the cervix closes
and secretes
mesh mucus
to seal the womb

endometrium
(food lining)
develops

Fig. *Fertilisation conception*

bilizing transfer of the bacterial chromosome to an F- cell.

Fertility rate The annual number of live births per 1,000 women of child bearing age (15 to 49 years) in a defined population.

Fertility specialist An obstetrician/ gynaecologist who specialises in treating people with fertility problems.

Fetal alcohol syndrome A congenital disorder resulting from alcohol teratogenicity (i.e., the production, actual or potential, of pathological changes in the fetus, most frequently in the form of normal development of one or more organ systems; commonly referred to as birth defects), with the following possible dysmorphic categories: central nervous system dysfunction, birth deficiencies (such as low birth weight), facial abnormalities, and variable major and minor malformations. A safe level of alcohol use during pregnancy has not been established, and it is generally advisable for women to refrain from alcohol use during pregnancy.

Fetal alcohol syndrome A congenital disorder resulting from alcohol terato-genicity (i.e., the production, actual or potential, of pathological changes in the fetus, most frequently in the form of normal development of one or more organ systems; commonly referred to as birth defects), with the following possible dys-morphic categories: central nervous system dysfunction, birth deficiencies (such as low birth weight), fa-

cial abnormalities, and variable major and minor malformations.

Fetal death rate The ratio of fetal deaths to fetal deaths plus live births.

Fetal death Stillbirth, or death in utero; the failure of the fetus to show signs of respiration, heartbeat, or definite movement of a voluntary muscle.

Fetal distress Including slowed heartbeat or absence of fetal movement are watched for throughout labour. If a fetus's life is believed to be in danger, usually because of lack of oxygen, the immediate delivery of the baby is called for.

Fetal hypoxia Absence of sufficient oxygen to sustain life in a fetus.

Fetal material Any or all of the contents of the uterus resulting from pregnancy excluding the fetus (the placenta, fluids, and membranes).

Fetal monitor The device used to track a fetus's heartbeat and a woman's uterine contractions during labour.

Fetal monitoring Tracking the heartbeat of a fetus and a wom-

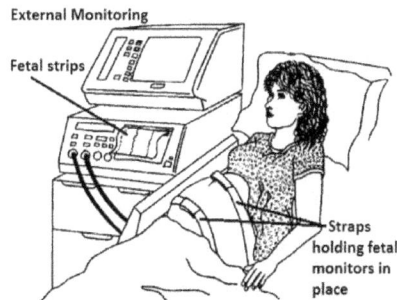

Fig. *Fetal monitor*

an's uterine contractions during labour.

Fetal mortality ratio The annual number of fetal deaths in a year as a proportion of the total annual number of births (live births and fetal deaths) in the same year.

Fetal tissue A part or organ of the fetus (e.g., the lungs or liver).

Fetal-maternal exchange The transfer of oxygen and nutrients from the mother to the baby and the transfer of waste from the baby to the mother.

Fetishism One of the paraphilias, characterized by marked distress over, or acting on, sexual urges involving the use of nonliving objects (fetishes), such as underclothing, stockings, or boots.

Fetoscopy is an endoscopic procedure during pregnancy to permit use of the fetus, the amniotic cavity, the umbilical cord, and also the fetal side from the placenta. A little (3-4 mm) incision is created in the abdomen,

as well as an endoscope is inserted through the abdominal wall and uterus into the amniotic cavity. Fetoscopy allows medical interventions such as a biopsy or perhaps a laser occlusion of abnormal arteries. Fetoscopy is really a process that employs a guitar known as a fetoscope to judge or treat the fetus while pregnant.

Fetus In humans, the embryo becomes a fetus after approximately 9 weeks in the uterus. This stage of development lasts from 9 weeks gestation until birth and is marked by the growth and specialization of organ function.

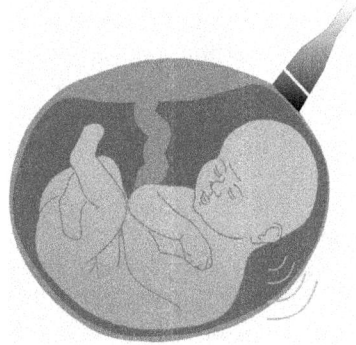

Fig. *Fetus*

Fetus, pre-viable A fetus that, although it may show some signs of life, has not yet reached the stage at which it is able to function as a self-sustaining whole independent of physical connection with the mother.

Fetus, viable A fetus that has reached the stage of maintaining the coordinated operation of its component parts so that it is capable of functioning as a self-sustaining whole independ-

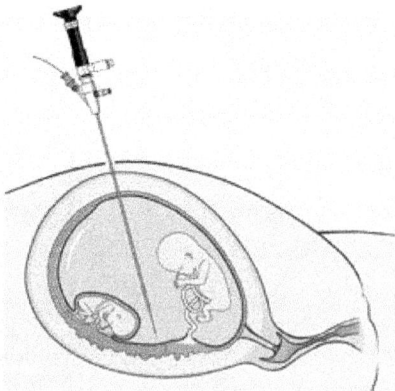

Fig. *Fetoscopy.*

ently of any connection with the mother.

Fever Fever occurs when body temperature rises above its normal level - usually defined as 98.6 degrees F/37 degrees C, although this varies by individual and time of day. A fever is a sign of the immune system at work and usually indicates an infection.

Fibre A substance found in foods that come from plants. Fibre helps in the digestive process and is thought to lower cholesterol and help control blood glucose (sugar). The two types of fibre in food are soluble and insoluble. Soluble fibre, found in beans, fruits, and oat products, dissolves in water and is thought to help lower blood fats and blood glucose (sugar). Insoluble fibre, found in wholegrain products and vegetables, passes directly through the digestive system, helping to rid the body of waste products.

Fibrillation Quivering of heart muscle fibres.

Fibrin Protein formed from fibrinogen by the action of blood clotting.

Fibrinogen Protein in the blood needed for blood clotting.

Fibrinolysis Breakdown of fibrin by enzyme action.

Fibrinolysis, secondary Process by which connective tissue is dissolved by the action of enzymes as a result of some disease process.

Fibrinolytic disorders Disease process characterized by dissolution of connective tissue by the action of enzymes.

Fibroblast A connective tissue cell, found in the skin. Fibroblasts also produce glycoproteins and polysaccharides for the ground substances, a gel-like material that surrounds collagen fibres of dense connective tissue, forming an "extracellular matrix",

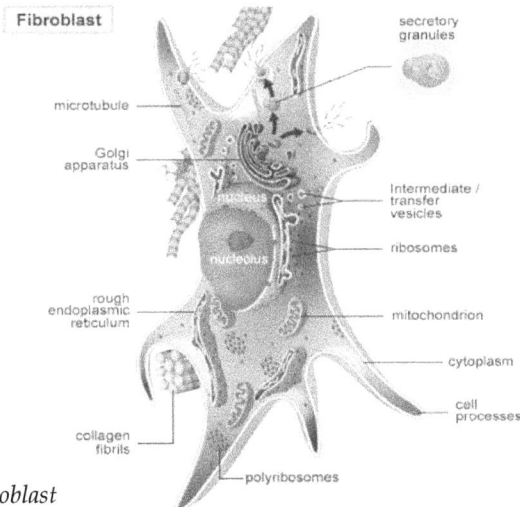

Fig. *Fibroblast*

which contributes to the structural integrity of ligaments and tendons, determines the physical properties of connective tissue.

Fibrocystic breast disease A common condition marked by benign (not cancer) changes in breast tissue. These changes may include irregular lumps or cysts, breast discomfort, sensitive nipples, and itching. These symptoms may change throughout the menstrual cycle and usually stop after menopause. Also called benign breast disease, fibrocystic breast changes, and mammary dysplasia.

Fibrocystic disease (Breast lumps) Disorder of the female breast characterized by nonmalignant lumps. Cause is unknown. Lumps may be accompanied by generalized breast pain, especially before menstrual periods.

Lumps often enlarge before menstrual periods, then shrink afterward.

Fibroids Abnormal growth of cells in the muscular wall of the uterus (myometrium). Fibroids are almost always benign (not cancerous). Fibroids can grow as a single tumour, or there can be many of them in the uterus. They can be as small as an apple seed or as big as a grapefruit. In unusual cases they can become very large. Fibroids also can put pressure on the bladder, causing frequent urination, or the rectum, causing rectal pressure.

Fibromas Benign neoplasm of fibrous or fully developed connective tissue.

Fibromatosis A condition in which multiple fibromas develop. Fibromas are tumours (usually benign) that affect connective tissue.

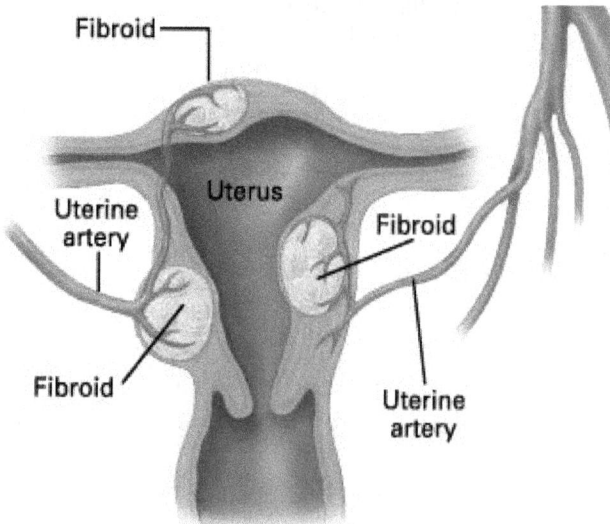

Fig. *Fibroids*

Fibromyalgia Condition that produces long-term pain all over the body and/or at tender points in soft tissues such as muscles, tendons and joints. The cause is unknown, but proposed triggers include trauma, sleep problems, an infectious microbe, depression, chronic back pain and hypothyroidism.

Fibronectin A plasma protein synthesized in the liver, which plays a variety of roles ranging from cell adhesion to enhancing the phagocytic clearance of parti-culate contaminants from the body.

Fibrosarcoma A type of soft tissue sarcoma that begins in fibrous tissue, which holds bones, muscles, and other organs in place.

Fibrosis Generation of fibrous tissue, such as in a scar.

Fibrous ankylosis Immobility and consolidation of a joint from disease caused by fibrous tissue.

Fibrous tissue Tissue that is made up of fibres.

Fibula The smaller of the two bones in the lower leg, located to the outside.

Fiduciary Relating to, or found upon, a trust or confidence. A fiduciary relationship exists where an individual or organization has an explicit or implicit obligation to act in behalf of another person's or organization's interests in matters which affect the other person or organization. This fiduciary is also obligated to act in the other person's best interest with to-tal disregard for any interests of the fiduciary.

Fifth disease Slapped cheek disease (erythema infectiosum) is also known as fifth disease because it was the last of five "red rash" childhood diseases to be defined after scarlet fever, measles, rubella, and roseola. It is characterised by fever and red cheeks.

Filaria Parasitic nematode worms, named for their threadlike appearance.

Filariasis Disease caused by the presence of parasitic worms or larvae in body tissue. Worms are round, long and threadlike. They are common in tropical and subtropical regions. They enter the body as microscopic larvae through the bite of a mosquito or other insect then infest the lymph glands and channels. Treatment is not very effective. After many years, this disease usually results in elephantiasis, characterized by tremendous swelling of the ex-

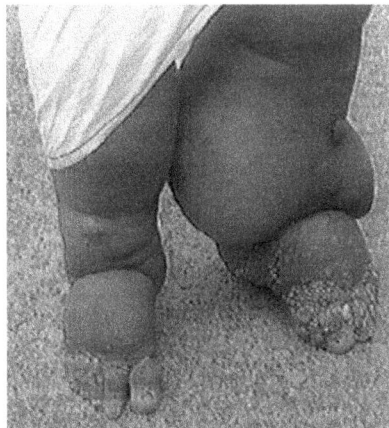

Fig. *Filariasis*

ternal genitals and legs. Overlying skin becomes dark, thick and coarse.

Fimbria Finger-like structures, such as the fringed entrance to the fallopian tubes.

Fimbrioplasty A surgical procedure to correct partial restriction of the fallopian tube.

Financial accounting standards board The FASB establishes voluntary standards designed to improve the accuracy, relevancy, and usefulness of corporate financial statements. FASB is proposing rules that would require the present employer liability for future retiree health expenditures to be reported in accounting records and financial statements.

Financing It refers to mechanisms through which money to pay health care providers for the delivery of health care services is delivered.

Fine motor skills The muscle control required to make small, precise movements, such as picking up a raisin or pushing a button.

Firearm A weapon from which a shot is discharged by gunpowder. The term firearm is usually used only when referring to small arms. The term firearms includes guns (defined as portable firearms).

First dollar coverage A feature of an insurance plan in which there is no deductible, and therefore the plan's sponsor pays a proportion or all of the covered services provided to a patient as soon as he or she enrolls.

First phase insulin release Release of insulin into the bloodstream from the beta cell within a few minutes after the blood glucose level rises. It is thought that this almost immediate release is due to release of insulin that was previously manufactured, and was being stored in the beta cell.

Fiscal intermediary Private health insurance company under contract with the Health Care Financing Administration (HCFA) to handle claims processing for Medicare Part A.

Fiscal note An analysis by the Legislative Budget Office of the financial impact of proposed state legislation.

Fiscal year A 12-month period in which an organization accounts for the use of its funds.

FISH A laboratory technique used to look at genes or chromosomes

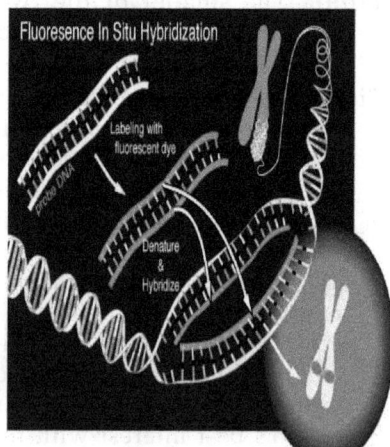

Fig. *FISH technique*

in cells and tissues. Pieces of DNA that contain a fluorescent dye are made in the laboratory and added to cells or tissues on a glass slide. When these pieces of DNA bind to specific genes or areas of chromosomes on the slide, they light up when viewed under a microscope with a special light. It is also called fluorescence *in situ* hybridization.

Fissures (i) Cleft or groove on the surface of an organ, often marking division of the organ into parts, as the fissures of the brain. (ii) Crack-like lesion of skin.

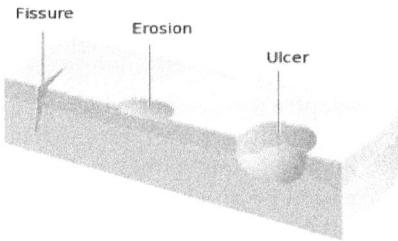

Fissure
Erosion
Ulcer

Fig. *Fissures*

Fistula An abnormal passage between two organs or from an internal organ to the surface of the body. It is generally a disease condition, but a fistula may be surgically created for therapeutic reasons. Fistulas can develop in various parts of the body.

Fitness for purpose Where goods are sold by a trader, they must be reasonably fit for the buyer's own particular purpose, provided the buyer made his purpose known (expressly or implied) and reasonably relied on the seller's expertise. Where goods are bought for their usual purpose, notification of the buy-

er's purpose is implied.

Fitness Usually defined as cardiorespiratory or aerobic fitness, but may also include muscle strength, muscle endurance, flexibility, and low body fat.

Five element acupuncture An ancient form of acupuncture based on the principle that there are five universal elements (wood, fire, earth, metal, and water) that affect a person's emotions, personality, health, and response to treatment. Each person is affected by one element more than the others. Also called traditional acupuncture.

Fixation In terms of vision, the eye's ability to maintain gaze upon an object.

Fixed costs An operating expense that does not vary, at least over the short term, with the volume of services provided.

Flashback Hallucinogen persisting perception disorder or posthallucinogen perception disorder; reexperiencing, after ceasing the use of a hallucinogen, one or more of the perceptual symptoms that had been part of the hallucinatory experience while using the drug.

Flat Absence or near absence of any signs of affective expression such as a monotonous voice and an immobile face.

Flexibility The ability of muscle to relax and yield to stretch force.

Flexibility exercise A general term used to describe exercise performed to passively or actively elongate soft tissues.

Flexible benefit plan A benefit programme that offers employees a number of benefit options, allowing them to tailor benefits to their needs.

Flexible worktime Structuring of individual work schedules so that they adapt to new, different, or changing requirements (e.g., of parents).

Flexion Bending a joint, as in flexing the arm or leg.

Flexor A muscle which upon contraction flexes or bends.

Flight of ideas An early continuous flow of accelerated speech with abrupt changes from one topic to another, usually based on understandable associations, distracting stimuli, or playing on words. When severe, however, this may lead to disorganized and incoherent speech. Flight of ideas is characteristic ofmanic episodes, but it may occur also in organic mental disorders, schizophrenia, other psychoses, and, rarely, acute reactions to stress.

Flight of ideas An early continuous flow of accelerated speech with abrupt changes from one topic to another, usually based on understandable associations, distracting stimuli, or playing on words. When severe, however, this may lead to disorganized and incoherent speech. Flight of ideas is characteristic of manic episodes, but it may occur also in organic mental disorders, schizophrenia, other psychoses, and, rarely, acute reactions to stress.

Floaters A dark or gray spot or speck that passes across your field of vision and moves as you move your eye. Floaters are very common and may look like clouds, strands, webs, spots, squiggles, wavy lines or other shapes. As your eye ages, the gelatinous vitreous humor begins to liquefy in the center of the gel. Floaters are caused by the undissolved vitreous humor that floats in the liquid vitreous. Sometimes, a "shower of floaters" is a sign of a serious condition, particularly if you also see flashes of light.

Flooding A behaviour therapy procedure for phobias and other problems involving maladaptive anxiety, in which anxiety producers are presented in intense forms, either in imagination or in real life. The presentations, which act as desensitizers, are continued until the stimuli no longer produce disabling anxiety.

Flooding(implosion) A behaviour therapy procedure for phobias and other problems involving maladaptive anxiety, in which anxiety producers are presented in intense forms, either in imagination or in real life. The presentations, which act as desensitizers, are continued until the stimuli no longer produce disabling anxiety.

Flower essences are intended to alleviate negative emotional states that may contribute to illness or hinder personal growth. Drops of a solution infused with the captured essence of a flower are placed under the tongue or in a beverage. The appropriate essences are chosen, focusing on the clients emotional state rather than on a particular physical condition.

Fluke The common name for a large number of species of parasitic flatworms that form the class Trematoda. It is also called flukeworms.

Fluoresce Emits light while exposed to light.

Fluorescein angiography An imaging test that involves first injecting fluorescent yellow-green dye into the veins. When the dye reaches interior regions of the eye, it provides opportunity for high contrast photography or other imaging of blood vessels. Fluorescein angiography particularly is useful in diagnosing conditions such as age-related macular degeneration, which in advanced forms can be characterized by abnormal growth of blood vessels in the retina.

Fluorescein Compound that becomes a bright, fluorescent yellow-green when in contact with alkaline substances. A fluorescein dye solution can help eye doctors see corneallesions or conduct tests for eye dryness.

Fluoridation The addition of a minute quantity of a fluoride (usually one part per million of fluoride ion) to drinking water supplies in order to protect growing children against dental caries. Fluoride can also be applied topically (in toothpaste and rinses).

Flux Excessive flow or discharge. For example, in dysentery or excessive menstruation.

Family nurse practitioner; Generally an acronym for a program name (e.g. FNP Program) or title; the credential is usually either APRN,BC (offered by the American Nurses Credentialing Center [ANCC]), or NP-C (offered by the American Academy of Nurse Practitioners [AANP] Certification Program).

Focal seizures Convulsions brought about by a disease process or injury to an identifiable part of the brain. Such seizures usually affect only one side or a specific area of the body as opposed to a generalized seizure, which is likely to involve all muscle groups in the body.

Foley catheter A tube which is inserted into the urinary bladder in order to drain urine. The urine drains through a tube and is collected in a plastic pouch.

Folic acid It is the B-complex vitamin which is essential for creating new blood cells, folic acid has been shown to reduce the incidence of neural tube defects such as spina bifida (incomplete closure of the spine) and anencephaly (partially or completely missing brain). It is recommended that all women trying to conceive should take a supplement of folic acid; good natural sources include liver, beans, and leafy green vegetables.

Folic acid supplements One of the B vitamins found in large amounts in spinach and liver.

Follicle An enclosed cluster of cells that protects and nourishes the cells within it, such as ovaries containing ova and hair follicles containing the roots of hair.

Follicles Each month several of these small, egg-containing cavities develop on the ovary of an ovulating woman. Each cavity contains a single immature egg; ovulation occurs when a follicle (or sometimes more than one) ruptures and releases an egg.

Follicles

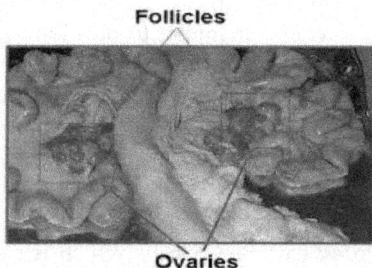

Ovaries

Follicle-stimulating hormone A hormone made in the pituitary gland. In females, it acts on the ovaries to make the follicles and eggs grow. In males, it acts on the testes to make sperm.

Followup inspection An inspection conducted by the Occupational Safety and Health Administration (OSHA) to verify employer abatement of a violation uncovered in a previous OSHA inspection.

Fontanelle Fontanelles are soft spots on a baby's head which, during birth, enable the soft bony plates of the skull to flex, allowing the head to pass through the birth canal. Fontanelles are usually completely hardened by a child's second birthday.

Foot care Taking special steps to avoid foot problems such as sores, cuts, bunions, and calluses. Good care includes daily examination of the feet, toes, and toenails and choosing shoes and socks or stockings that fit well. People with diabetes have to take special care of their feet because nerve damage and reduced blood flow sometimes mean they will have less feeling in their feet than normal. They may not notice cuts and other problems as soon as they should.

Forceps Surgical tool shaped like tongs, used for gripping.

Forceps delivery A delivery in which a hinged, tong-like instrument (called a forceps) is used to ease the baby's head through the birth canal.

Foreign body Something in or on the eye that doesn't belong there. Symptoms include foreign body sensation, eye pain or discomfort, a red or pink eye, tearing, frequent blinking, blurred vision, discharge, light sensitivity and vision loss.

Foreign body sensation Sensation that something is in your eye.

Foreign insurance company An insurance company that operates under the laws of another state.

Foreplay Sexual touching and play in the early stages of arousal that makes a woman and her partner more excited.

Foreskin The flap of skin which normally covers the head of the penis; it is removed when a baby is circumcised.

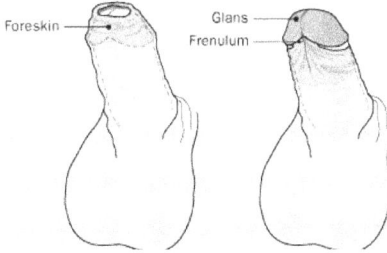

Fig. *Foreskin.*

Formula An alternative to breast milk, the baby formulas used in bottle-feeding are usually milk-based but can also be made from soya products.

Formula Grant Federal assistance to local governments in accordance with a distribution formula established by law or regulation. The actual payment is usually based on such factors as: population characteristics, per capita income, substandard housing, or rate of unemployment. Formulas indicate the total of which recipients are entitled if the requirements, regulations or other criteria of law are met. Also see categorical grant or block grant.

Formulary The panel of drugs chosen by a hospital or managed care organization that is used to treat patients. Drugs outside of the formulary are not used, unless in rare, specific circumstances.

Fornix A pathway that connects the hippocampus and the mamillary bodies.

Foundation for Accountability Independent national organization that has developed a quality system similar to *Hedis* that places more emphasis on outcomes, but does not take into account case mix.

Fovea A depression in the retina that contains only cones (not rods), and that provides acute eyesight.

Fractional urine Urine that a person collects for a certain period of time during 24 hours; usually from breakfast to lunch, from lunch to supper, from supper to bedtime, and from bedtime to rising. It is also called "block urine."

Fractionation Separation into components. When used in the context of blood products, a chemical process to separate various plasma proteins. In the United States, a cold-ethanol precipitation technique is the usual method of fractionation.

Fracture Breach in continuity of a bone. Most fractures are simple deep beneath the unbroken skin. If the skin is pierced by broken bone, the fracture is called compound or open. Either of these main types may be comminuted or impacted. A comminuted fracture occurs when the bone is crushed, splintered, or broken into more than two fragments. Types of fractures include— simple, compound, comminuted, greenstick, incomplete, impacted, longitudinal, oblique, stress or transverse. See fig. on next page.

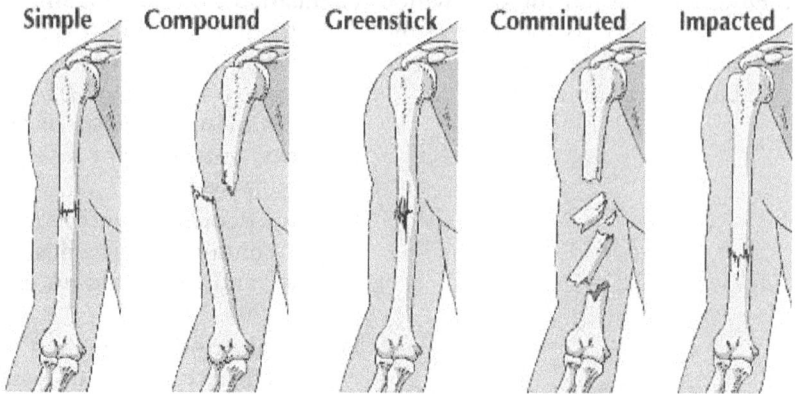

Fig. *fracture.*

Frail elderly Senior population with any combination of chronic conditions, dementia or ADL dependencies.

Fraternal twins Born at the same time but resulting from the fertilisation of two different eggs, fraternal twins are no more genetically similar than siblings; identical twins result from the division of one fertilised egg and are genetically identical.

Free clinic Typically freestanding community-based health services centers that developed in the late 1960s and ealy 1970s largely in response to the needs of substance-abusing youth, many of whom were alienated from society at large and were unable or unwilling to receive medical care from traditional sources. Free clinics do not set eligibility requirements or charge fees for services provided. In general, free clinic services are provided by volunteers, with agency activities coordinated by a core of paid staff.

Free look provision An insurance policy provision required by most states, allowing the policy owner to inspect the policy for a specified period of time. If desired the owner may return the policy to the insurer for a refund of the entire premium.

Free radicals Atoms or molecules with unpaired electrons that are highly chemically reactive. Free radicals are capable of causing tissue damage and accelerating the effects of aging through a process called oxidation.

Free standing emergency Medical Service Center. A health care facility that is physically separate from a hospital and whose primary purpose is the provision of immediate, short-term medical care for minor but urgent medical conditions. It is also called urgent care center.

Free standing facility Usually a specialty facility that is not part of a comprehensive care system. For example, a free-standing surgery facility or a free-standing assisted living facility.

Free standing outpatient Surgical Center A health care facility that is physically separate from a hospital, that provides pre-scheduled, outpatient surgical services. It is also called surgicenteror ambulatory surgical facility.

Freedom of choice In general, laws that permit enrollees to choose any provider and receive substantial reimbursement from their health plan. Also refers to a Federal medicaid rule requiring states to ensure that medicaid beneficiaries are free to obtain services from any qualified provider. Exceptions are possible through waivers of medicaid and special contract options. Also see any willing provider and point of service.

Free-look period After purchasing a policy, you usually have 30 days to review it. You may cancel the policy for a full refund during this time.

Freestanding facilities Health care facilities that are not physically, administratively, or financially connected to a hospital, such as a freestanding ambulatory surgery center.

Frequency of exposure The number of times a person or test animal is exposed to a chemical. Acute exposures are generally single exposures, whereas subacute, subchronic, and chronic exposures are repeated exposures.

Frequent replacement contact lenses It is also called planned replacement. Technically, this is any contact lens that is thrown away after a moderately short period of time. Among most eye care practitioners, "disposable" usage ranges from one day to two weeks, while "frequent replacement" lenses are discarded monthly or quarterly.

Fresh frozen plasma Plasma that has been frozen soon after collection to preserve the activity of the coagulation proteins.

Frontal lobe epilepsy Partial seizures beginning in the frontal lobe may produce weakness or the inability to use certain muscles, including the muscles that make it possible to talk. Sudden thrashing movements during sleep are also characteristic of frontal lobe epilepsy; as is posturing with the head jerking to one side, and the arm rising with it into a brief, frozen state. Sometimes a generalized convulsion follows the slow march of these movements. Complex partial seizures in the frontal lobe have some distinct features in contrast to those in the temporal lobes. They usually last less than a minute, are less likely to be followed by confusion or fatigue, and often occur in a series or cluster. Frontal lobe epilepsy has significant social effects because the seizures it generates are more likely to involve brief episodes of screaming, bicycling movements, or even movements suggestive of sexual activity. Treatment includes medication and, in some cases, surgery.

Frontal lobe The top, front regions of each of the cerebral hemispheres. They are used for reasoning, emotions, judgment, and voluntary movement.

Frontal lobe of the cerebrum The top, front regions of each of the cerebral hemispheres. They are used for reasoning, emotions, judgment, and voluntary movement.

Frontier counties Counties with population densities of 6 or fewer persons per square mile.

Frontal sinus One of the paired, but seldom symmetrical, air spaces located between the inner and outer compact layers of the frontal bone.

Frostbites is the medical condition where localised damage is caused to skin and other tissues due to freezing. Frostbite is most likely to happen in body parts farthest from the heart and those with large exposed areas. The initial stages of frostbite are sometimes called "frost nip". There are several classifications for tissue damage caused by extreme cold including—

Frostnip is a superficial cooling of tissues without cellular destruction.

Chilblains are superficial ulcers of the skin that occur when a predisposed individual is repeatedly exposed to cold.

Frostbite involves tissue destruction.

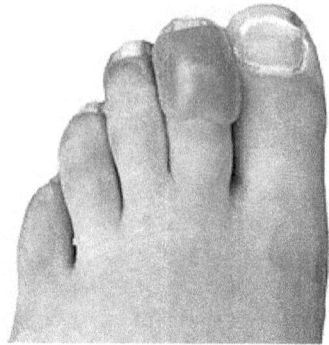

Fig. *Frostbites*

Fructosamine A term referring to the linking of blood sugar onto protein molecules in the bloodstream. The fructosamine value depends upon the average blood sugar level during the past three weeks. The fructosamine test could be viewed as complementary to the glycohemoglobin, as the two tests are different reflections of diabetes control: glycohemoglobin looks back approximately eight to twelve weeks, and the fructosamine test looks back about three weeks.

Fructose A type of sugar found in many fruits and vegetables and in honey. Fructose is used to sweeten some diet foods. It is considered a nutritive sweetener because it has calories.

Frustration The motivational and/or affective state resulting from being blocked, thwarted, disappointed or defeated.

FSH A hormone made in the pituitary gland. In females, it acts on the ovaries to make the follicles and eggs grow. In males, it acts on the testes to make sperm. Also called follicle-stimulating hormone and follitropin.

FSP (fibrin split products) Results from the breakdown of fibrinogen by plasmin (an enzyme).

Full-term A baby is considered full-term if born between 38 and 42 weeks' gestation.

Fulminating infection Infection that occurs suddenly, with great intensity.

Functional impairment A deficit in an individual's ability to function independently. Functional impairments in elderly people are often described in terms of deficits in activities of daily living (ADLs) and instrumental activities of daily living (IADLs).

Functional observational battery A collection of noninvasive tests to evaluate sensory, motor, and autonomic dysfunction in test animals exposed to substances or whose nervous systems have been damaged. FOBS are generally used to screen for neurotoxic substances.

Fundal height The distance between the top of a pregnant woman's uterus (called the fundus) to her pubic bone. It is measured to determine fetal age. The hight of the fundus at comparable gestational dates varies greatly from patient to patient. Those shown are most common. Convenient rule of thumb is that at five months' gestation, fundus is usually at or slightly above umbilicus.

Funding level The amount of revenue required to finance a medical care program. Under an insured program, this is usually premium rate. Under a self-funded program, this amount is usually assessed per expected claim cost, plus stop-loss premium, plus all related fees.

Funding method The means by which an employer pays for the employee health benefit plan. The most common methods are:

(i)   prospective and/or retrospective,

(ii)   refunding products,

(iii)   self-funding, and

(iv) shared risk management.

Fundus The larger part of a hollow organ that is farthest away from the organ's opening. The bladder, gallbladder, stomach, uterus, eye, and cavity of the middle ear all have a fundus.

Fundus of the Eye The back or deep part of the eye, including the retina.

Funduscopy A test to look at the back area of the eye to see if there is any damage to the vessels that bring blood to the retina. The doctor uses a device called an ophthalmoscope to check the eye.

Fungal keratitis eye infection The source of a 2006 outbreak of fungal eye infections among contact lens wearers is a fungus known as Fusarium, found in places such as soil, water, and organic matter including plants. Ordinarily, it is rare for this fungus to invade and damage the eye. But symptoms can be severe, and if untreated, the infection may become so eye-damaging that a corneal transplant is required.

Fungi Single-celled life forms that are larger than bacteria and have organelles (mini-organs) inside the cells. Fungi are an important group of living things. They get their food by breaking down the tissues of living or dead plants or animals. Many fungi can only be seen with a microscope. A few, such as mushrooms and toadstools grow much larger.

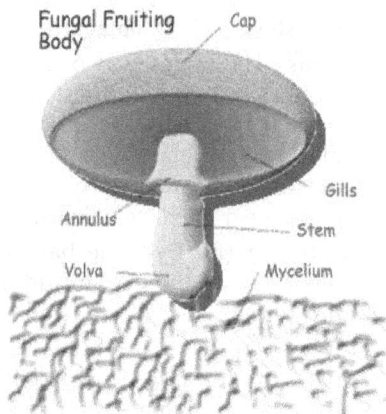

Fig. *Fungi*

Fungicidal An agent that kills fungi.

Fused kidney a single, anomalous organ produced by fusion of the renal primordia.

Fusiform cells of cerebral cortex Spindle-shaped cells in the sixth layer of the cerebral cortex.

Fusospirochetal disease Infection of the mouth and/or pharynx associated with fusiform bacilli and spirochetes, commonly part of the normal flora of the mouth.

Fusospirochetal stomatitis Generalized infection of the mouth with spirochetal organisms, usually in association with other anaerobes, especially fusiform bacteria.

Futile cycle A cycle of phosphorylation and dephosphorylation catalyzed by two enzymes that normally function in two different metabolic pathways; the net effect is the hydrolysis of ATP and the generation of heat, the futile cycle from the unregulated action of 6-phospho-fructokinase and fructose-1,6-bisphosphatase in muscle; such cycles may have an important role in heat production, in the fine-tuning of the regulation of certain pathways, and may be a factor in malignant hyperthermia.

G

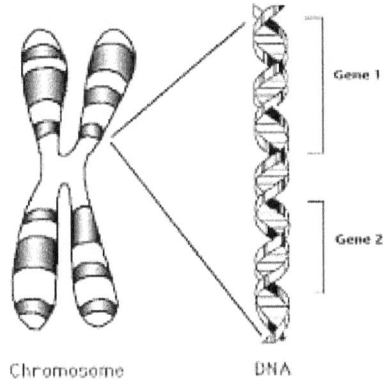

Chromosome   DNA

Gene 1
Gene 2

G phases The interval between two successive cell divisions during which the chromosomes are not individually distinguishable and DNA replication occurs.

G proteins Regulatory proteins that act as molecular switches. They control a wide range of biological processes including: receptor signaling, intracellular signal transduction pathways, and protein synthesis. Their activity is regulated by factors that control their ability to bind to and hydrolyze GTP to GDP.

G-6-PD (Glucose-6-phosphate dehydrogenase) Enzyme normally found in most body cells. Deficiency is inherited and makes red blood more prone to destruction.

GABA Agonist drugs that bind to and activate gamma-aminobutyric acid receptors.

GAD (Glutamic Acid Decarboxylase) A normal enzyme found in all cells that initiates the metabolism of a substance called glutamic acid. Glutamic acid is a component of all proteins and is also part of the cycle for the disposal of a waste product called ammonia. The presence of antibodies to GAD (called anti-GAD antibodies) in the blood is an early indication of the start of the autoimmune process in Type 1A Diabetes.

Gag-clause or Gag rule A provision in a provider contract with a managed care organization or insurer that prevents providers from discussing all available treatment options or financial incentives provided by the insurer with patients.

Galactorrhea Breast milk flow not associated with childbirth or breast feeding. It may be a symptom of a pituitary gland tumour.

Galactose A type of sugar found in milk products and sugar beets. It is also made by the body. It is considered a nutritive sweetener because it hascalories.

Galactosemia An inborn error of metabolism (genetic defect of an enzyme system) found in newborn infants, characterized by the inability to convert galactose, a milk sugar, into glucose (blood sugar). Symptoms of galactosemia include an accumulation of galactose and byproducts, leading to liver damage, cataracts, mental retardation, and death if untreated. Galactosemia can be detected in the first week of life through a newborn screening test, allowing treatment to be initiated before symptoms develop.

Gall bladder A small, sac-like organ located in the duodenum. The gall bladder is connected to the small intestine and the liver by the bile ducts. Gall bladder stores and concentrates bile. Bile is a fluid that helps us to digest food. Its main function is to break down fats in food. Bile is made by the liver and stored in the gall bladder.

Gall stone In gallbladder disease, bile in the gallbladder becomes concentrated and thickens. Gall-stones are born out of this sludge from cholesterol and bile salts. The end result of the disease process is inflammation (cholecystitis) or stones. A gallbladder attack occurs when the gallstone blocks the flow of bile from the gallbladder and is manifested as a pain in the right side, (sometimes perceived in the right shoulder because of referred pain) as severe as the excruciating pain of a heart attack.

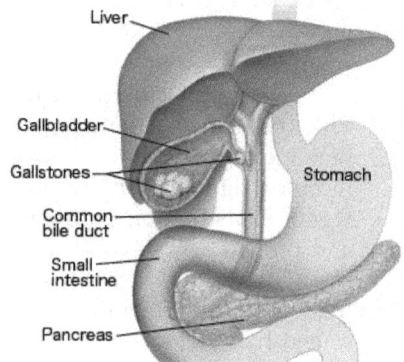

Fig. *Gall stone*

Gallbladder disease Any disease involving the gallbladder or biliary tract. The gallbladder is a reservoir for bile; the biliary tract is the passageway that transports bile to the small intestine. Gallbladder disease is a

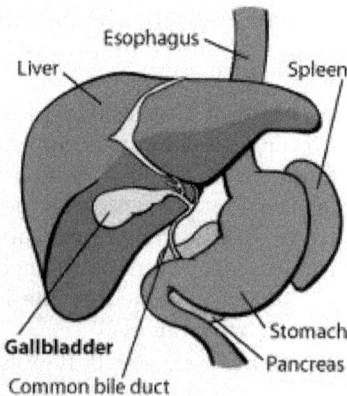

Fig. *Gall bladder*

175

common, often painful condition requiring surgery. It is commonly associated with gallstones and inflammation.

Gamekeeper's thumb Tear of the ulnar collateral ligament of the metacarpop-halangeal joint of the thumb.

Gametes Sperm and ova. Mature male or female reproductive cells (germ cells) with a haploid chromosome content (23 chromosomes in humans). Gametes of the opposite sex, when fused, lead to the formation of a new, diploid organism (a zygote).

Gamete intrafallopian transfer (GIFT) stands for "Gamete Intra-Fallopian Transfer." Gametes, i.e., the female's eggs and the male's sperm, are washed and placed via a catheter directly into the woman's fallopian tubes. This usually involves a minor surgical procedure which allows you to go home the same day with a minor degree of pain that lasts for just a few days. With GIFT, fertilization occurs inside the woman's body (not outside), and mimics the way a normally fertilized egg would begin its journey to the uterus for implantation.

Gametocyte A life cycle stage of Plasmodium, the malarial agent; this stage infects mosquitoes after the mosquito bites an infected human (or other mammal), and gives rise to the sexual stage of the parasite.

Gamma globulin A group of plasma proteins that have antibody activity and which in concentrated form may be used for passive immunization against a number of diseases and in the treatment of gamma globulin deficiency. Also called "immune globulins."

Gamma-aminobutyric acid An amino acid derivative that acts as an inhibitory transmitter

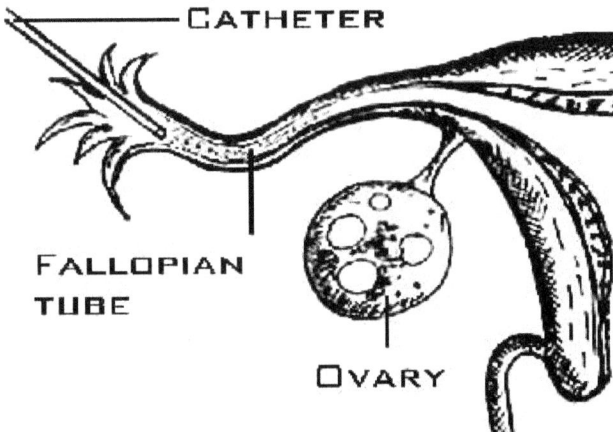

Fig. *Gamete intrafallopian transfer*

(i.e., inhibits signal transmission) in the nervous system.

Ganglia Clusters of multipolar neurons surrounded by a capsule of loosely organized connective tissue located outside the central nervous system.

Gangliocytomas A benign neoplasm that usually arises from the sympathetic trunk in the mediastinum. Histologic features include spindle cell proliferation (resembling a neurofibroma) and the presence of large ganglion cells. The tumour may present clinically with hormone syndrome or diarrhea due to ectopic production of vaso-active intestinal peptide.

Ganglion A group of neuron bodies (not in the brain or spinal cord)

Ganglioneuroblastoma Tumour of nerve cells.

Ganglioneuroma Benign tumour composed of nerve fibres.

Gangrene Dead tissue. Develops when a wound becomes infected or tissue is destroyed by an accident.

Fig. *Gangrene*

Gas chromatography/mass spectrometry A method of identifying specific substances (for example, drugs), in which a gas chromatography is coupled with a mass spectrometer. The gas chromatography is used to separate individual substances by the rate they traverse the chromatography column. As these compounds exit the chromatographic column, they may, for example, be bombarded with electrons, with each substance breaking up into characteristic pieces that can be identified with the mass spectrometer. A GC/MS can be calibrated to scan for many substances in a specimen, or to monitor for only a few masses that are characteristic of a particular substance.

Gastrectomy Excision of the whole (total gastrectomy) or part (subtotal gastrectomy, partial gastrectomy, gastric resection) of the stomach.

Gastric acid Hydrochloric acid present in gastric juice.

Gastric cancer Tumours or cancer of the stomach..

Gastric glands Surface epithelium in the stomach that invaginates into the lamina propria, forming gastric pits. Tubular glands, characteristic of each region of the stomach (cardiac, gastric, and pyloric), empty into the gastric pits. The gastric mucosa is made up of several different kinds of cells.

Gastric mucosa Surface epithelium in the stomach that

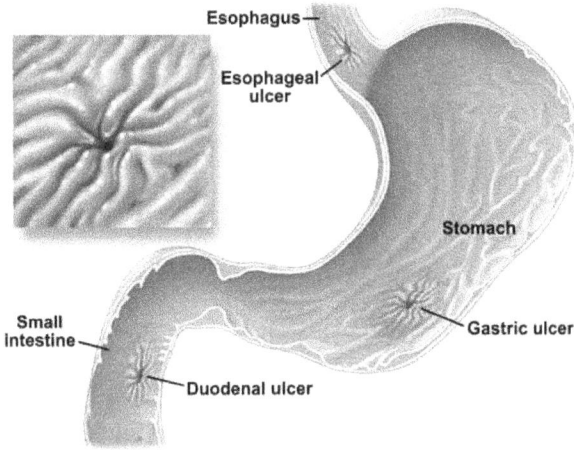

Fig. *Gastroduodenal ulcer*

invaginates into the lamina propria, forming gastric pits. Tubular glands, characteristic of each region of the stomach (cardiac, gastric, and pyloric), empty into the gastric pits. The gastric mucosa is made up of several different kinds of cells.

Gastrin Hormone that stimulates the production of gastric acid or stomach acid.

Gastrinoma Benign or malignant gastrin-secreting islet-cell tumour of the pancreas. There is an overproduction of gastric acid often resulting in an ulcer.

Gastritis Irritation, inflammation or infection of the stomach lining. Cause is sometimes unknown but may be due to excess stomach acid, food allergy, viral infection or adverse reaction to alcohol, caffeine or some drug. Symptoms may include nausea, diarrhea, abdominal pain, cramps, fever, weakness, belching, bloating and loss of appetite. Usually curable in 1 week, if cause is eliminated.

Gastroduodenal ulcer Ulcer that occurs in those portions of the alimentary tract which come into contact with gastric juice containing pepsin and acid. It occurs when the amount of acid and pepsin is sufficient to overcome the gastric mucosal barrier.

Gastroenteritis Inflammation of the stomach and intestines accompanying many digestive-tract disorders. Causes may include bacterial, viral or parasitic infections, food poisoning, food allergy, excess alcohol consumption or emotional upset. Symptoms are the same as gastritis. usually occurs within 1 week.

Gastroenterology A subspecialty of internal medicine concerned with the study of the physiology and diseases of the digestive system and related struc-

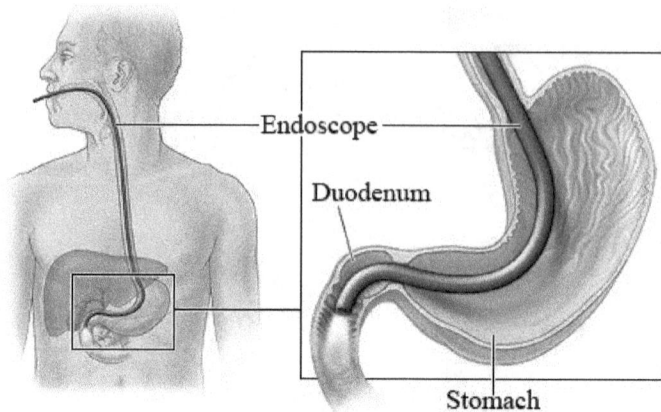

Fig. *Gastrointestinal endoscopy*

tures (esophagus, liver, gallbladder, and pancreas).

Gastrointestinal symptoms Any symptoms relating to the stomach or intestine. Some common GI symptoms include vomiting, diarrhea, constipation, bloating and heartburn.

Gastrointestinal disease Any disorder of the gastrointestinal tract, which includes the mouth, esophagus, stomach, duodenum, small intestine, cecum, appendix, the ascending colon, transverse colon, descending colon, sigmoid colon, rectum and anus.

Gastrointestinal disorders Any condition or disease relating to any part of the digestive system, including the mouth, esophagus, stomach, small intestine, large intestine and rectum. May also include some conditions relating to the liver, gallbladder and pancreas.

Gastrointestinal endoscopy An upper gastrointestinal endoscopy is a way for our doctor to look at the inside lining of our esophagus, stomach, and the first part of your small intestine (called the duodenum). The doctor uses a thin, flexible viewing instrument called an endoscope. With the endoscope, our doctor can check to see if we have any ulcers, inflammation, tumours, infection, or bleeding. This test is also known as an esophago-gastroduodenoscopy, or EGD.

Gastrointestinal hormones Hormones secreted by the gastrointestinal mucosa that affect the timing or the quality of secretion of digestive enzymes, and regulate the motor activity of the digestive system organs.

Gastroparesis A form of nerve damage that affects the stomach. Food is not digested properly and does not move through the stomach in a normal way, resulting in vomiting, nausea, or bloating and interfering with diabetes management.

Gastroscope Endoscopes used for examining the interior of the stomach.

Gastrostomy A surgical opening into the stomach. A gastrostomy tube allows food to be introduced directly to the stomach, bypassing the mouth and throat. A jejunostomy tube (which connects with the top of the large intestine) may also perform this function.

Gastrula The embryo in the early stage following the blastula, characterized by morpho-genetic cell movements, cell differentiation, and the formation of the three germ layers.

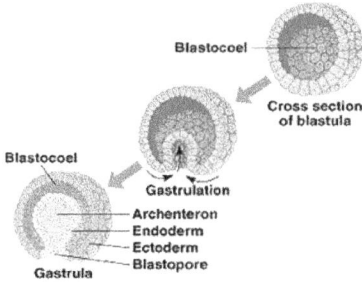

Fig. *Gastrula*

Gatekeeper A primary care physician responsible for overseeing and coordinating all aspects of a patient's medical care and pre-authorizing specialty care.

Gatekeeper programme A type of outreach programme used to identify isolated elderly people who may be in need of assistance.

Gatekeeping The process by which a primary care physician coordinates the use of all services required for a patient's medical care.

Gaucher disease An autosomal recessive genetic disorder of lipid metabolism that leads to the accumulation of a particular lipid (glucosyl ceramide) in internal organs, such as the spleen, liver, bone marrow, and lungs (and central nervous system in some forms of the disease), producing an enlarged spleen and liver and various neurological disorders. It is found with higher frequency among Ashkenazi Jews of Eastern European origin and their descendants. There are several different types, the two most

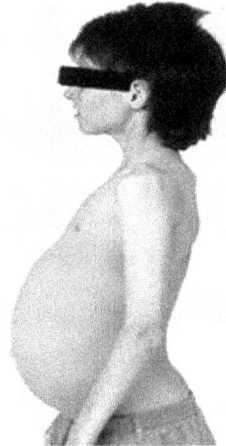

Fig. *Gaucher's disease*

GB hepatitis Viruses Proposed members of the family *Flaviviridae*. "GB" originated from the initials of a surgeon who supplied the serum that was passaged in primates.

Gel The semisolid jelly-like matrix used in electrophoresis to separate molecules.

Gender identity disorder One of the major groups of sexual and gender identity disorders, characterized by a strong and persistent identification with the opposite sex (cross-gender identification) and discomfort with one's assigned sex or a sense of inappropriateness in that gender role. Although onset is usually in childhood or adolescence, the disorder may not be presented clinically until adulthood. Manifestations include a repeated desire to be of the opposite sex, insistence that one has the typical feelings and reactions of the opposite sex, a belief that one was born the wrong sex, and transsexualism or preoccupation with one's primary and secondary sex characteristics in order to simulate the opposite sex.

Gene A linear sequence of nucleotides in DNA that is required to synthesize proteins and regulate cell functions; the fundamental physical and functional unit of heredity. Genes are the specific sequences of nucleotides along a molecule of DNA (or, in the case of some viruses, RNA) which represent the functional units of heredity. The majority of eukaryotic genes contain coding regions (codons) that are interrupted by non-coding regions (introns) and are therefore labeled split genes.

Gene expression The process by which the blueprint contained in a cell's DNA is converted into the structures and biochemical mechanisms present and operating in the cell; control of how active a gene is, measured by the amount of gene product (usually a protein or nucleic acid) made by the cell.

Gene family A group of related genes exhibiting a high degree of homology in function and nucleotide base sequence.

Gene library A collection of thousands of cloned DNA fragments in no obvious order whose position in the genome can be determined by physical mapping.

Gene pool The total genetic information possessed by the reproductive members of a population of sexually reproducing organisms.

Gene probe A molecule of known structure and/or function used to locate and identify a specific region or nucleotide sequence of DNA; usually a single stranded fragment of complementary DNA that has been labeled with a tracer substance, such as a dye or radioactive isotope.

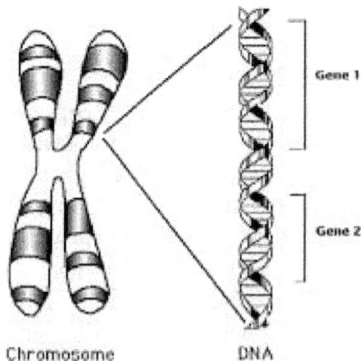

Chromosome   DNA

Fig. *Gene*

Gene supplementation A technique of genetic therapy in which "new" or repaired genes are introduced into a cell by microinjection or a similar process.

Gene surgery In molecular genetics, a laboratory procedure whereby a defective gene is excised and removed from a cell, and a normal gene substituted.

Gene therapy An experimental procedure to treat genetic disorders by inserting healthy genes into the body to replace damaged ones.

Gene transplantation A technique of moving an entire gene from one organism into another.

General anesthetics Agents that induce various degrees of analgesia; depression of consciousness, circulation, and respiration; relaxation of skeletal muscle; reduction of reflex activity; and amnesia. There are two types of general anesthetics, inhalation and intravenous. With either type, the arterial concentration of drug required to induce anesthesia varies with the condition of the patient, the desired depth of anesthesia, and the concomitant use of other drugs.

General duty clause (OSHA) Section 5(a)(1) of the Occupational Safety and Health Act (Public Law 91-596). This section provides that "each employer shall furnish...employment and a place of employment which are free from recognized hazards that are causing or are likely to cause death or serious physical harm to his employees." The Occupational Safety and Health Administration (OSHA) has used this clause for workplace conditions that present serious occupational hazards that are not

General hospital Large hospitals with a resident medical staff which provides continuous care to maternity, surgical and medical patients.

Fig. *General hospital.*

General practitioner A physician whose practice is based on a broad understanding of all illnesses and who does not restrict his/her practice to any particular field of medicine.

General ward Rooms occupied by one or more individuals during

Fig. *General ward*

a stay in a health facility. The concept includes aspects of environment, design, care, or economics.

Generalised headache Pain in the cranial region that may occur as an isolated and benign symptom or as a manifestation of a wide variety of conditions including sunarchnoid hemorrhage; craniocereral trauma; central nervous system infections, intracranial hypertension; and other disorders. In general, recurrent headaches that are not associated with a primary disease process are referred to as headache disorders (e.g., migraine).

Generation gaps The interactions between individuals of different generations. These interactions include communication, caring, accountability, loyalty, and even conflict between related or non-related individuals.

Fig. *Generation gaps*

Generic drug In cases in which the patent on a specific pharmaceutical product expires and drug manufacturers produce generic versions of the original branded product, the generic version of the drug (which is theorized to be exactly the same product manufactured by a different firm) is dispensed even though the original product is prescribed. Some managed care organizations and Medicaid programmes mandate generic substitution because of the generally lower cost of generic products.

Genetic code The sequence of nucleotides, coded in triplets, each of which specifies a single amino acid, along the DNA that determines the sequence of amino acids in protein synthesis. This code is common to nearly all living organisms.

Genetic counselling This form of counselling helps prospective parents to evaluate their risks of having a child with congenital abnormalities, and to understand their options for testing and treatment.

Genetic disorder A disease or condition which originates in the genes.

Genetic engineering Technologies (including recombinant DNA methods) used by scientists to isolate genes from an organism, manipulate them in the laboratory, and insert them stably in another organism.

Genetic inheritance The DNA that is passed from parents to children.

Genetic marker Any character that acts as a signpost or signal of the presence or location of a gene, chromosome, or hereditary characteristic in an individual, a population, chromosome or a DNA molecule. The phenotype of male sex, for example, is a reliable indicator of the presence of the gene for H-Y antigen, a cell surface protein found in males.

Genetic monitoring Periodic examination of samples of employees' blood cells to evaluate whether changes in the genetic material (e.g., chromosomal damage or increased frequency of mutations) have occurred during the course of employment where there may be exposure to mutagenic agents.

Genetic screening The search in a population for individuals with certain genetic traits known to be associated with disease in themselves or in their children. The main types of genetic screening include newborn screening (e.g., for PKU and other disorders); carrier screening (to identify couples at high risk for having children with serious genetic disease); prenatal screening (e.g., via amniocentesis for Down Syndrome); screening for disease later in life; and occupational screening (to detect certain inherited characteristics among employees or job applicants).

Genetic testing Technologies that determine a person's genetic makeup or that identify changes (damage) in the genetic material of certain cells. As used in the workplace, it encompasses both genetic monitoring and screening.

Genetic variance The fraction of the phenotypic variance due to differences in the genetic consti-

tution of individuals in a population. See phenotvpic variance.

Genetically engineered cell A cell into which new genes have been inserted.

Genetics The scientific study of heredity; how particular qualities or traits are transmitted from parents to offspring and how these traits are expressed in individuals.

Genital herpes Viral infection of the genitals transmitted by intercourse or oral sex. Genital herpes may increase the risk of cervical cancer. Symptoms include painful blisters on the genitals that can cause painful urination, fever, malaise and enlarged lymph glands. Currently incurable, but treatment can relieve symptoms.

Genital warts Bumpy growths in the moist areas in and around the genitals caused by the human papilloma-virus.

Genitals The external sex organs-the penis and testicles in a male and the labia in a female.

Genome All the genetic material contained in a single set of chromosomes (e.g., in the nucleus of a reproductive ceil).

Genomic library A collection of clones made from a set of overlapping DNA fragments representing the entire genome of an organism.

Genotype The genetic composition of an organism, as distinguished from its physical appearance (its . phenotype). For example, two individuals with

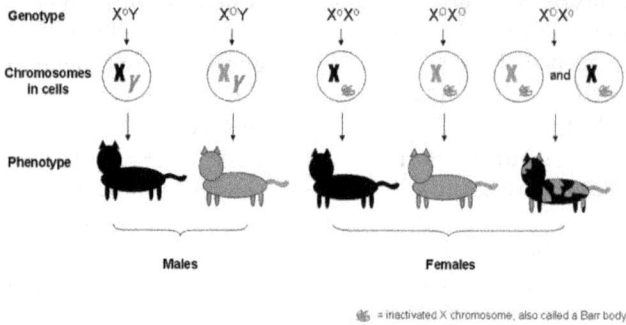

Fig. *Genotype*

the same phenotype (brown eyes) for eye colour may have. different genotypes for that colour: one may be heterozygous, possessing one allele for brown, which is dominant, and one for blue, which is recessive, while the other individual may be homozygous, possessing two alleles for brown eyes.

Genus (pI., genera) A taxonomic category that includes groups of closely related species of plants or animals.

Geographic atrophy Deterioration of tissue in the central portion of the retina, often associated with aging. Geographic atrophy (GA) is considered the end stage of a "dry" form of age-related macular degeneration, which occurs when tissue in the retina begins to break down and form yellowish spots known as drusen. GA can cause significant central vision loss.

Geographic multiplier A factor used to make geographic adjustments to the Medicare Fee

Schedule or any other fee schedule. The term "geographic factor" is also used.

Geographic practice cost index An index used by Medicare and some researchers to examine differences in physician practice costs across geographic areas. The index is based on per-unitcosts.

Geriatric nurse practitioner An RN with advanced training in geriatrics.

Geriatric research, education, and clinical centers Centers established at VA medical centers to provide basic and clinical research and education and training for clinicians and researchers in the field of geriatrics

Geriatrician A physician who specializes in the diagnosis and treatment of diseases of older persons.

Geriatrics The branch of medicine concerned with the physiological and pathological aspects of the aged, including the clinical problems of senescence and senility. "Geriatrics" is medical practice that addresses the

Fig. *Geriatrics*

complex needs of older patients and emphasizes maintaining functional independence even in the presence of chronic disease. It requires an interdisciplinary approach - we will work with other physicians, nurses, social workers, occupational therapists and family members, in order to provide comprehensive care for these patients with multiple needs. Geriatricians are primary care doctors for older patients and can also serve as consultants to other physicians and to hospital programmes that work with the elderly.

Germ cell A reproductive (egg or sperm) cell or its precursors. Compare somatic cell.

Germ cell tumours One of three types of cancer of the ovary. Arises in the ovum (egg). Prognosis is often poor because tumours tend to progress rapidly. Advances in chemotherapy may improve outcome.

Germ line The tissue or cell lineage that produces gametes and is used for reproductive purposes, as opposed to that tissue or those cell lineages (somatic tissue, or soma) producing the bodily structures and tissues used for functions other than reproduction. Also known as "germinal tissue."

Germinal mutations Mutations in the DNA of reproductive cells- egg or sperm. Germinal mutations can be passed on to the offspring only if one of those particular germ cells is involved in fertilization.

Germplasm The total genetic variability, represented by germ cells or seeds, available to a particular population of organisms.

Gerontology Social Science field studying the biological, psychological and social aspects of aging.

Gestalt theory A system which emphasizes that experience and behaviour contain basic patterns and relationships which cannot be reduced to simpler components; that is, the whole is greater than the sum of its parts.

Gestation The period of time a baby is carried in the uterus; full-term gestation is between 38 and 42 weeks (counted from the first day of the last menstrual period).

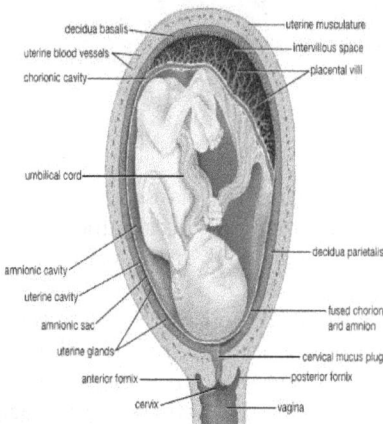

decidua basalis — uterine musculature
uterine blood vessels — intervillous space
chorionic cavity — placental villi
umbilical cord —
— decidua parietalis
amnionic cavity
uterine cavity
— fused chorion and amnion
amnionic sac
uterine glands
— cervical mucus plug
anterior fornix — posterior fornix
cervix — vagina

Fig. *Gestation*

Gestational age The number of completed weeks elapsed between the first day of the last normal menstrual period and the date of delivery. Full term babies are born at 40 weeks gestation.

Gestational diabetes mellitus A type of diabetes mellitus that can occur when a woman is pregnant. In the second half of the pregnancy, the woman may have glucose (sugar) in the blood at a higher than normal level. However, when the pregnancy ends, the blood glucose levels return to normal in about 95 percent of all cases.

Ggynaecological Having to do with the female reproductive organs.

Giant cell Multinucleated masses produced by the fusion of many cells; often associated with viral infections. In AIDS, they are induced when the envelope glycoprotein of the HIV virus binds to the CD4 antigen of uninfected neighboring T4 cells.

Giardia A genus of flagellate intestinal protozoa parasitic in various vertebrates, including humans. Characteristics include the presence of four pairs of flagella arising from a complicated system of axonemes and cysts that are ellipsoidal to ovoidal in shape.

Giardiases An infection of the small intestine caused by the flagellated protozoan Giardia lambia. It is spread via contaminated food and water and by direct person-to-person contact.

Gigantism Condition in which the body or a body part grows excessively, sometimes due to an overactive pituitary gland.

Gilbert's disease Benign hereditary condition characterized by jaundice and high bilirubin levels in the blood.

Gingival fistulas An abnormal passage in the oral cavity on the gingiva.

Gingivitis An inflammation of the gums that if left untreated may lead to periodontal disease, a serious gum disorder. Signs of gingivitis are inflamed and bleeding gums. The control of gingivitis is predominantly in our hands. In fact unless we want to have our teeth cleaned professionally on a weekly basis, this study indicates we will have some level of gingivitis if we don't brush and floss routinely.

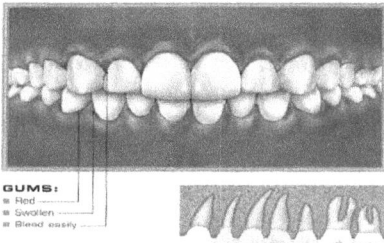

GUMS:
■ Red
■ Swollen
■ Bleed easily

Fig. *Gingivitis*

Gl tube A tube inserted surgically through an opening in the stomach. GI tubes offer another means of nutritional sustenance for those individuals unable to take these substances by mouth.

Gland A group of special cells that make substances so that other parts of the body can work. For example, the pancreas is a gland that releases insulin so that other body cells can use glucose (sugar) for energy.

Glandular fever A viral illness characterised by severe fatigue, swollen glands, sore throat, and fever.

Glandulars Freeze-dried animal glands, processed into pill form and taken to provide the body an extra dose of a hormone. Typically made from cow, sheep, or pig glands, glandulars on the market include adrenal, testicular, ovary, pancreas, pituitary, prostate, and thymus

products. Critics point out that these supplements are unlikely to boost gland function because digestion breaks down and inactivates the DNA in a glandular. In addition, using glandulars may encourage your own glands to reduce hormone production. Other risks include bacterial contamination of the product, and the antibiotics and pesticides present in the glands of the livestock they are taken from.

Glanzmann's thrombosthemia Rare, inherited hemorrhagic disease. Platelet cells cannot cluster normally; clots do not form and hemorrhage occurs. Transfusion with platelets is usually effective in stopping any bleeding.

Glargine Insulin glargine is the generic name for Lantus, a long acting insulin analog.

Glaucoma Disease characterized by elevated intraocular pressure, which causes optic nerve damage and subsequent peripheral vision loss. Most people have no initial symptoms of chronic (open-angle) glaucoma, but you can develop peripheral vision loss, headaches, blurred vision, difficulty adapting to darkness and halos around lights. Other forms of glaucoma (e.g., closed-angle glaucoma) may have additional symptoms such as eye pain, a pupil that doesn't respond to light, redness, nausea and a bulging eye.

Glenohumeral The shoulder socket, containing the glenoid, the humeral head and the labrum.

Glenoid A cavity of the scapula into which the head of the humerus fits to form the shoulder joint (the shoulder socket).

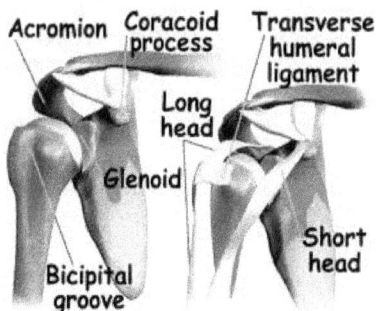

Fig. *Glenoid*

Glial cell, glia A special connective tissue cell of the central nervous system, comprising 40 percent of the total volume of the brain and spinal cord. Glial cells are involved in nutrition of neurons, insulation (through the production of myelin), and structural support.

Global budgets Global budgets or expenditure limits are prospectively defined caps on spending for some portion of the health care industry. Several industrialized countries have applied global budgeting in various forms. Many of these systems (e.g., France, Australia, Sweden, and Switzerland) concentrate their global budgets solely on hospital operating budgets treating capital expenditure outside the annual budget process. Others, including Canada and the United Kingdom, have global budgets that cover both hospital and physician expenditures. Global budgeting in the U.S. as envisioned by most proponents would establish binding targets for permissible growth in the U.S. health care system. Many issues remain unclear, however. In particular, the scope of services to be included (e.g., public vs. private sector programmes), and the method for enforcing budget caps (e.g., price controls, premium controls, etc.).

Global service A package of clinically related services treated as a unit for purposes of billing, coding, or payment.

Globin A class of proteins most often associated with processes of oxygen or other gas transport (e.g., hemoglobin or myoglobin).

Globulins Class of proteins that are insoluble in water but soluble in saline solutions.

Glomerular Of or pertaining to a glomerulus.

Glomerular filtration rate Measure of the kidneys' ability to filter and remove waste products.

Glomeruli Network of tiny blood vessels in the kidneys where the blood is filtered and waste products are removed.

Glomerulonephritis Inflammation of glomerulus. Damaged glomeruli cannot effectively filter waste products from the blood. Acute glomerulo-nephritis may follow streptococcal infection of the throat or skin. Kidney symptoms usually begin 2 to 3 weeks after strep infection.

Glomerulus Tiny structure composed of blood vessels. One of several structures that make up a nephron in the kidney. There are about 1.25-million nephrons in each kidney that filter the blood and remove wastes.

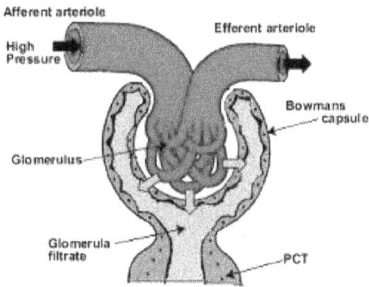

Fig. *Glomerulus.*

Glucagon A hormone that raises the level of glucose (sugar) in the blood. The alpha cells of the pancreas, in areas called the islets of Langerhans, make glucagon when the body needs to put more sugar into the blood. An injectable form of glucagon is available as a prescription item, for use to treat severe insulin reactions. The glucagon is injected and raises blood glucose levels within a half-hour. It is frequently recommended that people with Type 1 diabetes, and other people taking insulin injections, have a family member learn how to administer glucagon.

Glucagonoma Glucagon-secreting tumour of the islet cells of the pancreas. Glucagon increases blood sugar.

Glucocorticoids Hormones naturally produced by the cortex of the adrenal glands. Natural or synthetic glucocorticoids can influence a wide spectrum of physiologic functions, including suppression of inflammation, metabolic changes, psychological effects, blood pressure changes, and physical changes.

Glucocortocoid deficiency Decreased amount of hormone from the adrenal gland that increases production of glycogen.

Gluconeogenesis The formation of glucose from protein within the liver.

Glucosamine sulphate A natural amino sugar found in joint spaces. As a dietary supplement, it is said to stimulate the repair of arthritic joints by building up the protective cartilage that arthritis destroys.

Glucose tolerance test A test to see if a person has diabetes. The test is given in a lab or doctor's office in the morning before the person has eaten. A first sample of blood is taken from the person. Then the person drinks a liquid that has glucose (sugar) in it. After one hour, a second blood sample is drawn, and, after another hour, a third sample is taken. The object is to see how well the body deals with the glucose in the blood over time.

Glucose A simple sugar found in the blood. It is the body's main source of energy; also known as dextrose.

Glue ear The condition, also called otitis media, meaning inflammation of the middle ear, is the most common cause of hearing impairment in children.

In Glue ear, the inflammation often begins when infections that cause sore throats, colds, or other breathing problems spread to the middle ear (the part of the ear that lies behind the eardrum). There are many reasons why children are more likely to suffer from otitis media than adults.

- Children have more trouble fighting infections, partly because their immune systems are still developing.
- Also the passageways connecting the ears to the throat are small and can get blocked meaning any fluid cannot drain and will collect in the ear.
- As the fluid increases, the child may have trouble hearing because the eardrum and middle ear bones are unable to move as freely as they should.

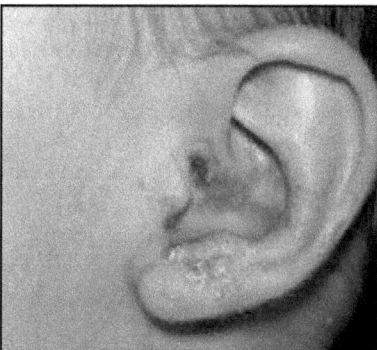

Fig. *Glue ear*

- As the infection worsens, the fluid gets thicker and glue-like and many children also experience severe ear pain.

Eventually, too much fluid can put pressure on the eardrum and tear it.

Gluten-sensitive enteropathy Coeliac disease or gluten-sensitive entero-pathy is an inherited disease caused by an allergic reaction to gluten, a protein found in wheat, rye, and barley. The immune system attacks the lining of the intestines in response to the allergy. This common disease, if left untreated, can leave the intestine unable to absorb essential nutrients and vitamins leading to anaemia, bone disease and, rarely, forms of cancer.

Glycemia A medical term that indicates the level of glucose in the blood.

Glycemic index A method of ranking foods in terms of how quickly they affect blood sugar levels. For example, foods with high glycemic index rankings (processed foods such as white flour, sugar, etc.) can cause unhealthy spikes in blood sugar. Foods with lower glycemic index rankings, such as whole grains, create more stable blood sugar levels.

Glycemic response The effect of different foods on blood glucose (sugar) levels over a period of time. Researchers have discovered that some kinds of foods may raise blood glucose levels more quickly than other foods containing the same amount of carbohydrates.

Glycogen Substance formed from glucose, stored chiefly in the liver. When the blood-sugar level is too low, glycogen is converted back to glucose for the body to use as energy.

Glycogenesis The process by which glycogen is formed from glucose.

Glycogen-storage disease Any of a group of inherited disorders of glycogen metabolism. An enzyme deficiency causes glycogen to accumulate in abnormally large amounts in the body.

Glycoprotein A protein with attached sugar groups.

Glycosuria, Glucosuria Having glucose (sugar) in the urine.

Glycosylated hemoglobin test A blood test that measures a person's average blood glucose (sugar) level for the 2- to 3-month period before the test.

Glycosylation The attachment of a carbohydrate molecule (glycogen) to another molecule, such as a protein.

Gerontological nurse practitioner; Generally an acronym for a programme name (e.g. GNP Programme) or title; the credential is usually APRN,BC (offered by the American Nurses Credentialing Center (ANCC).

Goiter Enlargement of the thyroid gland, which causes a swelling in the front part of the neck.

Golgi body It is also called the Golgi apparatus or Golgi com-

plex. It is a flattened, layered, sac-like organelle that looks like a stack of pancakes and is located near the nucleus. It produces the membranes that surround the lysosomes. The Golgi body packages proteins and carbohydrates into membrane-bound vesicles for "export" from the cell.

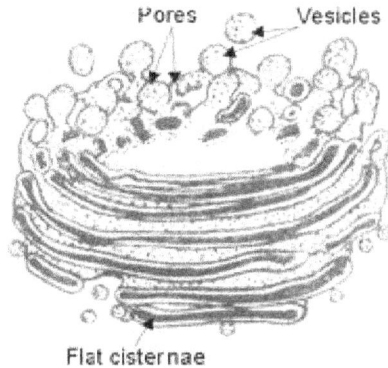

Fig. *Golgi body*

Gonad Organs (ovary or testis) that produce reproductive cells (ova and spermatozoa) and that release hormones that control secondary sexual characteristics.

Gonadal Pertaining to gonads.

Gonadal impairment Decreased function of the gonads.

Gonadotropin A group of hormones secreted by the anterior pituitary gland that stimulate reproductive activity of the testes and ovaries. Examples are follicle-stimulating hormone, human chorionic gonadotropin, human menopausal gonadotropin, and Iuteinizing hormone. These can be administered in cases of ovulatory dysfunction to directly stimulate the ovary.

Gonadotropin releasing hormone (The hormone released from the hypothalamus that causes secretion of gonadotropin from the pituitary gland.

Gonorrhoea Infectious disease of the reproductive organs and other body structures that is sexually transmitted (venereal disease). The most prominent symptom is a thick, green-yellow discharge from the penis or vagina. Antibiotics usually effect a cure.

Good laboratory practices Rules adopted by FDA in 1978 requiring that all regulated parties conducting nonclinical laboratory studies keep records and permit audits of such studies. The GLP rules also contain specific provisions for animal housing, feeding, and care. In 1983, EPA issued similar GLP rules for its toxic substances and pesticides research programmes.

Good manufacturing practices Requirements regarding the manufacturing, processing, packing, storage, and other practices involving products under the jurisdiction of the Food and Drug Administration (foods and food additives, cosmetics, drugs, biologics, and medical devices).

Gout happens when uric acid crystals build up in the joints. This causes the joints to be inflamed. If the crystals build up in the kidneys, kidney stones may re-

sult. It typically occurs if you have high levels of uric acid in your blood. A high level of uric acid in the blood is identified by the term hyperuricemia. However, you could also have normal uric levels and still have gout.

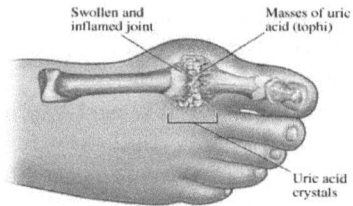

Fig. *Gout*

Grace period A set number of days past the due date of a premium payment during which medical coverage may not be canceled and through which the premium payment may be made.

Graduate medical education Medical education as an intern, resident or fellow after graduating from a medical school.

Graduation rate Graduation rates are calculated by dividing the number of high school graduates by the ninth grade enrollment 4 year earlier. Graduation rates by State are calculated by the U.S. Department of Education for public schools only because data on private high school graduates are not available by State. Compare dropout rate.

Gram A unit of weight in the metric system. There are 28 grams in 1 ounce. In some diet plans for people with diabetes, the suggested amounts of food are given in grams.

Gram-negative/positive A classification of bacteria based on differential staining utilizing the Gram- Wiegert procedure. Primarily as a result of an organism's cell membrane structure, Gram-negative

Grandfathering When rules change, current participants remain unaffected and the new rules only apply to new participants.

Grandiose delusion An exaggerated belief of one's importance, power, knowledge, or identity.

Granulocyte Any cell containing granules; refers specifically to a white blood cell containing granules in its cytoplasm.

Granulomas Nodule of firm tissue formed as a reaction to chronic inflammation, such as from foreign bodies or bacteria.

Granulomatosis Formation of multiple granulomas. Each has nodules of granulated tissue forming a tumourlike mass.

Grasping reflex This reflex is seen when a newborn baby grabs at an object, such as a finger, when it touches her hand. Her hold may be strong enough for you to pull her to a sitting position. The reflex lasts until a baby is three or four months old.

Graves' disease A form of thyroid disease, with overactivity of the thyroid function, enlargement of the size of the gland, and bulging eyes (exophthalmos) being common features. Named after a 19th century Irish physician. *Graves'* is autoimmune in nature. It is found somewhat more com-

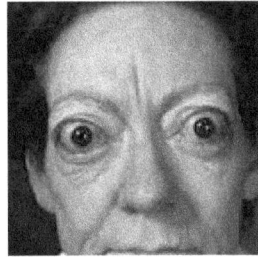

Fig. *Graves' disease*

monly than expected in people with type 1 diabetes.

Graves' ophthalmology Auto-immune eye disorder usually associated with abnormalities of the thyroid gland; symptoms include eyelid retraction, bulging eyes, light sensitivity, eye discomfort, double vision, vision loss, a red or pink eye and a limited ability to move the eyes.

Gravida The medical term for a pregnant woman.

Gray matter Central nervous tissue that is relatively dark in colour (in contrast to white matter) because of the relatively high proportion of nerve cell nuclei present

Greatest economic need The need resulting from an income level at or below the poverty threshold established by the Bureau of the Census.

Greatest social need The need caused by non-economic factors which include physical and mental disabilities, language barriers, and cultural or social isolation including that caused by racial or ethnic status which restricts an individual's ability to perform normal daily tasks or which threatens his or her capacity to live independently.

Grievance The process by which an individual can air complaints and seek remedies.

Grievance procedure The process by which a health plan member or participating provider can air complaints and seek remedies.

Groin The upper and inner thigh where the adductor muscles originate that are responsible for moving the leg in an inward or adduction direction.

Grommets A grommet is a plastic tube which is slipped through a tiny incision in the eardrum. It acts as a pressure-equalisation tube for the child providing a temporary, extra Eustachian tube to allow bacteria and fluid to drain from the middle ear.

Gross and flagrant violation under medicare A violation that presents an imminent danger to the health, safety, or well-being of a Medicare beneficiary or that unnecessarily places the beneficiary at riskof substantial and permanent harm. Utilization and quality control peer review organizations (PROS) identify potential violations and recommend sanctions, but the Office of the Inspector General of the U.S.

Gross motor skills The ability to make movements which use the large muscles in the arms, legs, and torso - such as running and jumping.

Gross patient revenue Consists of the full amount of revenue from services rendered to patients, including payments received from or on behalf of individual patients.

Group health insurance Health insurance purchased through a group that exists for some purpose other than buying insurance, such as a workplace, labor union, or professional association.

Group insurance Any insurance policy or health services contract by which groups of employees (and often their dependents) are covered under a single policy or contract, issued by their employer or other group entity.

Group model HMO An HMO that contracts with a multi-specialty medical group to provide care for HMOmembers;

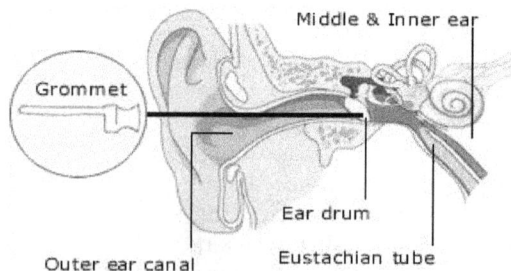

Middle & Inner ear
Grommet
Ear drum
Outer ear canal
Eustachian tube

Fig. *Grommets*

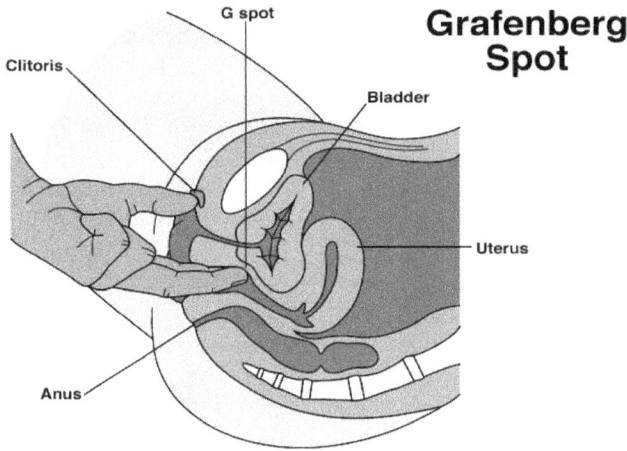

Fig. *G-spot*

members are required to receive medical care from a physician within the group unless a referral is made outside the network.

Group practice association A formal arrangement of three or more physicians or other health professionals providing health services. Income is pooled and redistributed to the members of the group according to a prearranged plan.

Group purchasing Organization (GPO) An organization that pools purchasers working together to provide larger potential purchases and therefore lower costs.

Group therapy A type of psychotherapy in which the focus is on helping individuals develop healthier ways of relating to other people (although therapy groups serve other purposes).

Growth hormone deficiency Deficiency of hormone that results in dwarfism.

G-spot The area at the top of the vagina where the back of the clitoris meets the vaginal wall; stimulation of this area may cause female ejaculation

Guaranteed issue The requirement that an insurer or health plan accept everyone, regardless of health, income or age, that applies for coverage and guarantees the renewal of that coverage as long as the premium is paid.

Guaranteed renewability The requirement that each insurer and health plan continue to renew health policies purchased by individuals as long as the person continues to pay the premium for the policy.

Guardian An adult who has been given legal responsibility for a minor in place of the biological parents.

Guardianship A legal mechanism that involves the appointment by a court of an individual or institution (the guardian) to protect and take care of the person and/or property of a person who is found incapable of managing his or her own affairs (the ward).

Guillain-barre syndrome A rare form of peripheral nerve damage that causes weakness of the limbs. Also called acute febrile polyneuritis. The relative risk of contracting Guillain-Barré syndrome was significantly greater among people who received swine flu vaccine (killed influenza A/New Jersey/1976) during the 1976 vaccine programme. Such an association has not been observed with subsequent influenza vaccines.

Gynaecologist A doctor who specialises in women's reproductive health.

Gynecology The study of diseases peculiar to women, that is, disorders of the ovaries, Fallopian tubes, uterus, vagina, and vulva. It is also a medical-surgical specialty concerned with the physiology and disorders primarily of the female genital tract, as well as female endocrinology and reproductive physiology.

Gynecomastia Excessive development of the male mammary glands, even to the functional state.

Gyrus These are high areas on the brain that are separated by fissures.

H

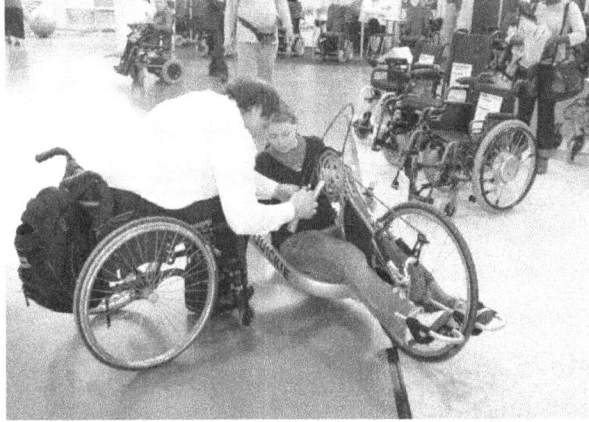

h

Habilitation Programmes and activities designed to help individuals maximize their independence.

Haemolytic It is also called Rhesus disease or erythroblastosis, haemolytic disease results when a woman who is Rh-negative (meaning she does not carry the Rhesus protein in her blood) has a fetus who is Rh-positive and her immune system makes antibodies against the fetus's blood. The disorder is treated with a compound which prevents the woman's immune system from making antibodies.

Haemophilia A genetic blood disorder, almost always in males, in which blood does not clot properly as a result of an enzyme deficiency.

Haemophilus influenza b (Hib) One of six types of infection with Haemophilus influenza b, a parasitic bacterium that occurs in an encapsulated form. In children and in debilitated older adults, infection may result in destructive inflammation of the larynx, trachea, and bronchi, and may also cause subacute bacterial endocarditis and purulent meningitis. Immunization against Hib is available through inocculation with anti-Haemophilus influenza serum.

Haemorrhoid Haemorrhoids are swollen blood vessels around the anus. They are caused by increased blood volume and pressure from the uterus on the veins in the legs and pelvis, and are common during pregnancy. Sometimes they swell so that the vein walls

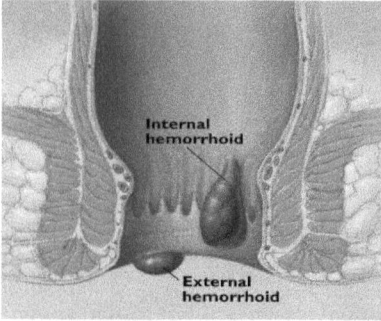

Fig. *Haemorrhoid*

become stretched, thin, and irritated by passing bowel movements. Constipation can also cause (or compound) the problem.

Hageman factor (Factor XII) Deficiency of this factor results in prolonged bleeding

Half-life The time initial value.

Hallucination involve sensing things while awake that appear to be real, but instead have been created by the mind. It can occur in any sensory modality — visual, auditory, olfactory, gustatory, tactile, proprioceptive, equili-brioceptive, nociceptive, thermoceptive and chronoceptive.

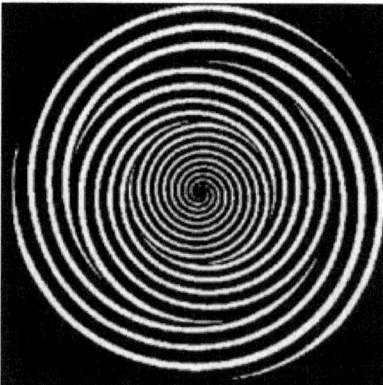

Fig. *Hallucination*

Common hallucinations include—

• Feeling bodily sensations, such as a crawling feeling on the skin or the movement of internal organs

• Hearing sounds, such as music, footsteps, windows or doors banging

• Hearing voices when no one has spoken (the most common type of hallucination). These voices may be critical, complimentary, neutral, or may command someone to do something that may cause harm to themselves or to others.

• Seeing patterns, lights, beings, or objects that aren't there

• Smelling a foul or pleasant odour

Hallucinogens A required for the activity of a given quantity of radioactive material to decay to half its perception that occurs without external stimulus (e.g., Hallucinations are symptoms of various disorders, such be caused by hallucinogenic drugs. group of heterogeneous compounds inducing heightened auditory hallucinations (the as schizophrenia, dementia, awareness of sensory input, often accompanied by an enhanced sense of clarity, and loss of boundaries. It is also known as psychedelics.

Hamster-oocyte penetration test A test that evaluates the ability of human sperm to penetrate an ovum by incubating sperm with hamster oocytes that have had their outer layer removed. Normal sperm will penetrate the eggs. The reliability and significance of this test are controversial.

Hamstring Muscle running from the buttocks to behind the knee. Often injured as a result of improper conditioning or lack of muscle flexibility. Muscle responsible for flexing the knee joint.

Handedness The preference for using one hand over the other. Most people are right-handed, about 10% are left-handed, and others, who don't favour a hand, are ambidextrous.

Handicap Inability to perform one or more life functions (e.g., eating, conversing, working) at a "typical" level, caused by the interaction of an individual's disability with the physical and social environments in which that person is functioning or expected to function.

Hand-Schueller-Christian disease Group of three symptoms that may occur in any of several disorders. Symptoms include marked protrusion of eyeballs (exophthalmos), diabetes insipidus and bone destruction..

Haploid A single set of unpaired chromosomes. Reproductive cells, or gametes, have a haploid set of DNA. Fertilization of an ovum by a sperm produces a full set (diploid number) of chromosomes in the zygote.

Hard contact lenses Rarely worn now, these are the small, hard lenses made of PMMA material that many people wore in the '70s and '80s. Compared with modern soft and rigid lenses, they are less healthy to wear long-term, since the material doesn't allow oxygen to reach the surface of the eye.

Hartnup disease Hereditary disease that causes skin rash, unsteady gait and excess amino acids in the urine.

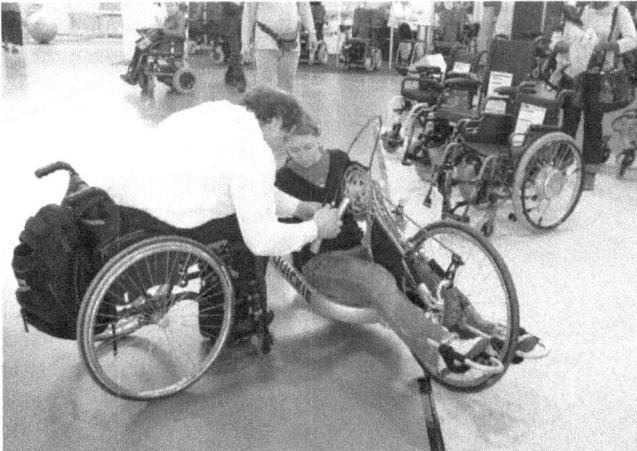

Fig. *Handicap*

Harvard mouse A transgenically engineered mouse, developed at Harvard and patented in April 1988, the first animal ever to be patented. The harvard mouse was engineered to be unusually susceptible to cancer and was developed for use in the testing of carcinogens and cancer therapies.

Hashimoto's thyroiditis is an inflammation of the thyroid gland that frequently results in hypothyroidism (lowered thyroid function). Chronic thyroiditis or Hashimoto's disease is a common thyroid gland disorder that can occur at any age, but it is most often seen in middle aged women. It is caused by a reaction of the immune system against the thyroid gland. It may be associated with other endocrine organ deficiencies such as diabetes mellitus or Addison's disease. It produces atrophic changes with regen-

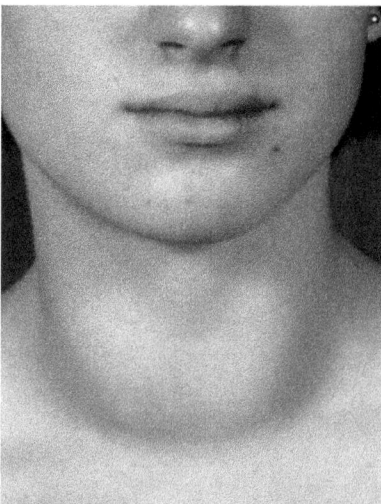

Fig. *Hashimoto's thyroiditis*

eration. This can lead to a goitre forming. Patients with Hashimoto's thyroiditis are usually hypothyroid or euth-yroid. However, they may have an initial thyrotoxic phase at presentation.

Hazard A factor or exposure that may cause disease; also an adverse chance or danger of injury, loss, or acquiring disease.

HCF Diet A high-carbohydrate, high-fibre diet.

HCFA generic quality screens The list of occurrences applied by utilization and quality control peer review organizations (PROS) to select cases that may have quality problems and that merit scrutiny. Because these screens generate a large portion of false positives, their application is only the first step in a multistage review process.

HDL High density liproprotein

Head start A federal programme begun in 1965 that provides educational, social, nutritional, and medical services to low-income preschool children. The programme is overseen by the Administration for children, youth and families (DHHS), but it is administered at the local level by head start agencies.

Healing touch is practiced by registered nurses and others to accelerate wound healing, relieve pain, promote relaxation, prevent illness and ease the dying process. The practitioner uses light touch or works with his or her hands near the client's body in an effort to restore balance to the client's energy system.

Health Most broadly, a state of optimal physical, mental, and social well-being, and not merely the absence of disease and infirmity.

Health alliances Nonprofit agencies that act as the health insurance purchasing agent for consumers under a system of managed competition, organized at either the state or regional level, or by employer groups. These alliances negotiated with provider networks to get the best plan at the lowest cost and would serve defined regions or classes of customers.

Health and human services, Department of An executive department of the federal government that is responsible for the oversight of the medicare and medicaid programmes.

Health and safety committees Groups made up of both management and labor within a plant that meet to discuss and take mutual action to resolve health and safety problems.

Health and welfare fund Health care benefit funds established under provisions of the Taft-Hartley Act, financed through employer and employee contributions, and administered by a board composed equally of representatives from labour and management.

Health care and social service professionals Physicians, nurses, social workers, psychologists, physical therapists, speech therapists, occupational therapists, and other professionals who provide health care, health-related, and social services.

Health care coalition Voluntary alliance of discrete interests sharing the principal objective of improving access to high quality health care services provided in a cost effective manner.

Health care data base Collection of information on health care episodes, such as utilisation, costs, or charges.

Health care decision counseling services, sometimes provided by insurance companies or employers, that help individuals weigh the benefits, risks and costs of health care tests and treatments. Unlike case management, health care decision counseling is non-judgmental. The goal of health care decision counseling is to help individuals make more informed choices about their health and medical care needs, and to help them make decisions that are right for the individual's unique set of circumstances.

Health care delivery system That combination of insurance companies, employer groups, providers of care and government agencies that work together to provide health care to a population.

Health care directive A written legal document which allows a person to appoint another person (agent) to make health care decisions should he or she be unable to make or communicate decisions.

Health care expense, direct All direct expenditures associated with promoting, maintaining, and restoring the health of a defined population. For employers, this frequently includes but is not limited to the design and communication of the benefit plan(s); plan administration; financing the plan(s), which may include medical, dental, vision, and pharmaceutical programmes; short and long term disability programmes; sick pay; payroll taxes attributable to state and general health programmes (e.g., worker's compensation, medicare, medicaid; and philanthropy). This may also include expenses for health promotion and wellness activities and on-site medical facilities.

Health care financing administration (HCFA) An agency within the U.S. department of health and human services that is responsible for the administration of the medicare and medicaid programmes.

Health care power of attorney The appointment of a health care agent to make decisions when the principal becomes unable to make or communicate decisions.

Health care prepayment A health plan with a Medicare cost contract to provide only Medicare Part B premiums. Some administrative requirements for these plans are less stringent than those of risk contracts or other cost contracts.

Health care prepayment system (HCPP) A cost contract with HCFA that prepays a health plan a flat amount per month to provide medicare-eligible Part B medical services to enrolled members. Members pay premiums to cover the medicare coinsurance, deductibles and co-payments, plus any additional non-medicare covered services that the plan provides. The HCPP does not arrange for part–A services.

Health care provider An individual or institution that provides medical services.

Health care proxy A health care proxy is recognized in some states as an alternate method for naming a person to act on one's behalf in health care decision making. In a few states, a health care proxy may be included as part of a living will.

Health care reform Changes in the organization, delivery and financing of health care to improve access, quality and to reduce the cost of care.

Health education A planned, sequential, K-12 curriculum that addresses the physical, mental, emotional and social dimensions of health. The curriculum is designed to motivate and assist students to maintain and improve their health, prevent disease, and reduce health-related risk behaviors. It allows students to develop and demonstrate increasingly sophisticated health-related knowledge, attitudes, skills, and practices.

Fig. *Health education– with live-demonstration to students of the teaching college*

The comprehensive health education curriculum includes a variety of topics such as personal health, family health, community health, consumer health, environmental health, mental and emotional health, injury prevention and safety, nutrition, prevention and control of disease, and substance use and abuse. Qualified, trained teachers provide health education.

Health fraud False or unsupported claims for a medical treatment's effectiveness.

Health hazard evaluation A hazard identification service provided by the National Institute of Occupational Safety and Health. After receiving a request from employees or an employer, a team of NIOSH researchers evaluate a workplace to determine the toxicity of substances or processes.

Health insurance A mechanism to spread the risk of unforeseen expenditures across a broad base to protect the individual from personal expenditures for health care services. Health insurance may be purchased individually or on a group basis. It may be custom designed to cover specific services and procedures and include requirements to control the level of use

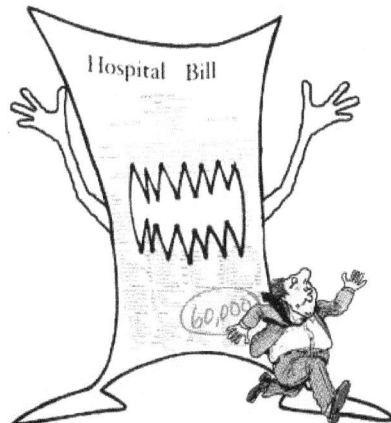

Fig. *Health insurance*

and payment for these services. An employee health insurance benefit is a nontaxable form of compensation to the employee in lieu of taxable salary or wages, provided through employment. Various types of insurance, such as accident, disability income, medical expense, dental, vision, hearing, and accidental death and dismemberment may be made available through employment. Benefits may be available to dependents of active employees, retirees, spouses, survivors, and dependents through employment. Benefits for classes of active and retired employees and their dependents need not be uniform. The employer may purchase benefits or the costs may be shared between the employer and employee.

Health insurance association of american A corporate member trade association of health and accident insurance companies; based in Washington, D.C.

Health insurance claim number The number listed on the beneficiary's medicare card consisting of nine digits followed by one or more letters. The nine digits represent the social security number of either the beneficiary or their spouse depending upon whose income it is based upon.

Health insurance portability and accountability act The 1996 Federal legislation that makes long-term care insurance premiums tax deductible if non-reimbursable medical expenses, including part or all of long-term care premiums, exceed 7.5% of an individual's gross income. HIPPA also excludes long-term care insurance benefits from taxable income. Not all long-term care insurance coverage qualifies for this benefit.

Health insurance trust fund The federal hospital insurance trust fund is a fund of the treasury of the United States in which the monies collected from taxes on the annual earnings of employees, employers, and self-employed people covered by social security are deposited. Disbursements from the fund are made to help pay for benefit payments and administrative expenses incurred by the hospital insurance programme (medicare part A).

Health insuring organization A hybrid of a state-funded health plan and a health maintenance organization. It is usually a public corporation that pays for medical services provided to recipients in exchange for payment of a premium or subscription charges paid for by the corporation that assumes the underwriting risk.

Health level seven (HL7) An existing formatting and protocol standard, that acts as an interface specification operating at the application level for transmitting health-related data. This standard has largely been used for transmission of data among departments within institutions for orders, clinical observations, test results, etc. Specific parts of HL7 have applicable CHIN use where such data needs to be transmitted between institutions and systems.

Health maintenance organization A health care organization that, in return for prospective per capita (cavitation) payments, acts as both insurer and provider of comprehensive but specified health care services. A defined set of physicians (and, often, other health care providers such as physician assistants and nurse midwives) provide services to a voluntarily enrolled population. Prepaid group practices and individual practice associations, as well as "staff models," are types of HMOS.

Health manpower shortage area An area or group which the U.S. Department of Health and Human Services designates as having an inadequate supply of health care providers. HMSAs can include:

(i) an urban or rural geographic area,

(ii) a population group for which access barriers can be demonstrated that prevent members of the group from using local providers, or

(iii) public or non-profit private residential facilities.

Health manpower shortage area placement opportunity list–A. List of the most needy health manpower shortage ar-

eas used by the National Health Service Corps. in the placement of volunteer and obligated personnel.

Health manpower shortage areas Areas, population groups, and facilities designated by the federal government as having shortages of health personnel. HMSAS, which are currently designated for primary care, dental, and psychiatric personnel, are determined primarily by population-topractitioner ratios.

Health outcome A measure of the effectiveness of preventive or treatment health services, typically in terms of patient health status, but sometimes in terms of patient satisfaction. Attributing changes in outcomes to health services requires distinguishing the effects of care from the effects of the many other factors that influence patients' health and satisfaction.

Health plan employer data and information sets A set of performance measures designed to standardize the way health plans report data to employers. HEDIS measures five major areas of health plan performance: quality, access and patient satisfaction, membership and utilization, finance, and descriptive information on health plan management.

Health professional shortage area (HPSA) A geographic area, population group, or medical facility that DHHSdetermines to be served by too few health professionals of particular specialties. Physicians who provide services in HPSAs qualify for the medicare bonus payments, re-payment of medical school loans or other incentives.

Health promotion Process of fostering awareness, influencing attitudes, and identifying alternatives so that individuals can make informed choices and modify their behavior in order to achieve an optimum level of physical and mental health.

Most broadly, a philosophy of health or a set of activities that takes as its aim the promotion of health, not just the prevention of disease. Sometimes narrowly defined as the set of prevention efforts aimed at changing individual behavior compare health education, health protection, and preventive services.

Health protection Strategies for health promotion and disease prevention related to environmental or regulatory measures that confer protection on large population groups.

Health services The health care services or supplies covered under the plan contract.

Health services corporation (HSC) General term to refer to a provider of an array of health services. Sometimes used in the insurance field to designate organizations that are required to meet special licensure requirements.

Health services system Traditionally, the aggregation of diagnostic and treatment services delivered by health care professionals, including physicians, physician assistants, nurses, nurse-practitioners, psychologists, and health educators.

Health status goals (of the report "Healthy People 2000") Goals defined in terms of a reduction in death, disease, or disability (e.g., "Reduce deaths among youth aged 15 through 24 caused by motor vehicle crashes to no more than 33 per 100,000 people" [Healthy People Objective No. 9.3b]).

Health system All the services, functions and resources for which the primary purpose is to affect the health of the population.

Health visitor A health visitor is a registered nurse with qualifications in obstetrics and midwifery, who visits new mothers and babies at home.

Healthcare financial management association (HFMA) The HFMA is the nation?s leading personal membership organization for more than 35,000 financial management professionals employed by hospitals, integrated delivery systems, long-term and ambulatory care facilities, managed care organizations, medical group practices, public accounting and consulting firms, insurance companies, government agencies, and other healthcare organizations. Offices located in Westchester, IL and Washington, DC.

Healthy start A medicaid programme that provides health care for pregnant women and children who are at or below a specified level of income and age.

Heat cramps Heat cramps are a form of heat illness. Heat illness occurs when a person's core body temperature rises above a safe level of the body's internal temperature range.

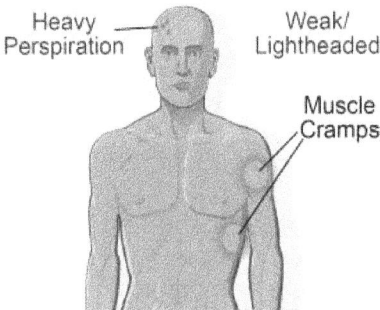

Fig. *Heat cramps*

Heat cramps are loss of salt in the body due to excessive perspiring causes the painful, involuntary muscle spasms. If the person does not take precautions to cool off and rehydrate at this point, more severe stages of heat illness will occur in a rapid progression, resulting in a potentially life-threatening situation.

Heat exhaustion Heat exhaustion is caused by the depletion of both water and salt due to excessive sweating during periods of work or exercise. Athletes are particularly prone to heat exhaustion. An effect of excessive exposure to heat, marked by—abnormally high body temperature, dehydration, diz-ziness, headache and some-times nausea.

Heat stroke is an extension of heat exhaustion, and it happens when the body's mechanisms responsible for temperature regulation fail. Signs and symptoms of heat stroke are— high body temperature, sweating, nausea and vomiting, rapid breathing, headache.

Fig. *Heat stroke*

Heinz bodies Granular deposits in red blood cells from precipitation of proteins. They are present in certain hemolytic anemias.

Hellerwork A system of somatic education and structural bodywork which is based on the inseparability of body, mind & spirit, making the connection between movement, body alignment and personal awareness. During sessions, the structural balance of the body is realized through the systematic release of muscle and connective tissue to restore the body's optimal natural balance, posture and flexibility. Myofascial release, movement awareness and dialogue are the essence of the sessions enabling one to move more fluidly, and have increased stamina, strength and energy.

Helminth Any parasitic worm.

Hemagluttination The agglutination, or clumping, of red blood cells, which may be caused antibodies, certain virus particles, etc.

Hemangioma Benign tumour made up of a mass of blood vessels.

Hematocrit: The volume occupied by the cellular elements of blood in relation to the total volume.

Hematoma A tumour-like mass produced by an accumulation of coagulated blood in a cavity.

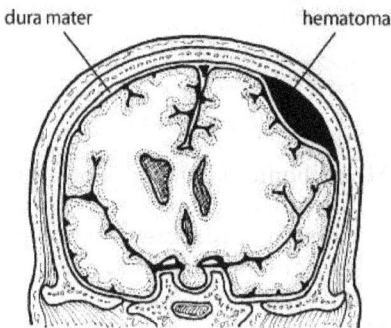

Fig. *Hematoma*

Hematuria The abnormal presence of blood in the urine, caused by various disorders of the urinary tract (e.g., cystitis, urethritis, prostatis, cysts, tumours, kidney or bladder stones, or glomerulonephritis).

Hemifacial spasm Involuntary muscles twitches on one side of the face, typically caused by compression of the seventh (facial) cranial nerve by a neighboring blood vessel somewhere in the brain.

Hemochromatosis A disease with excessive storage of iron, especially in the liver and other tissues, including the pancreas and skin; it may be genetic or the result of repeated transfusions. Pancreatic involvement may sometimes lead to destruction of islet cells and to a secondary form of diabetes. Sometimes called "Bronze Diabetes" because of the association of discoloration of the skin and diabetes.

Broadly, It is a pathological condition characterized by abnormal deposits of iron throughout the body; signs and symptoms include defects of the liver, glucose metabolism, and heart function.

Hemoconcentration Decrease of the fluid content of the blood, with resulting increase in concentration of blood cells.

Hemodialysis A procedure in which wastes or impurities are removed from the blood; used in treatment of renal insufficiency or failure and of various toxic conditions. In hemo-dialysis, a patient's blood is shunted through a machine for diffusion and ultrafiltration, where, by diffusion and osmosis, waste products and other molecules pass through the semipermeable membrane. The blood is then returned to the patient's circulation.

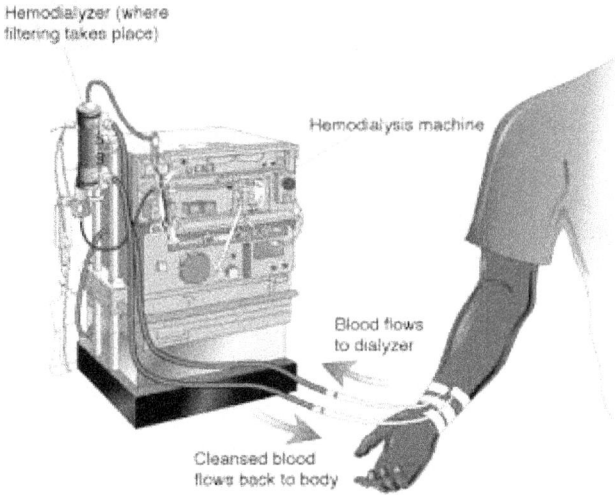

Hemodialyzer (where filtering takes place)

Hemodialysis machine

Blood flows to dialyzer

Cleansed blood flows back to body

Fig. *Hemodialyzer*

Hemodialyzer A device used to effect hemodialysis that consists of a compartment for the blood, a compartment for the dialysate, and a semi-permeable membrane separating the two. The three principal types are coil, hollow fibre, and parallel plate.

Hemodialysis uses a man-made membrane (dialyzer) to remove wastes and extra fluid from the blood. It also restores the proper balance of certain minerals in the blood (electrolytes). The fluid used to filter or clean the blood is called dialysate. Hemodialysis is usually done in a hospital or dialysis center.

In hemodialysis, the patient's blood is passed through a tube into a machine that filters out waste products. The cleansed blood is then returned to the body.

Hemodilution Increase in fluid content of blood, with resulting decrease in concentration of blood cells.

Hemoglobin A1C (HbA1C) The substance of red blood cells that carries oxygen to the cells and sometimes joins with glucose (sugar). Because the glucose stays attached for the life of the cell (about 4 months), a test to

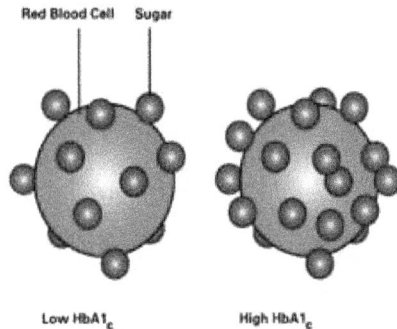

Red Blood Cell   Sugar

Low HbA1$_c$ High HbA1$_c$

Fig. *Hemoglobin A1C (HbA1C).*

measure hemoglobin A1C shows what the person's average blood glucose level was for that period of time.

The diagnosis of diabetes mellitus (type 2 diabetes) is based on two separate fasting plasma blood glucose (sugar) readings greater than 125 mg/dl. Or a hemoglobin A1c (average measure of plasma glucose over the past 2-3 months) equal to or greater than 6.5%.

Hemoglobin A protein found in red blood cells that serves as the primary oxygen transport vehicle in vertebrates. Hemoglobin is composed of an iron-containing molecule (heme) surrounded by four globin molecules, two each of two different types (two alpha globins and two beta globins in adults).

Hemoglobin-C disease Inherited blood disorder characterized by a moderate, chronic hemolytic anemia and associated with the presence of hemoglobin C, an abnormal form of the red cell pigment.

Hemoglobin-C trait Relatively common abnormal hemoglobin in which lysine replaces glutamic acid in the hemoglobin molecule.

Hemoglobinopathies A group of genetic disorders of hemoglobin structure and/or function. Examples are alpha thalassemia, beta thalassemia, and sickle cell anemia.

Hemolysis Process by which red blood cells breakdown and hemoglobin is released. Occurs normally at the end of the life span of a red blood cell. It may also occur abnormally with certain diseases or conditions such as hemolytic anemia.

Hemolytic Condition in which red blood cells break down and release the hemoglobin they contain. One example is hemolytic anemia. .

Hemolytic disease Disorder characterized by the premature destruction of red blood cells. May or may not result in anemia, depending on the ability of the bone marrow to increase production of red blood cells.

Hemolytic episode Separation of hemoglobin from red blood cells.

Hemolytic jaundice Jaundice caused by severe hemolytic anemia, which results in high levels of unconjugated bilirubin. Leads to a jaundiced appearance

Hemolytic transfusion reaction An antigen-antibody reaction in the recipient of a blood transfusion. It results in the destruction of red blood cells. The reaction typically occurs when there is incompatibility between donor red blood cells and recipient plasma, usually caused by an ABO mismatch. The symptoms range from fever or chills, to chest pain, shock, and renal failure.

Hemophilia Inherited deficiency of a blood clotting factor that may result in bleeding episodes. Characterized by bleeding into joints, muscles and skin, excessive bleeding from minor cuts, nosebleeds and blood in urine. Hemophilia is a rare, genetic bleeding disorder distinguished by a deficiency of one or more blood coagulation factors (e.g., Factor Vlll (hemophilia A) or Factor IX (hemophilia B)) leading to prolonged bleeding following injury to spontaneous bleeding in the muscles and joints. The genes for hemophilia are recessive and are found on the X-chromosome; as a result, hemophilia is usually found in males and is most often transmitted to children by asymptomatic (carrier) females.

Hemophilus influenzae type-B Bacteria that causes numerous diseases in children. Two of these diseases are especially serious. Meningitis (infection of the brain and spinal cord) can cause death or permanent brain damage. Epiglottitis is a condition of the throat in which the child can choke to death.

Hemoptysis Coughing up blood from the respiratory tract. Blood-streaked sputum can occur with minor upper respiratory tract infections. A greater amount of blood may indicate a serious disease or infection.

Hemorrhage The escape of blood from the blood vessels, either into surrounding tissues or into the environment.

Hemorrhagic Referring to the loss of a large amount of blood in a short period of time.

Hemorrhagic disease Medical problem accompanied by un-controlled bleeding. Hemorrhagic disease of the newborn is rare because it is customary to give vitamin K to the mother just before delivery or to the infant immediately after birth.

Hemorrhagic fever A severe complication of some viral diseases that involves internal or external bleeding. Some arboviruses can cause epidemic outbreaks of hemorrhagic fever.

Hemorrhagic gastritis Inflammation of stomach accompanied by bleeding from stomach lining.

Heparin An anticoagulant substance occurring in various tissues (lungs, blood vessels) or produced artificially that prevents the formation of blood clots.

Heparin therapy Course of treatment with medication that prolongs blood clotting time. Used to prevent or treat blood clots.

Heparinized To render blood non-clottable with heparin. For example, tubes used to collect blood often have heparin in them so blood does not coagulate.

Hepatic Of or affecting the liver

Hepatic coma Stupor or coma caused by waste products in the blood that are toxic to the brain. Normally, waste products are neutralized by the liver, but due to extensive liver damage they continue to circulate in the blood. Can cause death.

Hepatic disease Any disease involving the liver, including many types of hepatitis and cirrhosis.

Hepatic dysfunction Poor liver function

Hepatitis A Viral hepatitis, type A. An acute inflammation of the liver caused by infection with hepatitis A virus, which is transmitted by fecal contamination of food or water (e.g., through infected people handling food), or through parenteral infection (by contaminated needles or administration of blood products). Formerly known as "infectious hepatitis."

Hepatitis B A blood-borne virus (for which there is a vaccine) which primarily affects the liver and, like HIV, has few or no symptoms immediately after infection. It can be passed from mother to child during pregnancy, and can cause cirrhosis, chronic active hepatitis, and liver cancer.

Hepatitis B vaccine The vaccine against hepatitis B, a virus which primarily affects the liver.

Hepatitis Inflammatory liver condition characterized by jaundice, enlarged liver, loss of appetite, abdominal discomfort, abnormal liver function, dark urine and clay-coloured stool. It can be caused by bacterial or viral infection, parasites, alcohol, drugs or blood transfusions with incompatible blood. Symptoms may be mild, severe or life-threatening.

Hepatitis profile Blood tests performed include hepatitis-B surface antigen, antibody to core antigen and antibody (IgM) to A virus. These are all covered under Antibody Screening.

Hepatocellular injury Injury of liver cells.

Hepatomas (Malignant liver tumor; hepatocellular carcinoma) Malignant tumour that begins in the liver (primary site of cancer), as opposed to liver cancer that has spread from another site.

Hepatotoxicity Tendency of a substance, usually a medication or alcohol, to have a destructive effect on the liver.

Herbal medicine Herbal medicine uses plants or plant extracts (typically the whole plant or herb is used for the greatest effect) to treat conditions. Herbalists, like many other complementary therapists, treat the whole person and look for underlying problems, rather than specific symptoms.

Herbal treatments Treatments based on the therapeutic use of plant products.

Herbalism uses natural plants or plant-based substances to treat a range of illnesses and to enhance the functioning of the body's systems. Though herbalism is not a licensed professional modality in the U.S., herbs are prescribed by a range of practitioners, from holistic M.D.s to acupuncturists to naturopaths.

Herbalist A practitioner who prescribes plant-derived medicaments.

Herd immunity The level of immunity that must be attained to prevent epidemics of communicable diseases in a specific population.

Hereditary Transmitted genetically from generation to generation. In narrow sense, the passing of a trait such as colour of the eyes from parent to child. A person "inherits" these traits through the genes.

Hereditary anti-edema Inherited condition that prevents accumulation of fluid.

Hereditary spherocytosis Inherited disorder characterized by small, spherical red blood cells, leading to anemia because abnormal cells are fragile. See Anemia.

Herfindahl index A measure of economic market concentration that is calculated by summing the squares of the market shares of the firms in the market. Higher values of the index indicate a greater degree of concentration and a less competitive market structure.

Hernia Protrusion of an internal organ through a weakness or abnormal opening in the muscle around it. A hernia occurs when an organ or fatty tissue squeezes through a weak spot in a surrounding muscle or connective tissue called *fascia*. The most common types are — *inguinal* (inner groin), *incisional* (resulting from an incision), *femoral* (outer groin), *umbilical* (belly button), and *hiatal* (upper stomach). Umbilical hernias

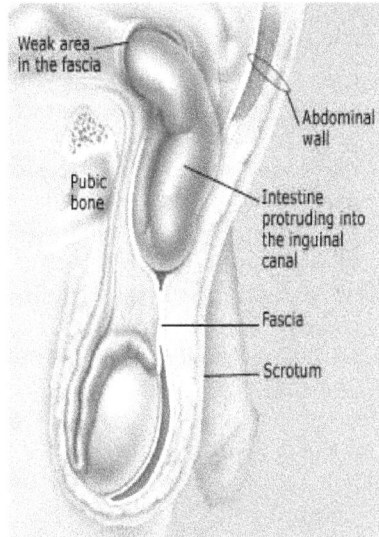

Fig. *Hernia*

rarely require surgery. Other hernias are usually curable with surgery.

Heroin An addictive psychoactive substance derived from opium. Heroin is administered mainly intravenously.

Herpes Herpes type-1 causes common cold sores, which appear around the mouth. Herpes type-2 (HSV-2) is a viral infection of the genitals transmitted by sexual intercourse. Type-2 herpes infection can be transmitted to a newborn from an actively infected mother. It can be fatal to the child.

Heterochromia Condition where one eye is a different colour from the other, or one eye is more than one colour.

Heterosexual A man or woman who is sexually attracted to someone of the opposite sex.

Heterozygote An individual who has two different alleles of any one particular gene. For instance, an individual who has one copy of the gene for thalassemia at the locus for beta globin and one copy of the gene for normal beta globin is heterozygous for thalassemia.

Heterozygous Having different alleles at a given locus. Compare homozvgous.

Hiatal hernia Abnormal weakness or opening in the diaphragm. Allows a portion of the stomach to protrude through the diaphragm. If symptoms occur (often there are none), they usually appear at least 1 hour after eating and may include heartburn, belching and sometimes difficulty swallowing. Treatment usually relieves symptoms. Surgery is rarely required.

Hib vaccine A vaccine given to protect against haemophilus influenzae type b (Hib), a serious bacterial infection which causes ear and airway infections and is the leading cause of meningitis in children under two years of age.

Hib vaccine is an inactivated vaccine. The Hib conjugate vaccine is made chemically by bonding a polysaccharide (sugar) to a protein. The sugar is one that makes up the surface capsule of the bacterium. Hib-polysaccharide conjugate to diphtheria toxoid (PRP-D), a diphtheria toxoid-like protein (PRP-HbOC), tetanus toxoid (PRP-T), or meningococcal outer membrane protein (PRP-OMP) are also available.

Hierarchy of controls The preference for using engineering controls to reduce or eliminate hazards. This preference, long a tenet of professional health and safety practice, has been followed by the Occupational Safety and Health Administration (OSHA). For example, to reduce exposures to air contaminants, OSHA requires that employers use engineering controls except when those controls are not feasible, not capable of reducing exposures to the required levels, or while they are being designed and installed.

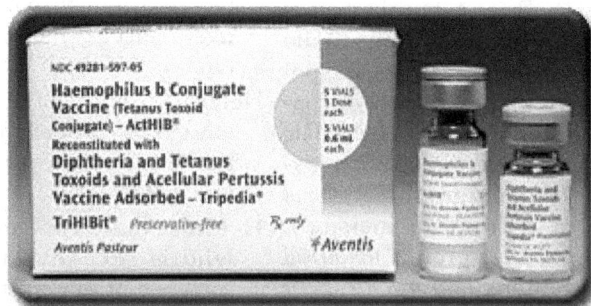

Fig. *Hib vaccine*

High 'Interosseous' ankle sprain
An injury to the Interosseous membrane, which is the fibrous tissue that stabilizes the two bones of the shin (tibia and fibula). This injury is usually due to excessive ankle rotation along with accompanied trauma to the ligamentous structures of the ankle joint.

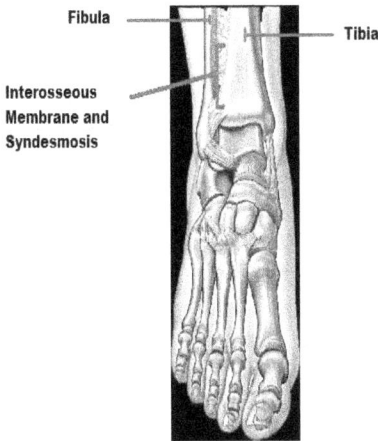

Fig. High 'Interosseous' ankle sprain

High blood pressure When the blood flows through the vessels at a greater than normal force. High blood pressure strains the heart; harms the arteries; and increases the risk of heart attack, stroke, and kidney problems. Also called hypertension.

High copy number plasmid A plasmid present in multiple copies within a single host bacterium. Copy number (single, low and high) is dependent on both plasmid and host cell factors.

High level care High-level care is for people who need 24-hour nursing care, nurses do tasks as laundry, cleaning and personal care.

High performance liquid chromatography (HPLC) A technique used to separate a complex mixture of unknown composition by passing it through a glass column packed with a silica gel or alumina. The components of the mixture are isolated as they travel through the column at different rates. Unlike the old gravity-dependent columns, HPLC operates under pressure and has better resolution with a shorter analysis time.

High risk At greater than normal risk of contracting a specific disease or condition.

Higher-order aberration Irregularity of the eye other than a refractive error (myopia, hyperopia or astigmatism). Higher-order aberrations sometimes affect your vision (such as decreasing contrast sensitivity), and sometimes do not.

High-index Type of lens with a higher index of refraction, meaning that light travels faster through the lens to reach the eye than with traditional glass or plastic. It is denser, so the same amount of visual correction occurs with less material (whether glass or plastic) - so the lens can be thinner.

High-mortality outliers Providers with mortality rates that are higher than expected after adjustment for patient or other characteristics.

High-purine diet Diet of foods that are high in purines, including anchovies and sardines, organ meats, legumes and poultry. Increased intake of purines may lead to development of uric acid stones (a type of kidney stone). .

High-risk babies This term describes those babies who have a greater likelihood of developing an illness or dying within the first few months of life. High-risk babies include those born to mothers infected with HIV or to mothers who have a drug or alcohol dependency.

High-risk pregnancy A pregnancy with a higher than normal risk of developing complications. Such pregnancies include those with multiple fetuses or Rhesus incompatibility, or when the mother has had problems with miscarriage, premature labour, or placenta praevia in earlier pregnancies.

Hilar Referring to the anatomic area where the bronchus, blood vessels, nerves, and lymphatics enter or leave the lung.

Hill Burton Act federal Legislation enacted in 1947 to support the construction and modernization of health care institutions.

Hill-Burton programme Federal programme created in 1946 to provide funding for the construction and modernization of health care facilities. Hospitals which receive Hill-Burton funds must provide specific levels of charity care.

Hip pinter Contusion to the iliac crest.

Hippocampus A curved structure (in the limbic system) at the core of the brain that is important for learning, the conversion of short-to long-term memory, and the expression of emotional responses.

Hispanics Persons who identify themselves as of Hispanic origin, or, less typically, individuals with Hispanic surnames identified by others (e.g., health care providers identifying patients in surveys) as of Hispanic origin. Hispanics can be those whose families have emigrated directly from Spain, or from Cuba, Central or South America. Persons of Hispanic origin can be of any race (white, black, American Indian); most are white.

Histamine A protein that can be released as part of the body's immune system responses during an allergic reaction. Presence of histamine can lead to inflammation and swelling, which is why antihistamines often are prescribed for allergy symptoms.

Histidinemia Hereditary defect of metabolism marked by excess histidine (an amino acid) in the blood and urine. Many people with this defect show mild mental retardation and improper speech development.

Histiocytosis Abnormal proliferation of histiocytes (immune system cells). Common symptoms include bone tumours and skin rashes. If histiocytosis affects the eyes, it causes bulging.

Histocompatibility The extent to which individuals (or their tissues) are immunologically similar, the extent to which tissue from one individual or organism is accepted or tolerated by the immune system of another individual or organism.

Histology The study of the minute structure, composition, and function of body tissues by using special staining methods making cell structures visible under light and electron microscopy.

Histoplasmosis Fungal infection from breathing dust that contains fungus spores or through direct contact into an open skin wound. Fungus is found in the feces of birds and bats and in soil contaminated by feces. In the U.S., disease is most prevalent in the Mississippi and Ohio River Valleys. Although the acute disease is benign, other forms are very serious and may be fatal. Usually curable with 3 months of treatment using antifungal drugs.

Historical controls In nonrandomized clinical trials, individuals treated with a 'control treatment" outside the study proper, at some time previous to the trial, against which the experimentally treated one individuals are compared.

Historical cost depreciation An estimate of depreciation based on the original cost of the fixed asset.

Histo-tech Cuts and stains vary thin sections of body tissue for microscopic examination by a pathologist.

HIV therapies Practitioners offer a range of therapies that aim to treat the human immuno-deficiency virus, AIDS, or its' symptoms. Due to the life-threatening nature of this disease, these therapies are often used as complements to conventional approaches to HIV.

Hives (Urticaria) A skin reaction that results in slightly elevated patches that are redder or paler than the surrounding skin and often are accompanied by itching. Hives come from histamine that is released into the bloodstream resulting in an allergic reaction to something. There are certain areas where it gathers and this is what causes the welts and the itching rash. There are many people who experience allergic reactions to certain triggers in the environment.

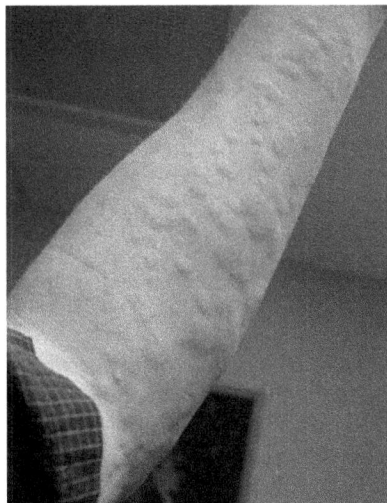

Fig. *Hives*

Human leukocyte antigen A pattern of cell surface proteins that identifies the cell to the immune system as 'self' or 'non-self'. Certain patterns (haplotypes) as defined by DNA analysis can indicate a susceptibility to Type 1 diabetes.

HMO lookalike This is a product where the benefit design looks much like that of an HMOwith coverage for preventative care services and dollar co-payments rather than percentage co-insurance. However, services are not restricted to network providers and there is no primary care physician requirement.

HMO, closed panel physicians Employed or contractually obligated exclusively or primarily to see the patients of an ADFS health plan.

HNC, hyperbaric nurse clinician; A credential offered by the Baromedical Nurses Association (BNA).

Hodgkin's disease Malignant tumour of the lymph glands characterized by progressive enlargement of the lymph nodes, loss of appetite, weight loss, fever, itching skin, night sweats and anemia.

Hold harmless A clause frequently found in managed care contracts, whereby the HMO and the physician agree not to hold each other liable for malpractice or corporate malfeasance if either of the parties is found to be liable. It may also refer to language that prohibits the provider from billing patients in the event a managed care company becomes insolvent.

Holistic An adjective meaning targeted to the whole person - mind, body, and spirit. Wholistic medicine considers not only physical health but also the emotional, spiritual, social, and mental well-being of the person.

Hollow fibre dialyzer A dialyzer containing thousands of hollow fibres bundled within a compact . cylinder. Blood flows through the semi-permeable hollow fibres.

Home and community based waiver Medicaid waiver that provides a menu of community long term care services as an alternative to nursing home care. Limited to a specified number of slots in each state. The waiver generally provides a more liberal eligibility level than state plan Medicaid services.

Home and community-based services Programmes which provide services in the home or at a convenient location in the community. Commonly these programmes provide assistance with meals, transportation or homemaking.

Home blood glucose monitoring A way a person can test how much glucose (sugar) is in the blood. Also called self-monitoring of blood glucose.

Home care In contrast with inpatient and ambulatory care, home care is medical care ordinarily administered in the house setting when a patient is not sufficiently ambulatory to make frequent office or hospital visits. With these patients, intravenous therapy for example is administered at the patient's residence, usually by a health care professional. Home care reduces the need for hospitalization and it's associated costs.

Home care services The provision of health, social, and supportive services in the home by outside organizations or individuals. Services can range from sophisticated (e.g., administering intravenous drugs) to relatively simple (providing home-delivered meals). Common, home care services include skilled nursing care, physical and occupational therapies, personal care, home health aide, homemaker, paid companion, and housekeeping services.

Home delivered meals A programme authorized under Title III-C-2 of the Older Americans Act which provides, five or more days a week, at least one home delivered hot or other appropriate meal per day to older persons who are home bound, lack the capacity to prepare meals independently, or for whom congregate meal facilities are not available.

Home health agency An agency that provides medical services in a home setting. Services may be provided by a nurse, occupational, speech or physical therapist, social worker, or home health aide.

Home health aide A person who is paid to provide health-related services in the home. The services provided by a home health aide may include assistance with medications and exercise, assistance with personal care (e.g., bathing, dressing, and feeding), and light household tasks. The term is sometimes used synonymously with the term homemaker, but some agencies and othes make a distinction between the two terms.

Home health care Medical and related services provided in the home.

Home health services Performed at an individual's home including a wide range of skilled and non-skilled services, including part-time nursing care, various types of therapy, assistance with activities of daily living and homemaker services such as cleaning and meal preparation. For Medicare purpose, this term refers specifically to intermittent, physician-ordered medical services or treatment.

Home medical equipment Durable medical equipment prescribed by a physician for use by a patient at home. It is a means of continuing access to health care without remaining in the hospital. Such equipment may help the patient function more independently, it may assist recuperation, or it may be palliative. The equipment may be leased or purchased. These costs may be covered by a health plan.

Home-based (mental health) services Crisis-oriented work intensively with children and families in their homes. timeliness, accessibility, and intensity.

Home-delivered meals Meals prepared at a central location and delivered to homebound people on a daily or less frequent basis.

Homemaker A person who is paid to provide in-home services, such as assistance with personal care (e.g., bathing, dressing, and feeding), household tasks, meal preparation, and shopping. The term is sometimes used synonymously with the term home health aide, but some agencies and others make a distinction between the two terms.

Homeopathy A philosophy of treatment founded by Samuel Hahnemann (1755-1843), in which microdoses of medicines are believed to stimulate the body's vital force. Some of these medicines are not known to contain even one molecule of the original compound per dose, but are considered by the homeo-path to be extremely powerful. The power of these doses is enhanced by "succession" (violent shaking) performed at various stages in their preparation.

Homeopathy is a medical system that uses infinitesimal doses of natural substances to stimulate a person's immune and defence system. Homeopathic remedies are named for the plant or animal ingredient they are made from. Homeopathy uses highly diluted preparations which correspond to symptoms, clinical signs and pathological states. Homeopathy is based on the theory of similars - that symptoms can be cured with a small dose of that substance which causes the symptom.

Homeostatis When the body is working as it should because all of its systems are in balance.

Homocysteine An amino acid containing sulfur. A high homocysteine level in the blood is a possible risk factor for heart disease. One major study indicates that lowering homocysteine lev-

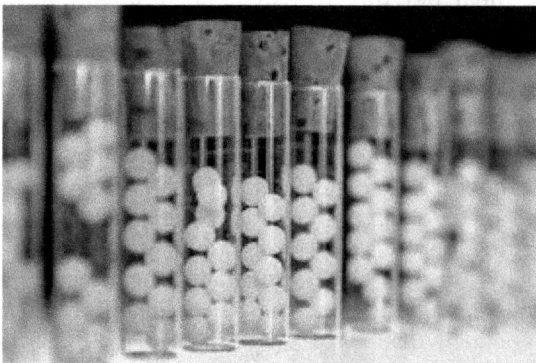

Fig. *Homeopathy*

221

els through vitamin B supplementation might help prevent diseases associated with impaired function of small blood vessels, such as macular degeneration.

Homocystinuria A congenital disoder caused by a deficiency of one of the enzymes involved in the metabolism of the amino acid homocystine. If left untreated, homocystinuria can lead to lifethreatening episodes of vascular thrombosis; most untreated survivors go on to have mental deficiency, and half of them may die in early adulthood.

Homologous sequence DNA or RNA segments having an identical or nearly identical linear order of nucleotide base pairs

Homology The correspondence among organisms of structures and functions derived from a common evolutionary origin (e.g., a common gene structure).

Homophobia Fear of lesbians and gay men

Homozygote An individual with the same alleles responsible for a particular protein, trait, or feature.

Homozygous Having identical alleles at a given genetic locus in the DNA.

Honeymoon period The period of time shortly after the diagnosis of Type 1 diabetes during which there is some restoration of insulin production and the blood sugar levels improve to normal, or near-normal, levels. Unfortunately, like other honeymoons,

this diabetes honeymoon doesn't last forever; it may last for weeks, months, or occasionally, years.

Hopelessness The state of being without one's own home, either on one's own, with one's family, living on the street or in a shelter or other temporary situation (e.g., with relatives or friends).

Horizontal integration Consolidation or merger of organizations that provide similar types of care. Also see vertical integration.

Horizontal transfer The passage of genetic material from one organism to another via nonsexual mechanisms.

Hormone A chemical released by special cells to tell other cells what to do. For instance, insulin is a hormone made by the beta cells in the pancreas. When released, insulin tells other cells to use glucose (sugar) for energy. Examples of such hormones include insulin, sex hormones, adrenaline, and thyroxine. Hormones were first discovered by the British scientists William Bayliss and Ernest Starling in 1902.

Hormone replacement therapy Supplements of the hormones which regulate the female reproductive system; these supplements may be taken during and after menopause to reduce the symtoms of menopause and the risk of some diseases such as osteoporosis

Horner's syndrome Condition characterized by a small pupil, ptosis and an abnormal lack of facial perspiration (all on the same side of the face); Horner's syndrome is caused by injury to the sympathetic nerves of the face.

Hospice Hospice/palliative care is provided to enhance the life of the dying person. Often provided in the home by health professionals, today there are many nursing facilities and acute care settings that also offer hospice services. Hospice care, typically offered in the last six months of life, emphasizes comfort measures and coun-seling to provide social, spiritual and physical support to the dying patient and his or her family.

Hospice care The provision of short-term inpatient services for pain control and management of symptoms related to terminal illness.

Hospice services Medical, nursing, counseling, and other supportive services rendered to termi-nally ill people and their families. Hospice care is intended to be palliative and to improve quality of life rather than to cure disease or extend life.

Hospital An institution whose primary function is to provide inpatient diagnostic and therapeutic services for a variety of medical conditions, both surgical and non-surgical. In addition, most hospitals provide some outpatient services, particularly emergency care. Hospitals may be classified by length of stay (short-term or long-term), as teaching or non-teaching, by major types of services (psychiatric, tuberculosis, general, and other specialties, such as maternity, pediatric, or ear, nose and throat), and by type of ownership or control (Federal, State, or local government; for-profit and non-profit).

Hospital affiliation A contractual relationship between a health insurance plan and one or more hospitals whereby the hospital

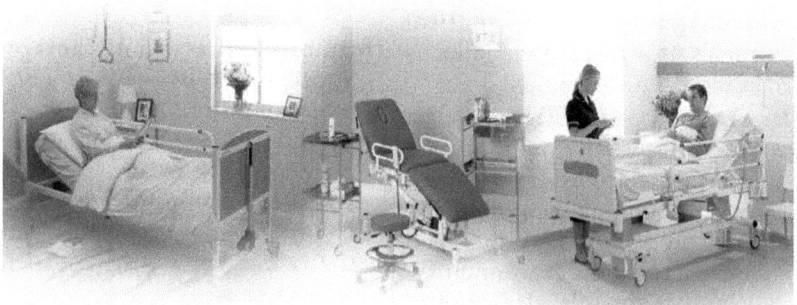

Fig. *Hospital*

223

provides the inpatient benefits offered by the plan.

Hospital alliance A group of hospitals that have joined together to improve competitive positions and reduce costs by sharing common services and developing group purchasing programmes.

Hospital discharge planner A person who arranges post-discharge care for hospitalized patients.

Hospital insurance programme The compulsory portion of Medicare which relates to hospital care.

Hospital market basket Components of the overall cost of hospital care.

Hospital mortality rate Number of deaths as a proportion of the total number of hospital patients or admissions.

Hospital or health care district/ authority A geographic area created and controlled by a political subdivision of a State, county, or city solely for the purpose of establishing and maintaining medical care.

Hospital volume The number of particular procedures performed or conditions treated in a hospital during a given period of time.

Hospital-based geriatric assessment programmes Special hospital inpatient or outpatient programmes that use a multidisci-plinary team to evaluate elderly patients with complicated medical or psychiatric problems and to develop a co-

ordinated plan of care. Some also offer other services such as medical and psychiatric treatment, and rehabilitative services. Hospital-based geriatric assessment programmes include inpatient geriatric specialty units, inpatient geriatric consultation services, outpatient geriatric services, and inpatient and outpatient geropsychiatry services.

Hospitalist A hospital-based internist who can be used to assume management of adult admissions from the primary care physician (PCP), freeing the PCP to do more office-based work. Hospitalists act as the hospital gatekeeper, to provide a valuable service by assessing the clinical needs of patients presenting to the emergency room and supervising inpatient care for those patients who are more critically ill, thereby reducing hospital inpatient costs.

Host 1. In parasitology, a living organism that harbors a parasite. Definitive hosts harbor the adult or sexual stage of a parasite; intermediate hosts harbor the Iarval or asexual stages of a parasite. 2. In recombinant DNA technology, the organism used for growth and reproduction of viruses, plasmids, or other sources of foreign DNA.

Host resistance The ability of an organism to mount a successful immune response against diseasecausing antigens.

Housekeeper Non-skilled environmental services provided in the home including help with housekeeping, laundry, cleaning, shopping and meal preparation. Does not include any hands-on care such as personal care or assistance with activities of daily living.

Human chorionic gonadotrophin This hormone is produced by the placenta and triggers the release of oestrogen and progesterone. As it is excreted in urine, hCG is used in testing to detect pregnancy.

Human gene therapy Treatment of disease by insertion of new genetic material or permanent modification of existing genes. Gene therapy can take three forms: 1) gene addition (or insertion), in which new DNA is added without affecting the native gene; 2) gene replacement (or surgery) in which the native gene is removed before the new gene is inserted; and 3) gene modification (or modulation) in which the native gene's expression is irreversibly altered without directly altering its native structure.

Human genome project A large scale, cooperative research and technology development effort designed to map and sequence human DNA.

Human growth hormone The hormone secreted by the pituitary gland which stimulates and regulates growth.

Human immunodeficiency virus (HIV) A retrovirus that is the etiologic agent of AIDS and whose infection has been associated with depression of the immune system and various opportunistic diseases. HIV infects and disables the T4 subset of T-lymphocytes, which are key elements of the immune system.

Human insulin Man-made insulins that are similar to insulin produced by your own body. Human insulin has been available since October 1982.

Human leukocyte antigen (HLA) A series of four gene loci that code for a group of antigens present on the surface of cell membranes; important in determining the acceptance or rejection by the body of a tissue or organ transplant; successful tissue transplantation requires a minimum number of HLA differences between the donor's and recipient's tissues; individuals with identical HLA types are considered histo-compatible for the purposes of organ transplantation.

Human menopausal gonadotropin (HMG) Hormone that can be extracted from the urine of menopausal women and injected to stimulate ovaries and testes.

Humerus Bone of the upper arm

Humoral Relating to any fluid or semifluid of the body.

Humoral immunity Immunity associated with antibodies that circulate in the blood.

Huntington disease is a brain disorder that affects a person's ability to think, talk, and move. The disease destroys cells in the basal ganglia, the part of the brain

Huntington's Disease Affects the Brain's Basal Ganglia

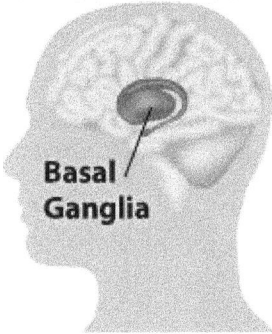

Basal Ganglia

Fig. *Huntington disease*

that controls movement, emotion, and cognitive ability. HD is caused by a mutation in a gene on chromosome

The disease is transmitted as an autosomal dominant trait, but usually does not manifest itself until middle age. Previously called "Huntington's chorea." Some of the symptoms include: poor memory, depression and/or mood swings, lack of coordination, twitching or other uncontrolled movements, and difficulty walking, speaking, and/or swallowing. In the late stages of the disease, a person will need help doing even simple tasks, such as getting dressed.

Huntington's chorea Rare, abnormal, hereditary condition characterized by involuntary, purposeless, rapid movements of various body parts, as well as progressive mental deterioration. Symptoms often appear in the 40s with death occurring about 15 years later.

Hybrid An offspring of a cross between two genetically unalike individuals.

Hybrid Model HMO A combination of at least two managed care organizational models that are molded into a single health plan. Since its features do not uniformly fit only one type of model, it is called a hybrid.

Hybridization The combining of materials from different sources. In molecular genetics, the process of joining two single-strands of RNA or DNA together so that they become a double-stranded molecule. For hybridization to occur, the two strands must be nearly or perfectly complementary in the sequence of the nucleotide base pairs,

Hybridoma A new cell resulting from the fusion of a particular type of immortal tumour cell line, a myeloma, with an antibody producing B lymphocyte. Cultures of such cells are capable of continuous growth and specific (i.e., monoclinal) antibody production.

Hydatidiform mole Disease occurring during early pregnancy resulting in death of the fetus and an overgrowth of tissue within the uterus.

Hydrocephalus Hydrocephalus is a relatively rare condition caused by swelling of the fluid-filled cavities in the brain (called ventricles). It is also called "water on the brain" . It is sometimes the first sign of spina bifida or can be caused by a tumour or surgery to close an open spinal column.

Hydrocephaly A defect marked by an unusual accumulation of spinal fluid in the ventricles of the brain. This fluid buildup causes enlargement of the head and usually retards brain development, often resulting in mental retardation and, in severe cases, early death. The condition can now be treated if diagnosed soon after birth.

Hydrogel (hydrophilic material) Highly water-absorbent, plastic material from which most soft contact lenses are made. The most commonly used of these materials is hydroxyethylmethacrylate (HEMA).

Hydrolysis A chemical process of decomposition involving the splitting of a chemical bond and the addition of the elements of water.

Hydronephrosis Caused by an obstruction in the tube that carries urine from the kidney to the bladder (ureter). Because urine cannot flow past the obstruction, it backs up into the kidney causing distention or dilation. Prolonged hydronephrosis eventually results in loss of kidney function; surgery to remove the obstruction may be necessary.

Hydrophilic Having an affinity for water (soluble in water). These substances may also be termed Iipophobic, or insoluble in lipids.

Hydrophobic Insoluble in water (or soluble in lipids).

Hydrosol The water that is obtained along with essential oil after plant materials are distilled. In distillation, plant materials are heated in water to release plant oils. The steam and vapor are channeled through a tube to a condensing coil, where they cool and return to liquid form. The essential oils float on top of the water. The hydrosol contains water-soluble plant constituents and trace amounts of essential oil. Hydrosols are sometimes used in aromatherapy together with the essential oils and may be spritzed in the air and on the face and body.

Hydrothorax An abnormal accumulation of watery fluid within the pleural cavity.

Hydroxyurea An experimental drug used to promote expression of hemoglobin F genes (to replace defective beta globin genes) in patients with thalassemia or sickle-cell disease.

Hymen The hymen is a thin piece of skin that surrounds and partially covers the vaginal opening (also called the introitus) in females. The main purpose of the hymen appears to be protection of the vaginal opening and the areas immediately surrounding the introitus during a female's early developing years. The hymen often, though not always, rips or tears the first time a woman has penetrative intercourse, which may cause some temporary bleeding and slight discomfort. The hymen may

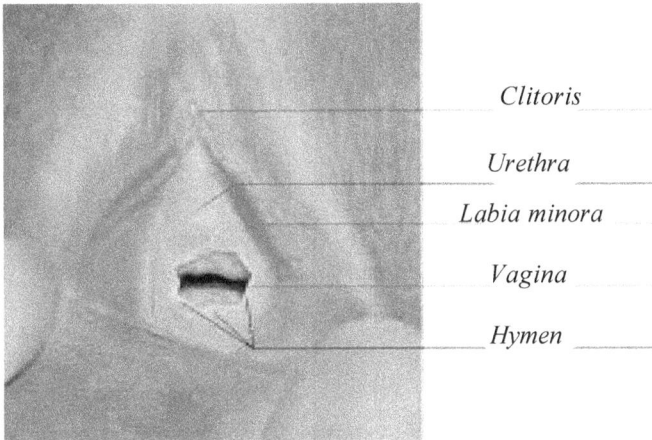

Clitoris

Urethra

Labia minora

Vagina

Hymen

Fig. *Hymen*

also tear prior to first inter-course due to athletic activity - some women may not be aware when their hymen tears, especially if it does not occur during sexual activity, because it may or may not cause bleeding or discomfort. The hymen has been and continues to be a source of intense concern in many cultures.

Hyper Abnormally increased; excessive.

Hyperactivity Excessive motor activity that may be purposeful or aimless; movements and utterances are usually more rapid than normal. Hyperactivity is a prominent feature of attention-deficit disorder, so much so that in DSM-IV the latter is called attention- deficit/ hyperactivity disorder (ADHD).

Hyperactivity Excessive motor activity that may be purposeful or aimless; movements and utterances are usually more rapid than normal. Hyperactivity is a prominent feature of attention-deficit disorder, so much so that in DSM-IV the latter is called attention- deficit/ hyperactivity disorder (ADHD).

Hyperalimentation Supplying total nutritional needs of patients who are unable to eat normally by intravenous feeding or by tube through the nose into the stomach. Provides nutrients containing essential proteins, fats, carbohydrates and vitamins.

Hypercalcemia Presence of excessive calcium in the blood. May result from tumour of the parathyroid gland (due to over-production of parathyroid hormone), Paget's disease, some cancers, multiple fractures or prolonged immobility. May also occur from excessive ingestion of calcium, such as overuse of antacids that contain calcium.

Hyperchloremia Presence of excessive amounts of chloride in the blood. May result from severe dehydration, complete shutdown of kidneys and primary aldosteronism.

Hypercholesterolemia (familial)

Hyperextension Extreme extension, or straightening, of a limb or body part.

Hyperfibrinogenemia Presence of excessive fibrinogen in the blood. See Fibrinogen. May indicate cancer of the stomach, breast or kidney or an inflammatory disorder.

Hyperfunctioning tumour Any tumour that leads to higher than normal action of the chemicals (usually hormones) usually secreted by the tissue from which the tumour arises. For example, hyperfunctioning tumour of the thyroid gland leads to an increase in thyroid hormone released.

Hyperglycemia Too high a level of glucose (sugar) in the blood; a sign that diabetes is out of control. Many things can cause hyperglycemia. It occurs when the body does not have enough insulin or cannot use the insulin it does have to turn glucose into energy. Signs of hyperglycemia are a great thirst, a dry mouth, and a need to urinate often. For people with Type 1 diabetes, hyperglycemia may lead to diabetic ketoacidosis.

Hyperinsulinism Excessive secretion of insulin. This term most often refers to a condition in which the body produces too much insulin. Researchers believe that this condition may play a role in the development

of noninsulin-dependent diabetes and in hypertension.

Hyperkalemia Abnormally high blood potassium level. May be seen in people who have suffered severe burns, crushing injuries, diabetic ketoacidosis or myocardial infarction. Also seen in those who have Addison's disease or kidney failure.

Hyperlipidemia Too high a level of fats (lipids) in the blood.

Hyperlipoprotenemia Condition in which excessive lipoproteins (cholesterol and other fatty materials) accumulate in the blood.

Hypermagnesemia Elevated levels of magnesium in the blood. Most commonly occurs in people with kidney failure.

Hypernatremia Excess of sodium in the blood, usually caused by excessive loss of water and electrolytes. Symptoms include mental confusion, seizures and eventually coma.

Hyperopia A defect in vision characterized by the inability of the eye to focus on near objects. It is also called farsightedness. Condition in which the length of the eye is too short, causing light rays to focus behind the retina rather than on it, resulting in blurred near vision. Additional symptoms include eye strain and squinting.

Hyperoxaluria Hereditary defect of metabolism, marked by excessive oxalate in the urine. May result in kidney stones, early onset of kidney failure (due to calcium deposits in the filtering system) and calcium-oxalate deposits in other areas of the body.

Hyperparathyroidism -- Excessive amounts of parathyroid hormone circulating in the blood. Excess amounts increase blood levels of calcium (hypercalcemia) and decrease blood levels of phosphorus (hypophosphatemia).

Hyperphosphatemia -- Abnormally high level of phosphates in the blood. May result from bone diseases, healing fractures, hypoparathyroidism, diabetic acidosis or kidney failure.

Hyperploidy Condition of having one or more chromosomes in excess of the normal number. The result is unbalanced sets of chromosomes. One example of hyperploidy is Down's syndrome.

Hyperprolactinemia The overproduction of the pituitary hormone prolactin, which can contribute to infertility. The causes of this condition are diverse and poorly understood. It can be treated with bromocriptine.

Hyperprolinemia, Type-A Disorder of amino acid metabolism.

Hypersensitivity In immunology, a state of heightened reactivity to a previously encountered antigen; may cause mild allergy or severe anaphylactic shock.

Hypertension Blood pressure that is above the normal range, or, Elevated pressure, usually referring to high blood pressure- a common and significant cardiovascular disorder character-ized by persistently high arterial blood pressure, usually greater than 140mm Hg systolic and 90mm Hg diastolic pressure.

Hyperthyroidism Overactivity of the thyroid, an endocrine gland that regulates all body functions.

Hypertonic Solution that contains substances that flow outward through a semipermeable membrane into a solution of lower concentration.

Hypertrophic anal papilla Excessive growth of the papilla of the rectum.

Hypertrophy Increase in the size of a cell or group of cells. Causes an increase in the size of an organ or part.

Hyperventilation Breathing so rapidly that carbon dioxide levels in the blood are decreased, upsetting normal blood chemistry. Can be caused by fever, heart disease, lung disease or severe injury. Can also be caused by anxiety. May be accompanied by numbness and tingling of mouth, hands and feet, weakness and faintness.

Hypervolemia An abnormal increase in the volume of circulating fluid (plasma) in the body.

Hypnosis Although the condition resembles normal sleep, scientists have found that the brain wave patterns of hypnotized subjects are much closer to the patterns of deep relaxation. Hypnosis is now generally viewed as a form of attentive, receptive, highly focused concentration in which external events are omitted or disregarded. Widely used by surgeons, dentists, and psychotherapists to relieve anxiety or as an anesthetic. Used to relax a patient, reduce resistance to therapy, facilitate memory, to address stopping smoking, eating less, or fighting fears.

Hypnozoite Forms of some species of Plasmodium, the cause of malaria, that remain dormant in liver cells, sometimes for many years, retaining their ability to activate an infection and cause acute malaria.

Hypo Deficient; beneath; under.

Hypoalbuminemia Abnormally low levels of albumin (protein) in the blood.

Hypoalderostonism Deficiency of aldosterone secreted by the outer layer of the adrenal glands. May result from Addison's disease, salt-losing syndrome and toxemia of pregnancy.

Hypocalcemia Abnormally low levels of chloride in the blood. Low chloride levels can occur from prolonged vomiting, intestinal fistula, chronic kidney failure and Addison's disease.

Hypofibrinogenemia Abnormally decreased level of fibrinogen in the blood. May result from disseminated intra-vascular coagulation, fibrinolysis, severe liver disease and some cancers.

Hypofunctioning tumour Tumour that causes the anatomical part it encroaches on to have less than normal function.

Hypogammaglobulinemia Abnormally low levels of gammaglobulins in the blood, which results in an immunity deficiency. This makes you more susceptible to infectious diseases. You can be born with this condition or it can result from other diseases, such as nephrosis.

Hypoglycaemia Too low a level of glucose (sugar) in the blood. This occurs when a person with diabetes has injected too much insulin, eaten too little food, or has exercised without extra food. A person with hypoglycemia may feel nervous, shaky, weak, or sweaty, and have a headache, blurred vision, and hunger. Taking small amounts of sugar, sweet juice, or food with sugar will usually help the person feel better within 10-15 minutes. Excessive insulin may be caused by a tumour, called an insuli-noma, that secretes too much insulin. May also result from kidney failure, liver disease, alcoholism or decreased food intake. The brain must have glucose available at all times.

Hypoglycemia unawareness A situation in which the usual epinephrine-induced symptoms of a fall in blood sugar are, for a variety of reasons, either not felt or not recognized. This situation may be dangerous, as the patient may go from functioning normally to unconscious within a short time. It is generally thought that if such a patient is allowed to maintain somewhat elevated blood sugar levels for several weeks, that the hypoglycemic unawareness may resolve.

Hypoglycemic syndrome Condition caused by low blood sugar, characterized by cold sweat, low body temperature, headache, confusion, hallucinations and ultimately (if left untreated) convulsions, coma and death.

Hypogonadism Decreased functional activity of gonads, with hindered growth and slowed sexual development.

Hypogonadotropism Abnormal condition caused by decreased production of gonadotropins.

Hypokalemia Below normal level of potassium in the blood. May result from aldosteronism, Cushing's syndrome, excessive loss of body fluids and licorice addiction.

Hypolipoproteinemia Abnormally low levels of lipoproteins in blood.

Hypomania A psychopathological state and abnormality of mood falling somewhere between normal euphoria and mania. It is characterized by unrealistic optimism, pressure of speech and activity, and a decreased need for sleep. Some people show increased creativity during hypomanic states, whereas others show poor judgment, irritability and irascibility.

Hyponatremia Less than normal concentration of sodium in the blood. Caused by excessive water in circulating blood or excessive loss of sodium from severe vomiting or diarrhea, or inadequate intake of sodium.

Hypooxaluria Decreased amount of oxalic acid in the urine.

Hypoparathyroidism Decreased production of hormones by the parathyroid glands, causing low calcium blood level.

Hypophosphatasia Inborn error of metabolism that causes difficulty building and healing bones.

Hypophysectomy Surgical removal of the pituitary gland.

Hypopituitarism Underactivity of the pituitary gland, resulting in inadequate hormone production.

Hypoplasia Incomplete development or underdevelopment of an organ or tissue, usually from a decrease in the number of cells.

Hypospadias A structural abnormality of the penis caused by an opening on the underside. It is a birth abnormality in which a boy's urethra, through which urine and semen pass, opens on the underside of the penis rather than at the end. It is almost always correctable with surgery.

Hypotension Low blood pressure or a sudden drop in blood pressure. A person rising quickly from a sitting or reclining position may have a sudden fall in blood pressure, causing dizziness or fainting.

Hypothalamus A region in the upper part of the brainstem that acts as a relay to the pituitary gland. It is located in the middle

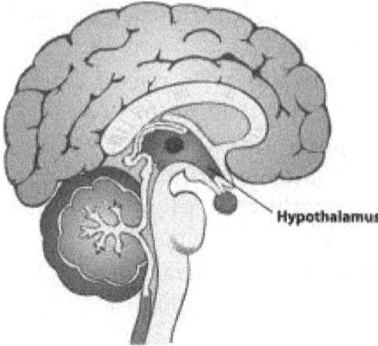

Fig. *Hypothalamus*

of the base of the brain, and encapsulates the ventral portion of the third ventricle. It controls body temperature, circadian cycles, sleep, moods, hormonal body processes, hunger, and thirst. The hypothal-amus is part of the limbic system and works with the pituitary gland.

Hypothyroidism Underactive thyroid gland, which results in decreased metabolic rate. Early symptoms may include decreased tolerance for cold, fatigue, unexplained weight gain, constipation and forgetfulness. If left untreated, the disorder may progress to myxedema and eventually coma. Treatment includes thyroid replacement hormones.

Hypotonia limp, slack muscles in a baby.

Hypotony Low intraocular pressure, often caused by eye surgery or trauma (e.g., open globe injury). Symptoms include blurred vision and eye pain or discomfort.

Hysterectomy Surgical removal of the uterus, in some cases also including the cervix, ovaries, oviducts, and pelvic lymph nodes.

Hysterosalpingogram A test used to evaluate the health and patency of the uterus and Fallopian tubes. Dye is injected into the uterus and an X-ray is taken. A hysterosalpingogram can locate blockages or tumours which may be treated with surgery or medication.

Hysterosalpingogram An x-ray study of the female reproductive tract in which dye is injected into the uterus while x-rays are taken showing the outline of the uterus and the degree of openness of the fallopian tubes.

Hysteroscopy Direct visualization of the interior of the uterus in order to evaluate any abnormalities that may be present. This is done by inserting a hysteroscope (a long, narrow, illuminated tube) through the cervix into the expanded uterus. Surgical procedures may also be performed using this method.

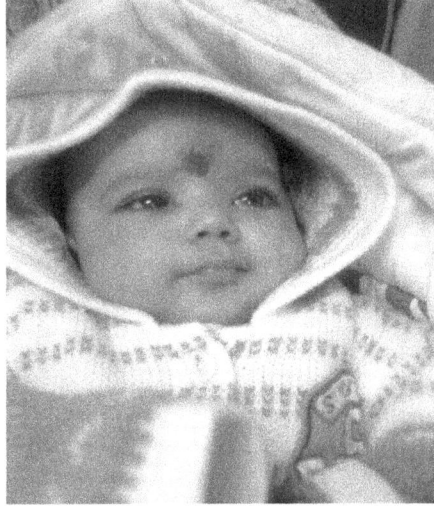

Ibandronate hormones A drug that is used to prevent and treat osteoporosis, and is being studied in the treatment of cancer that has spread to the bones. It belongs to the family of drugs called bisphosphonates.

Ibaril Topical anti-inflammatory glucocorticoid used in dermatoses, skin allergies, psoriasis, etc.

IBMFS Inherited bone marrow failure syndrome. A rare disorder in which a person's bone marrow is unable to make enough blood cells and there is a family history of the same disorder. There are several different inherited bone marrow failure syndromes. Patients with an IBMFS are at high risk of forming acute leukemia or certain solid tumors. Also called inherited bone marrow failure syndrome.

Ibritumomab tiuxetan A monoclonal antibody that is used to treat certain types of B-cell non-Hodgkin lymphoma and is being studied in the treatment and detection of other types of B-cell tumors. Monoclonal antibodies are made in the laboratory and can locate and bind to substances in the body, including cancer cells. Ibritumomab binds to the protein called CD20, which is found on B cells. It is linked to the compound tiuxetan. This allows certain radioisotopes to be attached before it is given to a patient. It is a type of monoclonal antibody-chelator conjugate.

IBS A disorder of the intestines commonly marked by abdominal pain, bloating, and changes in a person's bowel habits. This may include diarrhea or constipation, or both, with one occurring after the other. Also called irritable bowel syndrome, irritable colon, mucus colitis, and spastic colon.

Ibuprofen A drug used to treat fever, swelling, pain, and redness by preventing the body from making a substance that causes inflammation. It is a type of nonsteroidal anti-inflammatory drug (NSAID). Also called Advil and Motrin.

ICD A small device used to correct a heartbeat that is abnormal (too fast, too slow, or irregular). The device is placed by surgery in the chest or abdomen. Wires are passed through a vein to connect the device to the heart. When it detects abnormal heartbeats, it sends an electrical shock to the heart to restore the heartbeat to normal. Also called implantable cardio-verter-defibrillator.

ICE An abbreviation for a chemotherapy combination that is used to treat non-Hodgkin and Hodgkin lymphomas that have come back and do not respond to other treatments. It includes the drugs ifosfamide, carboplatin, and etoposide. Also called ICE regimen.

Ice minus (ice-) One of several strains of bacteria that have been altered genetically to remove a functional gene coding for a protein that promotes the formation of ice crystals (an ice nucleating gene); used experimentally to inhibit frost damage to agricultural crops infected with these bacteria.

Ice plus (ice+) Bacteria with an intact, functional ice nucleating gene.

ICE regimen An abbreviation for a chemotherapy combination that is used to treat non-Hodgkin and Hodgkin lymphomas that have come back and do not respond to other treatments. It includes the drugs ifosfamide, carbo-platin, and etoposide. Also called ICE.

Ichthyosis Skin condition in which skin is dry, thickened and fissured, resembling fish scales. Usually appears at or shortly after birth; it may be associated with one of several rare syndromes. Treatment with ath oil or vitamin-A solution (retinoic acid) applied to the skin may help some types.

Ichythosis follicularis Skin disorder characterized by dryness, roughness and scaliness.

ICI 182780 A drug used to treat certain types of breast cancer in postmenopausal women. It is also being studied in the treatment of other types of cancer. ICI 182780 blocks estrogen activity in the body and is a type of anti-estrogen. Also called Faslodex and fulvestrant.

ICI D1694 An anticancer drug that stops tumor cells from growing by blocking the ability of cells to make DNA. It belongs to the family of drugs called thymidylate synthase inhibitors. Also called raltitrexed.

Icterus A clinical manifestation of hyperbilirubinemia, consisting of deposition of bile pigments in the skin, resulting in a yellowish staining of the skin and mucous membranes.

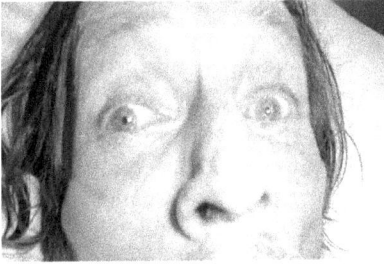

Fig. *Icterus*

Idarubicin An anticancer drug that is a type of antitumor antibiotic. Also called 4-demethoxy-dauno-rubicin.

IDEC-Y2B8 A radiolabeled monoclonal antibody that is used to treat certain types of B-cell non-Hodgkin lymphoma and is being studied in the treatment of other types of B-cell tumors. It is made up of the monoclonal antibody ibri-tumomab plus the radioisotope yttrium Y 90. It binds to the protein called CD20, which is found on B cells. The radiation in the yttrium Y 90 may kill the cancer cells. IDEC-Y2B8 is a type of radio-pharmaceutical. Also called Y 90 ibritumomab tiuxetan, Y 90 Zevalin, and yttrium Y 90 ibritumomab tiuxetan.

Identical twins Two offspring born at the same time who look exactly alike. Identical twins are also called monozygotic twins because they develop from the same egg: a single fertilised egg splits early in development and becomes two separate fetuses.

Fig. *Identical twins.*

Identity crisis A loss of the sense of the sameness and historical continuity of one's self and an inability to accept or adopt the role one perceives as being expected by society. This is often expressed by isolation, withdrawal, extremism, rebelliousness, and negativity, and is typically triggered by a sudden increase in the strength of instructional drives in a milieu of rapid social evolution and technological change.

Idiopathic Having an unknown cause. A medical condition that appears suddenly with no apparent explanation is considered idiopathic

Idiopathic cold-agglutinin diseases Disease of unknown cause associated with laboratory findings of an agglutinin that acts only at relatively low temperatures.

Idiopathic dementia Disorders in which the clinical symptoms of dementia (progressive intellectual deterioration) are present without the typical abnormal findings in the brain. This kind of dementia is found in approximately 5 percent of cases.

Idiopathic hypertrophic subaortic stenosis (IHSS) Chronic heart condition that produces an enlarged heart muscle, which restricts the amount of blood the heart pumps. Condition may be inherited, ut cause is usually unknown. Symptoms may include chest pain, shortness of breath, fainting, heart rhythm irregularity, heart murmur, swollen feet and ankles, and enlarged, tender liver. Usually curable with medication or surgery.

Idiopathic myelofibrosis A progressive, chronic disease in which the bone marrow is replaced by fibrous tissue and blood is made in organs such as the liver and the spleen, instead of in the bone marrow. This disease is marked by an enlarged spleen and progressive anemia. Also called agnogenic myeloid metaplasia, chronic idiopathic myelofibrosis, myelosclerosis with myeloid metaplasia, and primary myelofibrosis.

Idiopathic pneumonia syndrome A set of pneumonia-like symptoms (such as fever, chills, coughing, and breathing problems) that occur with no sign of infection in the lung. Idiopathic pneumonia syndrome is a serious condition that can occur after a stem cell transplant.

Idiopathic pulmonary fibrosis A disease in which the alveoli (tiny air sacs at the end of the bronchioles in the lungs) are overgrown with fibrous tissue. The cause of the disease is unknown and it gets worse over time. Symptoms include difficult, painful breathing and shortness of breath.

Idiopathic thrombocytopenic purpura (ITP) Bleeding into the skin and other organs due to a deficiency of platelets.

Idiopathic thrombocytopenic purpura A condition in which platelets (blood cells that cause blood clots to form) are destroyed by the immune system. The low platelet count causes easy bruising and bleeding, which may be seen as purple areas in the skin, mucous membranes, and outer linings of organs. Also called immune thrombocytopenic purpura and ITP.

Idiotype (or idiotope) An antigenic determinant specific for an individual immunoglobulin molecule; idiotypes are regions near the antigen binding site of an antibody that act as antigens themselves by stimulating the production of antibodies.

IgA deficiency A dysgammaglobulinemia characterized by a deficiency of Immunoglobulin A.

Ileostomy A surgical procedure used in colonic bypass operations or colonic resections to create an artificial outlet for the discharge of feces into a bag attached to the skin; involves

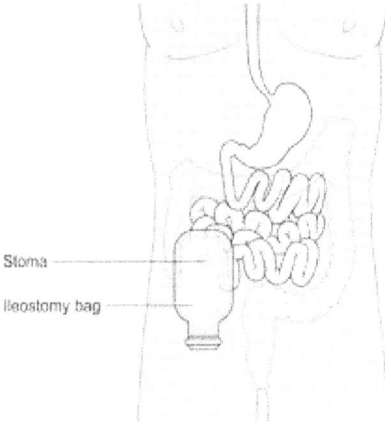

Fig. *Ileostomy*

bringing a loop or end of the ileum (the end portion of the small intestine) out through an opening in the abdominal wall to the outside of the body.

Ileum The last part of the small intestine before the large intestine begins.

Illusions The false perception of abstract information, leading to an incorrect or distorted interpretation of reality.

Immediate hypersensitivity Immune response mediated by antibodies, characterized by hives, wheezing, and/or abrupt changes in blood pressure, and occurring within a few minutes or hours after exposure to an antigen.

Immobilized enzymes Soluble enzymes encapsulated in an insoluble organic or inorganic matrix (such as glass) during chemical reactions, making them more stable and reusable after carrying out its catalytic functions.

Immune Resistance or protection against infection by the body's natural defenses. A person may be immune to one kind of infection but not immune to another. Some infections, such as measles or chickenpox, cause permanent immunity to that infection.

Immune deficiencies Any of a number of disorders (e.g., adenosine deaminase deficiency, purine nucleoside phosphorylase deficiency, AIDS) resulting from a failure or malfunction of the bodily defense mechanisms, or immune system.

Immune response A defensive reaction of the body in response to exposure to certain substances not recognized as normal body components (pathogenic microorganisms, transplanted tissue, etc.). Immune responses may involve the production of antibodies that react with antigens on the surface of the foreign substances to render them harmless, as well as a variety of physical and chemical responses from other cells of the immune system.

Immune serum Blood serum that contains immune globulins and can be used to confer passive immunity to a variety of diseases.

Immune system The integrated working of a number of the body's cells and organs to defend against infection.

In other words, it is the group of organs, specialized cells, and cell products that protect the

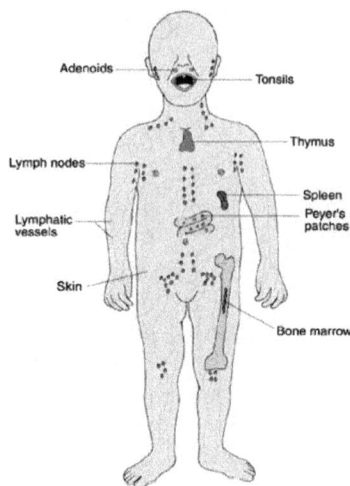

Fig. *Immune system*

body from harmful micro-organisms. There are a variety of things that can cause someone's immune system to weaken. Poor nutrition, chronic illness, heredity, injuries, allergies, and even some medications like certain antibiotics can leave your body open to illness and infection.

Immunisation Natural immunity provided by antibodies or induced immunity via inoculations.

Immunity The condition of being immune, or being protected against disease by the actions of the immune system. Immunity may be either innate or acquired; innate immunity is present from birth, having been passed to the baby from the mother during pregnancy; acquired immunity may be active (resulting from either previous exposure to the disease-causing agent or vaccination) or passive (resulting from the injection of pre-formed antibodies derived from an individual already immune to a particular antigen).

Immunization The deliberate introduction of an antigenic substance (vaccination, or active immunization) or antibodies (passive immunization) into an individual, with the aim of inducting immunity or resistance to disease.

Immunoassay A type of laboratory technique in which specific antibodies are used to identify and measure biological substances (e.g., the concentration of antibodies or hormones present in a sample of serum). Different types of immunoassay include radioimmunoassays (RIAs), in which antibodies or antigens are labeled with radioactive markers, and enzyme-linked immunoabsorbent assays (ELISA) in which the antibody is linked with an enzyme.

Immunodeficiency diseases Defects in the body's immune system. A healthy immune system protects the body against germs (bacteria, viruses, fungi), cancer (partial protection) and any foreign material that enters the body. When the system fails, the body becomes susceptible to infection and cancer. Can range from minor to very severe.

Immunogenic Able to cause an immune response.

Immunoglobin-deficiency disease Illness caused by deficiency of a protein molecule with known antibody activity.

Immunoglobulin Any of a group of specific defense proteins (produced by white blood cells) that react to the presence of a foregn antigen, react more quickly to a previously encountered antigen than to a new one, and under normal circumstances, do not respond to components of its own body. They are found in the blood plasma and lymph and in other body fluids and tissues. There are five basic classes .". of immunoglobulins-lgA, lgD, lgE, lgG, and lgM.

Immunological privilege The concept that part of the body (e.g., the central nervous system) is not as closely monitored by the immune system as the rest of the body and is therefore less susceptible to graft rejection.

Immunology The scientific study of the ability of organisms to identify and attack foreign substances, to distinguish self from nonself, to form antibodies and antigen-reactive lymphocytes, and to become hypersensitive to common allergens.

Immunomedicated disease Illness caused by medicines that decrease the efficiency of the immune system in preventing or decreasing severity of disease.

Immunoscintigraphy The use of external radioimaging techniques to locate tumors and to identify certain noncancerous diseases,

Immunostimulant Stimulating various functions or activities of the immune system.

Immunosuppression: Inhibition or suppression of the immunologic response (e.g., by infection, as in AIDS, or by the administration of drugs to prevent rejection of tissue grafts or transplanted organs, or by irradiation or biochemical agents).

Immunosuppressive Pertaining to or inducing the artificial prevention or diminution of the immune response.

Immunosuppressive Drugs Drugs that block the body's ability to fight infection or foreign substances that enter the body. A person receiving a kidney or pancreas transplant is given these drugs to stop the body from rejecting the new organ or tissue. Cyclosporin is a commonly used immuno-suppressive drug.

Immunosuppressive therapy Drugs used to prevent the body from forming a normal immune response. Therapy is used to treat diseases (especially when organs must be transplanted) when certain antibodies must be inactivated.

Immunotherapy is any medication or treatment that alters the immune system, such as vaccines. In a more general sense, Immunotherapy is a series of allergy shots given to gradually get your body "used to" an allergen or asthma trigger, so that you can build up a tolerance to it. Cancer treatment that produces antitumor effects primarily through the action of natural host defense mechanisms or by the administration of called *biotherapy* and biological therapy.

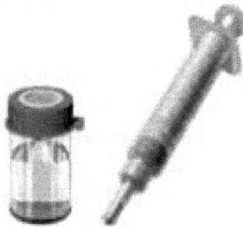

Fig. *Immunotherapy*

Immunotoxicant A substance that elicits an adverse immune response or damages the immune system.

Immunotoxicity An adverse or inappropriate change in the structure or function of the immune system after exposure to a foreign substance.

Impaired fecundity Categorization of infertility used by demographers to describe couples who are nonsurgically sterile, or for whom it would be difficult or risky to become pregnant.

Impaired Glucose Tolerance (IGT) Blood glucose (sugar) levels higher than normal but not high enough to be called diabetes. People with IGT may or may not develop diabetes. Other names (no longer used) for IGT are "borderline," "subclinical," "chemical," or "latent" diabetes.

Impaired physician A physician who does not have the ability to practice medicine with reasonable competence, skill, and safety to patients, because of physical or mental illness, including alcoholism or drug dependence.

Impairment Any loss or abnormality of psychological, physiological, or anatomical structure or function from injury or disease. It represents a deviation from the person's usual biomedical state.

Impingement syndrome Pinching together of the supraspinatus muscle and other soft tissue in the shoulder, which is common in throwing.

Implant When an egg attaches to the lining of the uterus.

Implantable insulin pump A small pump placed inside of the body that delivers insulin in response to commands from a hand-held device called a programmer.

Implantation Implantation occurs when a fertilised egg attaches itself to the lining of the uterus.

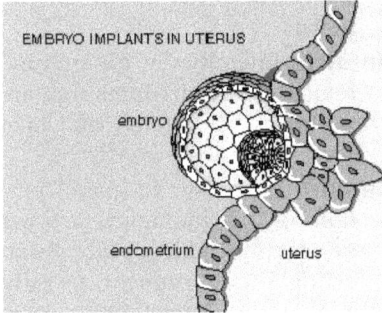

Fig. *Implantation*

Implantation and fertilization, events The morula floats in the uterus for 3 to 4 days, gaining in size and weight. At this time, the hollow fluid-filled morula, now called blastocyst burrows into the uterine lining.

(b). The outer surface of the blastocyst becomes covered with finger-like projections called chorionic villi. Chorionic villi aid in the process of implantation into the endometrium (decidua). Villi also manufacture human chorionic gonadotropin (HCG) which signal the corpus luteum within the ovaries to continue production of progesterone and estrogen to prevent menstruation.

(c). Implantation normally occurs in the upper, posterior wall of the uterus. The point of implantation becomes the origin for the placenta and umbilical cord.

Implicit review Review of the process of medical care using subjective criteria.

Impotence The loss of a man's ability to have an erect penis and to emit semen. Some men may become impotent after having diabetes for a long time because the nerves or blood vessels have become damaged. Sometimes

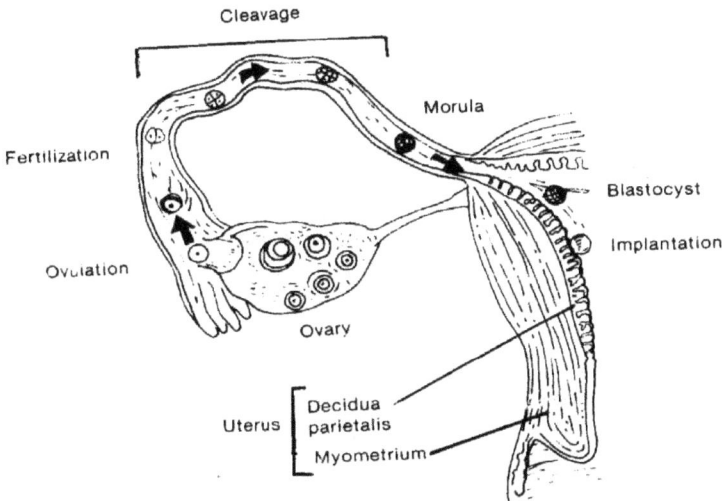

Fig. *Implantation and fertilization, events*

the problem has nothing to do with diabetes and may be treated with counseling.

Impulse control disorders Failing to resist an impulse, drive, or temptation to perform some act that is harmful to oneself or to others. The impulse may be resisted consciously, but it is consonant with the person', immediate, conscious wish. The act may be premeditated or unplanned. The person may display regret or guilt for the action or its consequences.

In loco parentis This is Latin for "in place of a parent", referring to the rights and duties of a guardian or organisation with regard to a child.

In situ hybridization A method to identify certain RNA or DNA segments, involving the use of radioactive-labeled probes.

In utero surgery This is surgery to correct an abnormality in a developing fetus, carried out while the fetus is still in the uterus.

In utero Literally, "in the uterus," referring to procedures that are performed or events that take place within the uterus.

In vitro Literally, "in glass," pertaining to a biological process or reaction taking place in an artificial environment, usually a laboratory. Sometimes used to refer to the propagation of cells from multicellular organisms under controlled laboratory conditions.

In vitro fertilisation IVF is an assisted conception treatment in which eggs and sperm are mixed in a petri dish in a laboratory in the hope that the eggs will be fertilised. Up to three develop-

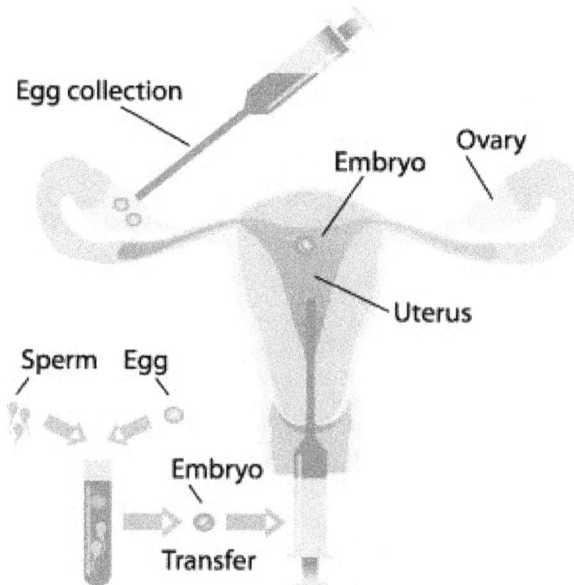

Fig. *In vitro fertilisation.*

ing embryos can then be transferred to the woman's uterus with the aim of achieving pregnancy. "In vitro" is latin for "in glass", and refers to the glass dish in which fertilisation takes place.In vitro fertilization is an option for many couples who cannot conceive through conventional therapies. These embryos are put back into the wife's uterus (womb) after 3 to 5 days of being in the incubator, hopefully they will then grow into a baby. The reasons IVF is done may include— poor sperm quality and/or quantity, obstructions between the egg and sperm, ovulation problems, and sperm-egg interaction problems. These problems can prevent couples having a baby naturally, and IVF helps to solve this specific conditions that might require IVF include— tubal blockage or failed tubal reversal, endometriosis, cervical factor, pelvic adhesions, male factor, unexplained infertility/ failed conventional therapy, genetic testing (PGD) for inheritable diseases, genetic testing (PGD) for possible reasons for multiple miscarriage

In vitro test Experimentation using cells, tissues, or explants grown in a nutritive medium rather than using living animals or human subjects.

In vivo Literally, "in the living," pertaining to a biological process or reaction taking place in a living organism. In biomedical research, used to describe experiments or processes in whole animals (e.g., mice, rats, humans), as opposed to those in a test tube or other experimental system.

In vivo fertilization The fertilization of an egg by a sperm within a woman's body. The sperm may be introduced by artificial insemination or by coitus.

In vivo genetic transfer The gene of a useful enzyme from one organism is recruited into a pathway of another organism via natural genetic processes such as transduction, transformation, and conjugation (facilitated by transmissible plasmids or transposons).

Inappropriate Discordance of voice and movements with the content of the person's speech or ideation.

Incentive plans Elements of health benefit plans that emphasize particular types of coverage and therefore serve to promote enrollee use of those benefits.

Incentives Economic benefits given to providers to motivate efficiency in-patient care management.

Incidence How often a disease occurs; the number of new cases of a disease among a certain group of people for a certain period of time. The frequency of new occurrences of disease within a defined time interval. Incidence rate is the number of new cases of a specified disease divided by the number of people in a population over a specified period of time, usually 1 year.

Incident reporting A system for collecting and reporting information about adverse events that affect patients in hospitals. Hospital personnel (most frequently nurses) complete forms when they observe an adverse event; the definition of an "incident" is subject to the discretion of the frontline health professionals who deal with patients. Examples of incidents include patient falls, medication errors, equipment failures, and procedure or treatment errors.

Incompetence Determined by a legal proceeding. Requires that the individual is incapable of handling assets and exercising certain legal rights.

Incompetent cervix It generally means that the muscles of the cervix are too weak to hold a baby in the uterus throughout pregnancy. A stitch may be placed at the opening of the cervix to keep it together.

In other words, when a woman's cervix is frail the baby is at risk of being born prematurely because the cervix shortens or opens too early. In order to prevent premature labor, a woman's doctor may recommend a cervical cerclage. A cerclage is used to prevent these early changes in a woman's cervix, thus preventing premature labour. The treatment consists of a stitch being inserted into and around the cervix early in the pregnancy, usually between weeks 12–14, and then removed towards the end of the preg-

nancy when the greatest risk of miscarriage has passed. It is also called *eager cervix*.

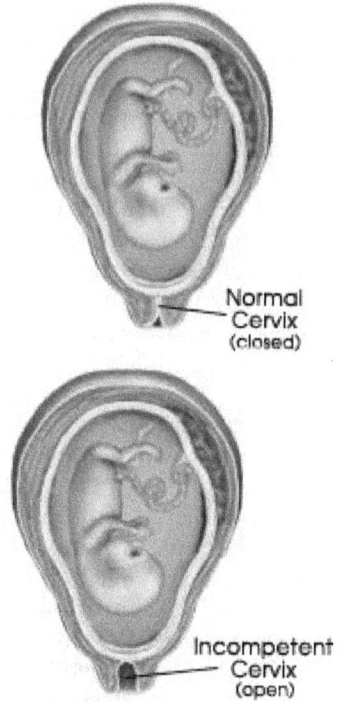

Fig. *Incompetent cervix*

Incontinence 1) Urinary incontinence is an involuntary loss of urine sufficient in quantity and/or frequency to be a social or health problem. Acute (urinary) incontinence is characterized by the sudden onset of episodes of involuntary loss of urine, and is usually associated with an acute illness or environmental factors that impair the mental or physical ability of the patient to reach a toilet or toilet substitute on time. Established urinary incontinence is characterized by repeated episodes of involuntary loss of urine not associated with an acute condition. Leakage of urine caused by chronic impairments of either mobility or mental function, marked by the inability or unwillingness of the patient to toilet himself or herself independently and a lack of sufficient help with this task, is termed functional incontinence. Leakage of small amounts of urine caused by anatomic obstruction to bladder emptying or inability of the bladder to contract is called overflow incontinence. Stress incontinence is leakage of urine, in either small or large amounts (e.g., during pregnancy or athletic activity, as intra-abdominal pressure increases). 2) Fecal incontinence is the involuntary excretion of stool sufficient in frequency to be a social or health problem.

Incontinent Partially or totally unable to control bladder and/or bowel functions.

Incubation In infectious disease, the time between infection by a disease-causing organism and the appearance of clinical symptoms of disease.

Incubation period Time during which a virus or bacteria develops in the body before symptoms appear

Incubator A box-like apparatus in which premature babies are kept at a constant and suitable temperature.

Incurred but not reported expenses (IBNR) This term refers to a financial accounting of all services that have been performed, but have not yet been invoiced or recorded.

Incurred claims A term that refers to the actual carrier liability for a specified period and includes all claims with dates of services within a specified period, usually called the experience period. Due to the time lag between dates of services and the dates claims payments are actually processed, adjustment must be made to any paid claims data to determine incurred claims.

Indemnity benefit A flat payment made directly to the policyholder, rather than to the provider for services rendered.

Indemnity health plan Similar to a fee-for-service plan in which the insurer pays for all or part of covered services that the patient chooses to purchase from health care providers.

Indemnity insurance Insurance providing a stipulated level of reimbursement for hospital/medical expenses, without regard to the actual expenses incurred during hospitalization.

Indemnity plans An insurance policy in which beneficiaries are allowed total freedom to choose their health care providers. Those providers are reimbursed a set fee each time they deliver a service. Reimbursement is usually limited to a percentage of customary and reasonable charges (which may be less than the billed amount).

Independent case management Comprehensive professional coordination of the health resources necessary to the support of the patient's diagnosis, treatment, and recovery, facilitating the ability of the patient to function with as much independence as possible through the convergence of physical, psychological, social, functional, and personal services. The case manager may organize services that are more cost-effective and appropriate to the needs of the patient that would not otherwise be covered under a beneficiary's health benefit.

Independent living Residential option where no assistance is needed with ADLs or most IADLs. A senior housing apartment complex is an example of independent living.

Independent medical evaluation An examination carried out by an impartial health care provider, generally board certified, for the purpose of resolving a dispute related to the nature and extent of an illness or injury.

Independent practice association Organization of physicians who have joined together for purposes of contracting with HMOs, PPOs, or other payers. IPA physicians continue to practice in solo settings or in groups, maintain their offices and regular practices, and usually are reimbursed on a fee-for-service basis.

Index of medical underservice (IMU) The sum of the weighted values of four indicators of unmet health care needs in an area (i.e., infant mortality rate, percent of the population 65 and older, percent of the population living in poverty, and population-to-primary care physician ratio) that is used to determine its status as a Medically Underserved Area. IMU values range from O to 100, with lower scores indicating increasing medical underservice.

Index of refraction A measure of how much a substance reduces the speed of light waves passing through it. The index of refraction (or refractive index) of a substance equals the ratio of the speed of light in a vacuum to its speed in that substance. Lenses or materials with a high index of refraction slow down and refract (bend) light more than materials with a lower refractive index.

Indian tribes Any Indian tribe, band, nation, group, Pueblo, rancheria, or community, including any Alaska Native village, group, regional or village corporation. A tribe may be federally recognized, State recognized, or self-recognized and/or federally terminated. In the context of the Federal-Indian relationship, tribes must be federally recognized in order to be eligible for the special programs and services provided by the United States to Indians because of their status as Indians.

Indigent medical care Care given by health care providers to patients who are unable to pay for it.

Indirect costs The costs that are shared by many services concurrently, for example, maintenance, administration, equipment, electricity, water.

Indirect immunofluorescence assay (IFA) A laboratory test to identify antibodies reactive against cellular antigens (e.g., HIV) in tissue sections, cells or bacterial samples, or cell suspensions, in which the antibody binds to a highly fluorescent compound (indicating the presence and position of the antigen when viewed under a fluorescent microscope).

Indirect reimbursement A situation wherein a health care practitioner can be reimbursed for his or her services, but can only obtain such reimbursement through the employing physician or health care facility.

Individual health care account A method of financing health care by giving tax advantage to individuals who establish and maintain personal accounts for health care purposes; similar to an Individual Retirement Account for retirement purposes. Also referred to as medical savings account.

Individual health care account A method of financing health care by giving tax advantage to individuals who establish and maintain personal accounts for health care purposes; similar to an Individual Retirement Account for retirement purposes.

Also referred to as medical savings account.

Individual health insurance Health services contract or insurance policy which is purchased by an individual and which covers the individual (and usually the person's dependents) in contrast to a group insurance.

Individual insurance Policies purchased without the benefit of group sponsorship that provide protection to the policyholder and/or his family. Sometimes called personal insurance.

Individual practice association (IPA) A type of HMO whose physicians usually practice in private offices and are paid by the HMO on a fee-for-service basis. Members, however, pay the HMO for coverage through cavitation payments. Also see health maintenance organization (HMO).

Individual tax credits Instead of employer or government health insurance coverage, all individuals would be required to purchase coverage directly from the insurer of choice. Individuals could participate in a group such as an Health Insurance Purchasing Cooperative (HIPC), where they can pay for their own insurance and receive a refundable tax credit to cover some portion of their health insurance costs. Low-income individuals with no tax liability may receive a voucher to purchase health insurance.

Individually underwritten groups Small employee groups that usually include no more than 50 individuals. Small group underwriting requires that individual group members provide a statement of health and evidence of insurability.

Induced abortion Induced abortion is the intentional termination of a pregnancy before the fetus can live independently. An abortion may be elective (based on a woman's personal choice) or therapeutic (to preserve the health or save the life of a pregnant woman).

Induced mutation A change in the structure of DNA or the number of chromosomes caused by exposure of the DNA to a physical or chemical agent.

Indwelling catheter A hollow, flexible tube inserted into the body to provide drainage or to administer drugs or nutrients (e.g., in the urinary system, a tube that is held in position in the bladder by a device resembling an inflated balloon).

Inert ingredient (of a pesticide) The solvent or "inactive" solid that dilutes or carries a pesticide; inert ingredients are so called because they have no effect on the targeted pest (not because they are inherently inactive). An inert ingredient as defined by EPA can, in some cases, cause adverse health effects in human beings.

Infant An infant is the very young offspring of a human. The term infant is typically applied to young children between the ages of 1 month and 12 months;

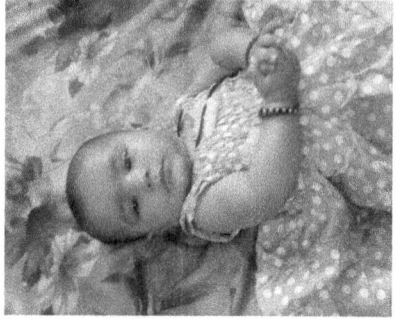

Fig. *Infant.*

however, definitions may vary between birth and 3 years of age. A newborn is an infant who is only hours, days, or up to a few weeks old. In medical contexts, newborn or neonate (from Latin, neonatus, newborn) refers to an infant in the first 28 days after birth; the term applies to premature infants, post-mature infants, and full term infants. Before birth, the term *fetus* is used.

Infant mortality Death in the first year of life, including neonatal mortality (birth to one month) and postneonatal mortality (one month to one year). About 1 percent of all babies born in the United States die in the first year of life.

Infant mortality rate Deaths in the first year of life per 1000 births. The infant mortality rate is the sum of two components: the neonatal mortality rate and the postneonatal mortality rate.

Infarction Tissue death due to the obstruction of blood to that tissue.

Infection Invasion and multiplication of pathogenic organisms, with or without clinical manifestations. The most common types of infectious organisms in human beings include bacteria, viruses, protozoa, nematodes (worms), and mycoplasma.

Infectious mononucleosis Infectious viral disease that affects the liver, respiratory system and lymphatic system.

Inferior colliculus A structure in the midbrain that is used in hearing

Inferior Lower, beneath, toward the bottom.

Inferior vena cava The inferior vena cava (or IVC), also known as the posterior vena cava. It is the large vein that carries deoxygenated blood from the lower half of the body into the right atrium of the heart. It is posterior to the abdominal cavity and runs alongside of the vertebral column on its right side (i.e. it is a retroperitoneal structure). It enters the right atrium at the lower right, back side of the heart. The IVC is formed by the joining of the left and right common iliac veins and brings blood into the right atrium of the heart.

Infertility Inability of a couple to conceive after 12 months of intercourse without contraception.

Inflammatory bowel disease Characterized by fever, pain, abscess formation, severe diarrhea, bleeding and ulceration of the intestine's mucous membrane lining. Cause is unknown. Treatment includes fluids, cortisone drugs, antibiotics, diet change and sometimes surgery.

Inflation protection An option offered on some long-term care policies which can increase the maximum daily and lifetime benefits to combat inflation. The protection is generally 5% per year, but varies from policy to

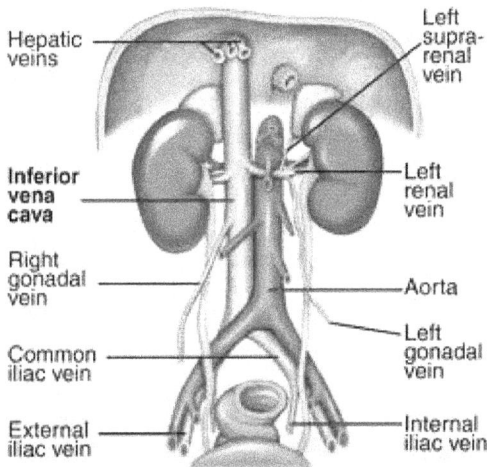

Hepatic veins
Left suprarenal vein
Inferior vena cava
Left renal vein
Right gonadal vein
Aorta
Left gonadal vein
Common iliac vein
External iliac vein
Internal iliac vein

Fig. *Inferior vena cava*

policy as to whether the increase is calculated at simple or compound interest.

Influenza Common, contagious respiratory infection caused by a virus. Incubation after exposure is 24 to 48 hours.

Informal care Care received at home from friends, neighbors or relatives who are not health care professionals. The vast majority of LTC services in the home are provided by informal caregivers.

Informal services Unpaid services provided for an impaired person by his or her relatives, friends, neighbors, or others.

Information and referral The provision of information about and referrals to specific services and sources of funding for services in a community.

Informed consent Informed consent is a legal term referring to the right of individuals to make informed medical treatment decisions. Under State law, informed consent typically includes the right to be told of one's medical condition and prognosis, the risks and benefits associated with a recommended procedure or course of treatment, and the risks and benefits of other available treatment options, including the option of refusing treatment. When a person becomes mentally incapacitated, his or her right to give or withhold informed consent typically passes to the person's legal representative, usually an agent or attorney-in-fact under a durable power of attorney, a court-appointed guardian, or a close family member.

Infusion A preparation made by soaking a plant part in hot water (or cold water, for a cold infusion); in essence, a "tea".

Ingestion Taking food, water, or medicine into the body by mouth.

Inhalant A substance that may be taken into the body through the respiratory system.

Inhalant use disorders In DSM-IV, this group includes inhalant dependence, inhalant abuse, inhalant intoxication, inhalant delirium, inhalant persisting dementia, inhalant psychotic disorder with delusions or hallucinations, inhalant mood disorder, and inhalant anxiety disorder.

In-home services Health care, long-term care, social, and other services provided in the home by a home health agency or other organization or individual.

Injection Injections are used to put medicine into the body via a syringe and a needle. A person with diabetes injects insulin by putting the needle into the tissue under the skin (called subcutaneous). Other ways of giving medicine or nourishment by injection are to put the needle into a vein (intravenous) or into a muscle (intramuscular).

Injection site rotation Changing the places on the body where a person injects insulin. Changing the injection site keeps lumps or small dents from forming in the skin. These lumps or dents are called lipodystrophies. However, people should try to use the same body area for injections that are given at the same time each day-for example, always using the stomach for the morning injection or an arm for the evening injection. Using the same body area for these routine injections lessens the possibility of changes in the timing and action of insulin.

Injection sites is an exact place within a given injection area. The injection site is the place within an area, were the needle will penetrate the skin into the subcutaneous tissue. Areas on the body where people can inject insulin most easily are:

A. The front and the outside of the thighs.

B. The abdomen, except the area around the navel. (2-inch circle).

C. The upper and outer areas of the arms.

D. The area just above the waist on the back.

E. The buttocks. These areas can vary with the size of the person.

These areas can vary with the size of the person.

In-kind resources Human, cash or other resources or capability located within an agency, organization or institution as opposed to originating in the outside environment. Often used as a match for other funds.

Inlier A patient whose length of stay or service cost resembles those of most other patients.

Innate immunity Inborn defenses against infection, including external barriers (e.g., skin, respiratory mucus, stomach acid, etc.), inflammatory response in the skin, phagocytic activity in the blood, and body substances (e.g., complement, interferon, etc.).

Innovation In the context of medical devices, any product or product modification that substantially improves the quality or decreases the cost of a product, while introducing a technology, material, or concept not previously found in any similar product on the market.

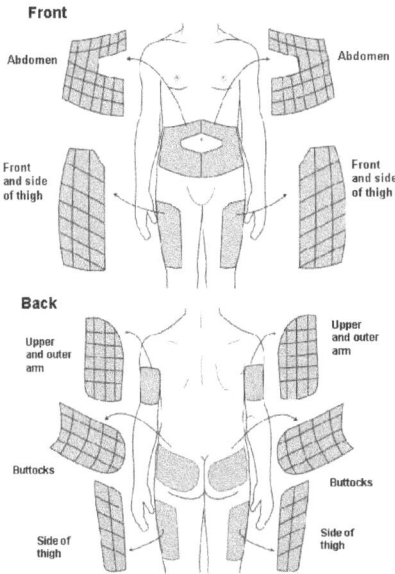

Front
Abdomen
Abdomen
Front and side of thigh
Front and side of thigh
Back
Upper and outer arm
Upper and outer arm
Buttocks
Buttocks
Side of thigh
Side of thigh

Fig.*Injection sites*

Inoculate To introduce immune serum, vaccines of various kinds, or other antigenic (foreign) materials into an individual for preventive, curative, or experimental purposes to stimulate the immune system to produce antibodies against substances and to protect against future microorganism infection.

Inoculum Material used for inoculation.

Inorganic Matter generally not containing carbon (i.e., not animal or plant matter).

Inpatient A patient who has been admitted at least overnight to a hospital or other health facility (which is, therefore, responsible for the patient's room and board) for the purpose of receiving a diagnosis, treatment, or other health services.

Inpatient care Care that includes an overnight stay in a medical facility.

Inpatient services Items and services furnished to a patient staying overnight in a hospital including bed and board, nursing and related services, diagnostic and therapeutic services, and medical or surgical services.

Insect vector An insect that can transmit a disease-producing organism from one human or animal to another.

Insecticide A substance capable of killing insects.

Insertion sequence (IS) One of a class of different nucleotide sequences found in bacteria that are capable of spontaneous movement from one chromosomal location to another. Chromosomal material may be mobilized during IS movement; movement may result in mutation at the original and/or new site(s) of insertion.

Inside limits Provisions that restrict the liability of an insurance plan. Various kinds of maximums can be imposed for specific services within a plan's overall limits. One example would be the limits on services for chemical dependency and mental illness in specific settings.

Institutional care Usually refers to nursing home or hospital care.

Institutional Review Board (IRB) A group established by an institution conducting medical research to assess the legal, ethical, and scientific aspects of that research on human subjects. IRB approval is required by the Department of Health and Human Services before proposals can receive Federal funding. IRBs must review research protocols on a regular basis, but not less than once a year.

Institutionalize To incorporate an act or practice into a structured, often formal, system.

Instrumental activities of daily living (IADLs) Activities related to independent living, such as preparing meals, doing laundry, managing money, shopping for groceries, cleaning the house, cooking, using a telephone, and taking medications.

Instrumental activities of daily living Normal day-to-day housekeeping activities such as cooking, cleaning, shopping, etc. with which functionally impaired individuals may need assistance.

Insufficient-capacity criteria: Criteria specific to primary care and dental HMSA designations that signify the inability to obtain health 'services in a timely fashion (e.g., unusually long waiting times for appointments, high percentage of area practitioners not accepting new patients).

Insulin A hormone that helps the body use glucose (sugar) for energy. The beta cells of the pancreas (in areas called the islets of Langerhans) make the insulin. When the body cannot make enough insulin on its own, a person with diabetes must inject insulin made from other sources, i.e., beef, pork, human insulin (recombinant DNA origin), or human insulin (pork-derived, semisynthetic).

Insulin allergy When a person's body has an allergic or bad reaction to taking insulin made from pork or beef or from bacteria, or because the insulin is not exactly the same as human insulin or because it has impurities. The allergy can be of two forms. Sometimes an area of skin becomes red and itchy around the place where the insulin is injected. This is called a local allergy. In another form, a person's whole body can have a bad reaction This is called a systemic allergy. The person can have hives or red patches all over the body or may feel changes in the heart rate and in the rate of breathing. A doctor may treat this allergy by prescribing purified insulins or by desensitization.

Insulin analog A synthetic modification of insulin where specific amino acids have been substituted for the natural ones at one or more places on the insulin molecule.

Insulin antagonist Something that opposes or fights the action of insulin. Insulin lowers the level of glucose (sugar) in the blood, whereas glucagon raises it; therefore, glucagon is an antagonist of insulin.

Insulin binding When insulin attaches itself to something else. This can occur in two ways. First, when a cell needs energy, insulin can bind with the outer part of the cell. The cell then can bring glucose (sugar) inside and use it for energy. With the help of insulin, the cell can do its work very well and very quickly. But sometimes the body acts against itself. In this second case, the insulin binds with the proteins that are supposed to protect the body from outside substances (antibodies). If the insulin is an injected form of insulin and not made by the body, the body sees the insulin as an outside or "foreign" substance. When the injected insulin binds with the antibodies, it does not work as well as when it binds directly to the cell.

Insulin Lispro Insulin lispro (marketed by Eli Lilly and Company as "Humalog") is a fast acting insulin analogue. Insulin lispro has one primary advantage over regular insulin for postprandial glucose control. It has a shortened delay of onset, allowing slightly more flexibility than regular insulin, which requires a longer waiting period before starting a meal after injection.

Insulin pen An insulin injection device the size of a pen that includes a needle and holds a vial of insulin. It can be used instead of syringes for giving insulin injections.

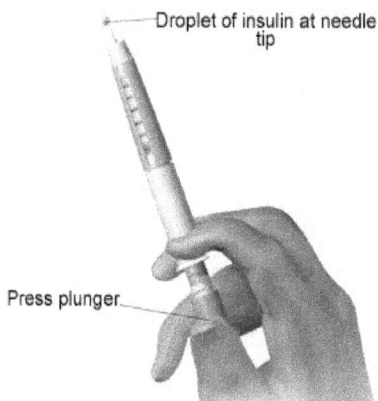

Fig. *Insulin pen*

Insulin pump A device that delivers a continuous supply of short-acting insulin into the body. The insulin flows from the pump through a plastic tube (called a catheter) that is connected to a needle inserted into the skin and taped in place. In-

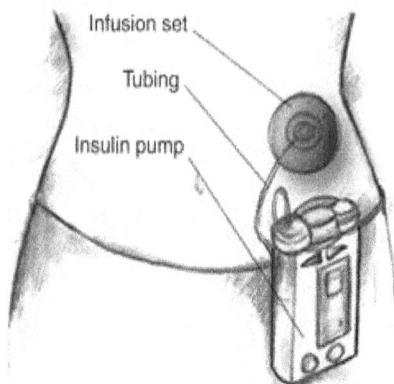

Fig. *Insulin pump.*

sulin is delivered at different rates, which can be either manually set or preprogrammed—a low, steady rate (called the basal rate) for continuous day-long coverage, and extra boosts of insulin (called bolus doses) to cover meals or when extra insulin is needed. Both the basal and bolus rates are adjustable by the user, in response to blood sugar tests done with standard methods; no available pump can measure the sugar level and calculate what changes to make in the insulin doses. The pump runs on batteries and can be worn clipped to a belt or carried in a pocket. It is usually used by people with insulin-dependent diabetes, although it is occasionally recommended for people with other forms of diabetes.

Insulin reaction Too low a level of glucose (sugar) in the blood; also called hypoglycemia. This occurs when a person with diabetes has injected too much insulin, eaten too little food, or exercised without extra food. The person may feel hungry, nauseated, weak, nervous, shaky, confused, and sweaty. Taking small amounts of sugar, sweet juice, or food with sugar will usually help the person feel better within 10-15 minutes.

Insulin receptors Areas on the outer part of a cell that allow the cell to join or bind with insulin that is in the blood. When the cell and insulin bind together, the cell can take glucose (sugar) from the blood and use it for energy.

Insulin resistance A state in which a given level of serum insulin produces a less than expected biological effect. Patients may vary from normoglycemic to severely diabetic despite large doses of insulin. Many people with Type 2 diabetes produce enough insulin, but their bodies do not respond to the action of insulin. This may happen because the person is overweight and does not respond well to insulin. Also, as people age, their body cells lose some of the ability to respond to insulin. Insulin resistance is also linked to high blood pressure and high levels of fat in the blood. Another kind of insulin resistance may rarely happen in people who take insulin injections. They may have to take very high doses of insulin every day (e.g., 200 units or more (in adults)) to bring their blood glucose down to the normal range.

This has also been called "insulin insensitivity."

Insulin sensitizer Any of several diabetes medications that reduce insulin resistance. Examples include metformin (Glucophage) and the thiazoli-dine-diones (or "glitazones") rosiglitazone (Avandia) and pioglitazone (Actos).

Insulin shock A term no longer used.

Insulin-dependent diabetes mellitus is a chronic disease characterized by hyperglycemia, impaired metabolism and storage of important nutrients, evidence of autoimmunity, and long-term vascular and neurologic complications. Insulin secretory function is limited. Cell membrane binding is not primarily involved. The goal of treatment is to relieve symptoms and to achieve blood glucose levels as close to normal as possible without severe hypoglycemia.

Insulin-induced Hypertrophy Small lumps that form under the skin when a person keeps injecting a needle in the same spot.

Insulin-induced atrophy Small dents that form on the skin when a person keeps injecting a needle in the same spot. They are harmless.

Insulinoma Benign (nonmalignant) tumor of insulin secreting cells of the islets of Langerhans in the pancreas. It results in excessive insulin production and is one of the main causes of hypoglycemia. It is a rare disease and very difficult to diagnose because symptoms are often vague and mimic neurologic and psychiatric disorders. Treatment is usually surgical removal of the tumor. Frequent high carbohydrate meals or medication may also be used.

Insulinoma A tumor of the beta cells in areas of the pancreas called the islets of Langerhans. Although not usually cancerous, such tumors may cause the body to make extra insulin and may lead to a blood glucose (sugar) level that is too low.

Insulin-resistant states Severe insulin dependent diabetes mellitus that no longer responds to treatment with insulin.

Insurance Sharing the costs of the risk of incurring losses, whether for health expenses or property and casualty losses, across a base large enough to protect any one entity against the actual costs of an incurred loss. The costs of spreading the risk are assumed to be less than the costs of an actual loss. The insured group or insurance company is at financial risk for assuming the guarantee against loss for the specific instance.

Insurance reform Changing insurance companies' practices that prevent some consumers from obtaining health care coverage.

Insurance market reform The goal of most insurance market re-

form initiatives is to materially change the nature of competition in health insurance markets by prohibiting, or severely limiting, the marketing, rating, and underwriting practices that identify and select the most favourable risks while rejecting the least favorable. Requirements that often accompany insurance market reform proposals include prohibition of experience rating in favor of modified community rating, open enrollment, use of a standard benefit package and elimination of preexisting conditions exclusions. Imposition of such regulations would have the effect of reducing the rate differential among groups, and among competing insurers. However, while premium costs would fall for some groups, they would rise for others.

Insured claims loss ratio The result of incurred claims divided by premiums. A defined time period is usually specified.

Insurer An insurance company, managed care plan, government program, or "self-funded" group responsible for providing coverage.

Integrated care An approach used to manage all aspects of health care including primary care, acute care and long term care.

Integrated delivery system Collaboration between physicians and hospitals for a variety of purposes. Some models of integration include physician-hospital organization, management-service organization, group practice without walls, integrated provider organization and medical foundation.

Integrated pest management (1PM) The use of a combination of biological and environmental measures to control vectors that transmit tropical diseases to humans or other animals. Also used in agriculture to control natural predators, parasites, and pest-resistant plants.

Integrated provider network A group of hospitals, physicians and ancillary providers which have joined together to create a system which provides comprehensive health care services through a coordinated, client-centered continuum designed to improve health care services in specified geographic markets also known as an integrated delivery system (IDS) or an integrated delivery and financing system, especially when the organization offers an insurance plan.

Intensive care Hospital service units designed to meet the special needs of patients who are seriously or critically ill or who otherwise need intense and specialized nursing care.

Intensive care units Highly specialized care requiring sophisticated technologies given to patients who are in danger of disability or death.

Intensive management A form of treatment for insulin-dependent diabetes in which the main objective is to keep blood glucose (sugar) levels as close to the normal range as possible. The treatment consists of three or more insulin injections a day or use of an insulin pump; four or more blood glucose tests a day; adjustment of insulin, food intake, and activity levels based on blood glucose test results; dietary counseling; and management by a diabetes team.

Intercostal Between the ribs.

Intercourse The penetration of the vagina with a penis. It plays a strong role in human bonding, usually being used solely for pleasure and commonly leading to stronger emotional bonds, and there are a variety of views concerning what constitutes sexual intercourse or other sexual activity.

Interim methadone A treatment program that provides methadone and HIV counseling without additional ancillary services to IV drug users (on waiting lists), until treatment space in a comprehensive program becomes available.

Intermediary The term used for Medicare contractors who process Medicare Part A claims.

Intermediate care A degree of nursing care evaluation that is less than that provided for skilled nursing care, but greater than that provided for custodial care. This level of care provides a planned, continuous program of nursing care that is preventive or rehabilitative in nature.

Intermediate care facility A facility providing an intermediate level of care to individuals who do not require the degree of care and treatment that a hospital or skilled nursing facility is designed to provide, but who do require care above the level of room and board.

Intermediate care facility for mentally tetarded persons (ICF/MR) Optional Medicaidservices which provide residential care and services for individuals with developmental disabilities.

Intermediate vision Generally refers to eyesight at approximately arm's length, used for tasks such as computer work and viewing the speedometer in a car.

Intermittent claudication Pain in the muscles of the leg that occurs off and on, usually while walking or exercising, and results in lameness (claudication). The pain results from a narrowing of the blood vessels feeding the muscle. Drugs are available to treat this condition.

Intermittent peritoneal dialysis (IPD) A form of peritoneal dialysis involving intermittent treatment three to four times per week. Typically, the patient is dialyzed for about 12 hours on each treatment.

Intermittent positive-pressure breathing therapy Form of treatment for disorders of the lungs using a sophisticated, expensive instrument that forces air into the lungs by controlled positive pressure. Treatment is usually given by a trained pulmonary therapist or technician.

Intern A physician in training in the first year after graduating from medical school.

Internal medicine Internal medicine in the United States differs from general and family practice mainly in not providing extensive training for pediatric and obstetric care and in providing more experience with severe and complex illness. General internal medicine differs from the subspecialties that have developed out of internal medicine (e.g., cardiology, oncology, hematology) by offering primary care, including first contact care and referrals to subspecialists when warranted.

Internal validity A measure of the extent to which study results reflect the true relationship of a "risk factor" (e.g., treatment or technology) to the outcome of interest in study subjects.

International classification of diseases, ninth revision, clinical modification (ICD-9-CM) coding A two-part system of coding patient medical information used in abstracting systems and for classifying patients into DRGs for Medicare. The first part is a comprehensive list of diseases with corresponding codes compatible with the World Health Organization's list of disease codes. The second part contains procedure codes, independent of the disease codes.

Internist A practitioner of internal medicine.

Interosseous membrane Uniting membrane between the tibia and fibula that forms a collagenous fibrous tissue. It has two functions—to serve as an origin for many of the muscles of the lower leg, and to transmit stress from the tibia to the fibula.

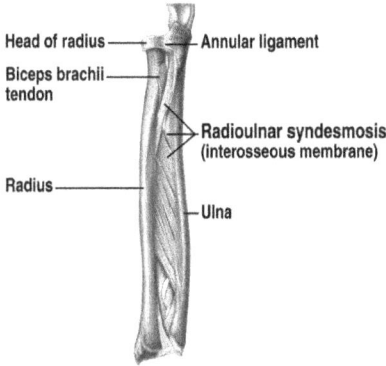

Head of radius — Annular ligament
Biceps brachii tendon
Radioulnar syndesmosis (interosseous membrane)
Radius
Ulna

Fig. *Interosseous membrane*

Interpersonal aspects of medical care The personal interaction-between patient and provider.

Interrater reliability Consistency of judgments among raters or sets of inters.

Interstate commerce Traffic, commercial trading, or the transportation of persons or property between States.

Interstitial fibrosis Formation of fibrous tissue between normal tissues.

Interstitial fluid Interstitial fluid (or tissue fluid) is a solution that bathes and surrounds the cells of multicellular animals. It is the main component of the extracellular fluid, which also includes plasma and transcellular fluid. The interstitial fluid is found in the interstitial spaces, also known as the tissue spaces.

On average, a person has about 11 liters of interstitial fluid, providing the cells of the body with nutrients and a means of waste removal.

Intervention strategy A generic term used in public health to describe a program or policy designed to have an impact on an illness or disease.

Intestinal fistula Abnormal opening leading from the intestinal

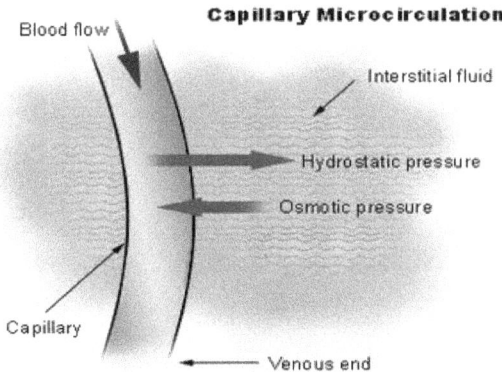

Capillary Microcirculation

Blood flow
Interstitial fluid
Hydrostatic pressure
Osmotic pressure
Capillary
Venous end

Fig. *Interstitial fluid*

tract to another abdominal organ or to the skin.

Intracervical insemination Artificial insemination technique in which sperm are placed in or near the cervical canal of the female reproductive tract, using a syringe or a catheter, for the purpose of conception.

Intracranial hemorrhage Bleeding in the brain.

Intractable pain Pain for which there is no cure.

Intracytoplasmic sperm injection An assisted conception treatment, undertaken as part of in vitro fertilisation (IVF) treatment, in which a single sperm is injected directly into the cytoplasm of an egg to achieve fertilisation.

Intraepithelial neoplasia Small tumor or cancer in the epithelial layer of the skin.

Intramuscular injection Putting a fluid into a muscle with a needle and syringe.

Intranatal care Care for a pregnant woman throughout labour.

Intraocular lens Artificial lens that a cataract surgeon places in a patient's eye after removing the eye's natural lens. Like a contact lens, it has a built-in refractive power tailored specifically to the patient's visual condition.

Intraocular pressure Eye pressure, as determined by the amount of aqueous humor filling it. High IOP (ocular hypertension) can be a sign of glaucoma.

Intrapartum care Medical care received during labor and delivery.

Intraperitoneal insemination An artificial insemination technique in which sperm are introduced into the body cavity between the uterus and the rectum, after ovulation has been induced, for the purpose of conception.

Intrarater reliability Consistency of judgments by a single inter.

Intrauterine device (IUD) A birth control method in which a small plastic or metal device is placed in a woman's uterus to prevent implantation of a fertilised egg. An intrauterine device (IUD) is

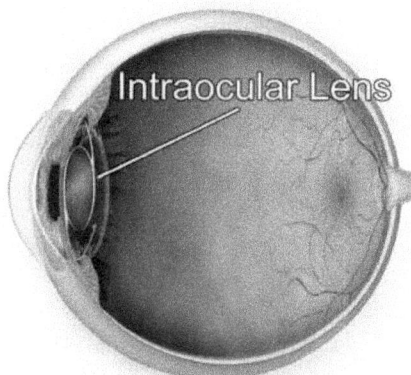

Fig. *Intraocular lens*

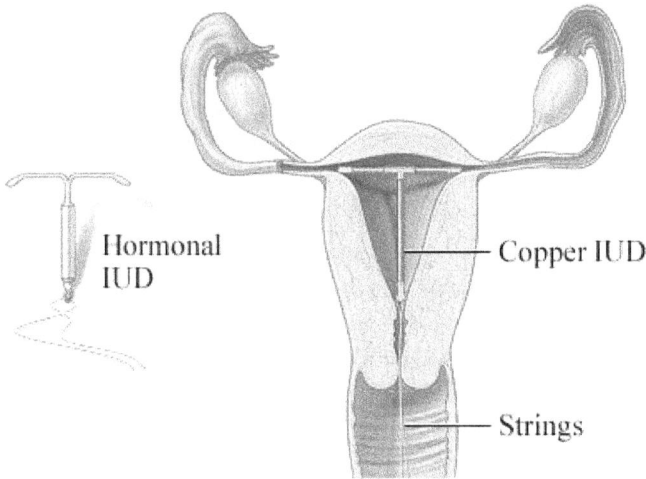

Fig. *Intrauterine device*

a small, plastic, T-shaped device that is inserted into the uterus to prevent pregnancy. IUDs contain copper or the hormone levonorgestrel (LNg). Plastic strings tied to the end of the IUD hang down through the opening of the uterus (cervix) into the vagina.

Intrauterine growth retardation The slow growth of a fetus in the uterus, possibly resulting in a low-birthweight baby.

Intrauterine insemination Artificial insemination technique in which sperm are deposited directly in the uterine cavity.

Intravenous(IV) Within a vein or veins. Intravenous (IV) medications are a solutions administered directly into the venous circulation via a syringe or intravenous catheter (tube). (ii) The actual solution that is administered intravenously. (iii) The device used to administer an intravenous solution, such as the familiar IV drip.

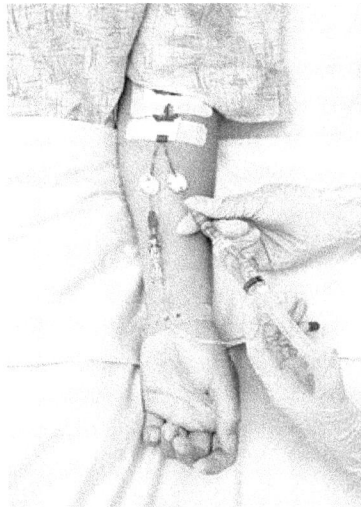

Fig. *Intravenous*

Intravenous injection Putting a fluid into a vein with a needle and syringe.

Intravenous therapies Nutrients, medications, or other treatments administered directly into the bloodstream (specifically, into a vein).

Intraventricular haemorrhage Bleeding into the cerebral ventricles, small cavities within the brain that secrete and convey cerebrospinal fluid. Common in premature babies.

Intrinsic factor levels Substance secreted by the stomach lining that is necessary for vitamin B-12 to be absorbed by the intestine. A deficiency of intrinsic factor results in pernicious anemia

Introgression The entry or introduction of a gene or genes from one population into another (most often in nature via sexual reproduction, or hybridization).

Introns The DNA sequences interrupting the protein-coding sequences of a gene that are transcribed into mRNA, but are cut out of the message before it is translated into protein. Also called intervening sequences.

Invasive medical tests Involve gaining entry into the body via a needle, tube, or hand.

Invertebrate An animal that lacks a backbone (e.g., worms, insects, and crustaceans). Invertebrates account for 90 percent of the Earth's non-plant species.

Investigational device exemption (IDE) A regulatory category and process under which the Food and Drug Administration permits limited use of an unapproved medical device in controlled settings for the purpose of collecting data on safety and effectiveness. This information may subsequently be used in support of a premarketing approval application.

Investigational new drug (IND) application An application submitted to FDA by any person or company for permission to conduct clinical research on an unapproved drug. If approved, the IND exempts the sponsor from the FDCA prohibition against shipping unapproved drugs in interstate commerce for the study or studies specifically described in the IND application.

Iodine-deficient goiter Enlarged thyroid gland due to too little iodine in the diet. Iodine is an essential trace element and is usually found in drinking water. Using small amounts of iodized table salt (if you live in an area with insufficient iodine in drinking water) prevents the occurrence of a goiter. A goiter causes a pronounced swelling in the front part of the neck.

Ion An electrically charged atom

Ipecac A syrup made from the dried rhizomes of two different species, Cephaelis ipecacuanha and C. acuminata. They contain eme-tine, cephaeline, psychotrine and other isoquinolines. Ipecac syrup is used widely as an emetic acting both locally on the gastric mucosa and centrally on the chemoreceptor trigger zone.

Iridology Diagnostic system based on the premise that every organ has a corresponding location within the iris of the eye, which can serve as an indicator of the organ's health or disease. Used by naturopaths and other practitioners, particularly when diagnosis achieved through standard methods in unclear.

Iris A pigmented membrane that lies between the cornea and the lens; it acts as a diaphragm to widen or narrow the opening called the pupil, thereby controlling the amount of light that enters the eye. It controls the amount of light that enters the eye by changing the size of the pupil

Iritis Inflammation of tissues that support the iris (the ring of colored tissue around the pupil of the eye). Symptoms include eye pain, sensitivity to light and blurred vision. May be caused by infection that spreads to the eye from other body parts, injury to the eye or an auto-immune reaction. Often cause is unknown.

Iron A mineral which works with protein in the body to make haemoglobin, essential for the blood.

Iron overload Too much iron in blood, liver or other organs.

Iron-deficiency anemia

Irritable bowel syndrome A digestive disorder that causes cramping pain and diarrhoea.

Ischemia Insufficient blood supply to meet the full physiologic needs of the tissue for oxygen (but short of the degree of Ischemla that results in necrosis), usually due to

atherosclerosis, but also due to Injury to blood vessels, muscle spasm, or inefficient pumping of the heart.

Ischemia poor blood flow. Obstructions such as clots in veins and arteries can block blood flow, depriving tissue of oxygen and nutrients. These blockages also can cause "eye strokes" and sudden vision loss.

Ischemic Condition in which there is decreased blood flow to a body organ or part.

Ischemic bowel disease Intestinal problems caused by inadequate supply of blood to the cells of the intestines.

Ischemic heart disease (IHD) A spectrum of conditions caused by insufficient oxygen supply to the heart muscle, and the leading cause of death in the United States. The most common manifestations of IHD are angina, acute myocardial infarction (heart attack), and sudden death.

Isichromosome Abnormal chromosome characterized by abnormal splitting of a chromosome during the process of duplicating itself. May cause inherited diseases or disorders.

Islet cell antibodies (ICA's) Specialized proteins, called antibodies, that are found in the blood of many people with Type 1 diabetes at the time of diagnosis. Most people with Type 1 diabetes have antibodies to a variety of islet cell proteins that are apparently released as a consequence of damage to the beta cells of the pancreas. The presence of these antibodies therefore is a useful indicator that the autoimmune process has begun. The antibodies that are presently routinely assayed include:

— IAA antiinsulin *GAD65 anti glutamic acid decarboxylase
— ICA512 a specific islet cell antibody
— EMA antiendomyseal antibodies (a test for celiac syndrome, another auto-immune disorder occurring in 5% of new-onset Type 1 diabetes)
— Anti 21-hydroxylase (a test for Addison's disease, also an autoimmune condition found in 2% of new onset Type 1 diabetes)

Islet cell transplantation Moving the beta (islet) cells from a donor pancreas and putting them into a person whose pancreas has stopped producing insulin. The beta cells make the insulin that the body needs to use glu-

cose (sugar) for energy. Although transplanting islet cells may one day help people with diabetes, the procedure is still in the research stage. Transplantation of the pancreas itself is surgically feasible, and is sometimes advised for some patients.

Islet cells (islets/islands of Langerhans) The clumps of cells within the pancreas that include those cells that make insulin and other hormones. The cells include several subvarieties, including:

— alpha cells, which make glucagon;
— beta cells, which make insulin;
— delta cells, which make somatostatin; and
— PP cells and D1 cells, about which little is known.

The islet cells appear under low-power magnification to be islands (islets) within the pancreas. First described by Dr.

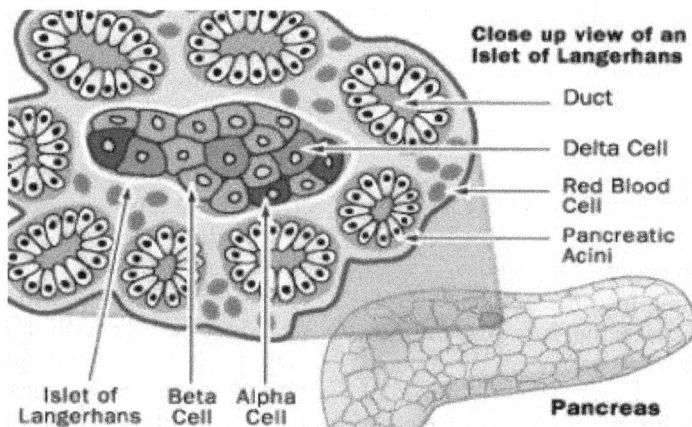

Close up view of an Islet of Langerhans

Duct

Delta Cell

Red Blood Cell

Pancreatic Acini

Islet of Langerhans   Beta Cell   Alpha Cell

Pancreas

Fig. *Islet cells*

Paul Langerhans in 1869, whose name is now associated with these islands.

Isoenzyme One of many forms of a protein catalyst differing in characteristics (chemical, physical, immunological) but catalyzing the same reaction. For example, lactate dehydrogenase may exist in five different forms.

Isograft Tissue transplanted from one identical twin to another; isografts pose no problem of rejection by the identical twin who receives the graft.

Isokinetic exercise A form of active resistive exercise in which the speed of movement of the limb is controlled by a pre-set rate-limiting device, such as Cybex, Bio-dex, etc.

Isolette Similar to an incubator

Isometric (static) Contraction A muscle contraction in which tension is developed but no mechanical work is done. There is no appreciable joint movement and the overall length of the muscle remains the same.

Isothermal infusion Injection with a fluid at the same temperature as the recipient.

Isotonic (dynamic) Contraction A concentric or eccentric muscular contraction that results in movement of a joint or body part (lifting a free weight).

IU A unit used to measure the activity of many vitamins, hormones, enzymes, and drugs. An IU is the amount of a substance that has a certain biological effect. For each substance there is an international agreement on the biological effect that is expected for 1 IU. It is also called International unit.

Infusion therapies The way that liquid solutions or liquid medications are administered directly into the blood stream through an intravenous catheter inserted in a vein in the body. Infusion therapies can include total parenteral nutrition, antibiotics or other drugs, blood, and chemotherapy.

Immunocompetence The capacity to respond immunologically to an antigen.

Immunodiagnosis A process used to detect and quantify antibodies or antigenic material in cells, serum, or biologic specimens, in the diagnosis of infections or other disorders.

J

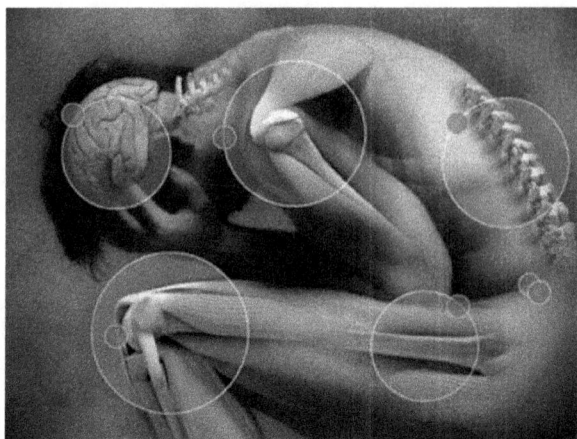

Jaagsiekte A contagious, neo-plastic, pulmonary disease of sheep characterized by hyperplasia and hypertrophy of pneumocytes and epithelial cells of the lung. It is caused by ovine pulmonary adenocarcinoma virus.

Jackknife seizure An epileptic syndrome characterized by the triad of infantile spasms, hypsar-rhythmia, and arrest of psycho-motor development at seizure onset. The majority present between 3-12 months of age, with spasms consisting of combinations of brief flexor or extensor movements of the head, trunk, and limbs. The condition is divided into two forms: cryptogenic (idiopathic) and symptomatic (secondary to a known disease process such as intrauterine infections; nervous system abnormalities; brain diseases, metabolic, inborn; prematurity; perinatal asphyxia; tuberous sclerrosis; etc.).

Jackson tracheostomy Tube Trademark for a silver tracheostomy tube with a rubber cuff built onto the tube. The design is intended to prevent accidental migration of the cuff off the end of the tube, causing interference with airflow to the patient.

Jacobson organ An accessory chemoreceptor organ that is separated from the main olfactory mucosa. It is situated at the base of nasal septum close to the vomer and nasal bones. It forwards chemical signals (such as Pheromones) to the central nervous system, thus influencing reproductive and social behaviour. In humans, most of its

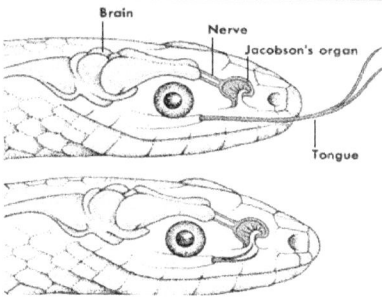

Fig. *Jacobson organ*

structures except the vome-
ronasal duct undergo regression after birth.

Jadassohn swebaceous nevus A
Syndrome characterized by lesions occurring on the Face,
Scalp, or neck which consist of
congenital hypoplastic malformations of cutaneous structures
and which over Time undergo
verrucous Hyperplasia. Additionally it is associated with
neurological symptoms and
skeletal, ophthalmological,
urogenital, and Cardiovascular
Abnormalities.

Jail fever The classic form of typhus, caused by Rickettsia
prowazekii, which is transmitted from man to man by the
Louse Pediculus humanus
corporis. This Disease is characterized by the sudden onset
of intense Headache, malaise,
and generalized myalgia followed by the formation of a
macular Skin eruption and vascular and neurologic disturbances.

Jacutin An organochlorine insecticide that has been used as a
pediculicide and a scabicide. It

has been shown to cause cancer.

Jaeger card Card with printed letters of varying sizes. Used to test
vision.

Japanese B Encephalitis A Mos-
quito-borne Encephalitis caused
by the Japanese B Encephalitis
Virus (Encephalitis Virus, Japanese) occurring throughout
Eastern Asia and Australia. The
majority of Infections occur in
Children and are subclinical or
have features limited to transient Fever and gastrointestinal
symptoms. Inflammation of the
Brain, spinal cord, and Meninges may occur and Lead to transient or permanent neurologic
deficits (including a Poliomyeli-
tis-like presentation); Seizures;
Coma; and Death.

Jaundice A clinical manifestation
of hyperbilirubinemia, consisting of deposition of bile pigments in the skin, resulting in a
yellowish staining of the skin
and mucous membranes. It is a
symptom of diseases of the liver
and blood caused by abnormally elevated amounts of
bilirubin in the blood. New-

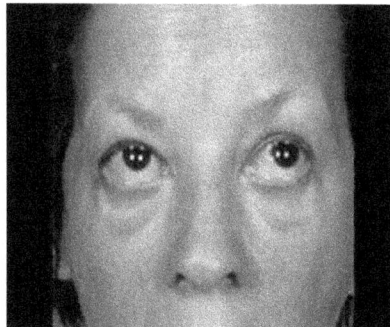

Fig. *Jaundice*

born jaundice usually begins on the second or third day of life and starts disappearing when the baby is 7-10 days old. It is sometimes corrected by special light treatment but it is harmless and soon passes.

Jaundice Yellow colouring in the skin and eyes caused by high levels of a pigment called bilirubin. Jaundice is associated with a variety of conditions involving the liver, gallbladder and bile ducts, including hepatitis and cirrhosis.

Jaundice, Neonatal A transient unconjugated hyperbilirubinemia that occurs between the second and fifth days of life because the hepatic enzyme Glucurono-syltransferase required for Bilirubin detoxification is inadquedate.

Jaundices, hemolytic Anemia due to decreased life span of erythrocytes.

Jaw Bony structure of the Mouth that holds the Teeth. It consists of the Mandible and the Maxilla.

Jaw cyst Saccular lesions lined with epithelium and contained within pathologically formed cavities in the jaw; also nonepithelial cysts (pseudo-cysts) as they apply to the jaw, e.g., traumatic or solitary cyst, static bone cavity, and aneurysmal bone cyst. True jaw cysts are classified as odontogenic or nonodontogenic.

Jaw abnormality Congenital absence of or defects in structures of the jaw.

Jaw Bony structure of the mouth that holds the teeth. It consists of the Mandible and the Maxilla.

Jaw fixation technique The stable placement of surgically induced fractures of the mandible or maxilla through the use of elastics, wire ligatures, arch bars, or other splints. It is used often in the cosmetic surgery of retrognathism and prognathism.

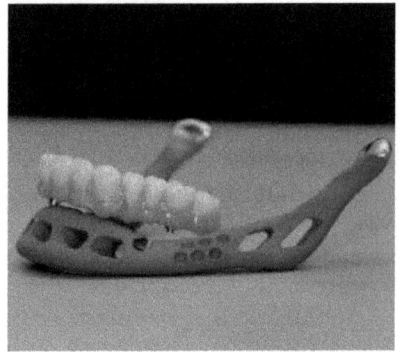

Fig. *Jaw fixation technique*

Jaw thrust maneuver The jaw thrust maneuver is a method of maintaining an open airway of an unconscious individual. Jaw thrust is used to open the mouth and lift the tongue which obstructs the patency of the airway. It is usually performed by placing on each side of the face, the index and middle fingers at the angle of the mandible. The thumbs are placed on the chin just below the lower lip. As the mouth is opened by exerting downward force on the chin, the index and middle fingers would lift the entire mandible anterior thus moving the base of the tongue out of obstruction.

JC polyomavirus A species of Polyomavirus, originally isolated from the brain of a patient with progressive multifocal leukoencephalopathy. The patient's initials J.C. gave the virus its name. Infection is not accompanied by any apparent illness but serious demyelinating disease can appear later, probably following reactivation of latent virus.

Jejunum The long, coiled mid-section of the small intestine; it is between the duodenum and the ileum.

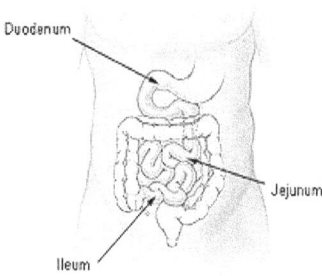

Fig. *Jejunum*

Jelly, Wharton Jelly-like connective tissue of the umbilical cord that contains mesenchymal stromal cells.

Jet injection The injection of solutions into the skin by compressed air devices so that only the solution pierces the skin.

Jet injector A device that uses high pressure to propel insulin through the skin and into the body. When used properly, injections are painless. However, the devices are more compli-

cated to use than a syringe and often require cleaning.

Jin shindo developed by a psychotherapist, it combines accupressure, Taoist yogic breathing and Reichian segmental theory (addresses how emotional tension affects the physical body) with the goal of releasing physical and emotional tension and armoring. Aims to promote a state in which the patient can address the emotional factors that underlie various physical conditions.

JME (Juvenile Myoclonic Epilepsy) A disorder characterized by the onset of Myoclonus in Adolescence, a marked increase in the Incidence of Absence Seizures, and generalized major motor Seizures. The myoclonic episodes tend to occur shortly after awakening. Seizures tend to be aggravated by Sleep Deprivation and Alcohol Consumption. Hereditary and sporadic Forms have been identified.

Jo 1 antigen An enzyme that activates Histidine with its specific Transfer RNA.

Job-lock The inability of individuals to change jobs because they would lose crucial health benefits.

Johne disease A chronic Gastroenteritis in Ruminants caused by Mycobacterium avium subspecies paratuberculosis.

Joint stiffness It is a common characteristic of arthritis. Joint stiffness can be one of the earliest symptoms of arthritis, a sign that you should see a doctor for

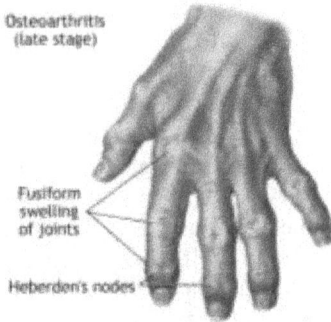

Fig. *Joint stiffness*

a thorough physical examination and accurate diagnosis. It is caused by inflammation in the synovium, the lining of the joint. The abnormal synovial lining is the cause of many types of arthritis. The only physical expression of synovial involvement may be joint pain, or there may be swelling, redness, and warmth associated with the affected joint. Joint stiffness can be a warning sign of an underlying problem that should be treated. A doctor should investigate any persistent stiffness. Heat application can often relieve stiffness and pain. People with morning stiffness due to rheumatoid arthritis or other rheumatic problems frequently feel better if they take a hot bath or shower just after getting out of bed.

Joint capsule The sac enclosing a joint. It is composed of an outer fibrous articular capsule and an inner synovial membrane.

Joint deformities, acquired Deformities acquired after birth as the result of injury or disease. The joint deformity is often associated with rheumatoid Arthritis and leprosy.

Joint temporomandibular TMJ is a synovial joint between condyle of the mandible an mandibular fossa on the under-surface of the squamous part of the temporal bone. The mandible is the single bone with the hori-

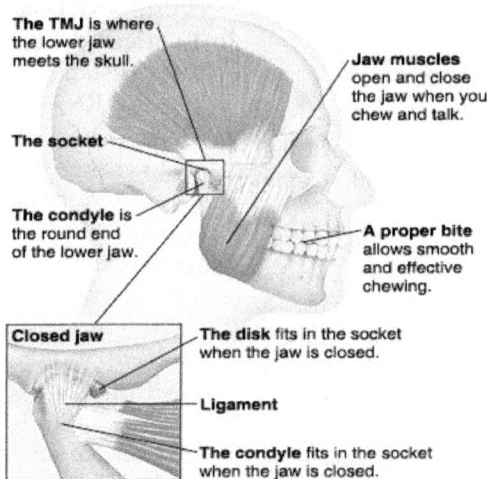

Fig. *Joint temporomandibular*

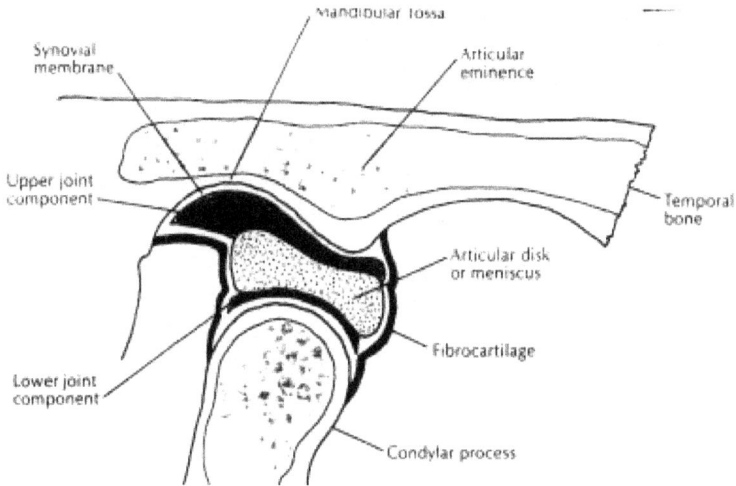

Fig. *Joint disc, temporomandibular*

zontal horse shoe shaped body, which is continuous at its posterior ends with a pair of vertical rami, each ramus is surmounted by a head or condyle. The temporomandibular joint allows opening and closing the mouth and complex chewing or side to side movements of the lower jaw.

Joint disc, temporomandibular A plate of fibrous tissue that divides the temporomandibular joint into an upper and lower cavity. The disc is attached to the articular capsule and moves forward with the condyle in free opening and protrusion.

Joint dysfunction syndrome temporomandibular (TMJD) is a broad term that refers to the dysfunction of the articulation between the mandible and the cranium – aka the TMJ or temporomandibular joint. TMJD is not exclusively a disorder of the bony structures, but may also be a result of hypertonic muscles which affect the joint and therefore cause symptoms.

Joint flexibility The distance and direction to which a bone joint can be extended. Range of motion is a function of the condition of the joints, muscles, and connective tissues involved. joint flexibility can be improved through appropriate muscle stretching exercises.

Joint instabilities Lack of stability of a joint or joint prosthesis. Fac-

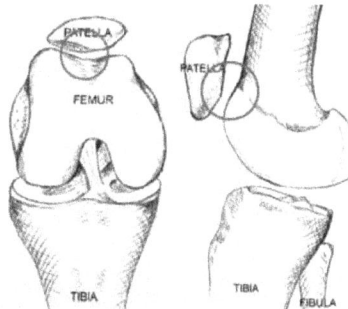

Fig. *Joint instabilities*

tors involved are intra-articular disease and integrity of extra-articular structures such as joint capsule, ligaments, and muscles.

Joint loose bodies Fibrous, bony, cartilaginous and osteocartilaginous fragments in a synovial joint. Major causes are osteochondritis dissecans, synovial chondromatosis, osteophytes, fractured articular surfaces and damaged menisci.

Joint pains can be caused by injury affecting any of the ligaments, bursae, or tendons surrounding the joint. Injury can also affect the ligaments, cartilage, and bones within the joint. Pain is also a feature of joint inflammation (arthritis) and infection, and can be a feature of tumours of the joint. Joint pain is also referred to as *arthralgia*.

Joint prostheses Prostheses used to partially or totally replace a Human or Animal joint.

Joint venture relationship in which two or more parties enter into a business as co-owners of a specific project(s) to share in profits and losses.

Joint venture, hospital physician A formal financial agreement made between one or more Physicians and a Hospital to provide ambulatory alternative services to those Patients who do not require Hospitalization.

Joint, acetabulofemoral The joint that is formed by the articulation of the head of Femur and the Acetabulum of the Pelvis.

Joint, ankle The joint that is formed by the inferior articular and malleolar articular surfaces of the Tibia; the malleolar articular surface of the Fibula; and the medial malleolar, lateral malleolar, and superior surfaces of the Talus.

Joint, carpal The articulations between the various carpal bones. This does not include the Wrist Joint which consists of the articulations between the radius; ulna; and proximal carpal Bones.

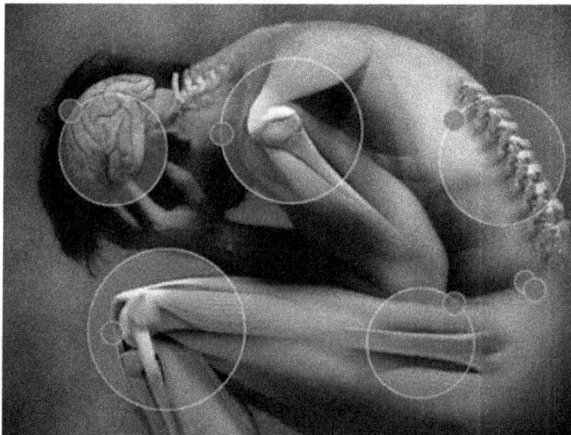

Fig. *Joint pains*

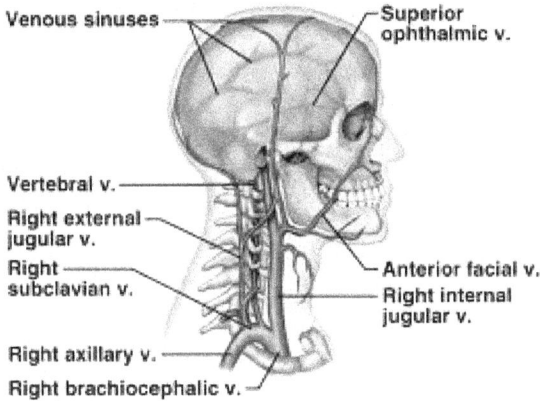

Fig. *Jugular veins*

Jugular veins Veins in the neck which drain the brain, face, and neck into the brachiocephalic or subclavian veins. The jugular veins are veins that bring deoxygenated blood from the head back to the heart via the superior vena cava.

Junctional nevus A type of nevus (mole) found at the junction (border) between the epidermis (outer) and the dermis (inner) layers of the skin. These moles may be coloured and slightly raised.

Juvenile justice facility Includes— (i) juvenile correctional facilities (facilities that hold juveniles after adjudication and are for the purpose of long-term commitment or placement for supervision and treatment); and (ii) juvenile detention facilities (facilities that are usually called juvenile detention centers or juvenile halls, and hold juveniles pending adjudication or after adjudication and awaiting disposition or placement). Both ju-venile correctional and juvenile detention facilities can be public (i.e., under the direct administration and operational control of a State or local government and staffed by governmental employees) or private (i.e., either profitmaking or nonprofit and subject to governmental licensing but under the direct administration and operational control of private enterprise; private facilities may receive substantial public funding in addition to support from private sources).

Juvenile justice system: The juvenile justice system includes law enforcement officers and othes who refer delinquent and maltreated juveniles to the courts, juvenile courts which apply sanctions for delinquent offenses and oversee the execution of child protective services, juvenile detention and connectional facilities, and, less frequently, agencies that provide protective services and care (e.g., foster care) for juvenile victims of abuse and neglect. The latter agencies intersect with the child welfare or social services system.

Juvenile myelomonocytic leukemia A rare form of childhood leukemia in which cancer cells often spread into tissues such as the skin, lung, and intestines.

Juvenile neurosyphilis Infections of the central nervous system caused by trponema pallidum which present with a variety of clinical syndromes. The initial phase of infection usually causes a mild or asymptomatic menin-geal reaction. The meningo-vascular form may present acutely as brain-infraction. The infection may also remain subclinical for several years. Late syndromes include-general paresis; tabes dorsalis; meningeal syphilis; syphilitic optic atrophy; and spinal syphilis. General paresis is characterized by progressive dementia; dysarthria; tremor; myoclonus; sezures; and Argyll-Robertson pupils.

Juvenile onset diabetes Former term for insulin-dependent or type 1 diabetes.

Juvenile parkinsonism A group of disorders which feature impaired motor control characterized by bradykinesia, muscle rigidity; tremor; and postural instability. Parkinsonian diseases are generally divided into primary parkinsonism, secondary parkinsonism and inherited forms. These conditions are associated with dysfunction of dopami-nergic or closely related motor integration neuronal pathways in the basal ganglia.

Juvenile pilocytic astrocytoma A slow-growing type of central nervous system tumour that forms from glial (supportive) tissue of the brain and spinal cord. Juvenile pilocytic astrocytoma usually occurs in children and young adults. It forms in the brain more often than the spinal cord.

Juvenile rickets A condition in children in which bones become soft and deformed because they don't have enough calcium and phosphorus. It is caused by not having enough vitamin D in the diet or by not getting enough sunlight. In adults, this condition is called osteomalacia. Also called infantile rickets, rachitis, and rickets.

Juvenile temporal arteritis A systemic autoimmune vasculitis occurring primarily in people over the age of 50. Pathologic features include a necrotizing pan-arteritis including granulomas and giant cells. There is a predilection for involvement of central nervous system blood vessels and the most frequent neurologic complication is an optic neuro-pathy, ischemic. Large blood vessels may become involved, including the aorta. Clinical manifestations may include myalgias, weight loss, headache, visual loss, necrosis of the skin or tongue, and chest discomfort. Superfi-

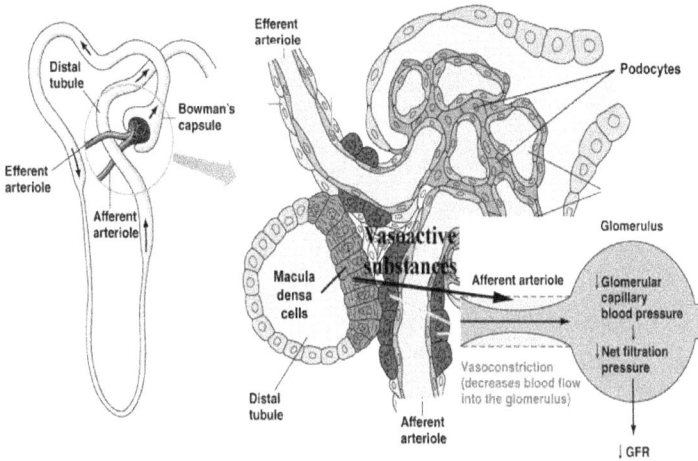

Fig. *Juxtaglomerular apparatus*

cial scalp arteries may become tender and enlarged. A related condition, juvenile temporal arteritis, tends to occur in the first or second decade of life.

Juvenile xanthoma Benign disorder of infants and children characterized by multiple nodules with lipid-laden, non-Langerhans-cell histiocytes.

Juxtacortical osteosarcoma A form of osteogenic sarcoma of relatively low malignancy, probably arising from the periosteum and initially involving cortical bone and adjacent connective tissue. It occurs in middle-aged as well as young adults and most commonly affects the lower part of the femoral shaft.

Juxtaglomerular apparatus The juxtaglomerular apparatus is a complex of structures associated with the vascular pole of each renal corpuscle. The juxtaglomerular apparatus has two principal components:

— The macula densa is a patch of densely-packed epithelial cell nuclei along the distal convoluted tubule, adjacent to the afferent arteriole at the vascular pole of the corpuscle from which the tubule arose. It may function as a sensor for sodium and/or chloride concentration.

— Juxtaglomerular cells ("J-G cells") in the wall of the afferent arteriole are specialized smooth muscle cells containing secretory granules, the source of the hormone renin.

— The juxtaglomerular region also includes extra-glomerular mesangial cells, also called lacis cells or cells of Goormaghtigh.

The juxtaglomerular apparatus is thought to participate in the regulation of blood flow through the glomerular capillaries (and hence the rate of urine formation).

K

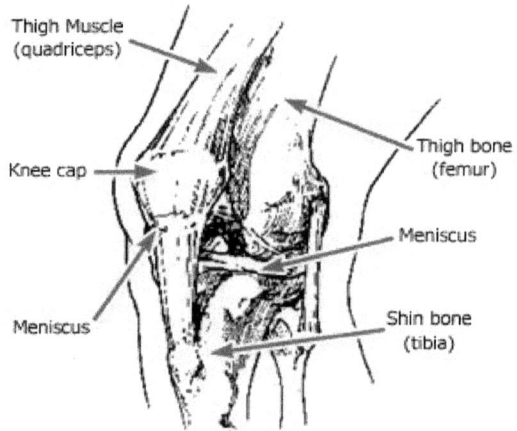

Thigh Muscle (quadriceps)

Knee cap

Meniscus

Thigh bone (femur)

Meniscus

Shin bone (tibia)

K

K cell Lymphocyte-like effector cells which mediate antibody-dependent cell cytotoxicity. They kill antibody-coated target cells which they bind with their Fc receptors.

K receptors, neuromedin A class of cell surface receptors for tachykinins that prefers neurokinin B (neurokinin beta, neuromedin K) over other tachykinins. Neurokinin-3 (NK-3) receptors have been cloned and are members of the G-protein coupled receptor super-family. They have been found in the central nervous system and in peripheral tissues.

Kabikinase Streptococcal fibrinolysin An enzyme produced by hemolytic streptococci. It hydro-lyzes amide linkages and serves as an activator of plasminogen. It is used in thrombolytic therapy and is used also in mixtures with strepto-dornase (streptodornase and streptokinase).

Kadipiro virus A genus of reviridae infecting Ixodidae ticks and transmitted by them to humans, deer, and small animals. The type species is colorado tick fever virus.

Kahler disease A type of cancer that begins in plasma cells (white blood cells that produce antibodies). Also called multiple myeloma, myelomatosis, and plasma cell myeloma.

Kahn test Serologic tests for syphilis.

Kala-azar A chronic disease caused by Leishmania donovani and transmitted by the bite of several sandflies of the genera *Phlebotomus* and *Lutzomyia*. It is commonly charac-

277

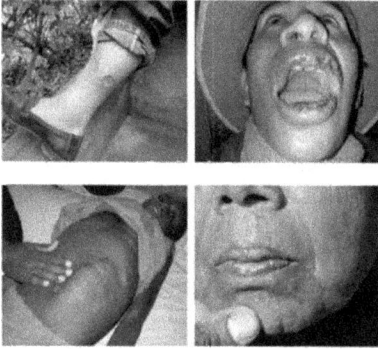

Fig. *Kala-azar*

terized by fever, chills, vomiting, anemia, hepato-spleno-megaly, leukopenia, hyper-gamma-globulinemia, emaciation, and an earth-gray color of the skin. The disease is classified into three main types according to geographic distribution—Indian, Mediterranean (or infantile), and African.Kala-azar is a vector-borne disease. Rodents are reservoir hosts and humans are incidental hosts for Leishma-niasis or Kala-azar .

Kaletra A combination of the drugs ritonavir and lopinavir. It is used to treat infection with HIV (the virus that causes AIDS). It is also being studied in the treatment of some types of cancer. Kaletra blocks the ability of HIV to make copies of itself and may help other anticancer drugs work better or may block the growth of cancer cells. Ritonavir blocks the breakdown of lopinavir. Kaletra is a type of anti-HIV agent and a type of protease inhibitor. Also called lopinavir/ ritonavir.

Kallidin A decapeptide brady-kinin homolog cleaved from kininogen by kallikreins. It is a smooth-muscle stimulant and hypotensive agent that acts by vasodilatation.

Kanpo Medicine System of herbal medicine practiced in Japan by both herbalists and practitioners of modern medicine. Kampo originated in China and is based on Chinese herbal medicine

Kaposi sarcoma karenitecin A drug being studied in the treatment of cancer. It is a type of topoisomerase inhibitor. It is related to the anticancer drug camptothecin.

Kaposi's sarcoma A multifocal, spreading cancer of connective tissue, principally involving the skin; it usually begins on the toes or the feet as reddish blue or brownish soft nodules and tumors. Previously seen in older men of Jewish or Mediterranean descent, Kaposi's sarcoma is now one of the opportunistic diseases occurring in AIDS patients.

KARMA Basic concept common to Hinduism, Buddhism, and Jainism. The doctrine holds that one's state in this life is the result of physical and mental actions in past incarnations and that present action can determine one's destiny in future incarnations. Karma is a natural, impersonal law of moral cause and effect.

Karnofsky performance status A standard way of measuring the ability of cancer patients to perform ordinary tasks. The Karnofsky Performance scores range from 0 to 100. A higher score means the patient is better able to carry out daily activities. KPS may be used to determine a patient's prognosis, to measure changes in a patient's ability to function, or to decide if a patient could be included in a clinical trial. Also called KPS.

Karotyping Determining the chromosome constitution of the nucleus of a cell. Useful in predicting abnormalities in a fetus before birth, using amniotic fluid to study cells.

Karyotype A photomicrograph of an individual's chromosomes arranged in a standard format, showing the number, size, and shape of each chromosome.

Keclor Semisynthetic, broad-spectrum antibiotic derivative of cephalexin.

Kegel exercises Exercises that may be used to strengthen the muscles surrounding the vagina. The pelvic floor muscles support the bladder, bowel and uterus. Kegel exercises are good preparation for childbirth and can help prevent urinary incontinence. It is a series of repetitive contractions of muscles of the pelvis maintain pelvic structure and to prepare for childbirth; also used in the incontinence in females. and vaginal wall to help management of stress. The role of these exercises is to reinforce the pelvic muscles. Results are visible after about 2-3 months of practice. The doctor is the one who guides patients on how to execute these exercises correctly. Unfortunately, one in three women use this technique without being guided.

Fig. *Kegel exercises*

Keloid Overgrowth of scar tissue at the site of a wound on the skin. Keloids are firm, rubbery lesions or shiny, fibrous nodules, and can vary from pink to flesh-coloured or red to dark brown in colour. A keloid scar is benign and not contagious, but sometimes accompanied by severe itchiness, pain, and changes in texture. In severe cases, it can affect movement of skin.

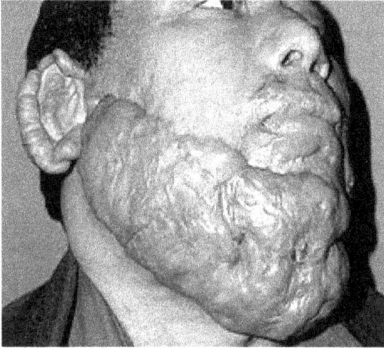

Fig. *Keloid*

Kemstro A drug that is used to treat certain types of muscle spasms and is being studied in the treatment of liver cancer. Kemstro relaxes muscles by blocking certain nerve receptors in the spinal cord. It is a type of antispasmodic. Also called baclofen and Lioresal.

Kepivance A form of keratinocyte growth factor (KGF) that is made in the laboratory. KGF stimulates the growth of cells that line the surface of the mouth and intestinal tract. Kepivance is used to prevent and treat oral mucositis (mouth sores) caused by high-dose chemotherapy and radiation therapy in leukemia and lymphoma. It is also being studied in the prevention and treatment of oral mucositis and dysphagia (difficulty swallowing) in other types of cancer. Kepivance is a type of recombinant human kera-tinocyte growth factor. Also called palifermin.

Keppra A drug used to treat seizures (involuntary muscle movements) caused by epilepsy (a group of brain disorders). Keppra is being studied in the treatment of seizures in patients with cancer that has spread to the brain. It is a type of anticonvulsant. .

Keratan sulfate A glyco-saminoglycan (a type of polysaccharide) found in cartilage and in the cornea of the eye.

Keratectomy Surgical removal of part of the cornea.

Keratectomy, photorefractive PRK, is a type of laser eye surgery used to correct mild to moderate nearsightedness, farsightedness, and/or astigmatism.

All laser vision correction surgeries work by reshaping the cornea, or clear front part of the eye, so that light traveling through it is properly focused onto the retina located in the back of the eye. There are a number of different surgical techniques used to reshape the cornea. During PRK, an eye surgeon uses a laser to reshape the cornea. This laser, which delivers a cool pulsing beam of ultraviolet light, is used on the

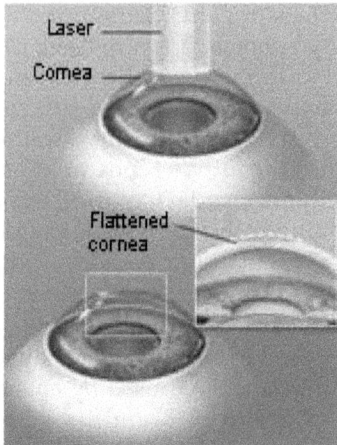

Fig. *Keratectomy, photorefractive*

surface of the cornea, not underneath the cornea, as in *lasik*.

Keratinocyte growth factor A natural substance that stimulates the growth of epithelial cells in the skin and in the lining of the mouth, stomach, and intestines. A form of keratinocyte growth factor made in the laboratory is called recombinant human keratinocyte growth factor. Also called KGF.

keratitis Inflammation of the cornea, caused by an infection or inflammatory process. Symptoms include eye pain or discomfort, light sensitivity, foreign body sensation, grittiness and tearing.

Keratoacanthoma A rapidly growing, dome-shaped skin tumor that usually occurs on sun-exposed areas of the body, especially around the head and neck. Keratoacanthoma occurs more often in males. Although in most patients it goes away

on its own, in a few patients it comes back. Rarely, it may spread to other parts of the body.

keratoconjunctivitis sicca Also called dry eye syndrome. Chronic lack of sufficient lubrication and moisture in the eye.

keratoconjunctivitis Inflammation of the cornea and conjunctiva.

keratoconus Degeneration and thinning of the cornea resulting in a cone-shaped bulge (a type of irregular astigmatism). The cause is unknown, but may be genetic. The first symptom is blurred vision that doesn't improve enough with glasses (contacts usually work well for a while). You may also have double vision or distorted vision.

keratometer An instrument that measures the curvature of the eye's clear, front surface (cornea). Keratometers help eye doctors collect information for contact lens fittings and surgical procedures. With keratometry, reflected images also can help identify dry eyes.

keratoplasty Any of several types of corneal surgery, such as shrinking the collagen to reduce farsightedness or transplanting a new cornea to treat keratoconus.

Keratosis Any horny growth, such as a wart.

Keratosis follicularis Uncommon hereditary skin disorder characterized by small, horny growths that grow together to form brown or black, crusted, wart-like patches. They can

281

spread rapidly, ulcerate and become covered with pus. Treatment includes large doses of vitamin-A by mouth, vitamin-A acid cream applied to lesions and sometimes steroids taken by mouth or applied to the skin.

Ketalar A drug used to cause a loss of feeling and awareness and to induce sleep in patients having surgery. It is also being studied in the treatment of nerve pain caused by chemotherapy. Keta-lar blocks pathways to the brain that are involved in sensing pain. It is a type of general anesthetic. Also called ketamine and ketamine hydrochloride.

Ketamine A drug used to cause a loss of feeling and awareness and to induce sleep in patients having surgery. It is also being studied in the treatment of nerve pain caused by chemotherapy. Ketamine blocks pathways to the brain that are involved in sensing pain. It is a type of general anesthetic. Also called Ketalar and ketamine hydrochloride.

Ketoacidosis Serious disorder that results from a deficiency or inadequate use of carbohydrates. Characterized by fluid and electrolyte disorders, dehydration and mental confusion. If left untreated, coma and death may occur. It is usually a complication of diabetes mellitus but may also be seen in starvation and rarely in pregnancy if diet is inadequate.

Ketoconazole A drug that treats infection caused by a fungus. It is also used as a treatment for prostate cancer because it can block the production of male sex hormones.

Ketone A type of chemical substance used in perfumes, paints, solvents, and found in essential oils (scented liquid taken from plants). Ketones are also made by the body when there is not enough insulin.

Ketone bodies Chemicals that the body makes when there is not enough insulin in the blood and it must break down fat for its energy. Ketone bodies can poison and even kill body cells. When the body does not have the help of insulin, the ketones build up in the blood and then "spill" over into the urine so that the body can get rid of them. The body can also rid itself of one type of ketone, called acetone, through the lungs. This gives the breath a fruity odor. Ketones that build up in the body for a long time lead to serious illness and coma.

Ketonuria Presence of ketone bodies in the urine. Usually seen in people with uncontrolled diabetes mellitus or as a result of starvation.

Ketorolac A drug that belongs to a family of drugs called nonsteroidal anti-inflammatory agents. It is being studied in cancer prevention.

Ketosis A condition of having ketone bodies build up in body tissues and fluids. The signs of ketosis are nausea, vomiting, and stomach pain. Ketosis can lead to ketoacidosis.

Ketotic hypoglycemia A poorly-understood disorder of childhood, marked by hypoglycemia and ketosis. There is carbohydrate deprivation, with consequent dependence on fat stores for energy. Ketotic hypoglycemia can often be effectively treated by simple dietary changes involving frequent feedings of carbohydrate and protein.

Keyhole limpet hemocyanin KGF A natural substance that stimulates the growth of epithelial cells in the skin and in the lining of the mouth, stomach, and intestines. A form of KGF made in the laboratory is called recombi-nant human keratinocyte growth factor. Also called keratinocyte growth factor.

Khellin A vasodilator that also has bronchodilatory action. It has been employed in the treatment of angina pectoris, in the treatment of asthma, and in conjunction with ultraviolet light A, has been tried in the treatment of vitiligo.

Khloditan A derivative of the insecticide DDD that specifically inhibits cells of the adrenal cortex and their production of hormones. It is used to treat adrenocortical tumors and causes CNS damage, but no bone marrow depression.

Kidney One of a pair of organs in the abdomen. Kidneys remove waste from the blood (as urine), produce erythropoietin (a substance that stimulates red blood cell production), and play a role in blood pressure regulation. The kidneys and urinary system help to excrete the waste products and also keep chemicals, such as potassium and so-

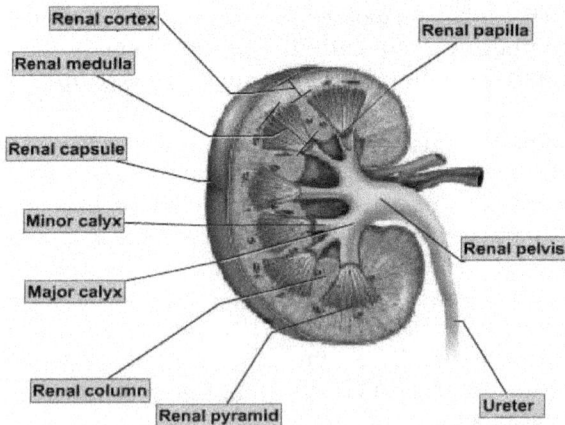

Fig. *Kidney*

dium, and water in balance by removing a type of waste, called urea, from the blood. Urea is produced when foods containing protein, such as meat, poultry, and certain vegetables, are broken down in the body. Urea is carried in the bloodstream to the kidneys. The kidneys also control the fluid and acid-base balance in the body

Kidney cancer that forms in tissues of the kidneys. Kidney cancer includes renal cell carcinoma (cancer that forms in the lining of very small tubes in the kidney that filter the blood and remove waste products) and renal pelvis carcinoma (cancer that forms in the center of the kidney where urine collects). It also includes Wilms tumor, which is a type of kidney cancer that usually develops in children under the age of 5.

Kidney disease Any one of several chronic conditions that are caused by damage to the cells of the kidney. People who have had diabetes for a long time may have kidney damage. Also called nephropathy.

Kidney failure A condition in which the kidneys stop working and are not able to remove waste and extra water from the blood or keep body chemicals in balance. Acute or severe kidney failure happens suddenly (for example, after an injury) and may be treated and cured. Chronic kidney failure develops over many years, may be caused by conditions like high blood pressure or diabetes, and cannot be cured. Chronic kidney failure may lead to total and long-lasting kidney failure, called end-stage renal disease (ESRD). A person in ESRD needs dialysis (the process of cleaning the blood by passing it through a membrane or filter) or a kidney transplant. Also called renal failure.

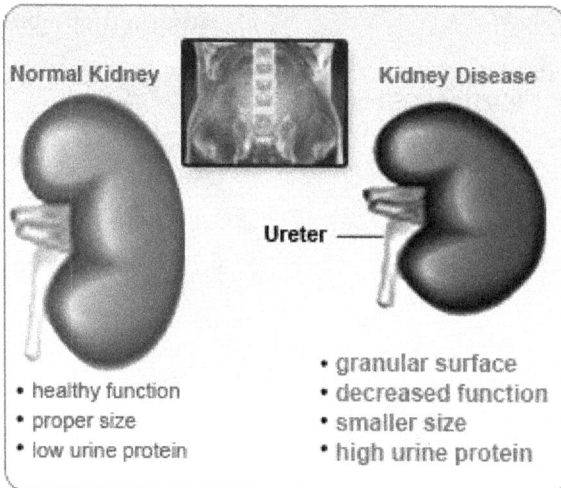

Normal Kidney   **Kidney Disease**

Ureter

• healthy function
• proper size
• low urine protein

• granular surface
• decreased function
• smaller size
• high urine protein

Fig. *Kidney disease*

Kidney function test A test in which blood or urine samples are checked for the amounts of certain substances released by the kidneys. A higher- or lower-than-normal amount of a substance can be a sign that the kidneys are not working the way they should. Also called renal function test.

Kidney shut down (Kidney failure; renal failure) Sudden failure of kidneys to function. Usually has a short, relatively severe course but is often curable.

Kidney stones Hard, unyielding material produced by the kidney. May lodge in the kidney or pass through the ureter, the bladder and finally the urethra to the outside of the body. Kidney stones form when there is a decrease in urine volume and/ or an excess of stone-forming substances in the urine. The most common type of kidney stone contains calcium in combination with either oxalate or phosphate.

Kidney threshold The point at which the blood is holding too much of a substance such as glucose (sugar) and the kidneys "spill" the excess sugar into the urine.

Killer T cell A type of immune cell that can kill certain cells, including foreign cells, cancer cells, and cells infected with a virus. Killer T cells can be separated from other blood cells, grown in the laboratory, and then given to a patient to kill cancer cells. A killer T cell is a type of white blood cell and a type of lymphocyte. Also called cytotoxic T cell and cytotoxic T lymphocyte.

Kindled model An animal model of epilepsy that is thought to be analogous to temporal in humans.

Kinesiology The study of muscles and their movement. Applied kinesiology is a system that uses muscle testing procedures, in conjunction with standard methods of diagnosis, to gain information about a patient's

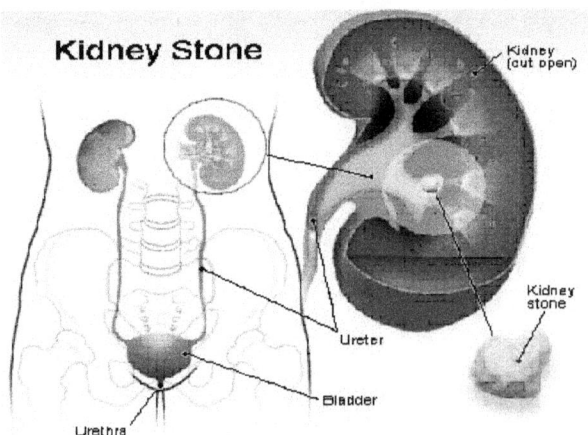

Kidney Stone

Kidney (cut open)

Kidney stone

Ureter

Bladder

Urethra

overall state of health. Practitioners analyze muscle function, posture, gait and other structural factors in addition to inquiring about lifestyle factors that may be contributing to a health-related problem.

Kinetoplastid Characteristic structure at the base of the flagellum in certain protozoa (e.g., Leishmania spp. and Trypanosoma spp.).

Klinefelter's syndrome A disorder in males due to a chromosome abnormality, present at birth but usually not clinically evident until puberty. The underlying abnormality is the presence of one or more extra X chromosomes in each cell (in contrast to the usual complement of sex chromosomes in males, one X and one Y). Clinical symptoms include androgen (male hormone) deficiency, infertility (due to impairment of sperma-togenesis and testosterone production), gynecomastia (breast development), and in some cases, character and personality problems related to the psychosocial consequences of androgen deficiency.

Knee injuries The knee is a complex joint with many components, making it vulnerable to a variety of injuries. Many knee injuries can be successfully treated without surgery, while others require surgery to correct. Many athletes experience injuries to their knee ligaments. Of the four major ligaments found in the knee, the anterior cruciate ligament (ACL) and the medial collateral ligament (MCL) are often injured in sports. The posterior cruciate ligament (PCL) may also be injured.

Knee medial ligaments The ligament that travels from the me-

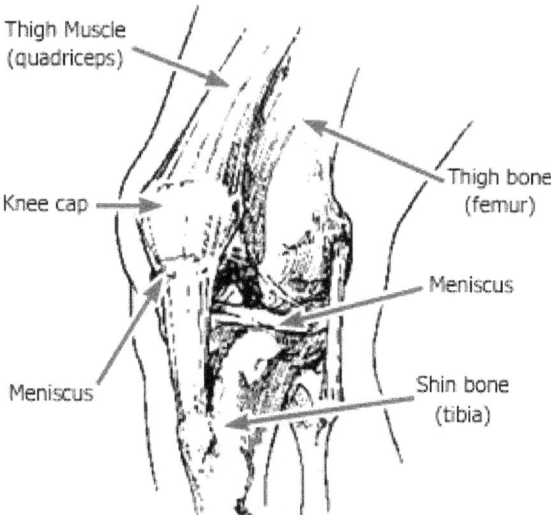

Thigh Muscle (quadriceps)

Knee cap

Meniscus

Thigh bone (femur)

Meniscus

Shin bone (tibia)

Fig. *Knee injuries*

dial epicondyle of the femur to the medial margin and medial surface of the tibia. The medial meniscus is attached to its deep surface.

Knee prostheses Replacement for a knee joint.

Kojewnikov epilepsy A variant of epilepsy characterized by continuous focal jerking of a body part over a period of hours, days, or even years without spreading to other body regions. Contractions may be aggravated by movement and are reduced, but not abolished during sleep. Electro-encephalography demonstrates epileptiform (spike and wave) discharges over the hemisphere opposite to the affected limb in most instances. The repetitive movements may originate from the cerebral cortex or from sub-cortical structures (e.g., Brain stem; Basal ganglia). This condition is associated with Russian spring and summer encephalitis; rasmussen syndrome; multiple sclerosis; diabetes mellitus; brain neoplasms;

and cerebro-vascular disorders.

K-ras gene A gene that may cause cancer when it is mutated (changed). The K-ras gene makes the KRAS protein, which is involved in cell signaling pathways, cell growth, and apoptosis (cell death). Agents that block the activity of the mutated K-ras gene or its protein may stop the growth of cancer. Also called Kras gene.

Kussmaul breathing The rapid, deep, and labored breathing of people who have ketoacidosis or who are in a diabetic coma. Kussmaul breathing is named for Adolph Kussmaul, the 19th century German doctor who first noted it. Also called "air hunger."

Kyphosis Abnormal condition in which the upper spinal column (between the neck and midback) curves outward excessively. Sometimes occurs in adolescents. Usually causes no symptoms and requires no treatment. Can be caused by rickets or tuberculosis of the spine.

L

Tonsils
Lymph vessels
Thymus
Spleen
Lymph nodes
Bone marrow

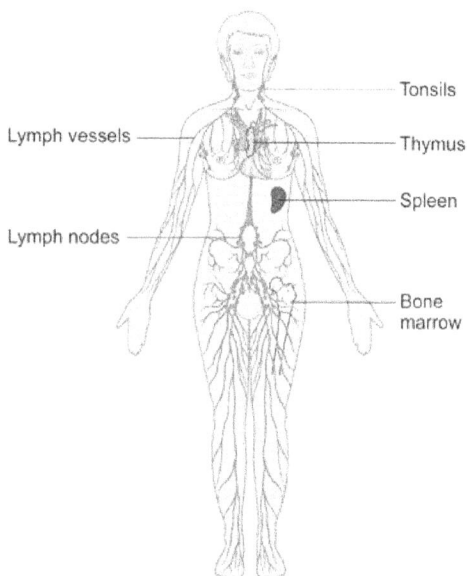

L/S ratio Ratio of lecithin to sphingomyelin. Abnormalities may represent the possibility of an immature or premature fetus.

Labeling standard The Hazard Communication standard of the Occupational Safety and Health Administration which requires that certain information be provided to workers about the identity of workplace chemicals and their hazards.

Labile Abnormal variability, with repeated, rapid, and abrupt shifts in affective expression.

Labile diabetes A term used to indicate when a person's blood glucose (sugar) level often swings quickly from high to low and from low to high. Also calledbrittle diabetes.

Laboratory supervisor Provides laboratory services to meet the

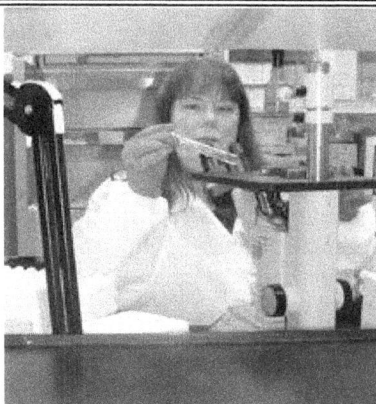

Fig. *Laboratory supervisor*

need of patients as ordered by the medical staff and performed in accordance with accepted standards and practices; directs, supervises, and coordinates functions and activities in any or all divisions of the clinical laboratories; Bacteriology, Blood Bank, Chemistry, Cytology, Hematology, Serology.

Laboratory test A medical procedure that involves testing a sample of blood, urine, or other substance from the body. Tests can help determine a diagnosis, plan treatment, check to see if treatment is working, or monitor the disease over time.

Labour The process of childbirth, from the dilation of the cervix to the delivery of the baby and the placenta.

Labour pain In the first stage of labour results from dilatation of the cervix and lower uterine segment and from distension of the body of the uterus by uterine contractions and is transmitted by afferent nerve fibers (accompanied by sympathetic fibers) of the 10th, 11th and 12th thoracic and 1st lumbar nerves.

Labour suite/room The labour suite is where a woman goes through labour and delivers her baby. If the mother is staying in hospital, she will then be transferred to a postnatal ward.

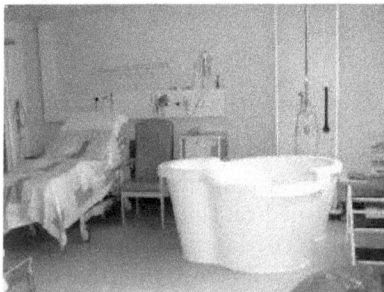

Fig. *Labour suite/room*

Lacrimal gland A gland that secretes tears. The lacrimal glands are found in the upper, outer part of each eye socket.

Lactase An enzyme that breaks down lactose, a type of sugar found in milk and milk products.

Lactate dehydrogenase One of a group of enzymes found in the blood and other body tissues and involved in energy production in cells. An increased amount of lactate dehydrogenase in the blood may be a sign of tissue damage and some types of cancer or other diseases. Also called lactic acid dehydrogenase and LDH.

Lactation The production of breast milk.

Lactic acid A substance made from sugars in milk, by the action of certain enzymes. It is used in skin care products to reduce wrinkles and soften the skin. It is also being studied in the treatment of hand-foot syndrome (a condition marked by pain, swelling, numbness, tingling, or redness of the hands or feet) in patients receiving chemotherapy. Lactic acid is also made in muscles in the body and is used in many chemical processes in the body. It is a type of alpha hydroxyl acid.

Lactic acidosis The buildup of lactic acid in the body. The cells make lactic acid when they use glucose (sugar) for energy. If too much lactic acid stays in the body, the balance tips and the person begins to feel ill. The signs of lactic acidosis are deep and rapid breathing, vomiting, and abdominal pain. Lactic acidosis may be caused by diabetic ketoacidosis or liver or kidney disease. Lactic acidosis is also a rare side effect of a diabetes medication called metformin.

Lactobacilli Bacteria that normally live in the vagina and produce lactic acid, which makes the vagina somewhat acidic. This helps control the growth of other bacteria.

Lactose A type of sugar found in milk and milk products (cheese, butter, etc.). It is considered a nutritive sweetener because it has calories.

Lactose intolerance A digestive disorder; the body is unable to break down milk sugar.

Laennec's cirrhosis Cirrhosis of the liver associated with alcohol abuse.

Laetrile Trademark name for l-mandelonitrile-B-glucuronic acid.

Lambda A bacteriophage that infects E. coli; used as a vector in gene cloning.

Lamina propria A type of connective tissue found under the thin layer of tissues covering a mucous membrane.

Laminaria An absorbent material made of seaweed, which is inserted in the cervix where it absorbs water and swells.

Lamivudine A drug used to treat infection caused by viruses.

Lamotrigine A drug that is used to help control some types of seizures. It is being studied in the prevention of peripheral neuropathy caused by some chemotherapy drugs. It belongs to the family of drugs called anticonvulsants.

Lancet A fine, sharp-pointed blade or needle for pricking the skin.

Landau's reflex When laid face down, a 3- to 12-month-old baby will arch his back and raise his head.

Lanugo Downy-like, fine hair on a fetus. Lanugo can appear as early as 15 weeks of gestation, and typically begins to disappear sometime before birth.

Laparoscope A thin, tube-like instrument used to look at tissues and organs inside the abdomen. A laparoscope has a light and a lens for viewing and may have a tool to remove tissue. It delivers a special kind of light to the body. It relieves pain by stimulating the release of endorphins. Endorphins are the body's own natural painkillers. Endorphins are very similar to morphine but are much more concentrated. Laser also calms nerves

Operating Laparoscope

Fig. *Laparoscope*

that send pain signals. Laser therapy stimulates healing and the growth of new, healthy tissue. Wounds, burns, sprains, and strains heal much faster with laser therapy.

Laparoscopic prostatectomy Surgery to remove all or part of the prostate with the aid of a laparoscope. A laparoscope is a thin, tube-like instrument with a light and a lens for viewing. It may also have a tool to remove tissue to be checked under a microscope for signs of disease.

Laparoscopic surgery Laparoscopic surgery is the technique of performing surgery by making small making small cuts (5-10 mm usually) over abdomen and inserting special instruments through them. Hence the name 'keyhole' surgery. The surgeon performs surgery using these special instruments, one of which is a camera, while looking at the image on a screen.

The advantage of this procedure over traditional surgery is that since there is absence of a large incision, pain is much less, recovery is faster, hospital stay is less, complications are less.

Nowadays, we perform almost all abdominal surgeries laparoscopically including those for appendicitis, gallstones, hernia, GERD (reflux disease), peptic ulcers, achalasia cardia, spleen removal, pancreatic surgery, liver surgery, surgery for cancers of stomach, foodpipe (esophagus), small intestine and large intestine (colon and rectal cancers), hysterectomy (uterus removal) and nephrectomy (kidney removal).

Laparoscopic-assisted colectomy Surgery done with the aid of a laparoscope to remove all or

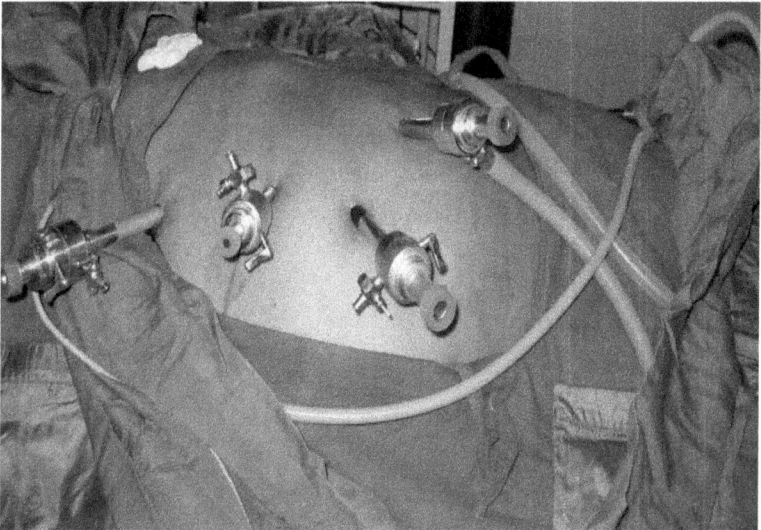

Fig. *Laparoscopic surgery*

part of the colon through several small incisions made in the wall of the abdomen. A laparoscope is a thin, tube-like instrument with a light and a lens for viewing. It may also have a tool to remove tissue to be checked under a microscope for signs of disease. The laparoscope is inserted through one opening to guide the surgery. Surgical instruments are inserted through the other openings to perform the surgery. When only part of the colon is removed, it is called a partial colectomy.

Laparotomy A surgical incision made in the wall of the abdomen.

Lapse Allowing insurance coverage to expire by not paying premiums.

Larvicide A substance capable of killing insect larvae.

Laryngeal cancer Cancer that forms in tissues of the larynx (area of the throat that contains the vocal cords and is used for breathing, swallowing, and talking). Most laryngeal cancers are squamous cell carcinomas (cancer that begins in flat cells lining the larynx).

Laryngeal Having to do with the larynx.

Laryngectomee A person whose larynx (voice box) has been removed.

Laryngectomy An operation to remove all or part of the larynx (voice box).

Laryngitis Inflammation of the larynx.

Laryngoscope A thin, tube-like instrument used to examine the larynx (voice box). A laryngoscope has a light and a lens for viewing and may have a tool to remove tissue.

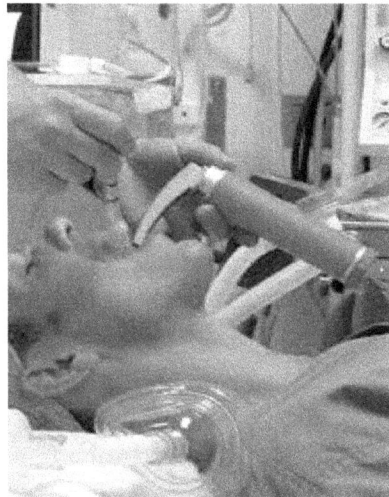

Fig. *Laryngoscope*

Laryngoscopy Examination of the larynx (voice box) with a mirror (indirect laryngoscopy) or with a laryngoscope (direct laryngo-scopy).

Laryngospasm Spasmotic closure of the larynx or voice box. When spasms occur, air cannot pass through the larynx properly. May occur with croup in infants, in tetany, caused by abnormally low calcium level in the blood, or in tetanus (lockjaw). Can be life-threatening if condition is severe.

Larynx The area of the throat containing the vocal cords and used for breathing, swallowing, and talking. Also called voice box.

Laser A device that forms light into intense, narrow beams that may be used to cut or destroy tissue, such as cancer tissue. It may also be used to reduce lymphedema (swelling caused by a buildup of lymph fluid in tissue) after breast cancer surgery. Lasers are used in microsurgery, photodynamic ther-apy, and many other procedures to diagnose and treat disease.

Laser acupuncture The use of a low-level laser beam instead of an acupuncture needle to stimulate an acupuncture point.

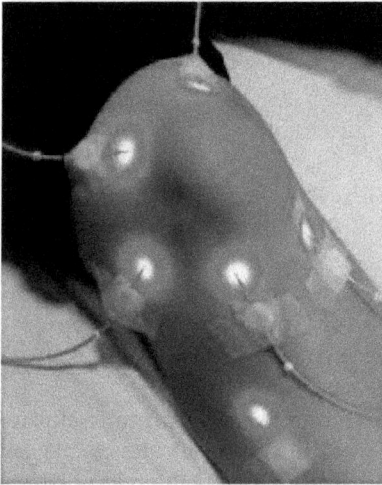

Fig. *Laser acupuncture*

Laser surgery A surgical procedure that uses the cutting power of a laser beam to make bloodless cuts in tissue or to remove a surface lesion such as a tumor.

Laser therapy It is a special kind of laser light that enters the body to produce pain relief and quick healing. It is also called *cold laser therapy* because no significant heat is produced either on the skin's surface or deeper inside the body. This new therapy is very effective at calming nerve pain and relieving chronic muscle pain. It has also been shown to be effective in the treatment of a number of other conditions, such as TMJ and headaches.

It is a painless, sterile, non-invasive, and drug-free technique.The high-intensity light used in cold laser therapy stimulates damaged cells to produce energy (ATP), which improves their function, assists their division, strengthens the body's immune system, and causes the secretion of various beneficial proteins, hormones, and endorphins. As a result, the body's tissues are healed, and pain is eased or eliminated. If damaged cells have died, the photons emitted by the cold laser help the division of neighboring cells to generate new healthy tissue, and thus bring about healing. Additionally, healthy cells treated with Cold Laser Therapy release healthy chemical substances

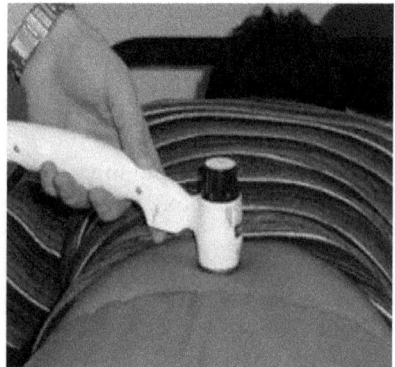

Fig. *Laser therapy*

into the blood and lymphatic systems that flow to other parts of the body. In this way, the effects of Cold Laser Therapy may not be only local, but can also achieve wide systemic benefits.

Laser treatment Using a special strong beam of light of one color (laser) to heal a damaged area. A person with diabetes might be treated with a laser beam to heal blood vessels in the eye.

Latching on To "latch on" to the breast, a baby needs to open his mouth wide. When a baby latches on to the breast successfully, he will be feeding from the breast and not just the nipple. It should not hurt when your baby feeds, although you may experience a strong sensation of sucking.

Late adolescence Occurs for those individuals, typically ages 18 to the mid-20s, who, because of educational goals or other social factors, delay their entry into adult roles. Compare early adolescence, middle adolescence, younger adolescents. and older adolescence.

Latent Autoimmune Diabetes in Adults (LADA) Autoimmune diabetes (Type 1A diabetes) occurring in individuals who are older than the usual age of onset of type 1 diabetes (that is, over 30 years of age at diagnosis). Sometimes, patients with LADA are mistakenly thought to have Type 2 diabetes, based on their age at the time of diagnosis. However, positive antibody tests would help make the diagnosis of LADA.

Latent diabetes Former term for impaired glucose tolerance.

Latent effect A reaction to a substance that is not immediately evident but that appears later in life; - also referred to as a silent effect.

Lateral collateral ligament Ligament of knee attaching lateral femoral condyle to the fibula head. It provides lateral stability to the knee.

Lateral sclerosis Degeneration of the lateral columns of the spinal cord.

Latex A type of rubber used to make male condoms and other methods of birth control Some people, particularly health care providers, develop allergies to this substance and must avoid birth control methods that use it.

LAV (Iymphadenopathy-associated virus) A retrovirus recovered from a person with Iymphadenopathy (enlarged lymph nodes) who was also in a group at high risk for AIDS; renamed Human Immuno-deficiency Virus (HIV) in 1986.

LD50 An indicator of the toxicity of new drugs, LD50 is the dose of a substance that causes death in 50 percent of a group of experimental animals exposed to a test substance. Exposure is often by ingestion.

LDL Low density lipoprotein.

L-dopa, Ievodopa The precursor of the neurotransmitter dopamine. L-dopa is the standard therapy for persons with Parkinson's disease.

Lead poisoning This occurs when lead is ingested in the body and damages organs.

Learning disabilities A person with learning disabilities is characterised by slower than normal or limited intellectual and emotional development.

Least restrictive environment Setting that provides the greatest opportunity for independence while ensuring the safety of the individual.

Left atrium The left upper chamber of the heart. It receives oxygen-rich blood from the lungs via the pulmonary vein.

Left hemisphere The left half of the cerebrum - it is the center for speech and language. In some left-handed people, however, the right hemisphere controls speech.

Left inferior lobe The bottom lobe of the lung on the left side of the body.

Left superior lobe The top lobe of the lung on the left side of the body.

Left ventricle The left lower chamber of the heart. It pumps the blood through the aortic valve into the aorta.

Leg cramps In order to move, we voluntarily contract and relax our muscles simultaneously. When a muscle or fibers of a muscle contract uncontrollably it causes a spasm. At times this muscle spasm is sustained over a period of time and it becomes a muscle cramp. A muscle cramp can be seen and felt in the hardening of a particular muscle. Leg cramps are involuntary

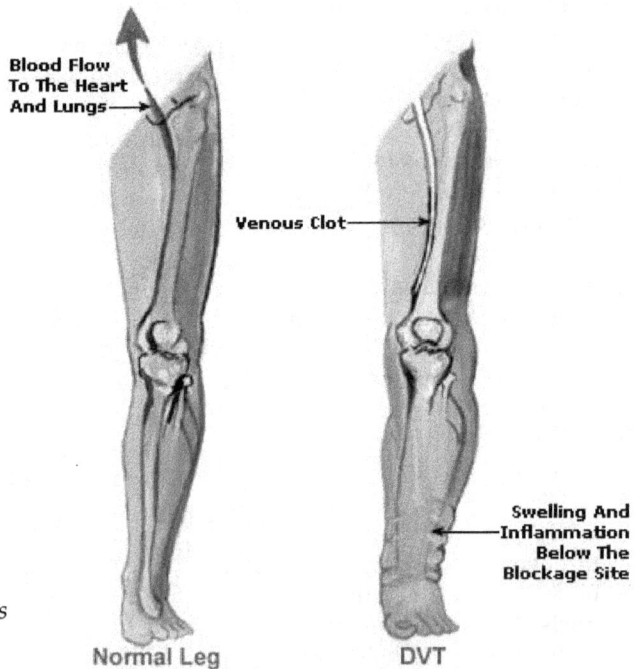

Blood Flow To The Heart And Lungs

Venous Clot

Swelling And Inflammation Below The Blockage Site

Normal Leg   DVT

Fig. *Leg cramps*

contractions of the leg muscles that can be very painful. Most leg cramps occur suddenly with warning signals that include tingling and twitching of muscles before an abrupt pain follows. Severe cramps can cause swelling and soreness and may require massage and rest to aid recovery.

Legal parent The parent who has legal charge and control of a child.

Legal services Assistance with legal matters, such as property disposition, transfer of assets, wills, living wills, powers of attorney, and guardianship.

Legend drug Drug that can only be obtained by prescription.

Leishmania A genus of flagellated parasitic protozoans that cause leishmaniasis.

Leishmaniasis Any of several infections caused by Leishmania spp., transmitted by sandflies. Cutaneous Ieishmaniasis is a skin ulcer caused by L. mexicana (New World) or L. tropica (Old World). Mucocutaneous Ieishmaniasis is an ulceration of the nose and throat caused by L. braziliensis, occurring in tropical America. isceral Ieishmaniasis, also called "kala-azar,w is a generalized and internal disease caused by L. donovani (New and Old World).

Length of stay The number of days a patient stays in a hospital or other health care facility.

Lens A crystalline structure located just behind the iris - it focuses light onto the retina

Lente insulin A type of insulin that is intermediate-acting.

Leprosy Chronic disease characterized by the production of fibrous connective-tissue lesions (granulomatous) of the skin, mucous membranes and peripheral nervous system (excluding the brain and spinal cord). It is not very contagious and requires prolonged, intimate contact to be transmitted to another person. The more serious form of leprosy may cause blindness and severe disfigurement. Treatment can result in improvement of skin lesions, but recovery of nerve damage is limited.

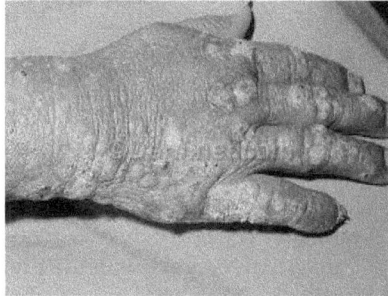

Fig. *Leprosy*

Lesbian A woman who is sexually attracted to other women.

Lesch-Nyhan syndrome An X-linked recessive genetic disorder characterized by compulsive selfmutilation and other mental and behavioral symptoms. It is caused by a defect in the gene that produces a particular enzyme hypoxanthine-guanine phosphoribosyl transferase) important in metabolism. In the absence of this enzyme, large amounts of uric acid accumulate in the blood, leading to gout. The causal relationship to the behavioral symptoms is not yet understood.

Lesion A general term for any abnormal structure or loss of function in the body (e.g., a wound, infection, tumor, abscess, or chemical abnormality).

Let-down Let-down is the release of milk in a breast-feeding mother as a response to the suckling of her baby. About 50% of women feel this as a tingling or warm sensation in the breast.

Leukaemia Cancers of the blood-forming organs, characterized by abnormal proliferation and development of leukocytes (white blood cells) and their precursors in the blood and bone marrow, and infiltration of lymph nodes, the spleen, liver, and other sites. The various forms of leukemia are classified according to the dominant cell type and course of the disease—chronic myelogenous leukemia (including myeloid, myelocytic, and granulocytic); hairy cell leukemia; chronic lymphocytic leukemia; and various types of acute leukemia. It is generally diagnosed in children aged between one and 14 years and is the most common cause of cancer-related deaths in children.

Leukemia, acute Malignant overgrowth of white blood cells in bone marrow or tissues that are part of the lymphatic system (lymph glands, spleen, liver). These excess cells accumulate and spill into the blood, eventually involving other tissues. Most common form of cancer in children.

Leukemia, granulocytic Malignant blood disease of granulocytes, a form of white blood cell.

Leukemia, lymphatic Very slow-growing cancer of blood-forming organs in older people. About 35% of all leukemia victims have this form of the disease. It is often discovered in a routine blood test for unrelated purposes.

Leukemia, monocytic Malignancy of blood-forming tissues in which the predominant cells are monocytes (a type of white blood cell). The disease has an erratic course characterized by malaise, fatigue, fever, weight loss, enlarged spleen, bleeding gums, anemia and unresponsiveness to therapy.

Leukemia, myeloblastic Malignancy of blood cells in which the predominant cells are myeloblasts (a form of white blood cell).

Leukemia, myelogenous

Leukemia, myeloid Malignancy of white blood cells with polymorphonuclear cells predominant.

Leukemia, myelomonocytic Malignancy of blood cells in which the predominant cells are monocytes and myelocytes.

Leukemia, myleocytic Disorder characterized by the unregulated, excessive production of myelocytes.

Leukoagglutinins Antibodies directed against white blood cells.

Leukocyte White blood cells (WBCs), including lymphocytes, monocytes, neutrophils, basophils, and eosinophils. WBCS are formed in lymph nodes and bone marrow and are present in the blood and lymphatic circulation. Their main function is to protect the body against infection and to fight infection when it occurs.

Level premiums The uniform raising of premium rates for an entire class of insurance with permission from the state Insurance Commissioner.

Liability Accountability and responsibility that are enforceable by legal sanctions.

Libido Interest in and desire for sex.

Lice Lice are tiny parasitic insects that feed on blood and are highly contagious through direct contact. Head lice are the most common.

Licensed practical nurse A licensed practical nurse administers treatment and medication under the direction of a registered nurse or a licensed physician. LPNs must complete coursework in a nursing school or vocational training school before they can be licensed by the state.

Licensure The legal authority, exercised by the State, for a health professional to practice, for a hospital or nursing home to operate, and for companies to produce and distribute biologic products.

Life-skills training The formal teaching of the requisite skills for surviving, living with others, and succeeding in a complex society. Life-skills training interventions emphasize the teaching of social competence, cognitive skills, and decision-making skills.

Life-sustaining treatment Drugs, medical devices, or procedures that can extend the life of a patient who would likely die within a foreseeable, though usually uncertain, amount of time. Examples include cardiopulmonary resuscitation, mechanical ventilation, renal dialysis, nutritional support (i.e., tube or intravenous feeding), and antibiotics to fight overwhelming infections.

Lift In the context of rehabilitation, the amount of weight a prosthesis will misc.

Ligament Band of fibrous tissue that connects bone to bone or bone to cartilage and supports and strengthens joints.

Lightening This occurs when a fetus positions itself lower in the pelvic cavity during the last few weeks of pregnancy.

Limbic system The interconnected areas of the brain that are used in emotions and some other behaviors.

Limited joint mobility A form of arthritis involving the hand; it causes the fingers to curve inward and the skin on the palm to tighten and thicken. This condition mainly affects people with IDDM.

Linea nigra A dark line which may develop during pregnancy, running from below the breasts, over the abdomen and the navel. It often fades after delivery but doesn't always disappear entirely.

Linear attenuation of X-rays: Partial absorption and partial transmission of X-rays.

Linkage In genetics, the physical proximity of two or more genes on the same chromosome, such that they are inherited together as a group and are unlikely to segregate independently during meiosis.

Liothyronine (T3) toxicosis Overactive thyroid function due to T3 poisoning.

Liotibial band A thick, wide facial layer from the iliac crest to the knee joint.

Lipid A term for fat. The body stores fat as energy for future use just like a car that has a reserve fuel tank. When the body needs energy, it can break down the lipids into fatty acids and burn them like glucose (sugar). The two most commonly measured kinds of lipids are triglycerides and cholesterol.

Lipid metabolism The process by which lipid molecules (fatty acids) are synthesized and broken down in the body.

Lipoatrophy Small depressions in the subcutaneous tissues just under the skin that form when a person keeps injecting insulin into the same spot. Injecting around the depressed area can very slowly fill in the depression (over a period of many months).

Lipodystrophy Lumps (lipohypertrophy) or depressions (lipo-atrophy) below the surface of the skin that form when a person keeps injecting insulin into the same spot. Both forms of lipodystrophies are harmless. People can decrease this problem by changing (rotating) the places where they inject their insulin. Using purified insulins may also help.

Lipohypertrophy Bulging of an area of the skin (due to fat accumulation) that forms when a person keeps injecting insulin into the same spot. Continued injection into these lumpy areas delays the absorption of insulin, and is not recommended even though injecting into the lumpy area is painless (as there are no nerve endings in the lump).

Lipophilic Having an affinity for lipids; that is, soluble in fat-like material. These substances may also be termed hydrophobic, or insoluble in water. Many toxic substances are lipophilic, making them especially dangerous to the nervous system.

Lipoprotein Compounds consisting of lipids (fatty substances such as cholesterol) and proteins, the form in which lipids are transported in the blood and lymph fluid. Lipoproteins form the main structural components of cell membranes and cell organelles. They are classified as very low-density (VLD), lowdensity (LD), and high-density (HD).

Liposome A structure with a lipid membrane (like that of a cell) that can be filled with specific substances and then used as a delivery vehicle to transport those substances to the interior of a target cell by fusion with the cell's own membrane, It is one of several potential delivery vehicles for use in gene therapy.

Lispro Insulin Lispro insulin is an insulin analog in which the position of two amino acids are switched. The resulting lispro insulin does not form hexamers (clumps of six molecules linked together) and is thus faster acting than regular insulin. It can be injected immediately before a meal, compared with regular which should be injected 30 minutes or more before a meal.

Lithotripsy A technique using ultrasonic waves to break up calculi (stones) (e.g., kidney stones, gallstones, and upper ureteral stones) for excretion in the urine (as in extracorporeal shock wave lithotripsy) or removal via minor surgery (as in percutaneous lithotripsy).

Lithotripter An instrument that fragments, erodes, or otherwise destroys calculi (stones) in the body.

Live birth The birth of an infant, regardless of the duration of gestation, that exhibits any sign of life (e.g., respiration, heartbeat, umbilical pulsation, or movement of voluntary muscles).

Liver The liver is the largest organ inside the body. In an adult it is about the size of a football and weighs close to three pounds. It is located behind the ribs in the upper right-hand portion of the abdomen. Shaped like a triangle, the liver is dark reddish-brown and consists of two main lobes. There are 300 billion cells in the liver that are connected by a well-organised system of bile ducts and blood vessels called the biliary system. It filters toxins from the blood, and makes bile (which breaks down fats) and some blood proteins.

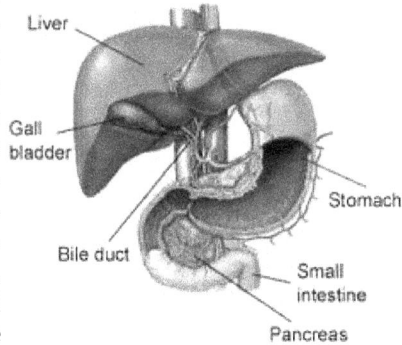

Fig. *Liver*

Liver and liver problems A healthy liver is soft and flexible. With chronic hepatitis B or C infection, the liver is constantly under attack and it can become hardened over time. Some of the changes and liver damage that can occur are described below:

(i) Fibrosis: After becoming inflamed, the liver tries to repair itself by forming tiny scars. This scarring, called "fibrosis", makes it difficult for the liver to do its job. As damage continues, many scars form and begin to join together, leading to the next stage, cirrhosis.

(ii) Cirrhosis: With chronic hepatitis B infection, large areas of the liver can become permanently scarred and nodules may form. Blood cannot flow freely through scarred liver tissue. This causes the liver to shrink and become hard, and can lead to serious bleeding from the gut.

Liver failure: If cirrhosis becomes very severe, liver failure can occur. This means the liver is unable to filter wastes, toxins and drugs from the blood. It can no longer produce the clotting factors necessary to stop bleeding.

Liver cancer Cirrhosis can sometimes set the stage for liver cancer. One explanation for this is that damage to liver cells may alter the genes inside the cells in such a way that they become cancerous. People living with chronic hepatitis B infection are at higher risk for developing liver cancer and must be monitored carefully.

Liver profile Cost is about $20.00. Blood tests performed include Bilirubin, Protein, LDL, Alkaline Phosphatase, SGOT, SGPT, Albumin, and Globulin.

Living will A written declaration by a competent adult outlining his or her wishes, especially the intent to refuse life-sustaining procedures, once he or she is in-

competent and death is imminent. Because these documents are frequently ambiguous, their legality may be unclear. They are not recognized in all States, and requirements and conditions vary from State to State.

LNCC Legal Nurse Consultant Certified; a credential offered by the American Legal Nurse Consultant Certification Board

Local health departments (LHDs) Municipal or county government-operated facilities providing basic personal and environmental health services.

Lochia This is the term used to refer to the vaginal discharge of mucus, blood, and tissue, which may continue for up to six weeks after delivery.

Locus In genetics, the position of a gene or a group of functionally-related genes on a chromosome.

Long term care insurance A policy designed to help alleviate some of the costs associated with long term care. Benefits are often paid in the form of a fixed dollar amount (per day or per visit) for covered expenses and may exclude or limit certain conditions from coverage.

Long term care The broad spectrum of medical and support services provided to persons who have lost some or all capacity to function on their own due to a chronic illness or condition, and who are expected to need such services over a prolonged period of time. Long term care can consist of care in the home by family members who are assisted with voluntary or employed help, adult day health care, or care in assisted living or skilled nursing facilities.

Long term home health care program A coordinated plan of care and services provided at home to invalid, infirm, or disabled persons who are medically eligible for placement in a hospital or residential health care facility for an extended period of time, but such a program was unavailable. Such a program is provided in the person's home or in the home of a responsible relative or other adult, but not in a private proprietary home for adults, private proprietary nursing home, residence for adults, or public home.

Long term rehabilitation program May be called Extended Rehabilitation. Have full range of rehabilitation services available. Frequently after initial year of rehabilitation when progress is slower. Generally not permanent placement. May be facility or community based.

Long terminal repeat (LTR) In genetics, a nucleotide sequence (at each end of a retroviral genome) that is involved in transcript initiation and regulation and contains signals for expression of the viral genome.

Long-distance caregiver An adult child or other relative or friend of an impaired person who lives in a different locality or area of the country but still tries to function as a caregiver for the person-often by trying to locate, arrange, and monitor services for the person.

Long-term care assessment and management program (LAMP) A program in Pennsylvania that contracts with local agencies (usually area agencies on aging) to provide case management for elderly people who are eligible for Medicaid-funded nursing home care but choose to remain at home. It is similar to Ohio's PASSPORT Program but is paid for solely with State funds.

Long-term care facilities A range of institutions that provide health care to people who are unable to manage independently in the community. Facilities may provide short-term rehabilitative services as well as chronic care management.

Long-term care services A variety of services that may be provided in a person's home, the community, or a residential or institutional setting, with the objective of maintaining and supporting a chronically ill or severely disabled individual.

Long-term care The provision of medical, social, and personal care services on a recurring or continuing basis to people who are chronically ill, aged, disabled, or mentally retarded. Long-term care services cay be provided in hospitals, private homes, nursing homes, board and care facilities, and mental health facilities, among other settings. Services include symptomatic treatment, maintenance, and rehabilitation for patients of all ages.

Lordosis Forward curvature of the lumbar spine (the small of the back).

Loss-control service Service provided by insurers to client companies. Loss-control specialists visit ' worksites and offer advice on the prevention of property loss and wok-related injuries and illnesses.

Lost-workday case As defined by the Occupational Safety and Health Administration and the Bureau of Labor Statistics, a work-related injury or illness that results in an employee missing time from work or that restricts the employee's work activity.

Low birthweight A term used to describe a full-term baby who weighs less than 5.5 pounds/3 kilograms at birth.

Low birthweight rate Percentage of live births with a birthweight of 2,500 grams or less.

Low birthweight Weight of a newborn infant that is less than 2500 grams (5 lb. 8 oz.)..

Low income Pertaining to an individual or family that is poor or near-poor.

LPN Licensed Practical Nurse (in some locations known as an LVN); a graduate from a (usually) one-year diploma/certificate program at a vocational/technical school.

LPN, CLTC Licensed Practical Nurse certified in Long-Term Care by the National Association for Practical Nurse Education & Service, Inc. (NAPNES).

LPN, NCP Licensed Practical Nurse certified in Pharmacology by the National Association for Practical Nurse Education & Service, Inc. (NAPNES).

Lubricant Any substances used to make the genitals slippery and ease sexual contact see What exactly is lube?

Lumbar puncture A procedure to draw spinal fluid from the spinal column to check for infections, tumours, and diseases such as meningitis.

Lumbar stenosis Narrowing or stricture in the lower part of the back.

Lumbosacral Region of low back comprised of lumbar and sacral spine.

Lupus erythematosus acutus An autoimmune disease where the body mistakenly attacks the connective tissue in the body.

Lupus erythematosus, systemic Inflammatory disease of connective tissue. Symptoms may include arthritis, swelling of the face and legs, anemia, mental changes, shortness of breath, hair loss and chest pain. Treatment usually requires immunosuppressive steroid and nonsteroid antiinflammatory drugs. It is not inherited or cancerous. Currently considered incurable.

Luteal phase defect (LPD) Failure of the endometrial lining of the uterus to develop properly after ovulation, leading to inability of a fertilized ovum to implant; a potential cause of infertility.

Luteal phase defect A luteal phase defect can refer to one of two problems with the luteal phase - the second part of the menstrual cycle, after ovulation has occurred. First, the phase itself may be too short (only ten days rather than the average 12 to 16), which does not give an embryo enough time to implant successfully. Second, progesterone production in this part of the cycle may be too low, meaning that the lining of the womb will not get thick enough for an embryo to implant before menstruation begins.

Luteinising hormone A hormone produced by the pituitary gland which stimulates other hormones of the reproductive system; it stimulates the development of the corpus luteum in women and testosterone in men.

Luteinization Process by which a follicle in the ovary transforms into a luteum.

Luteinized granulosa Thick, scarred, yellow lesion.

Luteinizing hormone (LH) A gonadotropin hormone, secreted by the anterior pituitary gland, that stimulates the secretion of sex hormones by the ovary and the testes and is involved in the maturation of ova and spermatozoa.

Luteum Yellow-colored cyst.

LVN Licensed Vocational Nurse (in some locations known as an LPN); a graduate from a (usually) one-year diploma/certificate program at a vocational/technical school.

LVN, CLTC Licensed Vocational Nurse certified in Long-Term Care by the National Association for Practical Nurse Education & Service, Inc. (NAPNES).

LVN, NCP Licensed Vocational Nurse certified in Pharmacology by the National Association for Practical Nurse Education & Service, Inc. (NAPNES).

Lyell syndrome An exfoliative disease of skin seen primarily in adults and characterized by flaccid bullae and spreading erythema so that the skin has the appearance of being scalded. It results primarily from a toxic reaction to various drugs, but occasionally occurs as a result of infection, neoplastic conditions, or other exposure.

Lymph Transparent, slightly yellow liquid found in lymph vessels throughout the body. Derived from tissue fluids.

Lymphadenitis Inflammation of the lymph nodes.

Lymphadenopathy syndrome (LAS) A condition characterized by persistent, generalized, enlarged lymph nodes that can occur along with various types of viral and bacterial infections, leukemias, and drug reactions, but which has recently become associated most closely with HIV seropositivity (in which it is usually called "persistent, generalized lymphadenopathy"). In HIV-infected individuals, it can occur during the acute phase of initial HIV infection as well as later on during HIV-induced immunosuppression in those with imminent AIDS.

Lymphadenopathy: Enlargement of a lymph node or lymph gland.

Lymphangiectases A transient dilatation of the lymphatic vessels.

Lymphangioma A benign tumor representing a congenital malformation of the lymphatic system and made up of newly formed lymph-containing vascular spaces and channels. Lymphan-gioendothelioma is a type of lymphangioma in which endo-thelial cells are the dominant component.

Lymphatic Pertaining to lymph system of the body.

Lymphatic drainage The movement of fluids, molecules, for-eign particles, and cells from various tissues in the body through the lymph system to the immune system; a means by which grafted cells reach the host's immune system and trigger rejection.

Lymphatic system The lymphatic system is a system of thin tubes that runs throughout the body. These tubes are called lymph vessels or lymphatic vessels.The lymphatic system is like the blood circulation - the tubes (vessels) branch through all parts of the body like the arteries and veins that carry blood. But the lymphatic system tubes are much finer and carry a colourless liquid called *lymph*. Lymph is a clear fluid that circulates around the body tissues. It contains a high number of

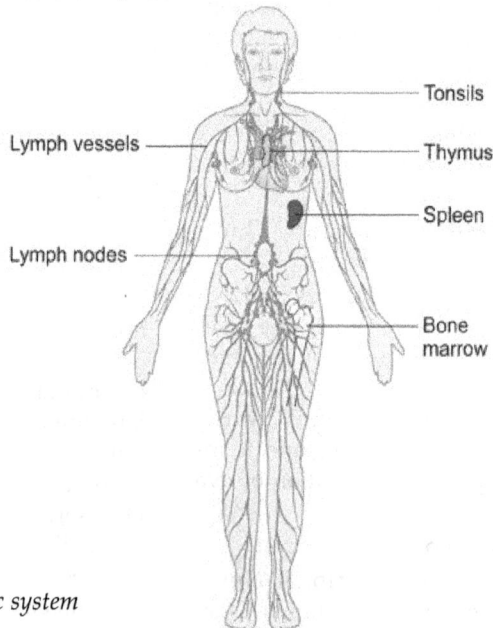

Tonsils

Lymph vessels

Thymus

Spleen

Lymph nodes

Bone marrow

Fig. *Lymphatic system*

lymphocytes (white blood cells). Plasma leaks out of the capillaries to surround and bathe the body tissues. This then drains into the lymph vessels.

Lymphatism Diseases of lymph or lymph vessels.

Lymphoblastic lymphoma (Lymphoblastoma; lymphoblastic lymphosarcoma) Malignant tumor of lymph tissue. Lymphomas are classified according to the predominant cell type causing the disease. Lymphoblastic lymphoma's predominant cell is structured similarly to the lymphoblast. Treatment for lymphoma includes intensive radiotherapy and chemotherapy.

Lymphocytes Specialized white blood cells involved in one type of immune response that does not depend directly on antibody attack (cell-mediated immunity). Lymphocytes originate from fetal stem cells and develop in the bone marrow. They normally comprise about 25 percent of the total white blood cell count and increase in number in response to infection.

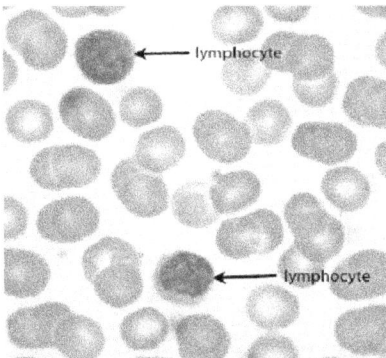

Fig. *Lymphocytes*

They occur in two forms—*B cells* and *T cells*. B cells, which circulate in an immature form and secrete antibodies that are carried on their surface membranes, search out, identify, and bind with specific antigens. T cells mature in the thymus gland and differentiate into thymocytes when exposed to an antigen; they divide rapidly and produce large numbers of new T cells sensitized to that antigen.

Lymphocytic proliferative disease Disease with an overproduction of lymphocytes, one form of white blood cells.

Lymphoid organs The principal organs of the immune system, including the thymus, bone marrow, spleen, lymph nodes, and tonsils involved in the production of lymphocytes and antibodies.

Lymphokine A type of soluble chemical factor produced and released by sensitized T-lymphocytes on contact with a specific antigen, including interferon gamma, interleukin 1, 2, and 3, tumor necrosis factor, colony stimulating factor, B-cell growth factor, and others. Lymphokines are involved in a number of essential immunologic functions, including attracting macrophages to the site of infection and inflammation and helping to produce cellular immunity by stimulating the activity of monocytes and macrophages.

Lymphoma Disorders involving new, abnormal growth or tumor of lymph tissue. Usually malignant but may be benign. Usually afflicts men.

Lymphomas Cancers of cells of the lymphoid tissue, found mainly in lymph nodes and the spleen; categorized as Hodgkin's lymphoma and various types of non-Hodgkin's lymphoma.

Lymphomatous meningitis A serious problem that may occur in leukemia or lymphoma. In lymphomatous meningitis, cancer cells have spread from the original (primary) tumor to the meninges (thin layers of tissue that cover and protect the brain and spinal cord). The cancer may cause the meninges to be inflamed. Also called leukemic meningitis.

Lymphopenia A condition in which there is a lower-than-normal number of lymphocytes (a type of white blood cell) in the blood. Also called lymphocytic leukopenia and lymphocytopenia.

Lymphoplasmacytic lymphoma An indolent (slow-growing) type of non-Hodgkin lymphoma marked by abnormal levels of IgM antibodies in the blood and an enlarged liver, spleen, or lymph nodes. Also called Waldenström macroglobulinemia.

Lymphopoietin-1 One of a group of related proteins made by leukocytes (white blood cells) and other cells in the body. Lymphopoietin-1 is made by cells that cover and support organs, glands, and other structures in the body. It causes the growth of T lymphocytes and B lymphocytes. Lymphopoietin-1 made in the laboratory is used as a biological response modifier to boost the immune system in cancer therapy. Lymphopoietin-1 is a type of cytokine. Also called IL-7 and interleukin-7.

Lymphoproliferative disorder A disease in which cells of the lymphatic system grow excessively. Lymphoproliferative disorders are often treated like cancer.

Lymphoreticular malignancy Cancer of the reticulo-endothelial cells of lymph nodes.

Lymphosarcoma Malignant tumor of the lymph glands. More common than Hodgkin's disease

Lymphoscintigraphy A method used to check the lymph system for disease. A radioactive substance that flows through the lymph ducts and can be taken up by lymph nodes is injected into the body. A scanner or probe is used to follow the movement of this substance on a computer screen. Lymphoscintigraphy is used to find the sentinel lymph node (the first node to receive lymph from a tumor), which may be removed and checked for tumor cells. Lymphoscinti-graphy is also used to diagnose certain diseases or conditions, such as lymphoma or lymphe-dema.

Lymphostatic elephantiasis A condition in which tissue or a limb becomes very swollen and thick, and changes color. It is caused by a block in the flow of lymph and a buildup of fluid in tissues. Also called stage III lymphedema.

Lynch syndrome An inherited disorder in which affected individuals have a higher-than-normal chance of developing colorectal cancer and certain other types of cancer, often before the age of 50. Also called hereditary nonpoly-posis colon cancer and HNPCC.

Lyophilized Freeze-dried.

Lyrica A drug used to treat nerve pain caused by diabetes or herpes zoster infection and certain types of seizures. It is being studied in the prevention and treatment of nerve pain in the hands and feet of cancer patients given chemotherapy. Lyrica is a type of anticonvulsant. Also called pregabalin.

Lyse To damage or rupture a cell membrane, allowing the release of cell contents into the extracellular medium.

Lysis In biology, lysis refers to the breakdown of a cell caused by damage to its plasma (outer) membrane. It can be caused by chemical or physical means (for example, strong detergents or high-energy sound waves) or by infection with a strain virus that can lyse cells.

Lysosomal storage diseases A group of genetic disorders resulting from a deficiency of specific Iysosomal enzymes needed to break down glyco-saminoglycans (previously called mucopolysaccharides), causing the accumulation of these substances in the Iysosomes (intracellular particles responsible for breaking down chemical substances, bacteria, etc.). Clinical severity of each type of disease depends on the degree of enzyme deficiency and the tissues most affected by the accumulation, but in general, these are chronic and progressive disorders that may be life-threatening at an early age. Examples of Iysosomal storage diseases include *Tay Sachs*, *Gaucher's*, *Hurler's*, and *Niemann-Pick* disease. Most disorders in this group are transmitted in an autosomal recessive inheritance pattern, although a few are X-linked.

Lysosome A sac-like compartment inside a cell that has enzymes that can break down cellular components that need to be destroyed.

Lytic Having to do with lysis. In biology, lysis refers to the disintegration of a cell by disruption of its plasma membrane. Lysis can be caused by chemical or physical means (e.g., high-energy sound waves) or by a virus infection.

M

m

M/R Coder Responsible for assigning diagnostic and procedure codes to the records of discharged patients and forwarding reports to insurance and governmental review boards as required. The coder also records and determines other required data such as attending physician, use of intensive care unit, number of consultations and referral source and requests diagnoses from physicians when not recorded.

Macroamylaemia Excess of starch in the blood.

Macrobiotics A lifestyle and diet adapted from the Far East and popularized in the United States by Michio Kushi and others. Macrobiotics has also been adopted by some cancer patients, although its promoters do not consider it primarily a treatment for cancer. The principles of the diet consist of balancing the "yin" and 'yang" energies of foods. Different types of cancer are considered either yin or yang and the macrobiotic programme is adapted to the particular type of cancer and to individual traits.

Macrocalcification A small deposit of calcium in the breast that cannot be felt but can be seen on a mammogram. It is usually caused by aging, an old injury, or inflamed tissue and is usually not related to cancer.

Macrocytic anemia A macrocytic class of anemia is an anemia in which the erythrocytes are larger than their normal volume. The normal erythrocyte volume in humans is about 80 to 100 femtoliters (fL= 10-15 L). In a macrocytic anemia the larger red cells are always as-

sociated with insufficient numbers of cells and often also insufficient hemoglobin content
per cell. Both of these factors
work to the opposite effect of
larger cell size, to finally result
in a total blood hemoglobin concentration that is less than normal (i.e., anemia).

Macroglobulinemia A condition in
which the blood contains high
levels of large proteins and is too
thick to flow through small
blood vessels. One type is
Waldenström macro-globu-
linemia, which is a type of cancer.

Macrophage A type of white blood
cell that surrounds and kills
microorganisms, removes dead
cells, and stimulates the action
of other immune system cells.

Macrosomia Abnormally large; in
diabetes, refers to abnormally
large babies that may be born
to women with diabetes.

Macrovascular disease A disease
of the large blood vessels that
sometimes occurs when a person has had diabetes for a long
time. Fat and blood clots build
up in the large blood vessels
and stick to the vessel walls.
Three kinds of macrovascular
disease are coronary disease,
cerebrovascular disease, and
peripheral vascular disease.

Macula The macula is an oval-
shaped highly pigmented yellow spot near the centre of the
retina of the human eye. It has a
diameter of around 1.5 mm and
is often histologically defined as
having two or more layers of

ganglion cells. Near its centre is
the fovea, a small pit that contains the largest concentration
of cone cells in the eye and is responsible for central, high resolution vision. The macula also
contains the parafovea and
perifovea.

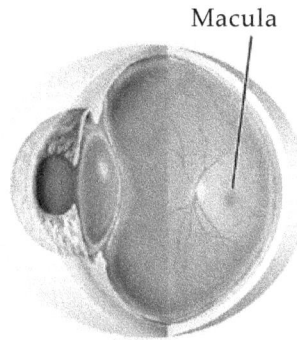

Fig. *Macula*

Macular degeneration A condition
in which there is a slow breakdown of cells in the centre of the
retina (the light-sensitive layers
of nerve tissue at the back of the
eye). This blocks vision in the
centre of the eye and can cause
problems with activities such
as reading and driving. Macular
degeneration is most often seen
in people who are over the age
of 50. Also called age-related
macular degeneration, AMD,
and ARMD.

Macular degeneration disorder It
is characterized by changes in
the eye's macula that result in
the gradual loss of central vision. The exact cause is unknown, but appears to be related to a genetic predisposition,
smoking and several other risk
factors. Central vision may be

blurred, distorted (metamorphopsia) or shadowy before vision loss occurs.

Macular disease Stain, spot or thickening of the cornea.

Macular edema Swelling of the central portion of the retina (macula), due to buildup of fluid leaking from retinal blood vessels. Causes temporary or permanent vision loss if untreated.

Macular hole A macular hole is a small break in the macula, located in the centre of the eye's light-sensitive tissue called the retina. The macula provides the sharp, central vision we need for reading, driving, and seeing fine detail. A macular hole can cause blurred and distorted central vision. Macular holes are related to aging and usually occur in people over age 60.

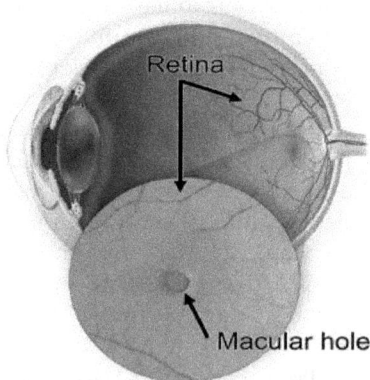

Fig. *Macular hole*

Maculopathy Any disease of the macula, the most sensitive portion of the central retina responsible for detailed vision and colour perception. One example

is age-related macular degeneration.

Madarosis Eyelash or eyebrow loss. Causes include infections, metabolic disorders, blepharitis, certain drugs, lupus erythematosus and trauma.

Mafosfamide A form of cyclophos-phamide that can be administered as an intrathecal infusion. Mafosfamide is being studied as an anticancer drug. It belongs to the family of drugs called alkylating agents.

MAGE-3 antigen A protein found in many types of tumours but not in most normal tissues. Vaccines using pieces of the MAGE-3 protein are being studied for their ability to boost the immune response to cancer cells in patients with cancer.

Magnesium In medicine, a mineral used by the body to help maintain muscles, nerves, and bones. It is also used in energy metabolism and protein synthesis.

Magnesium sulfate A drug used to treat pre-eclampsia and eclampsia (serious complications of pregnancy). Magnesium sulfate is also being studied for its ability to prevent the toxic side effects of certain drugs used to treat colorectal cancer. It is a type of anticonvulsant agent.

Magnetic field gradient A magnetic field that increases or decreases in strength in a given direction along a sample.

Magnetic resonance imaging A procedure in which radio waves and a powerful magnet linked to a computer are used to create detailed pictures of areas inside the body. These pictures can show the difference between normal and diseased tissue. Magnetic resonance imaging makes better images of organs and soft tissue than other scanning techniques, such as computed tomography (CT) or x-ray. Magnetic resonance imaging is especially useful for imaging the brain, the spine, the soft tissue of joints, and the inside of bones. Also called MRI, NMRI, and nuclear magnetic resonance imaging.

Magnetic therapy Magnetic field therapy or bio-magnetic therapy involves the use of magnets, magnetic devices or magnetic fields to treat a variety of physical and emotional conditions, including circulatory problems, certain forms of arthritis, chronic pain, sleep disorders, and stress.

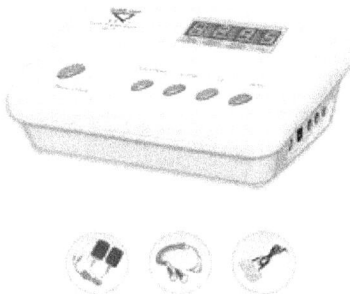

Fig. *Magnetic therapy*

Mail order pharmacy A source for brand name and generic prescription and over-the-counter medicines by mail, usually at lower unit prices than a retail pharmacy.

Mainstream health services Inpatient or outpatient care in acute care hospitals and ambulatory care in private office-based physicians' offices.

Maintenance of benefits Variation of coordination of benefits that allows benefits only up to a maximum allowed had the enrollee been covered only under one health plan. This approach subtracts charges paid by the primary plan from total eligible expenses, then applies the secondary plan benefits to the remaining costs.

Major activity In national health interview surveys such as DHHS'S National Health Interview Survey, persons are classified in terms of the major activity usually associated with the particular age group; attending school is considered the major activity for the age group 5 to 17. Persons are not classified as having a limitation in a major activity unless one or more chronic conditions is reported as the cause of the activity limitation.

Major diagnostic category A clinically coherent grouping of ICD-9-CM diagnoses by major organ system or etiology that is used as the first step in assignment of most diagnosis related groups (DRGs). MDCs are commonly used for aggregated DRG reporting. It is the 23 principal divisions in the DRG (diagnosis-related groups) patient classification scheme.

Major medical coverage Health insurance coverage that provides for an array of services and usually includes an annual deductible, coinsurance requirements, and maximum benefit limits. It is designed to offset heavy medical expenses resulting from catastrophic or prolonged illness by providing benefit payments of 75 to 80 percent of medical expenses above a certain base amount. By comparison, basic benefit plans usually provide first-dollar coverage but cover only a very narrow set of services (e.g., hospital, surgical).

Malabsorption syndrome A group of symptoms such as gas, bloating, abdominal pain, and diarrhea resulting from the body's inability to properly absorb nutrients.

Malabsorption syndromes Poor absorption of nutrients from the intestinal tract into the blood.

Malaise Vague feeling of body discomfort.

Malaria Any of a group of human febrile diseases caused by infection of red blood cells by protozoan parasites of the genus Plasmodium. Malaria is transmitted between people by a bite from an infected mosquito of the genus Anopheles or by blood transfusion or parenteral inoculation with infected blood. One of the most common infectious diseases worldwide, malaria is endemic in tropical areas of Central and South America, Africa, and Southeast Asia. Four species of Plasmodium cause malaria in humans: P. falciparum, P. vivax, P. mala-riae, and P. ovale. Once infection has occurred, it may persist in the body for years and recur peri-

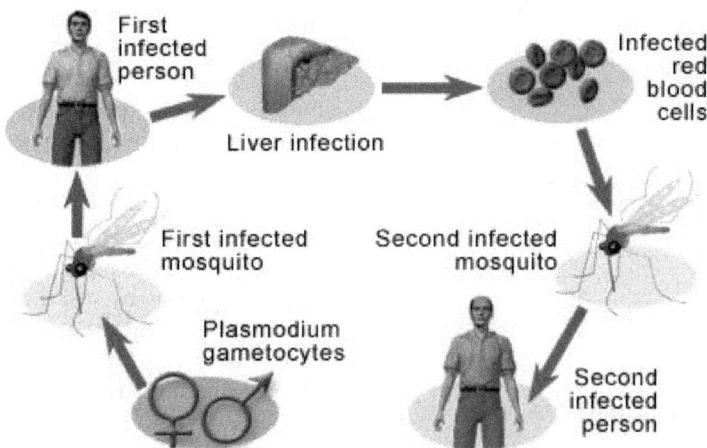

First infected person

Liver infection

Infected red blood cells

First infected mosquito

Second infected mosquito

Plasmodium gametocytes

Second infected person

Fig. *Malaria*

odically, resulting in chills, fever, anemia, and an enlarged spleen. The severity and manifestations of the disease largely depend on the particular infecting species (P. vivax and P. ovale have a persistent stage in the liver that causes relapses), the magnitude of the infection, and the cytokines released as a result of the infection.

Male breast cancer Cancer that forms in tissues of the breast in men. Most male breast cancer begins in cells lining the ducts. It is very rare and usually affects older men. Most cases of male breast cancer happen to men between ages 60 and 70.

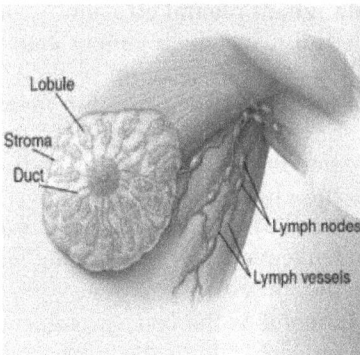

Fig. *Male breast cancer*

Male menopause Symptoms, such as depression, change in libido, impotence, in men at midlife. Many authorities claim no such condition exists.

Malignancy A term for diseases in which abnormal cells divide without control and can invade nearby tissues. Malignant cells can also spread to other parts of the body through the blood and lymph systems. There are several main types of malignancy. Carcinoma is a malignancy that begins in the skin or in tissues that line or cover internal organs. Sarcoma is a malignancy that begins in bone, cartilage, fat, muscle, blood vessels, or other connective or supportive tissue. Leukemia is a malignancy that starts in blood-forming tissue such as the bone marrow, and causes large numbers of abnormal blood cells to be produced and enter the blood. Lymphoma and multiple myeloma are malignancies that begin in the cells of the immune system. Central nervous system cancers are malignancies that begin in the tissues of the brain and spinal cord. Also called cancer.

Malignant Capable of causing destruction of normal tissue; may lead to death. Usually refers to cancer growth.

Malignant cancerous Malignant tumours can invade and destroy nearby tissue and spread to other parts of the body.

Malignant ascites A condition in which fluid containing cancer cells collects in the abdomen.

Malignant ectomesenchymoma A rare, fast-growing tumour of the nervous system or soft tissue that occurs in children and young adults. Malignant ectomesen-chymomas may form in the head and neck, abdomen, perineum, scrotum, or limbs. Also called ectomesen-chymoma.

Malignant fibrous cytoma A soft tissue sarcoma that usually occurs in the limbs, most commonly the legs, and may also occur in the abdomen. It is also called malignant fibrous histiocytoma.

Malignant melanoma A soft tissue tumour that begins in a tendon (tough, fibrous, cord-like tissue that connects muscle to bone or to another structure). Malignant melanoma of soft parts has certain markers that are also found on malignant melanoma (a type of skin cancer). It usually occurs in the leg or arm. Also called clear cell sarcoma of soft tissue.

Malignant meningioma A rare, fast-growing tumour that forms in one of the inner layers of the meninges (thin layers of tissue that cover and protect the brain and spinal cord). Malignant meningioma often spreads to other areas of the body.

Malignant mesothelioma A rare type of cancer in which malignant cells are found in the lining of the chest or abdomen. Exposure to airborne asbestos particles increases one's risk of developing malignant mesothelioma.

Malignant mixed Müllerian **tumour** A rare type of tumour that is a mixture of carcinoma and sarcoma cells. MMMT usually occurs in the uterus.

Malignant peripheral nerve sheath tumour A type of soft tissue sarcoma that develops in cells that form a protective sheath (covering) around peripheral nerves, which are nerves that are outside of the central nervous system (brain and spinal cord). It is also called MPNST.

Malignant pleural effusion A condition in which cancer causes an abnormal amount of fluid to collect between the thin layers of tissue (pleura) lining the outside of the lung and the wall of the chest cavity. Lung cancer, breast cancer, lymphoma, and leukemia cause most malignant pleural effusions.

Malleolus is the bony prominence on each side of the ankle. Each

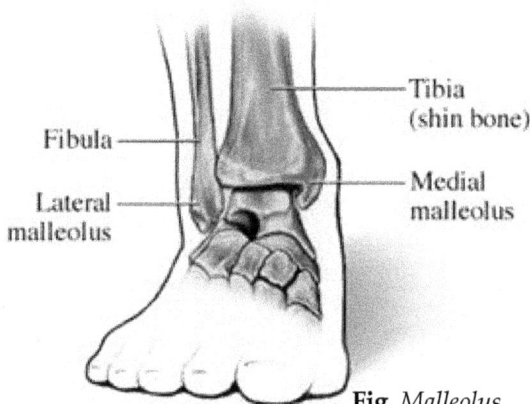

Fibula

Lateral malleolus

Tibia (shin bone)

Medial malleolus

Fig. *Malleolus*

leg is supported by two bones, the tibia on the inner side (medial) of the leg and the fibula on the outer side (lateral) of the leg. The medial malleolus is the prominence on the inner side of the ankle, formed by the lower end of the tibia. The lateral malleolus is the prominence on the outer side of the ankle, formed by the lower end of the fibula.

Mallory-Weiss Syndrome Condition characterized by massive bleeding following a tear in the mucous membrane at the junction of the esophagus and stomach. Tear is usually caused from prolonged vomiting, most common in alcoholics or people who have an obstruction preventing food from passing out of the stomach into the small intestine. Surgery is usually required to stop bleeding.

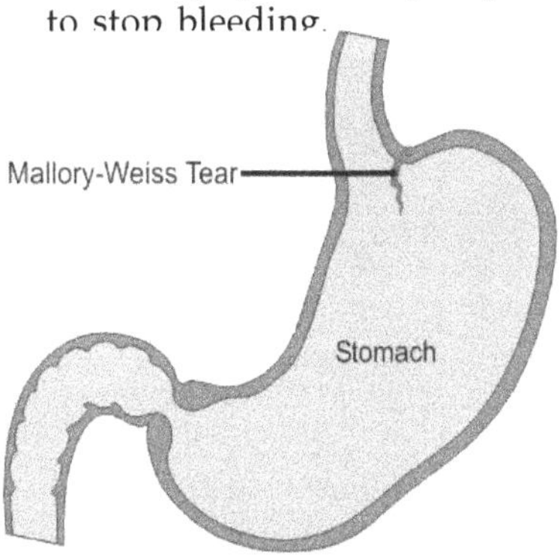

Fig. *Mallory-Weiss syndrome*

Malnourished Describes a condition caused by not getting enough calories or the right amount of key nutrients needed for health. Key nutrients include vitamins and minerals.

Malnutrition In broad sense, a condition caused by not getting enough calories or the right amount of key nutrients, such as vitamins and minerals, that are needed for health. Malnutrition may occur when there is a lack of nutrients in the diet or when the body cannot absorb nutrients from food.

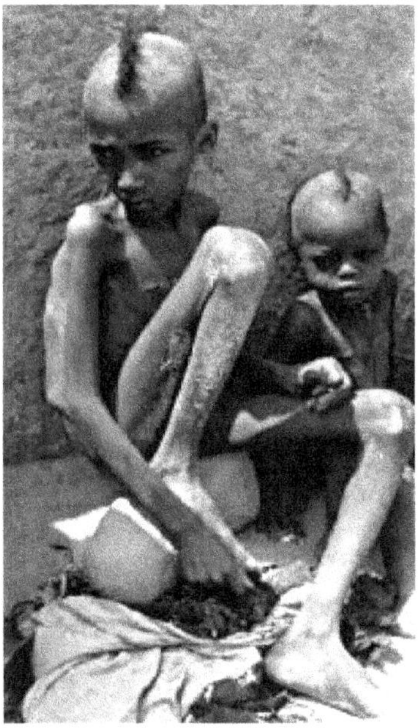

Fig. *Malnutrition*

Malpractice A dereliction from professional duty or a failure to exercise an accepted degree of professional skill or learning by one (as a physician) rendering professional services which results in injury, loss, or damage. Also an injurious, negligent, or improper practice.

Malpractice insurance Insurance purchased by doctors and other providers to cover them against malpractice lawsuits.

Maltreatment Physical, emotional, or educational neglect, or physical, emotional or sexual abuse, most often perpetrated by a family member.

Mammary dysplasia A common condition marked by benign (not cancer) changes in breast tissue. These changes may include irregular lumps or cysts, breast discomfort, sensitive nipples, and itching. These symptoms may change throughout the menstrual cycle and usually stop after menopause. Also called benign breast disease, fibrocystic breast changes, and fibrocystic breast disease.

Mammary Having to do with the breast.

Mammary gland   Glandular organ located on the chest. It is an organ in female mammals that produces milk to feed young offspring.The mammary gland is made up of connective tissue, fat, and tissue that contains the glands that can make milk. It is also called breast. A mammary gland is a specific type of apocrine gland specialized for manufacture of colostrum when giving birth.

Mammogram An X-ray of the breast.

Mammography X-ray examination of the breast, used as both a screening procedure on apparently healthy females and as a diagnostic procedure in clinical situations to detect breast pict.

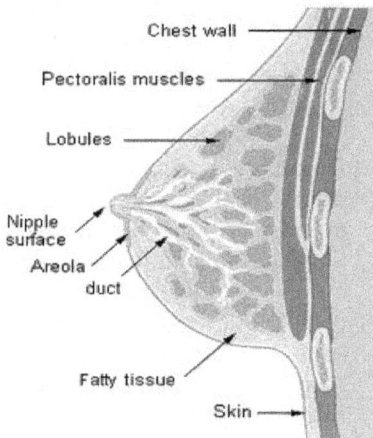

Fig. *Mammography*

The goal of mammography is the early detection of breast cancer, typically through detection of characteristic masses and/or microcalcifications. Like all X-rays, mammograms use doses of ionizing radiation to create images.

Mammotome A device that uses a computer-guided probe to perform breast biopsies. A Mammotome biopsy can be done on an outpatient basis

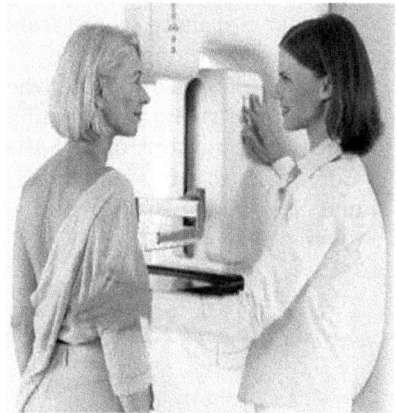

Fig. *Mammary gland*

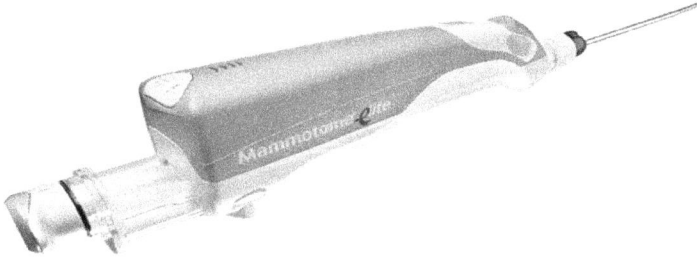

Fig. *Mammotome*

with a local anesthetic, removes only a small amount of healthy tissue, and doesn't require sutures (stitches) because the incision is very small.

Managed care A method of financing and delivering health care for a set fee using a network of physicians and other providers who have agreed to the set fees. Managed care may include pre-admission or pre-treatment certification, second surgical opinion programmes, fee or price negotiation, pre-treatment protocol review, pre-admission testing, continued stay review, discharge planning, and individual/large case management. Failure to comply with managed care requirements or decisions usually reduces health benefit coverage for claims. The penalties may affect both the patient and the provider(s).

Managed care organization An entity which provides or contracts for managed care. managed care organized programmes designed to control access to impatient and ambulatory health services, to ensure the medical necessity of the proposed service and the delivery of the service at the most efficient and cost effective level of care consistent with high quality. Managed care is essential to the structure of alternative delivery and financing systems, such as health maintenance organizations and preferred provider arrangements. The requirements can also be a component of traditional indemnity or fee-for-service health coverage.

Managed competition A series of financial structures and methods used to manage the process by which individuals select health insurance coverage in a competitive market. The goal of managed competition is to encourage cost-conscious consumer choice when individuals select a plan. This, in turn, is intended to strengthen financial incentives for plans to deliver services in the most cost-effective manner. The basic structures of managed competition include a national board which would make decisions affecting benefit design and market rules, "sponsors" which manage the process of individual health insurance choice, and integrated health care delivery networks which provide and manage care. These structures have been termed as a National Health Board, Health Insurance Purchasing Cooperative (HIPCs), and Accountable Health Partnerships (AHPs) in several reform proposals.

Managed fee for-service An insurance plan that works very much like normal plans except they have specific enforced utilization rules which include, but are not limited to: pre-hospitalization case review, prospective length of stay approvals, second opinions for surgery, current and previous records review, discharge planning and claims audits.

Management guidelines A practice guideline that covers the evaluation and management of patients who is known to have a particular condition.

Managerial technology Technology used to facilitate and support the prevision of health care services but not directly associated with patient care, including administration, transportation, and communication, both within and among health care facilities.

Mandated benefits Each state is responsible for the conduct of the insurance business within its boundaries rather than the Federal Government. Each state establishes its requirements for insurance company licensure. A

state may establish minimum health insurance policy coverage provisions, such as a specified scope of services and covered providers. A state may require that all insured benefit plans include specific benefits, or both approaches may be used, depending upon the specific coverage under consideration. ERISA exempts self-insured employers from state mandates.

Mandated benefits, federal preemption A legislative proposal that would require all employers to provide a minimum health benefit for all permanent employees as a condition of doing business. It would exempt employers meeting the Federal requirements from state mandated benefits.

Mandated employer insurance An insurance policy where employers are required to provide health benefit coverage for their employees.

Mandatory assignment A requirement that a physician agrees to accept the Medicare determination of approved charges as payment in full for medical services.

Mania Formerly used as a nonspecific term for any type of "madness." Currently used as a suffix to indicate a morbid preoccupation with some kind of idea or activity, and/or a compulsive need to behave in some deviant way. Some examples are as follows:

– egomania – Pathological preoccupation with self.

— erotomania : The delusion that one is loved by a particular person.

— kleptomania : Compulsion to steal.

— megalomania : Grandiose delusions of power, wealth, or fame.

— monomania : Pathological preoccupation with one subject.

— necromania : Pathological preoccupation with dead bodies.

— nymphomania : Abnormal and excessive need or desire in the woman for sexual intercourse;

— pyromania : Compulsion to set fires; an impulse control disorder.

— trichotillomania : Compulsion to pull one's own hair out; an impulse disorder.

Mania Bipolar disorder A mood disorder characterized by excessive elation, inflated self-esteem and grandiosity, hyperactivity, agitation, and accelerated thinking and speaking. Flight of ideas may be present. A manic syndrome may also occur in organic mental disorder.

Manic depression: Also called bipolar affective disorder, a mental illness whose symptoms involve abnormal mood swings cycling from a marked depression to uncontrollable feelings of elation and an expansive, euphoric mood (mania), with a return to normal behaviour between episodes. Its causes are complex and poorly defined, but may include biologic, psychologic, interpersonal, and cultural factors, with physical illness, certain drugs, and a familial pattern as possible contributors. Treatment includes the use of antidepressive, tranquilizing, and antianxiety drugs, long term psychotherapy, and lithium treatment to prevent relapse.

Manic episode A distinct period of time (usually lasting at least 1 week) of abnormally and persistently elevated, expansive, or irritable mood accompanied by suchsymptoms as inflated self-esteem or grandiosity, decreased need for sleep, overtalkativeness or pressured speech, flight of ideas or feeling that thoughts are racing, inattentiveness and distractibility, increased goal-directed activity (e.g., at work or school, socially or sexually), and involvement in pleasurable activities with high potential for painful consequences (e.g., buying sprees, sexual indiscretions, foolish business ventures).

Manic-depressive illness Term often used synonymously with bipolar disorder, as defined in DSM-IV.

Manipulation An application of manual force for healing. Term describes the techniques used in osteopathy, chiropractic, massage, and other bodywork therapies. Manipulation may involve various forms of massage, muscle pressure, and joint realignment or adjustment.

Mannitol A drug used to decrease swelling of the brain and to treat kidney failure. Mannitol can also be used to open the blood-brain barrier, which allows anticancer medicines to enter the brain and treat brain tumours.

Mantra In Hinduism and Buddhism, mystic word used in ritual and meditation. It is believed to have power to bring into being the reality it represents. Use of such mantras usually requires initiation by a guru, or spiritual teacher.

Manual rates Rates developed based upon the health plan's average claims data and then adjusted for group specific demo-graphics, industry factors, or benefit variations.

Manual wheelchair is a chair with wheels, designed to be a replacement for walking. Wheelchairs are used by people for whom walking is difficult or impossible due to illness (physiological or physical), injury, or disability. People with both sitting and walking disability often need to use a wheelbench. A basic manual wheelchair incorporates a seat, foot rests and four wheels: two, caster wheels at the front and two large wheels at the back. The two larger wheels in the back usually have handrims; two metal or plastic circles approximately 3/4" thick. The handrims have a diameter normally only slightly smaller than the wheels they are attached to. Most wheelchairs have two push handles at the top of the back to allow for manual propulsion by a second person.

MAO-B, monoamine oxidase B An enzyme, found in the liver and the nervous system, that catalyzes the oxidation of a large variety of monoamine, substances including epinephrine, norepinephrine, and serotonin. It can also convert

BASIC MANUAL WHEELCHAIR PARTS

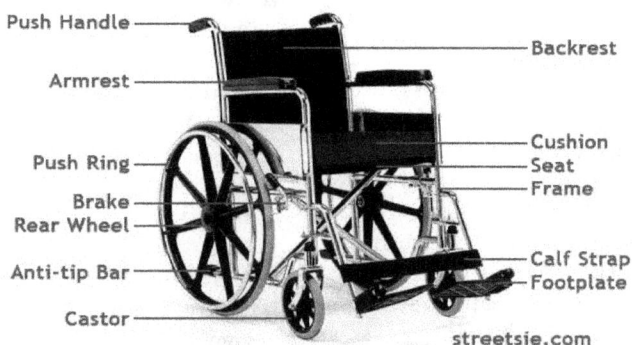

Fig. *Manual wheelchair*

other chemicals to toxins that destroy substantial nigra cells, thereby producing parkinsonism. Drugs that inhibit this enzyme in brain tissue are used as a treatment for depression.

Maple syrup urine disease (MSUD) A rare, autosomal recessive genetic disorder in which the enzyme necessary for the breakdown of three essential branched-chain amino acids (Ieucine, isoleucine, and valine) is lacking, resulting in the accumulation of these substances in the blood and urine. The disease derives its name from the characteristic odour of the urine of affected infants. Classic MSUD results in life-threatening acidemia and necrologic dysfunction in the newborn period, and is fatal if untreated or treated too late. It can be diagnosed before symptoms appear by a screening test in the first week of life. Treatment is based on rigid dietary control of these amino acids. Also called branched chain ketonuria.

Marasmus Marasmus is the predominant form of PEM throughout most developing countries. It is associated with the early abandonment or failure of breast-feeding. Infections, especially infantile gastroenteritis may then develop and worsen the malnutrition. Kwashiorkor is less common and is usually manifest as the intermediate marasmic kwashiorkor state. It tends to be predominant in those parts of the world (rural Africa, the Caribbean and Pacific islands) where staple and weaning foods such as yam, cassava, sweet potato, or green banana are protein deficient and excessively starchy.

Marfan syndrome A dominantly inherited connective tissue disorder associated with a variety of musculoskeletal abnormalities, including long, thin fingers, tall stature, scoliosis, ligament laxity, cardiovascular disorder, lens dislocation, and myopia. Its potentially fatal complication is aortic dissection and rupture, with the mean age of death before age 50. Also called arachnodacytly ("spider finge-redness").

Margin of safety Division of the NOEL or NOAEL by the current, desired, or most feasible human exposure level.

Marker In genetics, an identifiable physical location on a chromosome (e.g., a restriction enzyme cutting site) whose inheritance can be followed in family and population studies or linkage analysis. Markers can be expressed regions of DNA (genes) or some segment of DNA with no known coding function but whose pattern of inheritance can be determined.

Market area The targeted geographic area or areas of greatest market potential.

Market penetration The part of the total health care market that a managed care company has captured.

Market-based reform Reliance on competition in the health care market to assure services of acceptable cost and quality to consumers without government mandates or involvement in rate-setting, financing, or administration. If can also refer to the reduction of barriers in the operation of a health care market.

Marketplace medicine An attempt by purchasers to introduce competition for patients among providers and professionals as a cost containment mechanism.

Massage therapy This is a general term for a range of therapeutic approaches with roots in both Eastern and Western cultures. Involves the practice of kneading or otherwise manipulating a person's muscles and soft tissue.

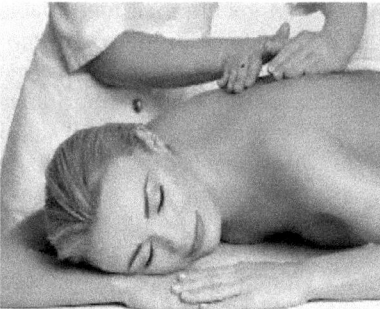

Fig. *Massage therapy*

Mast cells A mast cell is a resident cell of several types of tissues and contains many granules rich in histamine and heparin. Although best known for their role in allergy and anaphylaxis, mast cells play an important

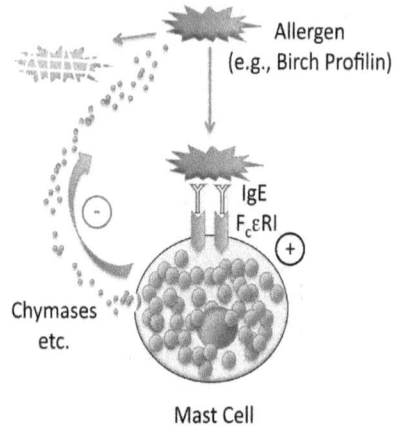

Fig. *Mast cells*

protective role as well, being intimately involved in wound healing and defence against pathogens. The mast cell is very similar in both appearance and function to the basophil, a type of white blood cell. However, they are not the same, as they arise from different cell lines.

Mastitis An inflammation of the breast, which sometimes develops into an infection. Symptoms include fever, soreness, and swelling.

Mastocytosis Overproduction of mast cells. May rarely infiltrate liver, spleen, bones, the gastrointestinal system and skin. May precede mast cell leukemia, which is a malignant disorder.

Masturbation is the sexual stimulation of one's own genitals, usually to the point of orgasm. The stimulation can be performed using the hands, fingers, everyday objects, or dedicated sex toys.

Match certain grants Requirement that the grantee contribute a percentage of the resources necessary for carrying out the grant programme. The usual resource is cash (hard match), but some programmes accept personal and/or facilities in lieu of cash (soft match). Material Safety Data Sheet (MSDS) The purpose of OSHA Hazard Communication Standard is to ensure the hazards of all chemical substances and mixtures produced or imported are evaluated and this hazard information is communicated by means of a printed written document called the MSDS. The MSDS must be written in English and contain certain required information including the chemical identity or common name, health hazards, emergency & first aid procedures, and safety precautions.

Maternal and child health (MCH) services block grant programme A Federal block grant programme authorized under Title V of the Social Security Act, that supports the provision of health services to mothers and children, especially those with low income or living in areas with limited availability of health services. Funds are provided to States, which in turn may provide them to local health departments. Created by the Omnibus Budget Reconciliation Act of 1981, the MCH block grant consolidated several categorical grant programmes into one block grant. The MCH block grant is administered by the Bureau of Maternal and Child Health in the Health Resources and Services Administration in DHHS.

Maternal deprivation syndrome A condition in a baby who has been physically and emotionally deprived. Symptoms include failure to thrive and slow growth and development. It may occur in cases of severe postnatal depression or in other cases when a parent may be unavailable.

Maternal mortality Maternal mortality includes deaths due to complications of pregnancy, childbirth, and the puerperium (the period of 42 days following the termination of pregnancy). Causes of maternal mortality include uterine hemorrhage, toxemia, and underlying medical conditions that complicate pregnancy such as diabetes and infections (e.g., tuberculosis, syphilis).

Maternal mortality rate The annual number of maternal deaths related to pregnancy as a proportion of the annual number of live births.

Maternity care Prenatal care and intrapartum care; medical services from conception through labour and delivery.

Maternity cycle The period of time from conception through to the first six weeks after the birth.

Maternity leave Paid or unpaid time off work after a mother has given birth or adopted a child.

Maternity stay legislation Governs the length of hospital stay for a mother and newborn following the newborn's birth. Most maternity-stay legislation follows guidelines jointly established by the American college of obstetricians and gynecologists (ACOG) and the American academy of pediatrics (AAP) which recommend that a woman and newborn receive a minimum of 48 hours of hospital care following an uncomplicated vaginal delivery and 96 hours of care following a C-section.

Maturation In evaluation studies, the impact on outcome of the passage of time, independent of the intervention being evaluated.

Maturity Onset Diabetes of the Young (MODY) A form of diabetes characterised by early age of onset (usually less than 25 years of age), autosomal dominant inheritance (that is, it is inherited by 50% of a parent's children) with diabetes in at least 2 generations of the patient's family. MODY diabetes that can often be controlled with meal planning or diabetes pills, at least in the early stages of diabetes. It differs from type 2 diabetes in that patients have a defect in insulin secretion or glucose metabolism, and are not resistant to insulin. MODY accounts for about 2% of diabetes worldwide and 6 genes have so far been found that cause MODY, although not all MODY patients have one of these genes.

Because MODY runs in families, it is useful for studying diabetes genes and has given researchers useful information about how insulin is produced and regulated by the pancreas.

Mauriac Syndrome A condition that occurs as the result of chronic poor control of diabetes. It leads to an enlarged liver due to excessive glycogen deposition, short stature and delayed puberty. There is usually a history of repeated hospitalizations for keto-acidosis and hemoglobin A1c tests can be as high as twice the upper level of normal. Kidney function is usually not affected although it may be an additional complication of poor control. Eating disorders are sometimes an accompaniment.

Maximal aerobic power The maximal volume of oxygen consumed per unit of time. An index of endurance potential.

Maximum allowable charge The largest dollar amount to which an insurance carrier will apply plan benefits.

Maximum allowable concentration (MAC) The limit on atmospheric contaminants in manned spacecraft for missions of up to seven days; set by the national aeronautics and space administration.

Maximum allowable costs list A list of prescription medications established by the health plan and distributed to pharmacies, which will be covered at a generic product level.

Maximum contaminant level (MCL) An enforceable standard set by EPA for pollutants in drinking water, to be set as close as possible to the maximum contaminant level goals.

Maximum contaminant level goal (MCLG) Nonenforceable goal set by EPA for pollutants in drinking water. MCLGS for carcinogenic pollutants are set at zero; goals for noncarcinogenic pollutants are set by establishing the lowest dose at which harmful effects can be observed, compensating for uncertainties, and calculating predicted human exposure from food and air.

Maximum out of pocket costs A limit on the total amount of co-payments, deductibles and co-insurance that a beneficiary is responsible for paying.

MDI Multiple daily injections (of insulin) One of several terms that are used to describe insulin programmes that are designed to obtain tight control of blood sugar by giving several shots every day.

MDS (Minimum data set) A core set of screening and assessment elements, including common definitions and coding categories, that form the foundation of the comprehensive assessment for all patients of long term care facilities certified to participate in Medicare and Medicaid. The items standardize communication about patient problems and conditions within facilities, between facilities and outside agencies.

Meal plan A guide for controlling the amount of calories, carbohydrates, proteins, and fats a person eats. People with diabetes can use such plans as the Exchange Lists or the Point System to help them plan their meals so that they can keep their diabetes under control.

Measles A highly contagious viral disease involving primarily a harassing cough with steadily mounting fever followed by the eruption of red papules on the skin. It is spread by respiratory contact, primarily airborne droplets of nasal secretions containing the virus. It can be prevented by the MMR vaccine.

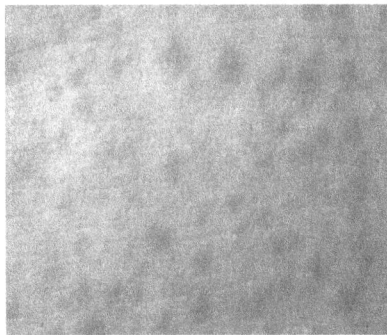

Fig. *Measles*

Measles, Mumps, Rubella (MMR) vaccine A combination vaccine composed of the three live, attenuated virus vaccines providing long term immunity against measles, mumps, and rubella; given by injection in a 2-dose schedule, usually at 15 months of age and again at school entry.

Mechanistic toxicology An approach to testing that focuses on the chemical processes by which a toxic effect occurs. Mechanistic toxicology testing relies heavily on physiology, biochemistry, and analytical chemistry techniques to monitor these processes.

Meconium Thick, sticky, dark-green material that collects in the intestines of a fetus and forms the first stools of a newborn.

Meconium aspiration Meconium is the first stool that a baby passes. This may occur before, during, or after birth. Stress may cause the baby to pass meconium before birth. Meconium then floats in the fluid in the womb. It can get into the baby's nose and mouth. It can even get into the baby's lungs, especially when the baby takes the first breath. There, the meconium can cause lung irritation and breathing problems. This is known as meconium aspiration syndrome. Depending on how much meconium is inhaled, the problem can range from mild to very severe.

When meconium gets into the baby's lungs, the airways (bronchial tubes) inside the lungs become inflamed (red and swollen). This makes breathing harder. Meconium can also get stuck inside the air sacs (alveoli) at the ends of the airways. This makes it harder for the baby to get enough oxygen. Meconium in the airways may also prevent air from leaving the lungs. This can cause the lungs to overinflate (fill with too much air) and lead to problems such as pneumothorax (a collapsed lung).

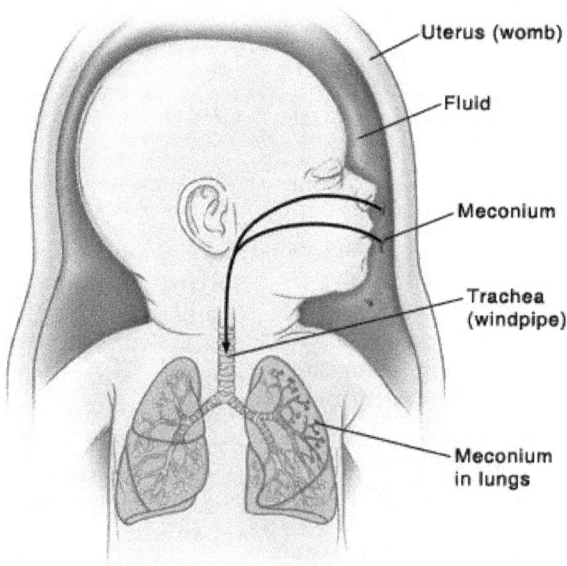

Uterus (womb)

Fluid

Meconium

Trachea (windpipe)

Meconium in lungs

Fig. *Meconium aspiration*

Meconium ileus Obstruction of the small intestine in the newborn caused by a plug of meconium. Often the plug may be dislodged by giving enemas. Rarely, surgery is required. Condition may be an indication of cystic fibrosis.

Medial collateral ligament Ligament of knee attaching to medial femoral condyle and to medial tibia. It provides medial stability to the knee.

Medial Pertaining to or near the middle.

Medial rectus muscle Muscle that moves the eye toward the nose.

Median When applied to numbers, a value that falls exactly in the middle of a specified range. Half of the numbers are above the median, and half of the numbers are below the median. As an example, "five" is the median of a range of numbers from one to nine.

Mediastinitis Inflammation of the mediastinum.

Mediastinum is an undelineated group of structures in the thorax, surrounded by loose connective tissue. It is the central compartment of the thoracic cavity. It contains the heart, the great vessels of the heart, the esophagus, the trachea, the phrenic nerve, the cardiac nerve, the thoracic duct, the thymus, and the lymph nodes of the central chest. The mediastinum lies between the right and left pleura in and near the median sagittal plane of the chest. It extends from the sternum in front to the vertebral column behind, and contains all the thoracic viscera except the lungs.

Mediastinal tumours are benign or cancerous growths that form in the area of the chest that separates the lungs. This area, called the mediastinum, is surrounded by the breastbone in front, the spine in back, and the

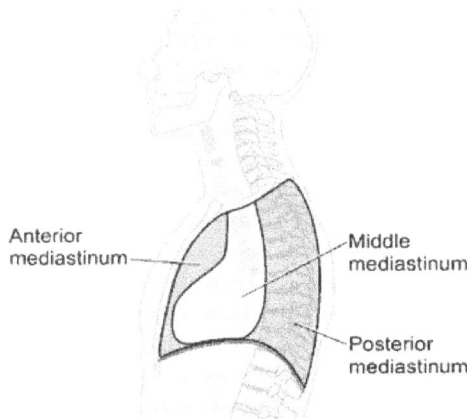

Anterior mediastinum

Middle mediastinum

Posterior mediastinum

Fig. *Mediastinum*

lungs on each side. The mediastinum contains the heart, aorta, esophagus, thymus and trachea.

- The anterior (front)
- The middle
- The posterior (back)

Mediastinum tumours are mostly made of reproductive (germ) cells or develop in thymic, neurogenic (nerve), lymphatic or mesenchymal (soft) tissue.

Medicaid The federally supported, state operated public assistance programme that pays for health care services to people with a low income, including elderly or disabled persons who qualify. Medicaid pays for long term nursing facility care, some limited home health services, and may pay for some assisted living services, depending on the state.

Medicaid (Title XIX) A joint federal-state programme that pays for medical and other services on behalf of certain groups of low-income persons. The following provisions of the social security act relate to managed care and long term care: 1902(r)(2) — section of the social security act which allows states to use more liberal income and resource methodologies than those used in determining SSI eligibility as the basis for setting medicaid eligibility. 1903(m) — section of the social security act which allows state medicaid programmes to develop risk contracts with

HMOs or comparable entities. 1929 — section of the social security act which allows states to provide a broad range of home and community care to functionally disabled individuals as an optional atate plan benefit (unpopular because of caps on federal participation).

Medicaid 2176 Home and Community-Based waiver A waiver obtained under the medicaid 2176 home and community-based waiver programme which allows States to provide a coordinated package of home and community-based services for individuals who otherwise would be at risk of nursing homeplacement or who are already in an institution. A State with a medicaid 2176 waiver may use medicaid funds to pay for services that are not ordinarily covered by medicaid; may pay for services for some medicaid beneficiaries and not others, so that benefits can be targeted; and may use a higher income standard to determine eligibility for the waiver programme than the standard used for other medicaid services.

Medicaid management information system The reporting system used by HCFA to gather data on medicaid use around the country.

Medicaid prudent pharmaceutical purchasing act Enacted as part of the omnibus budget reconciliation act of 1990, MPPPA provides that medicaid must receive the best discounted price of any institutional purchaser of pharmaceuticals. In doing so, drug companies provide rebates to medicaid equal to the difference between the discounted price and the price at which the drug was sold. This bill has resulted in cost shifting throughout the health industry.

Medicaid waivers An exception to the usual requirements of medicaid granted to a state by HCFA. The following numbers refer to the applicable section of the social security act—1115 – allows states to waive provisions of Medicaid law to test new concepts which are consistent with the goals of the Medicaid programme. System-wide changes are possible under this provision. Frequently used to establish medicaid managed care programmes. 1915(b) — allows state to waive freedom of choice. States may require that beneficiaries enroll in HMOs or other managed care programmes, or select a physician to serve as their primary care case manager. 1915 (c) – Allows states to waive various Medicaid requirements to establish alternative, community-based services for (a) individuals who would otherwise require the level of care provided in a hospital or skilled nursing facility, and/or (b) persons already in such facilities who need assistance returning to the community. Target populations for 1915 (c) waivers include older adults, persons with disabilities, persons with mental retarda-

tion, persons with chronic mental illness and persons with AIDS. Also known as a 2176 waiver in reference to the relevant section of the omnibus budget reconciliation act of 1981. 1915(d) –similar to 1915(c) waiver except that expenditures for nursing facility and home and community-based services for person 65 years and older cannot exceed a projected amount, determined by taking a base year expenditure (last year before the waiver), and adjusting for inflation. Also eliminates requirements that programmes be statewide and be comparable for all target populations. Income rules for eligibility can also be waived.

Medicaid-certified bed A nursing facility bed in a building or part of a building which has been determined to meet federal standards for serving medicaid recipients.

Medical aid unit A medical facility where ambulatory patients can be treated without an appointment, and receive immediate, non-emergency care. The medical aid units are not usually opened 24 hours a day; patients calling an HMO after hours with urgent, but not emergent, clinical problems, are often referred to these facilities. A similar facility is an urgent care centre or unit, which may be opened 24 hours a day.

Medical care evaluation studies The name given to a generic form of health care review in which problems in the quality of the delivery and organization of health care services are addressed and monitored.

Medical consumer price index An inflationary statistic that measures the cost of all purchased health care services.

Medical device Any instrument, apparatus, or similar or related article that is intended to prevent, diagnose, mitigate, or treat disease or to affect the structure or function of the body.

Medical director The medical director is the physician licensed in Florida, who is responsible for implementation of resident care policies and coordination of medical care in the facility.

Medical doctor (MD) A licensed physician who is a graduate of an accredited medical school and practices allopathic medicine.

Medical foundations (MF) An organization through which physicians, hospitals and other providers can integrate the delivery of medical service. Usually an MF is an affiliate of a hospital through a common parent organization or is a subsidiary of a hospital. In most cases MFs are non-profit entities that own and manages facilities, equipment and supplies of a medical practice. They usually contract directly with patients and third party payers and employ non-professional personnel as well as physicians.

Medical Illness Severity Grouping System (MEDISGRPS) A computerized data system devel-

oped by MediQual Systems, Inc., that categorizes patients' risk of dying or increased morbidity into four groups based on key physiological findings (e.g., seventy of illness upon admission to the hospital).

Medical indigence Inability to pay for needed medical care, whether through insurance, savings, current income, or borrowing against future income.

Medical injury An adverse medical outcome that could be either unavoidable or avoidable, i.e., negligently induced.

Medical IRA A tax-exempt account into which each household would contribute a limited amount of money to cover medical costs or buy insurance.

Medical laboratory technician Works under the direction of a registered medical laboratory technologist and performs many routine clinical laboratory procedures. These procedures include obtaining specimens, mounting tissue specimens and setting up and utilizing laboratory equipment.

Medical laboratory technologist Performs a variety of chemical, microscopic, and bacteriology tests and procedures and related duties, to obtain data for use in the diagnosis and treatment of disease.

Medical maintenance in the treatment of drug abuse, an approach that calls for stable, nondrug using, socially rehabilitative methadone-maintained patients to receive their total methadone dosage from a physician at a primary care setting at intervals as far apart as 28 days.

Medical malpractice Professional misconduct or unreasonable lack of skill by a physician or other health care provider a judicial determination that there has been a negligent (or, rarely, willful) failure to adhere to the current standards of medical care, resulting in injury or harm to the patient. Since the judgment of malpractice is social-legal and is made on a case by case rather than systematic basis, standards and processes for determining malpractice vary by area.

Medical practice act A State law that provides statutory authority for the State to license and discipline physicians and other health care professionals.

Medical protocols Medical protocols are the guidelines that physicians in the future may be required to follow in order to have an acceptable clinical outcome. The protocol would provide the caregiver with specific treatment options or steps when faced with a particular set of clinical symptoms or signs or laboratory data. Medical protocols would be designed through an accumulated database of clinical outcomes.

Medical record review Review of a patient's medical record to determine how the medical provider performed.

Medical record The file of information compiled by physicians or other medical professionals of patients' medical history, present illness, findings on examination, details of treatment, and notes on progress. The medical record is the legal record of care.

Medical records director/coordinator Plans and directs the activities and personnel of the department. Coordinates the management of resident medical records and the clerical needs of the nursing department.

Medical removal protection (MRP) A programme specified by the Occupational Safety and Health Administration's lead standard. It requires removal of workers from lead-contaminated environments when their blood lead levels exceed specified levels.

Medical savings account A method of financing health care by giving a tax advantage to individuals who establish and maintain personal accounts for health care purposes; similar to an Individual Retirement Account for retirement purposes. Also referred to as individual health care account.

Medical technology Includes drugs, devices, techniques, and procedures used in delivering medical care and the support systems for that care. There are no accurate estimates of how much new technology contributes to health spending.

Medical technology The drugs, devices, and medical and surgical procedures used in medical care, and the organizational and support systems within which such care is provided.

Medical tests These are procedures which enable medical experts to assess conditions in a patient. They range from non-invasive - listening to a heartbeat, for example - to invasive, such as injections or a spinal tap.

Medical transcriptionist Transcribes from dictating machine diagnostic work-ups, case histories, physicals, consultations, discharge summaries, and operations, using knowledge of medical terminology. Performs other routine clerical work.

Medical treatment case As defined by the occupational safety and health administration and the bureau of labour statistics, a work-related injury or illness that requires medical treatment beyond first aid.

Medical underwriting The evaluation process to determine whether the individuals or groups' health risk is acceptable. Individuals or groups may have to have their past experience or medical histories reviewed prior to coverage.

Medically indigent A category within the state medical assistance programme that defines an individual who is unable to pay for his/her health care.

Medically necessary A service or treatment which is appropriate and consistent with diagnosis, and which, in accordance with accepted standards of practice in the medical community of the area in which the health services are rendered, could not have been omitted without adversely affecting the member's condition or the quality of medical care rendered.

Medically needy Optional component of the Medicaid programme that allows states to offer Medicaid to persons who would otherwise be eligible, but whose incomes are too high. Such persons become eligible by spending a portion of their income each month on outstanding medical bills.

Medically underserved areas Areas determined by the Federal Government to have inadequate access to health care as determined by the Index of Medical Underservice(l M U) .

Medically undersexed populations Populations not meeting MUA criteria that are designated as undeserved based on unusual local conditions that may affect the area/population.

Medically unnecessary days A term used to describe that part of a stay in a facility deemed to be excessive to diagnose and treat a medical condition because the stay was either too long, or more appropriate care is available in a less costly or more efficient setting.

Medicare (Title XVIII) Federal programme that provides basic health care and limited long term care for retirees and certain disabled individuals without regard to income level. Beneficiaries must pay premiums, deductibles and coinsurance.

Part A —medicare hospital insurance that helps pay for medically necessary inpatient hospital care, and, after a hospital stay, and limited inpatient care in a skilled nursing facility, for limited home health care or hospice care.

Part B —medicare medical insurance that helps pay for medically necessary physician services, outpatient hospital services and supplies that are not covered by the hospital insurance.

Part C —medicare + Choice Also referred to as "medicare Part C," a medicare programme under which eligible medicare enrollees can elect to receive benefits through a managed care programme that places providers at risk for those benefits.

Medicare alzheimer's disease demonstration A demonstration programme, mandated by Congress in 1966, to determine the effectiveness, cost, and impact of providing comprehensive services for Medicare-enrollees who have Alzheimer's disease or a related disorder.

Medicare bonus payment An additional 10% payment to the physician above the allowed charge for services delivered to medicare beneficiaries in designated health professional shortage areas.

Medicare carriers Fiscal agents (typically blue shield plans or commercial insurance firms) under contract to the health care financing administration for administration of specific medicare tasks. These tasks include computing reasonable charges under medicare Part B, making actual payments, determining whether claims are for covered services, denying claims for noncovered services, and denying claims for unnecessary use of services.

Medicare conditions of participation Requirements that providers (including hospitals, skilled nursing homes, home health agencies, etc.) must meet in order to be allowed to receive payments for medicare patients. An example is the requirement that hospitals conduct utilization review.

Medicare cost HMO or contract Prospective payment for acute and primary health care (monthly fee per patient with settlement annually based on actual costs). Primarily used in rural areas where full capitation is not feasible.

Medicare cost report An annual report required of all institutions participating in the medicare programme. The MCR records each institution's total costs and charges associated with providing services to all patients, the portion of those costs and charges allocated to medicare patients, and the medicare payments received.

Medicare economic index The index that the medicare programme uses to set limits on physicians' prevailing charges, as specified by the social security amendments of 1972 (Public Law 92- 603). The MEI is based on estimates of the costs of producing physician office services and a measure of increases in earning levels in the general economy.

Medicare insured group Employer (or union) groups receiving a capitated rate from Medicare in exchange for integrating Medicare covered services into the employers own traditional retiree health plan.

Medicare intermediaries Fiscal agents (typically blue cross plans or commercial insurance firms) under contract to the health care financing administration for administration of specific medicare tasks. These tasks include determining reasonable costs for covered items and services, making payments, and guarding against unnecessary use of covered services for Medicare Part A payments. Intemediaries also make payments for home health and outpatient hospital services covered under Part B.

Medicare operating margin Revenues received by a health care provider from medicare less the provider's operating costs covered by medicare payments, divided by medicare revenues and multiplied by 100. medicare revenues and costs not covered under medicare's prospective payment system (e.g., capital expenditures, medical education costs) are excluded.

Medicare part A hospital insurance that helps pay for inpatient hospital care, limited skilled nursing care, hospice care, and some home health care. Most people get medicare Part A automatically when they turn 65.

Medicare part B Medical insurance that helps pay for doctors' services, outpatient hospital care, and some other medical services that Part A does not cover (like some home health care). Part B helps pay for these covered services and supplies when they are medically necessary. A monthly premium must be paid to receive Part B.

Medicare payment advisory commission A non-partisan congressional advisory body charged with providing policy advice and technical assistance concerning the medicare programme and other aspects of the health system. It conducts independent research, analyzes legislation, and makes recommendations to congress. The physician payment review commission (PPRC) has been merged with the prospective payment assessment commission (ProPAC) to create MedPAC.

Medicare provider analysis and review file A HCFA data file that contains charge data and clinical characteristics, such as diagnoses and procedures, for every hospital inpatient bill submitted to medicare for payment.

Medicare risk contract A contract between medicare and a health plan under which the plan receives monthly capitated payments to provide medicare-covered services for enrollees, and thereby assumes insurance risk for those enrollees. A plan is eligible for a risk contract if it is a federally qualified HMO or a competitive medical plan.

Medicare select A form of medigap insurance that allows insurers to experiment with the provision of supplemental benefits through a network of providers. coverage is often limited to those services furnished by the participating network providers and emergency out-of-area care.

Medicare self referral option A Medicare + Choice point of service option that allows enrollees in a medicare risk HMO to go out of plan at a higher cost.

Medicare supplemental insurance This is private insurance (often called medigap) that pays medicare's deductibles and co-insurances, and may cover services not covered by medicare. Most medigap plans will help pay for skilled nursing care, but only when that care is covered by medicare.

Medicare The federal programme providing primarily skilled medical care and medical insurance for people aged 65 and older, some disabled persons and those with end-stage renal disease.

Medicare vouchers A proposed alternative administrative change in the medicare programme in which each eligible person would be allowed a set amount of money to purchase medical care or health insurance.

Medicare waiver (222) Section of the social security amendments of 1972 allowing the federal government to waive medicare payment rules and allow alternative payment methods including capitation.

Medicare/Medicaid beneficiary One who receives coverage for health services under medicare or Medicaid.

Medicine holistic/wholistic Wholistic medicine is a broadly descriptive term for a healing philosophy that views a patient as a whole person, not as just a disease or a collection of symptoms. In the course of treatment, wholistic medical practitioners may address emotional and spiritual dimensions as well as the nutritional, environmental and lifestyle factors that may contribute to an illness. Many wholistic practitioners combine conventional forms of treatment with natural or alternative treatments.

Medigap A policy guaranteeing to pay a Medicare beneficiary's co-insurance, deductible and co-payments and will provide additional health plan or non-Medicare coverage for services up to a predefined benefit limit.

In essence, the product pays for the portion of the cost of services not covered by Medicare.

Medigap insurance A term commonly used to describe medicare supplemental insurance policies available from various companies. Medigap is private insurance that may be purchased by medicare-eligible individuals to help pay the deductibles and co-payments required under medicare. Medigap policies generally do not pay for services not covered by medicare.

Meditation refers to a broad variety of practices that includes techniques designed to promote relaxation, build internal energy (chi, ki, prana, etc.) and develop compassion, love, patience, generosity and forgiveness. A particularly ambitious form of meditation aims at effortlessly sustained single-pointed concentration single-

Fig. *Meditation*

pointed analysis, meant to enable its practitioner to enjoy an indestructible sense of well-being while engaging in any life activity. It often involves an internal effort to self-regulate the mind in some way. It can help clear the mind and ease many health issues, such as high blood pressure, depression, and anxiety to name a few (yoga journal).

Medline database The original, largest, and most utilized database in the National Library of Medicine's computerized retrieval and technical processing system. Medline contains references to biomedical and other literature relevant to health and health services.

Medulla Most internal part of a structure or organ.

Medulla oblongata The lowest section of the brainstem (at the top end of the spinal cord); it controls automatic functions including heartbeat, breathing, etc.

Meibomian gland Gland found in the eyelid that produces the oily outer layer of the three-layer tear film that lubricates the eye.

Meibomianitis Inflammation of the meibomian glands; rosacea is a common cause. Symptoms include red or pink eyelid margins, a red or pink eye, dryness, burning, blurred vision and a swollen eye.

Meiosis A type of cell division, unique to reproductive cells, by which chromosomes are duplicated and then reduced by half, giving rise to gametes each with half the chromosome number of the parent cells.

Melanin is a ubiquitous natural pigment found in most organisms. In animals melanin pigments are derivatives of the amino acid tyrosine. The production of melanin in human skin is called melanogenesis. Production of melanin is induced by UVB-radiation simulated by DNA, which is also a photo-protectan. In humans, melanin is the primary determinant of skin colour. It is also found in hair, the pigmented tissue underlying the iris of the eye, and the stria vascularis of the inner ear. In the brain, tissues with melanin include the medulla and pigment-bearing neurons wit-hin areas of the brainstem, such as the locus coeruleus and the substantia nigra. It also occurs in the zona reticularis of the adrenal gland.The melanin in the skin is produced by melanocytes, which are found in the basal layer of the epidermis.

Melanocytes are melanin-producing cells located in the bottom layer (the stratum basale) of the skin's epidermis, the middle layer of the eye (the uvea), the inner ear, meninges, bones, and heart. Melanin is the pigment primarily responsible for skin colour.

Melanoma Any of a group of malignant tumours, primarily of the skin, made up of melanocytes. Most develop from a pigmented mole over a period of several months or years.

Melanosis Condition characterized by melanin (pigment) deposits in the skin or eyes.

Melatonin Hormone produced by the pineal gland in the brain and released mainly at night in the absence of light on the retina. Regulates the onset and timing of sleep and seasonal changes in the body such as winter weight gain. Levels of melatonin decline with age. Melatonin is being investigated as a sleep promoter and to prevent or reduce jet lag. Synthetic melatonin and melatonin derived from bovine pineal glands are available as over-the-coun-

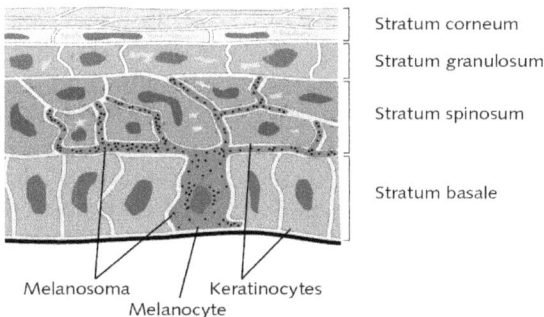

Stratum corneum

Stratum granulosum

Stratum spinosum

Stratum basale

Melanosoma / Keratinocytes
Melanocyte

Fig. *Melanocytes*

ter dietary supplements. Melatonin occurs naturally in some foods but in fairly small amounts. Reported side effects include reduced fertility, inhibition of male sexual drive, hypothermia, damage to the retina. Some physicians and scientists advise against taking melatonin as a long-term supplement.

Member A participant in a health plan who makes up the plan's enrollment.

Member month A unit of volume measurement. A member month is equal to one member enrolled in an HMO for one month, whether or not the member actually receives any services during the period. Two member months are equal to one member enrolled for two months or two members enrolled for one month.

Members per year The number of members effective in the health plan on a yearly basis.

Membrane fusion A process by which the membranes (outer walls) of two cells merge, thus creating one daughter cell from two parents. In contrast to fertilization by gametes, membrane fusion describesthe joining of somatic cells. One of the most productive results of membrane fusion technologies is the formation of hybridomas, wherein an antibody producing white blood cell (leukocyte) is fused with a tumour cell to produce a daughter cell that can generate large amounts of a specific antibody for use in diag-

nostic and therapeutic procedures (monoclinal antibodies).

Membranes The sac or "bag of waters" filled with amniotic fluid in which the developing baby grows. The "membranes" which make up the sac may occasionally rupture naturally as labour begins, but usually remain intact until the end of the first stage of labour. The membranes may also be broken by a midwife or doctor to speed up labour.

Memory The mental power that enables one to retain and to recall events, sensations, ideas, and information. There are several different forms of memory: immediate (remembering for a few seconds), short-term (remembering for a few months), and long-term (remembering material learned from year to year).

Mendelian In genetics, a term used to refer to a trait that follows the basic principles of inheritance described in the experiments of Gregor Mendel (1822-1884), the Austrian monk whose early research with garden peas laid the basis for modem genetics. Such traits are controlled by a single gene and follow a simple pattern of dominant or recessive inheritance. Mendel's laws include the Law of Segregation, which describes how each pair of alleles separates into different gametes, and the Law of Independent Assortment, which describes how different alleles are assorted inde-

Fig. *Gregor Mendel*

pendently of the other alleles in gametes and how the subsequent pairing of male and female gametes occurs at random.

Meninges are three layers of protective tissue called the dura mater, arachnoid mater, and pia mater that surround the neuraxis. The meninges of the brain and spinal cord are continuous, being linked through the magnum foramen.

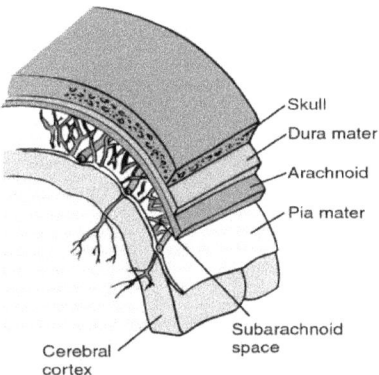

Fig. *Meninges*

Meningioma Hard, usually vascular tumour of the membranes covering the brain and spinal cord. Usually grows slowly. May invade the skull causing bone erosion and pressure on brain tissues. It occurs in adults, in some cases following head injury.

Meningitis Inflammation or infection of the meninges. It is contagious and may be caused by viruses, fungi or bacteria. Symptoms may include fever, headache, stiff neck, irritability, ensitivity of eyes to light, confusion, drowsiness or unconsciousness. Death or permanent brain damage may occur if treatment is delayed (especially in bacterial meningitis). Usually full recovery may be expected in 2 to 3 weeks, if there are no complications.

Meningo-encephalocele Hernia protrusion of the brain and its coverings through a defect in the skull.

Meniscectomy An intra-articular procedure at the knee by which meniscus (fibrocartilage) is removed surgically.

Meniscus Crescent-shaped cartilage of the knee located between the femur and the tibia bones.

Menke's kinky-hair syndrome Inherited disorder caused by a defect in intestinal absorption of copper. Characterized by the growth of sparse, kinky hair. Infants with syndrome suffer brain damage, retarded growth and early death.

Menopause Permanent cessation of menstruation. Occurs as early as age 35 or as late as age 55; usually spans 1 to 2 years. Menopause is only one event in the climacteric, a biological change in body tissue and body systems that occurs in both sexes between the mid-40s and mid-60s. It occurs when the ovary is virtually depleted of oocytes, but which may also result prematurely from illness or surgical removal of the uterus or both ovaries.

Menstrual Pertaining to menstruation.

Menstrual cycle The periodic cycling of events in the uterus of females of reproductive age, beginning at menarche and ending at menopause. Under hormonal control, the endometrial layer is bled, then regrows, proliferates, is maintained for several days, and sheds again at menstruation. Ovulation occurs at midcycle when an oocyte matures in a follicle produced on the surface of the ovary, which then ruptures, releasing the oocyte into the fallopian tube. The average length of one menstrual cycle is 28 days.

Menstrual magnification When an illness repeatedly becomes worse during the two weeks before a woman's period

Menstruating Normal discharge of blood and tissues through the vagina that come from the uterine lining. Lining builds up each month in preparation for a fertilized egg. If fertilization does not occur, lining is shed. This process is controlled by hormones and usually occurs about every 4 to 6 weeks.

Mental disorder For purposes of relevant OTA reports, any of the diagnoses classified as mental disorders by the American Psy-

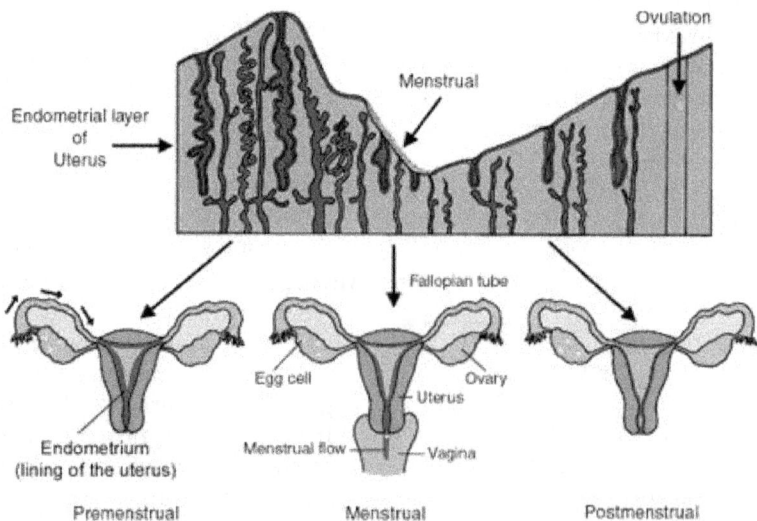

Fig. *Menstrual cycle*

chiatric Association in the Diagnostic and Statistical Manual of Mental Disorders (DSM-III). Generally, DSM-III defines a mental disorder as a clinically significant behavioural or psychological syndrome or pattern that occurrs in an individual and that is typically associated with either a painful symptom (distress) or impairment in one or more areas of functioning (disability). DSM V has been realeased in March 2013.

Mental disorders Dangerous, aggressive behaviour towards others, including non-communication, withdrawal, depression, and autistic, and psychotic tendencies.

Mental health A state of being that is relative rather than absolute. The best indices of mental health are simultaneous success at working, loving, and creating, with the capacity for mature and flexible resolution of conflicts between instincts, conscience, important other people, and reality.

Mental health promotion A broad range of efforts that seek to foster a healthy mental equilibrium and maintain emotional stability.

Mental health services Care for the treatment of mental health problems, third-party payment for which is usually limited to diagnosable mental disorders, and not available for subjective distress without an accompanying diagnosable mental disorder.

Mental retardation A term used for mental subnormality (i.e., a deficiency of intellectual function).

Mental status examination The process of estimating psychological and behavioural function by observing the patient, eliciting his or her self-description, and using formal questioning. Included in the examination are 1) evaluation and assessment of any psychiatric condition present, including provisional diagnosis and prognosis, determination of degree of impairment, suitability for treatment, and indications for particular types of therapeutic intervention; 2) formulation of the personality structure of the subject, which may suggest the historical and developmental antecedents of whatever psychiatric condition exists; and 3) estimation of the subject's ability and willingness to participate appropriately in treatment. The mental status is reported in a series of narrative statements describing such things as affect, speech, thought content, perception, and cognitive functions. The mental status examination is part of the general examination of all patients, although it may be markedly abbreviated in the absence of psychopathology.

Mentoring The practice of acting over time as a guide, tutor or coach, and sometimes as an advocate for another (typically not biologically related) person.

Merger (of health facilities) The union of two or more formerly independent institutions under a single ownership, accomplished by the complete acquisition of one institution's assets or stock by another institution.

Meridian One of a number of radially arranged imaginary lines, each of which passes through the centre of the pupil when viewing the eye head-on. Generally separated in one-degree increments, meridians are used to determine the location of the most- and least-curved sections of the cornea when prescribing lenses with cylinder power to correct astigmatism. Meridians are also used to describe the shape of corrective lenses.

Merozoite A life cycle stage of the malarial agent Plasmodium; this stage develops in the vertebrate host's liver, then enters the circulatory system and infects red blood cells.

Mesenteric adenitis Lymph glands in mesentery become inflamed. Symptoms may mimic appendicitis, but the pain is usually more generalized and does not become more severe.

Mesentery Membranous folds that hold and suspend the small intestines.

Mesothelioma A malignant tumour of the membrane that lines the lung and thoracic cavity, associated with prior exposure to asbestos.

Messenger RNA (mRNA) In molecular genetics, a type of RNA that transmits information from DNA to protein-synthesizing ribosomes of cells; ribonucleic acid that serves as the template for protein synthesis.

Meta-analysis A statistical process used to pool results from a number of studies (e.g., from many small randomized clinical trials), to enable the demonstration of statistically significant differences when the results are combined.

Metabolic alkalosis Too much base in the body due to loss of acid.

Metabolic disorders Metabolism is the process your body uses to get or make energy from the food we eat. Food is made up of proteins, carbohydrates and fats. Chemicals in your digestive system break the food parts down into sugars and acids, our body's fuel. Our body can use this fuel right away, or it can store the energy in our body tissues, such as your liver, muscles and body fat.

A metabolic disorder occurs when abnormal chemical reactions in your body disrupt this process. When this happens, might have too much of some substances or too little of other ones that need to stay healthy.

Metabolic syndrome A combination of health conditions that place a person at high risk for heart disease. These conditions are type 2 diabetes, hypertension (high blood pressure), hyperlipidemia (high levels of fat in the blood), and obesity.

343

According to theory, all of these conditions are associated with high blood insulin levels, and it is claimed that the underlying problem in patients with the metabolic syndrome is faulty insulin release from thebeta cells of the pancreas.

Metabolic treatment A non-specific term used by many unconventional practitioner to refer to a combination of unconventional approaches aimed at improving the physical and mental condition of cancer patients, sometimes including the concept of "detoxification."

Metabolism Sum of all the chemical and physical processes by which living substance is produced and maintained. Also includes the concept of the transformation by body cells by which energy is made available. Metabolism the term for the way cells chemically change food so that it can be used to keep the body alive. It is a two-part process. One part is called catabolism-when the body uses food for energy. The other is called anabolism-when the body uses food to build or mend cells. Insulin is necessary for the metabolism of food.

Metabolites Any substance produced by metabolism.

Metacarpals Five long bones of hand, just below fingers.

Metachromatic Ieukodystrophy A group of autosomal recessive genetic disorders characterized by the widespread loss of normal myelin (the protective sheath surrounding nerve cells), resulting from abnormally low activity of the enzyme aryl sulfatase A. Clinical symptoms appear in the first 10 years of life and lead progressively to dementia, convulsions, cranial nerve abnormalities, and finally severe spasticity and death.

Metamorphopsia Vision problem in which objects appear distorted. For example, straight lines may appear to be wavy, curved or bent, objects may appear to be larger or smaller than they actually are, or closer or farther away than they actually are. Metamorphopsia is typically caused by conditions or diseases that affect the eye's macula and retina.

Metastasis Process by which cancerous cells or infectious germs spread from their original location to other parts of the body.

Metastatic Pertaining to metastasis.

Metastatic cancer Cancerous cells that spread from their original location to other parts of the body.

Metastatic disease Disease that has transferred from an organ or body part not directly connected to a new location, due to transfer of the germ. For example, tuberculosis is usually found in the lungs but can spread to bones and other organs. In this case, the lungs are the primary site of disease, and the bones or other organs are the site(s) of metastatic disease.

Metatarsals Five long bones of foot, just below toes. The foot is made up of 26 small bones. The tarsus is the name for the seven bones that make up the hindfoot and the midfoot. The forefoot consists of the five metatarsals and the 14 phalanges. There are two phalanges in the big toe and three in each of the remaining toes. A foot fracture can happen in any foot bone, but metatarsal fractures are the most common.

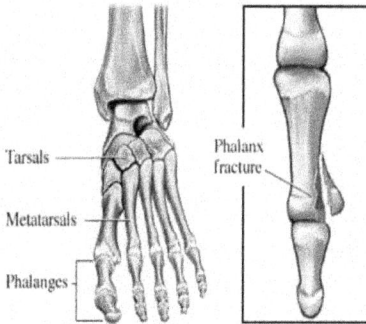

Fig. *Metatarsals*

Metatarsus valgus Out-turning feet. This condition generally corrects itself.

Metatarsus varus In-turning feet; commonly known as "pigeon toed". This condition generally corrects itself but may need surgery in severe cases.

Metformin A drug used as a treatment for Type 2 diabetes; belongs to a class of drugs called biguanides.

Methadone maintenance Pharmacotherapy for narcotics addicts that employs a synthetic opiate, methadone, to stabilize clients and help them to function in the community. In addition to daily oral doses of methadone, methadone maintenance programmes have traditionally included counseling and other support services.

Methylphenidate hydrochloride: A white crystalline powder, sold by the tradename Ritalin, used therapeutically as a mild stimulant for the central nervous system (e.g., in the treatment of attention deficit disorder in children and of narcolepsy in adults).

Me-too registration A regulatory practice by which subsequent products that are identical to an initial, registered product can be registered without undergoing regulatory tests.

Metropolitan statistical area As defined by the U.S. Office of Management and Budget, an MSA is a county or group of counties that includes either a city of at least 50,000 residents, or an urbanized area with at least 50,000 people that is itself part of a county or counties with at least 100,000 total residents.

mg/dl The unit of measurement of how much of a substance (such as sugar) is in a specific amount of fluid (such as blood or urine). Primarily used in the United States; most of the world uses mmol/L as the unit of measurement. (Note: To convert blood sugar to mg/dl from mmol/L, multiply by 18.)

Microalbumin Small amounts of protein in the urine that cannot be detected by the usual "dipstick" test done for routine urinanalysis testing for other reasons. Specialized dipsticks, or urine collections over a period of 12-24 hours, are used to measure the amount of microalbumin. If there is persistent microalbumin over several repeated tests at different times, the risk of diabetic nephropathy and macro-vascular disease are both higher.

Microaneurysm A small swelling that forms on the side of tiny blood vessels. These small swellings may break and bleed into nearby tissue. People with diabetes sometimes get microaneurysms in the retina of the eye.

Microbe Microorganism (small, living organism) capable of producing disease.

Microcephaly A small skull with small cranial capacity. Microcephaly usually indicates that a baby will have learning or developmental disabilities.

Microcornea Abnormally small cornea.

Microembolus A microscopic particle (such as a clot or other clump of cells) present in a blood vessel that obstructs the flow of blood; such particles can occur as a result of an accident or cardiovasculardisease.

Microfilariae Slender, motile prelarval forms of filarial nematodes, the parasites that cause filariasis.

Microglia A type of glial cell in the central nervous system thought to enter the immune system and initiate graft rejection.

Microinjection The technique of introducing very small amounts of material (DNA or RNA molecules; enzymes; cytotoxic agents) into an intact cell through a microscopic needle penetrating the cell membrane. In molecular genetics, the most commonly used technique for the insertion of genes from one animal into another, in which highly purified copies of a specific gene of interest are injected into a fertilized animal egg. The egg is then surgically implanted in a female animal's reproductive tract.

Microkeratome Small instrument that surgeons use to cut the cornea.

Micromelia A birth defect in which the arms or legs are abnormally short.

Micronuclei Result from the exclusion of fragments of/or whole chromosomes from nuclei formed at mitosis. Their presence can be taken as an indication of the previous existence of chromosomal aberrations.

Microorganism A minute, microscopic or submicroscopic living organism. Examples are bacteria, fungi, yeasts, mycoplasma, viruses, and protozoa.

Microphage A large, specialized immune cell that originates in the bone marrow and is involved in many stages of the immune response, including engulfing bacteria and other foreign particles.

Microphthalmia Congenital defect resulting in an abnormally small eye or eyes. The cause is usually unknown. Microphthalmia typically results in blindness or reduced vision, but normal vision is possible if the eyes are nearly normal in size.

Microsurgery is a general term for surgery requiring an operating microscope. The most obvious developments have been procedures developed to allow anastomosis of successively smaller blood vessels and nerves (typically 1 mm in diameter) which have allowed transfer of tissue from one part of the body to another and re-attachment of severed parts. Although microsurgery is used mostly in plastic surgery, microsurgical techniques are utilized by several specialties today, especially those involved in reconstructive surgery such as—general surgery, ophthalmology, orthopedic surgery, gynecological surgery, otolaryngology, neuro-surgery, oral and maxillofacial surgery, and pediatric surgery.

Microtrabeculum A shape. delicate surgical procedures performed with the aid of a microscope or other used primarily in ophthalmology, otology, gynecology, urology, and neurology. lattice of submicroscopic structures within cells that may serve to maintain cell.

Microvascular disease of the smallest blood vessels that sometimes occurs when a person has had diabetes for a long time. The walls of the vessels become abnormally thick but weak, and therefore they bleed, leak protein, and slow the flow of blood through the body. Then some cells, for example, the ones in the centre of the eye, may not get enough blood and may be damaged.

Midbrain A middle area of the brainstem that contains many important nerves (including the origins of the third and fourth cranial nerves which control eye movement and eyelid opening). The midbrain is the smallest region of the brain

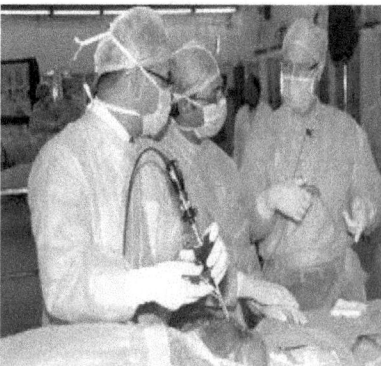

Fig. *Microsurgery*

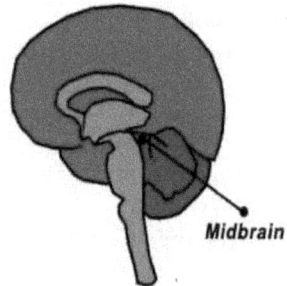

Midbrain

Fig. *Midbrain*

that acts as a sort of relay station for auditory and visual information.

It controls many important functions such as the visual and auditory systems as well as eye movement. Portions of the midbrain called the red nucleus and the substantia nigra are involved in the control of body movement. The darkly pigmented substantia nigra contains a large number of dopamine-producing neurons are located. The degeneration of neurons in the substantia nigra is associated with Parkinson's disease.

Midwife The word literally means "with woman". Midwives provide care to women during pregnancy, labour, birth, and postnatally - usually for the first ten days, although this can be extended to 28 days if the

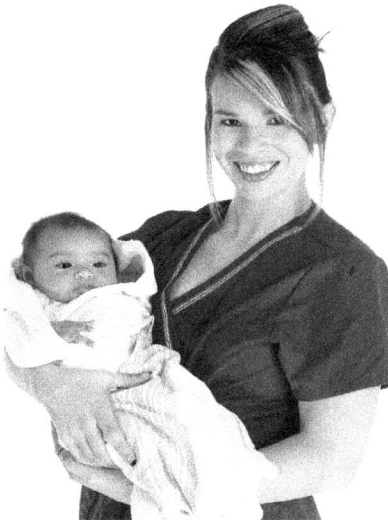

Fig. *Midwife*

new mother has particular needs. A health visitor then takes over care of the mother and baby. In other words, midwifery is a health care profession in which providers offer care to childbearing women during pregnancy, labour and birth, and during the postpartum period. They also help care for the newborn and assist the mother with breastfeeding.

Migraine Severe headache, sometimes accompanied by nausea and visual disturbances. Visual disturbances alone are also possible; this problem is called an ophthalmic migraine, or migraine without headache. Eye and vision symptoms include blurred vision, ptosis, halos around lights, light flashes, light sensitivity, eye pain or discomfort, vision loss (blind spots in central vision, tunnel vision or overall impaired vision), distorted vision and wavy lines in vision.

Migrant health centres Centres that provide primary health care to migrant and seasonal farm workers and their families and are part of the primary are programme administered by the Federal Bureau of Health Care Deliver and Assistance.

Milia Tiny, harmless white spots or pimples on a newborn. They usually go away by themselves.

Milia Raised tiny white bumps on the surface of the skin, often appearing on the eyelid and around the eyes and nose. Milia is caused when dead skin cells do not slough off properly and become trapped at the base of a sweat gland or hair follicle, forming a small keratin cyst. They are commonly seen in newborns, but also can affect adults of all ages.

Miliary tuberculosis Acute infection associated with the spread of tuberculosis throughout the body through the bloodstream. Tiny tubercles (small, rounded masses produced by infection with mycobacterium tuberculosis, the germ causing tuberculosis) are formed in a number of organs. If treatment is not delayed, the infection can usually be successfully treated with a combination of medications.

Miller trusts Commonly known as income sheltering devices, these trusts enable otherwise income-ineligible Medicaid applicants to qualify for Medicaid.

Minerals Essential elements in a diet needed to maintain health and well-being, including calcium, magnesium, potassium and so on.

Minification Making objects appear smaller; the opposite of magnification. Most lenses for nearsightedness make objects look smaller, and when the lenses are in eyeglasses, they also make the wearer's eyes look smaller. Aspheric lenses reduce this minification effect, for a more natural look.

Minimal risk Term used to denote that the chance of harm anticipated in proposed research is no greater than that encountered in daily life or during the performance of routine physical or psychological tests.

Minimization In randomized clinical trials, a method of patient allocation intended to minimize different distributions of prognostic factors between treatment groups without creating mutually exclusive subgroups.

Minimum data sets Federal data collection system for assessing nursing home patients. The MDS for nursing facility residents is a comprehensive resident assessment instrument (RAI) that measures functional status, mental health status, and behavioural status to identify chronic care patient needs and formalize a care plan in response to 18 Resident Assessment Protocols (RAPs). Under Federal regulation, assessments are conducted at a time of admission into a nursing facility, upon return from a 72-hour hospital admission, whenever there is a significant change in status, quarterly, and annually.

Minimum premium Financing mechanism for a medical benefit programme in which an employer remits only a portion of the conventional premium to the insurer to cover the cost of administering the benefits programme and to providing specific and aggregate stop-loss insurance. The employer funds a "bank account" which the insurer draws upon for payment of claims.

Minnesota care Minnesota's health care plan passed in April of 1992. This law is intended to provide health care to all of Minnesota's citizens while cutting health care costs. It includes cost-containment provisions for setting overall health care spending targets, monitoring providers, reviewing the distribution of new technologies, and evaluating methods for collecting health care data.

Minor offenses Federal Bureau of Investigation Part II offenses, which include abuse violations, weapons violations, assaults without weapons, disorderly conduct, involvement with stolen property, driving under the influence of alcohol or other drugs, and status offenses.

Minor A person who has not reached the age of majority, either age 18 or 19, depending on the State. Currently, the age of majority is set at age 18 in every State but Alaska, Nebraska, and Wyoming, where he age is 19.

Miscarriage The involuntary expulsion of a fetus before the 24th week. After that, the loss of a pregnancy is called a stillbirth.

Mitochondrion spherical to rod-shaped organelles with a double membrane. The inner membrane is infolded many times, forming a series of projections (called cristae). The mitochondrion converts the energy stored in glucose into ATP (adenosine triphosphate) for the cell. It contain enzymes involved in electron transport and in the citric acid and fatty acid cycles; contains self-replicating, extranuclear, circular DNA molecules.

Mitogen Substance that triggers mitosis.

Mitogenesis The initiation of cell division, or mitosis.

Mitosis Type of cell division in which the body produces new cells for growth and repair of injured tissues.

Mitral regurgitation Defective closure of the heart's mitral valve, which allows some of the blood to backflow or regurgitate. Normally, the mitral valve allows blood to flow from the top left

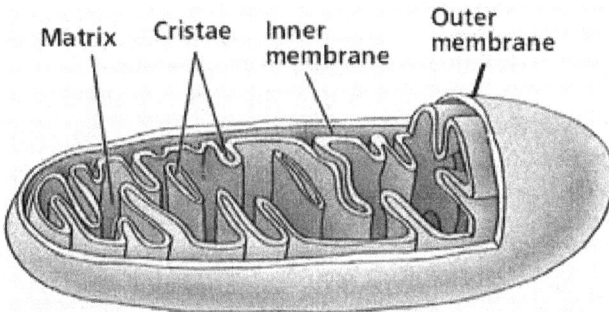

Fig. *Mitochondrion.*

350

chamber of the heart (atrium) to the bottom left chamber of the heart (ventricle), but prevents blood from flowing back into the left atrium. Although there are several causes, rheumatic heart disease is the single most common cause of this condition. Symptoms include fatigue and slight breathlessness. Eventually the condition may progress and result in severe congestion of lungs. Surgery to replace or repair the mitral valve is required in patients with severe symptoms.

Mitral valve Valves located in the heart between the left atrium and left ventricle.

Mitral valve prolapse Condition in which the mitral valve becomes floppy, resulting in mitral regurgitation.

Mittelschmerz German for middle pain, this refers to slight pains or twinges that some woman feel when they ovulate.

Mixed astigmatism Abnormal curvature of the eye's surface (cornea) that causes focusing problems at both near and distant ranges.

Mixed cell culture A culture of more than one type of cell.

Mixed connective tissue disease Disease affecting the entire body characterized by the combined symptoms of various collagen diseases. Symptoms may include joint pain, inflammation of muscles, non-deforming arthritis and swollen hands. May also affect esophagus and lungs.

Treatment often includes administration of corticosteroids.

Mixed dose Combining two kinds of insulin in one injection. A mixed dose commonly combines regular insulin, which is fast acting, with a longer acting insulin such as NPH. A mixed dose insulin schedule may be prescribed to provide both short-term and long-term coverage.

Mixed model HMO A health plan that includes more than one form of HMO within a single plan.

Mixed neuropathy: Degeneration of both sensory and motor neurons.

mmol/L (millimols per litre) The unit of measurement of how much of a substance (such as sugar) is in a specific amount of fluid (such as blood or urine). Most of the world uses mmol/L; however, in the United States, mg/dl is used as the unit of measurement. (Note: To convert blood sugar to mmol/L from mg/dl, divide by 18.)

Mobilization Passive stretching movements performed by a therapist at a speed slow enough that a patient can stop the movement.

Modality A method of application or use of any therapeutic agent, usually limited to physical agents.

Moderate handicaps (in infants) Disabilities that include moderate mental retardation (IQ or developmental quotient between 70 and 80).

Moderately low birthweight Birth-weight between 1,500 grams and 2,500 grams.

Modified community rating A separate rating of medical service usage in a given geographic area using age-sex data.

Modified fee for-service A system in which providers are paid on a fee-for-service basis, with certain fee maximums for each procedure.

Molecular biology The study of biochemical and biophysical aspects of the structure and function of DNA, proteins, and other cellular components.

Molluscicide Any chemical agent used to kill mollusks; in the 'context of tropical diseases, snails necessary in the life cycles of schistosomes are the most important targets.

Mongolian spot A large birth mark which looks light blue, usually on the lower body. It disappears or becomes less noticeable as the baby grows. They are more common in Asian and dark-skinned babies.

Monochromatic Refers to one wavelength of light, as opposed to the many wavelengths of light found in varying colours.

Monoclinal antibodies Artificially produced antibodies that recognize a single, specific antigen and are produced by a clone of specialized cells, used in the diagnosis and treatment of some forms of cancer. Commercial quantities of these molecules can be produced by hybridomas.

Monocytes Large mononuclear white blood cells that ingest bacteria and cell debris.

Monofocal Type of spectacle lens, intraocular lens (IOL) or contact lens design that has only one area through which the eye focuses. A multifocal lens has more than one focal area, enabling sight at multiple distances, typically for people with presbyopia.

Monomania Pathological preoccupation with one subject.

Monomer A chemical subunit, or a type of simple molecule capable of chemically bonding with others to form a polymer (a number of monomers bonded together).

Mononeuropathy A form of diabetic neuropathy affecting a single nerve. The eye is a common site for this form of nerve damage.

Monosomy Chromosomal abnormality characterized by the absence of one chromosome from the normally occurring pair of chromosomes. One example is Turner's syndrome.

Monovision Vision correction method for those with presbyopia in which one eye is corrected for near vision and the other for far, either through contact lenses or refractive surgery. Monovision eliminates the need for reading glasses, but does have some drawbacks, including decreased depth perception.

Mood disorders In DSM-IV, this category includes depressive disorders, bipolar disorders, mood disorder due to a general medical condition, and substance-induced (intoxication/withdrawal) mood disorder.

Mood swing Fluctuation of a person's emotional tone between periods of elation and periods of depression.

Morbidity The condition of being ill or otherwise afflicted with an unhealthful condition.

Morbidity rate The rate of illness in a population, calculated as the number of people ill during a time period divided by the number of people in the total population; used to refer to incidence or prevalence rates of disease.

Morning sickness The medical term for "Morning sickness" is "pregnancy related nausea and vomiting." For some pregnant women, the symptoms are worst in the morning and later ease up as day advances. The symptoms of nausea get initiated around six weeks of preg-

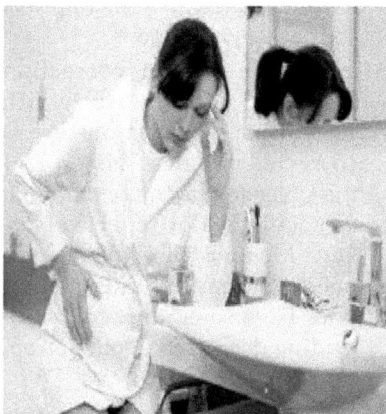

Fig. *Morning sickness*

nancy. In most cases, as pregnancy advances nausea will gradually disappear. However, though rare, in some women nausea will exist throughout the pregnant months.

Morning-after pill A pill (or pills) to prevent pregnancy, taken within hours of a woman having had unprotected intercourse.

Moro reflex If a newborn is startled by a sudden, loud noise, the Moro reflex will cause him to extend his arms, legs, and feet, arch his back and move his head back

Morphology The study of the physical form and structure of a specimen, plant, or whole animal.

Mortality Incidents of death in a defined group of individuals.

Mortality rate The death rate, often made explicit for a particular characteristic (e.g., age, sex, or specific cause of death). A mortality rate contains three essential elements:(i) the number of people in a population group exposed to the risk of death (the denominator); (ii) a time factor and (iii) the number of deaths occurring in the exposed population during a certain time period (the numerator).

Morula The solid mass of cells resembling a mulberry ("morula" in Latin) formed by the cleavage of a zygote; the stage before blastocyst.

Mosaicism Sometimes a baby who has a particular syndrome or disorder will have it in a mosaic form: some of the cells in the baby's body will have the extra genetic material which characterises the disorder, the others may be normal.

Most-favoured-nation clause A provision requiring the contracting physician, hospital or group to provide an issuer with the lowest price it charges any other insurer.

Motility disorders Any disorder or disease characterized by inability to remove intestinal waste contents efficiently.

Motoneurons (multipolar neurons) Neurons responsible for movement - the cell bodies of these neurons are located within the brain or spinal cord and the axons are located in muscle fibres.

Motor activity tests Observation and evaluation of the movements of test animals after acute or subchronic exposures to a substance; used as a screen for neurotoxic substances.

Motor cortex The part of both frontal lobes of the brain that controls voluntary muscle movements.

Motor neuron disease A type of neurodegenerative disease in which neurons in the central nervous system that control muscle movement are destroyed.

Motor skills Motions carried out by the combination of the brain, nervous system, and muscles.

Mouth The first part of the digestive system, where food enters the body. Chewing and salivary enzymes in the mouth are the beginning of the digestive process (breaking down the food).

MPTP, 1-methy-4-phenyl-1,2,3,6 - tetrahydropyridine A synthetic narcotic that can cause parkinsonism in humans.

Mucin Lubricant such as saliva that protects body surfaces. In the eyes, mucin is a tear layer that helps moisten and protect the eye's surface.

Mucocele Dilation of a cavity with accumulated mucus secretion.

Mucopolysaccharides Any of a group of genetic disorders caused by a defect in metabolism ofmucopolysaccharides. Characterized by skeletal changes, mental retardation, clouding of the cornea and xcessive mucopolysaccharides in urine. Currently there is no successful treatment.

Mucormycosis Fungal infection typically occurring in the sinuses or lungs and mainly acquired by those with compromised immune systems and by diabetics. Symptoms include sinusitis, eye and facial pain, fever, a bulging eye and vision loss.

Mucous membrane A wet layer of body tissue which lines internal parts of the body such as the nose and mouth.

Mucus plug A plug of mucus which blocks the cervix during pregnancy. It is often released with the onset of labour.

Multidimensional assessment: A client evaluation that focuses on many different aspects of the client's status (e.g., physical, mental, emotional, functional, financial, and social); conducted by individuals from various disciplines, usually including a physician, a nurse, and a social worker and, depending on the care setting, a physical therapist, a speech therapist, an occupational therapist, a psychologist, and various physician specialists.

Multidisciplinary team A team composed of individuals from various disciplines that provides comprehensive client assessments, care planning, and/or treatment. Multidisciplinary teams usually include a physician, a nurse, and a social worker and, depending on the care setting, may also include a physical therapist, a speech therapist, an occupational therapist, a psychologist, and various physician specialists.

Multifactorial traits Inheritance of traits that are not determined solely by a single gene. Multifactorial, or polygenic, traits have variable phenotypic effects that depend (for their expression) on the interaction of many genes and environmental influences (e.g., spina bifida and other neural tube defects).

Multifocal Type of spectacle lens, intraocular lens (IOL) or contact lens design that includes more than one area through which the eye focuses. such as bifocals or trifocals. Examples are bifocals or trifocals. This enables sight at multiple distances, typically for people with presbyopia.

Multihospital system Two or more hospitals that are owned, leased, sponsored, or contract-managed by a central organization (American Hospital Association definition).

Multi-infarct dementia An irreversible form of dementia resulting from many small strokes.

Multinodular goitre Enlarged thyroid gland causing a swelling in the front part of the neck. Swelling is very irregular (multinodular). Rarely toxic or malignant; may occur with chronic inflammatory thyroid disease.

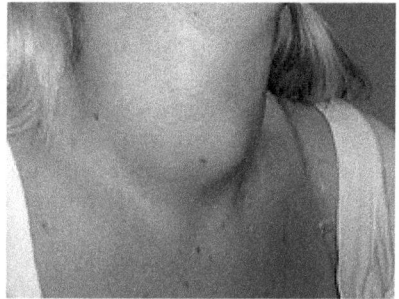

Fig. *Multinodular goitre*

Multiple birth A multiple birth occurs when more than one fetus is carried to term in a single pregnancy. Different names for multiple births are used, depending on the number of offspring. Common multiples are two and three, known as twins and triplets, respectively. These and other multiple births occur to varying degrees in most animal species, although the term is most applicable to placental species.

Multiple birth siblings are either monozygotic or poly-zygotic. The former result from a single fertilized egg or zygote splitting into two or more embryos, each carrying the same genetic material (genes). Siblings created from one egg are commonly called identical.

Multiple employer trust Legal trust established by a plan sponsor that brings together a number of small, unrelated employers for the purpose of providing group medical coverage on an insured or self-funded basis.

Multiple employer welfare Arrangement A group of employers joined together to offer employees health benefits comparable to traditional health insurance packages. Employers take part to reduce health insurance costs and spread the risk over a larger group of people.

Multiple myeloma Malignancy beginning in the plasma cells of the bone marrow. Plasma cells normally produce antibodies to help destroy germs and protect against infection. With myeloma, this function becomes impaired, and the body cannot deal effectively with infection.

Multiple option plan A health plan design that offers employees the option of electing to enroll under one of several types of coverage, usually from among an HMO, a PPO, and a major medical indemnity plan.

Multiple pregnancy A multiple pregnancy is one in which there is more than one fetus in the womb. Multiple pregnancy usually occurs when more than

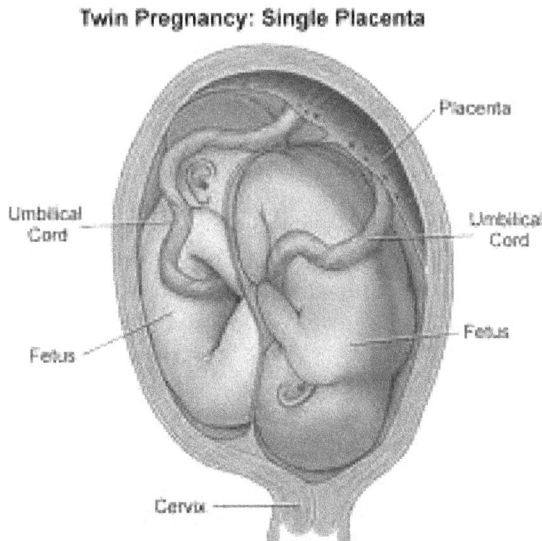

Fig. *Multiple pregnancy*

one egg is fertilized and implants in the uterus. This is called fraternal twinning and can produce boys, girls, or a combination of both. Fraternal multiples are simply siblings conceived at the same time. However, just as siblings often look alike, fraternal multiples may look very similar. Fraternal multiples each have a separate placenta and amniotic sac. Sometimes, one egg is fertilized and then divides into two or more embryos. This is called identical twinning and produces all boys, or all girls. Identical multiples are genetically identical, and usually look so much alike that even parents have a hard time telling them apart. However, these children have different personalities and are distinct individuals. Identical multiples may have individual placentas and amniotic sacs, but most share a placenta with separate sacs. Rarely, identical twins share one placenta and a single amniotic sac.

Multiple sclerosis Chronic disorder affecting many nervous system functions. Patches of white matter in the brain and spinal cord break down and cannot conduct normal nerve impulses. Usually begins in young adulthood. Early signs of the disease are often vague, including visual problems, abnormal skin sensations and muscle weakness or imbalance. Later, symptoms may include marked weakness, speech difficulty,

loss of bladder or bowel control, and extreme mood swings. Currently not curable. Symptoms can be relieved or controlled with treatment. One-third of MS patients have a mild, non-progressive disease. Another third worsen slowly. The rest worsen rapidly.

Multiple sclerosis A progressive, tippling disease of the central nervous system in which scattered patches of myelin in the brain, optic nerve, and spinal cord are destroyed, resulting in slowed nerve conduction; its cause is unknown, but may be related to an autoimmune process or an infectious agent. Clinical symptoms first appear in early adulthood and commonly include weakness, lack of coordination, speech and visual disturbances, numbness and tingling, incontinence, and paralysis.

Multipurpose senior centre A community or neighbourhood facility established for the organization and provision of a broad spectrum of supportive services, including health, social, nutritional, and educational services, and the provision of facilities for recreational activities for older individuals.

Multispecialty group A group of doctors who represent various medical specialties and who work together in a group practice.

Mumps is a viral disease of the human species, caused by the mumps virus. Before the devel-

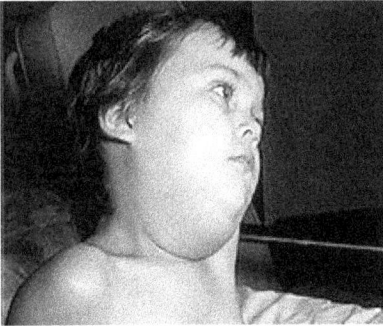

Fig. *Mumps*

opment of vaccination and the introduction of a vaccine, it was a common childhood disease worldwide. Painful swelling of the salivary glands – classically the parotid gland – is the most typical presentation. The symptoms are generally not severe in children. Fever and headache are prodromal symptoms of mumps, together with malaise and anorexia. Mumps is a contagious disease that is spread from person to person through contact with respira-

tory secretions, such as saliva from an infected person. When an infected person coughs or sneezes, the droplets aerosolize and can enter the eyes, nose, or mouth of another person. Mumps can also be spread by sharing food and drinks.

Murder and nonnegligent manslaughter The wilful (non-negligent) killing of one human being by another. Deaths caused by negligence, attempts to kill, assaults to kill, suicides, accidental deaths, and justifiable homicides, are excluded. Justifiable homicides are limited to: 1) the killing of a felon by a law enforcement officer in the line of duty, and 2) the killing of a felon by a private citizen.

Muscular dystrophy is the name given to a group of disorders which cause muscle weakness. There are many different types of MD. The different types vary

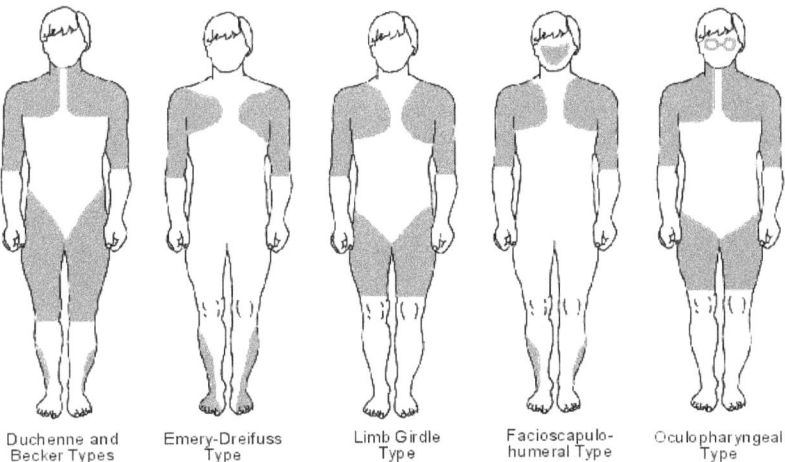

| Duchenne and Becker Types | Emery-Dreifuss Type | Limb Girdle Type | Facioscapulo-humeral Type | Oculopharyngeal Type |

Main areas of muscle weakness in different types of dystrophy

Fig. *Muscular dystrophy*

as to how mild or severe they are, and which muscles they affect. It is a genetic condition causing muscle weakness.

Mutagen An agent that induces chemical or physical changes in genetic material. Chemicals, viruses, and ionizing radiation can be mutagenic. Most carcinogens are mutagens, therefore many screening tests to detect carcinogens are designed to detect the mutagenic potential of the compound. Some mutagens act indirectly by requiring metabolic activation in the body before they exert their effects.

Mutagenesis The process of inducing mutations in the genetic material of an organism.

Mutagenic Causing increases in the mutation of genes.

Mutations Any change in the base sequence of DNA, classified according to size into gene mutations (changes within a single gene, such as nucleotide substitutions) and chromosome mutations (affecting larger portions of the chromosome, or the loss or addition of an entire chromosome). Heritable mutations are changes in DNA that are passed from parent to offspring and therefore were present in the germ cells of one of the parents. See induced mutation and spontaneous mutation.

Mutation rate The number of mutations per unit of DNA (e.g., per gene, per nucleotide, per genome, etc.) occurring per unit of time (usually per cell generation).

Mutism, selective Elective mutism; a disorder of infancy, childhood, or adolescence characterized by persistent failure to speak in specific social situations by a child with demonstrated ability to speak. The mutism is not due to lack of fluency in the language being spoken or embarrassment about a speech problem.

Myasthenia gravis Weakness of the voluntary muscles, believed to be autoimmune in nature. Symptoms include double vision and eyelid ptosis; patients

Fig. *Myxedema*

359

sometimes have non-eye symptoms as well, such as difficulty swallowing or using the arms and legs. It is an acquired autoimmune disorder in which the body reacts against its own acetylcholine receptors in the synapses between nerve and muscle ceils, resulting in chronic muscle weakness, especially in the face and throat, and fatigue.

Mycobacterial diseases A group of human and animal diseases caused by species of the bacterial genus Mycobacterium, Important human mycobacterial diseases are tuberculosis and leprosy.

Mycology The scientific study of fungi and fungoid diseases.

Mycoplasma The smallest free-living organisms, a genus of ultramicroscopic gram-negative organisms lacking a rigid cell wall; includes saprophytes, parasites, and pathogens (e.g., Mycocplasma pneumoniae).

Mycoplasma pneumonia Lung infection caused by germ mycoplasma.

Myelin A fatty substance (of which the myelin sheath surrounding axons is made) that acts as an electrical insulator which speeds the conduction of nerve impulses. Myelin is formed in the peripheral nervous system by Schwann cells and in the central nervous system by oligodendrocytes.

Myelin sheath A fatty substance that surrounds and protects some nerve fibres. The production of the myelin sheath is called myelination. In humans, the production of myelin begins in the 14th week of fetal development, although little myelin exists in the brain at the time of birth. During infancy, myelination occurs quickly and continues through the adolescent stages of life.

Myelocele Saclike protrusion of the spinal cord through a congenital defect in the spinal column.

Myelocytes Immature white blood cells normally found in bone marrow.

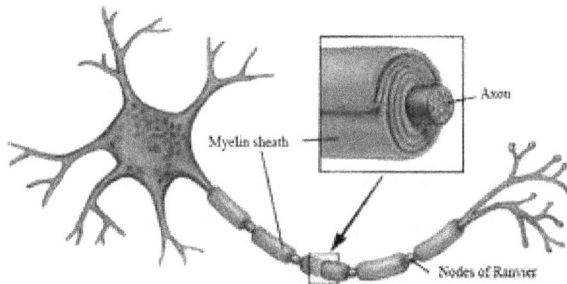

Fig. *Myelin sheath*

Myelogenous leukemia A form of cancer characterized by uncontrolled proliferation of granulocytes; includes acute and chronic myelocytic leukemia.

Myeloma A malignant tumour of an antibody-producing cell. In hybridoma technology, some of these tumour cells have been adapted to cell culture, and these cells contribute immortality to a hybridoma cell line.

Myelosuppressive Inhibiting bone marrow activity, resulting in the decreased production of blood cells and platelets.

Myocardial failure Condition that exists when the heart is no longer able to pump all the blood efficiently.

Myocardial fibrosis Formation of fibrous material in the heart.

Myocardial infarction Sudden necrosis (death) of tissue in the myocardium (heart muscle) characterized by severe, unremitting chest pain, leading to arrhythmias and/or heart failure; in most cases, caused by coronary atherosclerosis (insufficient blood supply to the heart).

Myocarditis Inflammation of the heart muscle (myocardium) that usually occurs as a complication of underlying illness, hypersensitive immune reactions, injury or radiation therapy. Symptoms may include fatigue, shortness of breath, irregular heartbeat and fever. Usually curable with detection and treatment of the underlying cause.

Myocarditis bacterial Inflammation of heart muscle (myocardium) caused by bacterial infection.

Myocardium Heart muscle

Myoelectric Controlled by electromyographic (EMG) signals.

Myofascial release Trauma, posture, or inflammation can create a binding down of fascia resulting in excessive pressure on nerves, muscles, blood vessels, osseous structures and/or organs. This hands-on technique seeks to free the body from the grip of tight fascia, or connective tissue, thus restoring normal alignment and function and reducing pain. Therapists apply mild, sustained hand-pressure in order to gently stretch and soften fascia. Treatment is used to treat neck and back pain, headaches, recurring sports injuries, and scoliosis, and other conditions.

Myoglobin Chemical stored in muscle that contains iron and oxygen.

Myo-inositol A substance in the cell that is thought to play a role in helping the nerves to work. Low levels of myo-inositol may be involved in diabetic neuropathy.

Myokymia Common eyelid twitch typically brought on by stress or fatigue.

Myopathy A disorder of the muscles characterized by wasting of muscle tissue and weakness.

Myopia Also called near-sightedness. Condition in which the length of the eye is too long, causing light rays to focus in front of the retina rather than on it, resulting in blurred distance vision. Additional symptoms include eye strain, poor night vision and squinting.

Myositis is a general term for inflammation of the muscles. Many such conditions are considered likely to be caused by autoimmune conditions, rather than directly due to infection (although autoimmune conditions can be activated or exacerbated by infections.) It is also a documented side effect of the lipid-lowering drugs statins and fibrates.

Myositis ossificans Inflammation in muscle resulting in the formation of bone-like substance.

Myxedema Condition of swollen lips, thickened nose, swelling of the skin and mental dullness caused by reduced function of the thyroid gland. Some examples are as follows:
  (i) Manic episode: A distinct period of time (usually lasting

at least 1 week) of abnormally and persistently elevated, expansive, or irritable mood accompanied by such symptoms as inflated self-esteem or grandiosity, decreased need for sleep, overtalkativeness or pressured speech, flight of ideas or feeling that thoughts are racing, inattentiveness and distractibility, increased goal-directed activity (e.g., at work or school, socially or sexually), and involvement in pleasurable activities with high potential for painful consequences (e.g., buying sprees, sexual indiscretions, foolish business ventures).
  (ii) Manic-depressive illness: A term often used synonymously with bipolar disorder, as defined in DSM-IV.
While IVF creates thousands of new families a year, multiple births carry special risks often overlooked in the desire to produce babies.

N

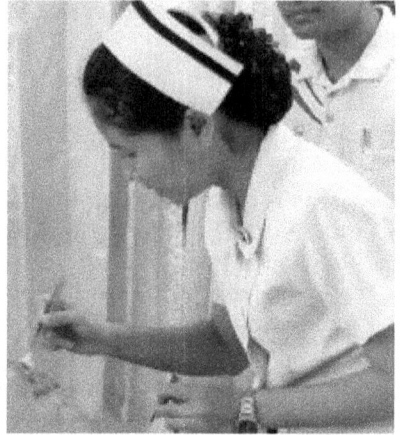

n

Naevus Birthmark, freckle or mole that is often brownish, but can be other colours as well. A nevus can occur on the skin or inside the eye and can become a melanoma, a type of cancerous growth.

Naltrexone A pharmacologic substance that is a narcotic antagonist.

Nanometer A measurement of length equal to one-billionth of a meter. Abbreviated as nm. Wavelengths of light are measured in nanometers. Eyeglass and sunglass lens manufacturers use nanometers to describe the different types of light that may pass through or be blocked by a lens, whether it be visible light, ultraviolet light, blue light, etc. For example, visible light has a wavelength range of 400 to 700 nm. The amount of light transmission itself is described as a percentage. For example, a dark sunglass lens might allow only 12 percent of visible light to pass through to the eye.

Naprapathy A system of treatment employing manipulation of connective tissue (ligaments, muscles, and joints) and dietary measures; said to facilitate the recuperative and regenerative processes of the body.

Narcosis Nonspecific, reversible depression of central nervous system function, marked by diminished reaction to stimuli, stupor, or unconsciousness; caused by the use of drugs with a depressant action on the nervous system, such as narcotics.

Narcotics A class of drugs that when administered therapeutically can lessen sensibility, relieve pain, and produce sleep. The term narcotic is used interchangeably with the term opiates. In a legal context, the term narcotics is used to refer to any substance that can cause dependence.

Nasal relating to the nose. Articulated by lowering the soft palate so that air resonates in the nasal cavities and passes out the nose.

Nasal bone Either of two small elongated rectangular bones that together form the bridge of the nose.

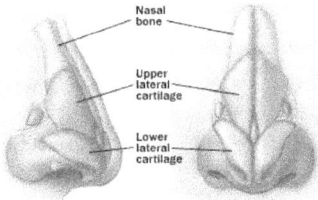

Fig. *Nasal bone*

Nasal cavities The proximal portion of the respiratory passages on either side of the nasal septum, lined with ciliated mucosa, extending from the nares to the pharynx.

The nasal cavity warms and moistens the air and filters it of impurities. Tiny hairs and sticky mucous membranes trap foreign materials before they can enter the delicate tissues of the lungs.

Nasal decongestants Drugs designed to treat inflammation of the nasal passages, generally the result of an infection (more often than not the common cold) or an allergy related condition, e.g., hay fever. The inflammation involves swelling of the mucous membrane that lines the nasal passages and results in inordinate mucus production. The primary class of nasal decongestants are vaso-constrictor agents.

Nasal lavage fluid The fluid obtained from flushing the nasal passages bronchoalveolar lavage fluid.

Nasal mucosa The mucous membrane lining the nasal cavity.

Nasal sinuses The sinuses are hollow areas, or cavities, in the bones of the skull that are lined with mucous membranes and that open into the nasal cavity. Air-filled extensions of the respiratory part of the nasal cavity into the frontal, ethmoid,

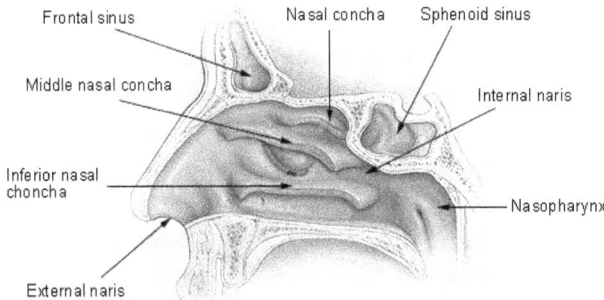

Fig. *Nasal cavity*

sphenoid, and maxillary cranial bones. They vary in size and form in different individuals and are lined by the ciliated mucous membranes of the nasal cavity.

The sinuses provide resonance for the voice. When the sinuses are inflamed and filled with mucus the voice has a different quality, often referred to as "nasal" in character.

Nasale, conchae The scroll-like bony plates with curved margins on the lateral wall of the nasal cavity.

Nasogastric Describes the passage from the nose to the stomach. For example, a nasogastric tube is inserted through the nose, down the throat and esophagus, and into the stomach.

Nasogastric tube A tube that is inserted through the nose, down the throat and esophagus, and into the stomach. It can be used to give drugs, liquids, and liquid food, or used to remove substances from the stomach. Giving food through a naso-gastric tube is a type of enteral nutrition. Also called gastric feeding tube and NG tube.

Nasonex A drug that is used in a cream to treat certain skin conditions and in a nasal spray to treat sinus problems caused by allergies. It is being studied as a way to treat inflammation of the skin caused by radiation therapy. Nasonex is a type of corti-costeroid. Also called Elocon, mometasone, and mometasone furoate.

Nasopharyngeal cancer Cancer that forms in tissues of the nasopharynx (upper part of the throat behind the nose). Most nasopharyngeal cancers are squamous cell carcinomas (cancer that begins in flat cells lining the nasopharynx).

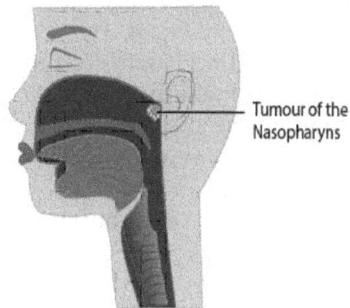

Fig. Nasopharyngeal cancer

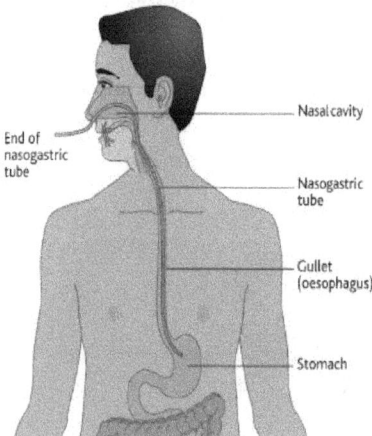

Fig. Nasogastric tube

Nasopharyngitis Inflammation of the nasopharynx.

Nasopharynx The area behind the nose and just above the back of the throat is called the naso-pharynx. An opening on each side of the naso-pharynx leads into the ear.

Nasoscope A thin tube-like instrument used to examine the inside of the nose. A nasoscope has a light and a lens for viewing and may have a tool to remove tissue. Also called rhinoscope.

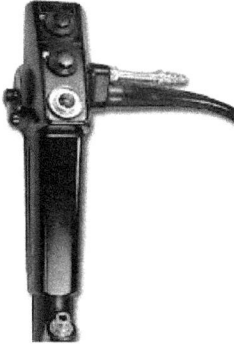

Fig. *Nasoscope*

Nasoscopy Examination of the inside of the nose using a nasoscope (or rhinoscope). A nasoscope is a thin, tube-like instrument with a light and a lens for viewing. It may also have a tool to remove tissue to be checked under a microscope for signs of disease. Also called rhinoscopy.

National drug code A national classification system for identification of drugs. Similar to the universal product code (UPC).

National fire protection association An association that develops standards related to fire protection. Fire departments usually adopt these standards into local regulations.

National health board The national health board has been described by most managed competition plans as an independent federal agency charged with implementation and oversight of the national health care plan. It would likely be responsible for developing the uniform benefits package, setting standards and registration requirements for AHPs and HIPCs, and any other tasks as designated by congress or the administration. Board members would serve staggered terms and be insulated from the executive and legislative branches. Membership would reflect provider, consumer and public policy interests.

National health insurance Proposed Federal programme that would use tax funds to finance the provision of comprehensive health benefits for the population. Scope of benefits, provider and beneficiary eligibility, financing, and ownership and control of resources, among other issues, must be defined.

National health interview survey A continuing nationwide sample survey in which data are collected through personal household interviews. Information is obtained on personal and demographic characteristics, illnesses, injuries, impairments, chronic conditions, utilization of health resources, and other health topics. For individuals under age 17, information is collected from a proxy respondent, typically a parent or guardian. The survey is conducted by the national centre for health statistics in DHHS.

National Institute of Diabetes and Digestive and Kidney Diseases (NIDDK) One of the 17 institutes that make up the national institutes of health, an agency of the public health service.

National institute on aging Federal agency within the national institutes of health that conducts and supports biomedical and behavioural research to increase knowledge of the aging process and associated factors resulting from old age. NIA conducts labouratory and clinical research at it Gerontology Research Centre in Baltimore, MD and its clinics. NIA funds research on aging at universities, hospitals, and other organizations.

National primary drinking water regulations Enforceable standards for contaminants in drinking water set by EPA that include maximum contaminant levels or required treatment techniques, or both. See maximum contaminant level.

National survey of family growth An interview survey, conducted by the national centre for health statistics in DHHS, of a sample of women ages 15 to 44 living in households. The purpose of the survey is to provide national data on the demographic and social factors associated with childbearing, adoption, and maternal and child health. These factors include sexual activity, marriage, unmarried cohabitation, divorce and remarriage, contraception and steri-lization, infertility, breastfeeding, pregnancy loss, low birthweight, and use of medical care for family planning, infertility, and prenatal care. Four "cycles" of the survey have been conducted, the latest in 1988.

Natural childbirth A general term for a labour and delivery which is free of medical intervention.

Natural family planning Contraception without the aid of drugs or devices, based on the rhythm method, basal body temperature, or the cervical mucus (Billings) method.

Natural history The course of a condition that occurs without any intervention.

Natural immunity Species-determined inherent resistance to an infectious disease agent, eg, resistance of humans to canine distemper virus.

Natural killer cell A type of lymphocyte that attacks cancerous or virus-infected cells without previous exposure to the antigen. Also called NK cell.

Natural selection The process by which simpler ancestral species of animals and plants evolve into new species, based on variations among traits in populations and differential reproductive success that selects for certain of those traits; described by Charles Darwin in 1858 in On the Origin of Species.

Naturopathy A system of disease prevention and treatment that avoids drugs and surgery. Naturopathy is based on the

Fig. *Naturopathy*

use of natural agents such as air, water, light, heat, and massage to help the body heal itself. It also uses herbal products, nutrition, acupuncture, and aromatherapy as forms of treatment. Naturopathic medicine is a centuries old system of medicine which honours seven tenets, the cornerstone of which is the 'healing power of nature'.

Nausea An unpleasant sensation in the stomach usually accompanied by the urge to vomit. Common causes are early pregnancy, sea and motion sickness, emotional stress, intense pain, food poisoning, and various entero-viruses.

Navel The impression or scar left on the outside of the abdomen after the umbilical cord falls off.

Naval medicine The practice of medicine concerned with conditions affecting the health of individuals associated with the marine environment.

Navelbine A drug used to treat advanced non-small cell lung cancer. It blocks cell growth by stopping cell division and may cause cancer cells to die. It is a type of vinca alkaloid and a type of antimitotic agent. Also called vinorelbine tartrate.

ND Doctor of Nursing

Near vision Eyesight used for reading and other close-up tasks, generally at a range of 12 to 16 inches from the eyes. See also: intermediate vision and distance vision.

Near-poor Pertaining to a family with an income between 100 percent and 150 percent of the official Federal poverty level. The Federal poverty level for a family of three was $10,560 in January 1990.

Nearsightedness Also called myopia. Condition in which visual images come to a focus in front of the retina, resulting in defective vision of distant objects.

Nebulizer A device used to turn liquid into a fine spray. While older children and teens can simply use a nebulizer with a regular mouthpiece, younger infants, toddlers, and preschoolers usually require a mask that fits over their mouth and nose to get an effective treatment.

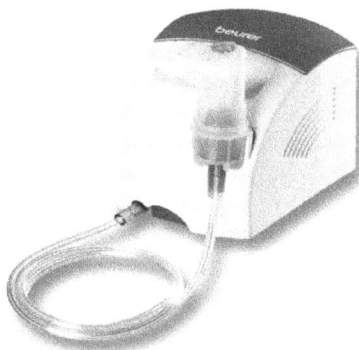

Fig. *Nebulizer*

Neck dissection Surgery to remove lymph nodes and other tissues in the neck.

Neck-righting reflex A newborn's reflex to turn his trunk and shoulders to the same side his head is turned.

Necrobiosis lipoidica diabeticorum A skin condition usually on the lower part of the legs. The lesions can be small or extend over a large area. They are usually raised, yellow, and waxy in appearance and often have a purple border. Young women are most often affected. This condition occurs in people with diabetes, or it may be a sign of diabetes. It also occurs in people who do not have diabetes.

Necromania Pathological preoccupation with dead bodies.

Needle biopsy The removal of tissue or fluid with a needle for examination under a microscope. When a wide needle is used, the procedure is called a core biopsy. When a thin needle is used, the procedure is called a fine-needle aspiration biopsy.

Needle exchange An organization that allows injection drug users to exchange used needles for clean ones in order to control infection.

Needling In acupuncture, the insertion of a thin needle into a specific place on the body to unlock qi (vital energy). The needle may be twirled, moved up and down at different speeds and depths, heated, or charged with a low electric current.

Negative operating margin A loss that occurs when costs of operation exceed revenues.

Negativistic personality disorder A type of passive-aggressive personality disorder characterized by passive resistance to demands for adequate social and occupational performance and a negative attitude. Typical manifestations include inefficiency, procrastination, complaints of being victimized and

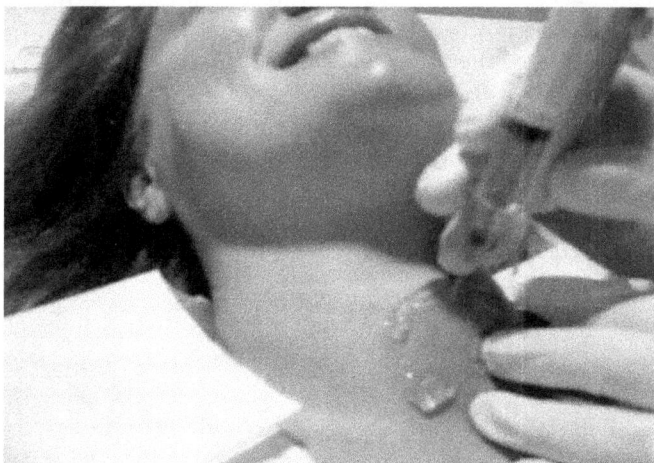

Fig. *Needle biopsy*

unappreciated, irritability, criticism of and scorn for authority, and personal discontent. The person with this disorder alternates between hostile assertions of independence and contrite, dependent behaviour.

Negotiated fee schedule Fees set through an organized bargaining process usually used to help determine a global budget. Also called negotiated payment schedule.

Negotiated settlement The resolution of a malpractice claim prior to a judicial determination.

Nematodes Elongated, cylindrical worms, many of which are parasites, including hookworm, porkworm (the worms that cause trichinosis), and filarial worms. Most infestations of nematodes are treatable with antihelmintic drugs. Also called roundworms.

Neonatal In medical contexts, newborn or neonate refers to an infant in the first 28 days after birth; the term applies to premature infants, postmature infants, and full term infants. Before birth, the term fetus is used.

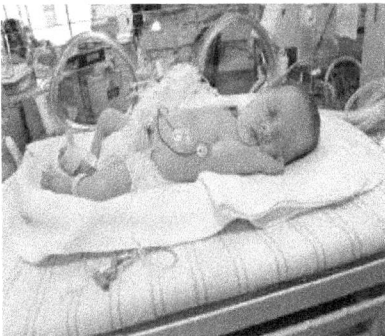

Fig. *Neonatal*

Neonatal care is the provision of nursing care for newborn infants up to 28 days after birth. Neonatal nurses are a vital part of the neonatal care team.

Neonatal intensive care unit A specialized hospital unit combining high technology and highly trained staff for the management and care of premature or seriously ill newborns.

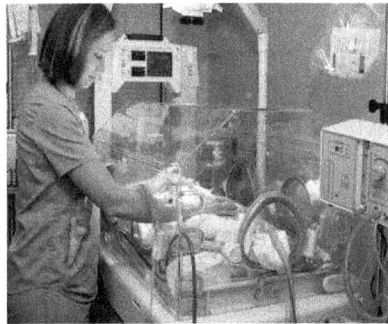

Fig. *Neonatal intensive care unit*

Neonatal mortality Death of an infant in the first 28 days of life.

Neonatal mortality rate The number of deaths among infants during the first 28 days of life in a given period (usually a year) per 1000 live births in that period.

Neonatal screening tests Initial tests on a newborn baby to determine any birth abnormalities or metabolic disorders.

Neonate A newborn infant less than 4 weeks old.

Neonatologist A doctor who specialises in the care of newborns.

Neonatology A subspecialty of pediatrics dealing with newborn care.

Neoplasia Abnormal and uncontrolled cell growth.

Neoplasm Uncontrolled and progressive growth of tissue, either benign or malignant; a tumour.

Neoplastic meningitis A serious problem that may occur in cancer in which cancer cells spread from the original (primary) tumour to the meninges (thin layers of tissue that cover and protect the brain and spinal cord). It can happen in many types of cancer, but is the most common in melanoma, breast, lung, and gastrointestinal cancer. The cancer may cause the meninges to be inflamed. Also called carcinomatous meningitis, lepto-meningeal cancer, lepto-meningeal carcinoma, lepto-meningeal metastasis, menin-geal carcinomatosis, and menin-geal metastasis.

Neovascularization Abnormal growth of new blood vessels, such as in an excessive amount, or in tissue that normally does not contain them, or of a different kind than is usual in that tissue.

Nephrectomy The surgical removal of a kidney.

Nephrolithotomy The surgical removal of a stone from the kidney.

Nephrologist A doctor who specializes in diagnosing and treating kidney disease.

Nephropathy Any disease of the kidneys. Kidney damage caused by diabetes, called diabetic nephropathy, can occur in several ways. The typical form of diabetic nephropathy, called diabetic glomerulosclerosis, has large amounts of urine protein, hypertension, and is slowly progressive. It usually doesn't occur until after many years of diabetes, and can be delayed by tight control of the blood sugar. Usually the best lab test for early detection of diabetic nephropathy is measurement of microalbumin in the urine.

Nephrostomy is an artificial opening created between the kidney and the skin which allows for the urinary diversion directly from the upper part of the urinary system (renal pelvis). A nephrostomy is performed whenever a blockage keeps urine from passing from the kidneys, through the ureter and into the urinary bladder. Without another way for urine to

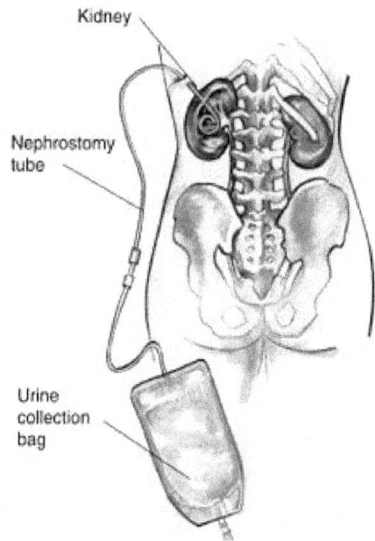

Fig. *Nephrostomy*

drain, pressure would rise within the urinary system and the kidneys would be damaged. The most common cause of blockage necessitating a nephrostomy is cancer, especially ovarian cancer and colon cancer. Nephrostomies may also be required to treat pyonephrosis, hydronephrosis and kidney stones.

Nephrotomogram A series of x-rays of the kidneys. The x-rays are taken from different angles and show the kidneys clearly, without the shadows of the organs around them.

Nephrotomy A surgical incision into the kidney.

Nephrotoxic Poisonous or damaging to the kidney.

Nephroureterectomy Surgery to remove a kidney and its ureter. Also called uretero-nephrectomy.

Nerve A bundle of fibres that receives and sends messages between the body and the brain. The messages are sent by chemical and electrical changes in the cells that make up the nerves.

Nerve block A procedure in which medicine is injected directly into or around a nerve or into the spine to block pain.

Nerve cell A type of cell that receives and sends messages from the body to the brain and back to the body. The messages are sent by a weak electrical current. Also called neuron.

Nerve conduction velocity Studies and Electromyography (EMG) Tests used to diagnose neuropathy and check for nerve damage. These tests are usually both run at the same time, using the same equipment.

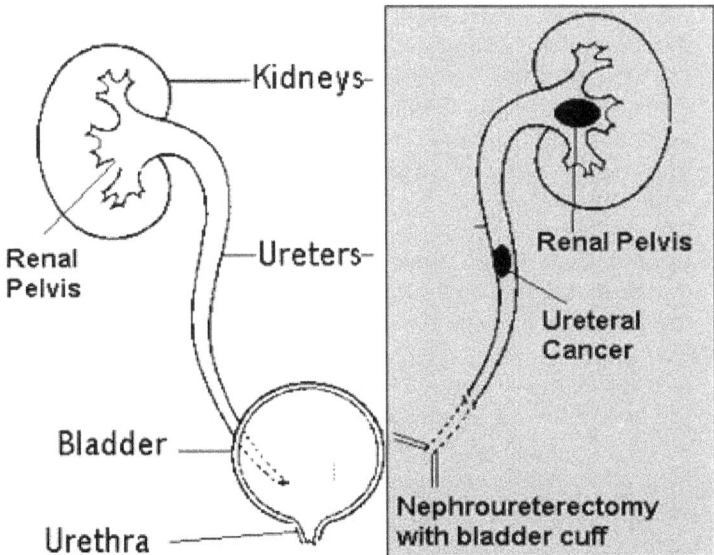

Fig. *Nephroureterectomy*

Nerve fibre An axon and its surrounding myelin sheath.

Nerve grafting Replacing a damaged nerve with a section of a healthy nerve that has been removed from another part of the body. This procedure is being studied in the prevention of erectile dysfunction in men having surgery for prostate cancer.

Nerve growth factor A protein that promotes axon growth in some areas of the peripheral nervous system and plays a role in the development of vertebrate sensory and autonomic systems. In 140 Office of Technology Assessment: Compilation of Abbreviations and Terms - September 1993 the central nervous system, it appears to protect from damage some populations of cells that synthesize acetylcholine.

Nerve root One of a collection of nerves that are attached to and demarcate the 30 segments of the spinal cord. Nerve fibres enter and leave the spinal cord at one of the 31 nerve roots. These fibres link the peripheral and central nervous systems, bringing sensory information from the body to the spinal cord and motor information from the spinal cord to the body.

Nerve-sparing radical prostatectomy Surgery to remove the prostate in which an attempt is made to save the nerves that help cause penile erections.

Nerve-sparing surgery A type of surgery that attempts to save the nerves near the tissues being removed.

Nervous system The organized network of nerve tissue in the body. It coordinates the voluntary and involuntary actions of the animal and transmits signals between different parts of its body. In most types of animals it consists of two main parts, the central nervous system (CNS) and the peripheral nervous system (PNS). The CNS contains the brain and spinal cord. The PNS consists mainly of nerves, which are long fibres that connect the CNS to every other part of the body. The PNS includes motor neurons, mediating voluntary movement, the autonomic nervous system,

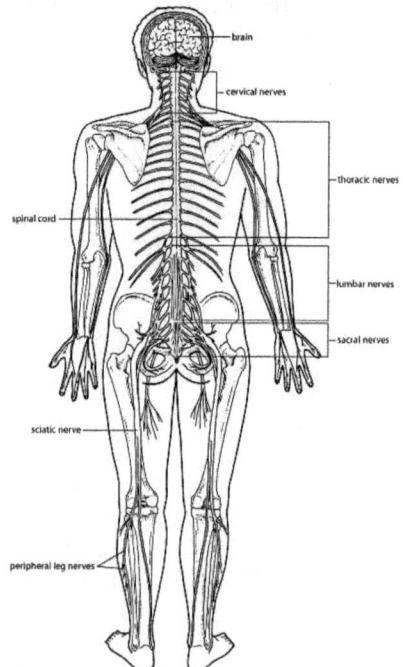

Fig. *Nervous system*

comprising the sympathetic nervous system and the parasympathetic nervous system and regulating involuntary functions, and the enteric nervous system, a semi-independent part of the nervous system whose function is to control the gastrointestinal system.

Nesidioblastosis A group of rare conditions occurring in infancy in which excessively large amounts of insulin are secreted by the beta cells in relation to the prevailing blood sugar level. Sometimes the condition occurs later in life, and sometimes it is due to an autosomal recessive genetic defect. Also called Persistent hyperinsulinemic hypoglycemia of infancy (PHHI).

Net efficiency The difference between direct benefits and direct costs, generally in regard to regulation.

Net Loss Ratio The result of total claims liability and all expenses divided by premiums. This is the carrier's loss ratio after accounting for all expenses.

Net patient revenue For a hospital or other health care facility, consists of gross patient revenue less ~ deductions for contractual adjustments (amounts of patient charges not paid by insurers), bad debts, charity, and other factors.

Net total revenue Consists of net patient revenue plus all other revenue of a hospital or other health care facility, including contributions, endowment revenue, government grants, and all other payments not attributable to patient care.

Network A set group of providers associated by contractual agreements that provide either specific benefits or a full choice of acute and long term care services.

Network chiropractic uses Network Spinal Analysis, a method characterized by the sequential application of a number of gentle, specific chiropractic adjusting techniques. Care progresses through a series of levels that parallel spinal and quality-of-life changes.

Neulasta A drug used to increase numbers of white blood cells in patients who are receiving chemotherapy. It is a type of colony-stimulating factor. Also called filgrastim-SD/01 and pegfilgrastim.

Neumega A drug used to increase the number of blood cells, especially platelets, in some cancer patients receiving chemotherapy. Neumega is a form of interleukin-11 (a cytokine normally made by support cells in the bone marrow) that is made in the laboratory. It is a type of biological response modifier. Also called oprelvekin, recombinant human interleukin-11, and rhIL-11.

Neural Having to do with nerves or the nervous system, including the brain and the spinal cord.

Neural grafting The transplantation (implantation) of cells or tissue into the brain or spinal cord, including various treatment goals (such as promotion of growth or provision of needed chemicals), materials (such as adrenal medulla or fetal central nervous system tissue) and methods (such as cell suspensions or cell lines) of grafting.

Neural therapy A form of therapy based on the idea that illness is the result of disruptions in biological energy and that the disruptions are caused by changes in the electric activity of the autonomic nervous system (which controls involuntary functions like breathing).

Neuritic plaque Abnormal cluster of degenerating neurons, other brain cells, and protein in the areas between neurons; found in the brains of persons with Alzheimer's disease.

Neuritis Inflammation of a nerve

Neurobehavioural Having to do with the way the brain affects emotion, behaviour, and learning. Some cancers or their treatment may cause neuro-behavioral problems.

Neuroblastoma Cancer that arises in immature nerve cells and affects mostly infants and children.

Neurocognitive Having to do with the ability to think and reason. This includes the ability to concentrate, remember things, process information, learn, speak, and understand.

Neurodegenerative disorder A class of neurological disease marked by loss of a particular population or populations of nerve cells in the central nervous system. Symptoms vary and depend on the neurons lost.

Neurodevelopmental outcome A measure of neurological and developmental status.

Neuroectodermal tumour A tumour of the central or peripheral nervous system.

Neuroendocrine Having to do with the interactions between the nervous system and the endocrine system. Neuro-endocrine describes certain cells that release hormones into the blood in response to stimulation of the nervous system.

Neurofibrillary tangle Accumulation of twisted protein filaments inside nerve cells; found in the brains of persons with Alzheimer's disease.

Neuroglia Connective or supporting tissues of the nervous system.

Neuroglycopenic Shortage of glucose in the nerve cells of the brain. Since the brain cells depends upon glucose as their main fuel, low blood sugars can quickly result in malfunction of the brain (with change in mental function, and possible loss of consciousness or seizures). In patients with Hypoglycemia Unawareness, where the patient may not recognize low sugar levels because other symptoms such as sweating, tremor, and rapid heart rate, are absent, the first symptoms are neuroglycopenic —namely, loss of mental functioning.

Neuroleptic A term used to describe any antipsychotic drug (e.g., certain tranquilizers) useful in the treatment of mental disoders, especially psychoses.

Neurological disorder Disease of, or injury to, the central nervous system.

Neurologist A doctor who specialises in treating and diagnosing disorders of the nervous system and brain.

Neuromodulator A substance (e.g., hormone or neuro-transmitter) that alters the transmission of nerve impulses; neuromodulators can regulate the strength of signaling between a neuron and another cell without acting directly on the receiving cell, either by regulating the amount of hormone present in the synapse or its receptor-binding capabilities.

Neuromuscular development The development of a child's control over gross and fine motor skills.

Neuron, nerve cell The fundamental conducting cell, a highly specialized type of cell capable of being stimulated and conducting electrical impulses along its axon. The neuron is typically composed of a relatively compact cell body containing the nucleus, several short radiating processes (dendrites), and one long process (the axon) with twig-like branches along its length and at its end. Information in the form of electrical impulses travels from the cell body along these processes to other cells. Sensory neurons send information to the brain and spinal cord; motor neurons send instructions to the muscles.

Neuronal ceroid lipofuscinosis Rare, hereditary, degenerative disease in which the body does not store pigments called lipofuscins properly; the disease is characterized by vision loss, seizures and dementia. Types include Santavuori-Haltia (infantile), Jansky-Bielschowsky (late infantile), Spielmeyer-Vogt (juvenile) and Kufs' disease

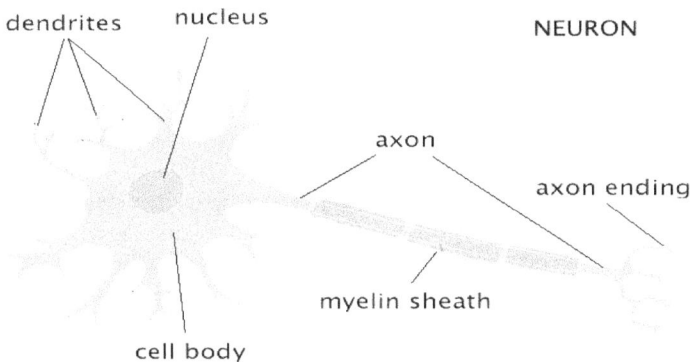

dendrites   nucleus   NEURON

axon

axon ending

myelin sheath

cell body

Fig. *Neuron, nerve cell*

(adult). Some types may also be called Batten disease.

Neuronopathy A primary damage to the nerve cell body which results in a rapid, but secondary degeneration of nerve process.

Neuro-oncologist A doctor who specializes in diagnosing and treating brain tumours and other tumours of the nervous system.

Neuro-otologist A doctor who specialises in ear and hearing problems affecting the acoustic nerve.

Neuropathological tests Postmortem examination of test animals in order to determine changes in the structure and function of the nervous system as a result of exposure to a toxic substance. These tests are used to screen for toxic substances. See screening tests.

Neuropathy (i) Disease of the nervous system. Many people who have had diabetes for a while have nerve damage. The three major forms of nerve damage are—peripheral neuropathy, autonomic neuropathy, and mono-neuropathy. The most common form is peripheral neuropathy, which mainly affects the feet and legs.

(ii) Degeneration of nerve cells; a general description for any disease of the peripheral or central nervous system.

Neuropeptide A general term for any short chain of amino acids found in the central nervous system that affects the behaviour of nerve cells, whether by acting

as a neurotransmitter, hormone, or neuromodulator (e.g., endorphins, enkephalins, vaso-pressin).

Neurophysiological tests Techniques for measuring the electrical signals, or evoked potentials, of charged ions; the measured potentials reflect the functioning of the neuron or neurons that generated them.

Neuroretinitis Inflammation of the optic nerve and retina, commonly caused by an infection. Symptoms include blurred vision, headache, floaters, eye pain or discomfort, vision loss and loss of colour vision.

Neuroscience The study of the brain and the nervous system.

Neurosis Currently there is no consensus in the mental health field as to the definition of neurosis, and the category neuroses was not included in the current diagnostic and statistical manual of the American psychiatric association (DSM-III), although it had been included in previous editions. The term neurosis is usually used to refer to emotional disoders caused by unconscious conflict and characterized chiefly by anxiety.

Neurosurgeon A doctor who specialises in surgery on the nervous system.

Neurotopic injection Treatment involves dozens of injections of small amounts (0.5 cc or less) of sterile saline solution (0.9 percent salt) into the muscles at both sides of the spine near the places where the nerves enter into the back muscles. According to this theory, salt injection helps the nerves function better, leading to improved circulation, control of pain, and healing of numerous disorders. Statistics on successful treatment of back and neck pain, sciatica, disk problems, headaches, arthritis, prostate and thyroid problems, asthma, and allergies have been presented at more than 15 international medical congresses. Technique is being evaluated in double-blind studies at the National College of Naturopathic Medicine in Oregon.

Neurotoxic effect An adverse change in the structure or function of the nervous system following exposure to a toxic substance.

Neurotoxic esterase assay A procedure for measuring the inhibition of the enzyme NTE in the brain or spinal cord of hens exposed to organophosphates. The test can be used to determine the delayed effects of acute and subchronic exposures to organophosphates.

Neurotoxicant, neurotoxic substance A chemical that adversely affects the nervous system.

Neurotoxicity The quality of exerting a destructive or poisonous effect on nerve tissue.

Neurotoxicology Study of the effects of toxic chemicals on the nervous system, including the modes by which neurotoxic substances enter the body, the effects these substances have on the nervous system, the biochemical and physiological mechanisms through which the effects occur, the prevention of damage to the nervous system, and the treatment of neurological and psychiatric disorders caused by exposure.

Neurotransmitter Specialized chemical messenger substances (e.g. acetylcholine, dopamine, norepinephrine, serotonin), synthesized and secreted by neurons, that transmit or modify nerve impulses from one nerve cell to another or from nerve cells to muscle fibres. Some types of neuro-transmitters are released into the synaptic space between neurons, bind to the dendrites of other neurons, and initiate a message in those neurons. Others (such as endorphins and vasopressin) transmit messages to receptors on distant cells.

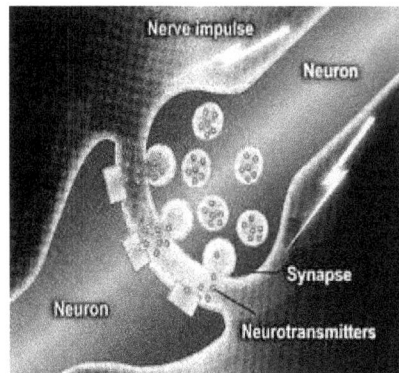

Fig. *Neurotransmitter*

Neurotrophic factor Chemical produced by some neurons and glial cells that affects the growth and development, maintenance of function, and response to injury of neurons.

New drug According to the FDA standard it is defined in part as— 'any drug...the composition of which is such that such drug is not generally recognized, among experts qualified by scientific training and experience to evaluate the safety and effectiveness of drugs, as safe and effective for use under the conditions prescribed, recommended, or suggested in the labeling thereof.'

New morbidities Illnesses and conditions caused by social and behavioural (rather than organismic) factors (e.g., outcomes of sex, drugs, and violence).

Newborn screening The process of routine testing of newborn infants with the goal of identifying cases for whom medical intervention can be provided to avoid devastating effects of untreated or late treated disease, or to detect individuals who will develop serious disease later in childhood.

NFPA Storage Codes National Fire Protection Association storage codes As fire departments inspect businesses, especially radiology departments, several questions arise including storage codes for x-ray films and chemicals.

Niacin Also known as vitamin B3. Niacin is a water soluble vitamin which cannot be stored by the body. Good sources include meat, flour, eggs and milk.

Nickel metallic element used mainly in alloys Many eyeglass frames are made of nickel alloy, so people who are allergic should choose a hypoallergenic substitute, such as titanium.

NIDDM Noninsulin-dependent diabetes mellitus

Nihilisitic delusion A conviction of nonexistence of the self, part of the self, or others, or of the world. "I no longer have a brain" is an example.

Nipple shield Flexible plastic covers which can be placed on the breast before feeding. Some women find they give temporary help for soreness but it is important long term to sort out the reason for the soreness. Check how well baby is latched on to breast. Nipple shields can cut down the amount of milk a baby takes at any one feed.

Nitrites "Poppers" or nitrite inhalants, including amyl, butyl, and isobutyl nitrite, that produce an intoxication characterized by a feeling of fullness in the head, mild euphoria, a change in the perception of time, relaxation of smooth muscles, and possibly an increase in sexual feelings. The nitrites may produce psychological dependence and may impair immune functioning, irritate the respiratory system, and induce a toxic reaction involving vomiting, severe headache, and dizziness.

Nitrogen fixation A biological process (usually associated with microorganisms in the soil) whereby certain bacteria convert free nitrogen in the air to ammonia and other forms usable by plants and animals for growth and development.

NOAEL, No observed adverse effect level — that dose below which no adverse effect is observed.

Nocturnal hpoglycemia Hypoglycemia occurring while the patient is asleep (between the evening injection and getting up in the morning). Nocturnal hypoglycemia typically has symptoms such as restlessness, nightmares, profuse sweating, and frequently is noted by the bed-partner or parent rather than by the sleeping patient, or sometimes is unrecognized.

Nocturnal penile tumescence The occurrence of erections during sleep.

NOD mouse A strain of mice in which the female has an especially high incidence of a diabetes similar to Type 1 in humans. Much used as a research model for prevention and new onset treatment.

Node of Ranvier are the gaps (approximately 1 micrometre in length) formed between the myelin sheaths generated by different cells. A myelin sheath is a many-layered coating, largely composed of a fatty substance called myelin, that wraps around the axon of a neuron and very efficiently insulates it. At nodes of Ranvier, the axonal membrane is unin-sulated and therefore capable of generating electrical activity.

Non-A, non-8 hepatitis A type of hepatitis (viral infection of the liver) in which both hepatitis A and hepatitis B virus infection have been excluded. Hepatitis C virus has been identified as the cause of a substantial portion of "non-A, non-B" hepatitis and is currently the major cause of post-transfusion hepatitis (since tests to screen donor units of blood for hepatitis C virus have only recently been instituted). Hepatitis C virus is also a common cause of hepatitis in needle users and accounts for 50percent or more of sporadic, or community-acquired, cases.

Noncoital reproduction Reproduction other than by sexual intercourse.

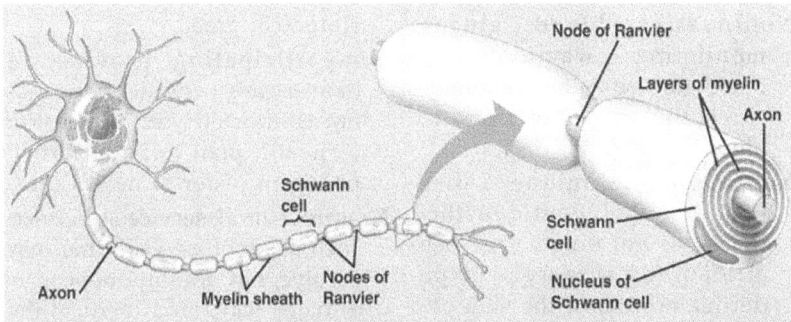

Fig. *Node of Ranvier*

Nonconjugative plasmid A plasmid incapable of initiating or directing the process of conjugation.

Noncontributory A situation in which the plan sponsor pays the entire cost or premiums for coverage. Employees do not contribute toward the cost of the coverage.

Nonforfeiture benefit All tax qualified policies offer a non-forfeiture benefit which provides a return of some premiums paid or a reduced benefit if the policyholder stops paying the premiums after some period of time.

Nonforfeiture feature A provision in some long-term care policies offering a guarantee that certain policy benefits will remain available even if the enrollee stops paying premiums. One type of non-forfeiture is a paid-up policy providing the same benefits for a shorter period of lower benefits for the same period as the original policy. Return of premium benefits are another form of non-forfeiture. Also known as lapsed coverage protection.

Noninvasive blood glucose monitoring A way to measure blood glucose without having to prick the finger to obtain a blood sample.

Noninvasive technique A diagnostic or therapeutic method that does not involve the penetration (by surgery or hypodermic needle) of the skin or a cavity or organ of the body to be entered.

Nonischemic heart disease Heart disease from causes other than coronary artery disease (e.g., congenital heart disease, myocadiopathy).

Nonketotic coma Hyperglycemic hyperosmolar nonketotic syndrome. A complication of diabetes caused by a lack of insulin and dehydration. It is diagnosed when the patient has: very high levels of glucose (sugar) in the blood; absence of ketoacidosis; severe dehydration; a sleepy, confused, or comatose state. Nonketotic coma is more likely to be associated with Type 2 diabetes, and is sometimes the initial presenting situation for Type 2 diabetes. Nonketotic coma is uncommon in Type 1 Diabetes.

Nonmaleficence Generally associated with the maxim 'primum non nocere" from Latin, meaning above all, do no harm. In ethics, it is the principle that one has a duty not to inflict evil, harm, or risk of harm.

Nonmetropolitan statistical area Any area not in a metropolitan statistical area.

Nonparticipating provider A health care provider who has not contracted with the carrier or health plan to be a participating provider of health care.

Nonprocedural service A service, such as an office visit, that may involve, but does not depend in a major way, on a medical device.

Nonself In immunology, cells or organs that are not recognized by an individual's immune system as being a natural constituent of that individual's body.

Nonspecific immunity Immunity that exists from birth and that occurs without prior exposure to an antigen; also called innate immunity. Compare acquired immunity.

Non-stress test A test on the fetus which is done by measuring the fetal heart rate in response to his or her movements.

Nontherapeutic abortion An induced abortion in situations other than when the woman's life is endangered by the pregnancy.

Nontherapeutic research Studies involving human subjects designed to further scientific knowledge about a disorder or process, with no anticipated direct benefit to the subjects themselves.

Nontoxic In general medical use, referring to treatments without adverse effects.

Normal birthweight Birthweight of 2,500 grams (5 lb., 8 oz.) or above.

Norplant Time-released birth control, administered through six tiny tubes which are implanted in a woman's upper arm. It remains effective for up five years.

Nose pad One of a pair of pads, usually clear, that rest on either side of nose and help to support glasses.

Nosocomial infection An infection that a patient acquires during hospitalization. The most common nosocomial infections are urinary tract infections, followed by surgical wound infections, pneumonia, and infections of the bloodstream. .

NOSODE A homeopathic remedy made from diseased tissue or bodily secretions rather than from a plant or animal. Taken like a homeopathic immunization to build up an immune response against a specific disease. Nosodes are often named for the disease present in the material they were made from - for example, the flu nosode and the infectious mononucleosis nosode.

Nostrum A medicine of secret composition recommended by its preparer but usually without scientific proof of its effectiveness.

No-threshold The situation in which any dose greater than zero increases risk.

Novelty One of the criteria used in the evaluation of patent applications. In order to be accepted on the grounds of novelty, the invention or discovery being evaluated must be new and must not have previously existed through the work of others.

NPH insulin A type of insulin that is intermediate-acting.

Nuchal cord Loop(s) of umbilical cord around the fetal neck, posing risk of intrauterine hypoxia, fetal distress, or death.

Nuchal fascia The fascia that encloses the posterior muscles of the neck.

Nuchal lucency Ultrasound finding of a lucent (anechoic) area behind the fetal neck early in pregnancy. An increase in the size of this area is associated with increased risk for Down syndrome, congenital heart disease, and other anomalies.

Nuchal translucency Ultrasonographic finding of a single nonseptated lucenty (anechoic area) projecting from the posterior aspect of the fetal neck; measured at menstrual age 11-14 weeks. Increased thickness of this area indicates increased fetal risk for aneuploidy and some nonchromosomal disorders.

Nuclear medicine technologist Operates radioscopic equipment to produce scanograms and measure concentrations of radioactive isotopes in specific body areas for diagnostic purposes.

Nuclear membrane The membrane that surrounds the nucleus. The nuclear membrane consists of two lipid bilayers—the inner nuclear membrane, and the outer nuclear membrane. The space between the membranes is called the perinuclear space, a region contiguous with the lumen (inside) of the endoplasmic reticulum. It is typically about 20–40 nm wide.

Nuclear Regulatory Commission A Federal commission created in 1974 to protect the public health and safety by regulating civilian uses of nuclear materials.

Nucleic acid Macromolecules composed of sequences of nucleotides that carry genetic information. There are two kinds of nucleic acids, occurring as double or single stranded molecules: DNA, which contains the coded instructions for an organism's development in the chromosomes and is transferred to daughter cells; and RNA, which helps transport, translate, and implement the DNA instructions, particularly the biosynthesis of proteins.

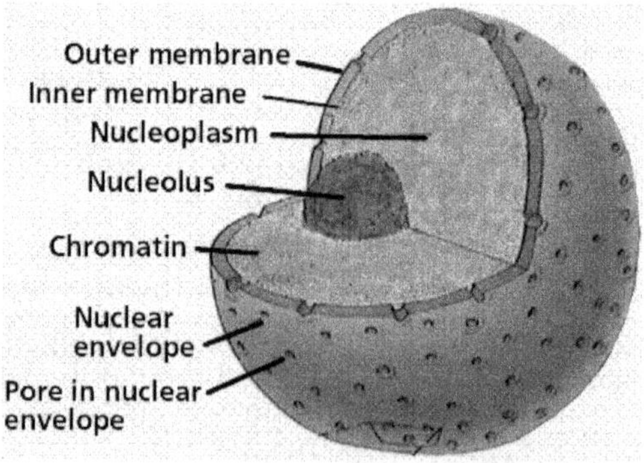

Outer membrane
Inner membrane
Nucleoplasm
Nucleolus
Chromatin
Nuclear envelope
Pore in nuclear envelope

Fig. *Nuclear membrane*

Nucleic acid hybridization A laboratory technique for identifying species and strains of organisms involving the matching of either DNA or RNA (depending" on the organism) from an unknown organism with DNA or RNA from a known organism.

Nucleolus An organelle within the nucleus - it is where ribosomal RNA is produced. Some cells have more than one nucleolus.

Nucleotide A subunit of DNA or RNA, consisting of a nitrogenous base (adenine, guanine, thymine, cytosine, or uracil), a phosphate molecule, and a sugar molecule (deoxyribose in DNA or ribose in RNA). The linkage of thousands of these subunits forms the DNA or RNA molecule.

Nucleus caeruleus A shallow depression, blue in the fresh brain, lying laterally in the most rostral portion of the rhomboidal fossa near the cerebral aqueduct; it lies near the lateral wall of the fourth ventricle and consists of about 20,000 melanin-pigmented neuronal cell bodies the norepinephrine-containing axons of which have a remarkably wide distribution in the cerebral cortex, dorsal thalamus, amygdaloid complex with the hippocampus, mesencephalic tegmentum, cerebellar nuclei and cortex, various nuclei in the pons and medulla, and the gray matter of the spinal cord.

Nucleus pulposus The soft fibrocartilage central portion of the intervertebral disc; regarded as a derivative of the notochord.

Nucleus reuniens A small cell group belonging to the midline group of thalamic nuclei and extending into the interthalamic adhesion (massa intermedia) when the latter is present.

Nucleus Spherical body containing many organelles, including the nucleolus. The nucleus controls many of the functions of the cell (by controlling protein synthesis) and contains DNA (in chromosomes). The nucleus is surrounded by the nuclear membrane.

Null cells Large granular lymphocytes that lack surface markers or membrane-associated proteins of either B or T lymphocytes.

Numbness Imprecise term for abnormal sensation, including absent or reduced sensory perception as well as paresthesias.

Nurse A legally qualified person who is licensed by the state to

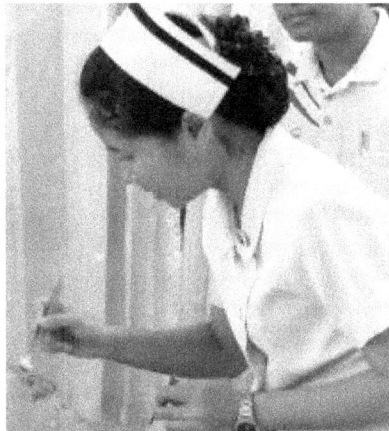

Fig. *Nurse*

provide nursing services. Also see registered nurse, licensed practical nurse, nurse practitioner, and advanced nurse practitioner.

Nurse assistant Performs a variety of routine duties for patients in caring for their personnel needs and comfort. Includes answering signal lights, baths, assists with personal hygiene, alcohol rubs, bed pans, takes and records temperatures, pulse, intake and output, gives enemas, etc.

Nurse epidemiologist A registered nurse with additional education in the monitoring and prevention of nosocomial infections in the client population in an agency.

Nurse manager Performs all the duties of an R.N., plus plans and supervises work of all nursing personnel within an assigned unit of the nursing department.

Nurse practitioner A registered nurse with additional specialized graduate level training. An NP performs physical exams and diagnostic tests, counsels patients, and develops treatment programmes.

Nurse, licensed practical A graduate of a state-approved practical nursing education programme, who has passed a state examination and been licensed to provide nursing and personal care under the supervision of a registered nurse or physician. An LPN administers medications and treatments and acts as a charge nurse in nursing facilities.

Nurse, registered Nurses who have graduated from a formal programme of nursing education (two-year associate degree, three-year hospital diploma, or four-year baccalaureate) and passed a state-administered exam. RNs have completed more formal training than licensed practical nurses and have a wide scope of responsibility including all aspects of nursing care.

Nurses aide Legally qualified person who is certified by the state to perform certain health care services, usually in the area of personal care or home health services. Also called certified nurses aid.

Nursing facility Nursing facilities are licensed to provide custodial care, rehabilitative care, such as physical, occupational or speech therapy or specialized care for Alzheimer's patients. Additionally, nursing facilities offer residents planned social, recreational and spiritual activities.

Nursing home A facility licensed with an organized professional staff and inpatient beds and that provides continuous nursing and other health-related, psycho-social, and personal services to patients who are not in an acute phase of illness, but who primarily require continued care on an inpatient basis.

Nursing homes are the residential care facilities that provide 24-hour supervision, nursing care, personal care, and other services. (see figure on next page)

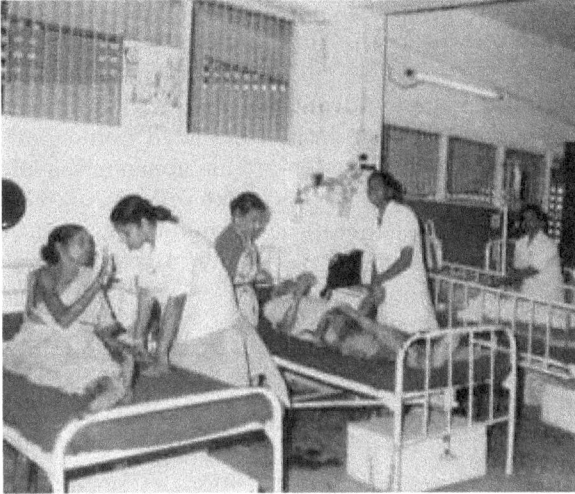

Fig. *Nursing home*

Nursing supervisor Responsible for reviewing specific problems with other nursing personnel; makes rounds to all nursing units, answers all Dr. Stat calls, assists physicians in these emergencies, develops and directs orientation programme for nursing service personnel, assumes administrative duties in absence of assistant director of nursing.

Nutrition The process by which the body draws nutrients from food and uses them to make or mend its cells.

Nutritional support The administration of nutrients in addition to, or instead of, food that a person can or would eat in a normal manner. Nutritional support is frequently used as an all-inclusive term for both parenteral nutrition (modification of the usual diet) and enteral nutrition (intravenous administration of nutrients). It is distinct from nutritional supplements, such as vitamins, added to the diet.

Nyctalgia Pain that characteristically occurs at night (nocturnal bone pain experienced by patients with syphilis).

Nyctalopia Decreased ability to see in reduced illumination. Seen in patients with impaired rod function; often associated with a deficiency of vitamin A.

Nymph The earliest series of stages in metamorphosis following hatching in the development of hemimetabolous insects (locusts); the nymph resembles the adult in many respects, but lacks full wing or genitalia development; it grows through successive instars without any intermediate or pupal stage into the imago or adult form.

Nymphomania An insatiable impulse to engage in sexual behaviour in a female; the counterpart of satyriasis in a male.

Nymphoncus Swelling or hypertrophy of one or both labia minora.

Nystagmus blockage syndrome Strabismus with eyes and head in a position to minimize associated nystagmus.

Nystagmus Rapid and involuntary eye movement that is oscillating and non-chaotic. Blurred vision may result.

Nystagmus typically affects infants and has a variety of causes.

Nystatin An antibiotic substance isolated from cultures of Streptomyces noursei, effective in the treatment of all forms of candidiasis, particularly candidal infections of the intestine, skin, and mucous membranes.

O

O

Obesity When people have 20 percent (or more) extra body fat for their age, height, sex, and bone structure. Fat works against the action of insulin. Extra body fat is thought to be a risk factor for diabetes. It can be also defined in different ways—(i) body mass index (BMl) (weight in kilograms divided by height in metres squared [m²]) greater than or equal to the 95th percentile of a similar population group (usually by age); or (ii) 20 percent or more over "normal" weight. More serious than overweight.

OBOB mouse (Obese-obese mouse) A variety of mouse that tends to be fat, and diabetic. A model for research on NIDDM.

Obsessive-compulsive disorder An anxiety disorder characterized by obsessions, compulsions, or both, that are time-consuming and interfere significantly with normal routine, occupational functioning, usual social activities, or relationships with others.

Obstetric care Medical care received during pregnancy, labour and delivery, and the period immediately following birth.

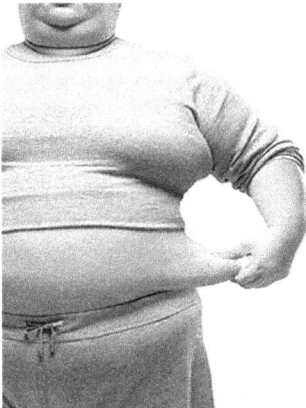

Fig. *Obesity*

Obstetrician A doctor who sees and gives care to pregnant women and delivers babies.

Occlusion In the context of the vascular system, the blocking off or obstruction of blood flow through a vessel.

Occupancy Ratio of the average number of inpatients (excluding newborns) receiving care to the average number of beds in a hospital set up and staffed for use (i.e., statistical beds) during a particular reporting period (American Hospital Association definition).

Occupational therapy Therapy provided to people who are physically or mentally impaired that is intended to improve functional abilities; provided by an occupational therapist.

Occurrence screen A list of criteria used to screen patients' medical records for occurrences. Examples of occurrences include deaths, unusually long lengths of stay, hospital-acquired infections, and unscheduled procedures, readmission, or transfers.

Ocular herpes Recurrent viral infection that can cause inflammation and scarring of the cornea. It is not sexually transmitted. There are various types of ocular herpes, ranging from herpes keratitis to more serious forms that can lead to blindness.

Ocular hypertension Condition in which the intraocular pressure of the eye is elevated above normal and which may lead to glaucoma.

Ocular migraine Visual phenomena that may accompany a migraine headache or that may occur without any headache. They include light flashes, spots, wavy lines, flickers, zig-zagging lights, semi-circular or crescent-shaped visual defects and distortions of shapes.

OD Abbreviation for "oculus dexter," the latin term for "right eye." Or, doctor of optometry.

Odds ratio A measure of association closely related to relative risk; the ratio of the odds of a disease occurring in individuals exposed to the risk compared to those unexposed.

Older adolescents As defined in most DHHS National Center for Health Statistics data analyses, adolescents ages 15 to 19.

Older Americans Act A law enacted in 1965 that established the Federal Administration on Aging and a programme of Federal grants to States for the development of a coordinated system of services for elderly people in their homes and communities. The act also required States to designate a single State agency-commonly referred to as a State unit on aging-to formulate a plan for developing the system of services envisioned in the act. The 1973 amendments to the act required each State to divide its jurisdiction into planning and service areas and to designate an area agency on aging to plan, co-ordinate, and arrange services for elderly people in each area.

Oligodendrocyte A type of glial cell that forms myelin in the central nervous system; oligo-dendrocytes appear to inhibit the regrowth of damaged axons in the central nervous system.

Oligomenorrhea Scanty or infre-quent menstruation, a problem found in about 20 percent of in-fertile women.

Oligonucleotide probe A short DNA sequence synthesized from a known gene or segment of a gene that can be either nor-mal or mutant.

Oligonucleotide A polymer made up of a few (generally fewer than ten or twenty) nucleotides; a short sequence of DNA or RNA.

Oligospermia Scarcity of sperm in the semen.

Onchocerciasis Commonly called "river blindness,". An infection of humans with the filaria worm Onchocerca volvulus, transmitted by the bite of blood-sucking blackflies. The disease is generally character-ized by skin nodules that can become fibrous and calcified. Also called "African river blind-ness," for the blindness that oc-curs when the worms invade the eye.

Oncogene One of several known genes, found in all cells, in-volved in one of the steps in the transformation from normal to malignant growth. Under nor-mal conditions, oncogenes play a role in the growth and prolif-eration of cells, but when acti-vated or altered in some way (e.g., by an environmental fac-tor) can cause a cell to become malignant. Such environmental factors include ultraviolet light, radioactivity, tobacco smoke, asbestos particles, carcinogenic chemicals, and certain viruses.

Oncogenesis The induction or for-mation of tumours.

Oncologist A physician who spe-cializes in the treatment of can-cer, usually referring to medi-cal oncology, which is a subspecialty of internal medi-cine.

One-stop shopping A setting for health care services that deliv-ers an entire set of comprehen-sive health (and, often, related) services. Currently an ideal rather than an actuality.

On-Lok senior health services An organization that plans, coordi-nates, and provides comprehen-sive health care, long-term care, social, and other services for about 300 very frail and se-verely impaired older adults in the Chinatown-North Beach area of San Francisco.

On-off phenomenon In Parkin-son's disease, alternating peri-ods in which the patient's mo-tor symptoms are under con-trol (on) or severe and uncon-trolled (off); the phenomenon occurs regardless of drug dos-age.

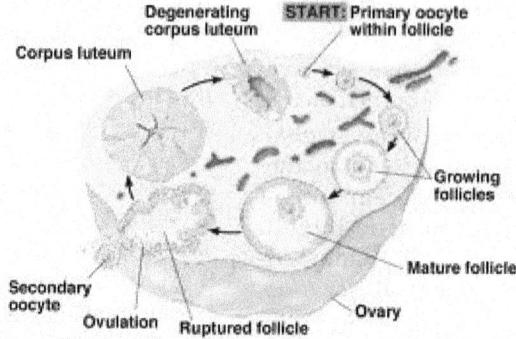

Fig. *Oocyte*

Oocyte A cell that develops into a mature ovum or egg, formed in an ovary and present from birth.

Open enrollment A health insurance enrollment period during which applicants need not meet any health status criteria. Open enrollment periods are characteristic of some blue cross/blue shield plans and health maintenance organizations.

Operating costs The ongoing expense of operating a health care facility.

Ophthalmologist A medical doctor (MD) who specializes in the eye. Ophthalmologists perform eye exams, treat disease, prescribe medication, and perform surgery. They may also write prescriptions for eyeglasses and contact lenses.

Ophthalmopathy Eye disease. There are several disorders that can affect vision in people with diabetes; the most severe is diabetic retinopathy.

Ophthalmoplegia Eye muscle paralysis. Causes include stroke, multiple sclerosis, a tumour, thyroid disease, migraines and progressive supranuclear palsies. Symptoms can include limited eye movement, blurred vision, double vision, nystagmus and ptosis. Tolosa-Hunt Syndrome, often called "painful oph-thalmoplegia," is characterized by intense pain behind the eye and a headache.

Opiate A narcotic drug derived from or similar to opium, extracted from the poppy plant. Opiate drugs (e.g., morphine, heroin) bind to specific receptors on nerve cells scattered throughout the brain to reduce 'pain and produce euphoria. Repeated use of these agents is associated with biological tolerance and addiction.

Opportunistic infection A disease or infection caused by a microorganism that does not ordinarily cause disease but which, under certain conditions (e.g., during treatment with immunosuppressive drugs or in immunodeficiency disorders), becomes pathologic.

Opportunity cost In economics, defined as the return available from the best alternative use of a particular resource, for example, the value of the other products that might otherwise have been produced by the resources used in the production of a particular good or service. Any single opportunity taken will have a cost in terms of an opportunity foregone.

Oppositional defiant order A patten of negativistic and hostile behaviour in a child that lasts at least 6 months. Symptoms may include losing one's temper; arguing with adults or actively refusing their requests; deliberately annoying others; being easily annoyed, angry, and resentful; and being spiteful or vindictive.

Opsoclonus Rapid and involuntary eye movement that is irregular and chaotic; sometimes called "dancing eyes." Typically seen in Opsoclonus-Myoclonus Syndrome.

Optic The rounded, central portion of an intraocular lens (IOL) used in cataract surgery. Optic also more generally refers to eyes or vision.

Optic nerve The optic nerve is a sensory nerve. Its basic responsibility is to transmit information received from rods and cones in the eye known as photoreceptors, and then deliver this information that is received from the retina. At the back of the eyeball, there is a gathering place for the optic

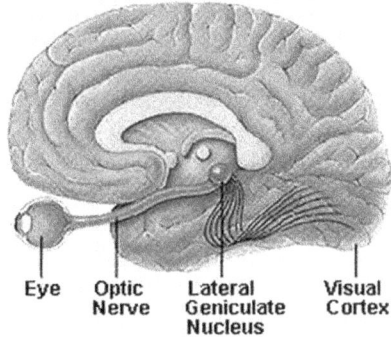

Eye Optic   Lateral   Visual
     Nerve   Geniculate   Cortex
             Nucleus

Fig. *Optic nerve*

nerves, and here, approximately 125 million nerve fibres which make up the optic nerve congregate.

Optic nerve head Also called optic disk. Circular area where the optic nerve enters the retina, and the location of the eye's blind spot.

Optic nerve problem The optic nerve (second cranial nerve) is the part of the eye that carries stimuli from the rods and cones to the brain. Problems such as inflammation (optic neuritis), tumours and swelling can lead to symptoms such as: blurred vision, loss of colour vision, floaters, headache, eye pain or discomfort, nausea and vision loss.

Optical coherence tomography A method of imaging that, in ophthalmology, uses light waves to provide cross-sectional views of interior eye structures. Also known as OCT.

Optician In the United States, opticians are not doctors, but in some states they must complete training and be licensed. And in some states they can, after special training, become certified to fit contact lenses. (Please visit the Opticians Association of America website for licensing requirements for various states.) Most opticians sell and fit eyeglasses, sunglasses, and specialty eyewear that are made to an optometrist's or ophthalmologist's prescription. Many also have equipment on the premises so they can grind lenses and put them in frames without ordering from a lab.

Optometrist Doctors of optometry (ODs) examine eyes for both vision and health problems, prescribe glasses, and fit contact lenses. They can prescribe many ophthalmic medications and may participate in your pre- and postoperative care if you have eye surgery. ODs must complete four years of postgraduate optometry school for their doctorate.

Oral Pertaining to the mouth, taken through or applied in the mouth as an oral medication.

Oral rehydration therapy (ORT) The treatment or prevention of fluid loss (dehydration) due to diarrhea by a specific water solution of electrolytes and glucose (salts and sugar) taken by mouth.

Oral glucose tolerance test A test to see if a person has diabetes. An oral glucose tolerance test a standard dose of glucose is ingested by mouth and blood levels are checked two hours later. Many variations of the glucose tolerance test have been devised over the years for various purposes, with different standard doses of glucose, different routes of administration, different intervals and durations of sampling, and various substances measured in addition to blood glucose.

Oral hypoglycemic agents Pills or capsules that people take to lower the level of glucose in the blood. The pills work for some people with Type 2 diabetes if their pancreas still makes some

The pathologist will give you:
75 ml glucose drink

Then ask you to:
Wait 2 hours

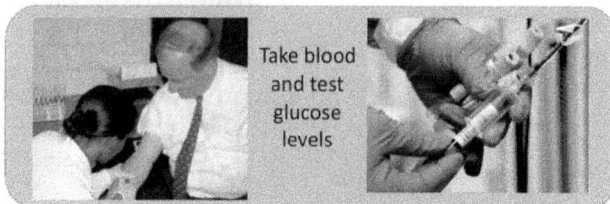

Take blood and test glucose levels

Fig. *Oral glucose tolerance test*

insulin. They can help the body in several ways such as causing the cells in the pancreas to release more insulin. Types of these pills for sale in the United States are: sulfonylureas (many varieties); biguanides: metformin (Glucophage); alpha-glucosidase inhibitors— acarbose (Precose); miglitol (Glyset); thiazolidinediones (or "glitazones"): rosiglitazone (Avandia); pioglitazone (Actos); meglitinides— repaglinide (Prandin); nateglinide (Starlix)

Oral polio vaccine The oral polio vaccine (OPV) was developed in 1961 by Albert Sabin. The vaccine is administered orally. OPV consists of a mixture of live, attenuated (weakened) poliovirus strains of all three poliovirus types. OPV produces antibodies in the blood to all three types of poliovirus. In the event of infection, these antibodies protect against paralysis by preventing the spread of wild poliovirus to the nervous system. OPV also produces a local, mucosal immune response in the mucous

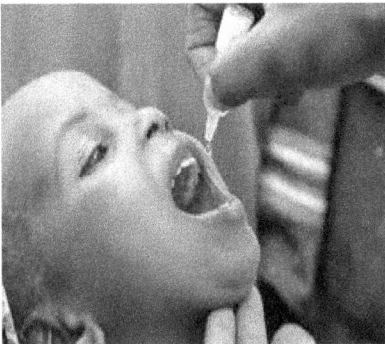

Fig. *Oral polio vaccine*

membrane of the intestines. In the event of infection, these mucosal antibodies limit the replication of the wild polio-virus inside the intestine. This intestinal immune response to OPV is thought to be the main reason why mass campaigns with OPV can rapidly stop person-to-person transmission of wild poliovirus.

Orbital cellulitis A sudden infection of the tissues immediately surrounding the eye, resulting in painful swelling of the upper and lower eyelid, and possibly the eyebrow and cheek. Other symptoms include bulging eyes, decreased vision, fever, and eye pain when moving the eyes. Bacteria from a sinus infection are a common cause; other causes include a stye on the eyelid, bug bites or a recent eyelid injury. Orbital cellulitis is a medical emergency and prompt IV antibiotic treatment often is needed to prevent optic nerve damage, permanent vision loss or blindness and other serious complications.

Orbital pseudotumour An inflammatory mass in the tissues around or behind the eye that looks like and mimics the symptoms of a tumour. The cause is unknown. The primary symptom is a painful, bulging eye. You may also experience pain or discomfort around the eye.

Organ culture The attempt to isolate and maintain animal or human organs in in vitro culture prior to transplantation to a suitable recipient. Long-term culture of whole organs is not generally feasible, but they can be sustained in cultures for short periods (hours or days).

Organelle A structure in the cytoplasm of a cell that is specialized in its ultrastructure and biochemical composition to serve a particular function (e.g., mitochondria, Iysosomes, centrioles, endoplasmic reti-culum, chloroplasts).

Organic Matter containing carbon (i.e., animal or plant matter). Compare inorganic.

Organic farming, organic production Farming without the use (or with limited use) of chemical pesticides or fertilizers.

Organic solvents Generic name for a group of simple, organic liquids that are volatile; that is, in the presence of air they change from liquids to gases, and are therefore easily inhaled.

Organoleptic Stimulating any of the organs of sensation or susceptible to a sensory stimulus.

Organophosphates, organophosphorous pesticides A class of pesticides with neurotoxic properties; organo-phosphates have also been used as nerve gases.

Organotypic culture A type of primary tissue culture in which the structure of the original organ is maintained in vitro. This method is useful in neuro-toxicity studies ecause the connections and spatial relations between neurons and glia can be maintained.

Ornithine transcarbamylase deficiency An X-linked genetic disorder of the urea cycle, involving a deficiency of an enzyme (transcarbamylase). Clinical symptoms, which result from the accumulation of toxic nitrogenous compounds (e.g., ammonium and glutamine) in the blood, include chronic ammonia intoxication, mental deterioration, and liver failure. Onset usually occurs in the neonatal

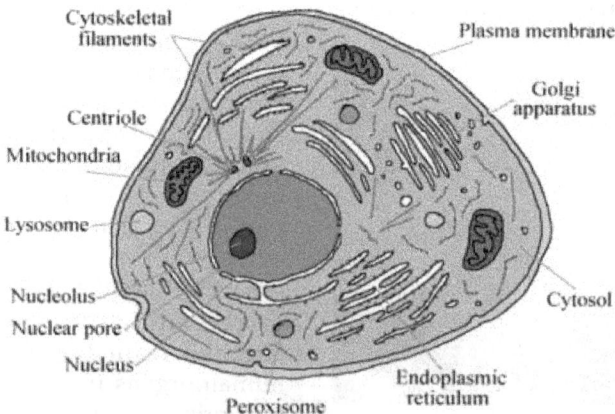

Fig. *Organelle of a cell*

period, but may also present later in childhood or in adulthood. Also called "trans-carbamylase deficiency."

Oropouche fever An arboviral disease transmitted by biting midges (Culicoides spp.). Symptoms include anorexia, rash, and joint and muscle pain.

Orphan drug A drug designated for treatment of a rare condition or disease that typically affects fewer than 200,000 U.S. residents. When the FDA grants orphan drug status, a company may be qualified for special grants, tax breaks or other incentives to help defray research and production costs. Without these incentives, companies would be unable to profit from development of orphan drugs because of limited demand.

Orphan Drug Act Public Law 97-414, which charges the U.S. Government with identifying and promoting orphan products, defined as drugs and devices for rare diseases.

Orthokeratology Procedure in which a doctor fits you with special gas permeable contact lenses to reshape your cornea and correct errors like nearsightedness. Often, patients wear the lenses just at night.

Orthomolecular medicine A form of nutrient therapy that uses combinations of vitamins, minerals, and amino acids normally found in the body to maintain good health and to treat specific conditions, such as asthma, heart disease, depression, and schizophrenia. "Ortho-molecular" means an approach based on a correct (ortho) balance of substances present in the body.

OS Abbreviation for "oculus sinister," the Latin term for "left eye."

Osteopathy A system of treatment founded by Andrew Taylor Still (1828-1917) based on the theory that the body is capable of making its own remedies against disease and other toxic conditions when it is in normal structural relationship and has favourable environmental conditions and adequate nutrition. It utilizes generally accepted physical, medicinal, and surgical methods of diagnosis and therapy, while placing chief emphasis on the importance of normal body mechanics and manipulative methods of detecting and correcting faulty structure. It works with the

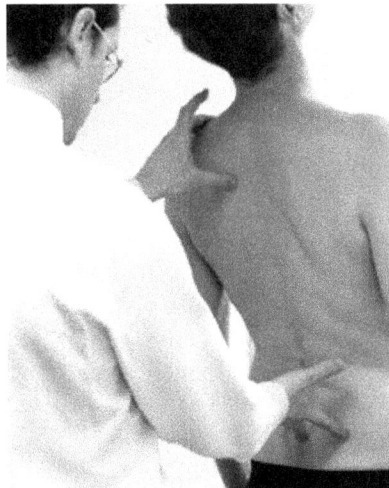

Fig._Osteopathy_

structure and function of the body, and is based on the principle that the well-being of an individual depends on the skeleton, muscles, ligaments and connective tissues functioning smoothly together.

Osteopetrosis literally "stone bone", also known as marble bone disease and Albers-Schonberg disease is an extremely rare inherited disorder whereby the bones harden, becoming denser, in contrast to more prevalent conditions like osteoporosis, in which the bones become less dense and more brittle, or osteomalacia, in which the bones soften. Osteopetrosis can cause bones to dissolve and break. Common symptoms include bone pain and fractures. Retinal degeneration may occur; it results in vision loss.

OU Abbreviation for "oculus uterque," the Latin term for "each eye," used in vision correction prescriptions to indicate both eyes. Also an abbreviation for "oculi unitas" or "oculi uniter," meaning both eyes working simultaneously together.

Outcome criteria to measure quality of care Criteria for measuring quality that focus on the outcome of care (e.g., the patient's health and functional abilities and patient and family satisfaction). The use of outcome criteria to measure quality assumes a direct link between the process of care and the outcomes of care.

Outmigration The movement by rural residents outside their communities (particularly to urban areas) to receive health care and other services.

Out-of-pocket costs Deductibles and copayments incurred by beneficiaries when health care services are rendered.

Outpatient care Care that is provided in a hospital, other medical facility, or other setting that does not include an overnight stay. Sometimes limited to care provided in a hospital setting that does not involve an overnight stay. Ambulatory care is the broader category, and includes outpatient care provided in a hospital setting. Outpatient care is often used as a synonym for ambulatory care (e.g., when referring to mental health services).

Fig. *Outpatient care*

Outpatient drug-free (ODF) programme A diverse group of drug abuse treatment programmes operating on an outpatient basis, with emphasis on counseling.

Outreach An active method to identify individuals and caregivers who need assistance but are unlikely to respond to public education programmes or to contact an information and referral source on their own.

Ovaries Paired female sex glands in which ova (eggs) are produced and stored and the hormones estrogen and progesterone are produced. The ovary (for a given side) is located in the lateral wall of the pelvis in a region called the ovarian fossa. The fossa usually lies beneath the external iliac artery and in front of the ureter and the internal iliac artery.

Overanxious disorder An anxiety disorder of childhood and adolescence, sometimes considered equivalent to the adult diagnosis of generalized anxiety disorder. Symptoms include multiple, unrealistic anxieties concerning the quality of one's performance in school and in sports; hobbies; money matters; punctuality; health; or appearance. The patient is tense and unable to relax and has recurrent somatic complaints for which no physical cause can be found.

Overconvergence Condition in which the eyes come too far inward when focusing on a near object, resulting in blurring.

Overflow tearing Common congenital condition in infants and developmental condition in older adults caused by a blocked tear duct. In infants, a membrane blocks the tear drainage duct, resulting in excessive tears and mucus. In adults, the cause of the blockage is usually unknown, but can be related to poor eyelid function.

Overhead costs Includes costs to a health care facility that are not direct labour (i.e., payroll expenses), such as employee fringe benefits and other expenses indirectly related to patient care operations.

Overt diabetes Diabetes in the person who shows clear signs of the disease such as a great thirst and the need to urinate often.

Overweight It can be defined as body mass index (BMI) (weight in kilograms divided by height in meters squared [m2]) greater

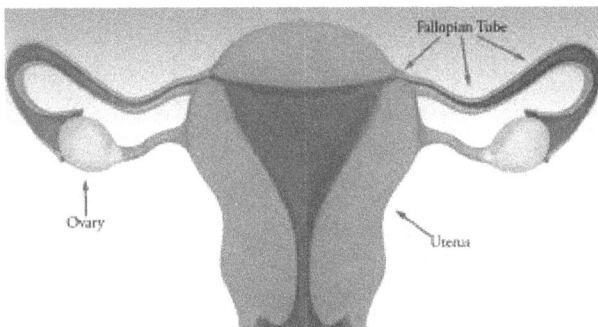

Fig. *Ovaries*

than or equal to the 85th percentile of a similar group. Compare obesity.

Oviduct Fallopian tube; the duct through which eggs pass from the ovary to the uterus.

Ovulation The release of an ovum from a woman's ovary into the Fallopian tube, generally around the midpoint of the menstrual cycle, as a result of cyclic ovarian and pituitary endocrine function.

Ovulation induction Treatment of ovulation dysfunction caused by such disorders as amenorrhea, oligomenorrhea, and luteal phase defect, using drugs that induce ovulation. These so-called fertility drugs include

clomiphene citrate and gonadotropin. Ovulation induction is also used as part of the artificial insemination, in vitro fertilization, and GIFT techniques.

Ovulation prediction kits Over-the-counter hormone monitoring kits that employ the enzyme-linked immunosorbent assay procedure to measure the midcycle increase in LH that indicates ovulation is taking place.

Ovum (pi. ova) The female egg released from the ovary at ovulation.

Ovum donor: A woman who donates an ovum or ova to another woman.

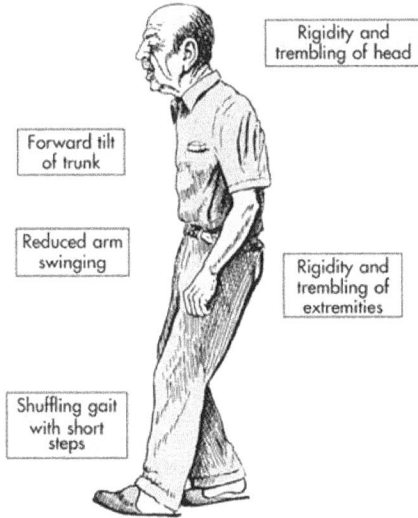

Rigidity and trembling of head

Forward tilt of trunk

Reduced arm swinging

Rigidity and trembling of extremities

Shuffling gait with short steps

Pancreas An organ behind the lower part of the stomach that is about the size of a hand. It has two major responsibilities: one part (the endocrine pancreas) makes insulin so that the body can use glucose (sugar) for energy. Another part (the exocrine pancreas) makes enzymes that help the body digest food. Spread all over the pancreas are areas called the Islets of Langerhans. The cells in these areas each have a special purpose. The alpha cells make glucagon, which raises the level of glucose in the blood; the beta cells make insulin; the delta cells make somatostatin. There are also the PP cells and the D1 cells, about which little is known.

Pancreas transplant A surgical procedure that involves replacing the pancreas of a person

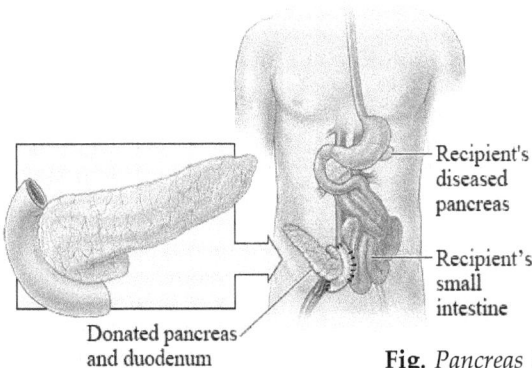

Recipient's diseased pancreas

Recipient's small intestine

Donated pancreas and duodenum

Fig. *Pancreas transplant*

who has diabetes with a healthy pancreas that can make insulin. The healthy pancreas comes from a donor who has just died or from a living relative. A person can donate half a pancreas and still live normally. At present, pancreas transplants are usually performed in persons with Type 1 diabetes who have severe complications. This is because after the transplant the patient must take immunosuppressive drugs that are highly toxic and may cause damage to the body. The donated pancreas is placed in the front part of the abdomen and connected to the lower abdominal blood vessels. The donated duodenum is attached to either the recipient's intestine or bladder so that pancreatic secretions can drain.

Pancreatectomy A procedure in which a surgeon takes out the pancreas.

Pancreatitis Inflammation (pain, tenderness) of the pancreas; it can make the pancreas stop working. It is caused by drinking too much alcohol, by disease in the gallbladder, or by a virus.

Panic attack A period of intense fear or discomfort, with the abrupt development of a variety of symptoms and fears of dying, going crazy, or losing control that reach a crescendo within 10 minutes. The symptoms may include shortness of breath or smothering sensations; dizziness, faintness, or feelings of unsteadiness; trembling or shaking; sweating; choking; nausea or abdominal distress; flushes or chills; and chest pain or discomfort. Panic attacks occur in several anxiety disorders. In panic disorder they are typically unexpected and happen "out of the blue." In social phobia and simple phobia they are cued and occur when exposed to or in anticipation of a situational trigger. These attacks occur also in posttraumatic stress disorder.

Papilla Small bump where the optic nerve exits the eye.

Papilledema Swelling with accompanying compression of the optic nerve head, which can be a medical emergency. Causes of papilledema can include bleeding near the vicinity of the optic nerve and abnormally high cerebrospinal fluid (CSF) pressure. Autoimmune disorders, trauma and infections of the central nervous system also can cause papilledema. Optic nerve swelling can result from central retinal vein occlusion or may occur as a side effect of medications such as lithium, tetracycline and corticosteroids.

Papilloma Usually benign tumour, such as a wart or a skin tag; papillomas may be raised or flat, and can be a variety of colours, such as skin-coloured, yellow, pink, brown or black. Eye papillomas are typically on the eyelid, but may also appear on the conjunctiva. The cause of papillomas is felt to be viral.

Parinaud dorsal midbrain syndrome Inability to look up, typically associated with a brain lesion, characterized by nystagmus and pupil unresponsiveness to light. Causes include hydrocephalus ("water on the brain") and tumours of the pineal gland.

Parkinson's disease Neurological disorder characterized by tremors, muscle rigidity, a shuffling walk and a mask-like appearance in the face. Parkinson's disease is a progressive nervous system disorder that affects how the person moves, including how they speak and write. Symptoms develop gradually, and may start off with ever-so-slight tremors in one hand. People with Parkinson's disease also experience stiffness and find they cannot carry out movements as rapidly as before this is called bradykinesia. The muscles of a person with Parkinson's become weaker and the individual may assume an unusual posture.

Parkinson's disease belongs to a group of conditions called movement disorders. Movement disorders describe a variety of abnormal body movements that have a neurological basis, and include such conditions as cerebral palsy, ataxia, and Tourette syndrome.

Pars plana Posterior part of the eye's ciliary body.

Patau syndrome It is also called Trisomy-13. Condition caused by an extra, third copy of chro-

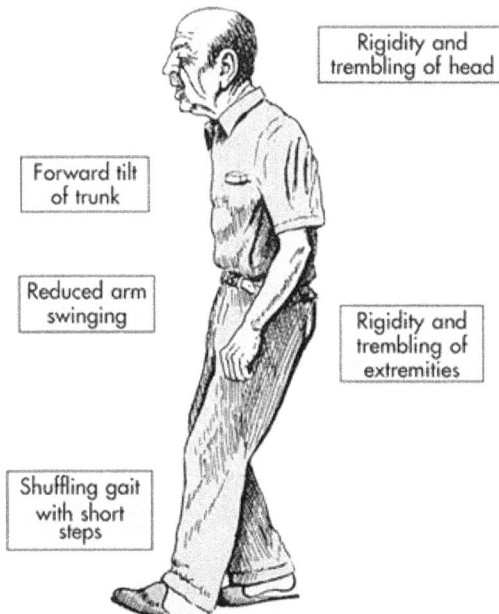

Fig. *Parkinson's disease*

mosome 13. Symptoms include severe mental retardation, a small head, microphthalmia, a cleft lip or palate, heart defects and extra fingers or toes; many patients also have an iris coloboma and retinal dysplasia (abnormal development). The majority of infants with Patau syndrome die within the first year.

Peak action The time period when the effect of something is as strong as it can be such as when insulin in having the most effect on lowering the glucose (sugar) in the blood.

Pediatric endocrinologist A doctor who sees and treats children with problems of the endocrine glands; diabetes is an endocrine disorder.

Pediculosis Lice infestation, typically caused by contact with an infected person or infected bedding. When lice infest the eyelid and eyelashes, they can cause

such symptoms as visible lice (white or gray), eggs called nits (white or gray) or feces (reddish-brown), blue bite marks, blepharitis and conjunctivitis. Some people also develop keratitis.

Penetrating keratoplasty A transplant procedure in which a circular area of surface eye tissue is removed from a healthy donor cornea and transferred to a recipient. A penetrating keratoplasty or corneal transplant may be needed in case of eye damage from injury or from eye diseases such as keratoconus.

Peptide Two or more amino acids linked together chemically. If the number of amino acids is relatively great, the string is sometimes called a polypeptide; a very long string of amino acids is called a protein.

Periodontal disease Damage to the gums. Periodontal disease is an infection of the gums and sup-

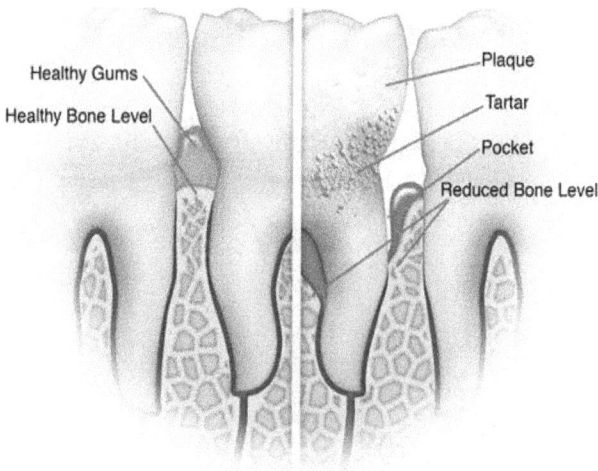

Fig. *Periodontal disease*

porting structures of the teeth that can only be diagnosed by dental professionals. The infection is caused by bacteria that live in dental plaque in and around the gum line in pockets that line the teeth. Even though it is often painless and may have few if any visible symptoms, if left untreated, periodontal disease frequently results in the loss of teeth. People who smoke are particularly vulnerable to periodontal disease. People who have diabetes are more likely to have gum disease than people who do not have diabetes.

Periodontist A specialist in the treatment of diseases of the gums.

Peripheral neuropathy Nerve damage, usually affecting the feet and legs; causing pain, numbness, or a tingling feeling. Also called "somatic neuropathy" or "distal sensory polyneuropathy."

Peripheral vascular disease Disease in the large blood vessels of the arms, legs, and feet. People who have had diabetes for a long time may get this because major blood vessels in their arms, legs, and feet are blocked and these limbs do not receive enough blood. The signs of PVD are aching pains in the arms, legs, and feet (especially when walking) and foot sores that heal slowly. Although people with diabetes cannot always avoid PVD, doctors say they have a better chance of avoiding it if they take good care of their feet, do not smoke, and

keep both their blood pressure and diabetes under good control.

Peripheral vision The edges of your visual field.

Peritoneal dialysis A way to clean the blood of people who have kidney disease.

Persistent hyperinsulinemic Hypoglycemia of Infancy (PHHI) An alternate term for Nesidioblastosis

Pet therapy A therapeutic approach based on the idea that expressing affection for a pet helps people feel happier, maintain a positive outlook, and therefore improve their health. According to several studies, having a pet can reduce stress, lower blood pressure, and ward off loneliness and depression. Many nursing homes and some prisons have developed pet therapy programmes, with excellent results.

Phacoemulsification Also called "phako," this in-office cataract surgery procedure involves using a device with a vibrating, ultrasonic tip to break up the cataract, then suctioning the pieces out with a tiny needle. Read our article about cataract surgery.

Phakic An eye that still has its natural lens. When an eye is aphakic, usually the lens has been removed during cataract or other eye surgery.

Pharmacist A person trained to prepare and distribute medicines and to give information about them.

Phobia Fear cued by the presence or anticipation of a specific object or situation, exposure to which almost invariably provokes an immediate anxiety response or panic attack even though the subject recognizes that the fear is excessive or unreasonable. The phobic stimulus is avoided or endured with marked distress. In earlier psychoanalytic literature, phobia was called anxiety hysteria. Two types of phobia have been differentiated—specific phobia (simple phobia) and social phobia. Specific phobia is subtyped on the basis of the object feared. The natural environment (animals, insects, storms, water, etc.); blood, injection, or injury; situations (cars, airplanes, heights, tunnels, etc.); and other situations that may lead to choking, vomiting, or contracting an illness are all specific phobias.In social phobia (social anxiety disorder), the persistent fear is of social situations that might expose one to scrutiny by others and induce one to act in a way or show anxiety symptoms that will be humiliating or embarrassing. Avoidance may be limited to one or only a few situations, or it may occur in most social situations. Performing in front of others or social interactions may be the focus of concern. It is sometimes difficult to distinguish between social phobia and agoraphobia when social avoidance accompanies panic attacks. Avoidant disorder has been used to refer to social phobia occurring in childhood and adolescence.

Fig. *Phobia*

Phoropter Device that provides various combinations of lenses used for tests of vision errors in eye examinations.

Photoablation Procedure in which a surgeon uses ultraviolet radiation to remove tissue.

Photochromic Able to change lens colour or darkness/density depending upon the degree of exposure to light.

Photocoagulation Use of heat from a high-energy laser to seal off bleeding in damaged tissue. Photocoagulation also may prevent formation of abnormal blood vessels (neovascu-larization) in eye diseases such as age-related macular degeneration or diabetic retinopathy. Photocoagulation also may be used to reattach a detached retina.

Photokeratitis "Sunburn" of the cornea; symptoms include discomfort, blurred vision, and light sensitivity. The temporary vision loss that can result is called "snow blindness."

Photophobia Discomfort from sun or other light. Photophobia has many causes.

Photopsia Flashes of light often noticed in the edges of the visual field. Photopsia can have many causes, including mechanical (rather than visual) stimulation of light-sensitive cells (photoreceptors) in the retina. For example, a detached retina can cause photopsia when the retina pulls away or detaches from tissue in the inner back of the eye. A vitreous detachment with accompanying photopsia can occur when the eye's gel-like interior begins to shrink and pull against the retina. Photopsia can be accompanied by a shower of spots and floaters.

Photoreceptor A light-sensitive cell found in the retina. Photoreceptors in the human retina are classified as cones and rods. Cones are located in the central retina (the fovea) and control colour vision. Rods are located outside the fovea and control black/white vision in low-light conditions.

Phytochemicals Chemicals found in plants that help protect against disease.

Pigment dispersion syndrome An eye condition where pigment granules that normally adhere to the coloured part of the eye (iris) flake off and adhere to the posterior surface of the cornea and other structures in the anterior chamber of the eye. If the pigment accumulates in the drainage angle of the anterior chamber, it can reduce the drainage of aqueous from the eye, causing ocular hypertension and (potentially) pigmentary glaucoma.

Pinguecula A yellowish, thickened lesion on the conjunctiva near the cornea. Pingueculae represent a benign degenerative change in the conjunctiva caused by the leakage and deposition of certain blood proteins through the permeable capillaries near the limbus.

Pioglitazone A drug used as a treatment for Type 2 (non-insulin-dependent) diabetes; belongs to a class of drugs called thiazolidinediones.

Pituitary gland is a roundish organ, about the size of a pea, located just behind the bridge of the nose in the centre and at the base of the skull/brain in a depression called the sella turcjca ("Turkish saddle"). It weighs about 1/2 gram (0.018 oz) produces 0.00001 grams of hormone per day, and is attached

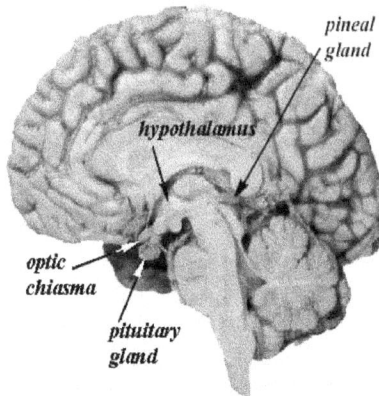

Fig. *Pituitary gland*

to the hypothalamus via nerve fibres. It is an important link between the nervous system and the endocrine system. The pituitary serves the body in many ways-in growth, in food use, and in reproduction.

Placebo A "false" but harmless treatment that has no proven medical value. Placebos usually are incorporated into clinical trials to measure how patients respond to an authentic therapy that is being tested. Some patients are given placebos, and others are given the actual therapy, to provide objective comparisons and assessments.

Plano A term eye care professionals use to describe lenses with no corrective power. The term is most often applied to nonprescription sunglasses or contact lenses that are worn for cosmetic purposes only.

Polymethyl methacrylate Old-fashioned hard contacts were made of PMMA, which is not oxygen-permeable; today's rigid lenses contain other polymers that allow oxygen to reach your eye. Some intraocular lenses are made of PMMA because the material is well tolerated inside the eye.

Podiatrist A doctor who treats and takes care of people's feet.

Podiatry The care and treatment of human feet in health and disease.

Point system A rarely-used system of meal planning for diabetes in which foods are rated based upon calorie content, regardless

of blood glucose effect or nutritional content. One "calorie point" equals 75 calories. The system may have a role to help with weight loss, but is not typically presently recommended for type 1 diabetes.

Polarity therapy based on a theory of energy flow in the body developed by Randolph Stone, a doctor of naturopathy, osteopathy, and chiropractic. Asserts that balancing the flow of energy in the body is the foundation of health. Specific points along the currents are said to hold positive or negative energies. Practitioners use gentle touch and guidance in diet, exercise and self-awareness to help clients balance their energy flow, thus supporting a return to health.

Polarized lenses Lenses that block light reflected from horizontal surfaces such as water, to reduce glare.

Polycarbonate Plastic that is very impact-resistant, and is thus sometimes used for spectacle lenses and frames.

Polycystic ovary syndrome A syndrome associated with bilateral polycystic ovaries and insulin resistance. Symptoms frequently include decreased menstrual flow, irregular menses, anovulation, and infertility.

Polydipsia Excessive thirst; may be a symptom of uncontrolled diabetes.

Polyphagia Excessive hunger; may be a symptom of uncontrolled diabetes.

Polyunsaturated fats A type of fat that comes from vegetables. These are triacylglycerols in which the hydrocarbon tails (caudae) of this ester constitutes polyunsaturated fatty acid.

Polyuria Excessive urination; may be a symptom of uncontrolled diabetes.

Poor man's pump (Basal/Bolus Insulin Administration) Using several daily injections of clear insulin (either Regular or Lispro), at mealtimes — the bolus doses — together with one or more daily injections of cloudy insulin (either NPH or Ultralente insulin) — the basal doses — to achieve blood sugar control in a manner similar to that used by people who use insulin pumps.

Porphyria Disorder in which the body produces too much of a compound called porphyrin and releases it in the urine, causing a reddish colour. Other symptoms include light sensitivity, skin that swells or is sensitive to sunlight, abdominal pain, blisters and muscle weakness.

Posterior capsular opacification Haziness that develops behind the artificial intraocular lens inserted during cataract surgery. A common complication following cataract removal, a PCO can be removed with a YAG laser capsulotomy.

Posterior chamber Part of the eye behind the iris and in front of the lens.

Postprandial Occurring after a meal. Example: Blood taken 1-2 hours after eating to see the amount of glucose in the blood would be called a postprandial blood glucose test.

Post-traumatic stress disorder An anxiety disorder in which exposure to an exceptional mental or physical stressor is followed, sometimes immediately and sometimes not until 3 months or more after the stress, by persistent reexperiencing of the event, avoidance of stimuli associated with the trauma or numbing of general responsiveness, and manifestations of increased arousal. The trauma typically includes experiencing, witnessing, or confronting an event that involves actual or threatened death or injury, or a threat to the physical integrity of oneself or others, with an immediate reaction of intense fear, helplessness, or horror.

Prana The yogic concept of a cosmic energy or life force, similar to the Chinese idea of chi, that enters the body with the breath. Prana is thought to flow through the body, bringing health and vitality. It is considered the vital link between the spiritual self and the material self.

Pranayama A term from Yoga and Ayurveda meaning breath control. Pranayama is a special form of breathing exercise. There are various forms of Pranayama. Though each form is done different, most of them have the following three steps in common:

- Rechaka (Exhalation)
- Puraka (Inhalation)
- Kumbhaka (Retention)

Fig. *Pranayama*

Prediabetes (i) Traditional definition: The stage before the development of diabetes, with normal glucose tolerance but with an increased risk of developing diabetes at some future time. Examples of increased risk might include family history of diabetes, prior diagnosis of gestational diabetes, presence of a positive antibody test for diabetes, or insulin resistance.

(ii) Revised definition: As of March, 2002, the American Diabetes Association has suggested a new definition for prediabetes: "Pre-diabetes is the state that occurs when a person's blood glucose levels are higher than normal but not high enough for a diagnosis of diabetes. Doctors sometimes refer to this state of elevated blood glucose levels as Impaired Glucose Tolerance or Impaired Fasting Glucose (IGT/IFG), depending on which test was used to detect it.

Pre-eclampsia A condition that some women with diabetes have during the late stages of pregnancy. Two signs of this condition are high blood pressure and swelling because the body cells are holding extra water.

Presbyope Person who has difficulty reading print and seeing near objects.

Presbyopia Condition in which the aging eye beginning at around age 40 is unable to focus at all distances, often noticed when print begins to blur. Additional symptoms include eye strain, headaches, and squinting.

Prescription lenses Lenses that provide vision correction as prescribed by an eye care practitioner.

Prevalence The number of people in a given group or population who are reported to have a disease.

Previous abnormality of glucose tolerance (PrevAGT) A term for people who have had above-normal levels of blood glucose (sugar) when tested for diabetes in the past but who show as normal on a current test. PrevAGT used to be called either "latent diabetes" or "prediabetes."

Prism In optics, a lens that can have precise geometric configurations enabling light to be bent or reflected in certain ways. A prism also can split white light into different wave lengths and colours.

PRK (Photorefractive Keratectomy) Surgical procedure in which an excimer laser is used to remove corneal tissue to correct vision problems.

Probiotics Substances such as acidophilus and bifidus that restore the beneficial bacteria normally present in the intestines. Stress, poor diet, antibiotics, and oral contraceptives can throw off the normal balance of bacteria and fungi. This imbalance may be manifested as a yeast infection, or in symptoms such as diarrhea or gastrointestinal disturbances.

Prognosis Telling a person now what is likely to happen in the future because of having a disease.

Progressive lenses Also called progressive addition lenses or PALs. Multifocal lenses whose corrective powers change progressively throughout the lens. A wearer looks through one portion of the lens for distance vision, another for intermediate vision, and a third portion for reading or close work. Each area is blended invisibly into the next, without the lines that traditional bifocals or trifocals have.

Proinsulin The initial protein made by the beta cells of the pancreas that later is broken into several pieces. Proinsulin consists of three parts: C-Peptide and two long strands of amino acids (called the alpha and beta chains) that later become linked together to form the insulin molecule. From every molecule of proinsulin, one molecule of insulin plus one molecule of C-Peptide are produced. (It may be noted that commercial production of exogenous insulin purifies the original insulin, and removes any residual proinsulin and C-Peptide that might have been initially present.)

Proliferative retinopathy A disease of the small blood vessels of the retina of the eye.

Proliferative vitreoretinopathy (PVR) A common complication of surgery for retinal detachment, which causes scarring of the retina. PVR may require a vitrectomy and intricate surgical removal of scar tissue.

Propionate A soft, flexible material that is sometimes used in goggles.

Prosthesis A man-made substitute for a missing body part such as an arm or a leg; also an implant such as for the hip.

Prosthetic Refers to a prosthesis, which is an artificial replacement for a part of the body. Read more about prosthetic contact lenses.

Protective eyewear Eyewear made with impact-resistant lenses, usually polycarbonate, that protects the eyes, especially in working situations or sports.

Protein Large, complex organic molecules found in all living cells. These molecules contain enzymes, antibodies, hormones and other elements that help organisms function. Proteins are made of amino acids, which are called the building blocks of the cells. The cells need proteins to grow and to mend themselves. Proteins are present in human tears and can collect on contact lenses, resulting in discomfort and cloudy vision. Protein is found in many foods such as meat, fish, poultry, and eggs.

Proteinuria Too much protein in the urine. This may be a sign of kidney damage.

Pruritus Itching skin; may be a symptom of diabetes.

Pseudoexfoliation syndrome A condition of unknown cause in which light gray, dandruff-like material forms on the pupil margin and anterior lens capsule in the eye. This material also can lodge in the trabecular meshwork, causing an increase in internal eye pressure and pseudoexfoliative open-angle glaucoma.

Pseudotumour cerebri A condition whose symptoms mirror those of a brain tumour—increased intracranial pressure, headache, nausea, brief periods of vision loss (graying or blurring) and double vision. The cause is unknown, but patients are often obese women.

Pterygium Triangular fold of tissue on the white of the eye that can eventually grow over part of the cornea; the cause may be irritation from sun (i.e., UV rays), dust and wind. Some people have no symptoms, while others may have redness or blurred vision. Pterygia that are chronically inflamed can become itchy.

Ptosis drooping eyelid Congenital ptosis is caused by a problem with the levator muscle (which lifts the eyelid). In adults, ptosis is commonly caused by the aging of the levator's connective tissue.

Puncta Tiny openings through which tears drain away from the eyes. Four puncta are in the nasal corner of the eye - two in the upper inner eyelid and two in the lower inner eyelid. Punctal plugs sometimes are used to block these openings so that more tears are retained as a treatment for dry eye syndrome.

Punctal cautery A procedure that uses heat or laser energy to permanently close channels from which tears drain. Punctal cautery increases the accumulation of moisture as a treatment for dry eye.

Punctal plugs Tiny inserts often made of plastic that are placed in channels or ducts of the eye where moisture drainage occurs. Punctal plugs can help stop excessive drainage to keep the eye moistened in conditions such as dry eye syndrome.

Pupil The round, dark centre of the eye, which opens and closes to regulate the amount of light the retina receives.

Pupillary distance This is the distance between the centre of each pupil. Opticians use a special ruler to measure your pupillary distance before ordering your eyeglasses. It is an essential measurement because the optical centre of each eyeglass lens must be positioned directly over the centre of each pupil. An incorrect measurement means you would have difficulty focusing when wearing the glasses.

Purified insulins Insulins with much less of the impure proinsulin. It is thought that the use of purified insulins may help avoid or reduce some of the problems of people with diabetes such as allergic reactions.

Q

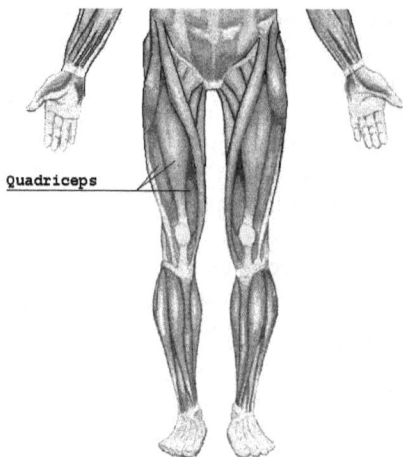

Quadriceps

q

Q enzyme In glycogen or amylopectin synthesis, the enzyme that catalyzes the transfer of a segment of a 1,4-alpha-glucan chain to a primary hydroxy group in a similar glucan chain.

Q fever An acute infectious disease caused by Coxiella Burnetti. It is characterized by a sudden onset of fever, headache, malaise, and weakness. In humans, it is commonly contracted by inhalation of infected dusts derived from infected domestic animals.

Q10 A nutrient that the body needs in small amounts to function and stay healthy. Q10 helps mitochondria (small structures in the cell) make energy. It is an antioxidant that helps prevent cell damage caused by free radicals (highly reactive chemicals). Q10 is fat-soluble (can dissolve in fats and oils) and is found in fatty fish, beef, soybeans, peanuts, and spinach. It is being studied in the prevention and treatment of some types of cancer and heart disease and in the relief of side effects caused by some cancer treatments. Also called coenzyme Q10, CoQ10, ubiquinone, and vitamin Q10.

Quackery A slang term used to describe medical treatments that are falsely described to be effective.

Quadriceps The four powerful muscles in the front of the thigh, responsible for extending the knee joint.

Quadriplegic Paralysis of all four limbs caused by damage to the spinal cord in the neck region.

Quality assessment An ongoing process to monitor and evaluate aspects of patient/medical care against pre-established criteria and standards to determine the medical necessity, appropriateness, and effectiveness of the services provided.

Quality assurance An interactive management process designed to objectively ensure the appropriateness and effectiveness of patient care. It includes identifying deficiencies, implementing corrective action(s) to improve performance, and monitoring the corrective actions to ensure that quality of care has been enhanced. In the broadest sense, this ongoing process should involve the medical and professional staff, the administration, and the governing body of the health care facility.

Quality assurance director Coordinates quality assurance programmes and policies for the facility. This person is responsible for quality assurance only and must be a licensed nurse.

Quality compass Quality assessment tool developed by the National Committee for Quality Assurance.

Quality improvement A continuous process that identifies problems in health care delivery, examines solutions to those problems, and regularly monitors the solutions for improvement.

Quality improvement system for managed care Guidelines established by the Federal government for quality assurance in Medicaid managed care plans.

Quality of care The degree or grade of excellence with respect to medical services received by patients, administered by providers or programmes, in terms of technical competence, need, appropriateness, acceptability, humanity and structure.

Quality of medical care: The degree to which actions taken or not taken increase the probability of beneficial health outcomes and decrease risk and other untoward outcomes, given the existing state of medical science and art. Which elements of patient outcomes predominate depends on the patient condition. Assessment of the quality of care involves evaluation of 3 groups of indicators—

(i) the structure of care, encompassing the resources and organizational arrangements in place to deliver care;

(ii) the process of care, referring to the activities of physicians and other health professionals engaged in providing care; and

(iii) outcomes of care, namely changes in patients' health status and quality of life.

Quality-adjusted life-year This unit of measure is one way to quantify health outcomes resulting from some type of intervention. The number of quality-adjusted life-years is the number of years at full health that would be valued equivalently to the number of years of life experienced in a less-desirable health state. For example, if a year of life confined to bed is considered on half as desirable as a year spent in full health, then 10 years of survival confined to bed would be counted as five quality-adjusted life-years.

Quality-of-life measures An assessment of patient's perceptions of how they deal with their disease or with their everyday life when suffering from a particular condition. It is subjective in the sense that the kinds of information cannot be measured objectively; however, it has been in health care literature for at least 20 years. It has been tapped in the area of pharmaceuticals most recently in the last five or six years. Through statistical means, the indices that have been developed to measure various aspects of quality of life have been validated over time, and we know that these measures are reliable and reproducible.

Quickening The first fetal movements felt by the mother-to-be; most commonly between the 16th and 20th weeks of preganancy.

Quinidine An alkaloid extracted from the bark of the Cinchona tree with class 1A antiarrhythmic and antimalarial effects. Quinidine stabilizes the neuronal membrane by binding to and inhibiting voltage-gated sodium channels, thereby inhibiting the sodium influx required for the initiation and

conduction of impulses resulting in an increase of the threshold for excitation and decreased depolarization during phase 0 of the action potential. In addition, the effective refractory period (ERP), action potential duration (APD), and ERP/APD ratios are increased, resulting in decreased conduction velocity of nerve impulses. Quinidine exerts its antimalarial activity by acting primarily as an intra-erythrocytic schizonticide through association with the heme polymer (hemazoin) in the acidic food vacuole of the parasite thereby preventing further polymerization by heme polymerase enzyme. This results in accumulation of toxic heme and death of the parasite.

Quinine A quinidine alkaloid isolated from the bark of the cinchona tree. Quinine has many mechanisms of action, including reduction of oxygen intake and carbohydrate metabolism; disruption of DNA replication and transcription via DNA intercalation; and reduction of the excitability of muscle fibres via alteration of calcium distribution. This agent also inhibits the drug efflux pump P-glycoprotein which is overexpressed in multi-drug resistant tumours and may improve the efficacy of some antineoplastic agents.

R

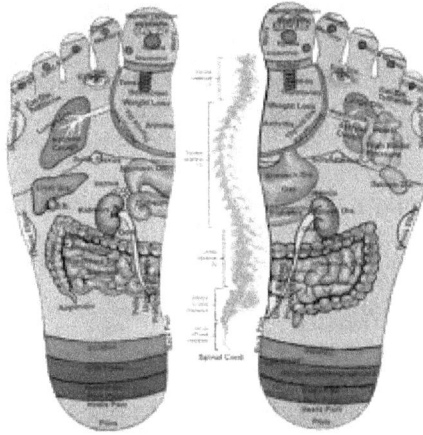

r

Race Races can be distinguished by usually inherited physical and physiological characteristics without regard to language or culture (caucasoids, negroid, mongoloid). By Census Bureau definition, the term race is used to distinguish among peoples who are white (caucasoid), black (negroid), or Asians or Pacific Islanders or American Indians (mongoloid).

Radiation therapy (Radiotherapy) Use of high-energy waves, generated by special x-ray machines, cobalt machines and other devices, to treat some forms of cancer. Radiation destroys cancerous tissue, but does little harm to healthy tissue.

Radiography Making x-ray films of internal structures of the body by exposure of film specially sensitized to x-rays or gamma rays.

Radio-immunoprecipitation assay An assay method based on antigen-antibody interactions, based on principles similar to enzyme immunoassay but using radioisotopes to measure the interactions.

Radioisotope Radioactive form of chemical normally present in the body. Chemical elements that give off radiation. A radioisotope of a chemical element normally present in the body, such as carbon, will mix with non-isotopes when it is injected into the body.

Radioisotope scan Radioisotope is given orally or intravenously and becomes concentrated in organs, such as the heart, lungs or brain. Instruments measure the radiation given off by the radioisotopes and create a photographic image of the organ being studied.

Radiotherapy is the medical use of ionizing radiation, generally as part of cancer treatment to control or kill malignant cells. Radiation therapy may be curative in a number of types of cancer if they are localized to one area of the body. It may also be used as part of curative therapy, to prevent tumour recurrence after surgery to remove a primary malignant tumour (for example, early stages of breast cancer). Radiation therapy is synergistic with chemotherapy, and has been used before, during, and after chemotherapy in susceptible cancers.

Random allocation In a randomized clinical trial, allocation of individuals to treatment groups such that each individual has an equal probability of being assigned to any group.

Randomized clinical trial An experiment designed to test the safety and efficacy of a medical technology in which people are randomly allocated to experimental or control groups, and outcomes are compared.

Rate setting system A method of payment in which a State regulatory body decides what prices a hospital, for example, may charge in a given year.

Rated premium A premium with an added surcharge that is required by insurers to cover the additional risk associated with certain medical conditions. Rated premiums are usually 25

to 100 percent higher than the standard premium.

Rational service areas To be proposed for health manpower shortage area (HMSA) designation, an area must be "rational" for the delivery of services based on criteria governing the size and boundaries of the area and consideration of such factors as established transportation routes and language barriers.

Raynaud's disease Primary disorder of the circulatory system that affects blood circulation to fingers and occasionally toes. Occurs mostly in people who smoke. This is different from Raynaud's phenomenon, which occurs as a complication of other diseases.

Raynaud's phenomenon Circulation system disorder affecting fingers and toes. A complication of an underlying disease or emotional disturbance. This is different from Raynaud's disease.

Reactive hypoglycemia A fall in blood sugar which causes symptoms during the period following meals. Simply put, the body has trouble braking the secretion of insulin after a meal, resulting in the blood sugar dropping further than it should. Reactive hypoglycemia is different from spontaneous hypo-glycemia, which is not assoi-cated with meal ingestion. Reactive hypoglycemia generally has a benign prognosis.

Reading glasses Also called readers. Glasses to help with close work, particularly for people who are presbyopic.

Readmission Admission to a hospital within a specified period of time after a prior admission or because of complications of a prior admission.

Reagent A substance that takes part in a chemical reaction.

Reagents strips Terms no longer used for diabetes blood and urine glucose or acetone test strips.

Real time ultrasound (B-SCAN) A device used to measure the anatomical structure of vessels by vibrations that are of the same physical nature as sound, but with frequencies above the range of human hearing.

Reasonable and necessary (Medicare) Criteria used by the Health Care Financing Administration or Medicare contractors to determine which services are eligible for Medicare coverage. Coverage is distinguished from payment in that coverage refers to benefits available to eligible beneficiaries, and payment refers to the amount and methods of payment for coverage. The criteria used to determine whether a service is reasonable and necessary are:
(i) general acceptance as safe and effective,
(ii) not experimental,
(iii) medically necessary, and
(iv) provided according to standards of medical practice in an appropriate setting.

Rebirthing Also known as conscious-connected breathing or vivation. A technique in which the therapist guides clients through breathing exercises to help them re-experience past memories — including birth — and let go of emotional tensions stored in the body.

Rebound A swing to a high level of glucose (sugar) in the blood after having a low level.

Rebound stimulation Response is reversed when stimulus is withdrawn.

Recalibration (Medicare) Periodic changes in relative prices of diagnosis-related groups (DRGs), including assignment of weights to new DRGs.

Receptor A protein embedded in the cell membrane to which a neuro-transmitter or other molecule can bind to excite or inhibit activity of the cell. An example is the acetylcholine receptor in muscle cells.

Recessive A genetic trait that is manifested phenotypically only when both alleles for a particular trait are present at a locus (e.g., the disease sickle cell anemia is manifest only when both copies of the gene for beta globin contain the betas mutation, whereas whe n individuals have only one copy of the betas gene, they do not develop the disease, but have sickle cell trait, a benign condition). X-linked traits generally act as if they were recessive in females and dominant in males.

Recombinant DNA (rDNA) technology Techniques involving the incorporation of DNA fragments, generated with the use of restriction enzymes, into a suitable host organism's DNA (a vector). The host is then grown in culture to produce clones with multiple copies of the incorporated DNA fragment. The clones containing this particular DNA fragment can then be selected and harvested. Also called genetic engineering.

Recombinant DNA Genetic material that contains DNA from different sources that have been combined by genetic engineering methods. Rearrangement of the genes is artificially induced using enzymes to break DNA into fragments, allowing recombination in different sequences.

Recombination In genetics, the rearrangement of genetic material within the chromosome (resulting in independent assortment of unlinked genes, crossing over of linked genes, and intragenic crossing over of nucleotides); usually applied to the process of meiosis, when the genetic material packaged into gametes is mixed and reconstituted in any number of possible combinations.

Recommended exposure limit (REL) Standard for maximum exposure of industrial workers to toxic substances, set by the National Institute of Occupational Safety and Health. Compare permissible exposure limit, threshold limit value.

Recommended maximum contaminant level Nonenforceable goals set by EPA for pollutants in drinking water renamed maximum contaminant level goal.

Recovered plasma Plasma removed from outdated blood or plasma not needed for other purposes.

Recrudescence The reappearance of a disease or its symptoms after a period of improvement.

Recurrence In cancer, the regrowth of tumour tissue after all evidence of it had apparently been eradicated either by surgery or other means (e.g., radiotherapy). A recurrence may occur at the site of the original tumour or elsewhere in the body, as metastatic disease.

Red book Published by the FDA center for food safety and applied nutrition, guidelines for toxicological testing of direct food additives and colour additives used in food under the federal food, drug, and cosmetic act.

Red cell indices Blood test that provides important information about the size, hemoglobin concentration and hemoglobin weight of an average blood cell. Aids in classification of anemias. Indices include mean corpuscular volume (MCV), mean corpuscular hemoglobin (MCH) and mean corpuscular hemoglobin concentration (MCHC). MCV expresses the average size of many cells and indicates whether most red blood cells are undersized (microcytic), oversized (macrocytic) or normal sized (normocytic). MCH is the hemoglobin-to-red-blood-cell ratio and gives the weight (concentration) of hemoglobin in an average red blood cell. MCHC defines the volume of hemoglobin in an average red cell and helps distinguish normally coloured (normochromic) red blood cells from pale (hypochromic) red cells.

Red measles (Rubeola) is a disease caused by the rubella virus. It is a common childhood infection that can sometimes be fatal usually with minimal systemic upset although transient arthropathy may occur in adults. Serious complications such as deterioration of the skin are very rare. Infection of the mother by Rubella virus during pregnancy can be serious; if the mother is infected within the first 20 weeks of pregnancy, the child may be born with congenital rubella syndrome (CRS),

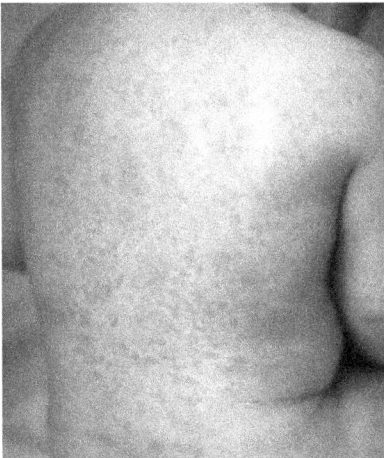

Fig. *Red measles*

which entails a range of serious incurable illnesses. Rubella, also known as German measles or three-day measles.

Reduviid bug A blood-sucking bug in the Reduviid family that is the vector of T. cruzi, the agent of Chagas' disease.

Reentry interval The time that must elapse between application of a pesticide and the return of agricultural workers to the treated area without special protection.

Reference dose (RfD) A term used to characterize risk and derived by applying safety factors to the highest level at which a substance produces no effect. If human exposure to a substance is below the RfD, no risk is assumed to exist; if exposure exceeds the RfD, risk is assumed to exist. The term may be used interchangeably with acceptable daily intake.

Reflexology is an alternative medicine involving the physical act of applying pressure to the feet, hands, or ears with specific thumb, finger, and hand techniques without the use of oil or lotion. It is based on what reflexologists claim to be a system of zones and reflex areas that they say reflect an image of the body on the feet and hands, with the premise that such work effects a physical change to the body. Reflexologists divide the body into ten equal vertical zones, five on the right and five on the left. Concerns have been raised by medical

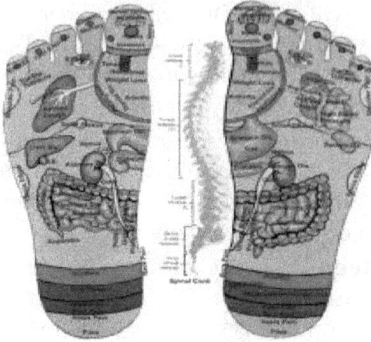

Fig. *Reflexology*

professionals that treating potentially serious illnesses with reflexology, which has no proven efficacy, could delay the seeking of appropriate medical treatment.

Reflux esophagitis Irritation of the esophagus from stomach acid splashing upward into the esophagus.

Refraction The test performed during an eye exam to determine the eyeglass lens powers needed for optimum visual acuity. An automated refraction uses an instrument that does not require the patient to respond. A manifest refraction is the manual way to determine the best lenses, by placing various lenses in front of the patient's eyes and asking, "Which is better, lens A or lens B?"

Refractive disorders Conditions of the eye in which the light-bending properties do not provide for clear focusing. Most common among these conditions are myopia (nearsightedness), hyperopia (farsightedness), and astigmatism.

Refractive error When light rays don't properly refract from the cornea to the retina, it is a refractive error. This can take the form of myopia (nearsightedness), hyperopia (farsightedness) or astigmatism.

Refractive surgery Surgery that corrects visual acuity, with the objective of reducing or eliminating the need for glasses and contacts. It Includes radial keratotomy, PRK, LASIK, and corneal implants.

Regeneration Repair or regrowth of a cell, tissue, or structure.

Regression psychological defence mechanism, viewed as a return to an earlier mode of behaviour, thought, or feeling. The unconscious process that helps the mind resolve conflicts or lessen anxiety by returning to forms of gratification previously abandoned.

Regression analysis A statistical procedure for determining the best approximation of the relationship between variables. Multiple regression analysis is a method for measuring the effects of several factors concurrently.

Regular insulin A type of insulin that is fast acting.

Reiki practitioners of this ancient Tibetan healing system use light hand placements to transmit healing energies to the recipient. While the practitioners may vary widely in technique and philosophy, Reiki is commonly used to treat emotional and mental distress as well as

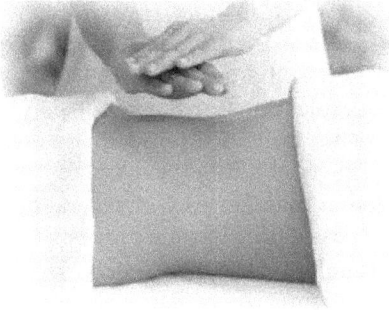

Fig. *Reiki*

chronic and acute physical problems, as well as to assist the recipient in achieving spiritual focus and clarity.

Reiter's disease Inflammatory disease caused by symptoms resembling those of arthritis, urethritis, conjunctivitis and psoriasis. The manifestations of Reiter's Syndrome include the following triad of symptoms: an inflammatory arthritis of large joints, inflammation of the eyes in the form of conjunctivitis or uveitis, and urethritis in men or cervicitis in women. It is also known as Reiter's Syndrome or Reiter's arthritis.

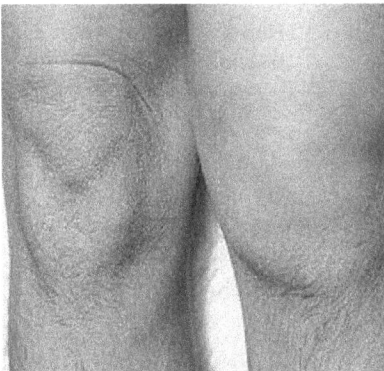

Fig. *Reiter's disease*

Rejection, graft rejection The destruction by the immune system of foreign tissue; specifically, destruction of foreign tissue transplanted into a recipient's body from a donor's body.

Related intervention A preventive or other service that may enhance health (e.g., social services, vocational training, educational services, food, housing, mentoring) but is not delivered in what is traditionally considered the health services system.

Relative value scale (RVS) A list of all physician services containing a cardinal ranking of those services with respect to some conception of value, such that the difference between the numerical rankings for any two services is a measure of the difference in value between those services.

Relaxation time characteristics In radiotherapy, the rate at which tissue hydrogen atoms, which have been excited to a higher energy state by radiofrequency energy, return to their lower energy (equilibrium) state.

Releasing factors Peptides secreted by the hypothalamus and released into the anterior pituitary that trigger the pituitary to release a specific tropic hormone (e.g., growth hormone releasing factor).

Reliability Refers to the reproducibility of results over repeated measurements, and relates to the lack of random error over these repeated measurements. Reliability is a prerequisite to validity.

Renal A term that means having something to do with the kidneys.

Renal artery normally arise off the side of the abdominal aorta, immediately below the superior mesenteric artery, and supply the kidneys with blood. Each is directed across the crus of the diaphragm, so as to form nearly a right angle with the aorta.

The renal arteries carry a large portion of total blood flow to the kidneys. Up to a third of total cardiac output can pass through the renal arteries to be filtered by the kidneys.

Renal hilum The renal hilum or renal pedicle of the kidney is the recessed central fissure. The medial border of the kidney is concave in the centre and convex toward either extremity; it is directed forward and a little downward. Its central part presents a deep longitudinal fissure, bounded by prominent overhanging anterior and posterior lips. This fissure is named the hilum, and transmits the vessels, nerves, and ureter.

Renal calix One of the finger-like projections of the renal pelvis that collect filtered urine and channel it into the kidney's core.

Renal disease Any of several diseases affecting the kidneys.

Renal glycosuria Glycosuria occurring when there is a normal amount of sugar in the blood, due to an inherited inability of the kidneys to reabsorb glucose completely.

Renal pelvis The hollow core of the kidney.

Renal plasma flow Rate of blood flow through the kidney.

Renal threshold When the blood is holding so much of a substance such as glucose (sugar) that the kidneys allow the excess to spill into the urine. This is also called "kidney threshold," "spilling point," and "leak point."

Renal tubular acidosis Loss of base or accumulation of acid in

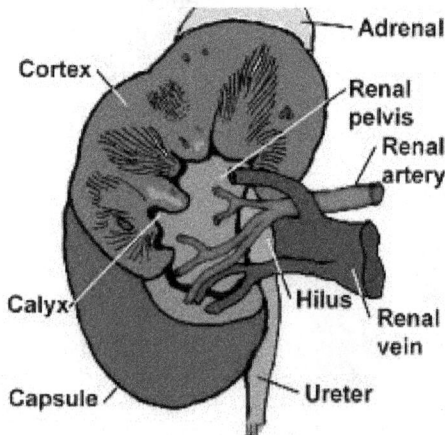

Cortex
Calyx
Capsule
Adrenal
Renal pelvis
Renal artery
Hilus
Renal vein
Ureter

Fig. *Renal artery*

423

the body due to disease of the kidney tubules.

Renal tubular acidosis Renal tubular acidosis is a medical condition that involves an accumulation of acid in the body due to a failure of the kidneys to appropriately acidify the urine. When blood is filtered by the kidney, the filtrate passes through the tubules of the nephron, allowing for exchange of salts, acid equivalents, and other solutes before it drains into the bladder as urine.

Renovascular hypertension (Portal hypertension) Abnormally high blood pressure within the vessels of portal circulation. Caused by compression or obstruction of a blood vessel(s) decreasing blood flow in this area. The portal circulation system is a network of veins that carries blood from abdominal organs to the liver. Portal hypertension is frequently associated with alcoholic cirrhosis, but also results from blood clots in the hepatic (liver) or portal vein, constrictive pericarditis or a defective tricuspid valve in the heart. Portal hypertension results in an enlarged spleen and ascites, and in severe cases, generalized high blood pressure and esophageal varices.

Reovirus Any of a group of relatively large, widely distributed, and possibly tumour-causing viruses with double-stranded RNA. Unlike retrovimses, which also contain RNA, reoviruses replicate in the cytoplasm of the cells they invade and do not produce DNA analogs to their RNA for incorporation into the host cell's genome. The genus name "reovirus" is derived from the term respiratory enteric orphan virus, to denote both respiratory and enteric trophism and isolation of the virus in the absence of known disease.

Repaglinide (Prandin) A drug used as a treatment for Type 2 (noninsulin-dependent) diabetes; belongs to a class of drugs called meglitinides.

Repeated-dose toxicity test Repeated or prolonged exposure to measure the cumulative effects of exposure to a test substance. These tests involve chronic, subchronic, or short-term exposure to a test substance.

Repetitive motion disorders Diseases caused by repetitive movement of part of the body. Some manual poultry processing tasks, for example, may lead to a disorder of the wrist known as carpal tunnel syndrome.

Replacement schedule How often you discard and replace your contact lenses: every day, week or two weeks (disposable); or every month, two months or calendar quarter (frequent replacement). It's important to differentiate between replacement schedule and wear schedule. Wear schedule is either daily wear (removed before sleeping) or extended wear (you may sleep with them in).

Replication (i) In genetics, the synthesis of new DNA from existing DNA. (ii) In epidemiology, repeating a study, usually with a different subject population, using the same methods as the original study in order to compare results (i.e., to see whether the results reasonably match the original results).

Replicon In genetics, a region of DNA that expands from a single origin; also, the minimum polynucleotide sequence that maybe replicated.

Reproductive health care Can include a wide range of services related to the male or female reproductive systems, including gynecological treatment services (i.e., examination and treatment of the female reproductive organs), and preventive services related to the use of contraception (e.g., counseling, prescribing contraceptive methods, dispensing contraceptives).

Reproductive-age of women: Women between and including the ages of 15 and 44 years.

Reservation state A State in which there is at least one federally recognized Indian tribe and in which the IHS therefore provides or finances health care for eligible Indians. There were 32 such States as of 1986.

Reservoir In infectious disease, an alternate host or passive carrier or a pathogenic organism sufficient to keep the organism alive and infective. Reservoirs can be living (e.g., animals, plants) or nonliving (e.g., soil).

Residential care facility A care setting in which the patient or client resides, such as a nursing home, a board and care facility, or a State mental hospital.

Residential treatment centers (RTCS) for emotionally disturbed children A residential organization, not licensed as a psychiatric hospital, whose primary purpose is the provision of individually planned programmes of mental health treatment services in conjunction with residential care for children and youth primarily under the age of 18.

Residual payer Refers to the Indian Health Service's position that other sources of payment available to the patient must be used first before IHS will pay for contract care services by non-IHS providers.

Respiration (i) In the occupational setting, an individually worn device designed to reduce the level of a toxic substance in the air breathed by a worker (e.g., dust masks, gas masks). (ii) In health care, a respirator is a device to substitute for or assist with the respirations of a patient who has difflculty with spontaneous breathing. A respirator may provide artificial respiration by exerting intermittent negative air pressure on the chest (the iron lung), or by forcing air into the lung by

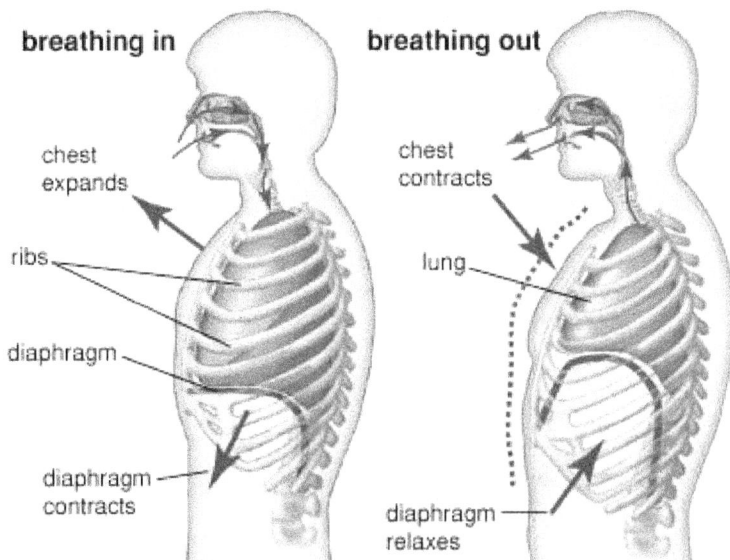

Fig. *Respiration*

positive pressure. Positive pressure devices are also referred to as ventilators.

Respiratory arrest is the cessation of normal respiration due to failure of the lungs to contract effectively. prevents delivery of oxygen to the body. Lack of oxygen to the brain causes loss of consciousness. Brain injury is likely if respiratory arrest goes untreated for more than three minutes, and death is almost certain if left untreated for more than five minutes. For the best chance of survival and recovery, immediate and decisive treatment is imperative.

Respiratory arrest is a medical emergency that, in certain situations, is potentially reversible if treated early. The treatment for respiratory arrest is artificial ventilation.

Respiratory distress syndrome (RDS) An acute lung disorder that causes difficulty breathing and a life-threatening deficiency of oxygen in the blood. Affects premature babies (caused by a deficiency of pulmonary surfactant, a chemical normally found in the lungs that keeps the alveoli open) and adults whose lungs have been damaged by illness (e.g., pneumonia, autoimmune disease) or injury (e.g., inhalation of irritant gas). Severe RDS often requires that patients get mechanical assistance to breathe.

Respiratory gating A technique in which image acquisition is coordinated with the breathing cycle.

Respiratory syncytial virus (RSV) The most important cause of lower respiratory disease (pneumonia and bronchiolitis) in infants and children under 2 years of age.

Respite care services Any shofi-term services that are intended to provide temporary relief for the primary caregiver of an impaired person. Such services may include in-home companion/sitter services, in-home personal care, adult day care, or short-term (e.g., overnight) stays in a nursing home.

Respite care The short term or intermittent provision of services to provide temporary relief for a family caring for a disabled or incapacitated individual. Respite programmes include in-home companion care, in-home personal care, adult day care, or short-term stays in a nursing home, hospital, or boarding home. Such services are not always publicly or privately funded and are often difficult for caregivers to find.

Restricted-activity day One of the following four types of days in which a person's activity is restricted—(i) a bed day, during which a person stayed in bed more than half a day because of illness or injury or was in a hospital as an inpatient; (ii) a work-loss day, during which a currently employed person 18 years of age and over missed more than half a day from a job or business; (iii) a school-loss day, during which a student 5- to 17-years-old missed more than half a day from the school in which he or she was cur-

rently enrolled; and 4) a cut-down day, during which a person cuts down for more than half a day on the things he or she usually does. Work-loss, school-loss, and cut-down days refer to the short-term effects of illness or injury. Bed days are a measure of both long- or short-term disability, however, because a chronically ill bedridden person and a person with a cold could both report having spent more than half a day in bed due to an illness.

Restriction enzyme recognition site The DNA site where a specific restriction enzyme cuts the DNA molecule.

Restriction enzyme An enzyme that has the ability to recognize specific short sequences of DNA (ranging from 4 to 12 base pairs in length) and cut or cleave the DNA where such sites occur. They are termed "restriction" enzymes because, occurring naturally in bacteria, they recognize foreign nucleic acid (e.g., the DNA of a bacterial virus as it begins to infect and destroy its host) and destroy it, thus restricting the ability of the virus to prey upon certain potential host strains. Over 400 different restriction enzymes are known, recognizing a great variety of different nucleotide base sequences. This has made possible the cutting and splicing together of nucleic acid within and between different organisms and species.

Restriction fragment length polymorphism (RFLP) The presence of two or more variants in the size of DNA fragments from a specific region of DNA that has been exposed to a particular restriction enzyme. These fragments differ in length because of a deletion or creation of a restriction enzyme recognition site. Polymorphic sequences that are responsible for RFLPs are used as markers on genetic linkage maps.

Restriction of activity As used in the DHHS National Center for Health Statistics National Health Interview survey, ordinarily refers to a relatively short-term reduction in a person's activities below his or her normal capacity.

Restrictive pericarditis Pressure develops when an increasing amount of fluid restricts the pumping action of the heart. Caused by development of fluid between the heart and the sac covering the heart. Treatment may include medication, aspiration of fluid from the sac using a needle or surgery to remove fluid from the sac.

Resuscitation The return to life or consciousness of one who is apparently dead or whose respirations have ceased.

Reticulocytes Young, immature red blood cells

Reticulocytosis Excess amount of reticulocytes in the blood.

Reticuloendothelial system Body system involved primarily in defence against infection and in disposal of products of the breakdown of cells. Made up of cells that are able to surround, engulf and digest microorganisms and cell debris (macrophages) and special cells in the liver, lungs, bone marrow, spleen and lymph nodes.

Retina (i) The center part of the back lining of the eye that senses light. It has many small blood vessels that are sometimes harmed when a person has had diabetes for a long time. (ii) The sensory membrane that lines the back of the eye. Cells in the retina called photoreceptors transform light energy into electrical signals that are transmitted to the brain by way of the optic nerve. (iii) A thin layer of neural tissue lining the back of the eye where light-sensitive receptor cells are located and where images are focused.

Retinal detachment Condition where the retina separates from the choroid. Retinal detachments have many causes, including aging, surgery, trauma, inflammation, high myopia and diseases such as diabetic retinopathy, retinopathy of prematurity and scleritis. Symptoms include light flashes, floaters, a shadow coming down over yourvision, blurred vision and vision loss.

Retinal pigment epithelium (RPE) A layer of pigmented cells found between the light-sensitive, inner back lining of the eye (retina) and the choroid, which contains blood vessels that supply nutrients and oxygen.

Retinal tear A tear or split in the retina typically caused by a vitreous detachment. Symptoms include floaters and light flashes.

Retinitis Inflammation of the retina. Symptoms include blurred vision, metamor-phopsia, floaters and vision loss.

Retinitis pigmentosa (i) Hereditary disease marked by progressive loss of retinal response, leading to partial or total blindness. (ii) Usually inherited condition characterized by progressive degeneration of the retina, resulting in night blindness and decreased peripheral vision.

Retinopathy is a dysfunction of the retina in which new blood vessels grow across the retina's surface. This growth causes the death of photoreceptors, the specialized cells (rods and cones) in the retina that receive lightwaves and convert them to nerve impulses for transmission to the brain. The blood ves-sels are also delicate and prone to bleeding, which further damages the surface of the retina. The most common forms of retinopathy are the following:

- Retinopathy of diabetes – results from chronically elevated blood *glucose* levels.
- Retinopathy of prematurity- occurs in some infants born earlier than 32 weeks of gestational age in whom the retinal blood vessels, which develop late in gestation, have not yet formed.
- Hypertensive retinopathy- develops as a consequence of untreated or poorly managed hypertension.
- Central serous retinopathy- in which fluid accumulates between the retina and the choroid, causes the retina to swell and lift up from the choroid.

Retinopathy of prematurity (ROP) A retinal disease affecting premature infants, particularly those weighing less than 1500

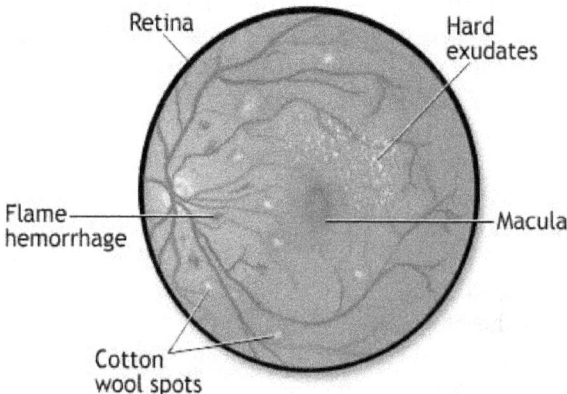

Fig. *Retinopathy*

grams who have received excessive amounts of oxygen therapy during the first two weeks of life to treat respiratory distress syndrome; ROP can lead to retinal scarring, retinal detachment, and blindness.

Retinopathy of prematurity An eye disease common in premature babies that involves abnormal growth of blood vessels in the inner back of the eye (retina). Also known as ROP.

Retinoschisis Condition in which the retina splits into layers, sometimes causing blurred vision. It is either inherited or acquired; the acquired form is caused by small cysts in the eye. You may also have floaters.

Retrobulbar hemorrhage Bleeding in the eye socket behind the eye. If untreated, can cause increased intraocular pressure (IOP), protrusion of the eyeball and permanent vision loss.

Retrocession The voluntary return of a contracted programme, or portion thereof, to the Federal Government pursuant to section 106(d) of the Indian Self-Determination and Education Assistance Act (Public Law 93-638).

Retrograde cell death The killing, due to axonal damage, of neurons located some distance away from the site of an injury in the central nervous system.

Retrograde ejaculation Abnormal discharge of semen backward into the bladder, rather than out through the penis.

Retrograde menstruation Menstruation that flows backwards through the Fallopian tubes into the peritoneal cavity; fragments of the endometrium shed during menstruation attach to the ovaries and other organs, which can cause endometriosis, a common cause of infertility.

Retroperitoneal Pertaining to organs closely attached to the abdominal wall, behind the peritoneum.

Retroperitoneal thrombosis Clotting of blood in the retroperitoneal space.

Retrospective cost-based reimbursement A payment method for health care services in which hospitals (or other providers) are paid their incurred costs of treating patients after the treatment has occurred. In this country, the term has traditionally referred to hospital payment, since other providers have generally been paid on the basis of charges instead of costs.

Retrospective study A study in which data that are already available are analyzed to test a hypothesis (e.g., inferences about exposure to a possible causal factor are derived from data on subjects who already have the disease in question, compared to other subjects who do not have the disease).

Retrovirus A type of virus that contains 2 identical single strands of RNA, not DNA, and that reproduces by making a double-stranded DNA transcription of itself in a process catalyzed by a virallyencoded enzyme known as "reverse transcriptase." The resulting DNA product may integrate into the cell genome (as a provirus) or may remain free in the nucleus (as an episome). Either way, it remains as a latent infection to be activated later (by a variety of factors) to a vim-producing form. Retro-viruses are found widely in nature and are associated with a variety of diseases, including cancer, neurologic disorders, and immunodeficiency syndromes, notably AIDS. Four well-characterized retroviruses are HIV-1 and HIV-2 (major causative agents of AIDS), and HTLV-I and HTLV-II (associated with T-cell leukemia and Iymphoma).

Reuptake Process by which neurotransmitters and their metabolizes are recycled.

Reverse transcriptase An enzyme occurring in retroviruses that produces a DNA transcript of its RNA counterpart, allowing a viral RNA genome to reproduce and integrate into cellular DNA. Also called RNA-dependent DNA polymerase.

Reweighing The adjustment of certain DRG weights to reflect changes in relative resource consumption.

Rewetting drops Eye drops designed to re-moisten and lubricate contact lenses while they are being worn, to increase comfort.

Reye's syndrome Disease in children and adolescents that involves brain and other major organs. Can cause permanent brain damage, coma or death due to pressure on brain. With treatment, most children survive and recover completely. Aspirin has been linked to influenza and various viral diseases as a possible cause. Children with influenza or chickenpox should not be given aspirin to reduce fever!

RGP (Rigid Gas Permeable) Type of contact lens made of breathable plastic that is custom-fit to the shape of the cornea. RGPs are the successor to old-fashioned hard lenses, which are now virtually obsolete.

Rh blood group Genetically determined immunologic antigens (referred to as D or Rh+) on the surface of red blood cells capable of inducing intense antigenic reactions when combined with blood cells lacking those antigens (no D or Rh-). The presence or absence of an Rh factor is especially important in blood transfusions (where it is a major cause of incompatibility) and in pregnancy when the mother is Rhand the fetus is Rh+, which, if untreated, can lead to hemolytic disease of the newborn. Also known as the Rhesus factor, since the antigens were first recognized in Rhesus monkeys.

Rhegmatogenous Arising from a break or tear, describing a common type of retinal detachment.

Rheopheresis is a method of blood filtration (apheresis) for treatment of dry age-related macular degeneration that removes large proteins and fatty components from the blood to improve circulation to macular cells at the back of the eye.

Rheumatic fever Inflammatory complication of Group–A strepococcal infections that affects many parts of the body, especially joints and the heart. Strep infections are contagious, but rheumatic fever is not.

Rheumatoid arthritis Illness characterized by joint disease that involves muscles, cartilage and membrane linings of the joints. Three times more common in women than men. Symptoms include red, warm, painful joints. Sometimes accompanied by weakness and fatigue. If disease is severe, permanent deformity and crippling may result.

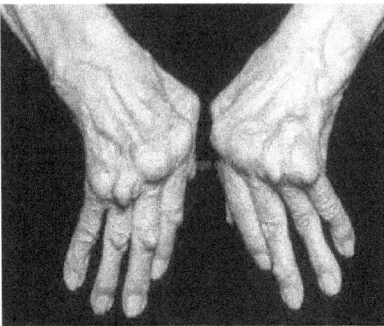

Fig. *Rheumatoid arthritis*

Rh-factor Symbol for rhesus factor. Antigens present on the surface of red blood cells.

Rhinitis Inflammation of the mucous membrane of the nose, caused by viral infection or allergy.

Rhinovirus One of many small RNA viruses that cause acute respiratory illness; responsible for 30 to 50 percent of cases of the common cold.

Rh-isoimmunization Development of agglutination against Rh-blood group antigens in an Rh-negative person in response to Rh-positive blood. It may lead to serious or fatal reactions to blood transfusion or development of erythroblastosis fetalis in the fetus of a subsequent pregnancy.

Ribosome An intracellular organelle, composed of RNA and protein, where protein synthesis occurs; they appear singly, in clusters (polyribosomes), or attached to the endoplasmic reticulum.

Rickets Condition caused by insufficient intake or absorption of vitamin D coupled with too little exposure to sunlight. Seen primarily in infants and small children. Characterized by abnormal bone formation. Symptoms include soft, pliable bones, enlarged skull, muscle pain and profuse sweating.

Rickettsia A group of rod-shaped bacteria, transmitted to humans by bites from lice, fleas, ticks, and mites, that are responsible for human diseases such as Rocky Mountain spotted fever and epidemic typhus.

Rickettsial disease Any disease caused by rickettsial microorganisms. Transmitted to humans by bites from infected lice, fleas, ticks and mites. Rickettsial diseases have been responsible for some of the worst epidemics in history.

Rickettsial germs Microorganisms smaller than bacteria and larger than viruses. Cause various diseases.

Rickettsial-collagen disease Connective tissue disease caused by rickettsial germs.

Right-to-know laws State and local laws requiring companies to identify the chemical names and hazards of their products to workers and the community.

Ring-chromosome formation Chromosome in which both ends have been lost; broken ends have reunited to form a ring-shaped figure.

Risk classification In insurance underwriting, the evaluation of an applicant to determine coverage on a standard or substandard basis, or not at all.

Risk factor Anything that raises the chance that a person will get a disease. With noninsulin-dependent diabetes, people have a greater risk of getting the disease if they weigh a lot more (20 percent or more) than they should.

Risk management Programmes that institutions, especially hospitals, undertake to prevent medical mishaps and to minimize the adverse effects of injury and loss to patients, employees, visitors, and the institution itself. Quality assurance is often considered a subset of the larger issue of risk management.

Risk reduction goal (of the report "Healthy People 2000") Defined in terms of prevalence of risks to health or behaviours known to reduce such risks (e.g., "Increase use of helmets to at least 80 percent of motorcyclists and at least 50 percent of bicyclists" [Healthy People Objective No. 9.13]).

Risk (i) A measure of the probability of an adverse or unfavourable outcome and the severity of the resultant harm to the health of individuals in a defined population; associated with the use of a medical technology applied for a given medical problem under specified conditions of use. (ii) The predicted or observed effects of exposures to toxic substances or harmful physical agents in the workplace, general environment, consumer products, etc. (iii) In insurance, the individual or property insured against loss from hazard. Risk assessment: The analytical process by which the nature and magnitude of risk are identified. Four steps make up a complete risk assessment— hazard identification, dose-response assessment, exposure assessment, and risk characterization.

Risk-benefit analysis A determination of whether the risks to health and the environment of using a chemical or drug exceed the economic benefits that accrue from its use. In the case of pesticides, benefits are measured in terms of the monetary value of crop yields; in the case of drugs, benefits are measured in terms of therapeutic efficacy.

Risk-taking behaviour An activity that may involve a risk to one's health. For adolescents especially, risk-taking generally carries a negative connotation, but some risk-taking is essential to the further development of competence, and thus some risk-taking can have positive health and other benefits.

River blindness Onchocerciasis is caused by a parasitic worm, which is spread in the human bloodstream through bites from blackflies and buffalo gnats found in parts of Africa, South America, and Central America. The worm's offspring cause inflammation, bleeding, and other problems in the eye. Without a 15-year regimen of annual doses of Mectizan, blindness will result. (Information supplied by ORBIS International.)

RK (Radial Keratotomy) Surgical procedure where cuts are made in the cornea in a radial pattern, to flatten the cornea and correct myopia. However, RK now is virtually obsolete as a corrective eye procedure.

RNA (ribonucleic acid) A type of nucleic acid that carries genetic instructions and assists in the assembly of proteins. RNA is a single-stranded chain of repeating units of adenine, cytosine, guanine, and uracil. Specialized types of RNA include: messenger RNA (mRNA), which car-ries a transcript of a DNA sequence to be used as a template for protein synthesis; transfer RNA (tRNA), which attaches the correct amino acid to the protein chain being synthesized at a ribosome; and ribosomal RNA (rRNA), a structural constituent of ribosomes. In some viruses, RNA contains the instructions for viral replication.

Rocky mountain spotted fever Caused by rickettsial germs transmitted by a tick bite. Symptoms include high fever, headache, body aches and skin rash. Tongue is covered with a thick, white coating that turns brown as the fever persists and rises. Fatal disease in 5% of those infected, especially anyone who delays treatment or is older. Incidence is increasing as camping and backpacking become more popular outdoor activities.

Rod A photosensitive receptor in the retina that helps you to see in low light.

Rolelessness The perception by adolescents (and many learned observers) that adolescents as a socially defined group do not have clear and useful roles to play in American society. That is, their function consists largely of being students and otherwise preparing themselves for the future, but there are few expectations for them to contribute to society while they are adolescents.

Rolfing Uses deep manipulation of the fascia to restore the body's natural alignment, which may have become rigid through injury, emotional trauma, and inefficient movement habits. The process, developed by biochemist Ida P. Rolf, involves ten sessions, each focusing on a different part of the body.

Rosacea Skin condition typically involving the face that is characterized by flushing, red bumps and telangiectasia (dilated, visible capillaries); it is most common among fair-skinned women, who develop it in their 30s through 50s.

Rosiglitazone (Avandia) A drug used as a treatment for Type 2 (noninsulin-dependent) diabetes; belongs to a class of drugs called thiazolidinediones.

Rotavirus Any of a group of viruses, containing double-stranded RNA in a double-shelled capsid, which are the major cause of diarrhoea in infants and children. The virus is transmitted by the faecal-oral route. It infects and damages the cells that line the small intestine and causes gastroenteritis.

Route of exposure The means by which a person or animal comes into contact with a chemical: namely intravenous (injected into the bloodstream), inhalation (through the lungs), oral (through . . ingestion), and dermal (through the skin).

Rubella (German measles) Mild, contagious viral illness. Likely to cause serious birth defects to an unborn baby of a pregnant woman who develops the disease in the first 3 or 4 months of pregnancy. Symptoms of

mother-to-be include fever, muscle aches, stiff neck, fatigue, headache, reddish rash that develops on the second or third day of illness and lasts only 1 to 2 days, and swollen lymph glands in the neck. Spontaneous recovery occurs in 1 week in children, longer in adults.

Rubenfeld synergy method Gentle touch, movement, verbal exchange, and imagination used to access memories and emotions locked in the body. Integrates elements of the Alexander Technique, Feldenkrais Method, Gestalt and Hypnotherapy. Combines bodywork and psychotherapy. May be used for physical or emotional problems or for personal growth.

Runaway A young person who is away from home at least overnight without the permission of a parent or caretaker.

Rural As strictly defined by the U.S. Census Bureau, rural refers to places of 2,500 or fewer residents. (Census-recognized 'places" are either (i) incorporated places such as cities, boroughs, towns, and villages; or (ii) closely settled population centers that are outside of urbanized areas, do not have corporate limits, and (unless they are in Alaska and Hawaii) have a population of at least 1,000.) The term "rural" is often used to refer to nonmetropolitan statistical areas (i.e., any area not in a metropolitan statistical area, which, as defined by the U.S. Office of Management and Budget, is a county or group of counties that includes either a city of at least 50,000 residents, or an urbanized area with at least 50,000 people that is itself part of a county/counties with at least 100,000 total residents).

Rural primary care hospital (RPCH) A newly designated type of rural hospital created by Congress in 1989 (Public Law 101-239). Limited to hospitals in only a few States, RPCHS will be small facilities that provide emergency and minimal inpatient care and will be eligible for special reimbursement under Medicare.

Rural referral centers (RRCS) Tertiary-care rural hospitals, usually large, that serve a wide geographic area. Hospitals that qualify as RRCS must meet certain size and referral characteristics, and are eligible to receive special considerations under medicare's prospective payment system.

S

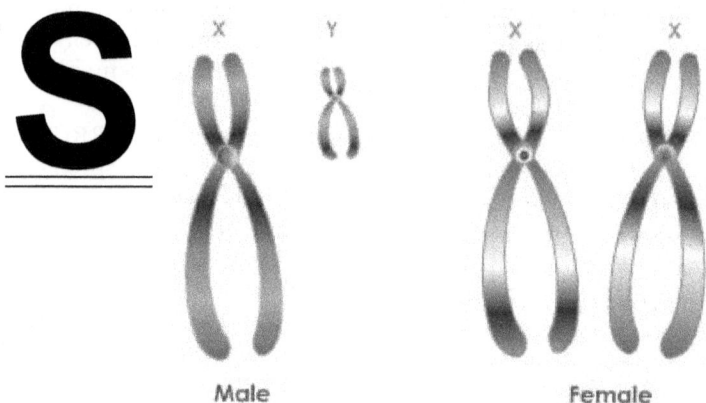

Male   Female

S

Saccharin A man-made sweetener that people use in place of sugar because it has no calories.

Safe harbor' regulations Regulations proposed by the U.S. Department of Health and Human Services that would specify which practices of hospitals and other health care providers would not be unethical under the Medicare and Medicaid anti-kickback provisions.

Safer sex practices Sexual practices designed to avoid actual and potential transmission of HIV infection and other sexually transmitted diseases (e.g., avoiding exchange of body fluids, use of condoms).

Safety A judgment of the acceptability of risk in a specified situation.

Salmonella A genus of bacteria that infect the small intestine, causing diarrhea by damaging the intestinal mucosa or by the action of bacterial toxins, and may also invade the surrounding tissue and infect the systemic circulation. Young children, the elderly, and people with certain disorders (e.g., sickle cell anemia, malaria, and immunodeficiency diseases) are particularly susceptible to salmonellosis. Most infections result from contamination of water or food, such as raw or undercooked animal foods. Some forms (e.g., Salmonella typhi) are particularly virulent and result in typhoid fever.

Salpingitis Inflammation or infection of the Fallopian tubes that may be the result of genital chlamydial or other bacterial infection. Common symptoms include lower abdominal pain, cervical tenderness, and fever. If the infection spreads, complications such as tubal scarring, ectopic pregnancy, and infertility can result.

Salpingostomy A surgical procedure, used to treat infertility, in which an opening is made in a fallopian tube that had been occluded as a result of infection, chronic inflammation, or abscess.

Sarcoidosis Disease in which granulomas (nodules of inflamed tissue) form in the lymph nodes, lungs, skin and other areas. The cause is unknown. Symptoms include fatigue, weight loss, fever, coughing, uveitis, cranial nerve palsies and skin lesions. Some patients also develop dry eyes.

Sarcoma A cancer of connective tissue of the body (e.g., bone, blood vessels, fibrous tissue, muscle, cartilage) classified into 4 main types: osteosarcoma, chondrosarcoma, Kaposi's sarcoma, and fibrosarcoma. Compare carcinoma.

Saturated fat A type of fat that comes from animals.

Scaling factor Weighting disparate measures of health outcomes for cost-effectiveness analysis on the basis of value judgments concerning their relative worth.

Schedule-controlled operant behavior (SCOB) A test in which an experimental animal's response to a stimulus is reinforced on a predetermined schedule in order to produce a predictable pattern of behaviour. SCOB is used to evaluate the effects of acute or chronic exposure to toxic substances on the rate and pattern of the animal's responses.

Schistosoma The genus of parasitic worms, known as "blood flukes," that cause schistosomiasis.

Schistosomiasis A chronic, debilitating infection in humans transmitted by one of the species of parasitic worms of the genus Schistosoma ("blood flukes"): S. mansoni, S. haematobium, or S.japonicum. Infection usually occurs via fresh water contaminated with human faeces.

Schizoid A disorder of childhood or adolescence, the essential feature of which is a defect in the capacity to form social relationships, particularly shown by a preference for being alone, self-absorption, and excessive daydreaming. The term schizoid was also used formerly to apply to individuals with various eccentricities of communication or behaviour, but they are now described as having Schizotypal Personality Disorder.

Schizophrenia Common (and professional) usage for what is most likely a group of disorders ("schizophrenic disorders") involving delusions, hallucinations, or certain disturbances in the form of thought; deterioration from a previous level of functioning in such areas as work, social relations, and self-care; duration of at least six months; and occurring before age 45, usually in late adolescence or early adulthood.

Schizotypal personality disorder Formerly referred to as schizoid, the essential feature is a personality disorder (i.e., a pervasive dysfunctional pattern of behaving) involving oddities of thought, perception, speech, and behaviour that are not severe enough to meet the criteria for schizophrenia.

Schlemm's canal A porous channel within the eye through which fluids drain. When drainage is blocked, high eye pressure can cause eye damage related to glaucoma.

School-based clinics Clinics in or near junior or senior high schools that typically offer a variety of health care services, including physical examinations, treatment for minor acute illness, preventive services, family planning, pregnancy testing, prenatal care, and screening for venereal disease.

School-linked health centres Refers to any school health centre for students (and sometimes the family members of students and/or school dropouts) that provides a wide range of medical and counseling services and is located on or near school grounds and is associated with the school.

School-loss day A day in which a student missed more than half a day from the school in which he or she was currently enrolled.

Schwann cell A glial ceil in the peripheral nervous system that produces myelin for the myelin sheath surrounding axons. Schwann cells also support regrowth of the axons of peripheral nerves.

Sciatic nerve The sciatic is the longest nerve in the body, beginning from nerve roots in the lumbar part of the spinal cord (lower part of the back) and extending through the buttock area to send nerve endings down to the legs. It connects the spinal cord and the leg/feet muscles. Pain resulting from irritation of the sciatic nerve is called *sciatica*. The clinical diagnosis of sciatica is referred to as a radiculopathy. Radiculopathy means that a disc has protruded from its normal position in the vertebral column and is

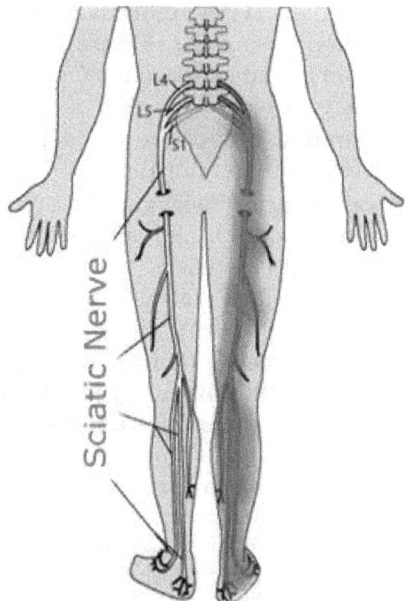

Fig. *Sciatic nerve*

putting pressure on the radicular nerve (nerve root) in the lower back, which forms part of the sciatic nerve. This is most commonly a result of a disc herniation, which compresses the L5 or S1 nerve root found in the lower spine but any other irritation or inflammation of this nerve can lead to the symptoms of sciatica. A mechanical compression of the siatic nerve as a result of spondylolisthesis, arthritis or spinal stenosis may also cause the pain.

When the sciatic nerve is pressed, the pain that radiates along its path is typically felt at the back of the thigh and is usually difficult to ignore. Depending on where damage to the nerve occurred, the pain may be accompanied by symptoms such as numbness or tingling, a burning sensation or general weakness in the leg.

There is no danger of paralysis because the spinal cord is not present in the lower (lumbar) spine.

Sclera (i) The elastic coating of connective tissues that covers the eye; includes the "white" of the eye. (ii) The outer coat of the eyeball that forms the visible white of the eye and surrounds the optic nerve at the back of the eyeball.

Scleritis Inflammation of the sclera. Autoimmune disorders are the most common cause. Symptoms include a red or pink eye, eye pain, light sensitivity, tearing and blurred vision.

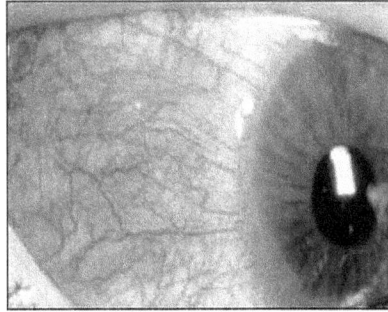

Fig. *Scleritis*

Scope of hospital services A structural measure of a hospital's quality of care that reflects whether the hospital has the resources-facilities, staff, and equipment-to provide care for the medical conditions it professes to treat or to care for the medical condition affecting a potential patient.

Scotoma Blind spot within the field of view.

Screening test Generally, a test used to sort out apparently well persons who probably have disease from those who probably do not. A screening test is not intended to be diagnostic. Compare diagnostic test and predictive test.

Seborrheic dermatitis Skin condition that causes scales, redness and itching; it commonly affects the scalp (dandruff), eyebrows, eyelids, nose, area behind the ears and sternum. It is associated with seborrheic blepharitis.

Second phase Insulin Release Delayed release of insulin into the bloodstream from the beta cell after the blood glucose level rises. It is thought that this delayed release is due to release of insulin that is manufactured in the beta cell after the blood sugar starts to rise.

Secondary diabetes When a person gets diabetes because of another disease or because of taking certain drugs or chemicals.

Secondary diagnosis Any medical condition of a patient other than the principal diagnosis.

Secondary infertility Infertility in those who have previously been fertile.

Secondary prevention An intervention that strives to shorten the course of an illness by early identification and rapid intervention.

Secrete To make and give off such as when the beta cells make insulin and then release it into the blood so that the other cells in the body can use it to turn glucose (sugar) into energy.

Sedatives Central nervous system depressants that produce relief from anxiety; includes barbiturates, metaqualone, and tranquilize.

Segment A part, as in the near-vision portion of a pair of bifocals.

Segmental transplantation A surgical procedure in which a part of a pancreas that contains insulin-producing cells is placed in a person whose pancreas has stopped making insulin.

Selection bias In studies of health interventions, a distortion of results and the comparability of the experimental and control groups due to the tendency of people with better than average health status to

Selective advantage In biology, an organism's increased probability of reproduction and producing offspring, conferred by its genetic characteristics.

Selective pressure In biology, the influence of factors extrinsic to an organism (i.e., environmental factors) on its ability to compete with other organisms for reproductive success.

Selective referral The referral or attraction of patients to physicians and hospitals with better outcomes.

Self-actualization Fully realizing one's individual human potential.

Self-awareness Self-conscious state of focusing attention on oneself.

Self-insurance Usually refers to the practice of employers, particularly large employers, of assuming the risks for the health care expenses of their employees instead of purchasing health insurance through insurance companies. Such employers often continue to contract with insurance companies or other organizations for claims processing and administrative services, as well as purchasing stop-loss insurance to limit the amount of their liability for medical claims. Similar arrangements exist in other lines of insurance (e.g., liability insurance).

Self-monitoring of blood glucose A way as person can test how much glucose (sugar) is in the blood. Also called home blood glucose monitoring.

Self-report data An indication of a survey respondent's attitudes, knowledge, or behaviour that is reported by the respondent him or herself.

Self-selection bias The likelihood that people who seek more or less health care, or different kinds of care, have inherently different health risks from those who do not.

Semen analysis Evaluation of the basic characteristics of sperm and semen, such as appearance, volume, liquefaction and viscosity, and sperm concentration and motility. The presence of bacterial infection and immunological disorders can also be determined by semen analysis. It is the fundamental diagnostic method used to evaluate male infertility.

Semen A fluid of the male reproductive organs consisting of secretions from the male's seminal vesicles, prostate, and from the glands adjacent to the urethra. Semen carries sperm and is ejaculated from the urethra during orgasm.

Senior centre A community facility for elderly people. Senior centres provide various activities for elderly people, including recreational, educational, cultural, or social events. Some centres provide adult, day care, congregate meals, health screening, and limited health care services.

Sensitivity analysis In cost-effectiveness and cost-benefit analysis, an analysis of the effect of changes in key assumptions or uncertainties on the findings and outcome of the overall study.

Sensitivity One measure of the validity (or accuracy) of a diagnos-

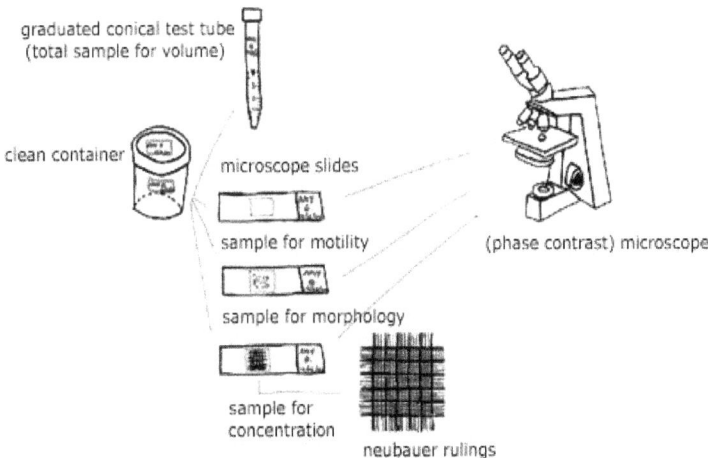

Fig. *Semen analysis*

tic or screening test: the percentage of all those who actually have the condition being tested for who are correctly identified as positive by the test. Operationally, it is the number of true-positive test results divided by the number of patients that actually have the disease (true-positives divided by the sum of true-positives plus false-negatives).

Sentinel health events Medical conditions that, population, indicate a lack of access to acceptable, by virtue of their presence or prevalence in a quality primary care services. Examples include dehydration in infants; measles, mumps, or polio in children; and advanced breast cancer or invasive cervical cancer in adult women.

Sentinel phenotypes A group of autosomal dominant or X-linked conditions that can occur sporadically, as a result of new germinal mutations in the parents' reproductive cells.

Separation anxiety disorder A disorder with onset before the age of 18 consisting of inappropriate anxiety concerning separation from home or from persons to whom the child is attached. Among the symptoms that may be seen are unrealistic concern about harm befalling or loss of major attachment figures; refusal to go to school (school phobia) in order to stay at home and maintain contact with this figure; refusal to go to sleep unless close to this person; cling-

ing; nightmares about the theme of separation; and development of physical symptoms or mood changes (apathy, depression) when separation occurs or is anticipated.

Sequelae After effects or secondary consequences of a disease, disorder, or injury.

Sequential design test The comparison of treatment groups at set stages of experimentation. Further experimentation at higher doses is undertaken only if there is no significant difference between the two groups.

Serious handicap in infants Disabilities that include severe mental retardation (IQ or developmental quotient below 70), cerebral palsy of significant degree, major seizure disorders, or blindness.

Serious offenses Federal Bureau of Investigation Part I offenses, which include specified violent offenses (i.e., murder and non-negligent manslaughter, forcible rape, robbery, and aggravated assault) and specified property offenses (i.e., burglary, larceny-theft, motor vehicle theft, and arson).

Seroconversion The initial development of antibodies specific to a particular agent.

Seropositive In the context of HIV, the condition in which antibodies to the virus are found in the blood.

Seroprevalence Prevalence based on blood tests.

Serotype The type of a micro-organism as determined by the kinds and combinations of constituent antigens present in the cell.

Serum triglycerides Neutral fats present in blood synthesized from carbohydrates for storage in animal adipose cells.

Service system An organizational entity that pools funds from several sources and integrates the functions of various agencies that provide services in a given geographic area. These entities are intended to create a consolidated system through which people are connected to services.

Service-connected disabilities With respect to the eligibility criteria for VA services, disabilities that were incurred or aggravated during military service. Veterans with a service-connected disability have priority for VA services.

Severely mentally ill A term that usually refers to individuals with a diagnosis of schizophre-

nia, a major affective disorder, psychosis, or a personality disorder and a recent history of psychiatric care that required more than voluntary outpatient treatment. The term is not usually used to refer to people with Alzheimer's disease or other diseases that cause dementia.

Sex chromosomes The X and the Y chromosomes, two of the 46 chromosomes in human cells, that determine the sex of the individual. Females have two X chromosomes, while males have one X and one Y chromosome.

Sexual abuse As defined by DHHS'S National Centre on Child Abuse and Neglect, sexual abuse can take three forms: actual penile penetration; molestation with genital contact; and other unspecified acts not known to have involved actual genital contact (e.g., fondling of breasts or buttocks, exposure), or inadequate or inappropriate

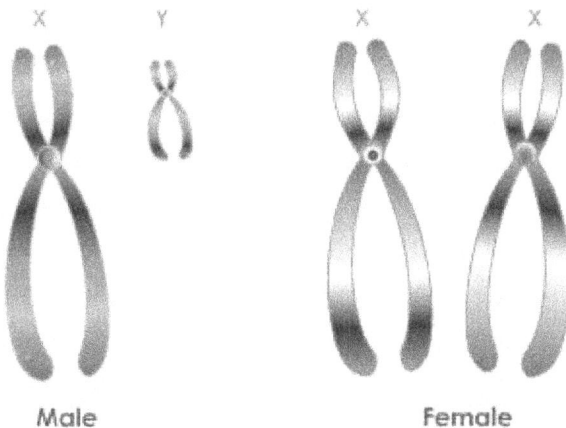

Male   Female

Fig. *Sex chromosomes*

supervision of a child's voluntary sexual activities.

Sexual activity rate As typically used in the literature, the number of individuals who have ever had sexual intercourse, per some population base.

Sexual dysfunction An alteration in sexuality (e.g., impotence, loss of libido) caused by pathophysiological, psychological, social, or behavioural reasons.

Sexually active As typically used in the literature, sexually active denotes ever having had sexual intercourse (as opposed to currently being sexually active).

Sexually transmitted diseases (STDS) Infectious diseases transmitted primarily by sexual contact, including syphilis, gonorrhea, chlamydia, herpes, and AIDS. Formerly (and sometimes, in law) called venereal disease.

Sham operation An operation that the patient believes was performed, but actually was not performed,for the purpose of creating a control group for experimental measure.

Shark cartilage A supplement touted as a cancer treatment. Sharks, whose frames are composed of cartilage not bone, get cancer infrequently. Proponents of this treatment claim sharks get cancer infrequently because something in their cartilage inhibits the ability of tumours to create the blood supply needed to continue growing. Shark cartilage is also promoted as an

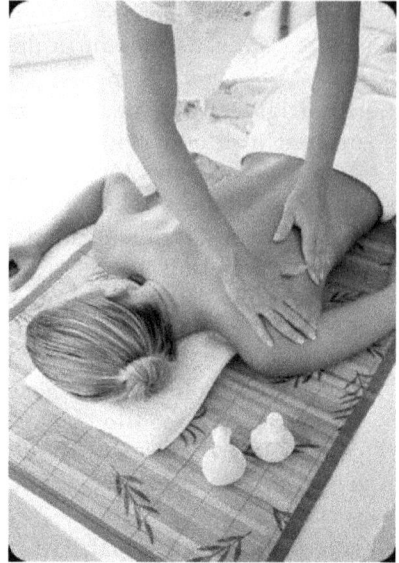

Fig. *Shiatsu*

immune system stimulant and remedy for joint pain, swelling, and stiffness.

Shiatsu A form of acupressure, used in Japan for over 1,000 years to treat pain and illness and for general health maintenance. Practitioners apply finger pressure at specific points on the body in order to stimulate chi, or vital energy. Used to treat stress, circulatory problems, depression, asthma, headaches, diarrhea, bronchitis.

Shift nursing Nursing provided in the home in hourly shifts (usually 8-hour shifts), as distinguished from nursing provided in visits (usually of an hour or less).

Shigella A genus of pathogenic bacteria, some of which cause gastroenteritis and bacterial dysentery.

445

Shock A severe condition that causes severe low blood pressure, decreased level of consciousness, and is a threat to life.

Shock, insulin A term no longer used.

Shooting gallery Location where drug abusers meet to inject (shoot) drugs, often sharing needles.

Short-stay hospitals Hospitals in which the average length of stay is less than 30 days.

Short-term toxicity test Repeated-dose toxicity test that involves exposure to a test substance over a period of 2 to 4 weeks.

Sibling species Independent, reproductive populations that are genetically distinct from one another yet very closely related, and often difficult or impossible to distinguish by morphological or other criteria.

Sickle-cell anemia An autosomal recessive genetic disorder of hemoglobin synthesis leading to the production of distorted and fragile red blood cells and severe, chronic anemia. Infants with sickle cell disease are at risk for overwhelming infection and sudden death in the first few years of life. In older individuals, the disease is characterized by painful episodes of vaso-occlusive crises (aggregation of misshapen red cells), joint pain, thrombosis, fever, chronic anemia, splenomegaly, lethargy, and weakness, although there is wide variability among patients. The disease is caused by a mutation in both copies of the gene for beta globin and is found with high frequency in some populations subject to malarial infections, such as people of African and Mediterranean descent.

Sickle-cell trait The asymptomatic condition shown by individuals carrying the variant globins gene as well as the normal globin-a gene, i.e., they are heterozygous for the sickle-cell gene. Two heterozygous parents have disease.

Silicone Type of flexible and comfortable plastic. Because it is commonly used in nose pads in eyeglasses, people who are allergic to silicone should ask their eye doctor for a different type of nose pad.

Single gene disorder A genetic disease caused by a single gene that shows a simple pattern of inheritance (e.g., dominant or recessive, autosomal or X-linked). Examples include Duchenne muscular dystrophy, retinoblastoma, and sickle cell disease. Also called "Mendelian disorder."

Single vision A lens that has the same power throughout the entire lens, in contrast to a bifocal or multifocal lens that has more than one lens power.

Single-vision disorder Hyperopia (hypermetropia), myopia, and other disoders that involve only one type of vision difficulty, rather than presbyopia, which involves difficulties with near vision as well as some general visual impairment.

Sinusitis Inflammation of the sinuses, due to an infection or an allergic reaction. Probably the most common cause of pain in and around the eye. Symptoms include head pain (headache, pain around the eyes, toothache, jaw pain), nasal discharge, postnasal drip, coughing, eyelid swelling, swelling around the eyes, a stuffy nose, fatigue, bad breath and a sore throat.

Sister chromatid exchange Crossing over between the sister chromatics (two daughter strands of a duplicated chromosome) during cell division (mitosis).

Sjogren's syndrome An inflammatory autoimmune disorder characterized by a dry mouth and dry eyes. Additional eye symptoms include burning, discharge, foreign body sensation, itching and light sensitivity.

Skilled nursing care Nursing care that requires highly technical nursing skills, including care provided by nonprofessionals (such as parents) trained in such skills.

Skilled nursing facility (SNF) A facility that provides skilled nursing care (see Iorm-term care). A "distinct part SNF" is a distinct unit within the hospital that provides such care (i.e., beds set up and staffed specifically for this service), is owned and operated by the hospital, and meets Medicare certification criteria.

Skin cancer Skin cancer is commonly caused by exposure to the sun's UV rays. Types include basal-cell carcinoma, squamous cell carcinoma and malignant melanoma. In carcinoma, you are likely to have a red or pink bump that bleeds, crusts and scales. In melanoma, the pigmented areas can be raised or flat; they are often brown or black, but can be (or include) other colours as well, such as blue, red, pink or white. Some raised moles are skin-coloured.

Sleep terror disorder One of the parasomnias characterized by panic and confusion when abruptly awakening from sleep. This usually begins with a scream and is accompanied by intense anxiety. The person is often confused and disoriented after awakening. No detailed dream is recalled, and there is amnesiafor the episode. Sleep terrors typically occur during the first third of the major sleep episode. Contrast with nightmare disorder.

Sliding fee scale A schedule of discounts in charges for services based on the consumer's ability to pay, according to income and family size.

Sliding scale Adjusting insulin on the basis of blood glucose tests, meals, and activity levels.

Smokeless tobacco Tobacco that is typically chewed or held in the mouth rather than smoked. Contains nicotine, a central nervous system stimulant.

Snellen chart Standard chart with letters, numbers, or symbols printed in rows of decreasing size used by eye care professionals in distance visual acuity testing. The chart was invented by Dutch ophthalmologist Hermann Snellen.

Snyder Act The basic authorizing legislation enacted in 1921 (42 Stat. 208; 25 USC section 13) for Federal health and social services programmes for Indians.

Social competence: Competence in aspects of interpersonal interaction, including: managing social transactions such as entry into social situations; ability to maintain satisfying personal and work - relationships; ability to resolve interpersonal problems so that there is both mutual satisfaction in the encounter and preservation of valued goals; ability to improvise effective plans of action in conflicted or disrupted situations; and ability to reduce stress and contain anxiety within manageable limits. The mediating factors affecting social competence that have been found to be susceptible to life-skills training include the individual's:

(i) motivation (i.e., to acquire knowledge and skills to enhance social competence);

(ii) knowledge base (i.e., about developmentally relevant health and social concerns); and

(iii) social skills (e.g., communication, empathy, ability to regulate one's own behaviour).

Social environment: The aggregate of social and cultural conditions that influence the life of an . individual or community. Aspects of the social environment particularly important to adolescents include the adolescents' families, other adults with whom adolescents come in contact, schools, workplaces, recreational facilities, and the media.

Social health maintenance organization An innovative organizational entity that offers voluntarily enrolled elderly Medicare beneficiaries a package of acute and long-term care services and operates on a capitated, prospectively fixed budget.

Social security disability insurance A Federal social insurance programme for workers who have contributed to the social security retirement programme and become disabled before retirement age. Beneficiaries receive monthly cash payments.

Social services block grant A Federal block grant to States for social services for elderly and disabled people and others. There are no Federal requirements for specific services that must be provided, but many States use a portion of their Social Services Block Grant funds for board and care, adult day care, home health aide, homemaker, and chore services. States determine the eligibility requirements for these services and may use a means test.

Social services Services provided in order to support the functioning of individuals or family units, including those services termed:

(i) "supportive" or "protective" services;

(ii) supplementary services such as financial assistance, respite care, home aid services (e.g., homemaker, caretaker, and parent aide services); and

(iii) 'substitute" services (e.g., shelter services, foster care, adoption).

Social support It can involve the provision of any or all of:

(i) supportive aid, including practical services and material benefits;

(ii) personal affirmation, including feedback that raises self-esteem and strengthens personal identity; and

(iii) supportive affect, particularly affection, caring, and nurturance.

Socio-economic status A synonym for income levels, typically those of an adolescent's family of origin, because adolescents are unlikely to have their own independent sources of income.

Soft contact lenses Contacts made of gel-like plastic containing varying amounts of water.

Sole community hospital A rural hospital, usually small, that is presumed to be the only source of local inpatient hospital care to area residents by nature of their isolated location, weather conditions, travel conditions, or absence of other hospitals. Federally designated SCHS receive special considerations under Medicare's prospective payment system.

Solid tissue graft A piece of tissue placed into the brain or spinal cord; such tissue contains more than one type of cell and therefore may be more likely than a cell suspension to provoke an immune response.

Solution Product used to clean, disinfect and store contact lenses.

Somatic A term used to refer to body tissues apart from reproductive (germinal) tissues.

Somatic cell Any cell in the body except reproductive cells and their precursors. It is any biological cell forming the body of an organism; that is, in a multicellular organism, any cell other than a gamete, germ cell, gametocyte or undifferentiated stem cell.

Somatostatin A hormone made by the delta cells of the pancreas (in areas called the islets of Langerhans). Scientists think it may control how the body secretes two other hormones, insulin and glucagon.

Somoclonal variation Genetic variation produced from the culture of plant cells from a pure breeding strain; the source of the variation is not known.

Somogyi effect A swing to a high level of glucose (sugar) in the blood from an extremely low level, usually occurring after an untreated insulin reaction during the night. The swing is caused by the release of stress hormones to counter low glucose levels. People who experience high levels of blood glucose in the morning may need to test their blood glucose levels in the middle of the night. If blood glucose levels are falling or low, adjustments in evening snacks or insulin doses may be recommended. This condition is named after Dr. Michael Somogyi, the man who first wrote about it. Also called "rebound."

Sorbitol A sugar alcohol the body uses slowly. It is a sweetener used in diet foods. It is called a nutritive sweetener because it has four calories in every gram, just like table sugar and starch. Sorbitol is also produced by the body. Too much sorbitol in cells can cause damage. Diabetic retinopathy and neuropathy may be related to too much sorbitol in the cells of the eyes and nerves.

Sounding the body A diagnostic and therapeutic technique used in sound healing. Sound healers read a patient's body by singing a series of tones and listening for imbalances in the natural frequencies of the body or its' energy fields. Imbalances are said to be indicated by changes in the tone of the healer's voice. To correct a problem, the sound healer applies sound to the patient's body by singing certain tones near the affected organ, or by applying tuning forks or electronic vibratory instruments to the body.

Southern blotting A laboratory procedure for transferring DNA fragments from an agarose gel to a filter paper without changing their relative positions; used to identify specific DNA fragments and to diagnose certain disorders associated with genetic changes (e.g., hemoglobinopathies and some forms of cancer).

Spatial frequency In optics and other fields, a measure of how often a repeating structure (such as a vertical line or bar) appears within a given unit of distance.

Spatial resolution The ability to distinguish two adjacent structures.

Specialty chemical A compound produced by only one company. Compare commodity chemical.

Species barrier The idea that there is a natural reproductive barrier between species that preserves their integrity or identity.

Species complex A group of two or more closely related species that can only be differentiated by cytogenetic analysis or cross-breeding experiments.

Species integrity The idea that a species has integrity as a biological unit. This would have to be based on the identity of the genetic material carried by the species. However, it is not clear how a species might be defined genetically, and this issue is the subject of debate among those seeking to understand the nature of species.

Species A category of living things subordinate to a genus and higher than a subspecies or variety, composed of individuals with common characteristics that distinguish them from other groups of the same taxonomic level; in sexually reproducing organisms, a group of interbreeding natural populations that are genetically distinct from other such groups.

Specificity One measure of the validity (or accuracy) of a diagnostic or screening test: the percentage of all those who do not have the condition being tested for who are correctly identified as negative by the test. Operationally, it is the number of negative test results divided by the number of patients that actually have the disease (tree-negatives divided by the sum of tree-negatives plus false-positives).

Spectrogram Graphic depiction of the individual components of nuclear magnetic resonance signals from phosphorous-containing compounds arranged according to frequency.

Sperm The male reproductive cell, or spermatozoon. Normal human sperm have symmetrically oval heads, stout mid-sections, and long tapering tails. They are produced in the testes and carried out in the semen. Sperm fertilize the female ovum during reproduction.

Sperm bank A place in which sperm are stored by cryopreservation for future use in artificial insemination.

Sperm motility The ability of a sperm to move normally.

Sperm washing The dilution of a semen sample with various tissue culture media in order to separate viable sperm from the other components of semen.

SPF (sun protection factor) Number representing the amount of sun something blocks. For example, if you nor-

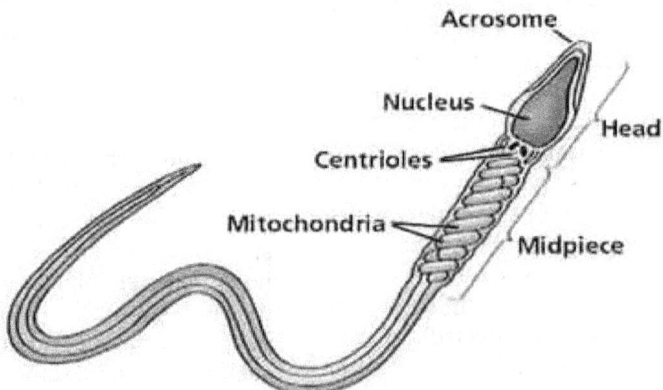

Fig. *Sperm*

mally begin to burn after half an hour in the sun, a sunscreen with an SPF of 2 should let you stay out twice as long (1 hour), SPF 4 should let you stay out four times as long, and so on.

Spherical A contact lens design that is like a sphere and is fairly common; in contrast, toric lenses for astigmatism are football-shaped and are less common.

Spherical aberration A common higher-order aberration of lenses or the eye that causes glare and halos around lights at night.

Sphincter A band of muscle fibres that constrict a passage or close a natural opening in the body (e.g., in the genito-urinary system, the ring-like band of muscular fibres around the urethra that constricts and relaxes to regulate the flow of urine).

Spilling point When the blood is holding so much of a substance such as glucose (sugar) that the kidneys allow the excess to spill into the urine.

Spin of one-half A quantum nuclear spin number of one-half to describe the rotation of the hydrogen nucleus.

Spina bifida A birth defect of unknown cause that results in incomplete or improper development of the spine, usually associated with the protrusion of the spinal cord through the bony spine.

Spinal cord The part of the central nervous system enclosed in the vertebral column extending

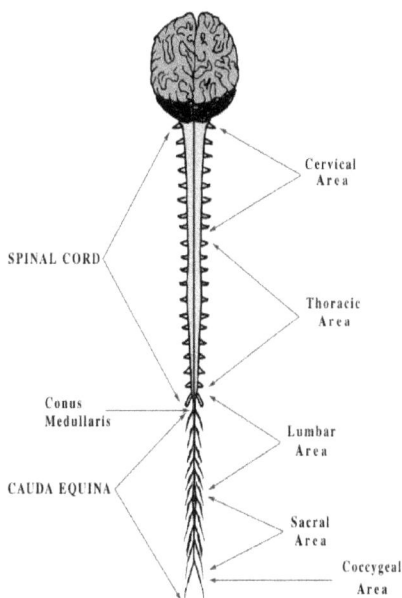

Fig. *Spinal cord*

from the medulla oblongata in the brain to the lumbar vertebrae, connecting all parts of the body with the brain; consists of 31 pairs of spinal nerves (motor and sensory nerves) arising from it and distributed to the body as the peripheral nervous system; contains a hollow core of grey matter surrounded by an outer layer of white matter, with its central cavity filled with cerebrospinal fluid.

Spin-casting A technique for manufacturing contact lenses, in which the lens material, in soft form, is placed in a cup-like mold, and the desired lens curvatures are achieved by spinning the mold at an appropriate speed.

Spiritual healing Practitioners who regard themselves as conductors of healing energy or sources from the spiritual realm. Both may call upon spiritual helpers such as power animals, angels, inner teachers, the client's Higher Self, or other spiritual forces. Both forms of healing can be used for a range of emotional and physical illnesses.

Split dose Division of a prescribed daily dose of insulin into two or more injections given over the course of a day. Also may be referred to as multiple injections. Many people who use insulin feel that split doses offer more consistent control over blood glucose (sugar) levels.

Spontaneous mutation In the absence of any known causative agent, a change in the structure of DNA or in the number of chromosomes. Also called a "background" mutation.

Spontaneous regression (or remission) In cancer, the disappearance (complete regression) or diminishing by at least 50 percent in size (partial regression) of a tumour without any identifiable cause (i.e., without medical intervention).

Sporozoite A life cycle stage of the malarial agent Plasmodium; this is the stage injected by the mosquito vector into the vertebrate host's bloodstream.

Spots Small, cloudy specks in the eye that become noticeable when they fall in the line of sight.

Spring hinge Type of hinge on eyeglass frames that is more flex-

ible than a regular hinge, making the frames more durable.

Staghom stone A large kidney stone that fills several calices, giving it a dramatic "staghorn" appearance in x-rays.

Staging The definition of distinct phases or periods in the course of disease. In oncology, the classification of cancer according to the size of the primary tumour, node involvement, and metastasis.

Standard Industrial Classification (SIC) codes A categorization of data on products and companies that is used by the U.S. Department of Commerce. Establishments (plants) are assigned to SIC "industries" on the basis of their primary line of business. However, SIC data on shipments of a specific product include all shipments of the relevant product, regardless of the "industry" in which the producing establishment is classified.

Standard risk In insurance, a person who, according to an insurer's underwriting criteria, is entitled to purchase insurance coverage without extra premium or special restriction.

Standard therapy Medical treatment or intervention currently being used and considered to be effective based on previous evaluation or common usage.

Startup standards (OSHA) The initial group of standards adopted by the Occupational Safety and Health Administration under section 6(a) of the Occupational Safety and Health Act (Public

Law 91-596). These consisted of established Federal standards and consensus standards.

State and county mental hospital A psychiatric hospital that is under the auspices of a state or a county government, or operated jointly by both a state and county government.

State medical boards' disciplinary actions The penalties imposed by state medical beads on physicians who have transgressed provisions in state medical practice acts. The penalties range from revoking licenses to practice medicine through lesser penalties such as suspension of licenses for a period of time; probation; stipulations; limitations and conditions relating to practice; reprimands; letters of censure and letters of concern.

State medical boards State licensing bodies and State disciplinary bodies. States exercise their authority to license physicians through State licensing boards. The disciplinary functions may be incorporated in the same body as the licensure function or in a separate body.

State mental health agencies (SMHAS) Agencies under the auspices of State governments, staffed through the State, and offering mental health services to any State resident in need of mental health care. State mental health agencies may supervise State mental hospitals, CMHCS, RTCS, and/or day treatment facilities.

State unit on aging A state agency designated under the provisions of the older Americans act to formulate a plan for developing the system of community services envisioned by the act and to oversee the use of older Americans Act funds in the state. Currently, there is a state unit on aging in each of the 50 states, the district of Columbia, and 7 territories.

States' regional Alzheimer's diagnostic and assessment centres Regional centres established by States to provide diagnosis, a comprehensive assessment, and a plan of care for people suspected of having Alzheimer's disease or a related disorder. Some also provide services, such as medical treatment, psychiatric treatment, adult day care, caregiver education and training, and caregiver support groups, and most centres assist in locating and arranging services for their clients. Many of the centres also conduct biomedical and clinical research.

Statistical conclusion validity The extent to which research is sufficiently precise or powerful to enable observers to detect effects. Conclusion errors are of two types: Type 1 is to conclude there are effects (or relationships) when there are not; Type II is to conclude there are no effects (or relationships) when in fact they exist.

Statistical power The probability of detecting a difference between the groups being compared when one does exist. Failure to detect an effect is called 'Type II error" or "beta," analogous to "falsenegative."

Statistically significant The likelihood that an observed association is not due to chance.

Status offenses Acts that are legal offenses solely because they are committed by a juvenile, such as running away from home and truancy. Statutes and other means, legally associated with the role of trustee, to recognize, and guides the axon by virtue of treaties, protect, and preserve tribal sovereignty and to protect; manage, develop and approve authorized transfers of interests in trust resources held by Indian tribes and Indian individuals.

Stem cells Undifferentiated cells in the bone marrow with the ability both to replicate and to differentiate into specific hematopoietic (blood) cell lines.

Stenosis A narrowing or constriction of a bodily passage or orifice.

Stereopsis Three-dimensional vision, enabling depth perception.

Stereotactic surgery A type of brain surgery; specifically, the implantation of tissue into the brain by means of a needle inserted through a small hole in the skull.

Stereotyped movement disorders Psychophysiological disorders characterized by involuntary movements of bodily parts (i.e., tics).

Steroids, anabolic Synthetic derivatives of testosterone used medically to promote protein anabolism. They can be drugs of abuse used to aid in body building. They sometimes produce an initial sense of well-being replaced after repeated use by lack of energy, irritability, and unhappiness. Continued use may lead to such serious complications as severe depression, outbursts of violence, and liver disease.

Stiff hand syndrome Thickening of the skin of the palm that results in loss of ability to hold hand straight. This condition occurs only in people with diabetes.

Stimulants Psychoactive substances that stimulate the central nervous system, including amphetamines, caffeine, and heroin.

Strabismus A misalignment of the eyes: the eye don't point at the same object together. Crossed eyes (esotropia) are one type of strabismus; "wall-eyes" (exotropia) are another. The exact cause is unknown, but appears to be a problem with the eye muscles. Strabismus can affect depth perception.

Strain A group of organisms of the same species having a distinctive quality or characteristic (biochemical, pathogenic, or other) that can be differentiated, but is not different enough to constitute a separate species.

Strategic planning A rational process by which a health care organization (e.g., hospital) determines its best course of action. This involves effectively balancing community needs for health services with the organization's strengths and ability to use available resources, and producing practical plans to implement strategies that are financially feasible and acceptable to consumer needs (American Hospital Association definition).

Stratification In randomized clinical trials, the categorization of individuals for the purpose of adjusting the groups to take into account unequal distribution of characteristics of prognostic importance. Stratifcation may be used during patient allocation, creating subgroups within which individuals are randomized to treatments; or stratification may be applied during data analysis to statistically adjust for differences between the groups.

Street kid A long-term runaway, thrownaway, or otherwise homeless child or adolescent who has become adept at fending for him or herself "on the street," usually by illegal activities.

Striatum, corpus striatum Part of the basal ganglia located in the cerebral hemisphere of the brain, consisting of the caudate nucleus and the Ientiform nucleus; the striatum receives dopamine from cells in the substantial nigra.

Stroke Loss of sensation, movement, or function caused by a sudden interruption of the blood supply or a leakage of blood in the brain. This can be caused by heart failure, blockage of arteries (cerebral thrombosis or cerebral embolism), or hemorrhage in the brain. Depending on the part of the brain affected, a stroke can cause a person to lose the ability to speak or move a part of the body such as an arm or a leg. Usually only one side of the body is affected. This condition is often followed by permanent neuro-

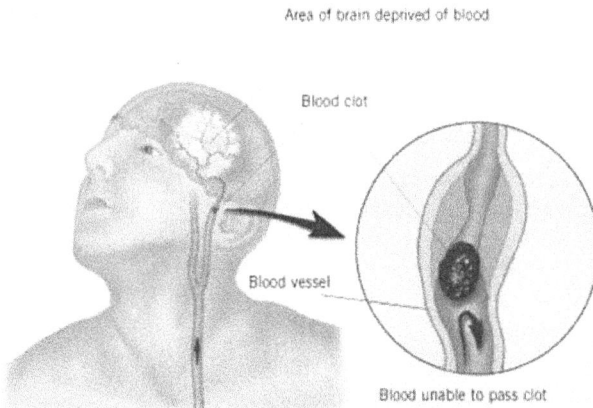

Area of brain deprived of blood

Blood clot

Blood vessel

Blood unable to pass clot

Fig. *Stroke*

logical damage and is a leading cause of death in developed countries.

Symptoms include weakness or numbness, particularly on one side of the body, a change in consciousness or mental status, vision loss, double vision, and limited eye movement. You may also blink frequently.

Stroma The cornea's middle layer; it consists of lamellae (collagen) and cells, and makes up most of the cornea.

Structural diagnosis An osteopathic diagnostic technique - involves a visual, hands-on assessment by an osteopathic physician of the skeleton, joints, muscles, ligaments, and tendons.

Structural measures of quality Measures of the resources and organizational arrangements that are in place to deliver medical care, such as the number, type, and distribution of medical personnel, equipment, and facilities. Underlying the use of such measures to assess quality is the assumption that such characteristics increase or decrease the likelihood that providers will perform well and in their absence, that providers will perform poorly. This assumption in turn raises the question whether specific structural characteristics are in fact associated with better processor outcome.

Structure-activity relationship The relationship between a chemical's structure and the biochemical changes it induces.

Stump The part of a limb left after amputation.

Sty A small red bump on the edge of the eyelid caused by an infected gland. Additional symptoms include eyelid pain, eyelid swelling, eye pain or discomfort, foreign body sensation, light sensitivity and tearing.

Subchronic toxicity test Repeated-dose toxicity test of intermediate duration, with exposure to a test substance for 3 to 6 months.

Subclinical diabetes A term no longer used.

Subconjunctival hemorrhage Bleeding from blood vessels on the surface of the eye that leaves a red patch. This common problem can be caused by sneezing, coughing, high blood pressure, trauma and more.

Subcutaneous injection Putting a fluid into the tissue under the skin with a needle and syringe.

Subcutaneous Beneath the skin

Subjective distress Feelings of sadness, hopelessness, discouragement, boredom, stress, dissatisfaction, or being worn out or exhausted, that are self-reported by individuals but are not necessarily symptoms of diagnosable mental disorders

Subluxation In chiropractic, a misalignment of bones within joints said to interfere with the flow of nervous impulses and diminish the body's ability to stay healthy.

Substance dependence A mental disorder in which a person has impaired control of psychoactive substance use and continues use despite adverse consequences. It is characterized by compulsive behaviour and the active pursuit of a lifestyle that centres around searching for, obtaining, and using the drug.

Substance use/abuse disorders In children, a set of mental disorders characterized by maladaptive behavioural changes resulting from regular use of substances that affect the central nervous system. In adults, the physical or mental problems resulting from overindulgence in and dependence on a stimulant, depressant, or other chemical substance.

Substance Term used for alcohol, tobacco, and illicit drugs.

Substandard risk A person that does not meet the normal health requirements of a standard health insurance policy and whose coverage is provided with a higher premium and/or exclusion waiver.

Substantial nigra A darkly pigmented structure in the brain containing a group of neurons that use dopamine as their transmitter in a projection to the basal ganglia (a structure involved in the coordination and initiation of movement). A deficit of dopamine in this projection is characteristic of Parkinson's disease and produces its motor symptoms.

Substantial violation A pattern of care over a substantial number of cases that is inappropriate,

Substantially equivalent device A device first marketed after the 1976 Medical Device Amendments (Public Law 94-295) that the Food and Drug Administration has found to be similar to a device already being marketed. To be found substantially equivalent, a post amendments device need not be identical to a pre amendments device, but must not differ markedly in materials, design, or energy source.

Subunit vaccine A vaccine that contains only portions of an antigenic molecule from a pathogen. Subunit vaccines can be prepared by using recombinant DNA technology to produce all or part of the antigenic molecule or by artificial (chemical) synthesis of short peptides.

Sucrose table sugar A form of sugar that the body must break down into a more simple form before the blood can absorb it and take it to the cells.

Suctioning Aspiration of fluid by mechanical means. For example, in children with breathing difficulties, suctioning is used to remove secretions from the airway and is particularly important when the child has a tracheotomy tube (artificial airway) that could be blocked by these secretions,

Sudden infant death syndrome (SIDS) The sudden and unexpected death of an apparently normal, healthy infant, usually during sleep, with no identifiable signs of illness or cause of death determined at autopsy. SIDS occurs in 1 in 300 to 350 livebirths. Multiple risk factors have been proposed, but none has yet been linked definitively with the syndrome.

Sugar A class of carbohydrates that taste sweet. Sugar is a quick and easy fuel for the body to use. Types of sugar are lactose, glucose, fructose, and sucrose.

Suicide The taking of one's own life.

Superior limbic kerato-conjunctivitis A condition characterized by episodes of recurrent inflammation of the superior cornea, the junction between the cornea and the sclera (the limbus), and the conjunctiva lining the superior sclera and inner surface of the upper eyelid.

SuperPRO An independent organization, working under contract to HCFA, that re-reviews a sample of - the patient records evaluated by each of the 54 PROS. The purpose of the SuperPRO reviews is to validate the determinations made by PROS, including the application of the HCFA generic quality screens.

Surgery complication Complications from cataract surgery, LASIK or other eye surgeries can result in a variety of symptoms, including blurred vision, ptosis, foreign body sensation, halos around lights, light sensitivity, eye pain or discomfort, red or pink eyes, vision loss and an iris defect.

Surrogate decision A decision made on behalf of another person, in particular a person who is decisionally incapable. Court rulings and legal analysis of decisions about the use of life-sustaining technologies have identified two standards to guide surrogate decisionmaking:

(i) the "best interest standard-(which requires the surrogate to make decisions from the perspective of a hypothetical reasonable person, using objective, societally shared criteria); and

(ii) the "substituted judgment standard" (which requires the surrogate to make decisions from the perspective of the patient, using the patient's personal values and preferences).

Surrogate decisionmakers Persons responsible for making decisions concerning an individual's health care, lifestyle, and estate once the individual is incapable of making those decisions. A surrogate decisionmaker can be a court-appointed conservator or guardian, or someone legally designated by the individual before he or she became incompetent. De facto surrogates (often spouses or other family members) assume these powers for an incapacitated individual without being formally or legally charged to do so. The limits on the types of decisions that can be made by surrogate decisionmakers vary from state to state.

Surrogate mother A woman who is artificially inseminated and carries an embryo to term, with the " intention of relinquishing the child at birth.

Surrogate gestational mother A woman who gestates and carries to term an embryo to which she is not genetically related, with the intention of relinquishing the child at birth.

Surveillance In epidemiology, ongoing scrutiny of a population for the occurrence and spread of disease.

Survival sex Engaging in sexual intercourse in exchange for food, shelter, money, or drugs.

Suspensory ligament It is also called zonule of zinn. Membrane of fibres (zonules) that holds the eye's lens in place.

Swing beds Licensed acute-care beds designated by a hospital to provide either acute or long-term care services. A hospital qualifying to receive Medicare and Medicaid reimbursement for care provided to swing bed patients must be located in a rural area (as defined by the U.S. Bureau of the Census), have less than 100 acute care beds, and when applicable must have received a certificate of need for the provision of long-term care services from its State health planning and development agency.

Swine flu Influenza virus common throughout pig populations worldwide. Transmission of the virus from pigs to humans is not common and does not always lead to human flu, often resulting only in the production of antibodies in the blood. If transmission does cause human flu, it is called zoonotic swine flu. People with regular exposure to pigs are at increased risk of swine flu infection.

Symbiosis In parasitology, the living together or close association of two dissimilar organisms.

Symptom A manifestation relating to the body or its functions that is suggestive of disease. Example: frequent urination is a symptom of diabetes.

Synapse An area across which signals are passed from the axon terminals of a neuron to the membrane of an adjacent neuron or effecter cell (e.g., muscle or gland cell). Synapses may be "chemical," using a neuro-transmitter to transmit the signal across a small gap between the membranes, or "electrical," in which the neuron's cytoplasm is actually joined with that of the adjacent cell, forming a bridge or "gap junction."

Synaptic cleft or space A narrow gap between two adjacent neurons into which neuro-transmitters are secreted.

Synaptic sprouting A process of limited regrowth following damage to the central nervous system whereby fibres from nearby, undamaged axons form new branches and establish new synapses to replace some of the lost ones.

Syndrome A set of signs or a series of events occurring together that make up a disease or health problem.

Syndrome X A older phrase describing a combination of health conditions that place a person at high risk for heart disease. These conditions are Type 2 diabetes, hypertension (high blood pressure), hyperlipidemia (high levels of fat in the blood), and obesity. According to theory, all of these conditions are associated with high blood insulin levels, and it is claimed that the underlying problem in patients with Syndrome X is faulty insulin release from the beta cells of the pancreas. Now usually called the Metabolic Syndrome.

Syphilis A sexually transmitted disease caused by the bacterial agent Treponema pallidum, resulting in symptoms including chancre (primary syphilis); skin rash, malaise, anorexia, nausea (secondary syphilis); and eventually, central nervous system abnormalities and other serious problems (tertiary syphilis).

Syringe A device used to inject medications or other liquids into body tissues. The syringe for insulin has a hollow plastic or glass tube (barrel) with a plunger inside. The plunger forces the insulin through the needle into the body. Most insulin syringes now come with a needle attached. The side of the syringe has markings to show how much insulin is being injected.

Systematic desensitization A behavior therapy procedure widely used to modify behaviours associated with phobias. The procedure involves the construction of a hierarchy of anxiety-producing stimuli by the subject, and gradual presentation of the stimuli until they no longer produce anxiety. Also called desensitization.

Systemic A word used to describe conditions that affect the entire body. Diabetes is a systemic disease because it involves many parts of the body such as the pancreas, eyes, kidneys, heart, and nerves.

T

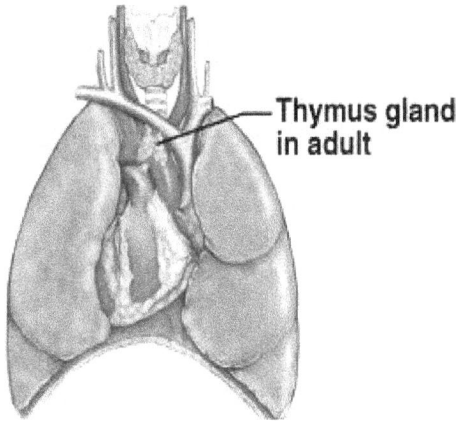

Thymus gland in adult

t

T cell A lymphocyte produced in the bone marrow that matures in the thymus and is integral to cellmediated immunity. T cells regulate the growth and differentiation of other lymphocytes and are involved in antibody production. See lymphocyte.

T4/T8 cell ratios The ratio of T4 lymphocytes (helper cells) to T8 lymphocytes (suppressor cells). Individuals with AIDS have a deficiency of T4 cells and a reversal of the usual ratio of T4 and T8 cells.

Tarasoff decision A California court decision that essentially imposes a duty on the therapist to warn the appropriate person or persons when the therapist becomes aware that the patient may present a risk of harm to a specific person or persons.

Targeted motility method An approach to quality assessment in which deaths in certain types of cases are targeted for review. Examples include deaths in primary procedures or diagnosis related groups (DRGs) with an average death rate of less than 5 percent, deaths occurring within 1 day of any procedure, and deaths in which bums are reported as a secondary diagnosis.

Tax-exempt revenue bonds Bonds generally are evidence of a debt in which the issuer (borrower) promises to repay the bond's holder. A revenue bond is issued by a government (borrower) to taxpayers (bondholder) to raise funds in anticipation of tax receipts, and then repaid from tax revenues once they are received. Most bonds issued by governments are tax-exempt, that is, the bondholder pays no Federal income tax on interest earned.

Taxonomy The study of naming and describing species of plants and animals and classifying them according to their presumed natural characteristics and relationships.

Tay-Sachs disease An autosomal recessive genetic disorder of lipid metabolism resulting in developmental retardation, paralysis, dementia, blindness, and death, usually before age three. It is caused by a mutation in the gene for hexosaminidase A, an enzyme that degrades certain sphingolipids in the brain. Symptoms are caused by an accumulation of cerebral gangliosides, fatty acid and sugar molecules found in the brain and nervous tisssue. The Tay-Sachs gene is found mainly among Ashkenazic Jews of Eastern European origin.

TDR diseases The six diseases singled out for attention by the Special Programme for Research and Training in Tropical Diseases (TDR): malaria, schistosomiasis, trypano-somiasis, filariasis, Ieish-maniasis, and leprosy.

Team management Describes a diabetes treatment approach in which medical care is provided by a physician, diabetes nurse educator, dietitian, and behavioral scientist working together with the patient.

Technical aspects of medical care The application of medical science and technology to a medical problem.

Technology The application of organized knowledge to practical ends.

Technology assessment In general, a comprehensive form of policy research that examines the technical, economic, and social consequences of technological applications. It is especially concerned with unintended, indirect, or delayed social impacts. In health policy, however, the term more often is used to mean any form of policy analysis concerned with medical technology, especially the evaluation of efficacy and safety.

Technology diffusion The diffusion or spread of a medical technology into the health care system.

Technology-dependent children Those children who use a medical technology (embodied in a medical device) that compensates for the loss of normal use of a vital body function, and who require substantial daily skilled nursing care to avoid further disability. Such care may be provided by nonprofessional caregivers, such as family members.

Temple The "arm" of a pair of glasses, running from the ear to the lens area.

Temporal subtraction The use of digital subtraction imaging (e.g., digital subtraction angiography) to show changes in the contrast appearance of the body part or tissues (e.g., arteries) overtime.

Temporo-mandibular joint disorder It is also called TMJ or TMD disorder. Problems with the jaw, jaw joint and surrounding muscles that control jaw movements such as chewing, which result in pain, swelling and difficulty with jaw movement. Other symptoms are toothaches, headaches and hearing problems. Causes include injury, teeth grinding/clenching, stress and osteoarthritis or rheumatoid arthritis.

TENS (Transcutaneous electrical nerve stimulation) Delivery of an electric current through the skin to the nerves. Used in physical therapy and to relieve painful conditions such as neuralgia, sciatica, and arthritis. The low voltage electric current blocks the nerves reception of pain signals and possibly stimulates the production of endorphins, the body's pain-killing chemicals.

Teratogen Physical or chemical agents, (e.g., thalidomide, radiation, alcohol, and certain viruses) that act on the fetus in utero to cause congenital malformations.

Teratogenic Capable of inducing the formation of developmental abnormalities in a fetus.

Terminal In cancer prognosis, forecasting death due to the growth and progression of the cancer.

Test rule A statement written by EPA of what chemical or chemicals in a compound must be tested by the manufacturer and how they are to be tested. Test rules are written under the Toxic Substances Control Act when it can be shown both that inadequate data on the effects of a compound exist and that testing is required to obtain such data.

Testes Also known as the testicles, the paired male sex glands in which sperm and the steroid hormone testosterone are produced. The testes like smooth, soft balls inside the baggy scrotum. At the top and to the back of each testis is the epididymis (this stores the sperm). This feels like a soft swelling attached to the testis, and can be quite tender if you press it firmly. Leading from the epididymis is the vas deferens.

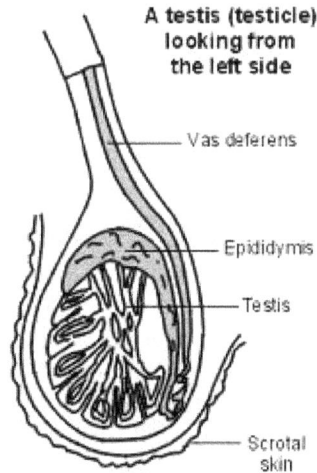

A testis (testicle) looking from the left side

Vas deferens

Epididymis

Testis

Scrotal skin

Fig. *Testes*

Testicular biopsy A testicular biopsy is a test to remove a small sample of tissue from one or both testicles and examine it under a microscope to evaluate

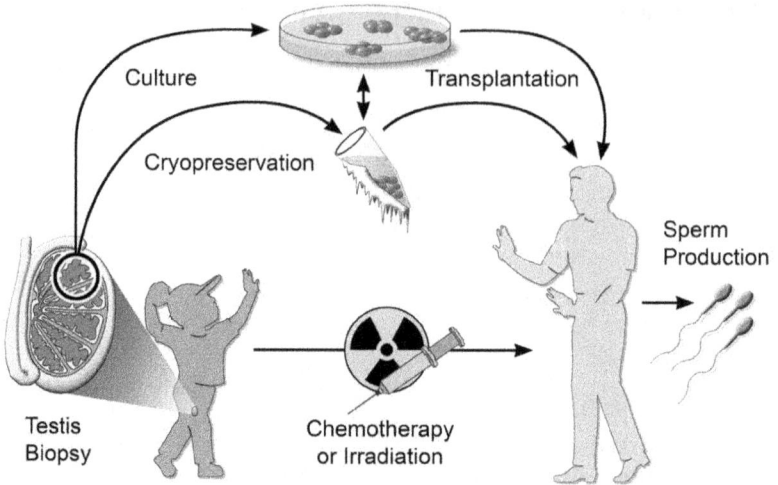

Fig. *Testicular biopsy*

a man's ability to father a child. The testicles (testes) are oval-shaped glands that hang in the scrotum beneath the base of the penis. The testicles produce sperm (necessary for reproduction) and male hormones, such as testosterone.

Testosterone A steroid hormone, or androgen, produced in the testes that affects sperm production and male sex characteristics.

Tetanus An acute, potentially fatal disease of the central nervous system caused by infection of a wound with spores of the bacterium Clostridium tetani; these spores release a poisonous neurotoxin that causes trismus ("lockjaw"), generalized muscle spasm, arching of the back, glottal spasm, seizures, respiratory spasms, and paralysis. Short-term immunity can be derived through vaccination.

Tetramer A molecule composed of 4 subunits (e.g., a protein such as hemoglobin composed of 4 globin chains bonded together).

Thalamus is a large, dual lobed mass of grey matter buried under the cerebral cortex. It is involved in sensory perception and regulation of motor functions. The thalamus is a limbic system structure and it connects areas of the cerebral cortex that are involved in sensory

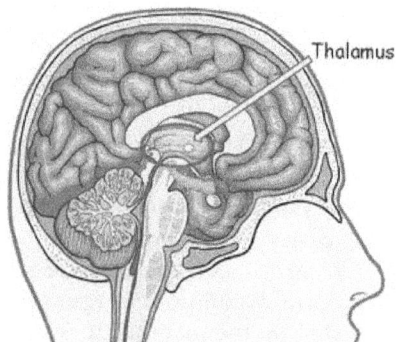

Fig. *Thalamus*

perception and movement with other parts of the brain and spinal cord that also have a role in sensation and movement. As a regulator of sensory information, the thalamus also controls sleep and awake states of consciousness.

Thalassemia A heterogeneous group of autosomal recessive genetic disorders of hemoglobin synthesis. The thalassemias are characterized by the absence or reduced output of one or more of the globin chains of hemo-globin, resulting in small, pale red blood cells, anemia, and the accumulation of unpaired globin chains. The *four* main categories are— alpha, beta, and delta-beta thalassemia, and hereditary persistence of fetal hemoglobin (HPFH). The thalassemias are found mainly in people of mediterranean, middle eastern, and Asian descent.

Therapeutic community Residential treatment programmes lasting approximately one year or more and characterized by a highly structured and confrontational approach. The TC philosophy views drug abuse as a reflection of personality problems and chronic deficiencies in social, educational, and marketable skills.

Therapeutic foster care A type of mental health care optimally involving the following features:

(i) placement of a child with foster parents who have specifically been recruited to work with an emotionally disturbed child or adolescent;

(ii) provision of special training to the foster parents to assist

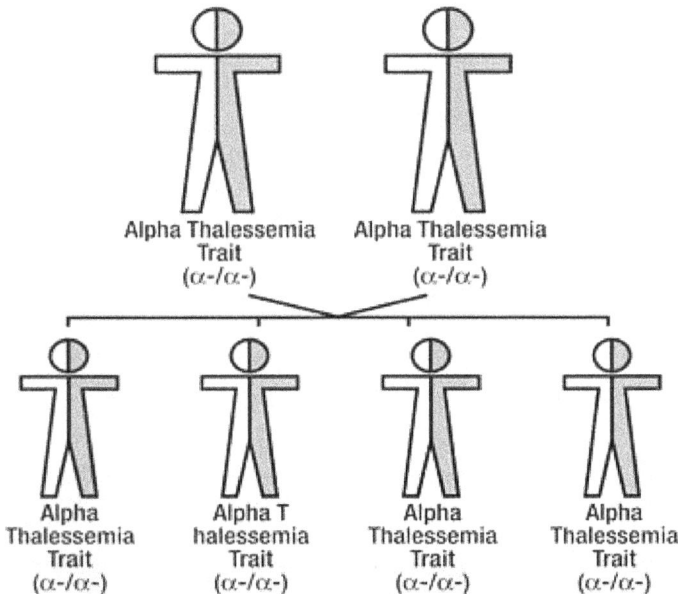

Fig. *Thalassemia*

them in working with the child;

(iii) placement of only one child in each special foster home (with occasional exceptions);

(iv) a low staff to client ratio, thereby allowing clinical staff to work very closely with each child, with the foster parents, and with the biological parents if they are available;

(v) creation of a support system among the foster parents; and

(vi) payment of a special stipend to the foster parents for working with the emotionally disturbed child or adolescent, and for participating in the training and other programme activities. Regarded as the least restrictive of residential mental health services.

Therapeutic group care A type of mental health care provided in homes which typically serve anywhere from 5 to 10 children or therapeutic environment.

Therapeutic technology A technology that cures or relieves the symptoms of a disease or other medical condition.

Therapeutic touch Practiced by registered nurses and others to relieve pain & stress. Practitioner assesses where a person's energy field is weak and congested, then uses his or her hands to direct energy into the field to balance it.

Therapy Treatment and care of someone to combat disease, injury, or mental disorder.

Thiazolidinediones One of several different classes of pills that lower the level of glucose in the blood. Used in Type 2 diabetes. There are several thiazolidinedione pills available. This class of medications is also called "glitazones." Each type of pill is sold under two names: one is the generic name as listed by the US Food and Drug Administration; the other is the trade name given by the manufacturer

Third-generation testing A level of testing that is three times as specific as the first test introduced.

Third-party administrators A term originally used in the Taft-Hartley legislation of 1947 to designate an entity that is neither union nor management but administers joint labour-management welfare and pension funds. In self-insured health plans, TPAs typically provide administrative services such as medical claims processing, utilization and charges review, and data processing and reporting.

Third-party payer Private insurers or government insurance programmes that pay providers for medical care given to patients they insure, either directly or by reimbursing patients for payments they make.

Third-party payment Payment by a private insurer or government programme to a medical provider for care given to a patient.

Thought disorder A disturbance of speech, communication, or content of thought, such as delusions, ideas of reference, poverty of thought, flight of ideas, preservation, loosening of associations, and so forth. A thought disorder can be caused by a functional emotional disorder or an organic condition. A formal thought disorder is a disturbance in the form of thought rather than in the content of thought (e.g., loosening of associations).

Threshold limit value That concentration (by volume in air) of a hazardous substance to which the majority of industrial workers may be repeatedly exposed every day without adverse effects; set by the American Conference of Governmental Industrial Hygienists. Compare reference dose (RfD).

Threshold In toxicology, the highest dosage at which no effect is observed. Compare no-threshold.

Thrombin An enzyme that induces blood clotting by converting fibrinogen to fibrin. Thrombin is formed in blood from prothrombin, calcium, and thromboplastin.

Thrombosis Blood clot. Such coagulation of the blood can occur anywhere in the circulatory system of the body, including the heart, arteries, veins and capillaries.

In other sense, It is the abnormal development of a blood clot (thrombus) inside an intact blood vessel, which can be life-threatening if it obstructs the blood supply to the brain (leading to stroke), heart (leading to myocardial infarction), or other organs (leading to tissue damage or loss of function); the presence of such clots also raises the risk that part of the clot (an embolus) may break off and travel to a dist 6Xoff an artery or vein, causing thrombophlebitis or deep vein thrombosis. Factors contributing to thrombosis include atherosclerosis, an increase in coagulation factors, or a deficiency of anticlotting factors in the blood.

Thrownaway A child or adolescent who has been told to leave the household, has been abandoned or deserted, or who has run away and no effort has been made to recover him or her.

Thrush An infection of the mouth. In people with diabetes, this infection may be caused by high levels of glucose (sugar) in mouth fluids, which helps the growth of fungus that causes the infection. Patches of whitish-coloured skin in the mouth are signs of this disease.

Thymus A ductless gland-like organ of the lymphatic system located in the upper chest region. As a central lymphoid organ, the thymus is necessary for the development and maintenance of immunologic competence. In infants, the development of lymphoid tissue and the immune response to foreign material occurs in the thymus. It later becomes the site for maturation and differentiation of T-lym-phocytes.

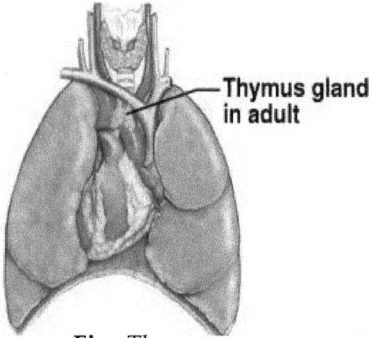

Fig. *Thymus*

Thyroid An endocrine gland located in the neck, that makes two hormones (T4 or thyroxine and T3 or triiodothyronine, which are frequently simply called "thyroid hormone") that regulate the body's metabolic rate. Overactivity of the thyroid gland is called hyper-thyroidism; under-activity is called hypothyroidism. Both hyperthyroidism and hypo-thyroidism may have an autoimmune basis, and both are somewhat more common in people with Type 1 diabetes.

Thyroid Stimulating Hormone (TSH) A hormone secreted by the anterior pituitary gland, that controls the production and release of the thyroid hormones (T4 and T3). Measurement of the TSH level in the bloodstream is commonly done as a screening tool for hypothyroidism and hyperthyroidism, and as an assessment of the adequacy of therapy in people who are taking thyroid hormone pills as therapy. Typically, high values of TSH are associated with hypothyroidism, and absence of TSH is associated with hyper-thyroidism.

Tic An involuntary, sudden, rapid, recurrent, nonrhythmic stereotyped motor movement or vocalization. A tic may be an expression of an emotional conflict, the result of neurologic disease, or an effect of a drug (espe-

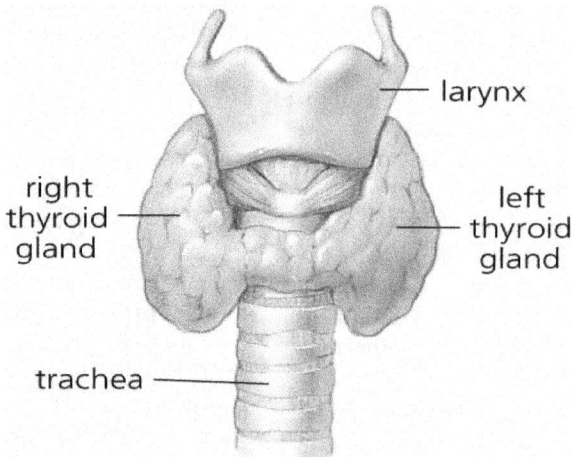

Fig. *Thyroid*

cially a stimulant or other dopamine agonist).

Tic disorders In DSM-IV, this category includes Tourette's disorder, chronic motor or vocal tic disorder, transient tic disorder, and tic disorder not otherwise specified; all beginning before the age of 18 years. Chronic tics may occur many times a day, nearly every day, or intermittently over a period of more than a year. Transient tics do not persist for longer than 12 consecutive months.

Time-weighted average An average, over a given (working) period of a person's exposure, as determined by sampling at given times during the period.

Tissue culture The propagation of collections of specialized cells (e.g., fibroblasts) removed from organisms in a laboratory environment that has strict sterility, temperature, and nutrient requirements; a tool for studying physical, biochemical, and genetic factors that determine growth and development of cells, both normal and transformed (cancerous).

Tissue plasminogen activator A clot-dissolving substance produced naturally by cells in the walls of blood vessels, acting by converting plasminogen to plasmin, which breaks down fibrin (the main component of clots); also manufactured synthetically by genetic engineering techniques; used therapeutically to remove blood clots in coronary arteries in patients with myocdial infarction, severe, progressive angina pectoris, and arterial embolism.

Titanium A type of metal alloy that is very strong. Eyeglasses made of titanium are lightweight, durable and often hypoallergenic.

Titer The lowest concentration (highest dilution) of an active substance (e.g., antibody in serum) that causes a discernible reaction with another substance; also a measurement of the concentration of a substance in a solution.

Tocodynamometry, ambulatory A device for detecting and recoding uterine contractions, used to detect premature labour in early stages when, theoretically, technologies for stopping labour may be more effective.

Tocolytic Stopping premature labour during pregnancy,

Tolazamide A pill taken to lower the level of glucose (sugar) in the blood. Only some people with noninsulin-dependent diabetes take these pills.

Tolbutamide A pill taken to lower the level of glucose (sugar) in the blood. Only some people with noninsulin-dependent diabetes take these pills.

Tolerance level In toxicology, the maximum permissible concentration of a toxic substance in or on food, water, or air as set by a regulatory agency.

Tolerance Increasing resistance to the effects of a drug. An outstanding characteristic of opiates and amphetamines, it results in a need for increasing dosage to maintain or recapture the desired drug effect.

Tomographic scan The x-ray image of a single cross-section of tissue from the body.

Tonic pupil Dilated pupil that reacts sluggishly to light, due to damage to the ciliary ganglion from trauma, viral infections or other causes. The cause is sometimes unknown ("Adie's tonic pupil").

Tonic Herbal remedy made from herbs taken to maintain health or ward off illness, rather than to treat an illness. Also known as a normalizer.

Toning In sound healing, projection of a nonverbal sound to balance the body's energy fields.

Toric A lens design with two different optical powers at right angles to each other for the correction of astigmatism.

Tort liability Liability imposed by a court for breach of a duty implied by law, contrasted with contractual liability, which is breach of duty arising from an agreement. A legal basis for compensation when property has been damaged or a person has been injured. The tort liability system determines fault and awards compensation for civil wrongs, including medical malpractice.

Total hospital margin A measure of hospital profitability, calculated as (total revenues minus total costs) divided by total revenues. Total revenues include private contributions and public subsidies as well as patient care and other revenue.

Tourette's disorder A tic disorder consisting of multiple motor and vocal tics that occur in bouts, either concurrently or separately, almost every day or intermittently over a period of more than 12 months.

Toxemia of pregnancy A condition in pregnant women in which poisons such as the body's own waste products build up and may cause harm to both the mother and baby. The first signs of toxemia are swelling near the eyes and ankles (edema), headache, high blood pressure, and weight gain that the mother might confuse with the normal weight gain of being pregnant. The mother may have both glucose (sugar) and acetone in her urine. The mother should tell the doctor about these signs at once.

Toxic dementia Dementia caused by exposure to toxic substances, such as alcohol (associated with over a dozen forms of brain disease), or chronic exposure to heavy metals.

Toxic Harmful; having to do with poison.

Toxicity The quality of being poisonous or the degree to which a substance is poisonous. Referring tomedical treatments, the degree to which they produce unwanted, adverse effects.

Toxicity testing The testing of substances for poisonousness to determine the severity of adverse effects or illness and to establish conditions for their safe use.

Toxicology The study of the harmful effects of chemical and physical agents on living systems.

Toxin A substance, produced in some types of microorganisms, that is toxic to other living organisms.

Toxocariasis Infection caused by Toxocara worms, which are typically found in cat and dog intestines. The form found in the eyes, ocular larva migrans, can cause vision loss.

Toxoplasmosis An infection caused by the Toxoplasma parasite, often from undercooked meat or contact with feces. It may occur in people with compromised immune systems. Symptoms are flu-like and can include swollen lymph nodes and muscle aches. Ocular toxoplasmosis causes inflammation of the eye's interior, leading to uveitis.

Trabecular meshwork The porous, spongy tissue within the drainage angle of the anterior chamber of the eye, through which the aqueous humor exits the eye.

Trachea The airway tube in the neck extending from the back of the mouth and nose to the bronchial tubes through which air is conveyed to the lungs. The trachea has an inner diameter of about 25 millimetres (1.0 in) and a length of about 10 to 16 centimetres (4 to 6 in). A flap-like epiglottis closes the opening to the larynx during swallowing to prevent swallowed matter from entering the trachea.

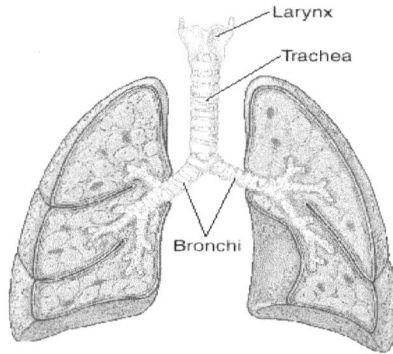

Fig. *Trachea*

Tracheotomy A surgical opening into the trachea through which an indwelling tube is inserted for attachment to a mechanical ventilator.

Trachoma Chronic infection of the eyelid and cornea caused by a microorganism that is spread by contact with eye discharge from an infected sufferer. Flies can also transmit the bacteria. Over time, the eyelid becomes scarred and turns inward. The eyelashes begin to scrape the eyeball and cornea, which eventually causes visual impairment and blindness. Worldwide, 84 million people are affected by trachoma. Clean water and good hygiene can prevent trachoma, while antibiotics can treat it early on. Inward-turning eyelids can be corrected with simple surgery performed by a nurse.

Trachoma A chronic, contagious disease of the eye caused by infection by the bacterium Clamvdia trachomatis. The disease is characterized by inflammatory granulations on the mucous membrane covering the inner surface of the eyelid and invading the cornea; if untreated, trachoma can lead to complications that cause blindness. Trachoma is a significant cause of blindness, particularly in hot, dry, areas.

Tracking The assigning of students to a particular curricular track, usually on the basis of estimated ability.

Trager bodywork Movement-education approach that gently rocks, cradles, and moves the client's body. Meant to promote relaxation, increase mobility and mental clarity. Used by athletes for performance enhancement and by people with musculoskeletal and back problems.

Trait A distinguishing feature; a characteristic or property of an individual.

Tranquilizer An agent that quiets, calms, and reduces anxiety and tension, with some alteration of the level of consciousness. Major tranquilizers include anti-psychosis drugs; minor tranquilizers include anti-anxiety drugs.

Transcription In genetics, the process by which RNA is formed from a DNA template during protein synthesis.

Transduction The process of genetic recombination by which DNA is transferred from one cell to another using a viral vector.

Transfer Act Legislation (42 USC sections 2001 et seq.) That transferred responsibility for Indian health care from the Bureau of Indian Affairs, in the Department of Interior, to the Public Health Service, in what is now the Department of Health and Human Services, creating the Indian Health Service in 1955.

Transfer RNA (tRNA) Any of 20 kinds of specialized RNA molecules that transfer the genetic code from messenger RNA to proteins by combining with a specific amino acid and bringing it to the ribosome where proteins are assembled.

Transferring A plasma protein essential for the transport of iron.

Transformation In genetics, the introduction and assimilation of DNA from one organism into another via uptake of naked DNA; in oncology, the process by which normal cells become malignant.

Transgenic animals Animals whose DNA has been altered by adding DNA from a another animal or a human, using recombinant DNA techniques.

Transient ischemic attack (TIA) Often called a "ministroke," a TIA is a short-lived blood clot-induced blockage of the blood supply to the brain. Vision may be blurred; other symptoms may include numbness on one side of the body, slurring of speech, dizziness and paralysis.

Transitional devices Devices that were regulated as new drugs before enactment of the 1976 Medical Device Amendments (Public Law 94-295). Such devices are automatically classified into Class Ill, which requires premarket approval, but maybe reclassified into Class I or Il.

Translation The process in which the genetic code contained in the nucleotide base sequence of messenger RNA directs the synthesis of a specific order of amino acids to produce a protein.

Transmissible dementia Dementia associated with diseases caused by unusual infectious agents. Examples are Creutzfeldt-Jakob disease, Gerstmann-Strassler syndrome, and kuru.

Transmission In infectious disease, the passage of a pathogen from one host to another host or from vector to host.

Transplantation With respect to human organs, the transplanting of a healthy organ (e.g., kidney, cornea, liver, skin, etc.) from one person to another (or from one body part to another) to replace a diseased organ or to restore functioning.

Transposable elements In genetics, a class of DNA molecules capable of being inserted into the chromosomes of the host organism at numerous positions, and of moving from one position to another. Speculation

on the origin of these molecules suggests that they may be derived from virus-like ancestors. They have been called "parasitic" DNA.

Transposase An enzyme involved in the movement of DNA segments from one site in the genome to another.

Transposon A gene or a group of genes that transfer genetic instructions (e.g., by spontaneously moving from one chromosome to another and from one position to another on the same chromosome).

Transurethral Through the urethra. Refers to treatment procedures that use instruments passed up the urinary tract, rather than through a surgical incision.

Trauma A wound, hurt, or injury to the body. Trauma can also be mental such as when a person feels great stress. Depending on the type of trauma, symptoms can include blurred vision, a bulging eye, burning, double vision, dry eyes, floaters, light sensitivity, pain or discomfort of the eye or around the eye, swelling, a pupil that is dilated or unresponsive to light, vision loss, limited eye or lid movement, ptosis, an iris defect and an eyelid cleft.

Traumatic brain injury Injury to the brain occurring as the result of impact.

Treatment IND A provision of the Federal Food, Drug and Cosmetic Act that allows patients with lifethreatening or serious diseases to obtain certain drugs that are in late stages of clinical testing, but have not yet been approved by FDA for marketing.

Treatment Interventions intended to cure or ameliorate the effects of a disease or condition once the condition has occurred.

Trematode Any of a group of parasitic flatworms, including the flukes, of the phylum Platyhelminthes. Schistosomes are important human trematode parasites.

Tribal trust land Lands held in trust for Indian tribes and administered for their benefit by the Federal Government.

Trichiasis Condition in which the eyelashes grow inwardly (towards the eye).

Trichotillomania Pathological hair pulling that results in noticeable hair loss. As in other impulse control disorders, an increasing sense of tension or affective arousal immediately precedes an episode of hair pulling, which is then followed by a sense of pleasure, gratification, or relief.

Trifocal A lens design that has three focal areas: a lens for close work or reading, a lens for mid-distance viewing or arm's length, and a lens for faraway viewing or driving.

Triglyceride A type of blood fat. The body needs insulin to remove this type of fat from the blood. When diabetes is under control and a person's weight is what it should be, the level of triglycerides in the blood is usually about what it should be.

Triplet In genetics, three consecutive nucleotide bases along a nucleic acid chain (DNA or RNA).

Trisomy The presence of an extra chromosome, resulting in three homologous chromosomes instead of two (e.g., Down syndrome can result from Trisomy 21, or the presence of an extra chromosome number 21 in each body ceil).

Troglitazone A drug formerly used as a treatment for Type 2 (noninsulin-dependent) diabetes; belongs to a class of drugs called thiazolidinediones. Withdrawn from the market in March, 2000 because of rare liver problems.

Trophic factor A chemical that promotes the growth of axons and the survival of neurons.

Trust responsibility The responsibility assumed by the Federal Government,

Trypanosoma A genus of slender, polymorphic, parasitic protozoans that cause trypanosomiasis.

Trypanosomiasis Any of several diseases caused by infection with species of the genus Trypanosoma. The important human diseases are African sleeping sickness (also called African trypanosomiasis) and Chagas' disease (also called American trypanosomiasis). African sleeping-sickness is caused by T. brucei rhodesiense in east Africa or T.b. gambiense in west Africa, both transmitted by the tsetse fly. Chagas' disease is caused by T. cruzi, transmitted by blood-sucking reduviid bugs.

Tsetse flies Tsetse are large biting flies that inhabit much of mid-continental Africa between the Sahara and the Kalahari deserts. They live by feeding on the blood of vertebrate animals and are the primary biological vectors of trypanosomes, which cause human sleeping sickness and animal trypanosomiasis, also known as nagana. Tsetse are crudely similar to other large flies, such as the housefly, but can be distinguished by various characteristics of their anatomy, two of which are easy to observe. Tsetse fold their wings completely when they are resting so that one wing rests directly on top of the other over their abdomen. Tsetse also have a long proboscis, which extends directly forward and is attached by a distinct bulb to the bottom of their head.

T-test: An estimate of the difference between the mean values of one parameter of two treatments. This test can be useful when the number of comparisons is small, but the potential for error increases with the number of parameters compared.

Tubal ligation The sterilization of a woman by tying and surgically dividing each Fallopian tube.

Tubercle bacillus A bacillus causing tuberculosis; usually refers to Mycobacterium tuberculosis, the principal cause of human tuberculosis.

Tuberculosis A chronic infectious disease of humans and animals caused by any of several species of mycobacteria. It usually begins with lesions in the lung, but can metastasize (spread) to other parts of the body.

Tumour marker assays Assays (e.g., immunoassay) that detect tumour-produced proteins.

Tumour A new growth of tissue in which the multiplication of cells is uncontrolled and progressive. Also called neoplasm.

T-wed testing A strategy for identifying the toxicological effects of a substance by proceeding from general toxicity tests to progressively more specific and sophisticated tests.

Twenty-four hour urine The total amount of a person's urine for a 24-hour period.

Type 1 diabetes mellitus Type 1 diabetes has been subdivided into:Immune-mediated diabetes (Type 1A). This form of diabetes results from a cellular-mediated autoimmune destruction of the beta cells of the pancreas. Markers of the immune destruction of the beta cell include islet cell autoantibodies and other antibodies. One and usually more of these auto-antibodies are present in 85 - 90% of individuals when fasting hyperglycemia is initially detected. Also, the disease has strong HLAassociations. Idiopathic diabetes (Type 1B). Some

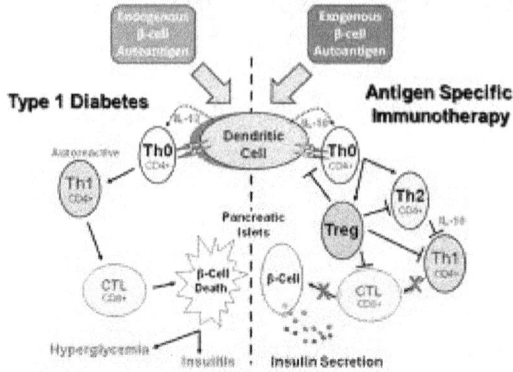

Fig. *Type 1 Diabetes mellitus*

forms of Type 1 diabetes have no known etiologies. Some of these patients have permanent insulin deficiency and are prone to ketoacidosis but have no evidence of autoimmunity. Although only a minority of patients with Type 1 diabetes fall into this category, of those who do, most are of African, Hispanic, or Asian origin. Individuals with this form of diabetes suffer from episodic ketoacidosis and exhibit varying degrees of insulin deficiency between episodes. This form of diabetes is strongly inherited, lacks immunological evidence for beta cell autoimmunity, and is not HLA associated. An absolute requirement for insulin replacement therapy in affected patients may come and go. Type 1 diabetes used to be known as insulin-dependent diabetes mellitus, juvenile diabetes, juvenile-onset diabetes, and ketosis-prone diabetes. Contrast with Type 2 Diabetes Mellitus.

Type 2 diabetes mellitus The most common form of diabetes mellitus; over 90 percent of people who have diabetes have Type 2 diabetes. The onset is usually in middle age and in most cases is thought to be due to some form of insensitivity to the action of insulin rather than to insulin deficiency. Many of the people who have this type of diabetes are overweight. Initial treatment is by weight reduction and excercise with the later addition of an increasing range of blood glucose lowering drugs. Ultimately it may be neccessary to give insulin. Increasingly, geneticists are defining specific subgroups such as maturity onset diabetes in the young; but to date, this has not led to any change in treatment plans. Type 2 diabetes used to be called noninsulin-dependent diabetes mellitus, adult-onset diabetes, maturity-onset diabetes, ketosis-resistant diabetes, and stable diabetes.

U

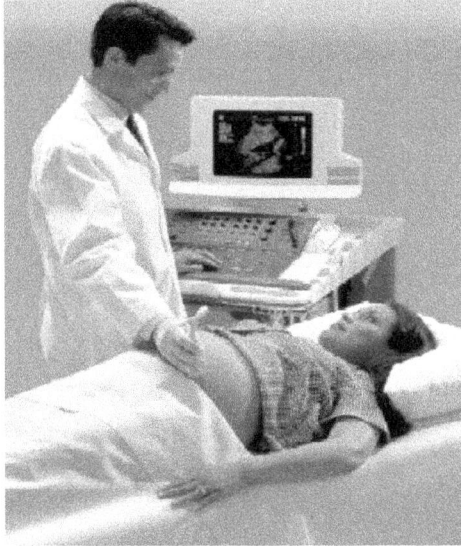

U-100 It is the most common concentration of insulin. U-100 means that there are 100 units of insulin per millilitre (ml) of liquid U-100. In the United States, insulin is labeled "U-100," which means there are 100 units of insulin per millilitre of fluid in the vial.

UB-82 The uniform billing form required by the Health Care Financing Administration for submitting and processing Medicare Claims. It merges billing information with diagnostic codes, including almost all the elements from the uniform hospital discharge data set.

Ulcer A break in the skin; a deep sore. People with diabetes may get ulcers from minor scrapes on the feet or legs, from cuts that heal slowly, or from the rubbing of shoes that do not fit well. Ulcers can become infected.

Ulcerated plaques Breaks in the yellowish plaque formed within the intima and inner media (innermost and middle coats of the blood vessels) of large and medium-sized veins.

Ulcerative colitis Ulcerative colitis is a disease that causes inflammation and sores, called ulcers, in the lining of the large intestine. The inflammation usually occurs in the rectum and lower part of the colon, but it may affect the entire colon. Ulcerative colitis rarely affects the small intestine except for the end section, called the terminal ileum. Ulcerative colitis may also be called colitis or proctitis.

It is an inflammatory bowel disease (IBD), the general name for diseases that cause inflammation in the small intestine and colon. Ulcerative colitis can be difficult to diagnose because its symptoms are similar to other intestinal disorders and to another type of IBD called Crohn's disease. Crohn's disease differs from ulcerative colitis because it causes inflammation deeper within the intestinal wall. Also, Crohn's disease usually occurs in the small intestine, although it can also occur in the mouth, esophagus, stomach, duodenum, large intestine, appendix, and anus.

Ulnar bone The longer of the two bones in the forearm. It is located in the bottom part of an arm.

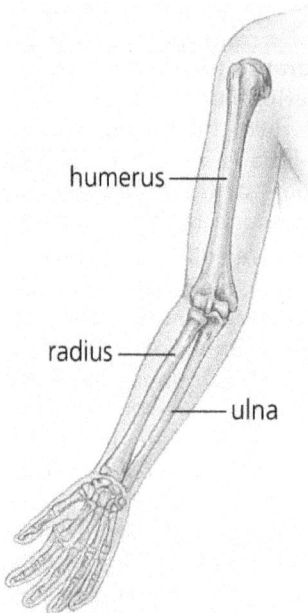

Fig. *Ulnar bone*

Ultrafast CT (computed tomography) Scan a type of radiology diagnostic procedure in which an x-ray beam moves in a circle around the body. This allows many different views of the same organ or structure, and provides much greater detail. The x-ray information is sent to a computer that interprets the x-ray data and displays it in 2-dimensional form on a monitor.

Ultralente insulin A type of insulin that is long acting. Ultralente insulin is a long acting form of insulin. It has an onset of 4 to 6 hours, a peak of 14 to 24 hours, and a duration of 28 to 36 hours

Ultrasound A diagnostic and imaging technique in which high-frequency sound waves are used to build a picture of internal organs or of a fetus. Ultrasound has many uses in obstetrics to view the uterus and fetus during pregnancy, and is also used in diagnostic radiology to detect abnormalities such as gallstones, heart defects, and tumours. Ultrasound is sent into the patient's body. Some of the ultrasound is reflected at each boundary between different tissues or organs.

The depth of each layer is calculated using the time taken for each reflected wave to return. The reflected waves (echoes) are usually processed to produce a picture of the inside of the body on a screen. The ultrasound waves used to image babies and soft tissue organs have small amplitude so are low energy. This makes it safer for the patient, as no damage is done to any living cells. See fig. on next page.

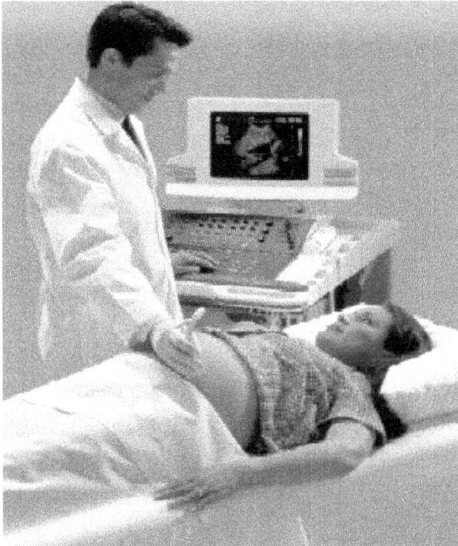

Fig. *Ultrasound*

Ultrasound technician Performs medical diagnosis using high frequency sound waves and imaging techniques to generate images of cross sections of organs. Works under the direction of a radiologist.

Ultraviolet radiation Invisible rays that come from the sun. UV radiation can damage the skin and cause melanoma and other types of skin cancer.

Ultraviolet (UV) The invisible part of the light spectrum whose rays have wavelengths shorter than the violet end of the visible spectrum and longer than X rays. UVA and UVB light are harmful to your eyes and skin.

Umbilical cord A rope-like cord connecting the fetus to the placenta. The umbilical cord contains two arteries and a vein, which carry oxygen and nutri-ents to the fetus and waste products away from the fetus.

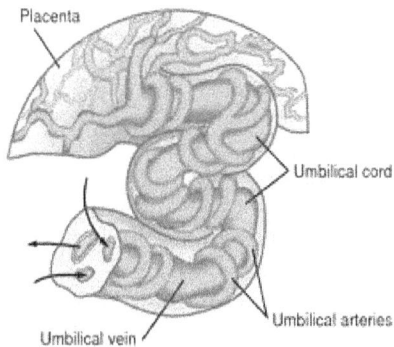

Fig. *Umbilical cord*

Umbilical hernia A weakness in the abdominal muscles. An acquired umbilical hernia directly results from increased intra-abdominal pressure caused by obesity, heavy lifting, a long history of coughing, or multiple pregnancies.

Unapproved drug A drug that has not been approved by the FDA for marketing in the United States.

Unassigned liability The difference, if any, between a physician's actual charge for a service on an unassigned claim and the Medicare approved charge for that service.

Unbundling Separating a service into its individual components and billing for each component separately. It is also refers to a trend in insurance benefits contracting where the purchaser unbundles or contracts separately for specific services.

Uncompensated care costs Deductions from patient care revenues that are attributable to charity care and bad debts (for which the health care facility never expects to receive payment).

Uncompensated care The charges for services rendered by providers which are not paid for by the recipient and for which there is usually no third-party coverage. Uncompensated care is usually either charity care or bad debt.

Unconventional cancer treatment A wide variety of treatments that fall outside the bounds of mainstream medicine. Other terms used by proponents of such treatments to describe all or some of these treatments include: alternative, complementary, non-toxic, holistic, natural, and non-invasive. Those used by the sharpest of critics include: unproven, question-

able, dubious, quackery, and fraudulent. The term unorthodox is used at times by both proponents and critics.

Undergraduate medical education The medical training provided to students in medical or osteopathy school.

Underinsured People with public or private insurance policies that do not cover all necessary medical services, resulting in out-of-pocket expenses that exceed their ability to pay.

Underwriting The process of examining and investigating an applicant for insurance to determine whether or not the insurance company is willing to provide insurance coverage and on what basis.

Uniform billing code of 1992 (UB-92) A revised version of the UB-92, a Federal directive requiring a hospital to follow specific billing procedures, itemizing all services included and billed for on each invoice, implemented October 1, 1993.

Uniform claim Form All insurers and self-insurers would be required to use a single claims form and standardized format for electronic claims.

Uniform health data act Amendment of this act ensures that discharge data currently required of hospitals resides with the state and can be publicly released without prior permission of the hospitals. In addition, the act calls upon the Delaware Health Care Commission to study the feasibility of broadening its scope to apply to other health care facilities, such as nursing homes and ambulatory surgical centres.

Uniform hospital discharge data set A defined set of data that gives a minimum description of a hospital discharge. It includes data on age, sex, race, residence of patient, length of stay, diagnosis, physicians, procedures, disposition of the patient and sources of payment.

Unilateral Affecting one side of the body. For example, unilateral kidney cancer occurs in one kidney only.

Uninsured People who lack health insurance.

Uninsured population An estimated 34 million Americans do not have health insurance. 56% are workers. 28% are children. 16.5% are non-working adults. 83% of workers have private health insurance.

Unit of Insulin The basic measure of insulin. U-100 insulin means 100 units of insulin per millilitre (mL) or cubic centimeter (cc) of solution. Most insulin made today in the United States is U-100.

Universal access Access to health insurance coverage for everyone.

Unprotected sexual intercourse Sexual intercourse without precautions taken to prevent pregnancy or the transmission of AIDS or sexually transmitted diseases.

Unsaturated fats A type of fat.

Unstable diabetes A type of diabetes when a person's blood glucose (sugar) level often swings quickly from high to low and from low to high. Also called "brittle diabetes" or "labile diabetes."

Unusually high-needs criteria Criteria specific to the type of HMSA (i.e., primary care, dental, psychiatric) that are indicative of an unusually high need for medical care (e.g., poverty rates, population without fluoridated water supply, and high prevalence of alcoholism).

Update factor DRG updating consists of an annual increase (or decrease) in all prices by an update factor that determines the overall generosity of the system. Inflation in the hospital sector and other factors not captured by inflation measures (known as the 'discretionary adjustment factor") are the two components of the update factor.

Upper brain The portion of the brain between the cerebral cortex and the brain stem.

Upper GI (gastrointestinal) Series (also called barium swallow) A diagnostic test that examines the organs of the upper part of the digestive system: the esophagus, stomach, and duodenum (the first section of the small intestine). A fluid called barium (a metallic, chemical, chalky, liquid used to coat the inside of organs so that they will show up on an x-ray) is swallowed. X-rays are then taken to evaluate the digestive organs.

Upper GI endoscopy Looking into the esophagus, stomach, and duodenum with an endoscope.

Upper respiratory tract infection An upper respiratory tract infection, or upper respiratory infection, is an infectious process of any of the components of the upper airway. The upper respiratory tract includes the sinuses, nasal passages, pharynx, and larynx. These structures direct the air we breath from the outside to the trachea and eventually to the lungs for respiration to take place.

Urban Indian programmes Programmes administered by urban Indian organizations and supported with Indian Health Service funds that operate health centres and help urban Indians gain access to other programmes for which they might qualify, such as Medicaid and other public assistance sources.

Urea breath test Test used to detect Helicobacter pylori infection. The test measures breath samples for urease, an enzyme H. pylori produces.

Urea One of the chief waste products of the body. When the body breaks down food, it uses what it needs and throws the rest away as waste. The kidneys flush the waste from the body in the form of urea, which is in the urine.

Uremia The presence of excessive amounts of urea and other waste products in the blood, an abnormality that occurs during renal failure.

Ureter One of the two tube-like structures that carry urine from the kidneys to the bladder.

Ureterocele The portion of the ureter closest to the bladder becomes enlarged because the ureter opening is very tiny and obstructs urine outflow; urine backs up in the ureter tube.

Ureterolithotomy The surgical removal of stones from the ureter.

Ureteroscope An optical device which is inserted into the urethra and passed up through the bladder to the ureter; to inspect the opening of the ureters.

Ureters two narrow tubes that carry urine from the kidneys to the bladder. The ureters tunnel through the wall of the bladder

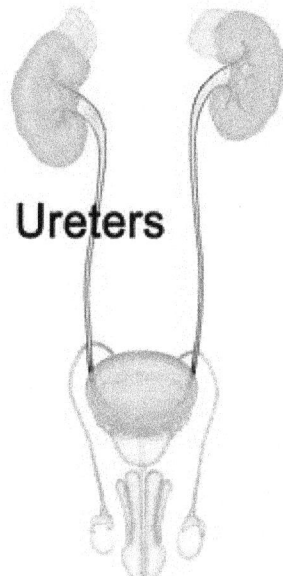

Fig. *Ureters*

at an angle to form a flap that acts as a valve. There is also a ring of muscle (sphincter) at the junction of the bladder and the urethra that stops urine leaking out in between pees. When peeing, the muscles of the bladder wall squeeze the urine out of the bladder, at the same time as the muscles in the sphincter need to relax to let the urine flow down the urethra. The valves between the ureters and bladder prevent urine flowing backwards into the ureters, so that all the urine in the bladder is passed in one go, as the urine cannot travel anywhere else. As the urine leaves the bladder at a high pressure, the valves stop this high pressure being passed on to the kidneys.

Urethra The tubular structure through which urine passes from the bladder out of the body; in males, also serves to transport semen. In females, the urethra is shorter and opens above the vaginal opening.

Urethritis Infection limited to the urethra.

Urge Incontinence the inability to hold urine long enough to reach a restroom.

Urgent care Centre or Unit

Urgent surgery An operation performed immediately as a result of an urgent medical condition.

Urinalysis Laboratory examination of urine for various cells and chemicals, such as red blood cells, white blood cells, infection, or excessive protein.

Urinalysis The loss of bladder control. A part of a urinalysis can be performed by using urine test strips, in which the test results can be read as colour changes. Another method is light microscopy of urine samples.

Urinary bladder The hollow, muscular organ that collects urine

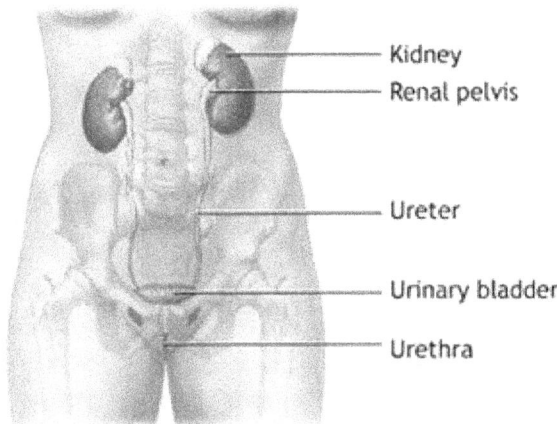

Kidney
Renal pelvis

Ureter

Urinary bladder

Urethra

Fig. *Urethra*

from the ureters and stores it until the urine is discharged through the urethra during urination.

Urinary incontinence An involuntary loss of urine sufficient in quantity and/or frequency to be a social or health problem. Also see incontinence for more information on the types of urinary incontinence.

Urinary retention The inability to empty the bladder.

Urinary tract infection (UTI) An infection that occurs in the urinary tract; often caused by bacteria such as Escherichia coli. A urinary tract infection often causes frequent urination, pain, and burning when urinating, and blood in the urine.

Urinary tract The organ system involved in the formation and excretion of urine; consists of the kidneys, ureters, bladder, and urethra.

Urine flow study A test in which the patient urinates into a special device that measures how quickly the urine is flowing. A reduced flow may suggest benign prostatic hyperplasia(BPH).

Urine testing Checking urine to see if it contains glucose (sugar) and ketones. Special strips of paper or tablets (called reagents) are put into a small amount of urine or urine plus water. Changes in the colour of the strip show the amount of glucose or ketones in the urine. Blood ketone testing can provide insight into the presence of ketones sooner than urine ketone testing.

Urodynamic testing Testing that pertains to the flow and motion of urine in the urinary tract.

Urogenital It refers to the urinary and reproductive systems.

Urologist A doctor who sees men and women for treatment of the urinary tract and men for treatment of the genital organs.

Urology The branch of medicine concerned with the urinary tract in both genders, and with the genital tract or reproductive system in the male.

Urticaria A condition in which red, itchy, and swollen areas appear on the skin - usually as an allergic reaction from eating certain foods or taking certain medications. It is also called *hives*.

Usher's syndrome A hereditary disease that affects hearing and vision.

Usual, customary, and reasonable charges In private health insurance, a basis for determining payment for individual physician services. This approach was developed in the early 1980s before the introduction of Medicare, and was adapted by Medicare as the model for CPR. 'Usualw refers to the individual physician's fee profile, equivalent to Medicare's "customary" charge screen. "Customary," in this context, refers to a percentile of the pattern of charges made by physicians in a given locality. "Reasonable" is the lesser of the usual or customary screens.

Uterine iavage A flushing of the uterus to recover a pre-implantation embryo.

Uterine prolapse Descension of the uterus down into the vagina, caused by weakening of the support ligaments and muscles that hold the uterus in place.

Uterine wall The wall of the uterus.

Uterus The uterus is a hollow, pear-shaped organ of the female reproductive system that is located in a woman's lower abdomen, between the bladder and the rectum. A "normal" uterus is typically the size and shape of an upside down pear and weighs somewhere around 6 ounces. Its dimensional size is about eight to ten centimeters by six centimeters (roughly 3-4 inches by 2 ½ inches).

Utilization and quality control peer review organizations (PROS) Organizations established by the Tax Equity and Fiscal Responsibility Act of 1982 (Public Law 97-248) with which the U.S. Department of Health and Human Services contracts to review the appropriateness of settings of care and the quality of care provided to Medicare beneficiaries.

Utilization management The process of evaluating the necessity, appropriateness and efficiency of health care services. A review coordinator gathers information about the proposed hospitalization service or procedure from the patient and/or provider then determines whether it meets established guidelines and criteria.

Utilization review Evaluation of the use of hospital services, including the appropriateness of the admission, length of stay and ancillary services. Review

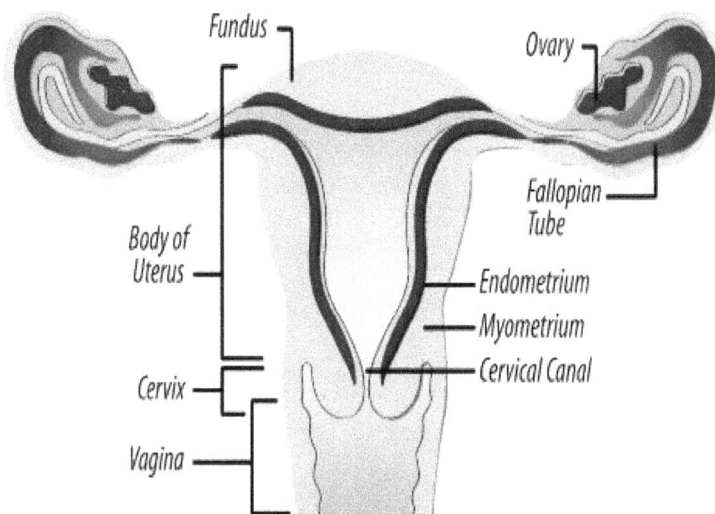

Fig. *Uterus*

may be conducted concurrently, retrospectively, or in combination. The process uses objective clinical criteria to ensure that the services are medically necessary and provided at the appropriate level of care. UR is conducted by the hospital for its own quality assurance and risk management system, using norms, criteria and standards adopted by its medical staff. Reports summarizing the findings and action taken as a result of the process are regularly provided to the hospital board.

Utilization The patterns of use of a service or type of service within a specified time, usually expressed in a rate per unit of population-at-risk for a given period (e.g., the number of hospital admissions per year per 1,000 persons in a geographic area).

Uvea Middle layer of the eye, below the limbus, and consisting of the iris, ciliary body and choroid.

Uveitis Inflammation of the uvea. In most cases, the cause is unknown, but infectious or immunological systemic disorders can cause uveitis. Symptoms vary depending on where in the uvea the inflammation occurs; they include mild to strong eye pain, redness, light sensitivity, blurred vision and floaters. You may also experience tearing, a pupil that responds poorly to light or squinting. Specific types of uveitis include iritis, iridocyclitis, cyclitis, pars planitis and choroiditis.

V

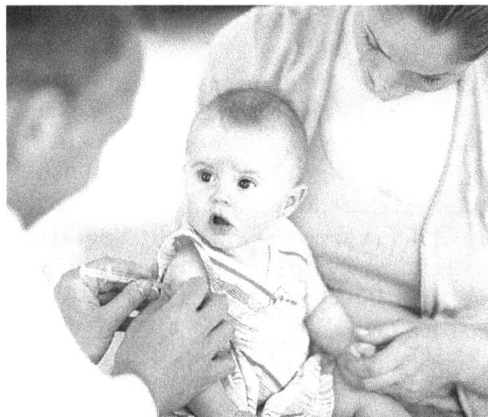

V

Vaccination The deliberate introduction of an antigenic substance (vaccine) into an individual, with the aim of producing active immunity to a disease.

Vaccine A preparation of living, attenuated, or killed bacteria or viruses, fractions thereof, or synthesized antigens identical or similar to those found in the disease-causing organisms, that is administered to produce or increase immunity to a particular disease.

Vaccinia virus The organism that causes cowpox; its injection into humans results in immunity to the related smallpox virus.

Vacuum aspiration Procedure in which a suction tube attached to a vacuum pump is inserted through the vagina into the uterus to loosen and remove its contents.

Vacuum extraction Procedure used to ease delivery by applying a metal or plastic cup to the baby's scalp and using suction to pull the baby gradually out of the vagina.

Vagina The part of the female genitals, behind the bladder and in front of the rectum, that forms

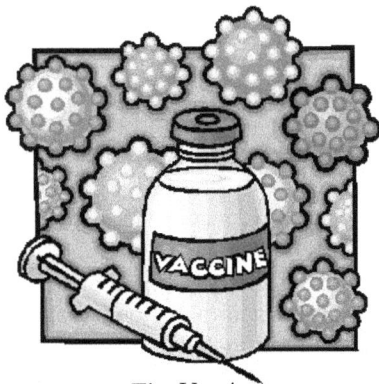

Fig. *Vaccine*

a canal extending from the uterus to the vulva.

Vaginal atrophy Often a symptom of menopause; the drying and thinning of the tissues of the vagina and urethra. This can lead to dyspareunia (pain during sexual intercourse) as well as vaginitis, cystitis, and urinary tract infections.

Vaginal hysterectomy The uterus is removed through the vaginal opening.

Vaginismus Painful, involuntary contraction or spasm of the muscles around the outer third of the vagina, interfering with sexual intercourse.

Vaginitis An infection of the vagina usually caused by a fungus. A woman with this condition may have itching or burning and may notice a discharge. Women who have diabetes may develop vaginitis more often than women who do not have diabetes.

Vaginitis, atrophic A form of noninfectious vaginitis which usually results from a decrease in hormones because of menopause, surgical removal of the ovaries, radiation therapy, or even after childbirth.

Vaginitis, Bacterial very common vaginal infection characterized by symptoms such as increased vaginal discharge or itching, burning, or redness in the genital area.

Vaginitis, noninfectious A type of vaginitis that usually refers to vaginal irritation without an infection being present. Most of-ten, the infection is caused by an allergic reaction to, or irritation from, vaginal sprays, douches, or spermicidal products. It may also be caused by sensitivity to perfumed soaps, detergents, or fabric softeners.

Vaginitis, Viral very common vaginal infection, often sexually transmitted, that is caused by one of many different types of viruses (i.e., herpes simplex virus, human papillomavirus).

Vagotomy Operation to cut the vagus nerve, which causes the stomach to produce less acid.

Vagus nerve Nerve that, in addition to other important functions, controls the production of stomach acid.

Valgus deformity A lateral inclination of a distal bone of a joint from the midline.

Validity A measure of the extent to which an observed situation reflects the "true" situation. Internal validity is a measure of the extent to which study results reflect the true relationship of a technology to the outcome of interest in the study subjects.

Values history document A document that expresses a person's wishes, values, and preferences with respect to his or her care.

Valve Fold in the lining of an organ that prevents fluid from flowing backward.

Valvuloplasty The repair of a heart valve using a balloon catheter inside the valve.

Varicella Chickenpox,

Varices Stretched veins, such as those that form in the esophagus from cirrhosis.

Varicocele An abnormal twisting or dilation of the veins surrounding the spermatic cord that carries blood from the testes back to the body; a varicose vein of the testis. It occurs more commonly in the left testis. Varicocele may result in a low sperm concentration in the semen and infertility in some cases.

Varicose veins Twisted, widened veins caused by swollen or enlarged blood vessels. The blood vessels have enlarged due a weakening in the vein's wall or valves.

Varus deformity A medial inclination of a distal bone of a joint from the midline.

Vas deferens The tubes leading to the testes. In males, the convoluted, narrow duct that carries and stores sperm from the testis and epididymis to the seminal vesicles.

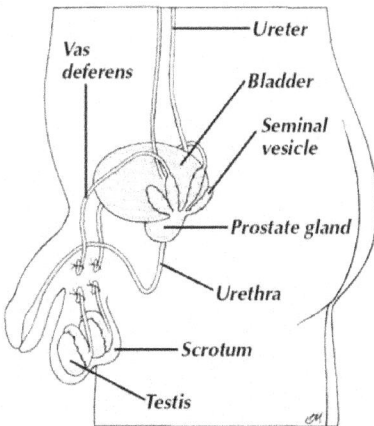

Fig. *Vas deferens*

Vascular Relating to the body's blood vessels (arteries, veins, and capillaries).

Vascular access site Pertaining to entry into the blood vessel system.

Vascular birthmark A pink, red or purple mark (flat or slightly raised), typically on an infant's face or neck, caused by a malformation of blood vessels. Types of vascular birthmarks include capillary hemangiomas ("stork bites" or "angel's kisses") and port-wine stains. Hemangiomas are a common vascular birthmark. Their cause is unknown. The colour results from the development of blood vessels at the site.

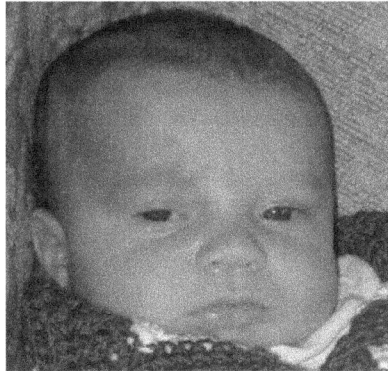

Fig. *Vascular birthmark*

Vascular dementia Dementia resulting from brain damages caused by cerebral infarction, or other diseases of disorder due to the blood vessels. Vascular dementia is the second largest cause of dementia in the United States.

Vascular problem Problems with your body's vascular system (i.e., blood vessels, arteries and so on) can include hardening of the arteries, high blood pressure, a clot, an aneurysm, an embolus, etc. These problems can sometimes affect the eyes, resulting in such symptoms as blurred vision, a bulging eye, double vision, eye pain or discomfort, a red orpink eye, eyelid swelling and vision loss.

Vasculitis Inflamed blood vessels.

Vasectomy A surgical procedure performed to make a man sterile, or unable to father a child. It is a permanent male birth control measure, and a means of contraception used in many parts of the world.

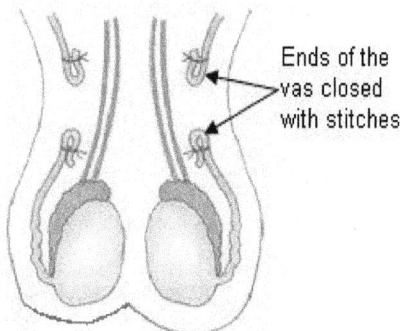

Ends of the vas closed with stitches

Fig. *Vasectomy*

Vasodilator A medication that dilates or widens the opening in a blood vessel.

Vasopressors A medication that raises blood pressure.

Vector bionomics The study of the habits (feeding, resting, and breeding) of vectors of disease and variations among different strains and in different locales.

Vector control technology A technology aimed at controlling vectors (that transmit disease) or other organisms (e.g., snails) that are not true vectors but serve as intermediate hosts of human or other animal disease organisms.

Vector In gene therapy, an agent such as a modified virus used to carry and transport genetic material that is then transferred into recipient cells in an organism.

It is a transmission agent—(i) a carrier of disease; usage commonly refers to arthropods (e.g., mosquitoes, sandflies, ticks) or rodents; (ii) in recombinant DNA technology, the DNA molecule used to introduce foreign DNA into host cells; vectors include plasmids, bacteriophages, and other forms of DNA.

Vector-borne disease A disease transmitted by an insect or other vector (e.g., malaria, trypanosomiasis, and arboviral infections).

Vein A blood vessel that carries blood from the body back into the heart.

Vein stripping Surgical removal of varicose veins;

Velocardiofacial syndrome Inherited disorder characterized by cleft palate, heart defects, characteristic facial appearance, minor learning problems, and speech and feeding problems.

Venipuncture Drawing blood with a needle from a vein usually in the forearm.

Ventilator A mechanical device that assists or replaces that natural mechanism for breathing.

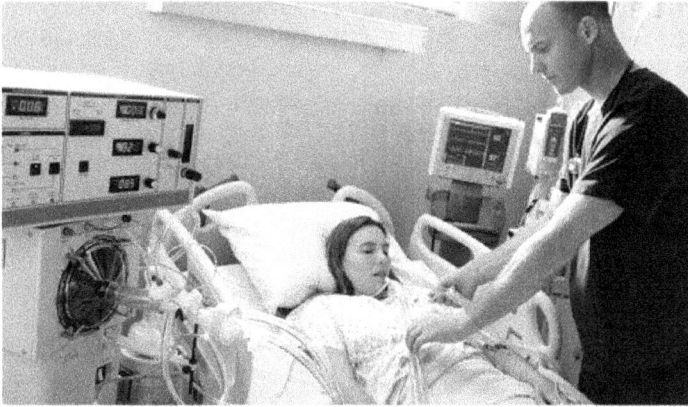

Fig. *Ventilator*

It is an automatic cycling device used to assist in or control respiration by delivering an appropriate volume of gas to the respiratory airways. Ventilators are classified according to the manner in which the air intake phase of the respiration cycle is ended-by reaching a predetermined volume of gases, by reaching a predetermined pressure, or by reaching a prescheduled time.

Ventilator dependent A person who must rely on a ventilator for survival, whether for a short time, or intermittent time but frequently, or constantly.

Ventricle A small cavity. Most commonly, the term is used to refer to the right and left ventricles of the heart. The left ventricle is the chamber from which blood is pumped to the aorta and then to the arteries (and therefore to the tissues of the body). The right ventricle is the chamber from which blood that has returned to the heart is pumped to the lungs to be oxygenated.

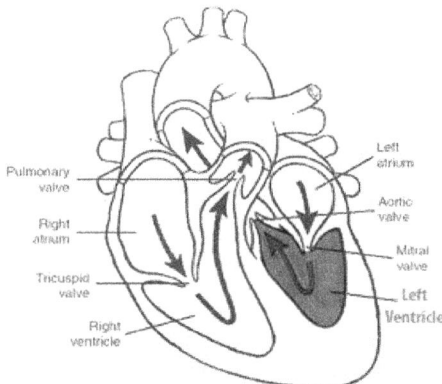

Fig. *Ventricle*

Ventricular angiogram A radiologic image of the ventricles of the heart obtained following the injection of a contrast dye.

Ventricular fibrillation A condition in which the ventricles contract in rapid and unsyn-chronized rhythms and cannot pump blood into the body.

Ventriculography Imaging of the ventricles of the heart.

Vergence disorder Vergence refers to the eyes' ability to turn either inward (convergence) or outward (divergence); convergence insufficiency is the most common vergence disorder. The disorders' exact causes are unknown. Symptoms include double vision, eyestrain, fatigue, headache, squinting and difficulty concentrating (particularly while reading).

Vernix caseosa A white substance that covers the skin of the fetus (while inside the uterus) and helps to protect the fetus. (also called vernix).

Vertebrae Bony structures that surround the spinal cord; also called the "back bone."

Vertical integration Consolidation or merger of organizations that provide different types of services in a hierarchical continuum such as a hospital acquiring a nursing home and a home health agency.

Vertical transfer The passage of genetic material from one organism to another through the germ line, (i.e., sexual mechanisms); in bacteria, through replication of genome and cell division.

Very low birthweight Birthweight of less than 1,500 grams (3 lb. 5 oz.).

Vesicoureteral reflux The abnormal flow of urine from the bladder back into the ureters; often as a result of a urinary tract infection or birth defect.

Vestibular neuronitis Infection at the vestibular nerve.

Vestibular system The vestibular and auditory senses are both part of the same organ – the inner ear. The purpose of the vestibular system is to check the position and motion of our head in space. There are two compo-

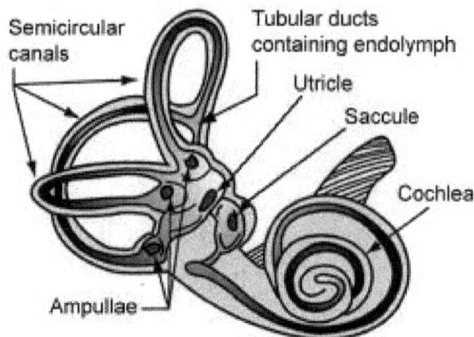

Semicircular canals
Tubular ducts containing endolymph
Utricle
Saccule
Cochlea
Ampullae

Fig. *Vestibular system*

nents, one detecting rotation through the three semicircular canals, the other detecting motion along a line through the utricle and saccule organs.

Vestibule Bony cavity of the inner ear.

Veterans administration A Federal agency responsible for veterans including VA hospitals and Veterans' benefits.

Vibrational healing Promotes healing by balancing the body's energy field. It can include acupuncture, homeopathy, flower essences, sound and colour healing, crystals, gems, aromatherapy, and energy-based bodywork (Reiki, Therapeutic Touch, Polarity Therapy).

Vibrio cholerae The bacterium that causes cholera.

Vibrotactile aids Mechanical instruments that help individuals who are deaf detect and interpret sound through the sense of touch.

Villi Tiny, fingerlike projections on the surface of the small intestine that help absorb nutrients.

Violent offenses According to the Federal Bureau of Investigation, serious violent offenses include murder and nonnegligent manslaughter, forcible rape, robbery, and aggravated assault. Minor violent offenses include assaults without weapons and weapons violations.

Viral hemorrhagic Fevers a term that refers to a group of illnesses caused by several distinct families of viruses. While some of these cause illnesses that are relatively mild, many cause severe, life-threatening diseases with no known cure, such as the Ebola virus.

Virology The study of viruses and the diseases they cause; also, the isolation and identification of viruses associated with specific infection.

Virulence The degree and severity of infection caused by a pathogen.

Virus Any of a large group of submicroscopic agents infecting plants, animals, and bacteria and characterized by a total dependence on living cells for reproduction and by a lack of independent metabolism. A fully formed virus consists of nucleic acid (DNA or RNA) surrounded by a protein or protein and lipid coat.

Visiting nurse A registered nurse who provides nursing care to an individual at home.

Visual acuity Sharpness of vision, usually as measured with the use of a Snellen eye chart. 20/20 is considered normal visual acuity, though some people can see even better (such as 20/15 or 20/10).

Visualization The use of mental imagery to create positive beliefs that will activate the body's defences against disease. In one type of visualization, patients are taught to see their cancer cells as vulnerable and disorganized, and their treatment as powerful and directed only at the cancer cells, sparing the healthy cells. They are also instructed to see their immune systems flushing away the cancer cells.

Vitiligo Smooth, white patches in the skin caused by the loss of pigment-producing cells.

Vitrectomy An operation to remove the blood that sometimes collects at the back of the eyes when a person has eye disease.

Vitrectomy Removing the gel from the centre of the eyeball because it has blood and scar tissue in it that blocks sight. An eye surgeon replaces the clouded gel with a clear fluid.

Vitrector Tiny, motorized cutting instrument used to remove the eye's gel-like vitreousduring a vitrectomy.

Vitreous body Part of the eye between the lens and the retina, containing a clear jelly called the vitreous humor.

Vitreous detachment Separation of the vitreous from the retina, caused by age-related vitreous shrinkage. Floaters are the typical symptom, but some people experience flashes of light as the vitreous tugs or causes traction on the retina prior to complete separation.

Vitreous hemorrhage Bleeding that goes into the vitreous from nearby parts of the eye, such as from leaking retinal blood vessels. Causes include diabetic retinopathy, trauma, a retinal tear or detachment, vitreous detachment and retinal vascular occlusion (blockage in the retina's vascular system). Symptoms include sudden

blurring or loss of vision, and new floaters.

Vitreous humor The vitreous is a water-based viscous jelly-like substance that fills the middle of the eye. It is transparent and also helps to keep the structure of the eye.

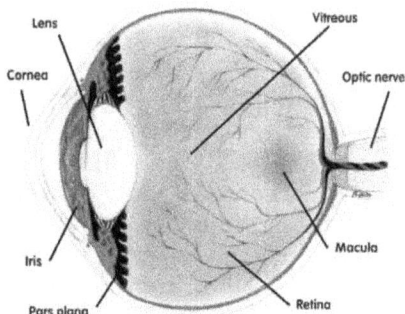

Fig. *Vitreous humor*

Vocal cords Muscularized folds of mucous membrane that extend from the larynx (voice box) wall; enclosed in elastic vocal ligament and muscle that control the tension and rate of vibration of the cords as air passes through them.

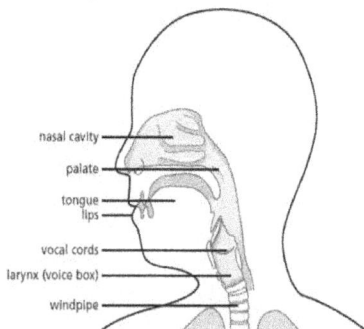

Fig. *Vocal cords*

Vocal cord paralysis Inability of one or both vocal folds (vocal cords) to move because of damage to the brain or nerves.

Vocal tremor Trembling or shaking of one or more of the muscles of the larynx resulting in an unsteady-sounding voice.

Vocational rehabilitation A programme of services designed to enable people with disabilities to become or remain employed. Originally mandated by the Rehabilitation Act of 1973, VR programmes are carried out by individually created state agencies. In order to be eligible for VR, a person must have a physical or mental disability that results in a substantial handicap to employment.

Voice disorders Normal pitch, loudness, or quality of the sound produced by the larynx (voice box).

Voice Sound produced by air passing out through the larynx and upper respiratory tract.

Void To empty the bladder in order to obtain a urine sample for testing.

Volume performance standard A mechanism to adjust Medicare physician fee updates based on how annual increases in actual Part B expenditures compare to previously predicted rates of increase.

Voluntary protection programmes (OSHA) Occupational Safety and Health Administration (OSHA) programmes designed to recognize the achievements of employers and to provide additional opportunities for OSHA-employer consultation and cooperation. The three programmes are called "Star," "Try," and "Praise."

Voluntary standards Product design specifications, product and worker safety standards, and so forth, developed by companies, trade associations, and professional organizations, but which do not have the force of law.

Volvulus Twisting of the stomach or large intestine.

Vomiting The release of stomach contents through the mouth; also known as throwing-up.

Vulva External, visible part of the female genital area.

Vulvitis An inflammation of the vulva, the soft folds of skin outside the vagina. This is not a condition but rather a symptom that results from a host of diseases, infections, injuries, allergies, and other irritants.

W

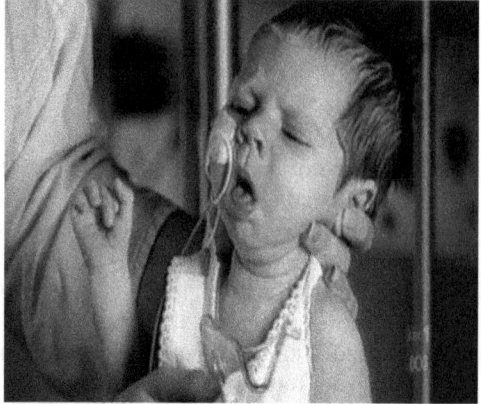

W chromosome The pair of chromosomes responsible for sex determination. In humans and most animals, the sex chromosomes are designated X and Y; females have two X chromosomes, males have one X and one Y chromosome In certain birds, insects, and fish the sex chromosomes are designated Z and W; males have two Z chromosomes, females may have one Z and one W chromosome, or one Z and no W chromosome.

Waardenburg syndrome Hereditary deafness that is characterized by hearing impairment, a white shock of hair, and/or distinctive blue colour to one or both eyes, as well as wide-set inner corners of the eyes; balance problems are also associated with some types of Waardenburg syndrome.

Wada test Unilateral internal carotid injection of amobarbital to determine the laterality of speech; injection on the dominant side causes transient aphasia or mutism; used prior to surgical treatment of epilepsy.

Waiting mode The waiting mode of health service delivery is characterized most strongly by professionals physically remaining within a service system and, indeed, waiting for clients, generally with chronic problems, to come to them. The waiting mode is distinguished from the "seeking mode" wherein professionals are usually physically operating outside the service system and seeking to intervene in problems before they become chronic. In practice, it is acknowledged that waiting/seeking is best thought of as a continuum, and less as a dichotomy.

Waiting period In some health insurance policies, a period during which no benefits are paid immediately after the policy goes into effect. Sometimes used incorrectly as a synonym for an insurance policy's elimination period.

Waiver of premium Any provision included within or as a rider to an insurance policy providing that, when specified conditions exist, the policy will continue in force without further premium payment. When the specified conditions no longer exist, the insured person resumes paying premiums.

Waldeyer sheath The tubular space between the bladder wall and the intramural portion of the ureter as it courses obliquely through this structure; actually a space and not a true sheath.

Wallet stomach A form of dilated stomach in which there is a general baglike distention, the antrum and fundus being indistinguishable.

Walsh-Healey Public Contracts Act A 1936 Federal law that directed the Department of Labor to issue requirements for safe work by Federal Government contractors and to "blacklist" contractors who did not comply with these requirements.

Wart A non-cancerous skin growth caused by a virus.

Watchful waiting Active surveillance (watchful waiting) is a good treatment choice for men who have prostate cancer that is low-risk and not likely to spread (early stage).

Water-borne disease A disease transmitted through contaminated water. Most diarrheal diseases can be water-borne.

Watermelon stomach Parallel red sores in the stomach that look like the stripes on a watermelon.

Wavefront Describes technology used to "map" how the eye processes images, enabling correction through surgery or lenses for obscure vision errors.

Wax A clear wax used to prevent your braces from irritating your lips when your braces are first put on, or at other times.

Wax bite A procedure to measure how well your teeth come together. You bite a sheet of wax and leave bitemark in the wax. The orthodontist looks at the bitemarks to see how well your teeth are aligned.

Weakness (i) Lack of strength or potency. (ii) Inability to perform normally.

Wear schedule How long you wear your contact lenses: either daily wear (you remove the lenses each night) or extended wear (you may sleep with them in). It's important to differentiate between wear schedule and replacement schedule - that is, how often you discard and replace your lenses.

Webbed fingers Two or more fingers united and enclosed in a common sheath of skin.

Webbed neck A neck that appears to be unusually broad because of bilateral folds of skin extending from the clavicles to the head but containing no muscles, bones, or other structures; occurs in Turner syndrome and Noonan syndrome.

Webbed penis Deficient ventral skin of the body of penis buried in the scrotum or tethered to the scrotal midline by a fold or web of skin. The urethra and erectile bodies are usually normal.

Wedge Resection of the lung a small, localized section of the lung is removed - often for a lung biopsy.

Well-baby care Services provided in the first year of a newborn's life to identify, treat and prevent health care problems.

Well-child care Periodic health supervision for children, including immunization, physical examinations and other tests that screen for illness or developmental problems, health education, and parental guidance.

Wellness A type of preventive medicine associated with an individual's lifestyle which, through a combination of exercise and diet, can reduce health care utilization and costs.

Wernicke-Korsakoff encephalopathy An acute brain disorder seen in association with chronic alcohol dependence (but can also accompany other conditions); caused by a dietary deficiency in addition to an inherited abnormality of thiamine (vitamin B1) metabolism. The disorder is characterized by encephalopathy and psychosis, and is treatable by thiamine supplementation.

Western blot A laboratory technique used to detect the presence of antibodies to specific antigens. The method is often used to check the validity of the ELISA test. Electrophoresis is used to separate proteins by their molecular weights, and each protein is identified through combining with its respective antibody or antigen. For example, in Western blot testing for HIV antibodies, the protein components of HIV are first separated electrophoretically, transferred to blots, then mixed with sera suspected of containing HIV antibodies. The presence of antibodies to specific proteins of HIV is revealed by the combination of antibodies with their specific protein components of HIV.

Wet cup A cupping glass applied to a part previously scarified or incised to draw and remove blood.

Wet dream A true physiologic orgasm during sleep including, in males, a nocturnal seminal emission usually accompanying a dream with sexual content.

Wet nurse A woman who is engaged to breast-feed another woman's infant.

Wet shock Severe hypoglycemia produced by administration of insulin, manifested by sweating, tremor, anxiety, vertigo, and diplopia, followed by delirium, convulsions, and collapse.

White dot syndrome One of a group of inflammatory conditions that are characterized by white dots in the retina and choroid. You may also hear these syndromes called by their specific names, such as acute posterior multifocal placoid pigment epitheliopathy, multiple evanescent white dot syndrome, birdshot chorioretinopathy or multifocal choroiditis and panuveitis. In some cases, the cause is unknown; in others, it's believed to be an autoimmune disorder. Symptoms can include blurred vision, loss of colour vision, floaters, light sensitivity, metamorphopsia and vision loss.

White matter Nerve tissue that is paler in colour than gray matter because it contains nerve fibres with large amounts of insulating material (myelin). The white matter does not contain nerve cells. In the brain, the white matter lies within the gray layer of the cerebral cortex.

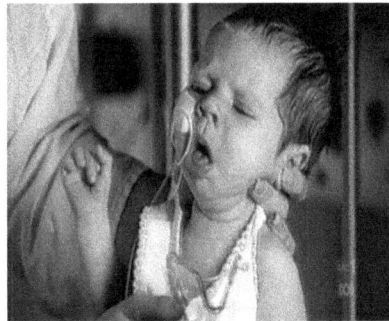

DORSAL ROOT (SENSORY FIBERS ENTER CORD)
DORSAL (BACK)
Grey Matter
(Cell bodies, synapses, dendrites, axon terminals)
White Matter
(Axons [=nerve fibers])
VENTRAL (FRONT)
VENTRAL ROOT (MOTOR FIBERS LEAVE CORD)

Fig. *White matter*

Whole blood Blood containing all its components, such as red and white blood cells, platelets and more.

Whole blood Blood from which none of the elements have been removed; used for transfusion.

Whooping cough It is an infection of the respiratory system caused by the bacterium Bordetella pertussis (or B. pertussis). It's characterized by severe coughing spells, which can sometimes end in a "whooping" sound when the person breathes in. It mainly affects infants younger than 6 months old before they're adequately protected by immunizations, and kids 11 to 18 years old whose immunity has started to fade.

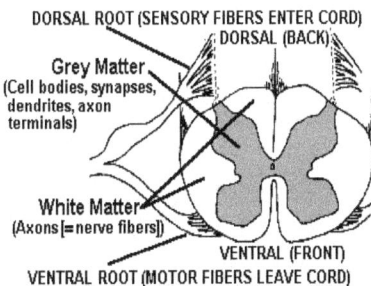

Fig. *Whooping cough*

The first symptoms of whooping cough are similar to those of a common cold, runny nose, sneezing, mild cough, low-grade fever.

Wild-type In genetics, the most frequently encountered phenotype in natural breeding populations.

Wilson disease Wilson's disease is an inherited condition in which copper is not excreted properly from the body. The excess copper can build up in the liver and/or brain causing liver damage and/or neurological problems. It can also collect in other parts of the body including the eyes and the kidneys.Copper begins to accumulate immediately after birth but the symptoms usually appear in the 2nd to 3rd decade. The first signs are hepatic (liver) in about 40% of cases, neurological (brain) in about 35% of cases and psychiatric, renal (kidney), haematological (blood), or endocrine (glands) in the remainder.

Treatment includes dietary restriction of copper and the administration of copper-binding drugs that allow it to be excreted from the body.

Withdrawal symptoms Symptoms associated with abstinence from a drug on which a patient is physically dependent.

Withhold fund The portion of the monthly capitation payment to physicians withheld by the managed care plan until the end of the year or other time period to create an incentive for efficient care. If the physician exceeds utilization norms for other members of his group or geographic region, he or she loses the fund or part of it. The principal of the withhold fund may be applied to hospital services, specialty referrals, laboratory usage, etc.

Wolff-Parkinson White syndrome An extra electrical pathway that connects the atria and ventricles and causes rapid heartbeat.

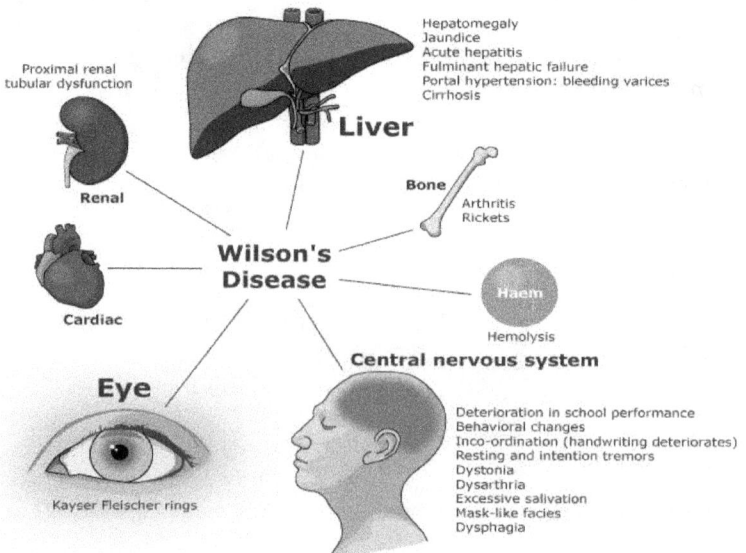

Fig. *Wilson disease*

Wolfram syndrome A syndrome comprising diabetes insipidus, a mild form of diabetes mellitus, optic atrophy, and deafness. It is an autosomal recessive inherited disorder, with the chromosomal abnormality on the short arm of chromosome 4. Also called DIDMOAD, for diabetes insipidus, diabetes mellitus, optic atrophy and deafness.

Work practice controls Methods of controlling hazards that involve only changes in job procedures and housekeeping.

Worker's compensation State-required insurance programmes that pay for medical costs and replace a portion of employees' wages lost due to work-related injury and illness.

Work-up The total patient evaluation, which may include laboratory assessments, radiologic series, medical history, and diagnostic procedures.

Wraparound Also called "wrap" for short. Type of eyeglass or sunglass frame that curves around the head, from the front to the side. Wraparound sunglasses offer extra sun and wind protection at the sides. Most cannot accept prescription lenses, because the curvature causes optical distortion. However, some of the newer styles have been engineered to overcome this problem.

Wraparound services A term used to denote a philosophy or practice of flexibly providing and funding mental health services that are designed to meet the unique needs of a particular adolescent, rather than (or in addition to) providing specified funding for particular settings or types of services (e.g., hospitals). The service package is developed by the child or adolescent's case manager and is purchased from vendors; when a service for a given child or adolescent is not available from an existing organization, funds are used to develop the service (e.g., flying in a consultant to treat a patient with schizophrenia rather than moving the patient to a hospital in another State).

X

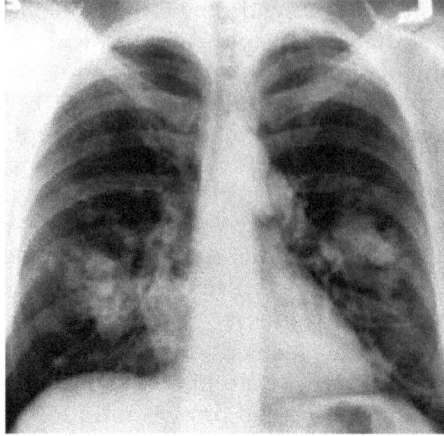

X

X disease One of several viral diseases of obscure etiology.

Xanthelasma A yellow, fatty spot or bump on the inner corner of either the upper eyelid, the lower one or both eyelids, often caused by a lipid disorder such as high cholesterol.

Xanthelasma palpebrarum Soft, yellow-orange plaques on the eyelids or medial canthus, the most common form of xanthoma; may be associated with low-density lipoproteins, especially in younger adults.

Xenobiotics Pertaining to organic substances that are foreign to the body, such as drugs or poisons.

Xenodiagnosis A technique in which an intermediate host or vector is used to diagnose the presence of parasites in humans (e.g., reduviid bugs are permitted to feed on someone suspected of having Chagas' disease, and later, the bugs are examined for the presence of Trypanosoma cruzi parasites).

Xenograft Living tissue transplanted from one species to another (e.g., animal organs transplanted into human beings).

X-linked gene A gene located on an X chromosome.

X-linked inheritance The pattern of inheritance that may result from a mutant gene on an X chromosome.

X-linked mutation A mutation that occurs on the X-chromosome.

X-linked A term used to refer to traits found on the X chromosome. X-linked recessive traits are seen far more often in males, who have only one X chromosome, than in females, who have two.

X-pattern esotropia Decreasing convergence from the primary position in both upward and downward gaze.

X-radiation Radiant energy from an x-ray tube.

X-ray Technician Performs in a technical position taking x-rays of patients upon the request of a physician. Prepares and administers barium and other medical preparations to assure x-ray pictures on specific tests. Assists physicians in performing special procedures.

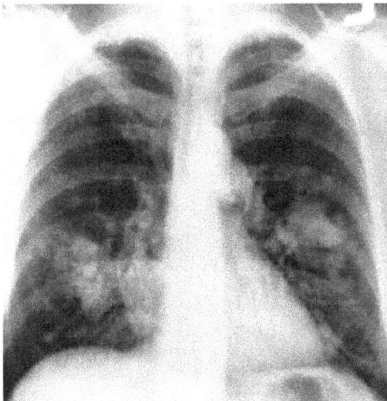

Fig. *X-ray*

Xylitol A sweetener found in plants and used as a substitute for sugar; it is called a nutritive sweetener because it provides calories, just like sugar.

Xylose test A laboratory aid in diagnosing alimentary or essential pentosuria, conditions in which xylose (a pentose) is excreted; the xylose may be identified by rapid reduction of Benedict solution, by nonfermentation by yeasts, or by a positive Bial test for pentose.

XYY syndrome A chromosomal anomaly with chromosome count 47, with a supernumerary Y chromosome; may be associated with tallness, increased physical activity, and a tendency to learning problems.

Y y

Yawn (i) To gape. (ii) An involuntary opening of the mouth, usually accompanied by inspiration; it may be a sign of drowsiness or of vital depression, as after hemorrhage, but is often caused by suggestion.

Yaws An infectious tropical disease caused by Treponema pertenue and characterized by the development of crusted granulomatous ulcers on the extremities; may involve bone, but, unlike syphilis, does not produce central nervous system or cardiovascular pathology.

Yellow bone marrow Bone marrow in which the stroma of the reticular network are largely filled primarily with fat; it replaces red marrow in the long bones after the fifth year of life.

Yellow cartilage Cartilage in which the cells are surrounded by a territorial (capsular) matrix outside of which is an interterritorial matrix containing elastic fibre networks in addition to type II collagen fibres and ground substance.

Yellow fever An acute febrile disease caused by an arbovirus that is transmitted by mosquitoes. Symptoms include a high fever, jaundice, black vomit, and anuria (absence of urine excretion). The virus that causes jungle/sylvan yellow fever is maintained in monkey reservoir hosts; urban yellow fever refers to transmission of the same virus to humans.

Yield ratio Ratio of profit to overall gross income for a given service, insurance product or other business venture.

Yin and Yang Chinese words for complementary and opposite

505

forces that make up the life force (Qi).

Y-linked inheritance The pattern of inheritance that may result from a mutant gene located on a Y chromosome.

Yoga Indian word for "union." Yoga is a posturing and breathing technique to induce relaxation.

Yoga therapy Emerging field of practices that use yoga to address mental and physical problems while integrating body & mind. Practitioners work one-on-one or in a group setting.

Younger adolescents As defined in most studies and data analyses, adolescents ages 10 to 14.

Fig. *Yoga*

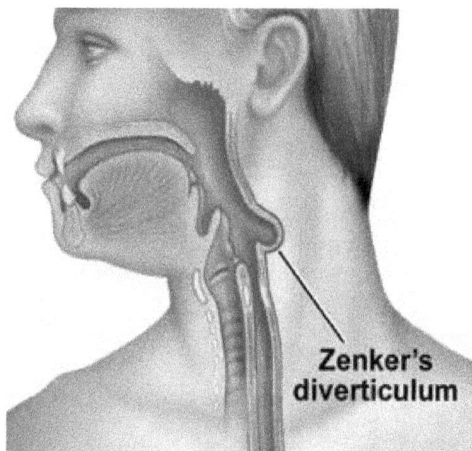

Z

Zenker's
diverticulum

Z

Z filament The thin zig-zag structure at the Z line of striated muscle fibres to which the actin filaments attach.

Z line Muscle fibres are multinucleated, with the nuclei located just under the plasma membrane. Most of the cell is occupied by striated, thread-like myofibrils. Within each myofibril there are dense Z lines. A sarcomere (or muscle functional unit) extends from Z line to Z line. Each sarcomere has thick and thin filaments. The thick filaments are made of myosin and occupy the centre of each sarcomere. Thin filaments are made of actin and anchor to the Z line.

Zeaxanthin A pigmented substance (carotenoid) found in yellow or orange plants, such as corn and squash, or in dark

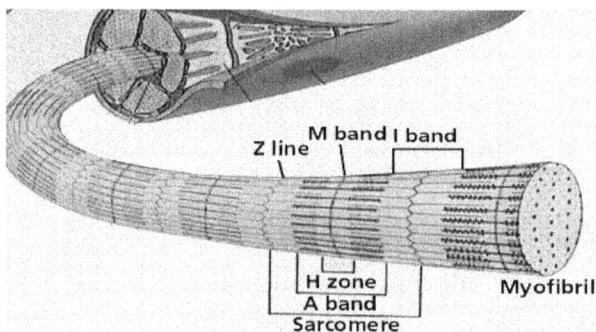

Fig. *Z line*

green, leafy vegetables. Zeaxanthin is being investigated for a possible association with promoting healthy vision.

Zenker diverticulum Pouches in the esophagus from increased pressure in and around the esophagus.

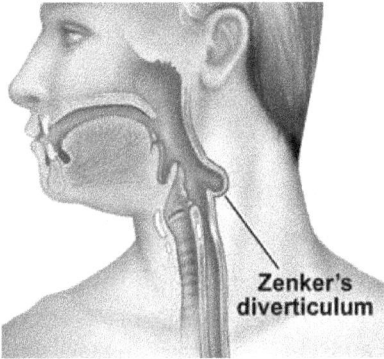

1. the corona radiata
2. the zona pellucida
3. the perivitelline space
4. the vitelline membrane

Fig. *Zona pellucida*

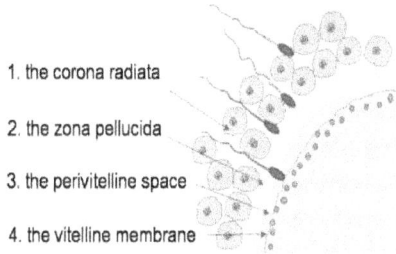

Zenker's diverticulum

Zero balancing Method for aligning body structure and body energy. Through touch akin to acupressure, practitioner seeks to overcome imbalances in the body's structure/energetic interface, which is said to exist beneath the level of conscious awareness. Zero Balancing is often used for stress reduction.

Zonula occluden cell Cell Junctions that seal adjacent Epithelial Cells together, preventing the passage of most dissolved molecules from one side of the epithelial sheet to the other.

Zona pellucida An extracellular coat, rich in glycoprotein, surrounding the oocyte; it contains microvilli of the oocyte and cellular processes of follicular cells and appears homogeneous and

translucent under the light microscope.

Zona striata The thickened cell membrane of the oocyte in forms, such as certain amphibians, in which it appears radially striated under the light microscope; with the electron microscope the striations can be seen to be microvilli.

Zona vasculosa An area in the external acoustic meatus where a number of minute blood vessels enter from the mastoid bone.

Zone therapy Another name for reflexology.

Zonography Tomography using x-ray transmission.

Zoology The study of animals - their morphology, growth, distribution, classification, and behaviour.

Zoonosis A disease primarily of animals that is transmissible to humans under natural conditions.

Zygomatic arch The arch formed by the temporal process of the zygomatic bone that joins the zygomatic process of the temporal bone.

Zygote A zygote is the initial cell formed when a new organism

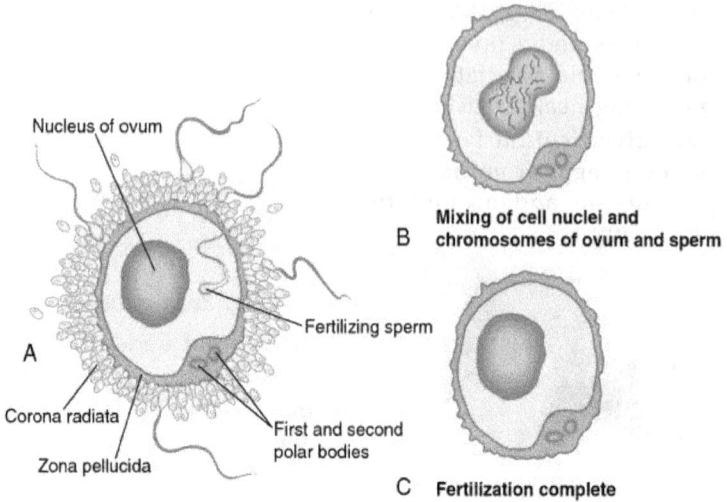

Fig. *Zygote*

is produced by means of sexual reproduction. A zygote is synthesized from the union of two gametes, and constitutes the first stage in a unique organism's development. Zygotes are usually produced by a fertilization event between two haploid cells - an ovum from a female and a sperm cell from a male - which combine to form the single diploid cell. Such zygotes contain DNA derived from both the mother and the father, and this provides all the genetic information necessary to form a new individual. The term zygote is also used more loosely to refer to the group of cells formed by the first few cell divisions, although this is properly referred to as a morula.

Zygote intrafallopian transfer A technique in assisted reproduction (Reproductive Techniques, Assisted) consisting of hormonal stimulation of the ovaries, follicular aspiration of pre-ovulatory oocytes, in-vitro fertilization, and intrafallopian transfer of zygotes at the pronuclear stage (before cleavage).

zyl Zylonite, or cellulose acetate, is a lightweight plastic often used in eyeglass frames. It often appears in laminated form, with layers in different colours, but it can also be made in mottled patterns to imitate natural tortoise shell or animal skins.

Zymogen The precursor of an enzyme, requiring some change (usually the hydrolysis of an inhibiting fragment that masks an active grouping) to render it active; pepsinogen, trypsinogen, profibrolysin.

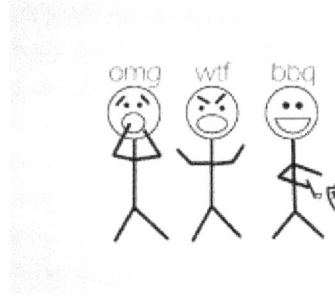

Glossary of abbreviation

A

ABG arterial blood gases

ac before meals

ACE angiotensin converting enzyme

ACL anterior cruciate ligament

ACTH adrenocorticotropic hormone

ADA American Diabetes Association

ADH antidiuretic hormone

ADL activities of daily living

AFB acid-fast bacilli

AFP alpha-fetoprotein

AGA appropriate for gestational age

AIDS acquired immune deficiency syndrome

AKA above knee amputation

ALP alkaline phosphatase

ALT alanine transaminase, alanine aminotransferase

AMA against medical advice

AMI acute myocardial infarction

AODM adult onset diabetes mellitus

AP apical pulse

APSGN acute poststrep-to-coccal glomerulonephritis

ARF acute renal failure

ASD atrial septal defect

AST aspartate amino-trans-ferase

ATN acute tubular necrosis

AU both ears

AVB atrio-ventricular block

B

BBS bilateral breath sounds

BE barium enema

BG blood glucose

BI brain injury

BID twice a day

B/K below knee

BM bowel movement or breast milk

BP blood pressure
BPH benign prostatic hypertrophy
BRM biologic response modifiers
BRP bathroom privileges
BS bowel sounds
BSA body surface area
BSE breast self examination
BT bowel tones
BUN blood urea nitrogen

C

C&S culture and sensitivity
Ca calcium, cancer, carcinoma
CABG coronary artery bypass graft
CAD coronary artery disease
CAPD continuous ambulatory peritoneal dialysis
CAT computerized tomo-graphy scan
CBC complete blood count
CBD common bile duct
CBE clinical breast examination
CBG capillary blood glucose
CBI continuous bladder irrigation
CBS capillary blood sugar
CC chief complaint
CCK cholecystokinin
CCPD continuous cyclic peritoneal dialysis
CEA cultured epithelial autograft
CFT complement-fixation test
CIN cervical intraepithelial neoplasm
CL cleft lip
CMS circulation, motion, sensation
CO cardiac output
COPD chronic obstructive pulmonary disease

CP chest pain, cleft palate
CPAP continuous positive airway pressure
CPD cephalo-pelvic disproportion
CPP cerebral perfusion pressure
CPPD chest percussion and post drainage
CRF chronic renal failure
CRRT continuous renal replacement therapy
CRT capillary refill time
CSF cerebrospinal fluid, colony stimulating factors
CT chest tube, computed tomography
CVA cerebral vascular accident, costovertebral angle
CVP central venous pressure
Cx cervix
CXR chest x-ray

D

DAT diet as tolerated
DC (dc) discontinue
DCCT Diabetes Control and Complication Trials
DEX (DXT) blood sugar
DIC disseminated intra-vascular coagulation
DKA diabetic ketoacidosis
DNA deoxyribonucleic acid
DNR do not resuscitate
DTR deep tendon reflex
DVT deep vein thrombosis
Dx diagnosis

E

EBV Epstein-Barr Virus
ECF extracellular fluid, extended care facility
EENT eye, ear, nose and throat
EMC ensephalomyocarditis

EMG electromyogram

ERCP endoscopic retrograde cholangiopancreatography

ESRD end stage renal disease

ET endotracheal tube

F

F & R force and rhythm

FA fatty acid

FBS fasting blood sugar

FD fatal dose, focal distance

FDA Food & Drug Administration

Fx fracture

FUO fever of unknown origin

FVD fluid volume deficit

G

GB gallbladder

GERD gastroesophageal reflux disease

GFR glomerular filtration rate

GGT gamma-glutamyl transferase

GI gastrointestinal

GOT glutamic oxalic transaminase

GU genitourinary

GVHD graft-versus-host-disease

H

HA headache

Hb hemoglobin

HCG human chorionic gonadotropin

HCO_3 bicarbonate

HCT hematocrit

HD hemodialysis

HDL high density lipo-protein

HEENT head, eye, ear, nose and throat

Hgb hemoglobin

HIV human immun-odefi-ciency virus

HRT hormone replacement therapy

HS bedtime

Hx history

I

IBC iron binding capacity

IBD inflammatory bowel disease

IBS irritable bowel syndrome

IBW ideal body weight

ICCE intracapsular cataract extraction

ICF imtermediate care facility

ICP intracranial pressure

ICS intercostal space

ICT inflammation of connective tissue

ICU intensive care unit

IDM infant of diabetic mother

IDDM insulin dependent diabetes mellitus

IE inspiratory exerciser

IH infectious hepatitis

IHD ischemic heart disease

IIP implantable insulin pump

IM intramuscular

IMV intermittent mandatory ventilation

INR international normalization ratio

IPD intermittent peritoneal dialysis

IPPB intermittent positive pressure breathing

ITP immune thrombo-cytopenic purpura

IV intravenous

IVF in vitro fertilization

IVP intravenous pyelography

I

JAMA Journal of the American Medical Association

JVP jugular venous pressure

K

K potassium

KCl potassium chloride

KI potassium iodide

KUB kidney, ureter, bladder

KVO keep vein open

L

L & A light and accommodation

LAD left anterior descending (artery)

LB large bowel

LDL low density lipoprotein

LE lupus erythematosus

LFTs liver function tests

LIJ left internal jugular

LLQ left lower quadrant

LMP last menstrual period

LP lumbar puncture

LSC left subclavian

LUQ left upper quadrant

M

MAP mean arterial pressure

MAR medication administration record

MCL modified chest lead

MDI multiple daily vitamin

MI myocardial infarction

MLC midline catheter

MM mucous membrane

MoAbs monoclonal antibodies

MOM Milk of Magnesia

MRDD mental retarded/ developmentally disabled

MRI magnetic resonance imaging

MRM modified radical mastectomy

MS multiple sclerosis, morphine sulfate

N

Na sodium

NaCl sodium chloride

NED no evidence of disease

NICU neonatal intensive care unit

NIDDM noninsulin dependent diabetes mellitus

NKA no known allergies

NKDA non-ketotic diabetic acidosis

NKMA no known medcation allergies

NPD nightly peritoneal dialysis

NPO nothing by mouth

NSAID nonsteroidal anti-inflammatory drug

NTD neural tube defect

NV nausea & vomiting

NYD not yet diagnosed

O

OD right eye

OGTT oral glucose tolerance test

ORIF open reduction internal fixation

OS left eye

OU both eyes

P

PABA para-aminobenzoic acid

pc after meals

PCA patient controlled analgesia, posterior communicating artery

PCN penicillin, primary care nurse

PCV packed cell volume

PD peritoneal dialysis

PDA patent ductus arteri-osus, posterior descending artery

PDD pervasive development disorder

PDR physician's desk reference

PEG percutaneous endosco-pic gastrostomy

PEJ percutaneous endosco-pic jejunostomy

PERL pupils equal, react to light

PERRLA pupils equal, round, re-act to light, accommodation

PET positron emission tomography

PFT pulmonary function test

PG prostaglandin

PH past history

PI present illness

PICC peripherally inserted central venous catheter

PID pelvic inflammatory disease

PMI point of maximal impulse

PNH paroxysmal nocturnal hemoglobinuria

PO by mouth

PRBC packed red blood cells

PS pyloric stenosis

PSA prostate specific antigen

PT prothrombin time

PTT partial thromboplastin time

PUD peptic ulcer disease

PVD peripheral vascular disease

Px pneumothorax

Q

QD everyday

QID four times a day

qns quantity not sufficient

QOD every other day

qs quantity sufficient, quantity re-quired

R

RA rheumatoid arthritis

RAD reactive airway disease

RAI radioactive iodine

RAIU radioactive iodine uptake

RCA right coronary artery

RDW red cell distribution width

REEDA redness, edema, ecchymosis, drainage, approxi-mation

RHD rheumatic heart disease, relative hepatic dullness

RIJ right internal jugular

RLQ right lower quadrant

RM respiratory movement

ROM range of motion

ROS review of systems

RSC right subclavian

RUQ right upper quadrant

Rx prescription, pharmacy

S

S/S signs & symptoms

SAB spontaneous abortion

SAST serum aspartate amino-transferase

SB spina bifida

SBO small bowel obstruction

SGPT serum glutamic-pyru-vic transaminase

SLE systemic lupus erythe-matosus

SNF skilled nursing facility

SOB short(ness) of breath

SR sedimentation rate

SS social services

STD sexually transmitted disease

STH somatotropic hormone

STM short term memory

SUI stress urinary incontinence

SVR systemic vascular resistance

Sx symptoms

T

T3 triiodothyronine

T4 thyroxine

TBSA total body surface area

TCDB turn, cough, deep breathe

TED (hose) thrombo-embolism deterrent

TEP transesophageal puncture

THR total hip replacement

TIA transient ischemic attack

TIBC total iron binding capacity

TID three times a day

TIL tumour infiltrating lymphocytes

TKR total knee replacement

TNF tumor necrosis factor

TNM tumor, node, meta-stases

TNTC too numerous to mention

TP tuberculin precipitation

TPN total parenteral nutrition

TTN transient tachypnea of the newborn

TTP thrombotic thrombocytopenia purpura

TUPR trans-urethral pros-tatic resection

TUR (or TURP) trans-urethral resection of the prostate

TWB touch weight bear

TWE tap water enema

Tx treatment, traction

U

UA urinalysis

UAO upper airway obstruction

UBW usual body weight

UGI upper gastrointestinal

UPJ ureteropelvic junction

URI upper respiratory infection

US ultrasonic

UTI urinary tract infection

UVJ ureterovesical junction

V

VA visual acuity

VBAC vaginal birth after caeserean

VF/Vfib ventricular fibrillation

VLDL very low density lipoprotein

VMA vanillylmandelic acid

VSD ventricular septal defect

VT/Vtach ventricular tachycardia

VW vessel wall

W

W/C wheelchair

WBC white blood cell

WD well developed

WHO World Health Organization

WN well nourished

WNL within normal limits

Appendices

LABORATORY VALUES AND TESTS

COMPLETE BLOOD COUNT

A complete blood count, often referred to as a CBC, is a common blood test. A CBC provides detailed information about three types of cells in your blood: red blood cells, white blood cells, and platelets. These blood cells are made in the bone marrow, the spongy tissue filling the centre of your bones. Bone marrow in the skull, sternum (breast bone), ribs, vertebral column (backbone), and pelvis produces these blood cells. Each type of blood cell plays an important role in our body's normal function.

A complete blood count includes five major measurements:

WHITE BLOOD CELL (WBC) COUNT

White blood cells fight infections. They are measured in thousands per cubic milliliter (K/uL) of blood. The normal range for the white blood cell count varies between laboratories but is usually between 4,300 and 10,800 cells per cubic millimeter of blood. This can also be referred to as the leukocyte count and can be expressed in international units as 4.3 - 10.8 x 109 cells per liter.

A low white blood cell count is called leukopenia. A high white blood cell count is termed leukocytosis.

RED BLOOD CELL (RBC) COUNT

Red blood cells carry oxygen to and remove waste products from the body's tissues. These cells also contain hemoglobin. Red blood cells are measured in millions per cubic millimeter (mil/uL) of blood.

HEMOGLOBIN (HGB) VALUE

Hemoglobin gives red blood cells their colour. Hemoglobin carries oxygen from the lungs to the tissues and takes carbon dioxide (the waste products) from the tissues to the lungs. From the lungs, carbon dioxide is exhaled. Hemoglobin is measured in grams per deciliter (g/dL) of blood.

HEMATOCRIT (HCT) VALUE

The hematocrit is the percentage of red blood cells in relation to your total blood volume.

PLATELET COUNT

Platelets help to stop bleeding by forming blood clots. They are measured in thousands per cubic millimeter (m/uL) of blood. Normal platelet counts are in the range of 150,000 to 400,000 per microliter (or 150 - 400 x 109 per liter). These values many vary slightly between different laboratories.

COMPLETE BLOOD CELL COUNT

Red blood cells (RBC)	4.25-6.1 x 10/ml (males)
	3.6-5.4 x 10/ml (females)
White blood cells (WBC)	5000-10,000/mm3
Hemoglobin (Hgb)	13-18 g/dl (males)
	12-16 g/dl (females)
Hematocrit (Hct)	45%-54% (males)
	37%-47% (females)

COAGULATION

Platelet	150,000-350,000/ml
Prothrombin time (PT)	10-14 sec
Partial thromboplastin time (PTT)	30-45 sec
Thrombin time (TT)	Control ± 5 sec
Fibrinogen split products (FSP) Negative reaction	at >1:4 dilution
Iron/ferritin (Fe) (deficiency)	0-20 ng/ml
Reticulocyte count	0.5%-1.5% of RBC

URINE ELECTROLYTES

Sodium (Na+)	40-220 mEq/L
Potassium (K+)	25-125 mEq/L
Chloride (Cl–)	110-250 mEq/L

BLOOD CHEMISTRY

Sodium (Na+)	135-145 mEq/L
Potassium (K+)	3.5-4.5 mEq/L
Chloride (Cl–)	98-106 mEq/L
Carbon dioxide (CO_2)	24-32 mEq/L
Blood urea nitrogen (BUN)	7-25 mg/dl
Creatinine (Cr)	0.7-1.3 mg/dl (males)
	0.6-1.2 mg/dl (females)
Glucose	70-110 mg/dl
Calcium (Ca++)	8.5-10.5 mg/dl
Magnesium (Mg)	1.3-2.1 mg/dl
Phosphorus	3.0-4.5 mg/dl
Osmolality	275-295 mOsm/kg
Bilirubin	
Direct	0-0.2 mg/dl
Total	0.2-1.0 mg/dl
Indirect is total minus direct	
Amylase	50-150 U/L
Lipase	0-110 U/L
Anion gap	8-16 mEq/L

NORMAL RANGES

PULSE
Normal Ranges with Averages

Infant	90-(160)-160 beats per minute
Child	80-(l00)-120 beats per minute
Adult	Female: 60-(80)-100 beats per minute
	Male: 55-(75)-95 beats per minute

RESPIRATION
Normal Ranges

Infant	30 to 70 respirations per minute
Child	20 to 30 respirations per minute
Adult	15 to 20 respirations per minute

BLOOD PRESSURE
Normal Averages (Systolic/Diastolic)

Newborn	65-90/30-60 mm Hg
Infant	(1 year) 65-125/40-90 mm Hg
	(2 years) 75-100/40-90 mm Hg
Child	(4 years) 80-120/45-85 mm Hg
	(6 years) 85-115/50-60 mm Hg
Adolescent	(12 years) 95-135/50-70 mm Hg
	(16 years) 100-140/50-70 mm Hg
Adult	(18-60 years) less than 120/80 mm Hg
	(60+ years) 120-140/80-90 mm Hg

PHYSICAL ASSESSMENT

APPEARANCE
Stage of development, general health, striking features, height, weight, behaviour, posture, communication skills, grooming, hygiene.

SKIN
Colour, consistency, temperature, turgor, integrity, texture, lesions, mucous membranes.

HAIR
Colour, texture, amount, distribution.

NAILS
Colour, texture, shape, size.

NEUROLOGIC
Pupil reaction, motor and verbal responses, gait, reflexes, neurologic checks musculoskeletal range of motion, gait, tone, posture.

CARDIOVASCULAR
Heart rate and rhythm, Homans' sign, peripheral pulses and temperature, edema.

RESPIRATORY
Rate, rhythm, depth, effort, quality, expansion, cough, breath sounds, sputum production (color and amount), tracheostomy size, nasal patency.

GASTROINTESTINAL
Abdominal contour, bowel sounds, nausea, vomiting, ostomy type and care, fecal frequency, consistency, presence of blood.

GENITOURINARY
Urine colour, character, amount, odour, ostomy.

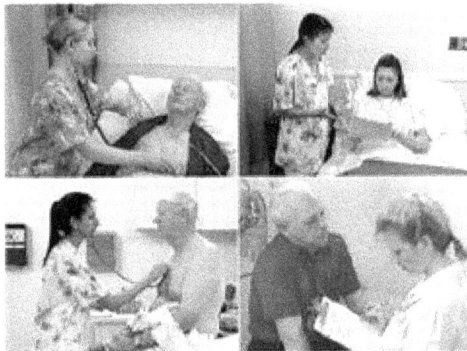

TEMPERATURE CONVERSION

$$F = C \times 9/5 + 32$$
$$C = F - 32 \times 5/9$$

Normal temperature:
98.6° Fahrenheit/37° Celsius (Centigrade)

°F	°C	°F	°C
70	21.1	94	34.4
75	23.8	95	35
80	26.7	96	35.6
81	27.2	97	36.1
82	27.8	98	36.7
83	28.3	98.6	37
84	28.9	99	37.2
85	29.4	100	37.8
86	30	101	38.3
87	30.6	102	38.9
88	31.1	103	39.4
89	31.7	104	40
90	32.2	105	40.6
91	32.8	106	41.1
92	33.3	107	41.7
93	33.9	108	42.2

BLOOD GLUCOSE TEST

The American Diabetes Association recommends frequent blood glucose checks for diabetics who are pregnant, taking insulin or diabetes pills, having low blood glucose levels without warning signs or after high blood glucose levels, and those having a hard time controlling their glucose levels. At-home devices that test glucose are called **glucometers** or glucose meters. Glucometers vary depending on the manufacturer, but they are generally compact and easy to use.

THINGS YOU'LL NEED:
- Glucometer glucose strips
- Lancet device
- Glucometer
- Gauze

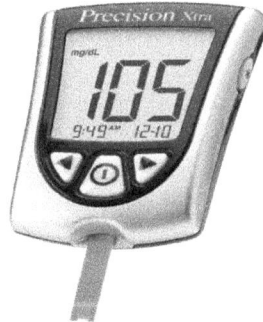

Fig. *Glucometer.*

INSTRUCTIONS
- **Step 1** Turn on your glucometer. Determine where you are going to puncture for blood, generally the fingertip.
- **Step 2** Wash your hands with soap and water and dry them. Insert a glucose test strip into the glucometer.
- **Step 3** Pierce the side of your fingertip with the lancet device to obtain a drop of blood. The size of the blood drop needed depends on the glucometer; consult the manufacturer's manual to determine how much blood you need to apply.
- **Step 4** Place your fingertip at the edge of the glucose strip and hold it to allow the strip to absorb the blood drop. Wipe any excess blood away with gauze.
- **Step 5** Read the glucose value that appears on the glucometer display. The typical range for diabetic glucose levels are 70 to

Fig. *Blood Sugar Test from Glucometer*

    130 mg/dL before a meal and less than 180 mg/dL after a meal.
- **Step 6** Record your glucose readings. It is important to write your glucose results down to monitor your condition and treatment and to discuss your plan with your doctor.

HOME PREGNANCY TEST

The home pregnancy test works by detecting a hormone called Human Chorionic Gonadotropin (hCG) in your urine. This hormone appears in a pregnant woman's urine, approximately 20 days after her last menstrual period. The levels then rise rapidly, reaching a peak in the next 60 to 80 days.

HOW IS THE TEST PERFORMED?

Try to perform the test first thing in the morning for optimal results, though this is not mandatory.

- Pregnancy tests are usually stored in the refrigerator. So, make sure you bring the test kit to room temperature before you use it.
- Collect urine in a clean, dry glass or plastic container. Ensure that there is no detergent residue in the container.
- Take out the pregcolor card (see image below) and place it on a flat surface.
- Draw out a little urine with a dropper (provided with the kit) and put just two drops in the circular test well that is usually marked 'S'. Do not spill urine on the reading strip.
- Wait for three to five minutes (depending on manufacturer's instructions) and then read the test results. Trying to read the results before the stipulated time or waiting too long, can both lead to inaccurate readings.

Some newly launched pregnancy test kits (for example, Clearview) can be held directly in the urine stream and do not require you to collect urine in a container. These kits are usually more expensive (around Rs 150).

HOW TO INTERPRET THE RESULTS?

- Look at the regions marked 'C' and 'T' on the test card. 'C' indicates a control. This band must always appear because this is the comparison band. 'T' indicates the test sample.
- If only one pink/purple band appear, in the region marked 'C', it means that the test is negative for pregnancy.
- If two pink/purple bands appear, one in the region marked 'C' and the other in the region marked 'T', it means that the test is positive for pregnancy.

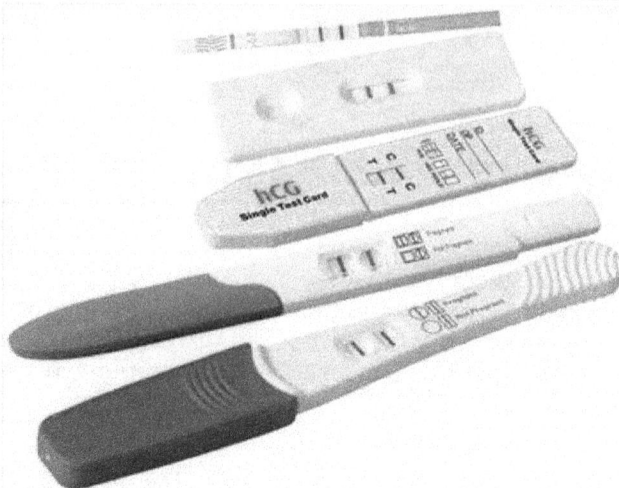

- In case no bands appear, then the test is invalid. Repeat the test with a new pack of pregcolor cards after 72 hours.
- If the line formed in region 'T' is faint, this could be due to low levels of hCG hormone. In case of a faint band, repeat the test with a new pack of pregcolor cards after 72 hours.

Note: In most cases, the test is sensitive enough to detect pregnancy even on the day of the missed period. In some women though, the levels of hCG are not detectable so early in the pregnancy. If the test is negative, you might want to try and repeat it after 72 hours.

THYROID FUNCTION TEST

INDICATION

Hyperparathyroidism and hypothyroidism.

PHYSIOLOGY

A butterfly like gland with two lobes extending around trachea and produces thyroxine. It exists as total T4,T3,free T4 and TSH.It affects cellular growth and metabolism.

NORMAL RANGE

T4-60-140nmol/L,T3-1.2-1.8nmol/L, TSH-0.1-6IU/L.

INTERPRETATION

Total T4-Increased levels are seen in graves disease,cancer of thyroid as symptoms of hyperthyroidism.low lwvels are seen in hypothyroidism whose symptoms are myoxyedema hashmito disease and pituatry disorders. T3 Increased levels are seen in hyperthyroidism and decreased levels are seen in hypo-thyroidsm.TSH-High in hypothyroidism and low in hyper-thyroidism.

SEX HORMONE TEST

INDICATION

Menstural problems,fertility problems, pregnancy delayed problems.

PHYSIOLOGY

The hormones include estrogen,testosterone ,progesterone. Estrogen stimulates sexual maturity,female sterlity. Progesterone stimulates pregnancy main-tenance.Androgen stimulates male fertility and secondary sexual chaarcters.

NORMAL RANGE

Estrogen	24-149pg/ml,
Testosterone	300-1200ng/dL,
Progesterone-menopausal women	150ng/Dl-2000ng/dL,
Premenopausal	1500-2000ng/dL.

INTERPRETATION

Increased levels of estrogen indicate early onset of puberty, male having female characters.low levels of estrogen indicates pregnancy failure.Increased levels of progesterone indicates cancer of ovary and cysts formation in ovary.Decreased levels are found in abortion. Higher levels of testosterone are seen in tumor of testes and encephilitis decreased levels are seen in genetical disorders like Down and Knilfilter syndrome.

TB S*KIN* T*EST*

INDICATION

Tuberculosis.

PHYSIOLOGY

This test is otherwise called as mantou test or tuberculin skin test. A purified protein derivative is injected under the first layer of the skin in the hand.

NORMAL RANGE

Negative.

INTERPRETATION

The appearance of red swollen around the injected area after 72 hours indicates the positive reaction for tuberculosis.

*I*NFLUENZA TESTS

INDICATION
　Flu fever

PHYSIOLOGY
　Flu fever is caused by influenza virus and it is a respiratory infection. It causes chilness, fever, coughs. A nasopharyngeal swab sample is required.

NORMAL RANGE
　Negative

INTERPRETATION
　The positive flu test indicates influenza virus infections.

BRONCHIECTASIS TEST

INDICATION

Severe cough, shortness of breath

PHYSIOLOGY

It is the destruction and abnormal widening of the air passages of the lungs.It is caused by continous infections of the nasal passages.

NORMAL RANGE

Negative

INTERPRETATION

A positive sputum culture growth indicates the presence of bronchiectasis.

PULMONARY TUBERCULOSIS TEST

INDICATION

Fatigue, weight loss, severe cough, loss of blood in cough and chillness.

PHYSIOLOGY

Pulmonary tuberculosis is caused by Mycobacterium tuberculosis. It primarily involves lungs and extend to other parts of the body.

NORMAL RANGE

Negative

INTERPRETATION

A positive sputum culture growth indicates positive test.

STOOL CULTURE TEST

INDICATION

Screen for pathogenic bacterial organisms in the stool, diagnose typhoid fever, enteric fever, bacillary dysentery, salmonella infection.

PHYSIOLOGY

Diarrhea is common in patients with AIDS. It is frequently caused by the classic bacterial pathogens, as well as, unusual opportunistic bacterial pathogens and parasitic infestation. Indications for stool culture are bloody diarrhea, fever, tenesmus, severe or persistent symptoms, bacterial infection, presence of fecal leukocytes.

NORMAL RANGE

Negative for pathogens

SAMPLE

Stool, rectal swab

TEST METHOD

Aerobic culture on selective media.

STOOL CULTURE, DIARRHEAGENIC E.COLI TEST

INDICATION

Establish diarrheagenic E.coli as the cause of clinical illness.

PHYSIOLOGY

Four major categories of Diarrheagenic E.coli are Enterotoxigenic (ETEC)-Travelers diarrhea and infant diarrhea in less developed countries. Enteropathogenic (EPEC) - Infant diarrhea. Enterohemorrhagic (EHEC) - Hemorrhagic colitis, Hemolytic uremic syndrome, Thrombotic thrombocytopenia purpura. Enteroinvasive (EIEC) - Dysentry.

NORMAL RANGE

Normal colinc flora

SAMPLE

Rectal swab, fresh stool

TEST METHOD

culture in macconkey agar

RELATED TESTS

Methylene blue stain, Stool culture

STERILITY CULTURE TEST

INDICATION

Confirm that adequate sterilization conditions have been attained.

PHYSIOLOGY

Biological indicators must be used at least once weekly with the steam autoclaves and with every load with the ethylene oxide sterilizer.

NORMAL RANGE

No growth in test strips

SAMPLE

Three strips (one control and two test strips)

TEST METHOD

Indicator strips impegrenated with spores of Bacillus stearothermophilus are used with steam autoclaves.

BLOOD VOLUME OR
PLASMA VOLUME TEST

A blood volume test (also called a plasma volume test or a red cell mass test) is a nuclear lab procedure used to measure the volume (amount) of blood in the body. The test also measures the volume of plasma and of red cells in the blood.

A blood volume test can be used in the diagnosis of these conditions:
- Hypovolemia (low blood volume)
- Hypervolemia (high blood volume)
- Anemia (low red cell volume)
- Polycythemia (high red cell volume).

A blood volume test may be used in the evaluation of these treatments:

Kidney dialysis

Pre-operative hemodilution (blood dilution) therapy

Pre- and post- evaluation of fluid status

Pseudo-anemia detection secondary to fluid retention

Blood transfusion therapy/precise volume replacement

INDICATION

The test measures the patient's total circulating volume of blood and/or fractions of the blood volume.

PHYSIOLOGY

A component of the blood (e.g., Albumin) is labeled using a radioisotope. The dilution of the label is inversely proportional to the size (Volume) of the compartment in which it has been diluted.

NORMAL RANGE

Normal values	Men ml/kg	Women ml/kg
Blood volume	61.54 ± 8.59	58.95 ± 4.94
Erythrocyte volume	28.27 ± 4.11	24.24 ± 2.59
Plasma volume	33.45 ± 5.18	34.77 ± 3.24

INTERPRETATION

This test differentiates relative from absolute polycythemia. Polycythemia is increased red cells and is opposite to anemia. Polycythemia is usually considered when hemoglobin is 18g/dL, hematocrit is 52% and RBC count is 6 million/mm3.

TEST RESULTS

Dilution Technique using 125I – tagged albumin and/or 51Cr-tagged Red Blood Cells.

RELATED TESTS

Erythropoietin Test, Hematocrit Test, Peripheral Blood, Red Cell Mass.

BLOOD TEST

Blood test results, made possible by the taking of Blood tests, are one of the most important tools that your doctor uses in evaluating your health status. It is important to realize that your Blood test result may be outside of what is called the 'normal range' for many reasons. Blood tests, including various Blood chemistry and hematology 'Blood tests' offered by most test labs, represent an economical way by which quality information about a patient's physical condition, at the time of the Blood testing, can be made available to the physician. These Blood test results, after review and interpretation by a qualified Blood professional, play an important part in an overall diagnosis. Blood test results are important in Blood disorders in Blood tests and a Blood test with Rare Blood types. Blood test results are compared and measured in 'normal ranges' for a given population group. Low cost Blood tests, discount Blood testing and even free Blood tests are available and listed in your local community.

A large number of laboratory Blood tests are widely available. Many Blood tests are specialized to focus on a particular disease or group of diseases. Many different Blood tests are used commonly in many specialties and in general practice.

Because most Blood test reference ranges (often referred to as 'normal' ranges of Blood test results) are typically defined as the range of values of the median 95% of the healthy population, it is unlikely that a given Blood sample, even from a healthy patient, will show "normal" values for every Blood test taken. Therefore, caution should be exercised to prevent overreaction to mild abnormalities without the interpretation of those tests by your examining physician. Again, a Blood test, though important, is only a part of the final diagnosis of a health problem. Often, you can get your Blood tested at the Bloodmobile.

Physicians rely on "clinical laboratory diagnostic Blood testing to diagnose medical conditions. From this Blood testing the medical professional then prescribes therapies and remedies, based on those

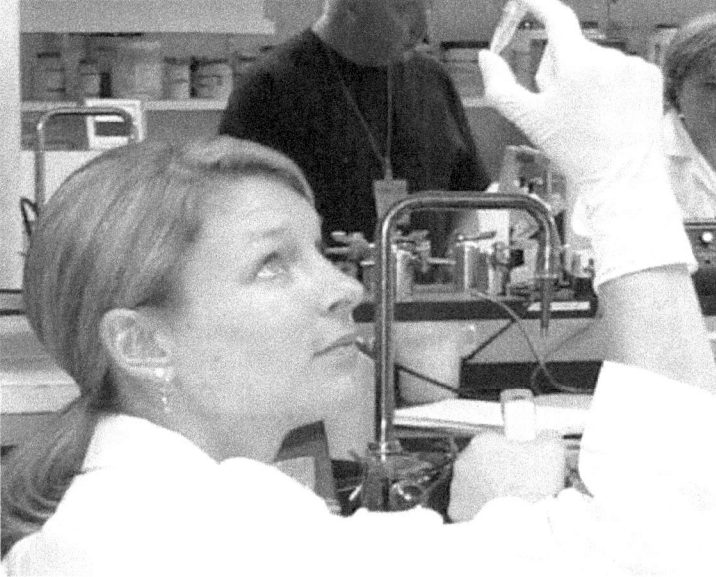

Fig. *Blood test in lab.*

Blood tests. Blood test results reveal Blood disorders in Blood tests and also with a Blood test with Rare Blood types. Good Blood tests make possible state-of-the-art lab procedures that can be provided directly to the public in private and these Blood tests can be provided affordably. Some of the most common Blood tests are: Blood Test Results, Blood test, rare Blood types, Blood disorders.

- Allergy Blood Testing.
- Blood Tests for Autoimmune Diseases.
- Blood Diseases Testing.
- Cancer Detection Blood Testing.
- Blood Cholesterol Test.
- Diabetes Blood Tests.
- DNA, Paternity and Genetic Testing.
- Blood Tests for Drug Screening.
- Environmental Toxin Blood Testing.
- Fitness, Nutrition and Anti-Aging.
- Gastrointestinal Diseases Revealed by Blood Tests.
- Blood Testing for Heart Health.
- Hormones and Metabolism.
- Infectious Disease Blood Tests.
- Kidney Disease Blood Test.
- Liver Diseases Blood Testing.

- Sexually Transmitted Diseases (STD's) Blood Tests.
- Thyroid Disease Blood Tests.

Screening Blood tests are used to try to detect a disease when there is little or no evidence that a person has a suspected disease. For example, measuring cholesterol levels helps to identify one of the risks of heart disease. These screening tests are performed on people who may show no symptoms of heart disease, as a tool for the physician to detect a potentially harmful and evolving condition. In order for screening tests to be the most useful they must be readily available, accurate, inexpensive, pose little risk, and cause little discomfort to the patient. Coupons for DNA and Cancer Blood tests.

Diagnostic Blood tests are utilized when a specific disease is suspected to verify the presence and the severity of that disease, including allergies, HIV, AIDS, Hepatitis, cancer, etc.

What is a Blood test

Blood tests are an essential diagnostic tool. Blood is made up of different kinds of cells and contains other compounds, including various salts and certain proteins. Blood tests reveal details about these Blood cells and, Blood compounds, salts and proteins.

The liquid portion of the tested Blood is plasma. When our Blood clots outside the body, the Blood cells and some of the proteins in Blood turn into a solid. The remaining liquid is called serum, which can be used in chemical tests and in other Blood tests to find out how the immune system fights diseases. Doctors take Blood samples and grow the organisms, found in Blood tests, that cause illness, to evaluate each, microscopically.

How is a Blood test carried performed?

Blood samples taken for Blood testing can be taken either from a vein or from an artery. A few drops of Blood are needed, most of the time. It is often enough to take a small drop from the tip of your finger and then squeeze the Blood out for Blood testing. Most Blood tests are taken from a vein (veins carry Blood *from* the heart,) most often from those veins near the elbow. First a tourniquet is tied around the upper arm to make the vein easy to find and take the Blood for the Blood test.

The place where the injection is to take place is then made sterile and then a hollow needle is put into the vein. The needle will be attached either to a Blood test sample bottle or to a syringe where the plunger is pulled back to create low negative pressure. When the needed amount of Blood for testing has been removed from the vein, the needle is removed. The area is then re-cleaned and pressure is placed on the area with a small ball of cotton. This is pressed against the area for a couple of minutes before applying a bandage. Blood test results are important in Blood disorders in Blood tests and a Blood test with Rare Blood types. Blood tests are relatively painless.

BLOOD TEST REFERENCE RANGE CHART

Test	Reference Range (conventional units*)
17 Hydroxyprogesterone (Men)	0.06-3.0 mg/L
17 Hydroxyprogesterone (Women) Follicular phase	0.2-1.0 mg/L
25-hydroxyvitamin D (25(OH)D)	8-80 ng/mL
Acetoacetate	<3 mg/dL
Acidity (pH)	7.35 - 7.45
Alcohol	0 mg/dL (more than 0.1 mg/dL normally
indicates intoxication) (ethanol)	
Ammonia	15 - 50 µg of nitrogen/dL
Amylase	53 - 123 units/L
Ascorbic Acid	0.4 - 1.5 mg/dL
Bicarbonate	18 - 23 mEq/L (carbon dioxide content)
Bilirubin	Direct: up to 0.4 mg/dL
Total: up to 1.0 mg/dL	
Blood Volume	8.5 - 9.1% of total body weight
Calcium	8.5 - 10.5 mg/dL (normally slightly higher
in children)	
Carbon Dioxide Pressure	35 - 45 mm Hg
Carbon Monoxide	Less than 5% of total hemoglobin
CD4 Cell Count	500 - 1500 cells/µL
Ceruloplasmin	15 - 60 mg/dL
Chloride	98 - 106 mEq/L

Complete Blood Cell Count (CBC) Tests include: hemoglobin, hematocrit, mean corpuscular hemoglobin, mean corpuscular hemoglobin concentration, mean corpuscular volume, platelet count, white Blood cell count

Copper	Total: 70 - 150 µg/dL
Creatine Kinase (CK or CPK)	Male: 38 - 174 units/L
	Female: 96 - 140 units/L
Creatine Kinase Isoenzymes	5% MB or less
Creatinine	0.6 - 1.2 mg/dL

Electrolytes Test includes: calcium, chloride, magnesium, potassium, sodium Erythrocyte Sedimentation Rate (ESR or Sed-Rate)

	Male: 1 - 13 mm/hr
	Female: 1 - 20 mm/hr
Glucose Tested after fasting:	70 - 110 mg/dL
Hematocrit	Male: 45 - 62%
	Female: 37 - 48%
Hemoglobin	Male: 13 - 18 gm/dL
	Female: 12 - 16 gm/dL
Iron	60 - 160 µg/dL (normally higher in males)
Iron-binding Capacity	250 - 460 µg/dL
Lactate (lactic acid)	Venous: 4.5 - 19.8 mg/dL
Arterial:	4.5 - 14.4 mg/dL
Lactic Dehydrogenase	50 - 150 units/L
Lead	40 µg/dL or less (normally much lower in
children)	
Lipase	10 - 150 units/L
Zinc B-Zn	70 - 102 µmol/L

Lipids:

Cholesterol Less than 225 mg/dL (for age 40-49 yr; increases with age)

Triglycerides

10 - 29 years	53 - 104 mg/dL
30 - 39 years	55 - 115 mg/dL
40 - 49 years	66 - 139 mg/dL
50 - 59 years	75 - 163 mg/dL
60 - 69 years	78 - 158 mg/dL
> 70 years	83 - 141 mg/dL

Liver Function Tests include bilirubin (total), phosphatase (alkaline), protein (total and albumin), transaminases (alanine and aspartate), prothrombin (PTT)

Magnesium	1.5 - 2.0 mEq/L
Mean Corpuscular Hemoglobin (MCH)	27 - 32 pg/cell
Mean Corpuscular Hemoglobin Concentration (MCHC)	32 - 36% hemoglobin/cell
Mean Corpuscular Volume (MCV)	76 - 100 cu μm
Osmolality	280 - 296 mOsm/kg water
Oxygen Pressure	83 - 100 mm Hg
Oxygen Saturation (arterial)	96 - 100%
Phosphatase, Prostatic	0 - 3 units/dL (Bodansky units) (acid)
Phosphatase	50 - 160 units/L (normally higher in infants and adolescents) (alkaline)
Phosphorus	3.0 - 4.5 mg/dL (inorganic)
Platelet Count	150,000 - 350,000/mL
Potassium	3.5 - 5.0 mEq/L
Prostate-Specific Antigen (PSA)	0 - 4 ng/mL (likely higher with age)
Proteins:	
Total	6.0 - 8.4 gm/dL
Albumin	3.5 - 5.0 gm/dL
Globulin	2.3 - 3.5 gm/dL
Prothrombin (PTT)	25 - 41 sec
Pyruvic Acid	0.3 - 0.9 mg/dL
Red Blood Cell Count (RBC)	4.2 - 6.9 million/μL/cu mm
Sodium	135 - 145 mEq/L
Thyroid-Stimulating Hormone (TSH)	0.5 - 6.0 μ units/mL
Transaminase:	
Alanine (ALT)	1 - 21 units/L
Aspartate (AST)	7 - 27 units/L
Urea Nitrogen (BUN)	7 - 18 mg/dL
BUN/Creatinine Ratio	5 - 35
Uric Acid	Male 2.1 to 8.5 mg/dL (likely higher with age) Female 2.0 to 7.0 mg/dL (likely higher with age)
Vitamin A	30 - 65 μg/dL
WBC (leukocyte count and white Blood cell count)	4.3-10.8 × 103/mm3
White Blood Cell Count (WBC)	4,300 - 10,800 cells/μL/cu mm

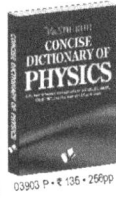

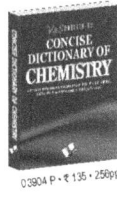

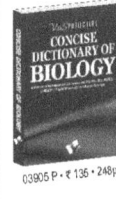

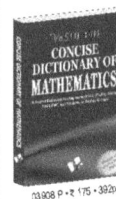

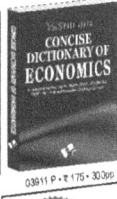

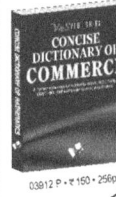

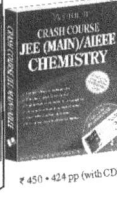

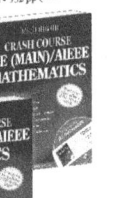

www.ingramcontent.com/pod-product-compliance
Lightning Source LLC
Chambersburg PA
CBHW072038020426
42334CB00017B/1313